The Long Voyage

Selected Letters of Malcolm Cowley, 1915–1987

EDITED BY HANS BAK

FOREWORD BY ROBERT COWLEY

Harvard University Press

Cambridge, Massachusetts
London, England
2014

Book design by Dean Bornstein

Library of Congress Cataloging-in-Publication Data

Cowley, Malcolm, 1898–1989.
  The long voyage : selected letters of Malcolm Cowley, 1915–1987 /
edited by Hans Bak ; foreword by Robert Cowley.
      pages cm
  Includes bibliographical references and index.
  ISBN 978-0-674-05106-5 (alk. paper)
  1. Cowley, Malcolm, 1898–1989—Correspondence.   I. Bak, Hans, editor of
compilation.   II. Title.
  PS3511.A86Z48 2014
  813'.52—dc23
  [B]

                                                                    2013012605

FOR ELLA AND SASKIA

Contents

Foreword: Beyond the Dry Season

ROBERT COWLEY

There are moments when I am convinced that the letters written by my father, Malcolm Cowley, constitute his most noteworthy literary achievement. He might have denied that claim, arguing that the letters were mainly a convenient way of persuading, explaining, and advising, and were intended as nothing more. What literary merit they had, he might have added, was merely a natural byproduct of clear thinking and writing of the English language in equal parts. As for their extraordinary number, blame it on the happy accident of a long life. That may be true, but reading through this selection, I have become increasingly impressed. It is also true that his literary generation, not a "lost" one by a long stretch, was a generation of letter writers: people like Robert Penn Warren, Allen Tate, and Edmund Wilson were correspondents whose daily output was as varied and prolific as my father's.

Still, when I saw that windowless manuscript vault in the Newberry Library in Chicago, I was unprepared for the bounty of documents that confronted me. All my father's papers, which include not just his own letters, manuscripts, working files, and family photographs but also letters written *to* him, fill 178 gray archival cartons stored on open shelves; if you were to place them side by side, they would extend for seventy-seven feet. (There are even more of my father's papers in other archival collections, including those at Yale and Princeton.) The editor of this book, the indefatigable Hans Bak, and the archivists at the Newberry estimate (as he writes elsewhere) that my father's letters in the Newberry collection alone add up to some 25,000 items. If, from that total, you subtract Christmas cards, directions on how to find my father's house in western Connecticut, and recommendations about where to spend the night, still hundreds, indeed thousands, of substantial letters remain. That does not count the much larger number of letters my father received from correspondents literary and otherwise for over seventy-five years. You can consider the entire collection a matchless portrait of the literary situation in the twentieth century. This book is, to be sure, a selection only of my father's letters, but it is a selection large enough to represent a significant contribution to American literary history.

It may sound curious, but, growing up, I was never that impressed by my father's zeal for letter writing: obsession is too strong a word, especially when you consider how much else he wrote in his long lifetime. Maybe I took it for granted. I often carried two or three envelopes, always with neatly typed addresses, down to the mailbox by Church Road in Sherman, long before the postman's car arrived around eleven. By that time (if it was summer), my father was finished with his letters for the day—he made a habit of attending to them first—and was out in his garden, adjusting the water flow from a hose at the head of a pole-climbing line of Kentucky Wonder beans or enveloping his tomatoes in clouds of wholesomely toxic dust. His thoughts had now turned to whatever piece he was writing. When the mail arrived, I would bring it up our hill, along with the daily *New York Herald Tribune* (which he preferred to the starch-impregnated conservatism of the *Times*). I'd try to steal a peek at the baseball scores before I handed him the paper and the mail. He tended to read every word—or so it seemed to the boy waiting impatiently for his father to disgorge the sports section. For years I cared about little else.

I do remember a day in 1977 when I came into his study and found it full of cartons. He told me that they were an installment of his papers, which he had sold to the Newberry, and that they were headed there. He had made the arrangement after notably happy months in 1954 spent in Chicago on a Newberry fellowship. A first collection of his papers had gone off that year, and there had been intervening shipments since. He described this particular shipment to his sometime Stanford colleague the novelist and teacher Wallace Stegner: "So far I have filled seven whisky cartons and I think there are still two to come." My father, I came to understand then, was a man of letters in every sense.

· · ·

My father was older than most of the fathers of my friends—at least he seemed, and acted, older. He was thirty-six when I was born, middle aged. Maybe it was his trademark mustache that added to his *gravitas*. I never knew him to not have that mustache. It makes its first appearance in a recently discovered passport photo taken before he sailed for France in June

1921. The way he spoke produced the same effect of slightly premature aging. There was a deliberate hesitation of his enunciation, as if he was carefully composing each sentence he uttered. He thought in paragraphs. His words were muscular but deceptively loose-limbed. They gave the impression of a taller, leaner man. Perhaps that is what led his *New York Times* obituary to describe him as "rangy." It was obvious that the writer had not met him. Though my father was strong, and would thump the tips of his stubby fingers on a tabletop to make a point, rangy he was not. He was 5'10" tall, with a potbelly that he never lost, even when a mild heart attack on New Year's Eve 1950 obliged him to go on a protein diet. The pot remained. He inevitably demanded a second helping.

That was the man I knew. Those were my first memories of him, the ones that lasted.

Why not begin, then, at the point where I first became aware, dimly to be sure, of the travails that shaped my father's career and forced him (as the cliché puts it) to reinvent himself? Those would be the years, roughly from 1940 to 1951, when the downs sometimes seemed more numerous than the ups—though, in the end, it was the ups that would prevail. Reading through the decades in this book, I find that these are the letters, so crucial to his life, that most affect me.

The downs, personal and institutional, began in the late fall of 1940, when doctors discovered that my mother was suffering from breast cancer and performed a mastectomy; she nearly died. I had nightmares and refused to eat. As if his wife's illness and his son's fears weren't worry enough, the backers of *The New Republic,* where he served as literary editor, chose this time "to have a great shake-up and shakedown," as he wrote to his oldest friend, Kenneth Burke. "For a time the atmosphere around the office was like Moscow during the purges." Until then my father had been one of the most powerful figures in literary New York. As Alfred Kazin described him in his memoir, *Starting Out in the Thirties,* he was "the last *New Republic* literary editor who dominated 'the back of the book,' and who week after week gave a continuing authority to his judgments." My father was displaced, and retired permanently to the country. He still wrote a weekly book review. But a book he was planning, a sequel to *Exile's Return,* the story of what he called "the writers' crusade of the 1930s," died, stillborn, yet another dreary milestone in a period that was turning calamitous.

I noticed the difference: he no longer spent three days a week in New York City, and there was no excited meeting him every Thursday night at the train station. The years 1939–1940 were not a good time for my family, or for the world in general. My father, in a letter to Burke in January 1941, characterized those two years as the period "when everything ended—the Spanish Republic (February), Czechoslovakia (March), the Federal Theatre (June), the People's Front (August), the long armistice (September)—then Poland (October), the illusion of Russia as a non-imperialist power (November), free Norway and Denmark (April), the French Republic (May and June)—did you ever stop to think how all our world crashed in those few months?"

In November 1941, Archibald MacLeish, the poet and confidant of FDR, persuaded my father to come to Washington. MacLeish headed the Office of Facts and Figures, the principal government propaganda organization. Washington was preparing for a war that was by then all but inevitable. (The better known Office of War Information would replace it the following summer.) "If the need is urgent," my father wrote MacLeish on November 16, "I could come on very short notice." Eight days later he was on his way. He spent almost two months in a rooming house, missing Christmas with the family. ("If you ever want to be really lonely," he told Burke in a letter not included here, "live alone in a room furnished with two double beds.") Hired as a chief information analyst, my father wrote and edited propaganda brochures, and contributed to policy speeches. FDR had apparently used a few of his lines.

The war came, and a month after Pearl Harbor, my mother drove me to Washington, where we met my father. We would be there just three months. I was too young to understand, or even recognize, the swirl of events that would seize my father, toy with him, and finally destroy his brief career in government.

· · ·

Almost as soon as we had arrived, it seemed, we were on our way home. On January 13, 1942, when my mother and I had been in Washington for just a week, "the storm broke" (my father's phrase). In the letters reprinted here, you can get a fair sense of what happened and of the way political opportunists can devour a reputation. Congressmen denounced my father and his past radical connections on the floor of the House. The Hearst press went after him. In a violent attack on the leftist associations that he had disavowed, the ex-Communist Whittaker Chambers, an influential editor at *Time*, ran an anonymous attack in the magazine on my father's little sheaf of poems *The Dry Season*. By obvious design, the review appeared not under Books but in the National Affairs section. A handful of lines, my father wrote MacLeish, were "shamelessly" taken out of context and "given a political meaning they do not possess." The article overlooked what has to be one of the great patriotic poems in the American language, "The Long Voyage:"

> Not that the pines were darker there,
> nor mid-May dogwood brighter there,
> nor swifts more swift in summer air;
>   it was my own country . . .

In the larger political scheme of things, my father was expendable. He was caught in a riptide of antileftist sentiment that, as early as 1942, was already gathering force. On March 12, he submitted an official letter of resignation to his old friend MacLeish, which you can read in these pages. We were back in Sherman by the beginning of April.

Almost forty years later, in the fall of 1981, a few months before he died at ninety, I interviewed Archibald MacLeish at his home in Conway, Massachusetts. He was still a handsome man, who spoke with quiet force and without letup—"ers" or "ums" or stammers were never a presence in his emphatic sentences. Nor was memory a problem. I think he only consented to the interview because I had been a student in his English S at Harvard, an advanced writing course, and because of my father. We had been talking all morning when we stopped for lunch. He asked me to turn off my tape recorder—and then confessed how close he had come to joining the Communist Party in the early thirties, even though he was writing for, and advising, Henry Luce and his new magazine, *Fortune*. "For a brief time," he said, "the Communists were the only ones who seemed to have an answer." He didn't join the Comrades, of course, and neither did my father, who had felt the same way. It was somehow comforting that the two men, both poets and persuaders, had shared the same dilemma. "You know,"

MacLeish said, "one of my greatest regrets is that I didn't stand up more for Malcolm."

That he didn't, as it turned out, may have been all for the good.

. . .

I have few distinct images of my father in the months after Washington. He was there—and yet he wasn't. When he had gone to work for the government, he had burned his bridges, and now they had to be repaired and restored. It wasn't easy. "I'm back in Connecticut—back writing for *The New Republic*—and apparently it's as if I had never been in Washington," he wrote MacLeish soon after his return. "But it gives me a terrific feeling of frustration to think that all the hell I went through was for nothing or next to nothing." At the end of June, he confessed to Burke that he was "feeling pretty low but not so low as last month or the month before, and I think that by fall I'll be writing again." Nearly a year after his resignation, he could report to MacLeish that his recovery was still tentative: "I took a pretty bad financial licking in Washington, and somewhat of a moral licking too, so that I retired into a state of estivation last summer, something like a bear's hibernation—but then in the fall I got back to work." He complained to his friend Newton Arvin, one of the pre-eminent authorities on American literature at the time, that the world was passing him by: "From me there isn't much to report, since Sherman, Connecticut, might as well be the Hermit Kingdom."

My father seemed constantly abstracted and, though I was too young to recognize the symptoms, probably depressed. Was it a coincidence, or just my growing awareness, that in those months I first noticed his advancing deafness? I see it now almost as a symbol of his rejection by Washington. He was broke. He spent an inordinate amount of time in his gardens. He had three, all large, as well as two beehives, which kept the family from going hungry that summer. My mother canned . . . and canned. Meat rationing was in effect now, but what little could be had was, in any event, an unaffordable expense. My father and his painter neighbor, Peter Blume, hunted. The season for game birds like pheasants lasted for only a few weeks in the fall; then they were off limits. But squirrels and rabbits were another matter, prey for all seasons. Rabbit could be tasty and tender; squirrel, dusted in flour and fried, looked like chicken parts and made a passable dinner. My mother once served a woodchuck that my father had shot. My parents tried to brave it through the meal, but I announced that the critter was stringy and bitter, and after an initial attempt to swallow a mouthful, spit it out. You might say that the taste of woodchuck was, for my family, the essence of 1942.

For my father, the humiliating reverses continued. Even a year later, there had been little measurable improvement in our finances. At the end of October 1943, we packed up, shut down the house, and went to New York. My father did have work as a staff critic for *The New Republic*, not the exalted and supremely influential position he had once held but at least a job, if not one that could support the three of us. At least in New York my father could make useful contacts, ones that might pay off in the future. Housing was tight and expensive in wartime Manhattan, and necessity and an empty exchequer forced us to share an apartment with our former neighbors up the road, Elsa Coates and her son, Tony, who had long been my best friend. The apartment was on the corner of Seventy-Second Street and Second Avenue, over a Schulte tobacco store. Elsa and her husband, Bob, were now living apart. She was older than her husband, and hadn't aged well: years of isolation in Sherman had taken a toll. Her heavy drinking, which had grown worse with time, didn't help. Their relationship was at an end— and, indeed, a couple of years later Bob would marry Boo Meighan, who had been married to a radio actor when Bob had begun seeing her in New York, when he was away from Sherman, working at *The New Yorker*. His short stories appeared regularly in the magazine, and he was also its art critic. (It was Bob who coined the phrase "abstract expressionism.") He was a large man with not just a shock but a throb of thick crinkly red hair, whose quiet wry humor and kindness were concealed behind a self-effacing stutter.

My parents slept in a windowless inner room next to the one I shared with Tony; curtained glass doors separated us. Around Christmas, my mother developed pneumonia. Doctors showed up—they still made house calls in those days. The bleak time continued. For Tony's sake, Bob spent Christmas Eve and most of Christmas day at Seventy-Second Street. After the lights went out at our end, I could hear Bob and Elsa, a little the worse for a long night's alcoholic wear, quarreling. Christmas morning came, and before it was light, Tony and I were up and heading for the tree in the living room. Bob must have heard us moving packages around, trying to make out presents with our names on them. He turned on the light and whispered to us that we could take one present each. I reached for a wooden machine gun on a tripod—a perfect wartime gift—and dashed down the hall cradling it. I turned a crank, which caused a clack-clack-clack that reverberated through the apartment. Now everyone woke up. My father burst into the room, confiscated the gun, and ordered me to keep quiet around my sick mother. The year was ending not with a whimper but with the hammering imitation of an angry woodpecker.

Forget our somewhat grim situation. There was something special about the city that winter of 1943–1944. It was a time, my father would later write in *Exile's Return,* "when New York was what Paris had been in 1920, the place where every writer wanted to be, the capital of the literary world." Nothing was permanent, not even the cocktail parties that seemed to go on nonstop. (I only heard about them.) People were here today, gone tomorrow, off to war or to Washington or to cover the invasion of France and the opening of a Second Front that was bound to happen that year.

In the spring the family returned to Sherman. It was planting season, naturally. But more than that, my father's fortunes had begun to change.

·   ·   ·

One notable piece of writing, unlike anything he had written until then, and too often overlooked in his canon, did take shape in 1943, perhaps out of a desperate urge to expand his repertoire. That was my father's profile of the editor Maxwell Perkins, for *The New Yorker.* "Perkins, I discovered, is the nearest thing to a great man now existing in the literary world," he wrote on April 8, 1943, to William Shawn, then the managing editor of the magazine. "Legends are clustered around him like truffles round an oak tree in Gascony." (It was Perkins who shaved more than a foot from a two-foot-high typescript of a novel by Thomas Wolfe.) Perkins was a man who, my father wrote, dressed in "shabby and inconspicuous grays," wore a hat that came down around his ears, and wandered around the offices of Scribner's to ask questions "while he holds onto his coat lapels with both hands." Perkins had helped to launch the literary careers of F. Scott Fitzgerald, Ernest Hemingway, Thomas Wolfe, John P. Marquand, Erskine Caldwell, Marjorie Rawlings, and a legion of other distinguished writers published by Scribner's.

When my father handed in the article later that spring, Shawn did something that he was unprepared for: he rejected it. My father, he said, had skimped on facts. Had my father scraped bottom? But he persuaded a somewhat reluctant Shawn to let him have another try. He put in extra facts and interviewed people he had not bothered to contact earlier. The new research—I remember his taking constant train trips to New York that summer—and the rewriting consumed most of the year. As my father later wrote, he came away with "a new respect for small hard facts simply stated, a feeling that I was never to lose." It is a gift amounting to a birthright, not just respect but reverence for those "small hard facts," that my father passed on to me. When *The New Yorker* published the profile of Perkins in April 1944, it appeared in an almost unheard-of two parts.

There is a footnote to the story of my father and Perkins. The two men discussed William Faulkner. Was it Perkins who planted the seed that would bloom as one of the most inspired pieces of editing in its time, resuscitating in the process the reputation of an almost forgotten writer? Of Faulkner, Perkins wrote to my father on January 31, 1944, "I was most enthusiastic about his early books. . . . At one time he almost did join us as an author, and seemed anxious to do so, but circumstances prevented it." Clearly Perkins was reluctant to establish a connection with a writer who, by 1944, had practically disappeared from print. "My only fear about him now," Perkins added, "is that he has fallen into a certain position which is not nearly as high as it should be, and once that happens to a writer, it is extremely difficult to change the public's opinion."

That was a mission that my father would, before long, undertake.

· · ·

The award to my father of a Mellon grant in the spring of 1944—about the time the Perkins profile appeared—changed everything for our family. The equivalent in its day of a MacArthur "genius" grant, it was named after Mary Mellon, the wife of the financier Paul Mellon and a woman deeply involved in the promotion of literature and the arts. It lasted for five years. My father would no longer have to rely on a never-ending series of short articles and reviews for his livelihood and now could turn to bigger projects, most notably his studies of American letters and their chief practitioners, living and dead. I regard that as the most important outcome of the savaging he sustained for his former leftist connections. You might say that he now began a second career, one that he might never have followed had he not been hounded from Washington.

What if he had remained there, rising (as was his natural bent) to ever higher positions? What if he had supplied not just phrases and sentences to the president but paragraphs and entire speeches? Would he have had the time, let alone the opportunity, to assemble his imaginative and ingenious chronicle of Faulkner's Yoknapatawpha, his mythical Mississippi county? Would he have championed the unremembered 1855 edition of Walt Whitman's *Leaves of Grass*, which, with his backing and his learned introduction, became one of the true classics of American literature? Would he have made the thorough, patient assemblage of the stories of F. Scott Fitzgerald, a collection that had not yet been collected when it appeared in 1951? Would he have attempted his ambitious revision of his autobiographical work, *Exile's Return,* which had defined the American—key word—literary generation of the 1920s? To be sure, someone else might have gotten to these works, but not *all* of them—or framed them with such grace and understanding. As it was, he never had time enough. "The damned trouble with my life," he complained to his friend Wallace Stegner in 1964, "is that I get involved with too many things and end like a shattered prism." Though there was some truth in what he said, he was being overly hard on himself. How else did he manage to produce so much, and of such consistent quality?

Painful experience led him to observe a simple rule, and one that he passed on to me: beware of ideologies, whether they come from the Left or the Right. If he had one now, it was the primacy of our national literature.

· · ·

That same spring of 1944 another important event in our lives took shape, though I was too young—not yet ten—to be aware of it. I did know of the Mellon grant—how could I ignore the immediate changes in our family circumstances?—but the name Faulkner had no meaning to me. I was too involved in local drives to collect newspapers and discarded pots and pans, all to enhance the war effort, too entranced with the prospect of D-Day, to pay attention.

My father had caught the scent of an irresistible project. "Almost every critic," he wrote later, "dreams of discovering some great work that has been neglected by other critics. Some day might he come upon an author whose reputation is less than his achievement and in fact is scandalously out of proportion with it, so that other voices will be added to the critic's voice, in a swelling chorus, as soon as he has made the discovery? That is the dream."

"At least once in my critical career I had the good luck to find it realized."

Faulkner had, by 1944, published seventeen books, including eleven novels, four collections of short stories, and two of poetry. By the age of forty-six, he was effectively out of print. My father did have the good fortune to own many of the books, then so hard to find, which he had acquired while running the book review section of *The New Republic*. He decided that the time had come to write a long essay on Faulkner, and the Mellon money gave him the freedom to do so. He had noticed that the majority of the novels and stories took place in a fictional county in northern Mississippi, called Yoknapatawpha, and formed what he recognized as a single saga. As he wrote, "all the separate works are like blocks of marble from the same quarry: they show the veins and faults of the mother rock."

In January 1944, my father wrote to Faulkner at his home in Oxford, Mississippi, to propose the article and to ask his help. It was more than three months before he received an answer, from Burbank, California: most of Faulkner's income these days came from screen writing for Warner Brothers. (He had just started collaborating on the screenplay for Ernest Hemingway's *To Have and Have Not:* besides taking place on a fishing boat, the film bore no resemblance to the original novel.) Faulkner had a habit of dumping his correspondence in a desk drawer, which he opened on the average of twice a year. He didn't get around to writing my father until May. Faulkner told him "he would like the piece, except the biography part." An essay did appear, but it wasn't until 1945 that Viking Press suggested a Portable Faulkner. Viking Portables, highly popular at the time, were usually collections of a writer's "Best Of," including one complete work and long excerpts of others. This book was different. As the jacket announced, this was "THE FIRST CHRONOLOGICAL PICTURE OF FAULKNER'S MYTHICAL COUNTY IN MISSISSIPPI . . . IN EFFECT A NEW WORK, THOUGH SELECTED FROM HIS BEST PUBLISHED NOVELS AND STORIES." The Portable would amount to a history of Yoknapatawpha County, from Indian times to World War II.

"The job is splendid," Faulkner wrote my father in April 1946, as the book was about to come out. "Damn you to hell anyway. But even if I had beat you to the idea, mine wouldn't have been this good. By God, I didn't know myself what I had tried to do, and how much I had succeeded." The result had to be one of the most esteemed pieces of editing in the history of American publishing, catapulting Faulkner to the literary forefront. For the first and only time, a Portable received a coveted opening page in the *New York Times Sunday Book Review.* Before long the former has-been became an eminence in American letters. Four years later, Faulkner won the Nobel Prize in Literature.

. . .

History was always the lynchpin of his thinking, and certainly his awareness of its complex narrative relationships played a major part in his inspiration about Faulkner. What was history but the literature of what did happen? It was a perception, a guiding principle that he passed on to me.

History became a joint passion. There is a passage that he composed late in his life, in 1984, almost before he stopped writing altogether, that has a special meaning for me. It came from a speech about the writing of memoirs, "Looking for the Essential Me," that he delivered at New York University. (I should remember it: I delivered the response, which I called "Living with a Memoirist.") He talked about watershed moments, "the scenes or episodes after which one's thoughts flow in different directions." Such a moment had occurred when he was fourteen years old:

> I stood alone on the east bank of the Mississippi at Quincy, Illinois, where my grandmother lived. The river was a mile wide and from bank to bank its current moved past me, solidly, relentlessly. A hundred yards from shore a water-soaked log bobbed up and down while being carried onward.

The sight of that bobbing log haunted him, and he couldn't explain why. Later he dreamed about it:

> In the dream I had become that water-soaked log, but somehow the log had eyes to observe what happened on the bank as it was carried along. Still later, much later, I came to feel that I had found a guid-

ing metaphor. The river was history and we were all involved in it as objects on its relentlessly moving surface. It would never turn back.

So, too, history moved in a single direction. But what of events caught in its wash? Did they have to be dragged along in the same inexorable direction? History is our curse. It can also be our deliverance. That log would beach somewhere. Endings, short of death, are always unexpected.

. . .

My father did his best to break free of his radical past. It was not easy, especially in those years of a new Red Scare. He could not yet separate himself from the flotsam that clung to that log bobbing downstream, the detritus of ancient, but still recent, history. At a 1949 party, he ran into an acquaintance, the journalist A. J. Liebling. Liebling was collecting evidence for the upcoming trial of the head of the Carnegie Endowment for International Peace, Alger Hiss. Hiss had denied under oath the assertion by a former Communist, Whittaker Chambers, that he had been a Communist himself in the 1930s—and a Soviet spy—while serving in the State Department. (It was Chambers, remember, who had written that infamous review of *The Dry Season* for *Time*.) The government proceeded to charge Hiss with perjury. What had begun as a dramatic clash of testimonies was shaping up as one of the trials of the decade.

At the party, my father mentioned to Liebling a strange lunch with Chambers at the New Weston Hotel in December 1940, about a year before the publication of *The Dry Season*. Chambers had quizzed him at length about his chapbook—which was all that his slim collection of poems amounted to. He told Liebling that he had described this lunch in his notebooks. The lunch was full of paranoia and talk about Chambers's life in the Communist underground. "He paid for the luncheon, nearly $4 worth," my father had written in his notebook. "It will cost me a great deal more when the article comes out." He was right.

Liebling asked if he could read the entry. The Hiss legal team were trying, among other things, to build a case of psychological instability against Chambers.

In June 1949, my father went to New York to testify in the Hiss trial. Late in the afternoon my mother and I picked him up at the Pawling railroad station—which, the summer before, had been redecorated in premature anticipation of the election as president of a local weekend resident and gentleman farmer, Thomas E. Dewey. My father described the day: how he had read the entry from his notebooks, and how the prosecutor, a large man with a bushy mustache named Thomas F. Murphy, had tried to score points by harping on his deafness. Later, my father had lunch with Alger Hiss, whom he had never met before. We arrived home in time to listen to the CBS evening news on the radio in the kitchen, and hear the commentator, Eric Sevareid, announce, "At the Hiss trial today, a man named Cowley testified . . ."

"A man named Cowley." I was impressed. My father was approaching celebrity.

The next morning I bicycled to see Tony Coates, who was spending the summer in Sherman. Around lunchtime, as I was returning home, I passed a farm and crossed over a small brook. Two boys I'd known at the Sherman School rose up from a culvert. They hurled rocks at me; one barely missed my head. "Commie, Commie," they shouted, "Commie bastard!" I speeded up. The rocks kept coming, but they fell behind me now. I escaped. It was harder to outpeddle the shouts.

. . .

But you might say that my father had begun to outdistance the same sort of shouts. I never encountered them again. In the winter of 1950, while I was at Exeter, he took a lectureship at the University of Washington. The *Seattle Post-Intelligencer,* the local Hearst newspaper, in conjunction with the American Legion and the freelance Communist hunters of *Red Channels,* tried to force his dismissal. The university backed him, and the brouhaha soon died down. That ended the political drama in his life.

My father's life was nothing more subversive now than the championing of American literature. That summer he finished his collection of the short stories of Fitzgerald. I was by now old enough—fifteen—to look forward to sharing my father's discoveries. I gobbled up the photostats that he brought back from the New York Public Library, and let me read. It wasn't a rediscovery equal to his resurrection of Faulkner, but it was discovery enough. Readers were familiar with some of the stories, like "Babylon Revisited," Fitzgerald's elegy to departed boom times. ("The snow of twenty-nine wasn't real snow. If you didn't want it to be snow, you just paid some money.") Others, now famous, like "Bernice Bobs Her Hair," "The Diamond as Big as the Ritz," or "May Day," had languished in collections that had been out of print for so long that they had become unknown: they might as well have been new. Still others had never been collected. I think of Fitzgerald's first Hollywood story, "Magnetism," about a good man and a faithful husband, who happens to be a movie star: he can't keep women from falling in love with him. Or there was the 1930 "Bridal Party," which describes a wedding that was a last gasp of Jazz Age opulence.

Years later, this time in the summer of 1958, my father treated me to another of his literary discoveries, and one of the best, the 1855 edition, the first and purest, of the many versions of Walt Whitman's *Leaves of Grass*. It sold few copies at the time, and (my father reported) "has never been widely read, except in the special world of literary scholars." But the author did send one copy to Ralph Waldo Emerson, then "the most widely respected American man of letters and the man best qualified to understand what the new poet was saying." Emerson thanked Whitman. "I find it the most extraordinary piece of wit & wisdom that America has yet contributed." As my father wrote, Whitman, though often reviled, "would never again be merely a call in the midst of the crowd."

The Fitzgerald stories were published in 1951. That was the same year that my father's revised and expanded *Exile's Return* came out. The book, which he described as "something close to a collective novel about the members of my literary age group," had undergone a notable renovation. The original memoir, published in 1934, had been a book for its time, the early and radically hopeful thirties, in which Moscow seemed for many intellectuals the only dependable beacon in the gathering darkness of the Depression. The 1951 version had a broader appeal, and one from which politics had been abolished. Compare the two endings. The earlier book invokes "the struggles of the oppressed classes all over the world." The key word was "struggle." Those were the days when (if you were like my father) you marched in May Day parades and sang the "International," the Communist anthem, with tears in your eyes. "Artists," my father wrote in that final paragraph, "used to think that the world outside had become colorless and dull in comparison with the bright inner world they so tenderly nourished;

now it is the inner world that has been enfeebled as a result of its isolation; it is the outer world that is strong and colorful and demands to be imaginatively portrayed."

As he concluded: "There are great days ahead for artists if they can survive in the struggle and keep their honesty of vision and learn to measure themselves by the stature of their times."

Almost two decades later, events and bellicose splits had attacked that stature and forever diminished it. By 1951, a reversal had taken place. Like those Soviet photographs in which faces and the bodies they were attached to have been eliminated and the incriminating spaces retouched, the word "struggle" has been dropped from the vocabulary. The 1934 *Exile's Return* ends with an encomium to the future; the 1951 revision, with one to the past, the 1920s. Both books describe New Year's Eve 1930–1931, but how different the occasion, and what led up to it, seems. "It was an easy, quick, adventurous age, good to be young in; and yet on coming out of it one felt a sense of relief, as on coming out of a room too full of talk and people into the sunlight of the winter streets."

In the new age of the Cold War, in an uncertain world that was always on the edge of self-destruction, it seemed safer, and certainly more comforting, to dwell on events and feelings that we had left behind. For the next four decades, my father would stake out his claim to the American literary past, and we are the better for it.

Editor's Preface

Best known as chronicler of the "lost generation" (*Exile's Return*, 1934/1951; *A Second Flowering*, 1973), literary editor of *The New Republic* (1930–1940), and the critic whose *Portable Faulkner* (1946) helped pave the way to Faulkner's 1949 Nobel Prize, Malcolm Cowley (1898–1989) participated in many facets of twentieth-century American literary, intellectual, and political life. His long and varied career—critic and historian, poet, editor, translator, publisher's advisor, writers' confidant, and "middleman" of letters—reverberated almost seismographically with the major moments of American literary history: Harvard in the 1910s, American Field Service in World War I, Greenwich Village and expatriate Paris in the 1920s, radical politics in the 1930s, anticommunist backlash and literary rehabilitation in the 1940s and 1950s, the New Criticism, the Beat movement, the turbulent 1960s, and beyond.

Operating at the center of an extensive web of literary, political, and intellectual relations, Cowley played an often visible and public role in twentieth-century American culture, notably in the interbellum era and the Cold War years. He offered influential interpretations and promoted the reputations of the writers of his own generation (Hemingway, Faulkner, Fitzgerald, Hart Crane, Cummings, Dos Passos) and as advisory editor for Viking Press aided the careers of numerous younger writers, among them Jack Kerouac and Ken Kesey. A public intellectual with strong opinions and a wide readership, he befriended—sometimes antagonized—many of the significant writers and intellectuals of his time. For almost seven decades, Cowley held a place of influence and distinction that has been widely recognized and occasionally challenged but that has not, as yet, been properly documented and evaluated. Though he is often ranked with Edmund Wilson as a preeminent American "man of letters" of the twentieth century, the nature and extent of his significance as critic and public intellectual remain to be fully assessed. This collection of selected letters is intended to contribute to that end. Focusing on his intellectual, literary, and political life, it aims to illuminate the multifaceted scope of his "long voyage" through twentieth-century American letters.

Cowley's epistolary life is bracketed by two of the great cataclysmic events of the twentieth century. In 1917, toward the end of his sophomore year at Harvard, he volunteered with the American Field Service and transported barbed wire, trench floors, and munitions behind the Western Front in northern France. And 1989, the year of his death, saw the end of the Cold War, as the fall of the Berlin Wall signaled the collapse of Soviet Communism as a viable form of state government. In between, Cowley's literary life played out against the background of the conflict between the dominant political ideologies of the twentieth century: democratic capitalism and totalitarian communism. The conflict acutely affected Cowley's career in the 1930s, with the advance of international fascism and the ascendancy of Stalinist Russia; as his letters testify, it remained the dark shadow behind his lifelong literary endeavors.

In the early 1920s, once again in France, he served as an eyewitness to transatlantic modernism, in its many and confusing manifestations, meeting with Joyce, Pound, and Valéry in Paris, consorting with American expatriates (Hemingway, Harold Stearns, Matthew Josephson, Harold Loeb), and enjoying a well-publicized fling with Dadaism (Aragon, Tzara). An expert critic and translator of French literature, in the interbellum years he slowly evolved into the chronicler, advocate, and gatekeeper of what later he preferred to call the World War I Generation. During the 1930s, from his desk at *The New Republic,* he spoke out authoritatively, if also controversially, on matters of literature and politics, in a weekly book page that helped to set and enhance the standards of literary journalism, and in the words of Alfred Kazin, sought "to unite, through his love of good writing and his faith in revolution, the brilliant Twenties and the militant Thirties."

The 1930s had as profound an impact on Cowley's career and intellectual development as the prior decade. As it did for so many others, the economic crisis prompted a dramatic reorientation of his personal, literary, and political life. Convinced that the fate of American writing was inextricably linked to the future of American society, Cowley chose sides. Inspired by the utopian vision that America was marching collectively toward "the golden mountains" of a socialist future, he became deeply involved in public action on the left, and in 1935 helped found the League of American Writers, serving as one of its vice presidents until 1940. The strength of Cowley's convictions made him vulnerable to the lures and pitfalls of the Communist Party line. A fervent "fellow traveler" (he never became a Party member), he allowed himself to be seen as a figurehead of the Party and became deeply embroiled in the factional quarrels between Stalinists and Trotskyites. He was sharply berated, by friend and foe alike, for using his post at *The New Republic* to promote and defend a Stalinist position, and in a series of occasionally strained, defensive letters to Allen Tate, John Dewey, Hamilton Basso, and Edmund Wilson he was forced to account for himself. Reluctant to acknowledge the real nature of Stalinist oppression, Cowley failed to publish his growing doubts and reservations about communism, which he expressed only privately in his notebooks and, more sparsely, in his letters. As a result, he inadvertently ended up in a position of duplicity. This bad faith left him with an enduring "sense of guilt" about the late 1930s that inspired long letters of anguished and honest self-examination.

Cowley's letters tell the story of his (procrastination in) breaking with radical politics, his resignation from the League of American Writers in July 1940 over the issue of U.S. involvement in the war, and the "coup" that took place at *The New Republic* in December 1940, which led to his "deposition" as literary editor (though he continued to write a weekly book page until 1944). They also narrate his painful experiences in Washington, D.C., in 1941–1942, when at the invitation of Archibald MacLeish he went to work for the Office of Facts and Figures, but had to resign after being denounced on the floor of Congress by Martin Dies on the grounds of his (supposedly) seventy-two connections with radical organizations. After what he remembered as "the worst two years" of his life, he resolved to withdraw from politics completely, and to return to his forte: the writing of literary history and criticism.

Cowley's career after 1942 is a double tale, of success and failure. On the one hand, as Robert Cowley's foreword beautifully underscores, it is the story of his literary rehabilitation: on the basis of much-laureled projects like his 1944 *New Yorker* profile of Max Perkins, *The Portable Faulkner* (1946), his 1949 portrait of Hemingway for *Life*, his 1951 edition of Fitzgerald's stories (and, more controversially, his edition of *Tender Is the Night*), the revamping of *Exile's Return* (1951), and—more exceptional in its focus on older American literature—his "rediscovery" of the original 1855 edition of Whitman's *Leaves of Grass* (1959), Cowley rose to prominence and prestige as a leading authority on modern American literature. He was elected to the National Institute of Arts and Letters in 1949 and became a full-fledged member of the literary establishment. On the other hand, Cowley continued to be haunted by the specter of his radical past, which, in a Cold War climate of intolerance and suspicion, reared up at regular and often inconvenient moments—as during his testimonies at the Alger Hiss trials, the notorious Lowell affair at Yaddo, and red-baiting at the University of Washington, all in 1949. Cowley's political errors exacted a heavy price in the years after 1940, and his struggles to come to terms with his sins of the past echo through his postwar correspondence. Through the 1960s and into the 1980s, New York intellectuals and later neoconservatives recurrently charged Cowley with misremembering his past, as did Sidney Hook and Kenneth Lynn in reviewing *The Dream of the Golden Mountains* (1980). Though, in his later years, Cowley frankly owned up to his misjudgments of the infamous Moscow Trials—as he wrote to Lewis P. Simpson in 1983, "I have been blamed for that rightly, no more than I blame myself"—he never succeeded in finishing his memoir of the late 1930s, a book he had started in 1940 and was still working on shortly before his death in 1989.

This book also helps to illuminate Cowley's role as an influential "middleman" of letters, a dimension of his career not fully understood or widely appreciated. As an advisor and director at Yaddo from the early 1930s till the late 1970s, as publisher's scout and literary advisor for Viking Press from 1949 to 1980, as critic and confidant of countless novelists and poets, young and established, Cowley generously offered encouragement and advice, sometimes blunt, always honest and personal. Often he helped open the doors to publication, as when for example—preparatory to persuading Viking to accept *On the Road* (1957)—he managed to place an excerpt from Kerouac's seemingly unpublishable manuscript with *The Paris Review,* much to the author's delight: "Your letter made me feel good, and warm, and better than anything in years," Kerouac wrote to Cowley on July 19, 1955. "It was a lamp suddenly being lit in the darkness, like that. It was a selfless gift of kindness, as well as news of a definite gift being made to me [...]. A

Toast to Malcolm Cowley." John Cheever, the recipient of Cowley's consistent support and encouragement, also acknowledged his indebtedness, writing to Cowley in the early 1950s: "I wouldn't have had much of a career without you and such as it's been it would have been intolerable without your common sense and your magnanimity." Cowley's letters to Nathan Asch, John Cheever, Jack Kerouac, Tillie Olsen, and Ernest Gaines are little jewels of literary criticism; what he did for Kerouac's *On the Road* (1957) was characteristic rather than exceptional.

From the late 1940s on, Cowley's letters reflect his multifarious activities as a "worker at the writer's trade": he lectured at universities and writers' conferences around the country, scouted new talent for Viking, advised on admissions for Yaddo, and served on juries for literary prizes. Through the National Institute of Arts and Letters, of which he was president from 1956–1959 and 1962–1965, and the American Academy of Arts and Letters, of which was chancellor from 1966–1976, he sought to foster a sense of community in the "Republic of Letters." Always, as self-appointed advocate and chronicler, he spoke up in defense of the writers of his generation.

. . .

Among the large cast of his correspondents, four stand out as recipients of his most intimate and revealing letters. Cowley's letters to Kenneth Burke (1897–1993) form the indispensable backbone of any record of his literary and intellectual life. As Cowley observed to Burke, on November 27, 1922, "I came to regard my letters to you as a sort of record not of my life but of my intellectual life, which tacitly we regard as life." Cowley's father, Dr. William Cowley, had been the Burkes' homeopathic family physician in Pittsburgh, and Burke and Cowley knew each other from early childhood, attending elementary and high school together in Pittsburgh. In adolescence they sharpened each other's ambitions for the literary life. They began their long correspondence in the summer of 1915, after graduating from Peabody High School, as Cowley waited for word on a Harvard scholarship at the family farm in Belsano, Pennsylvania, while Burke worked as a bank clerk near his parents' home in Weehawken, New Jersey, before enrolling at Ohio State and, later, Columbia University. Close and intimate literary friends, they maintained a lifelong correspondence marked by scrupulous honesty, unpitying criticism, and deep concern for each other's well-being and careers.

Though they often spent time together in New York City or at Cowley's home in Sherman, Connecticut, physical distance fostered the letter writing habit. Eager to make an impact on their literary times—Burke would become one of the great influential speculative thinkers and critical theorists of the century—they carefully preserved each other's letters, building a unique record of a literary conversation that extended from 1915 to the late 1980s. When in the early 1930s Cowley came to write his personal chronicle of his generation's expatriate experience in *Exile's Return,* he drew on his letters to Burke. At critical or "watershed moments" in his personal and professional life, he would often turn to Burke first for consolation or illumination, as when, for example, in the early 1940s he embarked on a critical revaluation of "the writers' crusade" of the 1930s and probed the root causes of his political disaffection. Cowley's letters (and, more privately, his notebooks) thus served a crucial function in his career as chronicler and memoirist of his own and his contemporaries' literary life. In 1988 Viking Press published *The Selected Correspondence of Kenneth Burke and Malcolm Cowley, 1915–1981,* edited by Paul Jay; it focused on their most poignant moments of friendship and interaction. For this book, Cowley's letters to Burke have been edited from their originals at the Newberry Library in Chicago and may appear in abbreviated or otherwise variant form. Letters that also appear in Jay's book are here marked *"SC"* or "partly *SC*," followed by page numbers. Letters without such designation are here published for the first time.

Allen Tate and Conrad Aiken were also longtime and intimate Cowley correspondents. Cowley first met the southern poet, critic, and novelist Allen Tate (1899–1979) in 1924 when Tate, already a leading member of the Fugitive poets, visited New York City and fell in with Cowley's circle of friends, including Burke, the editor, translator, and biographer Matthew Josephson, and the poet Hart Crane, recently arrived from Ohio, who would soon be a close if difficult friend and companion of both Cowley and Tate. In 1925 Tate and his newly wed wife, the novelist Caroline Gordon, became part of the group that regularly convened in Greenwich Village at Squarcialupi's restaurant and got together for parties at Robber Rocks, the Connecticut home of the novelist William Slater Brown ("B" in E. E. Cummings's *Enormous Room*) and Susan Jenkins, a fellow student from Peabody. Struggling freelance writers in the 1920s, Cowley and Tate debated the nature of modernism and conjointly persevered in their uncompromised dedication to literature and the literary life. In the history of Cowley's voluminous correspondence, the friendship in letters with Tate was second in longevity and intimacy only to that with Burke. It was battered by, but weathered, the political storms of the 1930s, when Tate embraced Southern Agrarianism and Cowley became an impassioned fellow traveler of the Communist Party. In the 1940s the two men found common ground in their admiration of William Faulkner. Tate (conjointly with Robert Penn Warren) supported Cowley's efforts to boost Faulkner's reputation and in the process helped Cowley rehabilitate himself after his political faux pas of the previous decade. Eventually both Cowley and Tate became presidents of the National Institute of Arts and Letters, where they were able to advance their shared commitment to a "Republic of Letters." As his letters testify, Cowley's attachment to Tate deepened over time into an almost brotherly affection. When Tate—who had emphysema—was no longer able to leave his bed in his final years, Cowley's monthly letters made his ailing friend feel he was still a member of a living community of writers; and at an advanced age Cowley took great pains to sit at Tate's bedside in Sewanee.

In 1918, having resumed his studies at Harvard after his stint with the American Field Service, Cowley sought out Conrad Aiken (1889–1973) in Cambridge; they first met at the Hotel Touraine and kept in touch thereafter throughout Aiken's life. Aiken was eleven years older than Cowley and, like Amy Lowell, an influential mentor and role model for a fledgling young writer seeking to make his way in the literary world of publishers, editors, and agents. As far as I have been able to establish, Cowley's earliest surviving letter to Aiken dates from the mid-1930s. They continued to write and visit each other from the 1940s on, Aiken and his wife, Mary, often dividing their time between England (Jake's House, in Rye, Sussex) and a summer home on Cape Cod, for many consecutive years the site of an annual Cowley pilgrimage. Despite their different temperaments—Cowley thriving on literary contacts, Aiken prickly and willfully reticent, resistant to public exposure or self-promotion—the two men got along well. Cowley had a deep and sincere literary appreciation for Aiken's poetry, fiction, and autobiography (he rated his autobiography *Ushant* perhaps his greatest achievement) and proved a persistent critical champion of "our most neglected" American poet.

On Aiken's death, Cowley confessed that, after a literary acquaintanceship of fifty-five years, he had come to regard him as a "father figure."

Among critics slightly older, Edmund Wilson (1895–1972) came closest to acting as a role model. Though they were never close friends, Cowley and Wilson corresponded frequently in the years between 1927 and 1940, when both were connected with *The New Republic.* As early as 1923 Wilson had written a personal note of invitation to Cowley to submit his poetry to *Vanity Fair,* where Wilson was then on staff, but it was only in late 1927 that their correspondence became more regular. As an undergraduate at Harvard Cowley had written a few book reviews for *The New Republic* under Francis Hackett, but his close and long-term connection with the magazine did not start until the late 1920s, after Edmund Wilson had come on board first as an associate and then as literary editor. Wilson was eager to enlist Cowley as a regular contributor: "I consider you one of the best writers in the country," he wrote to him on October 26, 1927. Cowley, for his part, admired Wilson for accomplishing what he himself had not yet been able to do: as he told Wilson on February 13, 1929, "you're the only writer I know who has been successfully leading a double life—that is, who has been earning a living out of literature and at the same time writing good books." In the radical 1930s, a politically more percipient Wilson repeatedly cautioned the younger writer as he plunged into the fray. Cowley respected Wilson's judgment enough to open up to him in his letters, explaining his controversial stances on the Moscow Trials and Stalinist Russia.

In the postwar years, as Wilson moved into broader fields of literary scholarship, history, and economics, Cowley remained focused on the literary and social record of American literature. A barometric chronicler of his literary times—the Boswell of his generation—Cowley first predicted the arrival of a new order of American writers on the literary scene, and then in *Exile's Return* (1934) aimed to define its early achievements. At midcareer, in his essays and reviews, and in his editions of the writings of Hemingway, Faulkner, and Fitzgerald, he sought to establish his generation's connections to the "American tradition." He participated in the postwar revival of the 1920s and revised *Exile's Return* (1951) by divesting it of its radical politics and highlighting its underlying mythical pattern of "alienation and reintegration." Still later, speaking (in Robert E. Spiller's words) as "the Ishmael of his generation," he defended the achievements of the writers of his generation against detractors of various critical and political persuasions. At the end of a long career spanning seven active decades, Cowley would bask in the glow of the burnished reputations of those now "classic" writers he had championed.

. . .

After the expiration of a prestigious five-year Mellon Foundation grant in 1949, Cowley mostly worked as an independent professional writer from his home in Sherman, Connecticut. Though he entered into a part-time arrangement with Viking Press and accepted occasional lectureships at universities, he made his living from his writing. Working at home in the Connecticut countryside, he was an indefatigable correspondent, the writing of letters— to friends and acquaintances, to authors, editors, and publishers—serving as a lifeline to New York and to the larger world of letters. Through letters he built and maintained a vast network of literary friends and professional acquaintance across the United States and, to a lesser extent, in Europe. It may well be that Cowley's mounting deafness—he had hearing problems from the late 1930s onward, and they became more acute by the late 1940s— made him more dependent on letter writing as an instrument of communication with the world beyond Sherman. Writing letters, he observed to the poet Louise Bogan on March 9, 1941, he "sometimes [felt] closer to people [. . .] than if I sat in a room with them and tried to hear what they said with my one good ear." As he observed in 1953 to James Thurber, his partial deafness was perhaps a writer's blessing in disguise, as it kept him from being distracted from transcribing "the inner monologue, [. . .] that unspoken dialogue."

As Cowley's network widened and his reputation rose, the writing of letters consumed a growing part of his weekly working hours: his epistolary output is a significant part of his literary legacy. This selection of approximately five hundred letters represents a small fraction of Cowley's letters. An estimated 25,000 are housed at the Newberry Library alone. Cowley's meticulousness is a boon to his editor: with rare exceptions, he scrupulously dated his letters, a practice in keeping with his intuitive awareness of "living in history." Even his earliest surviving notes to his parents, hand-scribbled at age fourteen from the family farm in Belsano, are dated: "March the—, 1913" and "August 4, 1913." Cowley's early letters are mostly handwritten, with fountain pen or pencil, in a round, bold, legible hand. He began to use a manual typewriter as early as October 1916 and became a neat, punctilious, and fast typist—even the carbon copies he began to make systematically from the mid-1940s onward show remarkably few spelling mistakes or corrections. Occasionally, he wrote shorter notes or letters by hand, and throughout his life (from 1919 till 1983) he kept a series of handwritten notebooks, a mixture of diary (observations on the literary life, writers, and books; entries of honest confession or doleful self-evaluation) and working notes (a laboratory for testing out new interpretations, drafting essays, lectures or tributes).

Cowley's long and rich epistolary life can, for the most part, be remarkably well documented. Because both Cowley and Burke were persuaded at an early age of the singular value of their literary friendship and were so self-consciously ambitious, they carefully preserved their correspondence. As Cowley began to move in wider literary circles, his cast of correspondents expanded. Unfortunately, many of the letters for the years 1919–1929 do not survive. One possible reason for their absence is the disorderly life Cowley and his wife, Peggy, led in those years—in Greenwich Village, in Montpellier and Giverny, traveling through inflation-ridden Europe, struggling against poverty in Jazz Age New York City. Another is that Cowley was not yet in the habit of keeping (carbon) copies. For the years 1920–1940, insofar as their recipients saved them, Cowley's early letters—to notable correspondents like Amy Lowell, John Brooks Wheelwright, Harold Loeb, Allen Tate, Hart Crane, Edmund Wilson, Scott Fitzgerald, John Dos Passos, Newton Arvin, and Granville Hicks—survive in repositories across the United States, and more incidentally in Europe. (Cowley's letters to Tristan Tzara, for example, are in the Jacques Doucet Library in Paris; those to Louis Aragon have disappeared.) Robert Coates hardly saved any letters; most of those to Matthew Josephson were burned in the fire that destroyed his New York apartment in early 1930. As noted, no letters to Conrad Aiken survive before 1935.

Other significant gaps remain. The correspondence files of *The New Republic* for the 1930s do not survive: to save space, the archives were periodically purged by the magazine's business manager, Daniel Mebane, and destroyed or sold for waste paper. As a consequence, most of the incoming correspondence to the magazine was lost, "a holocaust," as Cowley wrote to me on March 1, 1978, "like the burning of the great library at Alexandria." Most of Cowley's surviving outgoing correspondence represents only what was kept by recipients. Much of Cowley's editorial correspondence (only very selectively represented here) was dictated from his *New Republic* office desk and concerns the practical business of running "the back of the book"—soliciting reviews, suggesting cuts and revisions, negotiating rates of payment. The more intimate and more interesting letters sent to trusted friends and correspondents like Newton Arvin, Hamilton Basso, Kenneth Burke, Granville Hicks, John Dos Passos, Allen Tate, and Edmund Wilson were typically written from Sherman. These form the basis for the selection of 1930s letters presented here.

From the mid-1940s onward, Cowley kept carbon copies of almost all the typed letters he sent out from Sherman, now in the voluminous Malcolm Cowley Papers at the Newberry Library in Chicago. The majority of letters in this volume have been edited from these carbon copies; where possible, they have been checked against the originals in other collections (see Abbreviations). Letters edited from carbon copies are marked "cc," in combination with the standard practice of distinguishing handwritten from typed correspondence. Thus, a three-page typed letter edited from carbon copy is indicated as "tl/cc-3"; a three-page letter edited from a signed original as "tls-3"; a one-page handwritten letter edited from the signed original as "als-1." Postcards are indicated as "pc." Editor's ellipses within paragraphs are marked by three dots in square brackets: "[. . .]." Entire paragraphs eliminated are indicated by an indented "[. . .]." Cowley's own ellipses are marked by a series of dots as they appear in his letters: mostly ". . .". Obvious typing or spelling mistakes have been silently corrected, except where Cowley's intent is clearly playful or punning. Throughout, spelling has been brought in line with today's usage (as in "1930s" where the original might read "1930's"). Annotation has been limited to what a general reader minimally needs to know about correspondents and other people, places, and events.

This book is organized chronologically, with titled sections demarking key episodes in Cowley's career, to make a "life in letters." Occasionally, letters have been grouped together by correspondent (Hemingway, Kerouac, Olsen) or by theme or event (Hart Crane's death; the Yaddo affair; the

Fitzgerald revival), for greater narrative coherence. Each section is prefaced by a brief headnote that provides biographical and historical contexts for the letters that follow. Wherever possible, I have preferred to include complete letters, but elisions have been inevitable. Letters pertaining to personal or family affairs (except where they have literary bearings) have been mostly omitted. And with only a handful of exceptions, family letters have not been included. Reports on the weather or the state of the garden (Cowley was a diligent gardener and cherished his pine trees) have mostly been eliminated, as have been passages on such mundane affairs as travel arrangements, directions, or negotiations over reprint permissions, as well as bread-and-butter notes, well-wishings, and birthday greetings. Letters and passages on the trials and tribulations of aging have been kept to a minimum, except insofar as they reflect on Cowley's writing practice and ability. Cowley's wide-ranging literary activities are often represented only in exemplary or suggestive ways: his reports on manuscripts for publishers; his in-house memos for Viking Press; his often meticulously detailed letters of criticism, advice, or encouragement to poets, novelists, scholars, and biographers; the numerous recommendations for writers' fellowships or stays at Yaddo; his voting on candidates for literary prizes; and the many letters concerning National Institute and American Academy affairs. Many of these letters offer invaluable insights into the personal and working relations between editors and writers, the professionalization and economics of authorship, the politics of literary prizes and canon-formation, and the workings of important U.S. literary institutions, from publishers' meetings to honorary societies. They deserve fuller publication at some future time.

The vast majority of letters in this book appear here for the first time. A much smaller number have seen prior publication, often in books now out of print or difficult to locate. Cowley published his correspondence with Faulkner in *The Faulkner-Cowley File* (1966). Here, Cowley's letters to Faulkner appear in their original form, with textual deviations marked in italics within brackets. Part of a long letter to Edmund Wilson, of February 2/4, 1940, was incorporated in "A Personal Record" in —*And I Worked at the Writer's Trade* (1978); it here appears in full for the first time. Harold Loeb quotes some of Cowley's letters from the early 1920s in his memoir *The Way It Was* (1959); Cowley's letters to Hart Crane were printed in

Susan Jenkins Brown's *Robber Rocks: Letters and Memories of Hart Crane, 1923–1932* (1969); and two letters to F. Scott Fitzgerald appeared in *Correspondence of F. Scott Fitzgerald* (edited by Matthew J. Bruccoli et al.; 1980). Donald W. Faulkner included a small sampling of Cowley's letters to various correspondents in *The Portable Malcolm Cowley* (1990); and Cowley's letters to Robert B. Heilman appeared in *Robert B. Heilman: His Life in Letters,* edited by Edward Alexander et al. (2009). All previously published letters have here been edited anew from their originals or carbon copies in manuscript collections.

This selection aims to illuminate the role Malcolm Cowley played as an actor in and observer of American literary life and culture between 1915 and 1987. During his "long voyage" Cowley witnessed key events in cultural and political history, for many decades kept the pulse of contemporary American writing, cheered and critiqued, befriended and antagonized many of the stellar authors of the period, was a sensitive chronicler of major trends and tendencies in literature and publishing, and helped shape the canon of twentieth-century American literature. Cowley's efforts on behalf of American literature were part of a larger movement advancing American literature and American studies in the years after World War II. He reached a larger audience, and so in the end perhaps did more for American literature, than such luminaries as Alfred Kazin and Edmund Wilson. As he observed to James M. Kempf on November 23, 1974, his was an "18th-century ambition to write for the intelligent but unspecialized reader, the audience that Diderot had in mind for the *Encyclopédie.*" The focus of these letters, then, is what Cowley at age eighty-five retrospectively defined as a central theme in his long career as a man of letters: "to celebrate American literature and to defend American writers as a community within the larger community."

In seeking to illuminate the variegated roles of Malcolm Cowley, this selection imposes a rigorous selectivity. Priority has been given to letters that reveal Cowley's stance on literature and politics; offer astute (and often innovative) literary verdicts or appreciations; illuminate his practice and influence as literary critic and historian; evince the frictions and pleasures of his literary friendships; and show him at work as literary gatekeeper, canon-builder, and forger of reputations, as publisher's scout and critical advisor, as cheerleader of new (and older) talents, and as chronicler and memoirist. Conjointly, the letters included here suggest the contours and dynamics of Cowley's journey across the landscape of twentieth-century American letters, offering perspectives on its highs and lows, spectacular sights, and unexpected treasures. A prime criterion for selection has been the literary quality of the letters themselves—for Cowley was first of all a literary craftsman with a poet's sense of language, an artisan of words, and a seasoned practitioner of the art of writing letters.

Abbreviations

✣

Books

AMWH   *A Many-Windowed House: Collected Essays on American Writers and American Writing,* edited with an introduction by Henry Dan Piper (Carbondale: Southern Illinois University Press, 1970).

ASF   *A Second Flowering: Works and Days of the Lost Generation* (New York: Viking, 1973).

CFSF   *Correspondence of F. Scott Fitzgerald,* edited by Matthew J. Bruccoli et al. (New York: Random House, 1980).

CMC   *Conversations with Malcolm Cowley,* edited by Thomas Daniel Young (Jackson: University Press of Mississippi, 1986).

DGM   *The Dream of the Golden Mountains: Remembering the 1930s* (New York: Viking, 1980).

ER   *Exile's Return: A Literary Odyssey of the 1920s* (New York: Viking, 1951).

FCF   *The Faulkner-Cowley File: Letters and Memories 1944–1962* (New York: Viking, 1966).

FL   *The Flower and the Leaf: A Contemporary Record of American Writing Since 1941,* edited by Donald W. Faulkner (New York: Viking, 1985).

PMC   *The Portable Malcolm Cowley,* edited with an introduction and notes by Donald W. Faulkner (New York: Viking, 1990).

RBH   *Robert B. Heilman: His Life in Letters,* edited by Edward Alexander, Richard J. Dunn, and Paul Jaussen (Seattle: University of Washington Press, 2009).

RR   Susan Jenkins Brown, *Robber Rocks: Letters and Memories of Hart Crane, 1923–1932* (Middletown, Conn.: Wesleyan University Press, 1969).

SC   *The Selected Correspondence of Kenneth Burke and Malcolm Cowley, 1915–1981,* edited by Paul Jay (New York: Viking, 1988).

TBOU   *Think Back on Us: A Contemporary Chronicle of the 1930s,* edited by Henry Dan Piper (Carbondale: Southern Illinois University Press, 1967).

View   *The View from Eighty* (New York: Viking, 1980).

WT   *—And I Worked at the Writer's Trade: Chapters of Literary History, 1918–1978* (New York: Viking, 1978).

WW   Harold Loeb, *The Way It Was* (New York: Criterion Books, 1959).

Manuscripts

AA   Archives of the American Academy of Arts and Letters, New York City.

AB   Alan Barth Papers, Manuscripts and Archives, Yale University Library.

AG   Allen Ginsberg Papers, Rare Book & Manuscript Library, Columbia University in the City of New York.

AL   Amy Lowell Papers, MS Lowell 19 (275), Houghton Library, Harvard University.

AM   Archibald MacLeish Papers, Box 5, Manuscript Division, Library of Congress, Washington, DC.

ARVIN   Newton Arvin Papers, Mortimer Rare Book Room, Smith College, Northampton, Massachusetts.

ASCH   Nathan Asch Papers, Acc. 344, Louise Pettus Archives and Special Collections, Winthrop University, Rock Hill, South Carolina.

AT   Allen Tate Papers, Manuscript Division, Department of Rare Books and Special Collections, Princeton University Library.

BOYLE   Kay Boyle Papers, Morris Library, Southern Illinois University, Carbondale.

BR   Burton Rascoe Papers, Rare Book and Manuscript Library, University of Pennsylvania, Philadelphia.

CA   Conrad Aiken Papers, The Huntington Library, San Marino, California.

CB   Cleanth Brooks Papers, Yale Collection of American Literature, Beinecke Rare Book and Manuscripts Library, Yale University.

CC   Caresse Crosby Papers, Morris Library, Southern Illinois University, Carbondale.

CO   Charles Olson Research Collection, Archives and Special Collections at the Thomas J. Dodd Research Center, University of Connecticut Libraries, Storrs.

COLUMBIA   Rare Book & Manuscript Library, Columbia University in the City of New York.

CONTEMPO   *Contempo* Papers, Harry Ransom Humanities Research Center, University of Texas at Austin.

CPS   Chard Powers Smith Papers, Yale Collection of American Literature, Beinecke Rare Book and Manuscripts Library, Yale University.

CS	Carl Sandburg Papers (Connemara Accession), 1898–1967, University of Illinois Rare Book and Manuscript Library, University of Illinois, Urbana-Champaign.
DIAL	*Dial*/Scofield Thayer Papers, 1879–1982, Yale Collection of American Literature, Beinecke Rare Book and Manuscripts Library, Yale University.
DM	Dwight Macdonald Papers (MS 730), Manuscripts and Archives, Yale University Library.
EEC	E. E. Cummings Additional Papers, 1870–1969 (MS Am 1892–1892.11), Houghton Library, Harvard University.
EH	Ernest Hemingway Collection, John F. Kennedy Presidential Library, Boston.
EW	Edmund Wilson Papers, Yale Collection of American Literature, Beinecke Rare Book and Manuscripts Library, Yale University.
FBM	Fred B. Millett Collection, Yale Collection of American Literature, Beinecke Rare Book and Manuscript Library, Yale University.
FOM	F. O. Matthiessen Papers, Yale Collection of American Literature, Beinecke Rare Book and Manuscript Library, Yale University.
FSF	F. Scott Fitzgerald Papers, Manuscripts Division, Department of Rare Books and Special Collections, Princeton University Library.
GH	Granville Hicks Papers, Special Collections Research Center, Syracuse University Library.
GWA	Gay Wilson Allen Papers, David M. Rubenstein Rare Book and Manuscript Library, Duke University Libraries, Durham, North Carolina.
HB	Hamilton Basso Papers, Yale Collection of American Literature, Beinecke Rare Book and Manuscript Library, Yale University.
HC	Hart Crane Collection, Yale Collection of American Literature, Beinecke Rare Book and Manuscript Library, Yale University.
HL	*Broom* Correspondence of Harold Loeb, 1920–1956, Manuscripts Division, Department of Rare Books and Special Collections, Princeton University Library.
HOOK	Sidney Hook Papers, Hoover Institution Archives, Stanford University.
IS	Isidor Schneider Papers, Rare Book & Manuscript Library, Columbia University in the City of New York.

JB   John Berryman Papers, Literary Manuscripts Collection,
            University of Minnesota Libraries, Minneapolis.
JBW   John Brooks Wheelwright Papers, 1920–1940, Ms. 79.1,
            John Hay Library, Brown University, Providence, Rhode
            Island.
JCF   John Chipman Farrar Papers, Yale Collection of American
            Literature, Beinecke Rare Book and Manuscript Library, Yale
            University.
JCR   John Crowe Ransom Papers, Special Collections and Univer-
            sity Archives, Jean and Alexander Heard Library, Vanderbilt
            University, Nashville, Tennessee
JF   Joseph Freeman Collection, Hoover Institution Archives,
            Stanford University.
JK   Jack Kerouac Papers, The Henry W. and Albert A. Berg
            Collection of English and American Literature, New York
            Public Library, Astor, Lenox, and Tilden Foundations.
JP   James Purdy Papers, Yale Collection of American Literature,
            Beinecke Rare Book and Manuscript Library, Yale University.
JM   Josephine Miles Papers, BANC MSS 861107, the Bancroft
            Library, University of California, Berkeley.
KAP   Katherine Anne Porter Papers, Special Collections, University
            of Maryland Libraries at College Park.
KB   Kenneth Burke Papers, Rare Books and Manuscripts, Special
            Collections Library, Pennsylvania State University Libraries.
LAW   League of American Writers Archives, BANC MSS 721242,
            the Bancroft Library, University of California, Berkeley.
LB   Louise Bogan Papers, Amherst College Archives and Special
            Collections, Amherst, Massachusetts.
LH   Lillian Hellman Papers, Harry Ransom Humanities Research
            Center, University of Texas at Austin.
LG   Lewis Gannett Papers, MS Am 1888 (264), Houghton Library,
            Harvard University.
LR   *Little Review* Records, 1914–1964, Archives Department,
            University of Wisconsin-Milwaukee Libraries.
LT   Lionel Trilling Papers, Rare Book & Manuscript Library,
            Columbia University in the City of New York.
MARYLAND   Authors and Poets Collection, Special Collections, University
            of Maryland Libraries at College Park.
MJ   Matthew Josephson Papers, Yale Collection of American
            Literature, Beinecke Rare Book and Manuscripts Library, Yale
            University.

NHP	Norman Holmes Pearson Papers, Yale Collection of American Literature, Beinecke Rare Book and Manuscript Library, Yale University.
NL	Malcolm Cowley Papers, Roger and Julie Baskes Department of Special Collections, Newberry Library, Chicago.
NWW	New World Writing Records, Yale Collection of American Literature, Beinecke Rare Book and Manuscript Library, Yale University.
NY	*New Yorker* Records, Manuscripts and Archives Division, New York Public Library.
POETRY	Harriet Monroe Modern Poetry Manuscript Collection, Special Collections Research Center, University of Chicago Library.
POETRY BUFFALO	The Poetry Collection of the University Libraries, University at Buffalo, The State University of New York.
RES	Robert E. Spiller Papers, Rare Book and Manuscript Library, University of Pennsylvania, Philadelphia.
RH	Robert Herrick Papers, Special Collections Research Center, University of Chicago Library.
RJ	Randall Jarrell Collection of Papers, The Henry W. and Albert A. Berg Collection of English and American Literature, New York Public Library, Astor, Lenox, and Tilden Foundations.
RN	Ruth Nuzum–Malcolm Cowley Research Collection, Newberry Library, Chicago.
RP	Ronald Poteat, private collection.
RPB	R. P. Blackmur Papers, 1924–1965, Manuscripts Division, Department of Rare Books and Special Collections, Princeton University Library.
RPW	Robert Penn Warren Papers, Yale Collection of American Literature, Beinecke Rare Book and Manuscripts Library, Yale University.
RW	Richard Wright Papers, Yale Collection of American Literature, Beinecke Rare Book and Manuscripts Library, Yale University.
SCRIBNER'S	Archives of Charles Scribner's Sons, 1786–2003, Manuscripts Division, Department of Rare Books and Special Collections, Princeton University Library.
TO	Tillie Olsen Papers, Department of Special Collections and University Archives, Stanford University Libraries.

TT	Tristan Tzara Collection, Bibliothèque littéraire Jacques Doucet/Jacques Doucet Literary Library, Sorbonne University, Paris.
VFC	V. F. Calverton Papers, Manuscripts and Archives Division, New York Public Library.
VWP	Van Wyck Brooks Papers, Rare Book and Manuscript Library, University of Pennsylvania, Philadelphia.
WB	Witter Bynner Papers, MS Am 1891 (190), Houghton Library, Harvard University.
WCW	William Carlos Williams Papers, Yale Collection of American Literature, Beinecke Rare Book and Manuscripts Library, Yale University.
WF	Waldo Frank Papers, 1922–1965, Rare Book and Manuscript Library, University of Pennsylvania, Philadelphia.
WFC	William Faulkner Collection, Yale Collection of American Literature, Beinecke Rare Book and Manuscripts Library, Yale University.
WK	Weldon Kees Papers, The Jane Pope Geske Heritage Room of Nebraska Authors, Lincoln City Libraries, Lincoln, Nebraska.
YADDO	Yaddo Records, 1870–1980, Manuscripts and Archives Division, New York Public Library.
YUL	Manuscripts and Archives, Sterling Memorial Library, Yale University Libraries.
ZABEL	Morton Dauwen Zabel Papers, Roger and Julie Baskes Department of Special Collections, Newberry Library, Chicago

The Long Voyage

The Long Voyage

Not that the pines were darker there,
nor mid-May dogwood brighter there,
nor swifts more swift in summer air;
    it was my own country,

having its thunder clap of spring,
its long midsummer ripening,
its corn hoar-stiff at harvesting,
    almost like any country,

yet being mine; its face, its speech,
its hills bent low within my reach,
its river birch and upland beech
    were mine, of my own country.

Now the dark waters at the bow
fold back, like earth against the plow;
foam brightens like the dogwood now
    at home, in my own country.

MALCOLM COWLEY

PART I

Harvard, World War I, Greenwich Village, 1915–1921

Harvard, 1915–1917

A scholarship student from Peabody High School in Pittsburgh and a country boy from Belsano, Pennsylvania, Cowley entered Harvard in September 1915. He was young (he had turned seventeen on August 24), overly ambitious, and rather full of himself and determined to make an impact on Harvard's literary scene. His earliest letters from his Harvard years show his pride in having been admitted to "America's greatest university" and evince an eagerness to participate in Harvard's clubs and magazines. In March 1916 *The Harvard Advocate* accepted three of his poems, and it was not long before he gained admission to the magazine's inner circle; he served on the editorial board in his sophomore year and eventually became its president. He also joined the Harvard Poetry Society, through which he made the acquaintance of Amy Lowell, who would become a loyal if not uncritical literary mentor. Rubbing shoulders with Harvard's elite, Cowley did not rise above the snobbishness and anti-Semitism common at Harvard in those years.

Between 1915 and 1923 Cowley corresponded most frequently with his closest friend, Kenneth Burke, whom he had known since early childhood and with whom he had attended Peabody High. For all their temperamental and intellectual differences, they aided each other in their critical development and whetted each other's literary ambition. Cowley's early letters to Burke—blustering, unsparingly frank, yet deeply committed to a friendship that would last—form an irreplaceable record of his literary times and his emotional and intellectual life.

[NL ALS-10] [SC 10–11]
[TO: KENNETH BURKE]
Stillman Infirmary,
Harvard University
Cambridge, Mass.
Oct. 22, 1915

Dear Burke:

You always knew I was a damn fool, and I am beginning to suspect that fact myself. As you perhaps noticed we beat Yale 41 to 0. Cambridge was full all morning of Yale and Harvard graduates and undergraduates. Tickets for the game were selling as high as $75 a pair—damn fool that I am for not selling mine. The stadium was packed.

When Harvard made the first touchdown, the enthusiasm was wonderful to see, but after a while the matter of making touchdowns grew monotonous. Along with 2,000 other Harvard men, I threw my hat over the goalpost after the game—and lost it. So much for the day.

I don't want to tell you about the evening. It makes me sick to think of it. At the Woodcock I poured everything I could get my hands on down my throat. I drank cocktails, lacrima Christi, Moselle, Burgundy, sherry, champagne, beer, and ginger ale. I kissed two or three girls I never saw before and was rebuffed by more. I was happy. Thank God I was lost to the world before I started puking. Well, I began that at about 2 Sunday morning and continued it for twenty-four hours. And here I am now. I really am not at all proud of myself—for once.

So much for news. Now for a little dissertation. Man alive, there are only three Universities in the United States, and two of them aren't so awfully good. Harvard men can find an infinite number of faults with the University. But those faults, as any of them would tell you, have little bearing on the one shining fact that Harvard is America's greatest university.

If I only had a little time for outside activities, I would enjoy life better here. There is a remarkable lot of good verse written here—principally in the form of free verse and sonnets. There is even a Poet's Club. Just now I am competing in the dramatic club's publicity competition. It is an honor to belong to any of the clubs here. For example one must write a comic poem in German on special invitation before being eligible for membership in the Deutscher Verein. To belong to the Cercle Française, one must act in one of their French plays. Both these two organizations are infamous for booze and smutty stories. I must belong.

The "Advocate" is a remarkably poor magazine, publishing some good poetry. The "Monthly" has a lot of good stuff in it. The atmosphere of the "Crimson" office is invigorating. I would like to get on the staff of all these three papers. "Lampy" is independent in what it says, and is really one of America's best humorous publications, in or out of college. The "Illustrated" is not of much account, but the "Musical Review" publishes original compositions, and articles on Scriabin and on Mussorgsky's songs.

But in expatiating on Harvard I am forgetting my main theme, which is that America's only real universities are Harvard, Yale, and Princeton, of which Harvard is the only one possible for me—or you. You know that the names of Harvard, Yale, and Princeton are closely connected. The reason for this, I have lately discovered, is that the three universities are in somewhat the same connection that Cambridge and Oxford are in. Athletically, they treat all other colleges as outsiders. They have three covered debating meets. They play chess together. The University Press is a combination of the Harvard Press, the Yale Press, and the Princeton Press. Any custom that is successful at Yale or Princeton is sure to be followed here. Salesmen go from one university to another. And all these relations, coupled with the fact that prep school boys like to go to a famous school, have made the three universities what they are.

I have run out of paper.

Mal

[NL ALS-5]
[TO: KENNETH BURKE]
Gore E 13 Jan 26 [1916]

Dear Burke:

[. . .] I had a literary renaissance lately[1] [. . .]. Remember that awfully sensuous poem of mine—"In the Garden"? Distinguished, you told me, for immaturity—if you didn't tell me that, I did. I made over part of it. Here is one stanza:

Ah wonderful starless, moonless night,
Ah night of the blossoming South,
You hide the flower of my delight—
The heavy eyes that my eyes seek;
And the flush that comes and goes on her cheek,
And the warmth of her flowerlike mouth—
Ah the whispering silence of the night,
The starless night of the South.

You can only appreciate how good that stanza is if you remember the stanza I corrected. I renounce such poetry. After writing free verse, there seems to be something gaudy and cheap about this recurrent rhyme of the old lyrics. But I submit the stanza to you as a proof that my diction, even in the old poetry, is slowly maturing.

[...]

[...] I am coming to love the past—to love Oxford and Cambridge. Some of their lustre is reflected to Harvard—I know damn well that Ohio State[2] is free of it. You have heard of the masterful conceit of Harvard men. They all contemn any other college. Whatever big professors they have at Ohio State, they have bigger here. Prohibitionists are free. Boston has a disgustingly sensual night life which would inspire any decadent poet. And remember the inspiration of the place, and its reputation. Even street whores are highly respectful to Harvard men. The whole idea of going to Harvard is a paradox. Normal Americans go to Yale.

[...]

Mal.

P.S. Who says I can't be uninteresting?

———

[NL ALS-9] [PARTLY *SC* 18–19]
[TO: KENNETH BURKE]
The Harvard Union
[late January 1916]

Dear Burke:

I remember when I used to have stages—the vulgar stage, for example, the bored stage, the stage of love for the country, the stage of new theories of poetry, U.S.W. Now dammit I'd usually contrive to get a whim which you had already experienced. [. . .] Now I have revenge. You have been brazenly passing into my states of mind. You began to be vulgar—I exulted. You show a love for the country. I exult more. Finally you realize the inexpressibility of everything. I have been realizing that poignantly for the last month, and have had times in the past when the general inexpressibility of what I felt made me as desperate as some Latin Quarter Impressionist.

You want me to destroy your letters. We will compromise. I don't want to destroy them. Some day you might be famous. Your letters might be worth anything from $1.00 to $1.75 a piece. I might be damnably poor and want to sell them. Take another instance. You might fall out of literature and want to console yourself with the thought of your former ability. You will probably change your mind sometime in any case and want to read them again. Now if I were a tactful friend, I would tell you that I had destroyed your letters, and then file them away in some drawer. But I am not tactful. If either you or I had ever shown too much tact in our dealings with each other, we would have remained mere acquaintances. So I am telling you the truth. I am going to bundle your letters and file them away in a drawer—perhaps in two or three drawers.

You have been insulting me up and down lately. If I had more time, we might begin a contest in vilification. But such a contest would be against my dignity [. . .]. So I will merely write you one little ode. It is a poem combining all the best qualities of Henry James, W. S. Gilbert,[3] Rabelais and Charley Hill.

> Social lion, dull recluse,
> Tesselated hypertruse.
> Baudelaire's hypotenuse,
> Libidinous nonpareil—
> Sentimental formulator,
> Mysoginistic masturbator—
> Shit—O Hell.

[. . .] There is a crowd which is usually willing to enter into argument. We have, for example
An idealistic humanist
A defender of the double standard

A fellow who wavers between Orthodox Christianity, Unitarianism, Deism, Agnosticism, and Indifferentism

A skeptical Hedonist with a philosophy of negation—(High sounding words to describe me)

[. . .] With such a crowd we can occasionally have interesting discussions. I am occasionally lonely. I am sometimes forced to associate with Jews. But as long as I can talk—and I am naturally the best talker in the crowd—I am happy. [. . .] I should think that you would do better to get a job in New York than to go to Ohio State. Columbus is an unthinkable town and lacks a good library.

Mal.

[NL ALS-4]
[TO: KENNETH BURKE]
Belsano Pa. July 21 [1916]

Mon cher Burke,

[. . .]

450 pages of *Buddenbrooks* read.[4] Mon Dieu, what a colossus of fiction! I could write a whole letter about it—not that I am wild about it; just that the characters are as interesting as the people I meet, and much easier to understand. Isn't he good on the art-degeneracy theory. I think I am even a whole generation beyond little Hanno. For generations and generations our family has nourished artists, musicians, drunks, degenerates, insanity, and worst of all the religious spirit.[5] I ought to be a regular genius. [. . .]

[. . .]

Mal.

[NL TLS-1] [PARTLY *SC* 31–32]
[TO: KENNETH BURKE]
Russel 19, Nov. 1 [1916]

Dear Burke:

[. . .] Gad, I've been going through a kissing epidemic lately [. . .]. But anyway I have the girls for you whenever it suits you to come here and get them. Irish, you know, and the Irish don't have much social standing in Cambridge. Their male relatives are awful, true muckers. But then the girls themselves are so obliging; so affectionate. They kiss you readily at first, but my especial flame won't kiss me any longer. You see, I gave her a lecture on the dangers of indiscriminate kissing. I was out there last night till twelve o'clock; therefore the many mistakes and erasures today. All this proves is that you will find, if you come up here,[6] a bunch of rather agreeable youngsters to initiate you into the *ars amoris* as practised at present.

I am a snob—hurrah, a true snob. What pleasure it gives me to think that I can cut absolutely anybody I want to. What a feeling of superiority it gives me to have my boots blacked by the janitor of my Gold Coast dormitory instead of by an ordinary Dago. And just think—I hope to be invited to join a fraternity, and I am going to refuse—not because I don't want to join a fraternity, but because this one isn't good enough for me. Could anything be farther from the boy who used to associate with the social outcasts of a socially outcast highschool[?] I bought a fancy vest yesterday.[7]

[...]

Mal

The *Advocate* and *Monthly,* Burke, are cowardly, castrated sheets, but nevertheless there has been poetry at Harvard in the past, and there is poetry there now.

Cowley to Kenneth Burke, October 24 [1916] [NL]

[NL ALS-4]
[TO: KENNETH BURKE]
Russell 19, Dec. 14. [1916]

Dear Burke:

[. . .] Amy Lowell said that Snow[8] and I were the only two poets who wrote modern verse among the members of the Harvard Poetry Society. Snow's poem that called forth the comment follows:

The Pearl Diver
I dived, a bronze streak
Through the green depths of my mind,
To discover hidden pearls.

Mine was:

The Aesthete Discusses Kisses.
Like fox-grapes after the first frost,
Lucy's kisses are wholesome, and fragrant,
                    and a little tart;
Clara's sweetest kisses are sticky and
                    ostentatious,
Like shoeblacking.

The occasion was a meeting of New England Poetry Society, jointly with the Poetry Society here. New England Poetry Society is composed of Amy Lowell and her enemies. Chief of the opposite faction is probably Mrs. Marks (Josephine Preston Peabody). Formerly Amy was supported by Fletcher (John Gould Fletcher[9]—*Goblins and Pagodas*—but he has left Boston for the present[)].

Last night the poetry of the Harvard Poetry Club hopelessly outclassed that of the semi-professionals, except, I must admit, Amy. But as she said, most of it could have been written twenty years ago. A large part of the New England verse should never have been written.

And my Lord, those women were ugly. Amy stood with her back to the fire, puffing away at a Fatima, and looking very much like a volcanic mountain in eruption. Accent on mountain. She advised me to smoke Alfred Dunhill pipes. She had found, she said, that the vulcanized bits didn't bite through.

Sometimes as I look at her, I seem to see dear Miss Ruswinkle.[10] I like Amy, and because I like her, I am beginning to like her poetry. Besides her, there was an interminable bore, a man who wrote poetry about Calamity, five horribly ugly hags, and Amy's shadow. Amy's shadow is a woman, a fat woman, but Amy dwarfs her. Over in one corner, the mountain-queen would be haranguing a half dozen subjects and enemies. And in another corner, her shadow would be saying the same things to two or three.

Result—

> *To a Middle-Aged Poetess.*
> You catch the iridescent moments of life,
> Full of peacock-feather emotions—
> Intricate, that is, and vain, and changeable
> And set them down carefully in words,
> Merely to bore us to death.

Did you send anything to Jim?[11] I sent three poems, two sketches, and a tale.

[...]

And Burke, I have forgotten an important piece of news—important that is, for me only. My sterility has disappeared. I have found a subject of infinite interest. I am writing my own history. Try it yourself. No worry about form, no worry about plot, simply the almost unadulterated pleasure of sitting in an easy chair, a pad on the knee and a fountain pen in the hand, and scribbling interminably. Interminably—already I have written eleven pages.

R.S.V.P.

Mal.

[NL ALS-2]
[TO: KENNETH BURKE]
Russell 19, March 21 [1917]

Dear Burke:

[...]

Was taken on to the *Advocate* last night at a banquet. Good time. I wished that you were going on with me. We might turn it into a jolly sheet then in a couple of years, if tradition didn't prove too strong.

You know my Restoration Gentleman sonnet,[12] which you didn't answer even with a line, even with a protest against cribbing your verse, was a grand success here. Batty Wendell[13] said it was "literature." Bob Hillyer[14] gave it glowing praise in French last night while he was drunk.

And others likewise when sober. But I'm sterile now as a dried-up water hole.

[...]

Mal.

Dear Burke:

Just now I should be writing you a sentimental letter, because I am in just the mood to write a good one.[15] But mood does not supply effort. I'm packing. Did you ever do anything more sad than pack? Old letters, old poems, old faces. [...]

I received one most flattering commission. When one is leaving, one is always roundly flattered. Try it and see. To return to the subject, Freddie Schenk[16] gave me a soft-soaping to the head of the ambulance in America, and he asked me to write him letters about my experiences, the understanding being that if they are good enough, he will publish them. He has done that for several already.

Kirk[17] wrote me a letter of recommendation. In the note which accompanied it, he seemed very near to self-pity. Listen:

"I wish to God I were about twenty. I feel the blood and sauerkraut lust and would let some if I could do so."

That "God" there has a peculiar force coming from a professor. It seems to confess the full absurdity of having a man of Kirk's brains teaching stupid children in a stupid high school. A little more conceit and another university than Ohio State, and he could have been a Copeland.[18] Now dislike Copey if you care to, but Copey is almost a parent of present day American literature. Our writing today is done by Harvard men, and Harvard men of prominence in literature always take Copey's course. Yet he has no different mind, and only a little better rounded personality than the tyrant of the "Peabody."

[...] Please break your recent custom and write immediately. You shall be called upon to write me often when I am in the field. Oh shucks, don't I talk about it seriously? Perhaps I have a right to.

Mal.

France, 1917

From May until early November 1917 Cowley served as a volunteer camion driver with the American Field Service in northern France, transporting ammunition, barbed wire, and trench flooring, and reporting on the war and life behind the frontlines in letters home. As he observed the low morale among French soldiers—two regiments had mutinied—he found his national pride surfacing: "The chief thing I can see is that America is the best country in the world," he noted to Burke on June 20; "France, Germany, and England are simply busy cutting each others' throats. The fabled universal education and culture of France is fabled. But what is not a mere fable is their courage and endurance." On leave he sampled the sights and delights of Paris—bookstores and beer, wines and flirtatious *midinettes*—and explored the places in the Latin Quarter that would become the renowned hangouts of expatriates in the 1920s: the Café du Dôme and La Rotonde. Cowley's wartime letters from France constitute his first performance as chronicler of his generation. He reported on his discoveries of French literature and developed the "spectatorial attitude" that he posited as a hallmark of his generation's experience in *Exile's Return*. He wrote poems on his war experiences for *The Harvard Advocate* and reports for the *American Field Service Bulletin* and the *Pittsburgh Gazette* (his first income from writing). His letters to Burke and, less frequently, to his parents comprise an invaluable eyewitness account of his time on the Western front.

[NL ALS-3]
[TO: JOSEPHINE HUTMACHER COWLEY AND
DR. WILLIAM COWLEY (PARENTS)]
Somewhere in France
May 20, 1917

Dear Mother & Father,

In the last letter I told you I had changed to the Transport Service. Today I am in camp about fifteen miles behind the lines.[19] There are two aeroplane depots nearby—will the censor cross this out—and every minute almost we hear the buzzing of the Nieuports overhead. The German planes don't dare to venture around here.

There are eighty of us in camp—a section of thirty-six—chiefly from Cornell; several officers and non-commissioned officers, and the forty in our section—eighteen of whom are young buds of Yale's chief preparatory school—Andover. The Cornell men leave tomorrow and will soon be at the front.

[...]

We were out today to practice in the five ton Pierce Arrow trucks we are to drive. I did alright until I tried to back, and then managed to set the car wandering all over the road, much to the delight and fear of the spectators. But the work is going to be interesting.

Two days later—

I drove a car into the ditch yesterday, and it is still there. Otherwise I have been as happy as any well-fed person. We talk a great deal with the poilus, and receive sidelights about French life that I think the average tourist misses. But I am afraid I won't get out with this section.

Somehow there is too much to write. . . . Just as I wrote that sentence, platoon two was called out for driving. We went about six kilometers to an aviation camp. I drove, thank goodness, a little better than yesterday.

This evening, Will Irwin, reporter for *The Saturday Evening Post*,[20] called at the camp. You can read about us, probably, in the magazine. He is a rather mussy looking man who gave us some inside lights on the situation.

We hear a great deal of cannonading tonight. Probably you will have read, by the time you get this letter, that the French gained six hundred yards of trenches near—or—, or that a desperate German attack was repulsed. But all we know of it is that distant booming that sounds altogether like thunder, and a constant hum of aeroplanes.

Love to everybody,

Malcolm

If you ever get to feeling really generous, send me over a magazine to read—*Poetry, The Little Review,* if it is still running, *The Seven Arts,* or something of the kind. Also the last issue of the Sans Breeches[21] if there was one. ,

Cowley to Kenneth Burke, June 7, 1917 [NL]

[NL ALS-4] [SC 43–44]
[TO: KENNETH BURKE]
T.M.U. 527, June 26 [1917]
Convois Automobiles
Par B.C.M. Paris

Dear Ken:

· Me voici still in camp and destined to stay here for some months more. I read by the official communiqués that there is pretty violent fighting just north of us—German counterattacks, etc. And so, although we are loafing just now, there is work in store.

Bob[22] is to be chauffeur for one of the staff cars at the training camp. [. . .] Man, I was in for it at first. I was perhaps the poorest driver in camp, and everybody came to regard me as a general nincompoop. But a little judicious profanity and a great deal of silence, and above all our old friend Time have worked very well together.

As for cultivation of the region above the eyes, I have a splendid anthology of French verse from 1866 to 1888. There are Rimbaud, Verlaine, bawdy Baudelaire, all of whom I accept at the current estimate and don't think much about. There is also a certain Léon Valode whom I like very well indeed. Catulle Mendès, the same.

Apart from the French, I have read about half of that well known bastard piece of Dostoieffsky's. [in margin: "Tiens: *The Idiot*"] I thought it quite insane at first, but after three hundred pages I begin to discern the chaos becoming vertebrate. A novel by W. L. George—*The Strangers' Wedding,* I liked, and also [Arnold] Bennett's *These Twain.* In addition I was flattered to find that I could not swallow the same author's potboiler, *Buried Alive.* I think the difference between us two crystallizes about Dostoieffsky, however. In the quarrel between the latter and Turgenieff we should have taken different sides. But don't forget. Our differences, great as they are, are really insignificant compared with our similarities. I never realized that poignantly until I was left alone with fifteen jeering puppies from Andover. I think in a way we sometimes came as near to perfect frankness as one can get. You rather spoiled me for making friends. Since I left Pittsburgh, Bob is the nearest to a real friend I have had. [. . .]

[. . .]

You wonder no doubt how near we get to action. Twenty seven hundred yards. In other words, our farthest north is the third-line trenches. But considering that shells carry some twenty-four miles the third-line trenches are quite far enough. We take to dugouts occasionally, but Lord! there's not a chance of anyone's getting killed. Of course we all hope to get slightly wounded so that we can receive the croix de guerre, but no one has the slightest hopes of the croix de bois which is the meed of damned fools in any other arm of the service.

We have a wonderful opportunity here to learn the language (which sounds like a prospectus). Some of us are even trying to learn it. Even the dullest soak in a little, and one can hear ribald Chicagoans wandering about camp shouting at every opportunity.

"C'est beau ça. N'importe. C'est la guerre."

Moi aussi have studied a little. I am now perhaps as fluent as you were last summer. The lack of further progress is due to ignorance of Esperanto, Greek, and applied perversion, I am quite sure. Otherwise I should have to lay it to my own stupidity. But tiens! nous verrons. Now at last I know merdre, cocu, con, ordure, foutu, grand morceau de cul de cheval, and a few such expressions which your nasty mind had acquired il y a une année. I talked crops, forest fires, and express trains with a camion driver this afternoon for two hours.

For God's sake, write oftener.

Mal.

[NL ALS-4]
[TO: JOSEPHINE HUTMACHER COWLEY AND
DR. WILLIAM COWLEY (PARENTS)]
Our new address
Section–Groupe Américaine
T.M. 526 Peleton B
Par B.C.M. Paris.
June 30, 1917

Dear Mother and Father:

No letter from you now for three weeks. Have you forgotten me altogether, or has there been a mistake in my mail?

Life is very uneventful here in training camp. I have made only three trips up to date. There is some spice about them. One hears German shells whistling quite a bit, especially recently. One reads that they have transported a great many troops from the Russian front. A regiment which passed us yesterday on its way to forty-five days rest. They had captured three hundred and fifty German prisoners. These, we were told, were in very bad shape, and subsisted on black bread. If even the soldiers in the front line are underfed, the Boches must be in a bad way: But don't believe that the war is almost over. The United States is going to be in it head over heels before it ends. And you should be very glad that I am in a comparatively safer arm of the service. A great many of the fellows here are hunting something more risky. At the end of six months, twenty to fifty out of our three sections will go into aviation.

At our other camp we had plenty of opportunity to visit the men of the Lafayette Escadrille. They are a moderately wild bunch. The last time I came to their camp, half of them were getting drunk, and the other half were playing roulette. One, a nineteen year old from Iowa, was chased on his second trip out by seven Boche planes. One bullet went through his chest right above his heart. He went unconscious in the air. Just before he hit the ground, he came to and shut off the motor. The next time he regained consciousness, he was being carried back in a stretcher while heavy German shells were falling all around him. Four of our boys were over to see him at the hospital.

[. . .]

I have been picking up war relics. At present I boast of a German rifle in splendid condition, a French rifle, two bayonets, eight clips of German cartridge for my rifle, a shell basket, a French belt, and various other impediments.

Now please write me oftener.

Your loving son,
Malcolm.

Tell Ruth[23] I have her picture here with me, and look at it often. [. . .]

[NL ALS-4] [PARTLY *SC* 45–46]
[TO: KENNETH BURKE]
[American Field Service in France]
Note Bene
Section-Groupe Américaine,
TM526, Peleton B
Par BCM, Paris
July 4. [1917]

Dear Ken:

[. . .]

Since it suits you and Jim to take my trip merely as a holiday, please do so. (This is the sentence indicating great defiance.) And (this is the hissed *aside*) you won't be more than a hundred miles from the truth. Of course when I started, I was in the midst of a little throe of militarism. But since I'm over here, I find that as a camioniste I'm just as much of a slacker as Jim. The only difference is that I'm in a country new to me, doing work not very uncongenial—you know I always did like big lumbering things like camions—having my daily routine very faintly spiced with adventure, and above all seeing the events that are going to dominate the history of the world for the next century. [. . .]

[. . .] And you—I think you could write your novel about the world as it was very well indeed under the roar of the cannon that are destroying all the old order of things. For all we Americans realize too little that at the end of the war every nation—yes, even the United States—will be too exhausted in men and money, too much in need of quick recuperation, to go on with the old happy-go-lucky state of affairs. We Americans are fighting for personal liberty, and yet after the fighting is over, out of sheer need of efficiency, we shall have to forego it. And if the Germans win—oh gawd. In the captured portions of France, they are making even the little children work in the fields from five in the morning until seven at night. Imagine a regime like that for the world.

You asked for poetry about Paris. I gather that you are more anxious for dope on Paris. Well, in the first place, although whores are thick on the rue de Montmartre, they are much thicker around the Place de l'Opera, Café de la Paix, Boulevard des Italiens, etc. The great street for sporting houses is the rue St. Augustine.

The second hand book shops along the Seine are there just as described. But the Seine itself is in size something like the Youghiogheny.[24] Yet there is a great charm about all French rivers. They are all so swift, silent, and deep.

As for French women, as a rule they are much less pretty than American girls. But there is a certain class in Paris—the midinettes—who can dress according to the advertisements. [. . .] Bob and I met two of great charm on de Boulevard de Clichy very near La Chaumière, a pretty little cabaret where original music is played and original parodies recited. The whores there laugh tremendously, but my knowledge of argot is too limited to catch most of the allusions. Along the exterior boulevards, one meets few unprofessional women, but these two were exceptions. [. . .]

Today is July Fourth, and we have twenty-four hours' leave.[25] The amusements are of all sorts—tilting at a water bucket, egg and spoon races, Arab dances by some Tunisians stationed nearby, Arab music—unearthly stuff; fencing, baseball, a banquet, and champagne—beaucoup, beaucoup. Champagne, by the way, has gone up in price since the war and is now from three francs to eight francs fifty the bottle at our canteen. We drink a great deal of it. Of pinard we get a daily ration—a demi-litre. All this talk about temperance at the front—balls. Aviators are drunk half the time, and troops on repos make it a point to consume as much pinard as they can the first throw—all very far from talk about our fourth of July.

I have written two or three poems since I arrived; all quite gory. You ask me to write about the Luxembourg at dusk. I should do that, but only in its place. And its place is not fifteen miles from the front.

[...]

Another mélange in a couple of days.

M.

———

[NL ALS-3]
[TO: JOSEPHINE HUTMACHER COWLEY (MOTHER)]
Section-Groupe Américaine
T.M. 526 Peleton B
July 6, 1917

Dear Mother:

[...]

You seem to think that the camion service is dangerous. Guess again, Mamma. It holds even fewer risks than the ambulance. In fact I feel like a bally slacker for being here while men are dying like flies in the trenches just north of us.

[...]

About the war, everyone feels that it will last almost—well perhaps two years, perhaps only one. But it is pretty certain that the American conscript army will see service. And it certainly will be welcome. One doesn't realize in the United States what three years of war means to a people. I am enclosing a poem I wrote about the soldiers. You can't imagine how tired and stinking and dirty the war has made the best of them.

[...]

Your loving son,
Malcolm

Poilus

Regiments at a time pass through our village
And filthy with the caked mud of the front
They snore along the roadside or else hunt
Their quarters in dank cellars or in stables

And then, forgetting their abandoned tillage;
Their mining or their clerking or their law
They sleep like beasts together on the straw.

[NL ALS-4]
[TO: KENNETH BURKE]
Section-Groupe Américaine
TM 526 Peleton B
July 24. [1917]

Dear K:

[...]

We have been busy as the deuce lately. The papers tell of violent Boche attacks nearby. I know that the thirty-five odd miles of front which the American camions help to supply have kept us on the march. Our unhappy loafing of the first month is over.

[...]

I must [...] disappoint you in regard to my reaction from the war. Unlike Coningsby Dawson[26] I have not yet seen piled corpses. Here behind the lines one gets more the pictorial effects of war. On our night trips to the front, we can see star shells rising everywhere, and artillery flashing against the clouds very much like distant lightning. Once during a French attack, we saw the barrage fire from French 75's twinkling all over a wooded hillside. One could easily reduce it to miniature as fireflies in a twilight hedge.... Then there are German aeroplane raids. First come great blazes of red fire at the front as a warning. Then searchlights—hundreds of them—commence sweeping the skies. Sky rockets follow. Once the anti-aircraft guns catch sight of the Boche, they open up with shrapnel. Once in a while there will be the dull boom of dropping bombs. A hospital two miles from us seems to receive especially favorable notice from our German friends. Three nights ago one of its barracks was reduced to kindling wood and sausage meat—I mean the patients.

[...]

[...] I really am coming to think that this conflict is about as clear cut between right and wrong as any war ever is. The Russian revolution destroyed the last sound German argument. But all that, of course, is stale stuff. If I were you, however, I should believe the *New York World* with all its lies, sooner than *Staats*.[27]

[...]

One proposition. *Le Journal* publishes each day French war stories which have no American copyright. Why not translate them and sell them to American papers—this much I suggested before—n'est ce pas? [...]

M.

[NL ALS-5] [SC 49–51]
[TO: KENNETH BURKE]
Section-Groupe Américaine
TM 526 Peloton B
July 31, 1917

Dear K.

[...]

I thank God constantly that I have crossed the water. Not that my soul has been transformed with wonder, but just that I have been drawn out of my fixed orbit. Now I have the desire to wander, and think of Russia and Spain, and American lumber camps and wheat fields. There are so many sides of life which no one can afford to miss. Paris is one, and a dose of horrible, hectic Greenwich Village is another, and Chicago yet another.

At present, too, everyone should serve his time on the Western Front. That is the great common experience of the young manhood of today, an experience that will mould the thought of the next generation, and without which one will be somewhat of a stranger to the world of the present and the future. That is the real reason I should advise you to get over here.

No doubt you want to know the effect of the war on France. Downess—a very drunken aesthete who has been here often—says that the France of today is discouraging. There is not much intellectual life remaining. What there is seems to have accepted the war as the normal state of things, as you will gather from the stories [from *Le Journal*] I am sending you. All love stories are a result of permissions, or of letters from marraine to filleul.[28] Plays take the war for granted. Everyone longs for peace, but it seems so distant a possibility that no one dares to make it the condition, the background, of any literature. The most successful art exhibit recently was "Les Humoristes et la guerre."

I thought of writing you once that France as an average is no more intellectual than the United States. *La Revue de[s] Deux Mondes* costs three francs, and is not on sale everywhere. The other magazines are often childish; many of the people remind one strongly of our own familiar ditch-diggers, the Sicilians. But on the other hand, a little reading of French poetry reveals a difference. Just as a matter of statistics, the Librairie Delagrave compiled an anthology of poetry from 1866 to 1914. None of the contents were bad; some, of course, were unsurpassed in English. The collection amounted to 2,200 pages of fine print. As I said, just as a matter of statistics, could that be duplicated in England, or in America, or in both?

Again there is the matter of artistic innovation. As one reads from Baudelaire to Mallarmé, one gets the origin of all English verse movements, averaging ten to twenty years later. A lecture of Amy Lowell's on Vers Libre and the strophe—I saw where she stole it; from an exercise for his own methods written by Gustave Kahn in 1897.

Of course art movements would show an even more startling sameness in their origins, but of these I know little.

Yet I ask you for American magazines. Somehow I am not French, for all my intellectual admiration. I should like to be French before I come home—temporarily, of course. I think of living in a garret in Montmartre and of enlisting in the French artillery. But that is not yet. Meanwhile, remember that I am writing you frequently even if you don't get all my letters; that I have received all your letters up to June 28 (3), and that I am anxious for more.

M.

———

[NL ALS-8]
[TO: KENNETH BURKE]
[American Expeditionary Force]
Sept. 11, 1917

Dear Burke:

No news; bored to death. The camp has turned into a gambling hell; a true hell for me, because I have no money left to gamble with. [. . .] Christ,

I'm demoralized. [...] Anything, death included, is better than lying around camp, and hoping for enough money to play seven and a half. All this sounds suicidal and heroical, but I haven't decided on anything yet. If I do enter aviation or anything of general danger, I shall come home first.

As usual I can't escape publication. Piatt[29] put a couple of bad poems of mine into a bulletin published by the American Field Service, thereby advertising my shame. The *Poilu,* one of the innumerable French trench publications, is to publish an American page, and I shall contribute to it. Also—imagine—I am going to send a ballade to *Life.* Here it is, in all its naked shame.

> *We Held Great Argument*
> After a tardy sun had set,
> We four untried lieutenants chose
> The back room of the town *buvette,*
> And there, until the next sun rose,
> We each discussed in meaty prose
> The meaning of this firmament
> And all such things that no one knows
> That night we held great argument.
>
> It was no trouble to forget
> Dress and society and pose;
> The girls we knew; Marthe and Odette,
> Marie and Madelon and Rose;
> We did not give a thought to those;
> Or other things; War, or the Rent
> Our lives; the price of furbelows.
> That night we had great argument.
>
> A crimson sun rose like a threat;
> We drained our glasses and arose;
> Roused the good folk and paid our debt,
> And rode off northward towards our foes.
> Our feckless youth was at a close,
> And hell grew nearer as we went;

Yet life seemed good to us—because
That night we had great argument.

A German trench on the Aillette
Next day cost half our regiment,
And all my jolly friends—and yet
That night we had great argument.[30]

[...]

A Rebours[31] is Wilde exposed. Huysmans is terrible in his hates and his disgusts. Authors he doesn't like, he gives to his servants for toilet paper. He likes childish things, however; the pictures of Gustave Moreau; Poe, Baudelaire; trite English expressions because they are English. He demonstrates the banality of the whole decadent movement. There is some difference between him and the youth who smokes Fatimas instead of Camels because they are "distinctively individual," but not much. He is the sort of person who would have one wife in Turkey and eight in Massachusetts; who would read Arsène Lupin in the original French, if he is English, and Victor Hugo, and Dumas; he is in other words, an ass.

We roll at three o'clock and so I shan't trouble to fill another page.

M.

––––––––

[NL ALS-5] [SC 53–55] [PMC 469–470]
[TO: KENNETH BURKE]
Section-Groupe Américaine
TM 526 Peloton B
Oct. 9, 1917

Dear K.:

[...] Section 133 went up to a little advanced park some 800 meters from the lines, and underwent a severe bombardment, during the course of which one man had his hand shot off, and another was wounded in the body and the leg. A French ambulance section refused to bring back the wounded on account of the shelling, so the section chief got them in his Ford. For this, the first deed approaching heroism in the service, there was a meeting. Also a couple of our French captains received the Legion of Honor. [...]

In your letter you also asked for local color. I can give you that, and plenty. Zum beispiel, we leave camp at four o'clock on a rainy, windy afternoon, and go to the immense park at B. to have our camions loaded. The bearings are loose on the fan, and the steering gear doesn't work well, but then it is much too cold to leave the seat, so we smoke cigarettes and wonder what is going to happen in the night. The trip is for O—another of the dépôts avancés—some 1,500 meters from the lines.

That night we left the park at six. One of the other camions broke down after a two-kilometer ride, and that caused us a two-hour wait. When we finally climbed the hill above the Vesle, the night was so black that I was reminded of G. A. Henty[32] and the mythical nights through which his trappers and Indians used to crawl toward Fort George and Fort William. I rode on the dashboard and called out whenever Root[33] ran too near a ditch. Once I didn't call out in time, but we crawled out on first.

After that I had a great poetic emotion and lines kept running through my head like

"The jolly star shells rioted"

and

"And in the valley a river of mist"

or

"While a cold cynical moon looked down"

The cold cynical moon actually crept in just at that point, for in the battle of the cold wind and the cold rain, the cold wind proved the stronger.

How conventionalized the night seems now to me, after reading thousands of war diaries. [. . .] The only fresh note about it all, I think, was the barracks when we got home. From the outside these are plain wooden buildings, but inside at night, their shadowy length makes them as mysterious as ancient caves. Side by side a dozen lives—individual lives—go on. Some sleep, some sing, some read, some play cards. After five months of such a life, they all become at home in it, so that the requests to shut up or to shade a candle are merely perfunctory. In a way everyone has become a stoic, believing that no one else can harm him. And that night at two as we came in exhausted to drop into bed, one man was just getting up to go on guard while those others were still playing cards.

M.

[NL ALS-4] [SC 55]
[TO: KENNETH BURKE]
Royal Palace Hotel
[*Paris,*] *October 29, 1917*

Dear K.—

My letters to you for the past two months have been, as you have realized, masterpieces of futility. Things will change, however. I have things to talk about.

There was the offensive for one thing. For two months we had been expecting it. Toward the last the Aisne Front was clogged with batteries—all sizes. Then finally they opened up. Sixteen days and nights we had our ears battered and our sleep disturbed. Brother Boche opened up too, giving us lots of thrills at our different parks. Then one evening the relics and the prisoners came drifting back. The latter had strange stories. They had spent five days without food under a barrage [of] fire. At first they were trading gold watches and field glasses for loaves of bread.

Right in the middle of all this my time of service closed, and with a dozen others I packed up and came to Paris. [. . .]

In a way the decision of the next week will be very important in my life. If I should go into aviation, I should really be making a sacrifice, for even if I came out alive I feel I should be out of place at the end of the war. If I should go to Italy, I think that would start me on a career of roving. Finally, though, if I return to college for half a year I may find the old life again—and the old life a little broadened. This, I think, is what I shall do.

[. . .]

Mal.

[NL ALS-4 PENCIL]
[TO: KENNETH BURKE]
[Paris] [November 2, 1917]

Dear K:

The first time we saw her, Gaby said that she was an artist's model. This afternoon when we met again, it came out that her modelling was a thing of the past, though she still painted a little. Gaby is a whore. Moreover today she is a whore in trouble, because the poor girl's business is halted for three days on account of menstruation.

We talked it over, at the Café du Dome, losing half the pathos of it in the bière blonde and the petite gateaux. In a way Gaby's misfortune is fortunate for me, since I have always enjoyed being on simple terms of friendliness with a whore. Rather I have imagined it as a dream. And beside the American street woman, French cocottes are such a superior type. This one insisted that I give her a book I was reading—*Bubu de Montparnasse.*[34] Invited to a show, she suggested *The Merchant of Venice,* which I declined in favor of a revue at La Pie qui Chante or the Moulin de Chanson. And she approved of *Jean-Christophe,*[35] the one book to which I am giving my approbation today.

Anyway we have it all arranged that tomorrow [. . .] we will have tea at her studio together; dine at some funny Quarter restaurant, and in the evening go to a Montmartre cabaret. All that we would do today, but it is November 2, the day of the dead, and even the cinemas are closed.

[. . .]

November 3—

Well Gaby gypped me. I waited at the Café du Dome from three to four, enduring the stares of her sister harlots and consuming innumerable English cigarettes which cost me two francs the twenty. At last in desperation I marched over to the Bureau des Postes and telegraphed Marthe[36] that I'd meet her tomorrow.

Across the street at the Café à la Rotonde [*sic*], it is more gay, and there I went. Harlots and greasy Serbian artists passed me laughing. I even talked with a couple of Russians, who by the way, impressed me not at all favorably, though God knows they were interesting enough. [...] Both of them painted a little and made verses.

A la Rotonde, they told me, was very famous before the war. Serbians, Russians, Japanese, and Americans all made it their rendez-vous. Compared with those times it is sad these days—evidently, sad is merely a relative term in the Latin Quarter.

I can imagine you spreading yourself among the Russians and the whores of the Rotonde, combining always a desire to impress with a little contempt, because they take themselves so seriously. For my part I am awkward and aimless, and only blunder luckily into such places.

M.

Harvard and Greenwich Village, 1917–1921

Reluctantly fêted as a returning war hero, Cowley was back in Pittsburgh in December 1917. While there he began to render his war experiences in sketches and poems. On his way back to Harvard, he stopped over in Greenwich Village, where he explored bohemian hangouts like the Hell Hole and the Working Girls' Inn. Effectively, Cowley spent the years between 1918 and 1921 alternately in Cambridge and Greenwich Village, consorting with the crowd associated with the Provincetown Playhouse, and trying to launch himself as a poet and reviewer. As a Harvard undergraduate he placed work in the pages of *The New Republic, The Literary Review*, a weekly supplement to the *New York Evening Post, Poetry*, and *The Dial*, and, seeking out Conrad Aiken and Amy Lowell, e. e. cummings, and Van Wyck Brooks, began to build a network of literary friends that would serve him throughout his career. Making the acquaintance of Aiken in Boston was a catalyst: it propelled him away from Boston's literary conservatism and toward a distinctly modern poetry and triggered his ambition to launch a "post-bellum *Sansculotte*" to promote the new poetry produced by himself and his friends.

In the early months of 1919 Cowley fell in love with Peggy Baird, a Village artist he had met around Christmas 1918; soon the two were "living in sin" in her apartment at 107 Bedford Street. On August 12, 1919, they were married. Cowley's parents were shocked to learn he had wed a Village bohemian and never quite took to Peggy. The marriage was rocky from the start. While

Cowley was studying at Harvard, Peggy, a dyed-in-the-wool *bohémienne,* remained in New York. Not always faithful, she contracted syphilis and infected her young husband. Both underwent treatments at a New York clinic and were pronounced cured, but the experience (recaptured in Cowley's poem "Free Clinic") rankled. The few letters that survive from this period are silent on the topic.

Oscillating between Harvard and the Village, Cowley led a hectic, hungry, and disorderly life—perhaps as a result, much of his correspondence for the years 1919–1921 does not survive. Back at Harvard in the fall of 1919, he carried six courses in a single semester in order to graduate in 1920. He became president of the *Advocate* and cultivated his contacts with Amy Lowell, attending evenings at her salon, and inviting her to attend an evening with the Harvard Poetry Society. On graduation he returned to the Village, feverishly enjoying himself, scraping together funds through haphazard reviewing and coming closer to starvation than he imagined possible. Eventually he applied for a job as proofreader with a New York firm, adducing as his qualification his experience on the *Advocate* and providing Max Perkins of Scribner's as a reference. Eager to advance himself in the literary world, in late 1920 Cowley offered his services as reviewer to Van Wyck Brooks, who had recently launched *The Freeman*—with typical bluster, he presented himself as "the whole of the youngest generation of critics," giving Harold Stearns and John Dos Passos as references.

By the spring of 1921, repeated discouragement, persistent poverty, and his ongoing struggle to maintain "the integrity of an undisturbed life" (as he put it to Burke on June 19, 1920) made the prospect of a stay abroad increasingly tempting and urgent. Amy Lowell was a loyal supporter—"You are one of the people whom I count on for the future. See that you do not disappoint me," she wrote to Cowley on May 10, 1921—and provided introductions to Ezra Pound and the critic Jean Catel in France. By June 1921 Cowley was ready to turn his back on an American milieu that offered few opportunities to an ambitious young critic committed to the modern—as he told Burke on the eve of his departure: "nothing can save me now short of a new life."

Again I am one of the lick-the-Germans-first crowd. [. . .] Being in Pittsburgh seems a matter of "How did you like France?" "Did you see the real
stuff?" etc. etc. This being a bunk hero sickens me.

Cowley to Kenneth Burke, December 7, 1917 [NL]

[NL ALS-5]
[TO: KENNETH BURKE]
219 Wallace Bldg. Pittsburgh, Pa.[37]
Dec. 14, 1917

Dear K:

[. . .] To switch to the perennial self, I have turned vers librist just to
show that I can write the nasty stuff. I even do it well. Listen to this, for
example:

Ostel 1917.

By day
The town basks in the sun like some Aztec ruin.
There is quiet in the trenches nearby; quiet and
        strained watching.
The crumbling walls of the village are without
        habitant.

Everything changes with nightfall.
Hooded camions rumble up the street in convoy.
Out of holes in the ground come tired old men to
        unload them.
Artillery caissons strain towards the batteries
        and trains of pack mules
Down from the trenches stumble figures shrouded
        in mud.
Continually there are starshells
And the nervous hammer of machine guns
And ambulances.

Men work and talk; eat and dig graves;
The slow dawn comes, and everything disappears
Machines and men and animals
Like old-fashioned ghosts
At midnight

By day
There are only the dead.
And like vultures
The aeroplanes circling over them.[38]

[. . .]

Out of deference to your feelings, I refrain from war talk. Though if you had normal hearing, 20-20 vision, were six inches taller, and weighed fifty pounds more, I imagine you would be no more indifferent to the war than to a keg of powder on which you were sitting—especially if the fuse was lighted. [. . .]

Also the recent allied reverses impress me. I can't bear the idea of Germany's winning on a basis of spying, lying, and buying newspapers, atrocities aside.

M.

———

[NL ALS-6]
[TO: DR. WILLIAM COWLEY (FATHER)]
218 West 15th St.,
Jan. 25, 1917 [1918]

Dear Popsie:

[. . .]

I have certainly had a good time since coming here. The Greenwich Village section of New York provides as cheap living as one could desire. Also there are places of amusement like "The Working Girls' Inn" otherwise known as the Columbia Hotel, the saloon where John Masefield[39] worked when he was in New York, and the Golden Swan, called familiarly the Hell Hole, both of which places are the rendez vous of magazine writers, poets, dramatists, anarchists, and Tammany men belonging to the Hudson Dust-ers. Last night I ran into Gene O'Neill, a sailor who turned playwright, and who is at present one of the new wonders; Terry [Carlin], a labor agitator, and Hippolyte Havel, editor of the *Revolutionary Almanac*. They were discussing the relative merits of Paradise Street in Melbourne, Paradise Gardens in Liverpool, and Christ Street in Sydney, which they called the three wildest streets in the world. I didn't doubt them, although I thought that the Hell Hole was wild enough.[40]

[...]

You had better send me another five dollar check when you write me. I might need it.

Your loving son,
Malcolm.

And write soon please.

[NL ALS-4] [SC 61–62]
[TO: KENNETH BURKE]
Randolph 20, Cambridge Mass.
Feb. 25, 1918

Dear K:

[...]

Last Thursday night, I dined with Conrad Aiken. I should have written you immediately afterwards. In a last analysis, he scared me. He is a development, a successful development, of most of my present tendencies. Married and with two children, quiet, a bit shiftless, he devotes himself to the writing of remarkable poetry that doesn't sell. He agrees with me on a great number of points. In one, he surprised me. Without knowing a bloody thing about Wilkinson,[41] he is an enthusiastic admirer of the latter's two novels. He said that after reading *The Buffoon*, he was possessed by a fear that W. was the sort of man who writes only one book. *A Chaste Man* he wanted to send to all his chaste friends.

Aiken's own *Jig of Forslin* is something I wish you would read. It is a study in form; its verse is infinitely modified with each of the hundred moods. Aiken strung it out on a Freudian basis, which accounts for the large number of rapes, suicides, whores, vampires, etc., etc.

Coming home from a play the next night, I met Tim Whittlesey, a young poet who had been at Jouaignes with me. [...] Whittlesey took me to lunch at the Signet, a Harvard literary club, where I met the sons of various millionaires, who talked about going horseback riding just before tea. I think he will nominate me and fail. But the whole thing shows that my snobbery, which I thought I had conquered, still is quite powerful.

Nothing more. I just manage to be busy, and to go out evenings. Boston I am finding quite a tolerable town. There are saloons where Bass ale and Guinness stout are both on draught at a nickel a glass. There is a large Italian quarter and one Bolsheviki joint. So I can get along. But I wish they'd ship the Millay[42] family up here.

I don't want to discuss the German language except to say that my cheap sneers at it are really justified. Just now I am studying French literature. As I go along, I see brought out clearly what a consciously developed medium is the French language. Germany never had a Rabelais in the XVI century to introduce all sorts of Latin words, Greek words, technical words, manufactured words, or a preciose school in the XVII century to purify it; or an eighteenth century Voltaire to make clarity a deity. The chauvinistic attempt to make German a "pure" language, and the retaining of the declensional forms, are not the characteristics of a language of the highest development. Chaucer's English was structurally as advanced as modern German. And there was no imperially supported set of professors to forbid it to dip into the rich stores of other languages. Grillparzer[43] has been compared to Racine. My God to read the two at once! G. is wildly beautiful at times, it is true, but his diction sprawls all over itself like an adolescent elephant.

                                                                          M.

[NL TLS-2]
[TO: KENNETH BURKE]
Randolph 20, March 9, 1918

Dear K:

[...]

At the Common Cupboard (the girl who runs it is pretty; I go there often now) anyone who has lived in Greenwich Village and knows the name of the now defunct Romany Marie's,[44] is a little of the hero. Just to think of these miniature Greenwich Villages inhabited by Russians and Jews and Russian Jews, by syndicalists, socialists, anarchists, and those who like to think they are syndicalists, etc., and by students from the nearest university come to see Life. Gad they must be springing up all over the country these days. The Common Cupboard sports a Russian poet named Dave Gallick, an English poet named Bill King, various masculine and feminine social workers named Yesnofsky, Kasnofsky, Trechnofsky, and Davis, and in addition the charming proprietress, Rose Sullivan, de qui je suis épris.

Night before last I went to the New England Poetry Society with Foster Damon,[45] Royall Snow et alii. Amy Lowell has left it; Josephine Peabody Marks now presides. Her pet aversion is Aiken; my pet aversion is her. Afterwards I simply had to get drunk; a paper on the relation of painting and poetry by Mrs. Perry finished me. So Foster took us all to the Harvard Club and I did. Very morose yesterday. Royall Snow has joined the S.A.E;[46] is a wild, fruity aesthete in theory and a damned bourgeois in practice. Foster on the other hand is a very sound poetic workman outside of his decadent ideas. I am to dine with Aiken again this Wednesday.

Are you sending your White Oxen?[47]

M.

[NL TLS-2] [SC 62–63]
[TO: KENNETH BURKE]
Randolph 20, March 17, 1918

Dear K:

[...]

Last Thursday night I went to dinner with Aiken again. We had a charming conversation afterward—all about How To Sell Poetry. Kennerley[48] is a crook, although an altruistic crook. Macmillan doesn't accept anything unless he—she, rather, expects to sell two thousand the first year. Sherman French are damned Jews, but they have gone out of business, and a young altruist has taken their place. And so on and so on. I was entranced.

Aiken himself is now criticizing poetry for *The Dial*. He rips everybody to pieces; you must read him. He is getting so unpopular that he can't get anything published in a magazine. He decided to let his fortunes rise or fall with those of Edmund Brown of the Four Seas. The latter I went to see recently to get some books to review for the *Advocate*—a good graft, by the way. Young Brown has a head full of grand schemes: a popular literary weekly, a new *Yellow Book* for the Back Bay folk, etc., etc. So at least there is some literary gossip in this town.

[. . .]

God damn it, I wish the *Sansculotte*[49] would take down its breeches and get to work. There is a tremendous need for a magazine, not merely wild and Hebraic like *The Pagan;* not run by a temperamental woman, like *The Little Review,* and not inspired with nothing but love of the masses and other dirt, like *The Liberator,* but which would print decent stuff by (us) new men. Aiken would come in without hesitating. So, I think, would all the other contributors we need. And the money necessary is such a small sum.

The way A. puts it, there is a quiet conspiracy on now between Harriet Monroe and Braithwaite,[50] with the aid of almost all the critics, to stifle the new poetry at birth. For such rot as the cheap Semiticism of *The Pagan,* I don't blame them, but when it comes to passing Aiken and John Gould Fletcher and William Carlos Williams over in silence, it becomes too much. Gad, it sets me off toward writing criticism myself. But the best sort of critical encouragement is a magazine that publishes.[51]

And oh gad, read *Al Que Quiere!* (Williams). It is the framework and the suggestion of much good poetry, much excellent, superexcellent poetry. Only it is merely the framework.

Tell Sue[52] to write, Goddamnher. Tell Ellis[53] to go nut himself on a briar bush. I'll buy him a bottle of absinthe if you think that will hasten the end.

M.

[NL TLS-3]
[TO: KENNETH BURKE]
Randolph 20, March 25, 1918

Dear K:

[. . .]

Just now, quite in opposition to your verses, I am reading Pope, and meditating the establishment of a new classicism. Anybody with sufficient self-conceit to convince the world could do it. No more wild flights of fancy, no more exaggerated ego; a certain attendance to form, involving a perfect abandonment of 'poetic' language, inversions, etc., etc. Believe me, it can be done. I see clearly now that classicism isn't a matter of any particular rules, but just of Rules. Some of the maxims of the new classicism would be directly in opposition to those of Pope. However it still would be classicism.

[. . .]

Now to business. I am begging a favor from you. I can't get Tailhade's poems here except at the library, and they are good, damned good. Also Jammes. I suppose you read Ezra Pound's article in *The Little Review*.[54] Now I want you to make a pilgrimage of New York for me, and at any price get hold of *Poèmes Aristophaniques* (Tailhade), and *Le Triomphe de la Vie* (Jammes). Also if you can, get the *Oeuvres* of Rimbaud, which are in one volume. Everything is published by the *Mercure*. Rimbaud and Tailhade have a tremendously dirty view of life. Holy Thursday, Tailhade sees in the form of the faithful, who, by the beans of Lent, are now afflicted with constipation. Or again:

Des petits enfants—dirai-je masturbés—

He is a poet of barrooms, old women with ulcers on their anuses (though this particular observation was made by Rimbaud), old men whom the exhilaration of a shower bath sets running after little girls, the third sex, and other matters of the sort. All these are quite legitimate poetic subjects, and he executes them with power. Of Jammes, Amy spoke enough. Withal both Tailhade and Rimbaud write poetry that is not at all rough or uncouth. Rimbaud likes quatrains; Tailhade sonnets with a fifteenth line appended.

At any rate I beg for the books.

M.

[NL TLS-1]
[TO: KENNETH BURKE]
Randolph 20, April 27, 1918

Dear K:

[...]

I intended to write a criticism on Edna St. Vincent M. The reason I'm not is that on rereading, I decided definitely that the woman has been tremendously overrated. 'Freshness,' 'charm'—she borrows her freshness from the modern Celts and her charm from Sara Teasdale.[55] Continually she is talking baby talk. She thinks she has ideas. They disappear with a little analysis. "Renascence" is pantheism grown senile; the "Suicide" tells us that after laying down our task, we shall be punished by not being allowed to take it up again—a strikingly original conception, that; "Interim" says simply enough that she is sorry because someone has died, but must keep on eating and drinking nevertheless—perhaps the most poetic of all her ideas. And in her short lyrics, which should be absolutely perfect, she does not always attain perfection—she rouses at midnight, for example, "the falling fire to tend" just like any freshman at Vassar. She has magic, but it is rather thin, tarnished magic.

All of this does not prevent Edna from writing excellent sonnets. But most assuredly it takes a discomforting load off my mind.

[...]

M.

[AL TLS-1]
[TO: AMY LOWELL]
219 Wallace Bldg., Pittsburgh, Pa.
Nov. 1, 1918

My dear Miss Lowell:

I was very sorry to hear that you were ill, and just as glad to find out later from Foster that you were recovering safely. I also wish to congratulate you on your ability as a salesman. You have sold the impossible—namely three of my poems to Harriette Monroe.[56] She offered only twenty dollars, which seems niggardly, but no poet seems able to make his own terms—with one conspicuous exception.

Can Grande's Castle[57] was bully, especially the Bronze Horses.

And that is about all I have to tell you, except for the fact that I start out for camp this Thursday, to try for an artillery commission.[58] Germany looks to be on her last legs, and they are only leg-substitutes, so I mayn't be gone long.

Thanks again for your help,

Sincerely,
Malcolm Cowley

Released from service, Cowley lingered for some months in the intoxicating mood of an extended soldier's leave and plunged headlong into the distractions of Village life. A member of "the proletariat of the arts," as he recalled in *Exile's Return,* he subsisted on scanty meals and borrowed money, enjoying the hedonistic life and jeopardizing his health. He suffered badly in the epidemic of Spanish influenza, one day fainting in the street and realizing he must find a job. In the early months of that "long furlough" of 1919 he fell in love with Peggy and moved in with her in Greenwich Village. He found employment as a copyreader at *Iron Age Catalogue* and sought to establish a name as a poet outside the narrow circuit of Harvard's literary magazines. His first success came when, in the spring of 1919, he carried a poem to Margaret Anderson and Jane Heap, the editors of *The Little Review,* then established at the top floors of a red-brick bow-front house on West Sixteenth Street.[59]

[NL ALS-3]
[TO: KENNETH BURKE]
107 Bedford Street, New York City
June 10, 1919

Dear Kenny:

[…] Here in the city, I've been consoling myself with a backyard consisting of one potato, three rose bushes, a spirea, and a Spanish onion. Also three cats: Guinevere, Lilly May, and our newest and largest addition: Mister. He is yellow and sleek and amorously inclined; Lilly May has grown vain and washes herself continuously.

Lionel and Dorothy[60] are talking of going to Chicago. They remain loving. A publishing house, God knows which one, gave Dot $100 advance money on her unfinished novel, and it was spent riotously, the riot even involving Peggy. Meanwhile I was getting drunk with Christine and a bottle of Dago Red: very exciting evening. There was an attempted murder in front of our house last night, the attempter was Jim Cook, a gunman, who emptied his revolver and was attacked in turn. Much shouting and screaming; no fatalities, no arrests. *The Dial* published my third criticism (one I wrote last December);[61] there will be another, or rather 4 more, in the next issue. Cowley rampant.

Clara Tise has come to live in our house—you know, the illustrator—and Peggy is acting as her agent, collecting a royalty of 20% on the proceeds. We are both of us on the make; rush about all day; write an hour or so at night; and spend the remaining two hours before bedtime in floundering deeper into debt. [. . .]

[. . .]

Mal.

[NL TLS-1]
[TO: KENNETH BURKE]
107 Bedford Street, New York City,
July 8, 1919

Dear Kenny:

[. . .]

Several little exciting events have happened around the Village. Most interesting to you, perhaps, Matty[62] visited me Sunday night [. . .]. Chiefly Matty came to discuss poetry, and to tell me how good my verse was and how much like his.

New York is a wide-open town. Men in uniform now get liquor just as if they were honest citizens. Honest citizens order sherry, and get a brown liquid with a chaser for twenty-five a glass. But who ever heard of a chaser with a glass of sherry? The old crowd still hangs around O'Connor's; I broke the glass door there on "Prohibition" night, but fortunately no one informed John as to the identity of the culprit.

Above the eyes, I am a dead man. A little drink, a little sex; kaffeeklatsch and nine hours work a day for $42.50 a week; all that is the round of my existence. [. . .] I am still reading *Madame Bovary* occasionally; also the *Confessions of J. J. Rousseau* and *Coriolanus*. Also the *Tribune*, the *Call*, and *The New Republic*. And God I am dissatisfied with life. May be up in 3 weeks. Apologies for not writing. Mal.

———————

[NL ALS-6] [SC 68–70]
[TO: KENNETH BURKE]
Belsano, Pa., Aug. 30, 1919
[encircled: Pittsburgh from Sept. 4 to 9]

Dear Kenneth:

I received your Lines Written in Dejection near Weehawken on the Occasion of Receiving a Letter from a Friend. Ah! What a delightful Early Romantic title! What an interesting Neo-Romantic style! After a year of polite nothings, you reverted to form and spoke the sad, sad truth—which I never would have spoken. But you only spoke part of the truth. Here is the rest of us.

We have not lost the faculty of talking to each other. If we had anything to say, we could still say it—anything such as we once mumbled for hours. We haven't got it; measured by our ideals of adolescence, we are failures. [. . .]

We are both failures. Not on the basis of the work we have done, which is Promising, as anyone would tell us; rather because we have been caught up in the machinery of life. For two years or so you will be in what Mr. Harold Bell Wright[63] would call the Valley of the Shadow. In the same mail that brought your letter, I had an almost parallel communication from Peggy. She is having her troubles and discouragements and depends on me to carry her through. Little Does She Know that she is leaning on a Hollow Reed. [. . .]

We are failures in each other's eyes, that makes us uncomfortable. However we can still seek out some sub-Matty, who won't see through us and who will admire us as accomplished litterateurs. And I believe that the literary companionship of our respective wives[64] is just about on that order, which is a cruel thing to say and for God's sake don't repeat it. But such companionship—as far as writing and discussing the universe goes—won't satisfy us forever. Someday we are going to be able to talk again, and I think that the thing which now makes us uncomfortable is the high standards of past discussions. We haven't those things to say today; the platitudes stick in our throats.

But my solution of the matter isn't so drastic as yours. I don't know how much faith you have left in me, but I still believe that you are going to pull through. And if either of us becomes a success—even in his own eyes—our relationship can get back on a more comfortable basis. Meanwhile beer and poker and kaffeeklatsch; smuttitudes on married life, and discussion of salaries. I have a great feeling for institutions which you lack; our relationship had become institutional in my eyes, and even if I knew quite well it was hollow, I refused to speak. Now I suggest that we leave it on an institutional basis for a little while, counting on the chance—which is a good one—that it will swing around. Personally I don't feel capable of cutting apart from you. It would be too much of a blow at my self-respect. However if that is what you want, don't answer this, and we'll meet in a year with a fresher outlook.

Mal

[. . .]

[NL TLS-1]
[TO: KENNETH BURKE]
24 Mt. Auburn St., Cambridge, Mass.
October 23, 1919

Dear Kenneth:

[. . .] College is all that I hoped of it. Not intellectually, I mean; the advantages are physical and economic. I live in a charming little room with green painted walls and a student lamp—furnished, maid service, $7.00 a month. Meals at the Signet, at the Union, at Memorial averaging $1.25 a day. No leisure, but at least comfort, and assurance that my next meal will be waiting for me at six o'clock with a napkin ring beside my plate, a waiter at my elbow, and a flood of dull conversation sweeping over me, soothing as a bath in Lethe.

[. . .] A few tugs from Pegasus, tethered in the closet with a pile of dusty books, but the household cat will purr him to calmness.

College has incidentally been a study in *snobisme*, with myself as one of the principal actors. When I returned everyone seemed to hesitate a little before speaking to me. After all, you must know, I had been entangled in shady dealings . . . there were whispers of a woman. But my greetings were so artless and frank, my heartiness so aggressive that really . . . and I am once more a member, even though humble, of the Ruling Class. My dreams become circumscribed—Pegasus vs. Peggy, and a horse was never a match for a woman; he can fly but she can f. . . . 'I have a wife etc.'

[. . .] Now that Peggy is gone,[65] leaving a little more free time, I expect to write you oftener. I grow more attached to you as time goes on, not so much as a person as ideas. Seeing you I become inarticulate, puffing stolidly and wondering what to say next. Here in Boston, however, I hold many imaginary conversations. We are failures at twenty-one, but more and more I am emphasizing forty. At forty we shall be Somebodies, n'est-ce pas? Mediocrity never struggled harder than with me; its victory is still far from assured.

Mal.

[NL TLS-3]
[TO: KENNETH BURKE]
88 West Third Street, New York,
June 4, 1920

Dear Kenneth:

Joe Gould[66] is sitting behind me telling Peggy how he plans to go to the farm of the Self Masters tomorrow and be given free board. I hadn't seen him for two months; he was evidently a little afraid of me and always managed to come in while I was away. He has grown a T-shaped moustache and beard, is very thin, and seems to be straining even nearer to insanity. He was almost the medium of my making friends with Estlin Cummings; we met on the street and commiserated ourselves about Joe for half an hour. That day I had decided I must become more than an acquaintance of Estlin's; people who are producing anything are so rare in this town. [...]

These are details. My mind moves torpidly like a lizard in a stagnant pool; it attaches itself like a wood louse to the rush of events, trying to merge itself in the news of the Wood campaign, writing Youtellems for the *Journal,* anything to make thought less immediate. . . .

And so back to the letter after a dinner at Black Annie's, vin compris. This fonetic inglish of yurs is alright and DONT think imaking fun of it when i in this manner But others have tried it also and a use of large caps and a clever spacing on the typewriter like you know what; any forty a week fortyaweek forty count em 40 I count em copyreader can do it or any agency man with a fester of cortical matter under his kelly—yes i have noticed estlin cumMINGS hisself

> this
> but   is   eas
>   too   y
>   he
>   sang.

The letter meanders on over this nice white paper. I have discovered the secret of writing poetry—the fifth or sixth secret of writing poetry, I mean. You sit at the typewriter and let your subconscious run away with you. If your subconscious is running far enough and fast enough you produce pearls like this:

And then the quarrel over breakfast at eight fifteen

the hurry of the trip to the subway while the hands of the clock
        of the tower of the building of the Metropolitan Life In-
            surance company of the greatest city of the greatest country—
            God's country you know it

race past, like the Bronx express.

Or else in a more serious vein:

O tin alarm clocks exploding simultaneously in hall bedrooms
      from the Battery to Yonkers from coast to coast and agen-
      cies in all large foreign cities!

O explosive clocks you are very evidently the symbol of something.

But tonight my subconscious lags lamentably behind my typewriter, deflating itself between the clicks. [. . .] And now behind me a group forms gradually—the frances giffords, the minaloys, the Karl Kahlers, the peggys and duncans. They drink; the group identity is poured out of a bottle of sherry at two dollars behind a cellar door. And now they turn to gossip; the group focuses on Katherine Tyng—do her ears itch a[s] she psychoanalyzes herself in her Bedford street bed? My ears do ache, my stumick aches, my head vomits on this paper.
. . . . and the sun came up pustulently pimpling a brick wall . . . and probably the title of your opus nextum—"Vastitudes and Immensenesses."

[NL TLS-2][PARTLY SC 72–73]
[TO: KENNETH BURKE]
88 West Third Street, New York City,
June 9, 1920

Dear Kenneth:

In my pocket at present is a long letter which I am mailing you more for documentary purposes than for any other. To a certain extent it represents the history of an evening. I started it at eight o'clock; very bored and with nothing to say. People and booze drifted in; at intervals I returned to write a paragraph, each a little wilder than the last. And when it was finished, I could not even dare a signature.

And yet since that time there have been a great many things I have wanted to tell you. [. . .] The crowd that surrounds me is almost entirely different than the one that circulated when you left. At present the most assiduous visitor is Frances Gifford, a yellow-haired little roughneck of uncertain sexual—but not homosex—proclivities. Then there is Carl Kahler, an abstract painter. Do you know what it means to be an abstract painter? I don't, except that you make queer marks on canvas that don't represent anything except an emotion, and live on an allowance from your wife, who is in Paris, while you make love to the abovementioned Gifford. Charles Duncan is another abstract painter, only he supports himself by a membership in good standing of the signpainters' union. All these people are mentioned somewhere in the vastitudes of the accompanying letter. We go up to Haverstraw on Sundays and I fish for legendary trout in streams whose chief quality is their wetness.

I repeat that I have a great deal to tell you, but a certain inertia keeps me from hammering these recalcitrant keys. A proposition about Life; one about Art. Art first. I want to start a school with you. We might call it The Courve, as your manufactured word seems to express the school about as well as any. It exists in the fourth dimension; in other words in the time factor in measurement. Up to this time, practically all the motion expressed in art has been the motion of the object; the motion of the observer and its curious effects remain practically unwritten and unpainted. Also double motions and triple motions, as, for example, a subway express passing a local while the posts seem to stride backwards at a terrific rate.[67] Or the unrolling of a landscape like a reel of film. Or the queer going sour of a sound as your train moves away from it. My next poem will be concerned with a trip from New York to Pittsburgh; I shall dedicate it to the Pennsylvania Railroad just as the poem on Time was dedicated to the Ingersoll Company.[68]

But the school. We should have one or two poets, one or two prosateurs, a sculptor, a painter. And then hold an exhibit. The prose and poetry would be cast by the sculptor; for example a poem expressive of spiral motion would be engraved on a sort of circular staircase. Of course that part of it is freakish, but what sport. The sculpture would concern itself with moving trains, and perhaps we would even have a few pieces of real machinery. Man Ray's revolving doors should certainly be part of the exhibit. Also there is opportunity for a plentiful use of fonetty kinglish. Notice how well this new school would fit in with futurism and unanimism. Comments and suggestions are respectfully solicited address all queries to.

The Life idea is one that Peggy and I have worked out, and it should suit you as well as it does us. I decided against regular commuting, but around Haverstraw there is regular farming country and it is within thirty-five miles of 42nd street. Why not rent a house for ten or fifteen a month—it can be done—and live there during the summer, or perhaps during the whole year and raise a large vegetable garden. Peggy plans also to sell flowers. The little money necessary for existence can be raised through a carefully cultivated typewriter and one or two trips a week to the city. Think it over. Mountains, woods, groundhogs, trout, literature. If we are to undertake this vita nuova it will begin next spring very early.

[...]

Mal

[NL TLS-3] [PARTLY SC 76–77]
[TO: KENNETH BURKE]
88 West Third Street,
New York City
August 25, 1920

Dear Kenneth:

[...]

[...] [T]his fit of Viennese melancholy, this lavender-and-old-rose regret for other days, grows simply out of inability to adjust myself to my financial conditions. This week Peggy lost seven dollars, and as a result I had to hock four cameos and wrap the pawn ticket carefully around the fountain pen ticket and the ticket for my Phi Beta Kappa key. [. . .] Soon my salary goes up to fifty; I am to get ten a week extra from the *Post* for handling their briefer stuff, and yet I bet I am still the width of a bank vault from the nearest savings account. And therefore I continue to work on an architectural catalogue,[69] and the great drama of this age by Malcolm Cowley and Kenneth Burke will become, if finished, a rare tourdeforce by Kenneth Burke and Malcolm Cowley.[70] About said drammer, I continue enthusiastic, by the way. We lost our best chance for production when the Melomimes dissolved, but I think there is still a good chance with the comparatively conservative pp's.[71]

[...]

On the subject of poetry: I have written very little during the last months. [. . .] I was thinking that perhaps we could preempt a number of *The Little*

Review for our cute little movement, with your "Vomitory," my "Day Coach,"
the play, a Manifesto against Manifestoes, and a few drawings by Charley.
Think it over.

Yours, etc.

Mal

———

[VWB TLS-1]

[TO: VAN WYCK BROOKS][72]

88 West Third Street, New York City,

Nov. 27, 1920

Mr. Van Wyck Brooks,

Dear Sir:

I don't suppose that you are familiar with my name; it is too much to ask
that any one should be familiar with the whole of the youngest generation
of critics. And still there is a chance that you may have run across it in *The
Dial,* or the *Evening Post Literary Review,* or that you saw my initials somewhere in the back numbers of *The New Republic.* At any rate I have written
an appalling number of book reviews during the past year or two, and I am
even asking for the privilege of writing more.

It would be pleasant to write for *The Freeman.*[73] There is an agreeably ac-
rid taste about some of your reviews, and almost all of them manage to avoid
too much formality. When one writes for *The Nation,* one is pompous; one is
arty for *The Dial* and economic for *The New Republic.* For *The Freeman,*
however, one seems to be able to express one's own mind rather than the
personality of the editor.

As a reviewer I have specialized chiefly in modern literature: French, English, German, and American. By this I don't mean Bennett and Wells and
Cannan, but rather the generation that has followed them: James Joyce, T. S.
Eliot, Jules Romains; the crowd at the *Nouvelle Revue Française* and the
crowd that opposes them. I dislike most of the Georgian poets and delight in
a swashbuckling attack on them. Finally I review reviewers; in other words I
specialize in what Mr. [Francis] Hackett[74] calls "belette."

If you have any opening for a new reviewer, I should like an appointment with you. As a workingman my hours are few, but I could come around to the *Freeman* office any day between 12 and 2, or after 5 any day but Monday.

[Harold] Stearns or [John] Dos Passos, I think, would act as reference for me.

Very truly yours,
Malcolm Cowley

[NL ALS-4] [PARTLY *SC* 87–88]
[TO: KENNETH BURKE]
88 West Third Street.
New York City,
June 17, 1921

Dear Kenneth:

I have been unhappy—alas. I *am* unhappy—alas, alas. I don't know what it is; it resembles more than anything else the *mal du siècle* of the Romantics. One gets up, putters around the house, putters around the office, putters around the house, and goes to bed. One wakes suddenly and wonders when the devil it is all going to end. One tells a client professionally about a boom in building that one doesn't believe in—and while waiting for his reply wonders when the devil it is going to end. Not having any thoughts, one is afraid to be alone with them, and reads Mr. Hearst's *Journal,* and *The Saturday Evening Post,* and accounts of the coming fight at Jersey City (Put your money on Dempsey), and any other scrap of paper. And wonders vaguely "when in Christ's name is it . . . ?"

As you can see, the reason I haven't written you is that I haven't had anything to write. [. . .] I feel as if I were (was?) dying at the top; nothing can save me now short of a new life.

[. . .]

Things happen here of course. [. . .] The most profitable is the sudden interest which *The Dial* seems to have taken in my criticism. I have books for long reviews for the next 2 issues, and have written long reviews for the last 2 issues. Thayer[75] seemed pleased with them, but I wasn't.

The advertising manager for Moon-Glo silk wrote in to *The Dial* for a poet to do some work for them. I was recommended. I made him $35 as a submission price for a brief poem, and *$100* as acceptance price. The charge was ok'd, but as yet I have done no work on it. Only assets to date are: 1 lunch at Delmonico's; one supper (Peggy included) at Enrico & Paglieri's.

Djuna Barnes is going abroad
Harold Stearns[76]   ”   ”   ”
Ivan Opffer[77]   ”   ”   ”
Bill Brown[78]   ”   ”   ”
Estlin Cummings is already   ”
Dos Passos   ”   ”   ”
Dorothy Day   ”   ”   ”
Mary Reynolds[79]   ”   ”   ”   and oh God

I can't continue this list for weariness. I suppose Joe Gould will drop in on us at Montpellier to borrow money.

Have you read about the *Dial* prize of $2,000 to be given next January to a *young* author who has contributed to their paper? I really think that you and Estlin Cummings have the best chances—if the prize really goes to a *young* writer.

You should contribute to [Alfred] Kreymborg's magazine, *The Broom*. He pays. I will find you the address if I can. He's another of next week's departures for Europe.

Are you making any money, or living on your capital?

[...]

And even the recital of all this gossip leaves me empty and desolate. Maybe a sea voyage will be a tonic, but I doubt it.

Mal.

❦ PART II ❦

Pilgrimage to Holy Land—France,
1921–1923

The two years Cowley spent in France, from the summer of 1921 till the summer of 1923, were years of literary fermentation and intellectual ripening. His expatriate venture led him to a revaluation of the aesthetic potential inherent in American culture and prompted him to redefine his role as an American writer. His cast of correspondents expanded—he now wrote to editors, critics, and poets such as Harold Loeb, John Farrar, Burton Rascoe, Scofield Thayer, John Brooks Wheelwright, Tristan Tzara, and Hart Crane—but his letters to Burke remained the pivotal record of his intellectual life. Ten years later, the letters to Burke would provide the autobiographical framework for *Exile's Return,* Cowley's account of his expatriate years.

A young American writer of promise and ambition, Cowley aimed to make the acquaintance of a wide and varied circle of French writers, and was eager to place his work, and that of his contemporaries, with magazines that were committed to international modernism and the avant-garde—magazines such as *Broom,* edited by Harold Loeb in Italy; *Secession,* recently launched by Gorham B. Munson in New York; and (more staidly) *The Dial.* In Paris, the Cowleys at first found the American colony in Montparnasse little different from the Village they had just left behind, and soon they moved on to Montpellier, where Cowley was to spend a year as an American Field Service student at the university. En route, in Dijon, he wrote his first manifesto on "this youngest generation" for H. S. Canby's *Literary Review* of the *New York Evening Post.* The essay was promptly seized on by Munson as "an important origin and a general program" for *Secession.* Amy Lowell made good her promise to act as his "literary agent" and managed to sell his poems to *Poetry, The Dial,* and *North American Review.* In 1923 his verse was published for the first time in book form in the anthology *Eight*

More Harvard Poets, edited in Boston by S. Foster Damon, John Brooks Wheelwright, and Robert Hillyer.

In Montpellier, searching for a way of understanding the contradictory manifestations of modernism, Cowley was drawn to seventeenth-century French classicism. Judging contemporary literature by the precepts of Boileau, Molière, and Racine, he drew up a satirical "Ridicule of Current Aesthetics." His letters of this period evince a "new interest in form" that he saw as the hallmark of "this youngest generation" and show him groping toward a "pluralist esthetic." He was now developing many of the ideas (such as his notion of "the religion of art") that informed his interpretation of his generation in *Exile's Return.*

When his American Field Service fellowship was renewed for a second year, the Cowleys exchanged the rural quietude of Mediterranean Montpellier for the effervescent cosmopolitanism of Paris, the mecca of modernism. They settled in nearby Giverny, an artists' colony some fifty kilometers east of Paris. Cowley made regular expeditions to the city, where for the first time he encountered the Dadaists, "the most amusing people in Paris." As he was sucked into the city's infectious dynamism, he became a regular consort at the Dôme Café. From the French writers André Salmon, Louis Aragon, and Tristan Tzara, Cowley got "wonderful dope" on recent French literature. For *The Bookman* he interviewed André Salmon, Henri Barbusse, Georges Duhamel, and others. Meeting with Ezra Pound and James Joyce, he gained impressions he would later rework for *Exile's Return.*

In the summer of 1922 the Cowleys traveled through inflation-ridden Europe, profiting from the favorable exchange rate. The political and economic chaos (and poverty) in Austria stirred Cowley's humanitarian conscience and momentarily distracted him from his writing, but soon he was back to work on his poems, proofreading for *Secession* in Vienna, and negotiating writing and translating assignments with Harold Loeb, the editor of *Broom,* whom he met in Innsbruck, and again in Berlin. He was enthused to learn of Loeb's new plans for *Broom:* to make it a vehicle for revitalizing American literature, even as he sought to strengthen the magazine's international orientation and standing. In one significant sense Cowley remained a skeptical expatriate. As he wrote to John Farrar of *The Bookman* in October 1922, "the chief advantage of two years in France is to give you a taste for America." As the fortunes of *Broom* went up and down with the capricious fluctuations of European currency exchange values, Cowley found himself drawn more and more to *Broom*'s agenda of cultural nationalism: "America in the distance begins to loom up as a land of promise, something barbaric and decorative and rich," he wrote to Burke in early 1923.

Increasingly, however, Cowley saw his plans and ideals thwarted by frictions between Josephson, now a vociferous coeditor of *Broom,* and Munson, editor of *Secession*. Many of his letters (only exemplarily represented here) show him embroiled in unsavory and unproductive literary politics. As conflicts of personalities and programmatic ideals became more intrusive, Cowley found it hard to remain impartial. As he took on a more active part in editing *Broom,* his intuitive sympathies lay with Burke, Josephson, Loeb, and Crane, against those of Munson, Waldo Frank, and Paul Rosenfeld.

In the early months of 1923 Cowley was drawn more deeply into the orbit of the French Dadaists. Though there was much in Dada he disapproved of— its obscurantism, its lack of logic, its disdainful attitude to its audience—he was won over by its vitality and its iconoclastic spirit; as he wrote to Burke on February 8, 1923, "their love of literature is surprisingly disinterested. [. . .] They are a form of cocaine and personally take no stimulants except their own company." In particular, he fell under the spell of Louis Aragon, who had come to stay at Giverny. A brilliant talker, Aragon displayed disdain for the commercial mechanics of success and an intense commitment to literature. Struggling against precarious finances, Cowley wrote poems, satirical sketches, and reviews. As his letters to Scofield Thayer and Burton Rascoe demonstrate, he took care to maintain his connections with the New York literary market.

Cowley's French venture ended on a paradoxical note of rational humanism and Dadaist provocation: he published his first booklet, a long essay on Racine that celebrated the formal conventions of classical theater; and, "eaten with the desire to do something significant and indiscreet," he engaged in a "significant gesture" that stood as the culmination of his Dadaist desire to *épater le bourgeois:* on Bastille Day, he punched the café proprietor of La Rotonde in the face, was arrested, and spent a night in a Paris jail. Overnight, he became a Dadaist celebrity, on both sides of the Atlantic.

On July 28, 1923, the Cowleys sailed back to New York. "The famous two years is ending," Cowley reported to Burke, "with little accomplished and much learned. It seems to me that their great value was not so much what I learned about literature as the aid they gave me in developing a personal philosophy."

————

[NL ALS-2] [SC 95–96]
[TO: KENNETH BURKE]
Permanent address
c/o American University Union,
1, rue de Fleurus,
Paris (VIe), France
Aug. 10, 1921

Dear Kenneth:

[…]

Paris, as you may imagine by putting two together with two, has an American colony. That colony centers at the Rotonde, and at times straggles over to Boudet's. Members of that colony, when asked the location of the Louvre and of Montmartre, said, *"Anybody* can tell you where the Louvre is and *Nobody* goes to Montmartre." They don't go either place. They dine at Boudet's and sleep with one another, or, if they are not homosexual, with the tarts of the Quarter. It is Greenwich Village, only much more so than the Village. But if you don't go to the Rotonde, Paris is quite as charming as the guidebooks. One has to look at it historically. After going through the Musée Carnavalet, where all the antiquities of Paris are stored, you begin to realize the datelessness of all the people you see. The large man with one arm lost the other at Malplaquet.[1] The little *fille* seduced Napoleon when he was a student. Voltaire plays chess at this table in the Café Blank; here he comes now. Voilà l'aristo! His head will go through the Faubourg St. Honoré on a pike—past the dressmaking establishment of Mr. Paul Poiret,[2] whom I am to interview on Thursday.

In 1914 and in 1735 the English were very popular. 1918 (almost as much as 1779) was the year of Americans. We are still fairly popular; I should advise you to come over before the signs go up:

MAISONS FRANÇAISES
LES ALLEMANDS ET LES AMERICAINS
N'ENTRENT PAS ICI

[...]

Malcolm

[NL TLS-I]
[TO: KENNETH BURKE]
c/o American University Union,
1, rue de Fleurus, Paris, France,
August 17, 1921

Dear Kenneth:

[...]

Among the recent arrivals at Dijon are Mr. Malcolm Cowley and wife of New York, N.Y. They intend to remain a month.

So far they have spent their time beating the ancient cobblestones (dating from A.D. 1429) and getting themselves installed in a room where the brown-figured hangings and enlarged photographs date, unfortunately, from 1887. Already they begin to regret Paris. Or rather, one should say, they are still regretting Paris.

Paris, that is Greenwich Villagers [*sic*] as the founders of the Village desired it to be. In the first place (prime requisite of every Village) nobody works. Living is cheap, [()or rather restaurants are cheap). Liquor is cheaper. Talk is cheapest and most plentiful. At a recent soiree they noticed

Robert McAlmon (still married, still wearing a blue shirt)[3]

Mina Loy (en route to Florence)[4]

Djuna Barnes (to whom they did not speak. She is unhappy in France)

Lorimer Hammond (from my old office)[5]

Roy Snow (from Harvard)

Harold Stearns

Sinclair Lewis (who talks just like his book, only it is

    better in conversation. It is Middle West, with a twist.

    Sometimes he forgets the twist)

The party ended at five o'clock with onion soup at the market. Harold Stearns kept calling for a whore, kept protesting that he was to[o] bashful to speak to one. The woman having been provided, he was left with her at one o'clock and applied argyrol at seven.

Harold was the man who kept advising young Americans to be wicked and go to Europe.

It is hard to describe to you the Brevoortness, the O'Connorness of the Dome and the Rotonde. Only Julius has changed his name to Jean.

I believe that the Cowleys can get some work done at Dijon. Mr. Cowley is planning a story which is already half written. His muse seems to be tethered for the time being, at least it has attempted no ambitious flights.

He has received no letter from you and it's god damned near time that he should.

Mal

[AL TLS-1]

[TO: AMY LOWELL]

c/o American University Union,

1, rue de Fleurus,

Paris (VIe),

Aug. 30, 1921

Dear Miss Lowell:

You wonder, probably—in that compartment of your brain reserved for me—why I haven't written to my literary agent. I wonder too. I have said every day, "Tomorrow I will gather my poems and send them to Miss Lowell." [...]

There will be 28. You will say as you page them over, "This won't sell. . . . this one won't sell." When you say that of a poem, don't waste stamps on it.

There are some of them that will sell, I am almost certain. You can judge better than I.

The whole thing is very discouraging for two years' work.

I wonder what you thought of my review.[6] It was hard work writing it— hard to formulate my thoughts and to express them. It would have been much easier if I had disliked *Legends*, for it is always easy to pick the flaws. I worked three solid days, and at the end I didn't know the quality of the result. I worry a little now, because [John Gould] Fletcher picked quite a quarrel with me over the review I wrote of *Breakers and Granite*. Fortunately you aren't so touchy, so absurdly touchy, as your friend across the water. You quarrel, but only with your enemies.

In short I liked *Legends*, and I am afraid I didn't say so emphatically enough. I wrote like a lawyer, like a judge of the Court of Appeals.

[...]

News. Witter Bynner has fallen for Earl Roppel's verse.[7] Like ten tons of lead off the top of the Woolworth Building. And for Earl Roppel's *worst* work—not the dishpan poem or the Venice poem or the Arab sheik poem. For awful little things in rhyme. Encouraged by Bynner, one of the patriotic poems was set to music and sung by a trained choir of 3000 voices. Bynner wrote to the War Department, the Navy Department, the Candor Post Office, the Owego Free Library, and the Author's League of America— asking them all to find Earl Roppel. He was decent enough to send me all the correspondence. Earl Roppel, I think, is becoming a huge and legendary figure.

[...]

I suggest that if any of my poems sell, you take out the agent's customary 10 or 20 percent, and use it to start a fund for the Malcolm Cowley home for Indigent Poets. I will elect myself the first member. Not that I'm penniless, but just that I seem always trying to be.

[...]

Agréez, Madame, l'expression de ma vive gratitude—to use a courtly expression which my English won't allow me.

Malcolm Cowley

[JBW TLS-2]
[TO: JOHN BROOKS WHEELWRIGHT][8]
C.o. American University Union
1, rue de Fleurus, Paris, VIe
October 9, 1921

Dear Jack:

I wrote a story at Dijon with you very much in mind.[9] It was your passion for arbitrary and nonsensical events that fascinated me. But really
you'll have to read it to understand what I mean, and you can't read it till it's
published, for Art Moss possesses the only copy of it. He promised to print
it this month in his *Gargoyle* and to send me copies. And I shall forward a
copy to you, for I await anxiously your judgment.

Don't be scared; it's really a satire and not a fiction. Let me now repeat,
from the sanctuary of Montpellier, that after another year of New York I
should have been ready to saw off the part of me above the bridge of the
nose and bury it. A month in Dijon put some life into my decaying member
(let me call it a member, like the penis, for it is really with the brain that a
writer copulates). I corrected my poems. I wrote my satire, and three satires
in verse, and an essay on This Youngest Generation for the *Evening Post*.[10]
The essay should also interest you, if it gets into print, which it should. Peggy
painted.

The reason our family Wrote and Painted (like veritable Malcolm
Vaughns)[11] was this. Dijon is dull. There is a lot of Architecture, but one can't
drink Architecture. There are a lot of excellent drinks, but no company in
which to consume them. And even the excellent mustard of Dijon cannot
quite fill a life. There was nothing to do but work.

Montpellier, like all the towns of Midi, is gayer. Since one can't run up to
Paris for the week-end, one takes one's enjoyment at home. [. . .] Montpellier
is twenty minutes from the still bathable Mediterranean.

[. . .]

You might [. . .] look up Kenneth Burke. He is so much your opposite that
you should be great friends. This year he will arrive from Maine with a great
pack of manuscripts. But very hard-up, and, I imagine, rather alone, and with
nothing to occupy him but his feuds. He has a fantastic mind, usually in-

correct, I suppose, but always profound. His world exists in a bundle of theories, covering everything from hygiene to the proper way to develop a thought. He was much impressed by some of the things you said one night at McSorley's, but God knows what, for it is now three thousand miles ago.

[. . .]

[Malcolm]

———————

[NL ALS-2]
[TO: KENNETH BURKE]
Villa Marcel, rue Marguerite,
Montpellier (Hérault),
Oct. 27, 1921

Dear Kenneth:

[. . .]

Tonight I feel very discouraged. Namely because I have been quite unable to write a satisfactory poem since coming to France. [. . .] [In Montpellier] I have done nothing except a very mediocre article on the Rabelais fêtes, which the *Tribune* will probably turn down.[12]

And yet I look forward to an amusing year. Provincial towns are the same everywhere. The Midi hates Paris and is determined to prove that the intellectual center of France is south of the Loire. For which reason people here are aggressively intellectual. I met [Jean] Catel, who criticizes American poetry for the *Mercure*. He introduced me to a girl intellectual (a mouse) who is translating "Vote the New Moon."[13] They write for a literary paper published in Marseilles, which tries to patronize Picabia[14] and Tristan Tzara[15] equally. It is sanely progressive—you know, like Harriet Monroe. People do little sketches in Provençal or Languedoc or Catalan, and innumerable woodcuts. "Go to Paris and you gain wit in losing your own." But if they were a little richer, they would go to Paris.

Politics is more interesting. I have met a Royalist newspaperman. I read the legislative debates every morning. They move with the rapidity of a $1.90 novel, with duels, fisticuffs, hoots, and insults every five minutes. I am acting as American delegate to the Tenth Congress of the National Union of the Associations of French Students. I carry a big American flag. I sympathize with the French in their dislike for Britishers and swear the eternal amity of America. They know enough not to take things so seriously, whereby the game becomes amusing.

[...]

I thought tonight that I am one of those people who need a tradition to work in, who need a) a form and b) an audience before they can write. I regret again the Restoration drama.

Mal.

———————

[NL TLS-3] [PARTLY *SC* 107–108]
[TO: KENNETH BURKE]
Villa Marcel, rue Marguerite
Montpellier, Hérault,
Nov. 28, 1921

Dear Kenneth:

Please send me [Van Wyck] Brook's [*sic*] article against us;[16] I think I might be able to make something out of it.

You complain with utter justification about my letters which do not arrive. The University is open now, and most of my time is occupied with the mysteries of French pedagogy. [...] And naturally when I have finished paring my nails, poking the fire, rolling a cigarette, and trying to bite Peggy on the left buttock, I have expressed myself; there is nothing left to write.

[...]

I think it is about time we instituted a New Classicism. I have thought of reading Boileau[17] for this purpose, and of copying such of his maxims as still hold good. [...]

Dec. 1.

[...]

I bought a second-hand school text of Boileau for 2 francs. [...] there is obviously a great deal of Boileau that we can hang our hats on, perhaps even better than on the less venerable mahogany of Uncle Matthew [Arnold].

The whole of l'Art poétique seems to be a treatise directed against John Gould Fletcher. [...]

I feel at home in the seventeenth century, as if I had just been introduced to a very pleasant company of very kindred minds. The two sides of it: the grand tragedies in which one could say only noble words, and the low comedies in which one could say anything . . . there are two waterproof compartments in my mind like that, and I have always felt ashamed of their existence. How regally I should have licked King Louis' ass, meanwhile composing the satire for publication after his death. In you also I seem to detect the ruin of an excellent satirist: if Floyd Dell[18] had been Chapelain or Shadwell, you should already be enjoying a pension from His Majesty the second Charles or the fourteenth Louis.

[. . .]

M.

[AL TLS-1]
[TO: AMY LOWELL]
Villa Marcel, rue Marguerite,
Montpellier, Hérault,
Dec. 9, 1921

Dear Miss Lowell:

The portentously sealed envelope from *The Dial* contained a check for the equivalent of ten dollars, in francs.[19] [. . .]

But your criticism[20] touched me more than I could ever be touched by the lack of an editor. Was it really true that I was stinting work on my verse? I read my poems over and found that there were indeed many things to correct. Notably I eliminated half a dozen syllables from "For a New Hymnal" and made the meter more strongly and regularly trochaic.

[. . .]

To tell the truth, the meters that sing themselves in my head are rather against the traditions of English poetry. Since Coleridge, trimeter and tetrameter have been extremely free measures, but in pentameter there has always been a tendency to count the syllables. Our heroic line has been several times under the strong influence of the French alexandrine.

Now the measure which comes most naturally, and which carries the most force to me, is a line of five assorted accents. Even my free verse tends to fall into this pattern. To ears trained in the tradition of English poetry, the extra syllables are rather uncomfortable; the only other modern poet I can point to who uses this crowded and irregular pentameter is D. H. Lawrence. Perhaps that is why his verse has always fascinated me.

I am coming to think that his muddy ecstasy is a very bad influence for any one.

[...]

Sincerely,
Malcolm Cowley

[NL ALS-2]
[TO: KENNETH BURKE]
Villa Marcel, rue Marguerite,
Montpellier, Hérault,
Jan. 12, 1922

Dear Kenneth:

[...]

Lately I have begun to make Some Observations on Contemporary Aesthetics. I wish to hold the ideas of others and ourselves up to a mild ridicule; for example, the fashion in which Art is taking the place of religion— the desire that the artist should be poor and chaste. The Fear of Being Understood, which I wish to tie up with Rosicrucianism. The Search for Originality, and all these other ridiculous ambitions of our time. I am looking for documents—incidentally could you find me the manifesto of *Contact*?[21]

Boileau was not a damn fool: where did you ever get the idea? He was the theorician of the group which included Molière, La Fontaine, and Racine. Their practice has survived where much of his theory has died; nevertheless he was alive enough so that the first two pages of the *Art Poétique* would make a telling criticism of—let us say—D. H. Lawrence. His watchwords were Truth, Nature, Good Sense. We are changing all those watchwords, but we have to think carefully before denying them, and Boileau makes one think.

Evidently tonight I feel very argumentative.

Malcolm

[NL ALS-5] [PARTLY *SC* 109–110]
[TO: KENNETH BURKE]
Villa Marcel, rue Marguerite,
Montpellier, Hérault,
Jan. 23, 1922

Dear Kenneth:

[…]

A few days ago we had a stroke of luck. Stewart Mitchell[22] commissioned Peggy to do his portrait in water-colour and paid her $60 for the work, bringing our grand total to nearly $300. There it rests. *Broom* has bought another poem, but it pays in lire. I have done a translation of a silly article on Georges Braque, for which I demanded $30 (s'il plait à Dieu que je sois payé). My problem seems rather to write the stuff than to sell it; bankruptcy is the event of four months; life has been costing us 370 francs a week. So much for finances.

A propos of *Broom*. When I sent two poems lately, I addressed them with a personal letter to Kreymborg (who is a nice little chap and doesn't justify your polemics). Two weeks later I received a brief note from Loeb,[23] on paper which carried his name only as editor. Has Alfred been fired? (Just as I always blamed the *Dial's* shortcomings on Thayer, so I have been blaming those of *Broom* on the richer Jew. I should regret Kreymborg's demise).

[…]

My thoughts have been taken up increasingly with the theories of classicism. One night I even began drawing up an esthetic, but I walked too quickly, and I arrived home just before I should have succeeded in defining my subject. I had drawn up two principles: "Art is the creation of the beautiful," and "Beauty is the object of art." Since these two principles formed a circle, I had to abandon them both.

"To test whether a piece of prose is a work of art, it is only necessary to inquire whether it is disinterested." This proposition is a favorite one among amateur aestheticians; it applies to some cases but not to all. Machen's[24] theory of ecstasy is dangerous. When I arrived into my own gaslight I had not yet succeeded in stating the subject of my aesthetics, so that the laws themselves still remain in the air.

[. . .]

[. . .] [I wrote] a criticism of *Fir-Flower Tablets* for Art Moss.[25]

Really that book of Chinese poems produced a tremendous effect on me. Obviously classicism means clarity, honesty, and (as Ezra Pound added so sagely) freshness, and obviously these Chinese poems possess these qualities to the highest degree.

Do you know, I was always rather ashamed of myself because I wasn't sufficiently unintelligible. Now I see that the most ridiculous feature of modern writing is the fear of being understood. We wish to be the priests each of our own little sect, and each sect has its rosicrucian secrets, only to be revealed to the proselyte who has passed through the seven stages of the novitiate. Meanwhile the proselytes are too busy founding little sects of their own. And literature remains the art of conveying ideas and shows no disposition to adopt either Dada or Rosicrucianism.

I want instead to reduce everything to its simplest terms, and to build up subtlety by the opposition of simple statements.

I never had your passion for filling each page I began.

M.

[NL TLS-2]
[TO: KENNETH BURKE]
Villa Marcel, rue Marguerite,
Montpellier, Hérault,
Jan. 28, 1922

Dear Kenneth:

[. . .]

I feel more than ever the need of intelligent society. Not being a romantic I have no wish for magnificent solitude. I want to write comedies and satires, and comedies and satires require an audience.

Mr. T. S. Eliot named one of his pieces "Gerontion"; I never understood what he meant by it until I examined my Larousse. [. . .] If Mr. Eliot had named his poem "Pantaloon" he should have carried the same meaning to several times as many people; he preferred to be Rosicrucian, and I have no wish to be. I want an audience.

[. . .] This magazine that Gorham B. Munson is starting[26] may be the one we want—I don't know Gorham B. Munson, so I can't judge of it. The dozen or score of members for our society are already living and writing; it is only necessary to focus their activity. A focus is what I want. I want standards, common principles, a certain amount of common knowledge without which a classical literature cannot exist. I want a common language—English is a great heap of slime out of which each writer takes a shovelful; most of the words which we use have no established meaning.

[. . .]

I just finished [John Dos Passos's] *Three Soldiers*. It is overwritten, badly composed. On the other hand it is frank, accurate, splendidly malicious; it introduces half a dozen new characters to literature. I shall never carp against it, for it expresses Dos Passos' generation perfectly and comes too near to expressing our own. I shall never write that kind of novel; I never could. Nevertheless that novel aroused too many memories in me and too many fancies for me to object to it.

When Munson comes to New York find out whether his taste is to be trusted, and if it is entice him and his magazine into the green country. What do you know about him?

Mal

[WB TLS-1]
[TO: WITTER BYNNER]
Villa Marcel, Rue Marguerite,
Montpellier, Hérault,
Feb. 1. [1922]

Dear Bynner:

I recently received an invitation to join the Poetry Society of America. [. . .]

I don't want to join your frat. There would be only two possible reasons for my joining it—you and Miss Lowell; the other reasons resigned two years ago.[27] And even you and Miss Lowell aren't enough. I love poetry but I hate poets. When poets get together they are usually worse than a Methodist sewing circle, and in my one encounter with the Poetry Society of America I found it no exception to the rule. And yet I was glad to hear you had become president. If any one could save the poetry society you could—but I suspect that the task is even beyond your power. "Not that I am wicked, though my poems may sound that way, but somehow I just think that way which I know you will understand." Thus the lamented Earl Roppel, and thus I.

[. . .] Earl was a collaboration between Foster Damon and me, and it was Foster who wrote the poem that was sung by a choir of three thousand trained voices. We invented him partly for a joke and partly to ridicule certain common poetic abuses: false simplicity, easy quatrains, and rhymes like "girl" and "squirrel"; "roses" and "posies," "bowers" and "flowers." His seven best poems were written in one hour. Finally—as you yourself found in burlesque—we began to put too much of ourselves into him, Requiescat.

[. . .]

For God's sake don't divulge what I said about Poetry Society; it wasn't for publication; I just wanted to get it off my chest. Some day when you are its president no longer we will form a new society together, where [our] aim will be the extermination of poets for the advancement of poetry. I am already sharpening my critical tools: poets, beware![28]

Very truly,
Malcolm Cowley

———

[NL ALS-7]
[TO: KENNETH BURKE]
Villa Marcel, Rue Marguerite,
Montpellier, Hérault
March 5, 1922

Dear Kenneth:

[. . .] I went to visit Jean Catel the other day, the one who writes the American chronicle for the *Mercure*. I walked with him to his class at the Lycée; on the way he met the postman and a letter from Amy Lowell. The second paragraph was about me and he read it aloud, soon beginning to blush. It began, "Have you met my little friend Malcolm Cowley?"—Oh how we remember these attacks on our vanities. "He writes both criticism and poetry but I do not think he is a poet, although I do not like to say this to him as he hasn't found this out yet for himself." I listened and said nothing; perhaps Amy is right.

Certainly the remark is blatantly easy to make on my work of the last two years. For every hour on a poem I have spent at least ten on criticisms; it would be a sad commentary if my criticisms were not the better. But if any sentence would determine my career, a sentence like that would pig-headedly turn me into a poet.

Fortuitously it arrived just when I was working on a review of *Fir-Flower Tablets* for *The Dial*. My first impulse was of course to inject a little venom into the review, but I did not act on it for several reasons, among which was the fact that I had really liked the book. Instead I wrote poetry when I should have been developing my open career as a critic. [...]

[...]

March 13

[. . .] Tonight I am pretty nearly incapable of thinking, so I cannot make answer to your theories. Except this: both terms of any antinome tend to become of equal importance. Thus Good-Evil; as soon as one has admitted the existence of evil, one is led inevitably to a dualism and a balance. Form-Matter is the same kind of antinome. As soon as one has admitted the existence of matter—the independent existence thereof—it becomes just as important as form. The only way to make it less important is to resolve it entirely into smaller forms, thus building what one might call a Berkleyan Aesthetic. The other solution is to deny the existence of form: an aesthetic which might be called Neo-Realist or Dreiserian. Both these solutions are logical; neither is sensible. There remain the two illogical solutions. The one is the Dualism of Form and Matter; in this, as I said, both terms, despite one's efforts, tend to become equally important. The final solution is to split up the antinome into several terms; in other words to erect a pluralistic esthetic.

Form especially can be so divided. Thus, when we speak of the *form* of a poem, we mean one or all of the following:

1. Its *architectural* form (it is in this sense that we generally employ the term; rather let us say its *geometrical* form).
2. Its *motion*.
3. Its *rhythm*.
4. Its clarity or lack of it; in other words its *expression*. (sentence-structure, etc.)

Now if you proclaim that the *geometrical form* of a work of art is its most important feature, or if you proclaim that it should be judged by its motion, you are proclaiming something. But if you say that form is more important than matter you are adding only an individual affirmation to a dispute that has lasted since Plato.

My other thought is not original, but it is potent. "An artist should choose a form in which he can express all of himself." Imagine the poverty of a man who could express himself completely in poetry as it is written today.

[...]

I enclose the announcement of *Secession*. I don't like the name.

Mal.

———

[NL TLS-1] [SC 117–118]
[TO: KENNETH BURKE]
*Villa Marcel, rue Marguerite,
Montpellier, Hérault
March 30 (Ste. Amédée),
1922*

Dear Kenneth:

[...] I am going to write an article on the centenary of Murger[29] for *The Freeman*. I have it all doped out. A Brief History of Bohemia. Murger was the founder for the romantic Bohemia. Nothing has changed since his time, except that the artists and writers have gradually withdrawn from it, leaving it to people who paint on pottery, romantic fairies, and vendors of peanut novelties. Plea for classical life as a basis for classical art. Evidently the article will skim the edges of banality, but it is a case where my theory of "big subjects" applies; if I skim successfully it will be a very authoritative article. I want you to peddle it, and *definitely* to take out enough to pay for your trouble.

Cussy Wright[30] has taught me the new trick. Don't criticize current literature; write about Molière and Petronius. It's just as easy—or easier, because Cussy cribs most of his material—and it gives you a great deal more standing. If Murger goes I shall continue with Racine and Wycherley.

You and Jack Wheelwright, when you assigned me my precise niche in literature, were more kind than just to my poetry and more just than kind to the excellent tool which is my brain. It is perhaps true that by taking thought I shall add never a cubit to my stature, but by thinking I shall at least develop what I have. My brain is a practical brain, a brain that likes to work on definite lines, a brain that thinks about means rather than ends and that can make at least A- on any subject set for it. No one ever does justice to this type of brain. It is the classical brain which builds a perfectly proportioned edifice, which writes prose that is simple and clear, and poetry studiously incorrect. It does not question enough; it respects ability and authority. It is the brain of Boileau and Pope and Congreve; that is the real reason of my classical campaign.

62 days to starvation.

Mal.

[NL TLS-2]

[TO: JOHN BROOKS WHEELWRIGHT]

Villa Marcel, rue Marguerite,

Montpellier, (Hérault) France,

April 2, 1922

Dear Jack:

We have just returned (at six o'clock) from a luncheon with John Nef[31] and wife. They leave tomorrow morning to be at the Conference at Genoa. John is, as usual, very simple and very charming. His wife is more pert, more aggressive, more rude; determined (as are all recent wives) to be the perfect friend, the companion, the playfellow, and to share equally the erudition and the vices of the husband. Has no one called attention to the fact that happy marriages are becoming fashionable? We are living in an age of reaction.

—Back to Ingres, declare the painters.

—Classicism, say the writers; back to Racine, Molière, Ben Jonson, Congreve, Swift. (Nobody reads Greek these days, or we should hear more of Euripides).

The composers have discovered the music of seventeenth century Italy. The sculptors, most reactionary of all, will have nothing but Congolese idols.

A wonderful opportunity for satire; unfortunately I can't satirize it, since I feel too much that I am part of it. I feel too much classical myself. My mind is ordered, exact, and limited. It would have been more appreciated in the age of Congreve, and therefore I must strive diligently to resurrect that age. In some ways an impossible task.

I am convinced that another age will speak of ours as the logical unfolding of the romantic movement. In literature the work of William Carlos Williams, Dada, the Baroness Else von Freytag-Loringhoven—romanticism carried to the limit of formlessness, immediacy, and unintelligibility. In philosophy Bergson, in life Greenwich Village, in politics De Valera serenaded under the window of his prison, and the romantic nationalism of France, Albania, and the mythical Croatian Republic. Open diplomacy and secret diplomacy, the White Army and the Red—all equally romantic.

But everything I have said is utterly valueless without a definition of romanticism. I mean by it the idea that matter is more important than form, the emotions than the intellect, and complex and inexpressible concepts more than clear concepts. Thus democracy is the subordination of form to matter; mystical nationalism demands the slavery of the intellect; Freudianism is greeted as a final victory over conscious thought.

But I wander among grandiose ideas which are the opposite of the sober clarity I demand. I have a very shallow foundation for theories on society; among literary ideas I feel more certain. Let us demand a literature which preserves the virtues of classicism without its vices. A literature, in other words, which still possesses the sentiment of nature, which remains emotional and imaginative, but in which the emotions and the imagination are not given free licence. A literature which may strive for complex effects, but which gains them with sentences and paragraphs which are absolutely lucid. An architectural literature, from which is disengaged an impression of proportion (or studied disproportion) as from a fine building. A literature, finally, which is a literature and not a theft from life (of it one will never repeat the judgment; That's a fine novel; I know a man just like the hero).

I think we are all fools if we don't work and if we don't work together. The requisite for an intelligent literature (as distinguished from an emotional literature) is an intelligent society, and an intelligent society may consist of only half a dozen people. It would be a mistake to found a school: that would mean that these half dozen men had only one idea. One should aim rather at creating an atmosphere in which many ideas can be born and be polished by rubbing against each other.

American literature suffers just now from a lack of such ideas. One can reduce Harold Stearns, for example, to one syllogism—Puritanism is bad: America is puritan = America is bad. (Or—America is bad: America is puritan = puritanism is bad.) (Or—Badness is puritan: badness is American = puritanism is American.) Even this simplicity would be excusable if Stearns had ever defined puritanism—or badness. Mencken has perhaps two or three other ideas; Van Wyck Brooks may reach the complexity of six or seven. But most of our novelists have not even one. (And some one said that [Edmund] Wilson had a single-track mind!)

And yet America is not, like England, incongenial to ideas. It is a land of sunlight and clear forms—no fogs—and it welcomes clear ideas when it finds them. I think the haziness of our unintelligentzia is borrowed from a too-close reading of the London *Nation*.

Therefore let us to work for the clear play of ideas. We need a magazine (perhaps we can borrow one; that's better than paying for it ourselves. Let's see what sort of sheet Gorham B. Munson is getting out.) We need a theater (it should exist in some country barn, not in New York City.) We need a Maecenas,* but he should not be too rich; otherwise he would stifle our ventures. None of these essentials are impossible to find, if only we can get together.

While I nourish these ideals and others (my head has been abnormally busy these last two weeks) I myself am nearing my judgment day. June 1— the sun rising at 5:37, the moon being in its first quarter, and the administration republican—June 1, the day of brides and St. Pamphilius, I shall go inevitably bankrupt. I count, however, on only one starving month; if my fellowship is renewed, I shall receive more funds the first of July—life being not yet extinct.

Meanwhile with a full stomach I face the future bravely.

Malcolm.

[* autograph note in margin: "requirements for the post: he should *help* support the magazine; *help* the theatre; no personal gifts; it is dangerous these days for an artist not to support himself; he loses too much of his independence."]

[HL TLS-2]
[TO: MATTHEW JOSEPHSON]³²
Villa Marcel, rue Marguerite
Montpellier (Hérault)
May 10, 1922

Dear Matty,

When I wrote you my first letter, I was totally ignorant of the fact that you were Will Bray, especially since nothing you had written before—nothing which I had seen of yours, at least—resembled Will Bray's opinions. I think I said that they were the opposite of Kenneth's or mine, and that a magazine which published both of them, laid itself open to the very charges which Munson made against *The Dial*.³³ . . . And then I wondered at the choler of your reply, and would be wondering yet, if Kenneth hadn't casually spoken of the Bray article as being yours.

I was certainly right when I said that our attitudes were opposite; our last two letters have made that clear enough. And I can hardly answer you, for one can't argue about attitudes. If someone says to me, "I don't like Italian art," he has stated an attitude, and I have nothing to reply to him. But if he tells me the facts which have led him to dislike Italian art, he gives me something of more than personal interest. He gives me, in other words, a criticism.

[. . .]

You say, "An attitude can be expressed in a few sentences." True; it can even be expressed in one sentence or one word. It can be put on and off like a necktie. Any number of the young ladies of both sexes who hang around la Rotonde have attitudes which make those of Joyce or Apollinaire seem naive. Most of your letter is the expression of an attitude, which is why I can only pick a sentence here and there to answer.

Z.b. "Are you futuristic or are you not?" No, Hermione, I'm a proof-reader. Two years ago I wrote a poem which I said was futuristic. Two years ago I believe you were fond of Remy de Gourmont.

"André Gide who with Apollinaire is the only French writer of the pre-war and war periods that counts." Cf. Ezra Pound: "These four lines are worth the forty volumes of Maurice Barrès."

I have lent all my copies of *Secession,* so I can't reread the fragment by Aragon. But as far as the "central directing brain" in Proust, I think you would have noticed if you had read on (and his third volume is much easier to read) that he selects his experiences with much care. In the case of "Day Coach" [. . .] I was trying to define not motion in general but the motion of a particular person between two definite points. If my subject had been different, I should have chosen a different set of experiences, but the "central directing brain" would apply equally in both cases. Writing today I should certainly choose a different subject, and probably it would please you less.

"Brain detached from experience. . . ." It doesn't exist: where are your four years of philosophy; in what particular latrine did you vomit them?

The provinces, as you say, are not stimulating and I shall be glad to get to Paris for a visit. On the other hand the provinces are safer as a permanent residence—for me, that is; each organism has its proper environment. Their very lack of stimulation is perhaps their most valuable feature. . . . I hope your trip through the Tyrol is successful; I envy you. Only I doubt that you will find a good English-printing printer at Innsbruck; you may have to go to Vienna again. Still, they didn't do a bad job on Joyce at Dijon, and Innsbruck should be just as intelligent. Good luck.

Malcolm

[RP TLS-2]
[TO: DR. WILLIAM COWLEY (FATHER)]
Villa Marcel, rue Marguerite,
Montpellier (Hérault) France
May 19, 1922

Dear Popsie:

The news about the [American Field Service] fellowship came today. I had been dogging the steps of the mailman for a week, and I had hardly been able to do any work on account of the suspense. You see, everything depended on it, and I faced the alternatives of an immediate and difficult return to New York, or another year in France. . . . Oh, yes, I forgot to say that the fellowship was granted.

In the same mail I found that Van Wyck Brooks had accepted the two articles which Kenneth had sent—for me—to *The Freeman*. Brooks said that my style had a "mallic clarity" (what in the deuce did he mean by that?);[34] also that nobody he had known in college could write like me. Since he liked my articles, a new magazine is opened to me, and *The Freeman,* which is published every week, can buy four times as much as *The Dial*. . . . Meanwhile *The Dial* printed one of the most boring criticisms I ever wrote (May issue). *The Dial* speaks—in conversation, not in print—of Kenneth and me as their 'youngsters,' and seems to forgive us a lot, although Kenneth says they think we should be spanked sometimes. Especially they think this lately, since we have become tangled up with a new magazine which spends most of its energy in ripping *The Dial* up the back and stealing its contributors (*Secession,* I mean; I think I wrote you about it.) Finally, *Broom* accepted a sketch I wrote, called "Young Man with Spectacles." With all these articles appearing about the same time, I should begin to be well known. And that is my object in remaining in France—so that when I return I can live by writing and not by proofreading for an architectural catalogue.

I told you that I had corrected 18 of my poems and sent them to Jack Wheelwright for a book he is publishing of Eight More Harvard Poets. He objected flatteringly that my poems would outweigh the others in the book, and so wished to substitute for some of them certain more immature poems that I wrote in college. He says he will use 14 of my poems, whereas no one else in the volume will have more than 10. But I hate to see my old work dragged out of the *Advocate* files, where I hoped it had definitely been put to an oblivious sleep.

I am surprised at the number of people who are willing to help me; either by publishing my work, or by giving me fellowships. I suppose the explanation is not difficult; America has arrived at a stage where it is anxious to possess literary men, and anyone who shows the least talent is pushed forward willy nilly. Tonight after this overwhelming amount of news I feel very flattered, but not really happy.

[...]

Your son,
Malcolm

[NL TLS-2] [PARTLY *SC* 120–121]
[TO: KENNETH BURKE]
Villa Marcel, rue Marguerite,
Montpellier (Hérault), France,
May 20, 1922

Dear Kenneth:

Your letter arrived yesterday in the same mail as the announcement of the renewal of my fellowship. [...] My sentiments about it are mixed. Latterly I have been frightfully homesick for a country where No Trespass signs can be disregarded, and where there are trout streams. Also at times my head becomes frightfully empty, and I lie around the house in a frenzy of idleness. My talent is not cosmopolitan, and I have no desire to spend my life in France. On the other hand this existence in the French provinces—like that in the Argentine or a Chinese river town—gives an excellent perspective on America, and under its influence my ideas seem to be clarifying slowly.

[...]

Broom bought "Young Man with Spectacles,"[35] which was the first work I did with any of the material on the ridicules of contemporary esthetics. It was a voluble little portrait, all concerned with the conversation of a young writer who must have read the letters of K. Burke and M. Cowley. The whole thing was a little too pat, but it was the first sketch of that nature which I had written. Why don't you send more things to *Broom?* I thought that Kreymborg's departure would leave it in the hands of the Louis Untermeyers,[36] but on the contrary Loeb seems moving more towards the younger writers. Especially he seems interested in ideas. He publishes bad things and good things with more indiscriminacy than *The Dial,* but he is a market—one cent a word—for the old things which you have not published.

   [...]

Malcolm.

<hr />

[NL ALS-2] [SC 122–123]
[TO: KENNETH BURKE]
c/o American University Union,
1, rue de Fleurus, Paris (VI e),
July 2, 1922

Dear Kenneth:

   I haven't written you, and God knows how I'm able to write you now. Paris is like cocaine; either it leaves you tremendously elated or sunk in a brown fit of depression. I begin now to understand its fascination, and I subscribe to the opinion of the ten thousand Matty Josephsons: you must come to Paris. Only, you mustn't stay here.

   Paris has rarely or never produced great literature. There are rare exceptions: Baudelaire, Verlaine, but the rule is pretty safe. However, Paris has been the condition of great literature. Occasionally a man tears himself away from it and writes like—George Moore, James Joyce. He never writes till he goes, or if he does it is *genre boulevardier; pour épater les* etc. As witness Aragon, Cocteau, all the rest.

   We have been doing the Dôme as usual. The crowd: Art Moss, Percy Winner,[37] several nice boys, several Jewish girls, Ivan Opffer. This time, however, I was luckier. Ivan has a commission for *The Bookman,* to draw great European Men of Letters. Under cover of his commission, and to do the accompanying interviews, I have met Barbusse, Paul Fort—nice but no good to me—finally André Salmon, who was just what I was looking for.[38]

   Salmon is nice. He is forty, and belongs to the generation of Apollinaire, Picasso, Max Jacob—which means that he was very closely associated with them, and that his work bears the strong influence of Apollinaire, the great man of that group. More particularly he is interested in literary history, and he gave me wonderful dope on the last twenty years, which I will pepper-and-salt through a dozen articles. [. . .] Salmon has almost a superstitious reverence for Apollinaire, who, he says, originated all the tendencies which are occupying French literature today.

There was a dance Friday at the Bal Bullier which was very Webster Hall, except for one nude lady. I got drunk and enjoyed myself. Met Nina Hamnett, an English portrait painter, who knows more dirty songs than Lionel Moise. The rest is a dull catalogue of books and bridges.

When I think over your last letter, I shall be able to answer. Your last trinity: life, style, art, is very satisfactory to me, more so than the *Freeman*'s check for $20. [. . .]

                                                                                              Mal.

————————

[JCF TLS-1]
[TO: JOHN C. FARRAR,[39] *THE BOOKMAN*]
American University Union,
1, rue de Fleurus, Paris, VIe,
July 27, 1922

Dear Mr. Farrar:

Two days ago I finished an article on Duhamel[40] and mailed it to him with instructions to forward it to you. I wanted to be sure all my facts were straight, and when one is handling a writer as meticulously accurate as Duhamel, one can take no liberties with the facts.

By the time you read this latest article you will have a good idea of what I am trying to do. I am trying to *define* each man I treat and to give a personal impression of him. I am trying, in addition, to give the sort of data that cannot be found in New York; in other words, to make my interviews exclusive. That is why they should interest you.

[. . .]

I spoke of writing five interviews in all: the three I sent you already and two more, Salmon and Mac Orlan. For the last named I think I shall substitute an impression of James Joyce, whom Ivan has drawn already. An

'impression,' I say, for Joyce doesn't give interviews. He made that statement to me several times in the course of a two-hour conversation. I am at
liberty, in other words, to write about Joyce and to quote him, but not to
call my article an interview.

    [. . .]

Faithfully yours,

Malcolm Cowley

[HL TLS-1]

[TO: HAROLD LOEB, *BROOM*]

c/o American University Union,

1, rue de Fleurus, Paris (VIe),

July 27, 1922

Dear Mr. Loeb,

    We managed at last to tear ourselves from Paris, and now we're spend-
ing a week in Brussels. Afterwards to Austria.

    In Paris my strongest impression was gained from the watercolours of
Jules Pascin.[41] No exaggeration. I had seen a couple of reproductions in *The
Dial*—bad reproductions—but I had no idea of the amount or quality of the
work he had done on his American trip. It is caricature of the highest sort,
savantly distorted; civilization revealed by the line of a uniform and race by
the colour of an eyeball. Sure choice of the picturesque: Mexicans in Texas,
niggers in Florida, Jews in New York, Irish in Boston. Stevedores on the
docks shooting craps; a hand reaches out for the money; that hand is the
spirit of gambling personified and still remains a lean nigger hand. Travel-
ling salesman enters the washroom of a pullman, his collar draped round a
brown derby. . . . After Waldo Frank[42] and Mr. Stearns, here at last is a worthy commentary on American civilization.

    [. . .]

    And what's my ante? [. . . .] I want to do a brief article about them,
that's what. I'm going to write it anyway but, quite disinterestedly, I
want to see those pictures reproduced. They deserve a book to themselves, a "Your America," and some day they're going to have it. Some

day in the future. Meanwhile *Broom* has the opportunity to introduce them.[43]

Pascin's address at Paris is 36, Boulevard de Clichy.

Faithfully,
Malcolm Cowley

[NL TLS-1]
[TO: KENNETH BURKE]
c/o American University Union,
1, rue de Fleurus, Paris (VIe)
August 20, 1922

Dear Kenneth:

I came to Austria to get some work done, and thereby made a mistake. One lives cheaply here—perhaps not so cheaply as in Germany—but being sensitive one does not write (not being sensitive one is not a writer).

All I can think about is poverty, political economics, and the exchange.

The Austrians (poor people, they are paid in kronen) haven't enough to buy food. Here in Imst even, where conditions are much better than in Vienna or Innsbruck, I see them dining on a slice of rye bread washed down with water. Water is plentiful. They confide to you how dear things are, and you have to agree with them, although personally and familially you are spending less than a dollar a day at the best hotel. Every day you read the paper to see how much more the krone has fallen, and every day it surprises you. I enclose one to satisfy your curiosity. Seventy-four thousand notes like this would be worth a dollar—today. Laid end to end they would reach from Times Square to the village where the prohibition law is enforced. One of them still buys a match in Austria, and twenty-five will buy a cigarette.

Despite reports to the contrary, tourists are not particularly popular here, and they are growing less popular daily. Revolution is spoken of, with violence to foreigners. If I had enough money to move, I'd move—this despite the fact that the country is the most agreeable, or rather the most grandiose, I have ever seen. I should be happier in Italy or France—somewhere

I felt more welcome. Meanwhile I do exactly what any one else would do under my circumstances. I stuff myself, fill out gaps in my wardrobe, swim, climb mountains. Instead of writing I brood about politics. I don't see how such a thing as pure literature can come out of Austria for the next ten years.

[...]

When we arrived in Imst, Matty had gone already to Reutte, a cheaper town some thirty miles away. He is there with Tzara and a couple more Dadas; at least he was there. I wrote him a note but so far have received no answer. He fights with hotel keepers.

Soul is not functioning.

M.

———————

[NL TLS-3]
[TO: KENNETH BURKE]
c/o American University Union,
1, rue de Fleurus, Paris (VIe)
September 10, 1922

Dear Kenneth:

[...] [H]aving a headache, an eyeache, a toothache, constipation, and a touch of influenza, I pass my leisure building ragtime lyrics. If you have leisure you might write music to them, but I fear you have no leisure.

Or else I meditate about Edna Saint Vincent Millay. She was a famous lesbian when we first met her, so they say. When Floyd [Dell] undertook to lead her into a better path, the first time Floyd led her into a better path, she rolled from her back to one tired delicate side where the skin was white and crushed like violets that children have plucked and thrown away, she rolled over on one wood-violet side and said,

—Floyd, I shall have many lovers.

Meeting Kitty Cannell[44] once in Paris she quoted those lines of Verlaine, "With anyone, at any place, at any time," and said grandiloquently, "Kitty, you know, I think those lines were written just for me." And now she is married to a young boy, a nice boy, and a boy I pity. He too will grow up into a minor poet, and no doubt a fruiter. I wish I knew his name; I should write him and condole. Edna liked you once, didn't she?

Kitty Cannell, by the way, is the mistress of the editor, therefore the editrix of *Broom*. Her taste is pretty sound, sounder than Loeb's, and I believe much stronger. Last week I made a trip into Innsbruck to meet them.

Loeb is thirty years old. His family is somewhat of the type of the Rothschilds: a Jewish family which has possessed money not for one generation but for six or seven, a family with relatives and connections in almost every country. My first year's roommate at Harvard—John Rothschild—familiarized me a little with the type. They have the feel of money and possess it no longer. They put up at the best hotels or the fourth-best hotels, buy and lend generously, support philanthropy or art, and somehow manage to finance everything, although they are always pleading poverty.

At college Loeb was a wrestler, captain of the Princeton wrestling team. He was invited five or six years ago with his wife to the Mowbray Clarke's,[45] near Haverstraw. It was a pre-Rape-and-Raphael sort of circle, but honestly interested in art, and art was a new world to this accomplished wrestler. Dr. Ananda Coomaraswamy[46] was also a member of the circle; he preached Indian negativism; as a result Mr. Mowbray Clarke ran off with another wife than his own and the circle disbanded. Loeb remained artistic and near Haverstraw. He ran The Sunwise Turn, which paid for itself.

I have met another man—of more ability—who became aesthetic late in life. Georges Duthuit[47] adopted a whole philosophy at once and writes brilliantly in that philosophy. Loeb was never sure of his tastes. He came to Europe with Kreymborg to run a magazine, thinking that Kreymborg would edit a vastly superior *Others*. As a matter of fact Kreymborg became scared and conservative, and accepted every ms. submitted from England, rejecting K. Burke and M. Cowley. (Loeb admits to being lukewarm on both "Day Coach" and "Yul";[48] if Kreymborg had pressed he would have accepted them; as soon as they appeared in *Secession,* he kicked himself, and set out immediately to add us to his staff.) [. . .]

[. . .]

Now picture Loeb under the successive influences of Mowbray Clarke, Kreymborg, Kitty Cannell. Josephson has also influence, but no so strong as Kitty's; he doesn't sleep with Loeb. Picture Loeb then; is he a perpetual straw, or is he developing, comparatively late in life, his own opinions? After two days with him, I incline slightly to the second view. He is still very young, much younger in spirit than Charlie Ellis and he is Jimmy Light's grandson at least. He is developing slowly an ability as an essayist; even now he is infinitely more logical than Matty. He does things. He may be material for our Academy. Meanwhile there is always *Broom*.

And, *Broom* existing, I think you ought to write for it. *Broom* is now in a frame of mind to accept almost anything you send it, providing that anything can escape the American censorship. *Broom* has one advantage over *Secession:* it pays. It is a good tool, probably, against *The Dial* (which still has never printed, I believe, the "Portrait of an Arrived Critic," and which uses you too much as a critic and translator).

You are fundamentally a critic, but I still believe I am a better critic because I started out as a poet. You are an infinitely better narrator than I because your basis is criticism.

Broom is damned hard up for American fiction. Send them—him—it—a story.

[. . .]

Perhaps all this is a partial justification of my own for taking a job with *Broom*. Not an important job; just the one Matty had last year. It pays badly: 12 francs a page for translation, $4 a page for prose, $6 a page for poetry, but Loeb seems willing to print damned near anything I give him. Also we concur in our attitude as expatriates expatiating on America as a literary subject. [. . .] I shall translate Salmon and Max Jacob and have a comfortable lever for meeting any one I want to know in Paris.

. . .

I have now the following prose markets:

Dial for literary ideas.

Freeman for political ideas (and I have them).

Broom for cultural ideas.

All I need is the ideas. I feel now as if I had room to turn round in, an opportunity to express myself, which is really, even if the Villagers think so, the only satisfaction in life.

. . .

Secession for me means poetry and polemic.

[. . .]

M.

———

[NL TLS-2] [SC 125–126]
[TO: KENNETH BURKE]
c/o American University Union,
1, rue de Fleurus, Paris (VIe),
September 25, 1922

Dear Kenneth:

I just blew in from Vienna, where I corrected the proof sheets of *Secession* 3. I swore lustily as I corrected. Kenneth, that number stinks of bad writing, Dada and the ghetto. The story by Waldo Frank is abominable. The story by Matty is abominable. The comment is the abomination of abominations. In this same issue is printed a solidly perfect piece of architecture, a romanesque church by Kenneth Burke.[49] It rises out of a huddle of wooden tenements. Possibly they may burn, destroying the church also.

Possibly the whole number may be suppressed. Certainly it will be if the postal authorities happen to read that story by Waldo Frank. Let us hope they do.

[. . .]

The whole weakness of *Secession* is the fact that it is supposed to be a group organ and that the group falls apart in the middle. I often contradict myself, but if there's one thing I believe in, it is good writing. With you I have been trying to work towards solidity and elegance, towards a to-some-extent classical reaction against the muds and fogs of contemporary literature. And then I stand sponsor for the Austrian child which is of high import psychologically. I repeat that the third number of *Secession* has got to be suppressed and that Matty alone cannot edit another number. Otherwise to save our self respect we have got to secede from *Secession*.

[. . .] *Secession* should be a group organ, but I doubt whether it can be the organ of a group of fifteen, because I doubt whether there are fifteen young and intelligent writers in the United States. Talent is cheap but intelligence is rare, and *Secession* has more need of intelligence than talent. However it may, if it is successful, form a group of five or six, which is quite enough.

Secession should not be a dignified medium for perfect stories and elegant poems which will be discovered ten years from now. What's the use. All those stories and poems could be published today—in *Broom* if nowhere else. The purpose of *Secession* is not really to be the organ of a group but to form a group which as yet does not exist. The purpose of a group is to be an audience for poetic drama and to make intelligent literature possible. The way *Secession* can form a group is by publishing both literature and polemic.

[. . .]

You mentioned jealousy, speaking of Matty. At present any jealousy between you and me would be suicidal, because as things have worked out I think our fortunes are rather intertwined. For our own times, which are the only times that matter, we go up or down together.

                                                                M.

———

[HL TLS-3] [PARTLY *WW* 134–135]
[TO: HAROLD LOEB]
c/o American University Union,
1, rue de Fleurus, Paris (VIe),
September 27, 1922

Dear Harold:

When a magazine is founded it has neither a body of writers nor a public, and I suppose of the two the body of writers is harder to create. You must have found it so.

Broom is an international magazine of the arts. You have assembled a staff of translators who find you very good international material. That much of your problem is on the way to solution. But *Broom* is also, by reasons stronger than any of us, an American magazine of the arts. As such it has to represent a definite attitude and a set of definite ideas. It needs a sort of manifesto, which I always thought was lacking.

But by God it isn't any longer, not since your article on the Mysticism of Money.[50] There was a set of clear ideas, ideas which are fresh to American literature and which ought to revitalize it. Of course in *Soil*[51] they were implicit, but you have drawn the implications out of *Soil*. Here is *Broom*'s declaration of principles; all that remains is to apply them.

[. . .] The examples of American art were excellently and justly chosen. The article on the whole was bully. I make a more personal comment on it when I say that it affected my own thinking.

I have gone to the length of developing your antepenultimate sentence into a sketch of my own. I just finished the first draft of "Young Mr. Elkins," which is a portrait of the American intellectual, the sort of person who wants to turn New York into a larger Paris. Venom and bile against the generation of Harold Stearns. Twelve hundred words of fine hate. You'll see it soon, or maybe I can give it to you personally in Berlin.[52]

[. . .]

I found a certain fitness in the fact that the photographs of archaic sculpture were in the same number as your essay. Along side of them you should have reproduced a damned good advertisement as another example of archaic art. [. . .]

Then the sound, informative, technical articles on photography, advertising, typography. Incidentally Marianne Moore's article on George Moore was sound, informative, technical. You might get her to write the same sort of article on poetry, as pendant to the article on photography you are publishing. Matty's summary of *Ulysses*, with its account of Joyce's trade-secrets, was sound, informative, technical; probably the most valuable piece of prose he ever wrote. All this suits excellently with the new *Broom*.

Again, you can develop the internationalism of *Broom* still farther. Make your staff of translators write brief notes on the state of art and literature in their respective capitals. Not the conventional London Letter, Paris Letter, with its vague summary of events, but something more vivid and condensed. Lozowick's[53] Russian Berlin, though written with a sort of high-school cleverness, exactly-balanced cleverness;—Lozowick's note was a step in the right direction. [. . .] Perhaps L.R.,[54] with her politics, would be dangerous for New York, but she should be interesting. Why not write a New York Letter yourself, from Berlin, drawing a picture of the literary New York which you imagine after an absence of sixteen months?

[. . .]

I received a bunch of material from Paris, but not much of it was suitable. Really I should be there myself. I have seen two things that I think *Broom* should print. One is an essay on Whitman by George Duthuit; it must be cut. The other is "L'Extra," by Louis Aragon. Josephson mentioned that story to me; perhaps he has translated it already.[55] I haven't had any reply from [André] Salmon; maybe my letter went astray. Nothing from *La Négresse du Sacré-Coeur*[56] stands alone. If I still had my copy of *À Bord l'Étoile Matutine*,[57] I should translate one of those episodes; unfortunately I sent it to America.

[. . .]

Faithfully,
Malcolm Cowley

Joyce isn't a man you write about casually. You handle him with care and gloves and an eraser.

Cowley to John Farrar, November 12, 1922 [CF]

[JCF TLS-I]
[TO: JOHN C. FARRAR, *THE BOOKMAN*]
American University Union,
1, rue de Fleurus, Paris, VIe,
October 28, 1922

Dear Mr. Farrar:

[. . .]

Joyce has been getting a lot of publicity these days, and I believe you will want something pretty fresh about him; certainly not the conventional article on *Ulysses*. I am going to write up Joyce from the standpoint of his audience; his reaction on the people who know him; a collection of the bromides that one hears in a Parisian conversation on *Ulysses*. My aim as usual will be to send you something that couldn't be written in New York.[58]

In spite of the note about me in the Contributor's Column of *The Bookman*, I have joined no band of expatriates and show every intention of returning to New York. Only, I came to France on a two-year's fellowship from the American Field Service and shall stay until the second year is up. The chief advantage of two years in France is to give you a taste for America. It does.

Not that I have no fondness for French people and French literature, but I happened to be born on the other side of the water and it will be a sad day when I forget it. The only expatriates in Paris are the people who arrived on the last boat and Harold Stearns. As for the rest . . . say, if you want to hear good, nasal, limey-hating Amurricns, if you want to hear Amurricn spoken in all its ungrammatical purity, come to Paris.

Anyway, Paris is a great town to come to. For two years.

[. . .]

Yours faithfully,
Malcolm Cowley

[NL TLS-2] [PARTLY *SC* 128–129]
[TO: KENNETH BURKE]
Chez Tellier,
Giverny par Vernon, Eure,
November 27, 1922

Dear Kenneth:

I came to regard my letters to you as a sort of record not of my life but of my intellectual life, which tacitly we regard as life. Therefore during those relatively long periods when my brain ceases to function, I have written you little. And sometimes even when I was thinking, I wrote little, because I had come to regard only certain departments of the intellect as being of interest to you. Whereas you write me not more conscientiously but with a different sort of conscience; you are capable of making literature out of your household chores; mine I have never succeeded in intellectualizing. It is like the French and German armies during the war; the French, even after four years, never succeeded in regarding the war as something permanent; they lived in makeshift hovels and complained because the roof leaked; the Germans built concrete palaces. I have always regarded chores as being something which in a perfect but attainable state could be avoided entirely; you, like the Germans, have made the best of them and even elevated them into the intellectual life; chores persist and your course is so much the wiser that I shall try to imitate it.

Having decided that the intellectual life was the only real life, I drew such restrictions about it that I entered it seldom, thus only living at moments.

The class will now read the above paragraphs aloud. What comments do you make? Kenneth, I see you raising your hand; what is it? Yes, you are right. The author has been reading Marcel Proust.

Proust bathes everything in some luminous mental fluid which does not alter the facts but makes them stand out in unfamiliar relief, as if seen by moonlight. He is jealous. His brain is incapable of altering his jealousy, but it can make his jealousy effective. He loves. His brain cannot destroy his love, but it can define the exact nature of his passion. The brain of Proust is a tool which he has fashioned to serve his egoism. It is the sharpest of tools; nevertheless Proust belongs to an inferior category of artists; whatever type he belongs to, he is its foremost specimen.

His one novel is not a work of art but a gallery in which the separate portraits are works of art. You walk around observing them; you do not begin at the beginning and read through. The second chapter of the first volume is the finest thing he has written; nevertheless even a busy editor should read everything as far as the first part of *Sodome et Gomorrhe*; *Sodome et Gomorrhe II* is inferior to everything else he has written.[59]

[...]

Giverny is hardly a winter resort. The north winds are cold and wet, the south and west winds warm and wet; only the east winds are cold and dry, and the east wind seldom blows. Fogs and mud. However our apartment is warm and comfortable; the country is genuine, and life costs considerably less than at Montpellier.

A long hill running east and west, with little copses and wheatfields. A huddle of stone cottages. A little river bordered with poplars, damp green fields, then finally the Seine. Giverny should be familiar to everybody; it has been painted for the Luxembourg, the Metropolitan, the Autumn Salon, and the Independents; by Cézanne, Monet, T. E. and J. Butler and Robert W. Chambers. Incidentally there is a wine merchant here who imports an astonishingly good wine from his brother's vineyard in the Bordelais.

Here in Giverny we shall spend the winter and the spring. I shall make fortnightly trips to Paris, one visit to London, perhaps a trip to Montpellier in the spring. I want to write a thesis, prepare a book of poems, write some more portraits for *Broom* and criticisms for *The Dial,* make enough money to go home. I want to do too much. If I had come here to write a novel or a thesis, I should write it. Under the circumstances, with divided aims, I shall probably accomplish little. But more, by God, than I did last year. By God.

M.

———

[NL TLS-1]
[TO: KENNETH BURKE]
Chez Tellier,
Giverny par Vernon, Eure,
Dec. 17, 1922

Dear Kenneth:

This is a fifteen-minute letter. Matty and Hannah are coming to see us, and as soon as I address the envelope I must rush off to meet them. Four days ago we saw them in Paris and Matty took me around to visit his friends the Dada.

He is right about them; they are the most amusing people in Paris. [. . .] [André] Breton, their present *chef d'école*, had discovered a play of which he approved. At least he was not half-hearted in his approval. He brought around his twenty friends with their wives and mistresses to applaud along with him. He attended the rehearsal. The first night. The second night. The third night. When I attended with him it was the fourth night, and Dada still possessed its twenty seats in the balcony. That fourth night they even paid for seats. *Attention, attention* says the hero, and Dada burst into a storm of applause. *Mais ils ne comprendront jamais.* At this remark, which might apply to any book, to any story by any member of the crowd, they applaud so loudly and interminably that the police interferes. Breton orates for half an hour to the parquet. The audience separates into little groups of arguing men. Really it is huge fun.[60]

I met Ford Madox Hueffer in the Dome. He is pathetic and sympathetic. He is so used, from infancy, to the company of great men that he mistakes his every table companion for a great man and bows to his beliefs. He says: "You won't be interested in this, but . . . All this must bore you." Any one who mentions the word "bore" is mistaken for one, and Hueffer has suffered that common fate. Unjustly, for he is charming. He adores Ezra Pound and believes that everything living in English literature comes, like Pound, from America.

[...]

Malcolm

[NL TLS-4] [PARTLY *SC* 129–131]
[TO: KENNETH BURKE]
Chez Tellier,
Giverny par Vernon, Eure,
January 6, 1922 [1923]

Dear Kenneth:

Loeb sails tomorrow for New York to try to arrange for the financing of *Broom,* and he will have landed already by the time you receive this letter. He says he will visit you at the *Dial* office.[61] He will expect you to tell him what you think of *Broom,* and to give him advice as to his future policy. He expects that of every one he meets. He almost always takes the advice. [...]

What is the "modern" note that distinguishes authors of the present "advance guard?" Those terms are so distasteful to me that I can't repeat them without quotes, and yet I possess the current weakness for modernity. And the modern note at present is the substitution of associational for logical thought. Carried to its extremity among the Dadas, the modern note is the substitution of absurdity for logic. You were most "modern" at the time you wrote "My Dear Mrs. Wurtelbach," and boasted of your calculated errors. "First Pastoral" and "Prince Llan" are both individual and traditional. [...]

[...]

Personally I have done little work since I sent the Proust to *The Dial.* [...] Here in Giverny we have had a succession of visitors, each of whom has done his or her little to prevent me from working, and all with the best intentions. Bob Coates[62] and Elsa Petersen were here for a week. Coates has been improved by his year in France. He writes stories without punctuation, but he is beginning not to need this camouflage of modernism; he begins to have ideas. He is a nice boy—six feet—astonishing red hair—freckles—sings Don't Strike Your Mother Boys Just 'Cause She's Old. He is going home at the end of March and I have asked him to look you up. [...]

[. . .] I am working on a "Portrait by Leyendecker," an attempt to describe the life of the man who is advertised in *The Saturday Evening Post*. I try a lot of stunts, slice off on unrelated tangents, end with a long speech to the Chamber of Commerce, which becomes more and more incoherent and ends with a poem made entirely of advertising slogans, which I tried to combine so as to give an atmosphere of inexplicable sadness. Thus:

> *fresh* from the factory
> watch their eyes open
> are you covered?

Are you the ten-pin or the ball? How fast do you think? IS
YOUR BODY THEN YEARS OLDER THAN YOU ARE? Do you like
fine things?

are you covered?

> you and your family need it now
> *you and your family need it now*
> YOU AND YOUR FAMILY NEED IT NOW

> are you covered?

The Sunshine of the Night—Makes the Easiest Way the Best Way—
From Sheep's Back to Yours—Keeps You Warm as Toast—No Metal
can Touch You

are you covered?

> give him the gift you'd like to
> get it not in sale in your vicinity
> write for complete catalog and you
> will avoid imitations and substitutes
> if you are covered.

EAT TWO OR THREE CAKES A DAY
RELAX TENSE NERVES YES MY
BODY IS TEN YEARS OLDER AND
A HANDY PLACE TO THROW TRASH

goodbye old flannel lining
    goodbye, goodbye
old flannel lining goodbye[63]

Since writing "Two American Poets"[64] I have evidently right about faced on the question of the importance of American material. The change is largely psychological. America in the distance begins to loom up as a land of promise, something barbaric and decorative and rich. The form-matter pendulum has taken another stroke, and I begin to believe strongly in the importance of using contemporary material. [. . .]

Mal.

[NL TLS-2]

[TO: KENNETH BURKE]

Giverny, January 11 [1923]

Dear Kenneth: —What's all this row between Munson and Matty? I get echoes of one side of it only. [. . .] Is *Secession* a Cause, a Movement? Are we going to post the Village, advising young writers to "jump on the *Secession* bandwagon?" What's all this pink tea stuff?

I wish Munson would write and give me the other side of the case. Frankly, I begin to be prejudiced against him. I get the distant impression that he is climbing into Olympus over our several backs. His bandwagon stunts have done us this much good: that we can now write for several more magazines per each than we could last winter, and have a respected organ of our own. But when literary politics pass this point, they begin to do more harm than good. We are both of us going to be successful to a certain point, and our success should not come too early; otherwise in ten years, when success should begin, it will have grown stale. And Munson wants to make us, but himself especially, successful NOW.

Perhaps there is something sound in Matty's instinct when he tries to shock people.

Matty has several appealing qualities, chief of which is a lively interest in literature. I hate to admit it, but at present he is really less venial than either of us. He is sure that he will never starve to death, and can afford a certain independence. He is uncompromising and compromising; I mean that he would compromise even the Holy Ghost or Charles Evans Hughes. He treads where angels fear to, being ignorant. In a fight between Munson and Matty I should instinctively support the latter, just as surely as I should support you against Matty. But I am making my judgment on insufficient evidence. Can you send me more?

[...]

Mal

[JBW TLS-2] [NL TYPED COPY-2]
[TO: JOHN BROOKS WHEELWRIGHT]
Giverny par Vernon, Eure
January 14, 1922 [1923]

Dear Jack:

[...]

I hear rumors that you are spending a wildish winter in New York with the *Secession* crowd. Don't let 'em play too many literary politics. It's a good thing not to arrive at successes too quickly in New York, for successes fade more rapidly than they are attained. Every friend you make means one sure and ten potential enemies. It is almost safer to begin by antagonizing people, for every enemy you make is apt to mean potential friends.

There is a fundamental weakness in *Secession:* namely, that it doesn't agree with itself. Munson believes in the sanctity of criticism. Josephson believes in criticism as a burlesque. Brown seems to work on a basis of Joyce, and everyone else to believe that Joyce is an expression of the last generation. Munson, Our Founder, reveres Waldo Frank, a sentiment which I should hardly share. I like Sinclair Lewis, have begun to potter with Amurricn material, think that among the Dadas Louis Aragon has really accomplished something, have been changing my ideas rapidly, don't know just where I stand. However I believe in good writing and believe equally that neither Munson nor Josephson writes good prose. The title of this chapter is A House Divided.

[...]

Mal

[NL TLS-3] [SC 134–136]
[TO: KENNETH BURKE]
Giverny par Vernon–Eure–France–January 28–1923

Dear Kenneth:

[. . .] I want to quote a sentence from your paragraph on quality and quantity in America:

"There is, for example, not a trace of that really dignified richness which makes for peasants, household gods, traditions. America has become the wonder of the world simply because America is the purest concentration point for the vices and vulgarities of the world."

That really dignified richness—Shit, Kenneth, since when have you become a furniture salesman. You seem to have the disease of the American lady I met in Giverny. "You know, in America the wallpaper hardly seems to last a minute it fades or peels off so quickly, but heah the good European papuh dyed with European dyes and put on with *that good European glue.* . . . It just seems to last forevuh." . . . Let me assure you that the chiefest benefit of my two years in Europe was the fact that it freed me from the prejudices of that lady—whose European flour paste was so much better than the American product—and of Harold Stearns. America is just as God-damned good as Europe—worse in some ways, better in others, just as appreciative, fresher material, inclined to stay at peace instead of marching into the Ruhr. I'm not ashamed to take off my coat anywhere and tell these cunt-lapping Europeans that I'm an American citizen. Wave Old Glory! Peace! Normalcy . . . America shares an inferiority complex with Germany. Not about machinery or living standards, but about Art. *Secession* is less important than *Littérature*[65] because it is published in New York. Marin,[66] being American, is a minor figure even beside such a minor French watercolourist as Desnoyers de Segonzac. The only excuse for living two years in France is to remove this complex, and to discover, for example, that Tzara, who resembles you like two drops of water, talks a shade less intelligently than you. To discover that the Dada crowd has more fun than the *Secession* crowd because the former, strangely, has more American pep. That people who read both Suares[67] and Waldo Frank from a sense of duty bracket them together but think that Frank is superior. THE ONLY SALVATION FOR

AMERICAN LITERATURE IS TO BORROW A LITTLE PUNCH AND CONFIDENCE FROM AMERICAN BUSINESS. American literature—I mean Frank, Anderson, Oppenheim,[68] et al.—is morally weak, and before it learns the niceties of form its morale has to be doctored, or all the niceties in the world will do it no good at all.[69]

[. . .] A single electric light on Broadway has the same value as a single lower-case 'e' in *Hamlet*. As for America being the concentration point for all the vices and vulgarities of the world—shit. New York is refinement itself beside Berlin. French taste in most details is unbearable. London is a huge Gopher Prairie. You give me a pain in the ass. Mr. Burke, meet Mr. Stearns. You'll be crazy about each other. You have *so* much in common.

I get carried away. I intended to write only a short note. Honestly, I hate to see you falling for this American Civilization by Thirty Prominent Americans.[70] Let us repeat in chorus that if I were in New York or if you were here in Giverny the disagreement would hardly exist. We are both showing ourselves the rebellious slaves of environment, even our rebellion being determined by our slavery.

[. . .]

Mal

[JBW TLS-2]
[TO: JOHN BROOKS WHEELWRIGHT]
Giverny par Vernon, Eure,
January 30, 1923

Dear Jack

—O shit, Jack—you're getting this serious critic bug, like a very Munson. How long will it be till you begin making a pompous distinction between destructive and Constructive criticism, electing the latter as your High life work? Of course I am answering your objections to the smartness of my criticism of Aiken and Sandburg, a smartness which, incidentally, it took me a month to elaborate. [. . .]

[. . .] My general aim in the review was to place the generation of 1914 in history—something which critics have neglected to do; also to shovel away some of the hooey which surrounds them; also and incidentally to show

how they had pre-empted the adjective American for their own purposes, when its proper meaning is both broader and narrower than the limits of their work.

"Two American Poets" was written in August. Since then I have greatly changed my attitude toward American traditions. I should no longer say that there is no American poetry in the sense that there is French or Chinese poetry. I even disagree with you when you state that America begins with the Civil War, and I think if you re-read *Huckleberry Finn* or the beginning of *Moby Dick* you would revise your statement. From certain documents it would even seem that American characteristics were already pretty well defined in Revolutionary days. I begin to admire Sinclair Lewis, having recently read *Main Street* and *Babbitt,* and I do not think that critics are at all discerning when they say that he writes from hate only. He has done more than Whitman to create a national consciousness. Nationalism is not a spook. Spooks don't hit you on the head with a brick or prevent you from eating in restaurants. Nationalism does just that to the French in Munich. Nationalism is just as real as bricks or restaurants. A few of its manifestations are desirable.

[...] Gossip: We met Clive Bell,[71] who is a bounder, Hueffer, who is a dear, Joyce, who has limp white hands. Seldes[72] arrived in Berlin and had tea with the Bonis and Josephsons. The latter, during their visit to Paris, introduced me to the remainder of the Dada people, young men with a great deal of vitality and charm. Tzara just spent the week-end with us. Stewart Mitchell wrote from Cambridge. The Nefs, who passed through Paris recently, entertained us regally.... Ideas: Mine, after a long period of mist and fog, are beginning to clarify slowly. You will note a greater interest in things American, which is the normal result of two years in Europe.... We expect to return in the early summer. [...]

Normally,
Mal

[TT ALS-2]
[TO: TRISTAN TZARA]
Giverny par Vernon, Eure,
le 8 février, 1923

Cher ami,

Le jemenfoutisme absolu c'est le seul état d'ésprit vraiment logique. Un écrivain vraiment dada s'en fout de l'activité collective comme de tout autre agissement sur l'ésprit de publique. Et moi, néanmoins, n'étant pas vraiment logique, j'aime l'activité en groupe et j'éspère que le groupe dada puisse se reconstituer.

Merci pour votre lettre. Merci également pour le livre de Miss Bitch. [. . .]

Je crois que j'ai oublié une livre chez vous: *Pavannes and Divisions*, par Ezra Pound. Si vous le trouvez, pouvez-vous me l'envoyer?

Il faut arranger un temps pour venir chez nous [. . .]. Nous avons la chambre; vous pouvez y travailler, et nous serons heureux de vous voir, tous les deux.

Tâchez d'envoyer la photographie de passeport à Peggy pour qu'elle puisse achever le dessein [*sic*].

Je vous enverrai un mot avant devenir à Paris. En attendant,

bien cordialement votre

Malcolm Cowley

. . .

Dear friend,

This I-could-not-care-less-attitude is the only really logical state of mind. A writer truly dada does not care about collective action any more than he cares about influencing the general public's state of mind. As for me, nevertheless, not being a logical being, I like group activities and I hope that the dada group will reconstitute itself.

Thanks for your letter. Thanks, also, for the book of Miss Bitch.[73] [. . .]

I believe I've left a book with you: *Pavannes and Divisions,* by Ezra Pound. If you find it, could you send it to me?

We should make arrangements for you to visit us [. . .]. We have a room; you could work there, and we should be happy to see you, both of us.

Try to send the passport photograph to Peggy so she can complete the drawing.[74]

I will send you word before coming to Paris. Meanwhile,

Cordially yours,
Malcolm Cowley

———————

I haven't swallowed Dada hook and sinker; my instincts are classical and intellectual; I'll save my soul if it can be saved.

Cowley to Kenneth Burke, March 18, 1923 [NL]

[NL TLS-3] [PARTLY *SC* 136–138] [PARTLY *PMC* 471–472]
[TO: KENNETH BURKE]
Giverny par Vernon–Eure–February 8–1923

Dear Kenneth:

Paris is a town I enter with joy and leave without regret: I repeat that experience weekly and have repeated it since November 1917. I can't imagine people living in Paris. It is a town where one spends week-ends which occasionally last a lifetime.

My last voyage was spent chiefly with Dadas. The crowd is trying to re-create itself. Tzara, Rigaut, Breton, Ribemont-Dessaignes, Aragon, Picabia were assembled together for the first time in eighteen months. They fought but finally decided to stage a joint manifestation. About twenty of us signed a paper. I suppose I am now officially a Dada, although none of them greet me with great warmth except Aragon and Tzara. A poem of mine is to be engraved in the program of the Russian Ball, along with Tzara, Ribemont-Dessaignes and thirty others. Tzara is translating "Valuta"[75] for *les feuilles libres*. At the same time I lunch with the hated enemies of the Dada group: Salmon and MacOrlan, and interview in the most fraternal manner the enemies of Salmon, MacOrlan and the Dada group, like Vildrac and Duhamel. Like Matty last year I am being received into the complex life of Paris. To become a true citizen of that fantastic and unlivable city, I should only have to steal the mistress of, let us say,

Vitrac,[76] and to hand on Peggy to, let us say, Tzara. I have no wish to be a citizen of Paris.

Dada c'est le jemenfoutisme absolu. It is negation of all motives for writing, such as the Desire for Expression, the Will to Create, the Wish to Aid. A Dada has only one legitimate excuse for writing: because he wants to, because it amuses him. Therefore the movement becomes a series of practical jokes. Dada c'est le seul état d'esprit vraiment logique.

But not entirely logical. A writer who was truly dada would disdain collective action as he would disdain any other attempt to influence the mind of the public. The actual Dadas, on the contrary, try to accomplish things which are sometimes serious. They try to work together.

Their love of literature is surprisingly disinterested. At their memorable meeting it was proposed that none of them should write for any except dada publications during the next three months. No dada publication is widely read or pays. The proposal would have been carried except for the objection of one man out of twenty.

Their commerce is tiring and stimulating. I left Paris with fifty new ideas and hating the groupe dada. They are a form of cocaine and personally take no stimulants except their own company. Last Wednesday all the Americans I knew went to a tea and got divinely drunk. The French had a three-hour meeting at which not even water was served. And much more excitement than at the tea where gin only was poured from the pot.

They take their wives and mistresses everywhere but in the sole quality of wives or mistresses. This, perhaps, is a valuable suggestion for the *Secession* group. Our anti-feminism went the wrong way to achieve its ends.

Talent ... we have as much as they, perhaps more, but less vitality, less courage. Because we write for other aims we achieve less fun out of our writing, which is often equally true of our readers.

They live in Paris. That is my final criticism. They are over-stimulated, living in a perpetual week-end. I like to meet them on week-ends.

I have grown very fond of Tzara.

Will any of them ever accomplish anything? Yes, but not while they remain in the group. As they grow more powerful they will break away, as Soupault[77] has done already. Aragon is immensely talented but follows the stronger and less talented Breton with a sort of canine devotion. Till he breaks away he will write interesting sketches. Tzara speaks well of Éluard and Ribemont-Dessaignes,[78] but I am unfamiliar with their work.

Whatever my judgment they have affected not my thinking but my writing profoundly. I wish you could meet them because I think you would react in somewhat the same way to the stimulus.

[...]

Loeb came back from New York with the impression that Matty had made himself vastly unpopular. The fate of *Broom* is in the balance; it may end with the next issue and may go on with more money. . . . Matty's own personality is a puzzle I can no longer solve. You would understand him better after meeting the Dadas, whom he apes down to their methods of conducting a quarrel and their need for quarreling. His most charming quality is his willingness to compromise himself. [...]

[Written in margin:] Letter from Loeb this morning: *Broom* ends with March issue short of a miracle, thus depriving me of the second magazine which would publish anything I wrote, and the first which would pay me for it . . . I suppose Matty will come to Paris before sailing. *Tell nobody as yet and especially not Munson.*

[...]

                                                                        M.

——————

If *Broom* had no rudder, or too many of them, its course was always interesting. It was the appearance of *Broom* which made the Viennese letters of Hugo von Hofmannsthal appear so hopelessly stodgy. It was less dignified than *The Dial* and wrong more often, but more interesting (I repeat the word).

Cowley to Kenneth Burke, March 11, 1923 [NL]

[HL TLS-2] [PARTLY *WW* 156]
[TO: HAROLD LOEB]
Giverny par Vernon, Eure, Feb. 9, 1923

Dear Harold: —It was a tough blow but you had been expecting it so long that it lost much of its force. Write *finito* on *Broom,* probably the most interesting magazine which Americans ever published. Its poetry from the first outranked every other American magazine—or English—; its reproductions were vastly superior; it translated what nobody else dared to translate. Its native fiction was weak, but that could hardly be called your fault. See how many complete files of *Broom* you can collect; they will be valuable.

[. . .]

[. . .] It's a damned shame that *Broom* should be stopping just now, but then . . . oh hell . . . . . . O . . . . . . HELL.

Malcolm

[BR TLS-1]
[TO: BURTON RASCOE, EDITOR, NEW YORK TRIBUNE]
Giverny par Vernon, Eure,
March 25, 1923

My dear Mr. Rascoe:

From time to time, even in Europe, I see a copy of the Sunday *Tribune,* and I always turn to the book section first. You have done wonders with it. It was fun to write for, even in the old days when everything was vastly haphazard. Now it is a magazine for which one can write intelligently.

I wonder whether I could write anything from over here. [. . .] There is Ezra Pound, for example; nobody has yet undertaken to describe the curious situation he occupies in Paris, where the young men avoid him as being too conservative. What comedy and pathos! And there is Tzara . . . did anybody ever tell you why the Dada movement broke up, or what the ideas really were which brought it into being? And Giraudoux,[79] who has just been published in New York.

[. . .]

[. . .] I don't think that any one has translated the feeling of exhilaration that one gets in the Parisian literary world today; I should like to do it in these articles.

Yours faithfully,
Malcolm Cowley

[DIAL TLS-1]
[TO: SCOFIELD THAYER, *THE DIAL*]
Giverny par Vernon, Eure,
May 18, 1923

Dear Mr. Thayer:

Time is up; within six weeks I'll be having to leave France. Before going I should like to talk several things over with you. [...]

Principally I should like to know what you think about my work in *The Dial*. Kenneth wrote that you liked the essay on Proust. For the rest I have no idea. Some of the later criticisms were pretty experimental, like almost everything else I have been writing. Being very doubtful whether I should ever be given two years more of free time, I tried to make the best of these two years by learning as much as possible and by doing nothing twice. For me an admirable course, but perhaps risky for the magazines to which I contribute. Therefore I ask your advice.

After three years of the new *Dial* it seems hard to imagine a world in which *The Dial* did not exist. It is the rock of American literature, on which schools, movements and other magazines are founded. It has been called conservative, and that is perhaps its greatest triumph. Imagine anybody's calling it conservative three years ago. The public which could call *The Dial* conservative was formed by reading *The Dial*.

I think there was never a period in American literature which promised more. Not because the public taste in general is better, but because there have risen in the last three years a number of special publics, and because there are a couple of dozen capable writers who haven't been recognized yet. Recognition by the general public is our national form of artistic euthanasia.

[...]

Yours faithfully,
Malcolm Cowley

[DIAL TLS-1]
[TO: SCOFIELD THAYER, *THE DIAL*]
Giverny par Vernon, Eure, France,
June 2, 1923

Dear Mr Thayer:

[. . .] I am sorry, because I value your judgement, that you like my verse less than my prose. I am glad that you said 'verse' and not poetry. To me poetry is a quality that verse and prose may share equally. It bores me to write anything that lacks poetry, which must be one of two reasons you like my book reviews. I wish you could like the same quality in my verse, where it exists in a purer state, perhaps, and where certainly it has more music. The fatal weakness of book reviews is the fact that unless one cheats they die with the book reviewed. [. . .]

Sincerely,
Malcolm Cowley

———

[NL TLS-2]
[TO: KENNETH BURKE]
Giverny par Vernon, Eure,
May 20, 1923

Dear Kenneth:

Our French venture is smoked down to its butt-end. Within six weeks we should be sailing if we find the money to sail. It will have to be borrowed. [. . .]

[. . .] I am going over to the damned unconscious school of writers, having discovered that my best phrases are really inspiration. The plan, the structure, the criticism of faults are perfectly conscious, but the music of the best lines and the unity of the whole impression are not. It is almost an invariable rule with me that I create a poem by rewriting it. I have found the reason. By force of retyping the same page a dozen times I semi-hypnotize myself and suddenly find that words and ideas are flowing freely through this usually tongue-tied brain. But I also find that the things I do easily are the result of damned hard work at some previous time . . . . . . No, damnation, I am not going over to the unconscious school. I continue to abjure their

Franks and Andersons. But I have found that my own unconscious is often a shortcut to better work than I can do consciously, and I am trying to make the best use of this unexpected tool. Consciously.

[...]

Three or four days ago I visited Harold Loeb, who is preparing the first number of the new series of *Broom* and a good number it should be. [...] *Broom* in its next issue will contain an explanation and defense of its policy, in the course of which Loeb says that it exists as an organ for a certain group of writers, describing the characteristics of your work, mine and Matty's, and mentioning Coates, Crane,[80] Toomer,[81] Westcott,[82] Winters,[83] Wheelwright, etc. It means a direct bid for our own crowd with its far dependencies. If *Broom* gets into a position where it is sure to continue, I think the ideal solution is to make it the worthy paper, full of permanent work, while *Secession* becomes polemic, combative, stunty. Whether *Broom* continues at all depends largely on you and me, so think over your attitude carefully. The most difficult point in the program is to reconcile Munson and Loeb and to convince the two of them that both magazines are necessary.

[...] I had lunch with Cummings two days ago and found him charming. Before that I had never been sure whether he was a friend or an enemy. He said he was glad to contribute both to *Broom* and *Secession*. [...]

M.

[HC ALS-2] [RR 10]
[TO: HART CRANE]
Giverny par Vernon, Eure,
May 20, 1923

Dear Crane: —Thanks for your note in *S4N*,[84] which I thought the most intelligent criticism our book [*Eight More Harvard Poets*] received. I hope I was right. Anyhow you gave me a chance to tell you that I like your own poems. For several months I have been telling people how good they are, and perhaps I have made some impression. You write with a bombast which is not Elizabethan but contemporary, and you are one of two or three people who can write a twentieth century blank verse, about other subjects than love, death and nightingales and in other patterns than ti tum ti tum ti tum ti tum ti tum. Salutations.

"Poster," in *Secession* 4, was printed between Williams and [Wallace] Stevens, and was far better than either of them. *O brilliant kids* is the most simple, the most brilliant combination of noun and epithet that I have seen these many years.

I hope you don't rush to print a volume. If we all wait three or four years, till our public is formed, we can have a great deal more fun by publishing.

Mrs. Cowley and I are sailing in a few weeks. We hope to meet you when we get back.

Sincerely,
Malcolm Cowley

[NL TLS-2]
[TO: KENNETH BURKE]
Giverny par Vernon, Eure,
June 4, 1923

Dear Kenneth:

[...]

I have been intending to write you a letter about Aragon,[85] for his is a character which demands a long explanation. His influence is less literary than moral, and that is why he imposed all his ideas on Matty. Imagine this elegant young man, from a family whose social connections are above reproach: a young man so gifted that the word genius must have been used in his connection ever since the age of four, when he wrote his first novel. A brilliant career stretches in front of him. He has read everything and rejected it. Suddenly, at a certain age, he begins to reject all his family and social connections deliberately, and with a splendid disdain which he had acquired from his early successes, to tell everybody exactly what he thought. And still he was successful. He has so much charm when he wishes to exercise it, that it takes him years to make an enemy. But by force of repeated insults, he succeeds. He retains all the hatred of compromise which is the quality of a youth we never wholly possessed. He disapproves of the *Nou-velle Revue Française;* therefore he has refused to write for it, although he had already closed all the other channels of publication. He insults Rivière.[86] He throws up his job with *Paris-Journal.* Finally an old collector gives him 800 francs a month to write a literary history, and so he comes to Giverny, where he spends his time marching up and down country roads and reciting poetry, with gestures.

He lives literature. If I told him that a certain poem of Baudelaire's was badly written, he would be capable of slapping my face. He judges a writer largely by his moral qualities, such as courage, vigour, the refusal to compromise. He proclaims himself a romantic. As a romantic, his atti-tude to women is abominable. He cannot treat them as human beings: he is either reciting poetry to them, which bores them, or trying to rape them. He is always seriously in love; he never philanders. He is often a ter-rible bore. He is unbelievably energetic. He is an egoist and vain, but faithful to his friends. If he comes to America you will meet him and have a chance to judge him for yourself. There are other people I have met whose work is interesting, but Aragon is the only one to impose himself by his character . . . I forgot to say that he has a sort of dog-like affection for André Breton.[87]

My apologies for this long digression, but I think it will explain a great deal of Matty to you, and possibly some of myself, for I admit that Aragon has had a certain influence on me, which I have tried to keep in a moral sphere . . . The consciousness of returning to New York gives a relativity to everything I say, for I am certain that New York and the attempt to make money will change me again completely. Would it be better to have some stable envi-ronment in which one's ideas could develop in more orderly progression? Probably, but then it has been a mistake of yours and mine to avoid experi-ence. We have lost by it.

Malcolm

[NL TLS-2]
[TO: KENNETH BURKE]
Giverny par Vernon, Eure,
June 16, 1923

Dear Kenneth:

[. . .]

The rubies of my wisdom . . . I am working on the monumental Racine. I have written a long outline, several pages of notes, and five hundred polished words. Every night I recite verses to put myself to sleep. Racine can be tremendous [. . .]. It's something to tear the guts out of you. But to write an essay about it. . . . Anyhow, my essay is not on the beauty of Racine's diction but on the conventions of his theatre, suggesting that the existence of conventions is more important than their exact nature. I end with a discussion for the need of a historical definition of classicism, to place beside the historical definition of romanticism, suggest Racine as the classical type par excellence, and in a tangent point out that the whole classical movement is only a part of literature and not the ideal for everybody. Thirty-five hundred words at least.[88] Blooey.

In the mornings I write a little at Racine, but I find writing difficult, and divert myself with unpublishable matters such as An Open Letter to Gertrude Stein on Lesbian Literature, or such songs as:

> Battling Denver Benny
> The Rocky Mountain Jew
> Spent a pretty penny
> A lady for to screw
> Pimples were too many
> Charms alas too few
> —Denver O Battling Benny
> I shall never sleep with you
> We shall never never never
> Never never sleep together
I shall never never never sleep with you.

And I make no preparations whatsoever for returning to New York. They tell me there are houses in New York of 56 stories. Is it true?

M

[NL TLS-1] [SC 143]
[TO: KENNETH BURKE]
Giverny par Vernon, Eure,
June 29, 1923

Dear Kenneth:

    [. . .]

Yesterday, Kenneth, it struck me with the force of revelation that the time has come for us to write some political manifestos. We are not critics or short story writers; we are poets; in other words we are interested in every form of human activity. To be ticketed and dismissed as such-and-such sort of a writer makes my ass tired. Also I am eaten with the desire to do something significant and indiscreet. An Open Letter to President Harding. An Open Letter to the Postmaster General on the Censorship, in which I admit the right to censor, point out how dangerous my opinions are, and demand why I am not suppressed. And other manifestations: for example a call to voters to cease voting, an attack on the liberals, an attack on the socialists and communists. Imagine all these documents appearing together in a political number of *Broom*. What a stink. But the stink would mean something. In a country as hypocritical as the United States, merely to enumerate the number of laws one has broken would be a significant gesture. And if all the literary forces of law and order rose up against us, we could always return to farming or reading proofs. [. . .] And, Kenneth, I have the feeling that some such courageous and indiscreet step is required of us, if we are not going to resign ourselves to petty literary wars with Ezra Pound, Robert McAlmon, Floyd Dell.[89]

    I continue to work vainly on Racine, whom I admire more and more. [. . .]

Yrs.
Malcolm

[NL TLS-I] [SC 144]
[TO: KENNETH BURKE]
Giverny par Vernon, Eure,
July 5, 1923

Dear Kenneth:

[...]

[...] The famous two years is ending with little accomplished and much learned. It seems to me that their great value was not so much what I learned about literature as the aid they gave me in developing a personal philosophy. I haven't defined that philosophy, and I am even uncertain as to what manner of life it demands me to lead. I am considerably less anxious to be a hackwriter. My ideal would be to find somebody to pay my expenses for five years on condition that I published nothing during that time. The only important matters are friends, books, sex, the cultivation of the mind, but not especially in the order named. I can't write anything more tonight.

M.

❧ PART III ❧

The City of Anger—New York, 1923–1929

Dada in New York, 1923–1925

Back in New York in late August 1923, Cowley hustled to pay off his debts. Though he was ambitious to pursue a literary life without commercial compromise, he was soon forced to resume working as an advertising copywriter at *Sweet's Architectural Catalogue*. Meanwhile, he and Josephson were struggling to keep *Broom* financially afloat. Looking backward at his Paris experiences, he was determined to shake up what he now saw as a lethargic New York literary scene: "People need to be shocked, have pins stuck in their buttocks, made to think," he had written to Witter Bynner on May 20, 1923. Cowley wanted to inject into the New York scene some of the excitement that had so thrilled him in the Dada movement. In October 1923, discouraged by factional quarrels and the apathy of his literary friends, he called a "catholic" meeting—to be held in an Italian restaurant-annex-speakeasy on Prince Street—of all those who had contributed to either *Broom* or *Secession*. But the meeting ended in more disagreement and ill feeling. Disillusioned, and overcome by his unfocused and fragmentary life in the modernist city, he poured out his sense of dislocation and disorientation into his letters to friends.

———

[NL TLS-1]
[TO: KENNETH BURKE]
16 Dominick Street, New York City,
October 11, 1923

Dear Kenneth:

    Can you come into town next Fridaynight (Oct. 19th)? Me, I place great importance on your coming. *Broom* is near its close, which must not be ignoble. To die gently on an ebb tide is not my idea of death. Munson is meditating new plans for *Secession*. When they are ripe, I suppose he will present them to us and ask whether we should like to contribute to *his* magazine. Everybody else seems content to settle down to a winter of occasional drunks and conversation about living conditions. The greatest American writers are George Moore and Arthur Schnitzler.[1] Mr Kreymborg has licked enough asses to be published by Harcourt, Brace. The situation would be encouraging if anybody retained the capacity for indignation. If one hates a person violently, the strongest term one is allowed to employ is to say, "I take no interest in him."

Kenneth, I decided with Matty to call a meeting of everybody who had worked for *Broom* or *Secession,* a catholic meeting with Brown, Burke, Coates, Cowley, Crane, Frank, Josephson, Munson, Nagle, Toomer, Westcott, Williams, or such of them who are beyond taking-no-interest-in our immediate future. If we can get together in one room, we can at least define our positions, if we can make no plans to go ahead. Piddling Jesus. The people who can be content with art-for-art's-sake, three issues of a magazine composed of essays by GBM [Gorham B. Munson] and stories by WF [Waldo Frank] and an occasional glass of synthetic gin, will continue to be content. For God's sake let's brew some stronger liquor.[2] For God's sake, let's find out where people stand.

[. . .]

Bob Coates should be in New York in a couple of days. I haven't seen Seldes yet. I like Crane, but every time I see him we fight on another subject.

[. . .]

Snappy answer, kid.

M

[NL TLS-I]
[TO: JOHN BROOKS WHEELWRIGHT]
16 Dominick Street, New York City
Oct. 25, 1923

Dear Jack:

To publish a magazine is perhaps the easiest of the accepted ways of making enemies. [. . .]

Everything came to a head at a meeting we held last Friday (October 19). We wanted to learn whether people were willing to work together, whether they would support *Broom,* and whether they were willing to join in further manifestations. The answers in general were No. The question of personal quarrels seemed to overshadow everything else. Munson and his little gang were willing to work for *Broom* if Matty were forced off the board; they said so flatly. And my only possible answer was that if Matty, in a burst of generosity such as would be quite foreign to his nature, decided to resign from *Broom* for the common good, I should resign also to keep my hands clean. I decided to write for *Secession* no longer. Kenneth took a middle-of-the-road course which involved resigning from the board of *Secession,* leaving Munson as sole editor. At the same time it transpired that there were so many real differences of opinion between Munson and Brown-Josephson-Cowley that our co-operation in the same magazine would make it as meaningless as *The Dial.* I told Munson he should continue *Secession,* that its policy was so far removed from that of *Broom* that there was no real competition between the two. I said I hoped there would be no ill feeling. He said there would be. Awright.

[...]

Malcolm

[NL TLS-I] [SC 147]
[TO: KENNETH BURKE]
16 Dominick Street, New York City,
[November] 8, 1923

Dear Kenneth:

My head being empty, a letter becomes a catalogue of events. Eugene O'Neill, Mr. O'Neill the playwright, Gene, came to New York. We drank at Jim's. Peggy went back to Ridgefield with Gene and Agnes.[3] There was a Halloween party at our office, much dancing, pretty girls; my head still buzzes with jazz. (Rings with rag?) I went to Ridgefield, stayed till Sunday, went to Woodstock, stayed till Tuesday. We played hide and go seek. I wrote a jazz poem in jazzy prose and swore I should write no more verse. Matty is publishing [Apollinaire's] *The Poet Assassinated* to clear off some of *Broom's* deficit or pile it on—one becomes so confused. Munson seems to have Broken off Relations with me. Mr. O'Neill speaks a language so different from ours that I seemed to converse with him from different worlds. Cummings' book[4] appeared. The beer is getting poorer. New York has enveloped itself for me in a haze of ragtime tunes, a sort of poetry which leads me to a melancholic happiness. To work in an office is a refuge. Are the trees indeed bare? Who is this man Burke?

I dashed out of the subway and down 42nd Street. She was standing on the corner. So there are prostitutes in New York. I shall never speak to one, but the knowledge of them makes the city more livable. Behind swinging doors. Draw two. Did you hear about the new show? Matty has gone to Woodstock. The rumble of trucks is doom approaching. When the skyscrapers tumble, when cornices fall to crush the people in the street. Speed.

Speed. See people. Gossip. Drink. Smoke. There is a quieter land. Some day surely, and not too far in the future, we shall buy a farm. I am counting a great deal on your being here this winter. Violent physical exertion when drunk is the solution of every moral problem.

M.

[NL TLS-2]
[TO: WILLIAM SLATER BROWN]
16 Dominick Street, New York City,
November 14, 1923

Dear Bill:

It is only with the greatest difficulty and at the end of efforts whose poignancy leaves me exhausted that by the exercise of the conceptive powers which at an earlier age made my career spoken of as promising I succeed to a degree in bringing up a picture, its poetry is not that of definite concept but of the romantic haze, a hazy picture, I say, of the scene in Fisher's Field one day last week.[5] Blows fell with the accuracy of a description by Waldo Frank. I see two men who roll in the soft mud. Whose blood is that on a fallen leaf? No answer. The mist descends, and all the rest is literature.

People disgust me who try to carry physical matters into the domain of the intellect. Munson keeps repeating, in those letters the writing of which is his principal vice, that he won a "moral victory." If I remember my war, moral victories are the sort which precede strategic retreats. [. . .] I never saw a man of so little talent who possessed such a capacity for irritation. He never lies. He told Kenneth about hitting Matty, about rolling over on top of him, and ended by saying, "Fisher discreetly calls the fight a draw." All of these statements agree with Matty's; they must be gospel. But. The impression he gives is this: I defeated Matty clearly but Fisher, out of politeness, called the affair a draw. By a combination of truths he produces falsehood. Immediately on reading this, the fight changed its values for me. It had seemed a sorry spectacle, completely ridiculous; now suddenly I wanted to punch his pasty face myself.

[. . .]

M

[NL TLS-2]
[TO: KENNETH BURKE]
16 Dominick Street, New York City,
November 18, 1923

Dear Kenneth:

The function of poetry is to make life tolerable. New York was becoming more than I could bear. In the few moments when I was alone I found myself miserable to a degree which, in my case, you never seem to credit. The dance at our office was a partial salvation; it filled my head with ragtime tunes, with impossibilities and pretty girls, all of which is the strong and vulgar poetry peculiar to New York. Afterwards the irregular landscapes of Manhattan took a different meaning and I began to drink out of good nature. Drinking has left me miserable, establishing life's unalterable balance. I went to the museum.[6]

[. . .]

Walking home from the museum I drew two sentences from air and began to embroider on them. "Beauty is a by-product. I like the authors who build an emotion instead of expressing it."

At Giverny the buildings were ugly. The mill was an exception. Whereas the other builders had tried to create beautiful houses, and succeeded in summer villas, hideous, the owner of the mill had confined himself to lines which contributed to the utility of the building. *Beauty is a by-product.* Aesthetics has something to do with efficiency. The man who writes for eternity writes dullnesses. The man who attempts deliberately to create beauty is an artsy-crafts-man.

Literature is using words to make emotions. There is the literature of expression and the literature of creation. Personally *I like the writers who build an emotion instead of expressing it.* The test of a book is whether it is organic; whether it exists independently of the man who wrote it. Yet a bad man can not write a good book.

And so on, and so on.[7] There are logical weaknesses which my use of simple declarative sentences, without connectives, serves to cover over.

[. . .]

M

[HL TLS-2]
[TO: HAROLD LOEB]
16 Dominick Street, New York City,
November 22, 1923

Dear Harold:

It is terribly difficult to get time to write you. New York keeps one so busy there is no time for the simplest actions, the most simple emotions. Suddenly one discovers himself to be magnificently bored or sad or in the midst of a frantic good humor. I have undergone all of them. Yesterday a stenographer in the office came to me and said—Mr Cowley, what is a triste?—A what?—A triste, an engineering triste. While I explained to her that she meant an engineering treatise, I felt such an unutterable sadness that I crunched my teeth to keep from weeping. New York has several kinds of poetry, of which this sadness is one. The city is most bearable, however, to ragtime, cheek to cheek with a pretty stenographer. When looking at a Manhattan landscape one should hum Mamma went away, she didn't say where, she didn't say where. The brick house, the empty lot, the skyscraper, juxtaposed, become an organic whole. New York is also more amusing on payday.

[. . .] I personally should be very sorry to see *Broom* go under, for I think all of us need an organ in which to print. Much as you would like to hear it, I am not going to repeat the sordid details of my fight with Munson. [. . .] I got sick of him, and it is quite possible that under circumstances easily postulated I may save you the disagreeable job of changing his complexion from a pasty white to a pasty blue. [. . .] I should prefer to bury the affair. Meanwhile, I shall never write for *Secession*. Munson's friends are Frank, Crane, Toomer. He will also publish Westcott, Winters, and one more story of Burke's. Crane is the only one I grudge him. Burke is neutral but much more interested in *Broom,* to the next number of which he is contributing a fine story. The rest of us, sensationalists, apers of French dadaists, skyscraper primitives—we have been called a fine bunch of names—are in the position where, if we didn't want to continue *Broom*—and we do—we should be forced to by circumstances. [. . .] Harold, we've got to have a paper, and I am willing to spend considerable time, even money, to that end.

[. . .]

Our best to Kitty.

Yours,
Malcolm

─────────────

[VWB TLS-I]
[TO: VAN WYCK BROOKS]
16 Dominick Street, New York City,
December 18, 1923

My dear Mr Brooks:

In the next number of *Broom* we are publishing an attack on the *Dial* award.[8] In spite of our explicit language (Mr Brooks is a critic of integrity (# and worthy of any prize which *The Dial* may choose to give him) there are sure to be people who will interpret our open letter as an attack on you. Nothing could be more false. What we are attacking is the prize itself, pardon, the award, which by going to writers of different purposes, opinions and levels of ability, has lost all of its meaning. We think you deserve a more definite award.

Without doubt *The Dial* intended at one time to give the prize to Cummings. I have been given several reasons why they changed their minds, and naturally cannot repeat them. "Policy" was one, which is another name for lack of courage. If they had intended from the beginning to give you the award, we should have nothing but praise for their decision. Their change of mind was not unjust to Cummings but to you.

This letter is damnably difficult to write, and if I placed a lower value on your friendship, I should certainly keep silence. The people one can respect are so rare that they deserve complete explanations.

Respectfully,
Malcolm Cowley

(# "Integrity" was the word I chose, because it is the rarest quality in American letters. Ability is cheap; we all have it, and if I had said that you were able, merely, I should have been insulting.

The contents of the second paragraph is the only "confidential" part of this letter.

[NL TLS-2] [SC 155–156]
16 Dominick Street, New York City,
February 1, 1924

Dear Kenneth:

I live by clocks which deceive me. I rise at 8:45 and reach the office at 8:45. I rise at 9:05 and reach the office at 9:20. I rise at 8:00 and reach the office at 9:30. I never keep engagements, but on no principle. I have time for nothing.[9] What I lay down is never picked up again. Suddenly I had a hysterical desire to read Plato, and rushed to the library to consume *Phaedrus* and the *Banquet,* out of which latter I remember that Alcibiades compared Socrates to a flute-player, which I thought an obscene remark. As soon as I put off writing you so long that it became a duty, I did not write. Why is it that this fragmentary life puts me in extreme sympathy with you, so that my ambitions now are to read Plato and Goethe, and to write an esthetic in 96 theses to be nailed to some church door, perhaps *The Dial*'s, out of a sense of the necessary disproportion between end and means. [. . .]

[. . .]

Out of Paul Elmer More[10] I derived a statement of the great truth that the basis of philosophy is to attain ataraxy (free security, or more vulgarly (Oxford), stoical indifference, from *a*, not, and *tarasso*, disturb). Philosophy is the power of not being disturbed. After six months of New York, one takes refuge in such preoccupations, and the atmosphere of New York is mysticism or a (hysterical) classicism, to be distinguished from the classicism of the Mediterranean, which results from sympathy with one's environment instead of rebellion against it. Let us repeat, however, I AM NOT DISTURBED I AM NOT DISTURBED I AM NOT DISTURBED I AM NOT DISTURBED DISTURBED NOT AM I NOT DISTURBED NOT I AM NOT. NOT.

NOT.   neti   not. [. . .]

MC

During December, January, and February Cowley and Josephson struggled against all odds to keep *Broom* afloat. The death blow came when the January issue, containing a story by Burke, "Prince Llan," which referred to a woman's breasts in the plural, was classified as pornographic and confiscated by the postmaster general as unmailable under U.S. postal law. In March, Cowley reported to Loeb on the suppression of *Broom*.

[HL TLS-2] [PARTLY *WW* 205–206]
[TO: HAROLD LOEB]
16 Dominick Street, New York City,
March 14, 1924

Dear Harold:

You have a lot to forgive me, or rather, since forgiveness is a repulsive gesture, a great deal to understand. The key to ¾ of my actions at present is the fact that I have time for nothing; no time for a decent shave, for a haircut, to think, talk, write letters, or for more than a duty-bath at hebdomedary intervals. This evening, having stolen a moment to sit down at the typewriter, I'll try to make a brief report of the things which may interest you.

It would have been much better to suspend *Broom* after the November issue, when Geffen[11] withdrew his support. My personal plan was to devote the December issue to a closing gesture, a number composed of propaganda from all our contributors. However, the future did not look dark, and I agreed with Matty to go on. For two weeks we rushed about New York looking for money, and raised the price of a new issue, which by that time became the January *Broom*. Then Matty got his job on the Exchange, and everything ended. It took us some weeks to realize that everything was ended, but when letters piled up without our being able to answer them; when we were suppressed with a chance for big publicity, and could not take advantage of the chance, we began to see how hopeless was the affair. It is still a nightmare to me, for it was the first time I found myself absolutely impotent, absolutely unmeasured to the work in front of me, while Matty, threshing wildly about with stop orders in a falling market, could give no help at all. The January issue cost us about $260, of which Williams contributed $25, Stevens $15, myself $20, and Matty a little out of his own pocket, besides mulcting his friends, and me my friends, and paying all the debts I had in subscriptions to *Broom* and turning over the cash to the magazine. During those three weeks my bank account dropped from $120 to $30.

The suppression came about in this way: After the November issue had been mailed, somebody complained to the New York Post Office. They laid for the next issue, sent it on to Washington to be carefully examined, and Washington found that something was objectionable—probably one paragraph in Kenneth's story. Of course no reason was assigned for the suppression.

At present we plan to raise about $70 and print a small issue in Kingston to be distributed to subscribers only. [. . .]

[. . .]

On Washington's Birthday I made a trip to Woodstock to see Bill Brown, he lives alone in a shack, drinks hard cider, and writes as much as ten hours a day. He is writing with immense vigour, and for the moment seems the one man in whom there is hope. During three days with him I followed this schedule: chop wood in the morning, talk in the afternoon, drink at night. Since I had to leave at five on the third day, we telescoped the talking and the drinking with amusing results. Those three days have been the high light of a rather somber three months.

At the office we are publishing the *Engineering Catalogue*, a light undertaking compared with the huge architectural book, but one which keeps me working nights. The days pass and I do not know how. We see Coates, Matty, Burke, Crane with some frequency, and less often Sanborn, Peggy Loeb, Sue Light, Bendall.[12] The chief topic of conversation is wanting to be somewhere else, though I suspect that New York would be pleasant enough if I had ten thousand a year and no job. Coates, who is free-lancing, seems to be contented and says, "I am very happy in New York. I never look in people's faces."

[. . .]

Yours,
Malcolm

[HL TLS-4] [PARTLY *WW* 221–223]
[TO: HAROLD LOEB]
33 Bank Street, New York City,
September 15, 1924

Dear Harold:

I keep putting off the writing of a letter because I always hope that tomorrow there will be something new to report. There ought to be, tomorrow. I'm now trying to see Horace Liveright[13] in the very little time that remains to me after working 9—12—, 1—6—, 8—10 in the office to put the nineteenth edition of Sweet's on the press. [. . .]

It would amuse you both to hear that Munson is a gurgeyite, galooshiously gurgling Gurdjieff growling Gurdjieff gargling Gurdjieff.[14] At least so I hear, for he long ago passed out of my picture. My picture now exists in the limited frame of apartment and office, a condition which gives me a pain in the same place where the hickory switch once fell. And for this reason I decided to quit work next spring and let the future care for itself.

[. . .]

The only magazine of any interest now appearing is *1924*,[15] the life of which will be even briefer than its merit would promise. *1924*'s defect is a serious little editor and the omnipresence of Munson's influence. Its virtues to date have been an excellent story by Isidore Schneider[16] and promise of good material from Burke and Brown.

In general, Harold, I should find New York a very agreeable city if I had money and leisure. It has many charms, including good museums, good music, Central Park, with its tame mallards and down-at-the-heel menagerie, the Aquarium, negro musical comedies, the Palace, black-and-tan cabarets in Harlem, pretty women, bathing beaches, Coney Island, the American Radiator Building (of black brick with a gold dome twenty-four stories above the street), the Bronx Park Zoo, the American Museum of Natural History, a few fine Irish saloons . . .

I was drinking my beer today when I heard the old Irishman beside me say, ". . . now *I* wouldn't shoot the best woman that ever lived. A man's a fool to shoot a woman. She ain't worth it."

. . . also grain alcohol at eight dollars a gallon, which is drunk with sugar, water, ice and lemon-juice, a few streams within commuting distance where the trout still bite, sumac trees in the autumn, twenty-cents-a-mile taxicabs (almost as cheap as Paris), drinkable coffee and the noise of a black woman singing, in the shadows:

> I got nineteen men and I want one mo'
> I got nineteen men
>   and I want one mo'
> If I get that one mo' I will let the nineteen go!

At the Pennsylvania Station you board trains for Chicago and points West, St Louis and points West, Washington and points South, Montreal and points North. There is now dancing on the Boston boats, dancing on the Albany boats, dancing on the new Atlantic City boats. At Altoona they put an extra locomotive on the Commercial Limited for the long pull over Horseshoe Curve and the Alleghanies. Automobile racing at Altoona; driver and mechanician killed. Ku Klux picnic at Johnstown. Once I reached our farm I found all the letters Kenneth had written me for eight years back, and moved into my own adolescence. I picked out Chopin waltzes on the piano, caught four trout, and New York on No. 213 in the evening.

The disgusting feature of New York is its professional writers, who are venial to the last degree. Out of business, into literature, there is nobody to respect. One doesn't demand Apollinaire or the Dadas in every city, but there should be at least, in the older generation, a Paul Valéry. The Brouns, Boyds and Canbys[17] are international.

Harold, there would be all sorts of fun to be had with these straw figures of greatness if the business of living left one with any time. The atmosphere of this city is exhausting. I feel the need of nine hours of sleep, evenings at home, a mind walled up like the entrance to a deserted subway. I have done, during the year, nothing, and will do, during the year, nothing. To quit the job is my only hope, and that hope, considering the amount of hack work it involves, is not bright. Nowhere else in the world have I been brought so blankly against the mechanics of living. And for this reason, I do not advise you to come home. What I want to do is to join you in France. How?

[...]

Yours,
Malcolm

In the September issue of *1924* Waldo Frank argued that the slapstick iconoclasm of Dada had perhaps worked well in a moribund Europe, but had no relevance for the United States: "For America is Dada," he had written; "We are a hodgepodge, a boil. We are a maze of infernos and nirvanas. Our brew of Nigger-strut, of wailing Jew, of cantankerous Celt, of nostalgic Anglo-Saxon, is a brew of Dada." What America needed, he felt, was rather the "antithesis" of Dada: seriousness, order, tradition, a sense of wholeness rather than chaos, fragmentation, and arbitrariness.[18] Cowley retaliated with an open letter that, with a rejoinder by Frank, was printed in the November issue of *1924*.

[NL TL-2]
[TO: WALDO FRANK]
nd [late October, 1924]

Dear Mr. Frank:

The progress of literature (and here progress does not imply improvement) is in large measure a series of reactions: romanticism against classicism, realism against romanticism; aestheticism against realism; Dada against the aesthetes. But given the fact that the literature of each nation starts from a different point and has a different course, the reactions, at a given moment, can hardly be the same. Thus, for American writers to revolt against Remy de Gourmont or Anatole France, is quite as foolish as for the French to revolt against the Ku Klux. And in this measure, your protest against an imaginary group of writers (I never met them) whom you term the American Dadas, is perfectly justified.

However, the progress of literature is also a discovery of new truths and a rejection or re-affirmation of old principles. To this extent literature, like ethics and aesthetics, is international. If a Frenchman discovers a literary principle which is or seems new, and an American utilizes the principle, I can find no more objection to the act of the second than has been raised against Baudelaire's utilization of Poe.

[...]

Dada was in large measure a reaction against European writers whom you list as "the solemn romanticists, the shrill parnassians, the symbolists, the votaries of Bergson. . . . the pragmatists of Germany and the rhetoricians of Italy." Translate this process into American letters, where only a few of these existed, and you have less than nothing.

Dada was also a discovery: that nonsense is often the strongest form of ridicule, that associational processes of thought often have more place than the logical, that writing is often best when it is in the form of a play, that the language is capable of unexpected development, that the romantic movement is not dead, that defiance and assertiveness, carried to farthest extremes of bravado, are more to be admired than a passive mysticism, that what a man writes is a fundamental part of his life. And in this sense Dada is living still.

You have been to Paris and have brought back the gossip of Monsieur X the poet and Monsieur Y the novelist. I have been to Paris and met Messieurs X and Y. Other American writers have been to Paris. Some of them meet Paul Fort and write polyphonic prose in his manner, some meet Paul Valéry and become classicists, some meet Soupault, Aragon or Tzara and write a Yankee Dada, some meet Jules Romains and his serious little group, study his treatises on Unanimism, adopt his more solemn thoughts and some of his virtues and are proud to be called the Unanimists of America. There are also Americans who go to Paris, meet many people of many schools, take the best of each, and retain the conviction to write about their own surroundings in their own manner, but you, Mr Frank, are not generally considered one of their number.

Neither, in spite of my efforts to keep free of the ten schools and two academies, am I. In this day of advertising slogans one must have a little ticket which admits one to the Sunset Limited or the Oriental Express, blue or yellow, a slip of cardboard printed with the name. I was in doubt which name to adopt, but your article decides me. I, Mr Frank, am your butt, the clever but not coruscant smart or swift young man who clutters our serious magazines, the American Dada.[19]

[Malcolm Cowley]

[WF TLS-2]
[TO: WALDO FRANK]
33 Bank Street, New York City,
November 7, 1924

Dear Mr Frank:

Your reply to my open letter was very effective. I admired specially the last sentence,[20] in spite of not agreeing with it. And the angry tone was justified by my own. I think it would be better to let our published statements rest there, with the letter and reply; and to continue the discussion personally, if at all.

I should like to continue it, for your letter raised one or two more questions. The first is that of whether mysticism is fundamentally passive. Bertrand Russell and many other philosophers believe that it is. Certainly

Thomas Aquinas is not passive, but neither is he, in the strict sense of the word, a mystic. Note that after much debate the Catholic church became more Aristotelian than Platonic, having discovered that Platonism was encouraging mysticism, which, at least in its extremes, destroyed the activity of the church. I wish you would refer back to any history of medieval philosophy, as I shall certainly do myself, my own memories of Philosophy B having become a little vague.

An "active mysticism" is almost a paradox in words; so at least Russell believes. However, Calvin, Pascal and Bergson are all active mystics. It was for this reason—because an active mysticism does exist—that I used the epithet "passive." [...]

So much for mysticism. As for my making any definition of the "progress" of literature, I pointed out carefully that I did not mean to imply "improvement." What I meant was "course" or "history"; just as one would say, "The General's progress from Whitehall to 42nd Street was a continual ovation." That is at least the journalese of it.

Another question of fact is your list of "the solemn romanticists, the shrill Parnassians, the symbolists, the votaries of Bergson." Now the Parnassians disappeared from French letters many years ago. There are two or three remaining symbolists, but they are over sixty; men like Vielé-Griffin, of great integrity but little influence. The votaries of Bergson have so many powerful enemies that Dada never bothered with them. And as for reacting against the solemn romanticists, the Dadas I knew were always proud to be called solemn romantics. [...]

The last two paragraphs were the cheapest part of my letter. I'm sorry you chose them to answer, instead of replying to my distinction between the national and international elements of any literary movement. Please read it over; it seemed to me the argument was sound. And thank you for sending me your reply. I want to be a fair opponent and shall try, in the future, to be less personal in my arguments. Since Matty and I, as editors of *Broom,* were sponsors for most of the writing to which your article objected, you can hardly blame me for taking it personally.

Yours cordially,
Malcolm Cowley

Dear Mr Frank:

I was glad to receive your letter, which closed and opened interesting points of speculation. Indeed I failed to meet your article squarely, my answer to your main thesis being only an implication. This thesis (I write from memory) was that American civilization is essentially Dada, and that for this reason American authors who write a Dada are merely being submerged in its tide. My answer would be that American civilization is not essentially Dada. One phase of it seems to correspond with the most obvious phase of the early Dada movement, and that is all. Thinking back on the subject after a long time, it seems to me that Dada was essentially a theory of ethics, but to explain what I mean by this would exceed the limits of any ordinary letter. At least it is certain that Dada had many sides, of which the love of unreason to which you object on geographical reasons was only one.

The second part of your thesis was more forcefully stated in your open letter: that I was being beshat and befooled by the very elements of life which I profess to despise. To which I can only answer, Indeed yes. We are all beshat and befooled. The civilization of our nation is more powerful than any of us; we all try to fight its more sinister tendencies; in the meantime I also like to admire its value as a spectacle.

As for our dispute on mysticism, it was indeed a question of terminology. What you mean by mysticism is, I think, what I should mean by "deep religious feeling" [. . .]. On the other hand I understand by mysticism a current in the philosophy of all nations which can be found most explicitly in the writings of Lao-Tze, Gautama, Plotinus and Jacob Boehme. It is the stricter sense of the word, though both meanings are certainly correct.

By mystic I understand "one who seeks by contemplation and *self-surrender* to obtain union with or absorption into the Deity." I quote the Oxford dictionary, underlining the word which bears on my point. "Traditional mysticism," says Bertrand Russell, "is essentially a lazy man's philosophy."

[. . .]

As I write, I begin to question just what you mean by mysticism, any-how. Don't you take the word as simply an opposite of materialism and formalism? [. . .] This question of definition is only important because it bears on an understanding of your work.

Our correspondence has raised many hares; it has driven at least one of them to earth. I admit to misunderstanding—without intention of malice—your list of the conditions from which Dada revolted. In the case of the French Dadaists, however, their revolt was really much more nar-row; more against the stupidity and literary politics of their day; and never included an attack on Hugo or the greater romantics, whom they always admired.

Yours sincerely,
Malcolm Cowley

———

[NL TLS-2] [PARTLY SC 164–165]
[TO: KENNETH BURKE]
33 Bank Street, November 16, 1924

Dear Kenneth:

Now the latest news is that I'm out with *1924*. Not walked out, Kenneth, but kicked. At least so I interpret a tart letter from Seaver, refusing to make two changes I requested in the open letter to Frank. I answered him diplo-matically, because I don't want to quarrel. It is an excellent magazine, the most interesting we have at present. What disturbs me is the fact that it is continuing old quarrels instead of ending them. [. . .] Under the circum-stances it seems that the standard of selection is something else than liter-ary. And in this little teapot-tempest with Frank, he seems to be taking Frank's side, not only personally but as an editor.

Everywhere I turn, another fight. Meanwhile Hart, Matty and I had been making plans together. We decided to borrow *1924* for an issue which should be entitled Contributions to a Literary History of Our Times. We wanted to fill the issue with memoirs, letters, anything which bore on our thesis that the Great Literary Politicians of New York were a bunch of worms, afraid of shadows because they cast none, anxious to kiss the feet that trampled on them. [. . .]

This little rumpus with Frank [. . .] has been a great education. I find that it is forbidden to say a word against mysticism. [. . .] I gather the impression, at second hand through Tate,[21] that Frank, Munson and Crane have gone much deeper into Gurdjieff, Ouspensky, etc. than we ever suspected, and that any reference to mysticism outrages not an idea but a cult. Yeats swallowed any number of theosophies and continued to write well. I like Yeats but God knows I can't swallow theosophy. The only solution is to write. [. . .]

Yours,

M

Eager to resuscitate the spirit of his Dada days in Paris, Cowley plunged headlong into the irreverent polemics which he felt were needed to shake up New York's literary climate. The publication of Ernest Boyd's *Portraits: Real and Imaginary* (1924) was the occasion for a spoofing counter-polemics. *Aesthete 1925,* edited by the fictitious Walter S. Hankel, momentarily united Cowley's companions in a communal spirit of subversive buffoonery and cleared the air for serious literary discourse. In nostalgic retrospection Cowley referred to this as "the good winter" of 1924–1925, recaptured in his poem "The Flower and the Leaf."

[NL TLS-2]

[TO: KENNETH BURKE]

December 6 [1924]

[. . .]

Dear Kenneth:

The contributors to *Aesthete 1925*[22] have been lessened by one, and that one is Hart, and the cause of his departure is Jack Wheelwright, and the feelings remain good on all sides. [. . .]

Kenneth, for the moment the atmosphere of petty quarrels of which I complained so much has disappeared. Of course it will rise again, at some date, but in the mean time it is pleasant to talk to people, say what you think, without the fear of your remarks being repeated and garbled. The result is that conversations are turning from gossip to literature. The last

Saturday night drunk was devoted, between squirts of a siphon, to opinions on the romantic poets, and there is even much sober discussion of the same sort. [. . .]

We thought of giving ratings to the critics whom Jack is mentioning in his list. As nearly as I can remember, they are Brooks, Frank, Amy Lowell, Aiken, Van Doren, Santayana, More, Babbitt, Farrar, Rascoe, Broun, Eliot, Pound, Sherman, MacGowan, Mathews, Lewisohn, Canby, Mencken, Nathan, Littell. Percentages 0 to 100. Jack and I together thought that no one should receive over 80. Jack wished to give this grade to Santayana, and to give Eliot and More 75 each. On this basis we gave 2 to Farrar, 2½ to Broun, 2¾ to Rascoe, 3 to Van Doren, 42 to Aiken, 50 to Brooks and so on. Mencken was given −79 and Nathan −39½.

[. . .]

M.

Encouraged by the resuscitation of a cooperative spirit behind *Aesthete 1925,* Cowley hoped for a more earnest literary sequel. But the idea foundered on a lack of cooperation among his friends, and Cowley saw himself once again facing the challenge of a freelancing life in the "city of anger." In early April 1925, preparatory to a definitive move to the country, he and Peggy rented a house on Staten Island. Distrustful of the effect of city life, he decided to reroot himself in more rural environs, while maintaining his economic and literary ties to New York City. It set a pattern for life.

[NL TLS-2] [PARTLY *SC* 173–174]
[TO: KENNETH BURKE]
33 Bank Street, March 7. [1925]

Dear Kenneth:

[. . .]

I could do you a very pretty essay on Groups and Schools in Literature. Let us brief it, and make it autobiographical. Two years ago, walking down the gangplank of the Savoy, I wanted to help to start a—something—in New York that would incorporate the better features of Dada. The better features of Dada were its ethics, assertions and adventures. I hoped also to be able to find somebody to act as organizer, since I find any sort of leadership profoundly distasteful. These were not definite plans—I should be rather ashamed of them as such—but a sort of emotional direction which I can formulate now after two years.

The series of quarrels over Munson, with all the petty backbitings which followed, discouraged me more than now seems possible. This fall I was again cheered up. *Aesthete,* which I do not think was my idea, went through with much less quarreling than any one had thought possible. Everybody worked hard on it. Everybody met at Squarcialupi's, and the discussion was not entirely gossip. Here at last is a Group—but we never really wanted a group, except for social purposes. What we wanted was a direction. A group stares at its navel and lives in an atmosphere of self-congratulation. Its direction is centripetal.

People who live in cities have bright eyes like squirrels. They hop about incessantly. They never write letters, but they telephone. They diminish their interior resources. This is the first year I ever discovered in myself the inability to stay alone. Continuing the inventory, I cannot decide whether the friendship with other writers of my own age was good or bad. I am not thinking of you or Matty, friendships too old and tangled to be evaluated, but of the earnest ensemble which contributed to *Secession, 1924* and *Aesthete.* Certainly these magazines gave us more reliance; they hurt us with strangers by making it more difficult to think of each of us individually; this is not important; I think decidedly, that till everything we write can be published, we had better make every effort to continue some sort of magazine of our own.

But as for groups, their function is more social than literary, and as we grow older—man's brain is keenest at 16—we should limit them more to this social function. Living in Roseville, this question of the group-function never disturbs you. Living in the country, it won't disturb me.

We are going to try Staten Island. If we can find a cheap rentable house in the interior, where it is hilly and wooded, we shall be satisfied, for the cost of moving, carfare and telephone calls will be so much less that I can safely embark on my new freelancing career. [. . .]

M

Freelance, 1925–1928

At the end of June 1925 Cowley resigned as a copywriter for Sweet's Catalogue Service to become a full-time freelance writer. Over the next four years his literary output steadily increased: he wrote more than 125 essays and reviews, translated seven books from the French, and published some twenty-five poems (his first book of poems, *Blue Juniata,* would appear in 1929). A freelance writer of rising reputation, he now had access to more prestigious avenues of publication: his poems appeared in *The Dial, Poetry, The Little Review, transition, The Nation,* and *The Hound & Horn;* his articles and reviews in the *New York Evening Post, Herald Tribune Books, The Saturday Review of Literature,* and *The New Republic.* He was passionately committed to writing about the literature of his own times, and he found an appreciative audience; his skills as critic, translator, and ambassador of French literature also proved preeminently marketable—and influential. For all his productivity, however, he remained dogged by financial worries.

Cowley wrote on a wide array of topics in limpid prose he honed for a general audience. Through the late 1920s he fought to maintain the relative purity of a rural writing life against the compromises of an urban culture of consumerism. Still, there were good times galore, as Squarcialupi's "multicolored crew" reconvened for weekend parties at Tory Hill, near Patterson, New York, where Slater Brown and Susan Jenkins, now married, had purchased an old farmhouse nicknamed Robber Rocks. There Malcolm and Peggy Cowley regularly convened with Hart Crane, Allen Tate and Caroline Gordon, Matthew and Hannah Josephson, and, later in the decade, Robert and Elsa Coates, Nathan and Lysl Asch, and Peter and Ebie Blume—all friends (and often country neighbors) for life.

[LR ALS-1]
[TO: JANE HEAP, *THE LITTLE REVIEW*]
Everton Ave. and Woodrow Road,
R.D. Princes Bay,[23]
Staten Island, N.Y.
Oct. 24, 1925

Dear Jane:

I'd like to help you.[24] If you have some short pieces to translate—prose aggregating not over 2000 words or verse not over 100 lines—I'd like to work on it. The reason I set this arbitrary line is, well, I've got to eat and I eat by writing articles on Churches That Remember the Revolution, etc., which Aragon would consider very unethical. For Aragon life is a succession of ethical problems—for me of financial scrapes.

[...]

Yours,
Malcolm Cowley

[JBW TLS-1]
[TO: JOHN BROOKS WHEELWRIGHT]
Everton Ave. and Woodrow Road,
R.D. Princes Bay, Staten Island,
Nov. 28, 1925

Dear Jack:

I feel like a man who has just had a cataract removed from his eyes. They are open now, to the delights of alcohol. In a sober life, devoted to Art, Letters and Money, I have forgotten the strange countries which lie over the border of work and sleep. It was good to drink with you, to walk around Boston, and to talk of many things. However, since that time, I find it difficult to return to my practical affairs, which God knows are in a terrible state. I haven't been so poor since I left college, ill, with Peggy ill, and with just money enough for a train and a taxicab to Greenwich Village.

I am returning your latch key. This is not a symbolic gesture.

On the way home, before we crawled into our bunks, Matty and I were talking of the necessity of a salon—some place where people could meet once a week or once every two weeks, with a pretence of breeding and a reality of conversation. A salon has the effect of a whetstone; it sharpens people's minds against each other (one another, Mr. Woolley, the authority on English grammar would say). It is an opportunity for general conversation, which Plato believed to be the highest delight of life. Voltaire was of the same opinion. Personally I should rank it somewhat below sex, although I value it highly.

A salon requires a room, a bottle of Scotch, and a bottle of imported gin for people who drank Scotch the night before. It also requires intelligent people, but they are not so difficult to find. Finally it requires a hostess, and there our project fell apart. I suggested Leonie Sterner[25] as a vague possibility. She might possibly be interested in the project, as she seems to have a weakness for writers and artists. Should you think it wise to suggest the idea to her? I hardly know her well enough to do so myself. Or should you be interested enough to suggest other ladies who would like to invite the froth of the whipped cream of the Artists and Writers of the nation?

[. . .]

Yours,
Mal

[WCW TLS-1] [NL TL/CC-1]
[TO: WILLIAM CARLOS WILLIAMS, CONTACT COLLECTION]
Everton Ave. and Woodrow Road
R.D. Princes Bay, Staten Island,
January 3, 1925 [1926]

Dear Bill:

Here are two groups of poems.[26] They represent pretty well the sort of work I'm doing now, though sometimes I write blank verse or sonnets. I'm more interested in new forms of thought than new forms of verse. By new forms of thought I don't mean new ideas, but new ways of connecting ideas or impressions. Or images. Thus, in the Kenneth Burke poem, when I wrote:

> I shall heap your lap with pears
> oranges nectarines and rubies
> around your neck a chain of afternoons
> your head crowned with forgetfulness

etc., I was finding what for me was a new chain of impressions. This could be done in rhymed verse as well as in free verse; I'm trying to write both.

The poem about Munson appeared in *Broom*, in a slightly different form. An earlier version of the third part of "Leonora" appeared in *1924*. Otherwise none of these poems has been published. If you don't like them, write me and I'll leave all my manuscripts with Kenneth for you to make a choice. . . . As for *le bonheur*, Bill, you paint my existence in pastel shades. I just borrowed money to pay the rent, after worrying about the subject for two weeks. The uncertainty of existence keeps one whirling in nineteen directions. One direction, ahead, is the only possible way to get things done. Therefore I envy and have always envied your honorable profession. Give our best regards to Mrs Williams.

Yours,
Malcolm

————

[SCRIBNER'S TLS-1]
[TO: CHARLES SCRIBNER'S SONS]
Everton Ave. and Woodrow Road
R.D. Princes Bay, Staten Island,
March 8, 1926

Gentlemen:

I wonder whether you could help me arrange an interview with Ring Lardner. The occasion is this: I've been writing a series of literary portraits for *Brentano's Book Chat*.[27] In the beginning I thought I had a fairly original idea—to describe an author's work from the standpoint of his personality and his personality from the standpoint of his work—but I find that in practice my portraits read very much like a publisher's brochure, except that they're rather less blah. [. . .]

However, to return to Lardner . . . I suppose that if he consents to be interviewed I'll have to trot out to Great Neck, Little Neck, or wherever it is that he kennels the family wolf. You can tell him that I promise not to ask too many questions, not to treat him as one of the Seven Lively Arts, not to handle his Puppets with dirty fingers and not to drain the family cellar. Maybe on these conditions he'll consent to be talked to—before May 25, I hope, for I'm leaving New York at that time.[28]

Sincerely yours,
Malcolm Cowley

I have always counted you among the few American writers meant by the left oblique in Emerson's remark, 'There are persons born and reared in this country who culturally have not yet come over from Europe.'

Carl Sandburg to Cowley, May 18, 1926 [NL]

[CS TLS-1]
[TO: CARL SANDBURG]
R.F.D. Gaylordsville, Conn.,
October 6, 1926

Dear Mr. Sandburg:

Hal Smith, of Harcourt, Brace, was supposed to tell when or if you arrived in New York [. . .]. I've been looking forward to meeting you, and to writing an article about you as conclusion to a series of portraits of American authors which I have been contributing to *Brentano's Book Chat*. Portraits, I called them, but as a matter of fact the form, if it is a form, is a mixture of interview and literary appreciation, an attempt to show the relation between an author's personality and his work. So far I've written about Willa Cather, Sinclair Lewis, Eugene O'Neill, [William] Beebe and Ring Lardner, a very miscellaneous group chosen largely because they represented different forms and different tendencies. There isn't a poet among their number, nor any one who could write a really tremendous life of Abraham Lincoln . . .

So please, if you happen to be coming East within the month, don't fail to let me know.[29]

'There are persons born and reared in this country who culturally have not yet come over from Europe.' I haven't been able to find the quotation in Emerson, and so I don't know just how oblique the compliment was intended to be. Whether or not we have come over from Europe, there is one aim to which we might all subscribe. 'Not to be colonial:' either as a person or a writer, isn't this a very good secondary purpose?

Faithfully yours,
Malcolm Cowley

[NL TL/CC-I]
[TO: ERNEST BOYD, LITTLE, BROWN & COMPANY]
Everton Avenue, R.F.D. Princess Bay
Staten Island, N.Y.
March 13, 1926

Dear Mr. Boyd:

Thanks for writing me about "The International Men of Letters Series."[30] [. . .] As for writing one of these volumes myself, I should like nothing better. Stendhal would interest me most; after him (at a fairly great distance) Remy de Gourmont.

The man I am most anxious to write about is Baudelaire. Probably, the list having been made, it's too late to add another name, but I'll state my reasons notwithstanding. The first is that I believe him to be the great poet of his century, and one of the great precursors. The second is the interest of his background, which is rich in tragic, and even more in comic effects. French Satanism was ludicrous and terrible; there is a mass of material on the subject which has never been utilized. One of my professors at Montpellier—Monod, his name was—made a considerable research of the subject; his work was never published, but I think I could borrow the manuscript from his widow; he showed Baudelaire in the new role of a reformer, trying to get his friends to smoke a little less opium. They would stain their faces green, to look like Satan . . . From the publishers' standpoint, Baudelaire is also a good subject; people are always interested in his life, and there is no really good book about him, either in English or in French.

Stendhal would be less dramatic, but almost as interesting.

[...]

[Sincerely yours,
Malcolm Cowley]

———————

[AT TLS-4]
[TO: ALLEN TATE]
Everton Ave. and Woodrow Road,
R.D. Prince[s] Bay, Staten Island,
March 27, 1926

Dear Allen:

By searching the slopes of hills which face the north, one can still find little patches of snow, and in the depths of swamps the ground is still frozen. However, the rest of Staten Island is given over to King Mud. I walk in galoshes, but slip up to the knees sometimes. There must be hepaticas in the sheltered places; I haven't found them yet; we have carried azalea branches into the house and they will bloom tomorrow. Tomorrow the sun will be gentle and the sky pale. It is spring. The mail brings poems.

[...]

Personally, I am writing no poems. No stories. No essays of any value. I am writing a great deal. The *Charm*[31] reviews, with an occasional article. A series of interviews for *Brentano's Book Chat.* A new job also,—conducting "The Tower of Babel" for *Book Chat,* being four pages of reviews of French, German, Spanish and Italian books. Considering that my German is rusty, and that my Spanish and Italian are non-existent, this last job is something of a joke. [...] Besides this, I write reviews for the *Tribune* and *The Dial,* and a few publisher's reports for Harcourt, Brace, with promises of translations when they get the books. The work for Brentano's and for *Charm* brings in an assured income of $100 a month. The other jobs provide about as much more, if I work at them.

[...]

Allen, the last two paragraphs are a mass of unimportant details, but I offer them as giving the behavioristic portrait of a mind. Three years ago, when I came back from France, I had very different plans. I was going to take a job so that all my writing could be disinterested. I also felt (and feel today) that the grave weakness of the literary life in New York was the fact that it was unimportant. For unimportant read "had no moral value." Anything to which we attach importance becomes a moral question. We don't consider it a vice to do sloppy work—at least there is no form of opinion which condemns sloppy work—so evidently we consider the whole question as immaterial.

And we were going to change all that. [...]

According to my own standards, everything I'm doing now is rotten. The articles for *Charm* are rotten. The articles for *Book Chat* are rotten. The translation would have been respectable, but I let the publishers make so many expurgations, and made so many myself without being asked, that I feel as if even that job helped to dirty my hands. I want to write a book on Baudelaire, but oughtn't to be doing it for Ernest Boyd. I see nothing else to do but compromise. Some people are saved by a sort of divine dummness which makes them incapable—not morally, but intellectually—of successful hackwork. I've always lacked that defence.

Lack of talent isn't one of our chief problems. Almost any of our friends has as much talent as Andre Gidé or Joseph Conrad. The problem is living such a life as to develop our talents. Until forty, at any rate—afterwards things are easier. To reach forty with clean hands. I can't see myself doing it.
[...]
Peggy and I are anxious to hear whether we can rent a place in your vicinity.[32] [...]

Yours,
Malcolm

On May 1, 1926, Cowley contracted with Harrison Smith, then at Harcourt, Brace and Company, to undertake his most ambitious and influential translation from the French: *Variété,* a book of essays by Paul Valéry. Shortly afterward, he discovered that Valéry had asked Lewis Galantière to translate the book.

[NL TL/CC-2]

[TO: PAUL VALÉRY][33]

Everton Avenue,

R.F.D. Princess Bay,

Staten Island, N.Y.

May 7, 1926

My dear M. Valéry:

I remember—perhaps you remember also—a morning in July [1922] when I paid you a visit [in Paris]. I carried a letter of introduction from Georges Duthuit. I came from the University of Montpellier, where I had met your brother and your nephew. You talked to me about your poetry, and spoke of observing all the rules of verse as one would observe the rules of tennis. *Quand j'étais jeune*, I said, and you corrected me. *Quand j'étais garçon*, I continued. I still remember my embarrassment at this mistake, which was caused not by careless French, but by careless thought. I intended to write an essay on your work. The essay was never written, but when Messrs. Harcourt, Brace asked me to recommend a French book for translation, *Variété* was the first I mentioned; I was pleased and flattered when they asked me to translate it.

You don't mind, do you, my writing in English? This is a business letter, in spite of the beginning, and I find that I can think of business terms more clearly in my own language.

To continue: The publishers informed me this morning that they had received a letter from M. Galantière,[34] who said that you had asked him to do the translation. They had replied immediately, without consulting me; they said that the translation had already been arranged for. I think I can understand their action, due partly to the fact that I had recommended the book originally. Partly it was because I had already done a great deal of preliminary work, partly because they had made me an advance payment, and partly because they value my work as a translator. The element of time was also important. They plan to publish the book early in the autumn. To make this possible, the manuscript must be in their hands by July 20, and the proofs must be promptly corrected. With the translator in New York, this gives sufficient time, but owing to delays of the mail, the schedule is almost impossible to maintain if the translator stays in Paris.

I shall be deeply hurt if their choice of a translator runs counter to your wishes. However, I think I can assure you that whoever writes the translation, whether M. Galantière or I perform the work, its quality will be good. He is an excellent translator, and I have the highest respect for his work. I think he will tell you that my own translations have been good. I translated *À Bord de l'Étoile Matutine,* by Pierre MacOrlan, and Joseph Delteil's *Jeanne d'Arc;* both translations were very well received by the American critics.

In Messrs. Harcourt, Brace, you are dealing with the best of the American publishing houses. They are extremely honorable in all their transactions, have the best reputation for the quality of the books they publish, and are capable in their business dealings. One cannot expect a very wide sale for *Variété,* partly because the American public has no very deep interest in ideas, and partly because the ideas which do interest them are of a different intellectual order. However, you can be assured that Harcourt, Brace will take all possible care with the publication of *Variété,* and distribute the book to the widest possible audience. Later, I hope they can proceed with the publication of *Eupalinos* and of your *Descartes.*

[...]

I'm afraid that I have written you a very long and very boring letter. Writing from a point in space three thousand miles from Paris, I find it very difficult to explain the situation of American publishers. You can be sure, however, that *Variété* will be adequately translated and well presented to the public. And if any of the points I mentioned are not sufficiently clear, I'll explain them more carefully in other letters. I'm very anxious to see that this English version of your book complies with all your wishes.[35]

Sincerely yours,
Malcolm Cowley

[POETRY TLS-2]
[TO: HARRIET MONROE, POETRY]
R.F.D. Gaylordsville, Conn.,
June 3, 1926

Dear Miss Monroe:

We have just moved from Staten Island into Connecticut. [. . .][36] This is a magnificent country, full of deer, trout, granite and poison ivy. I hope I'll be able to stay out of the woods long enough to complete some work. "The woods" are not a figure of speech. They are acres of oak, elm, hemlock, black, white and yellow birch surrounding the bed of a stream where trout sleep in pools below the falls. Before writing the last sentence I looked out of the window, sniffed the breeze and decided the fish would be biting. Then, conquering temptation, I returned to the machine.

And first, after this peroration, I'd like to say that I was enormously pleased to hear you were publishing my poems, all of them.[37] To publish a few verses here, a few verses there, at the foot of the page, has very little effect. Especially in the case of long-winded, unemphatic, unfigured work like mine, where several poems together are required to create an atmosphere, to cause a state of mind. Next spring I want to publish a book, and the appearance of a group of poems in *Poetry* is the very best introduction to that book, the best assistance to its publication. And *Poetry* is indeed the best read of magazines. [. . .]

[. . .]

As for the title of the group of poems, and of the first poem, I was glad to hear your suggestion. Let's say "Blue Juniata" for the group, and "Bones of a House" for the first poem. When I publish a book, I want to call it "Blue Juniata," so I'll be glad to see this group of poems carry the same title.[38]

[. . .]

And, in answer to your question, I *am* in this country permanently, although I hope to spend another year in France before I finish this life of Baudelaire.[39]

Sincerely yours,
Malcolm Cowley

[NL TLS-2] [SC 175–177]
[TO: KENNETH BURKE]
R.F.D. Gaylordsville, Conn.,
July 26, 1926

Dear Kenneth:

[...]

[...] The Fourth of July party was rather less drunken and less successful than last year's, for me especially, because I couldn't drink. Jimmy [Light] was there with the manuscript of a new O'Neill play, which Sue says is the best he ever wrote. There was also a delightful flapper, Jig Cook's[40] daughter, who entered the world at the age of sixteen, provided only with a gold pessary (sp?) and a copy of the Kamasoutra. She speaks of Her Generation, which makes one feel very old. And it really is a generation, with marked characteristics, chief of which is a total lack of sexual scruples. Caroline got drunk. She and Allen, more than ever, give the impression of babes in the wood, unable to cope with the complexities of modern life. When the grocer refuses to extend them further credit, Allen writes an article, then settles back into inertia. [...]

To take stock. Twenty-eight, good biceps, bad constitution, nothing accomplished. Or seemingly nothing accomplished. What frightens me is that I have no margin. Having finished one poem or one essay, I have no plans for another; I am a perfect vacuum, like a man after copulation who is very doubtful whether he will ever be able to copulate again.

Have I ever talked to you of the Instrumental Mind?[41] It is one of my favorite conceptions. The instrumental mind has no objects of its own. Given an object it can attain it quicker than another mind, but it cannot create an object for itself. And without objects it rusts like an unused tool. Sue is an almost perfect example of such a mind. Myself also, to a lesser degree, for there are moments when I have convictions, dark and intense, for which I respect myself with involuntary mysticism, but I haven't the gift of spinning these moments into days or months.

And so, twenty-eight, an instrumental mind which I believe to be of excellent quality, though sometimes I doubt its quality for lack of objects. And to a certain extent the quality of the instrumental mind is determined by the objects given it; a poor object, such as my articles for *Charm,* will blunt the tool, and I wonder whether it hasn't been blunted already. Then add to this inertia. Couldn't one base a philosophy on inertia? Schopenhauer could see nothing between the two extremes of torture and boredom. Personally I am rarely tortured and very rarely bored; I often attain the almost perfect willlessness which he recommends, and that is a worse punishment than he was able to conceive. To be empty, to rust, to seek for the traces of desires . . .

And these traces of desires revolve in a circle, a narrow circle whose limits I fixed myself. Sex, money, writing, I can find no others. The first two require no further explanation. The third, at present, is limited to the wish to write a few essays and write them very well. At the same time believing that the essay is a minor form; that only poetry (the creation of emotions) and novels or the drama (the creation of characters plus emotions) are to be considered as final ends. Still, this is not so much a belief as a prejudice; I consider the example of Valéry, who made an end-in-itself out of the instrumentality of the mind; all his poems and essays are exercises, on themes dictated by circumstance . . . Then I begin to marvel at the kindliness of people like Hal Smith, who are willing to believe in me so much more than I believe in myself; certainly I shan't fail for want of opportunity.

In this state of mind I am seized, of course, by a naïve desire for self-improvement. I want to read books which, you know, make you think. One which I have desired for a long time is Richards' *Principles of Criticism.*[42] Maybe you could mail me your copy; is it too much to ask?

Behind my present discouragement lies the idea of the good life as one in which all one's powers are exercised to the most dangerous degree. Here the analysis ends.

Yours,

Mal

[NL TL/CC-2]
[TO: LEWIS GALANTIÈRE]
R.F.D. Gaylordsville, Conn.,
September 12, 1926

Dear Galantière:

By this time, you must have received the manuscript of *Variety*. Get down on your knees, and lift your voice to Heaven, saying, O Lord, I thank Thee that I didn't go ahead with that translation. . . . For, excepting the first two essays, which are comparatively easy, it's the toughest piece of work that one could hope to find. I slaved over it, wore out the binding of a thesaurus dictionary, spent nearly a week in the library checking up, finally turned in the manuscript last week (after being delayed a month by illness), and am far from satisfied with the result. It's a tremendously fine book, and the more time I spent with it, the more I admired it. However, I doubt whether I should, with my present knowledge, recommence the work.

Ordinarily I'd be furious to think that someone else was going over my translations. This time, on the contrary, I'm glad. It takes something of a collaboration to render Valéry into good English. And, from reading your Cocteau translations, I have a great deal of confidence in your judgement.

[. . .]

In some passages I departed pretty far from the original. [. . .] My aim was always to obtain greater clarity. I argued something like this: Valéry is difficult in French, because of his shortcuts and elliptical expressions, but in each case the reader is aided by a wealth of associations. To the American reader, these associations are lacking. Therefore, to translate literally is to make Valéry much more difficult than he is in the original. So when I felt sure of the meaning, I sometimes added words, and on four occasions, each time at the beginning of a paragraph, I added short transitional or thematic sentences. I note from reading the translation of Spengler, that this is a pretty general custom among translators of philosophic prose. It's a liberty which shouldn't be abused.

[. . .]

And I hope that Valéry has ceased to think that he's being treated cavalierly. We're all trying to do the best possible work with the English Version.

And nobody's making a profit out of it. The publisher isn't, you're not, and as for me, the time I've spent is entirely out of proportion with the money I'm receiving. We're all acting out of respect for a magnificent volume of essays.

How have you been? It's an age since I've had any news from Paris. Do you ever see Seldes and his menagerie of seven (7) arts? The publishers are prosperous, like this great obese country in general. The last virgin south of 182nd Street was lately captured. Someone put salt on her tail. Men are also being hunted down. The tame tribe of authors is growing more numerous. Are you writing a book? I am.

Yours,
Malcolm Cowley

———————

[HC TLS-I] [PARTLY *RR* 65–66]
[TO: HART CRANE]
R.F.D. Gaylordsville, Conn.,
October 8, 1926

Dear Hart:

I've spent the summer absorbed in two operations—slaving over Valéry and lying on my fanny to stare vaguely at the ceiling. "Septic condition" was the temporary diagnosis, but my trouble turned out to be a tumor on the bladder; there will have to be a not very dangerous operation some time this winter. [...] Today is one of a long series of days when I meant to write you an immense letter and didn't get around to it. I'll confine myself to saying that I think "The Bridge" a magnificent piece of work.

Here is a little joke. A ½ French ½ American poet named Eugene Jolas,[43] modernist in his sympathies, is compiling and translating an anthology of modern American poetry, to be issued in Paris. He must have read my poems in *The Little Review* and remarked, "Ah, magnifique! Here is a bloat who has prepared a little anthology of my own and saved me a great deal of work." So he up and sends me a sheaf of questionnaires. I'm enclosing the one addressed to you. Walter S. Hankel also received one of these forms.

I thought seriously of letting Jolas remain in ignorance, and of having us all prepare fictitious biographies to send to him. But the joke isn't worth the trouble, and besides, you ought to be present in this anthology with a poem of your own. So I've explained his mistake to Jolas, and told him that I'm asking you to send him some poem which you may think easy to translate. Can't you select some piece from *White Buildings*?

It looks as if the Patterson neighborhood will be deserted this winter. Can you imagine Allen as a janitor—"Yes, ma'am." What I'm going to do, God only knows. I'm dead broke, have to do a great deal of research and pay for an operation. Cripes. I wish I were living next to a breadfruit tree

> in savannas
> where bananas
> would grow all over me
> Jesus Christ how glad I'd be

Yours—M.

———————

[AT TLS-2]
[TO: ALLEN TATE]
R.F.D. Gaylordsville, Conn.,
November 24, 1926

Dear Allen:

To continue the discussion of my essay[44]—did you read hastily or did I fail to make myself clear? My paragraph on associationalism was not the technical definition of modernism; far from it. At the end of that paragraph I said, "Still (associationalism) is not the essential of the modern spirit. . . . Fundamentally, modernism is a state of mind, a certain moral attitude toward letters and the world. This is the only characteristic which all the poets I mentioned possess in common." And the rest of the essay was an attempt to define this moral attitude.

Remember that I'm talking about French poetry. In poets like Stevens or Eliot the moral attitude is different or lacking. Eliot impresses a French modernist as being pathetic or old-fashioned. Valéry, however, belongs to the modern spirit. Valéry attacks the trend toward subconscious writing. Evidently, then, subconscious writing—associationalism—isn't fundamental to the modern spirit.

Valéry is accepted as a modern largely because of the fashion in which he abandoned literature, then returned to it merely as an exercise. He is accepted because of his moral attitude—"the only characteristic which all the poets I mentioned possess in common."

If all this were pure theory, it would seem far-fetched. But I know it to be a fact. All I've done is to state the theory which is implicit in all the criticisms I've heard Louis Aragon making.

[...]

Coming down to specific instances, it would be hard to convince me that, in such romantic poems as "Don Juan," "Les Femmes Damnées" or "Ode to the West Wind," subject and vision weren't perfectly integrated. It would also be hard to convince me that there was any radical difference between the scientific spirit at its best and the spirit of poetry. Monks of art and monks of the laboratory—both are discoverers. Valéry speaks of "poets of the hypothesis"—not a bad phrase.

Your definition of classicism as "the state in which poetry more closely meets the spiritual structure of society" seems excellent. Do you mean also that the "subject" is this spiritual structure of society? Wouldn't that be straining the word? When "vision" moves away from this norm, doesn't "subject" (in the ordinary sense) move along with it?

It was partly the feeling of these difficulties that led me to define modernism on a more unsubtle basis. And, as I said, my definition, insomuch as it relates to French poetry, has an unquestionable basis in fact. With the possible exception of Horthy, I wasn't exaggerating when I said: "Rimbaud smuggling rifles into Abyssinia and Mussolini seizing a kingdom; Jarry's insolent life and the adventures of Admiral Horthy or Béla Kun; Sorel's *Reflections on Violence,* the *Seven Dada Manifestoes,* the Action Française, the latest riot of the Superrealists—all these events are related, at least in spirit, to such poetical works as *Le Bateau Ivre, Ubu Roi,* and the *Calligrammes* of Apollinaire."

[...] Today is Thanksgiving eve. A large turkey in the house, a small barrel of cider, guests for tomorrow, and sixty cents in cash. Money, money, money.

Yours,

Malcolm

I hope that Mr. [Hervey] Allen, being a poet himself, will consider Poe as a writer, instead of treating him as a psycho-analytic case.[45]

Cowley to Marianne Moore [Dial]

[DIAL TLS-I]
[TO: MARIANNE MOORE,[46] *THE DIAL*]
463 Central Park West,
New York City,
January 13, 1927

Dear Miss Moore:

To sum up my own feeling about the review of *Israfel,* I think that I advanced several ideas which are important as ideas, and ought certainly to be expressed before the present Poe controversy[47] dies down—but that I crowded too many of them into a space entirely too limited, and thereby made them appear noisy and ungracious. I can't help thinking of a large family in a kitchenette apartment.

One suggestion which I didn't make in conversation occurs to me now. I might mention the—is it Winston?—two-volume Poe, and Mr Krutch's study in abnormal psychology, and expand the review into an essay of, let us say, twenty-four hundred words, which would add a drawing room, and drawing-room manners, to our one room, kitchenette and bath. We could be urbane.

Sincerely yours,
Malcolm Cowley

———

One of Cowley's early and persisting historical interests was the slave trade, which he researched extensively in the late 1920s. In 1927 he proposed a project on the subject to the publishing firm of Boni & Liveright; in 1928 he contracted to edit *Adventures of an African Slaver,* for Albert & Charles Boni. Nearly thirty-five years later he edited and coauthored *Black Cargoes: A History of the Atlantic Slave Trade* (1962) for Viking Press.

[NL TLS-2]
[TO: T. R. SMITH, BONI & LIVERIGHT]
R.F.D. Gaylordsville, Conn.,
September 4, 1927

Dear Mr. Smith:

I want to suggest a book for the Black and Gold Library. It is "A New Account of Some Parts of *Guinea and the Slave Trade,*" by Captain William Snelgrave. It was originally published in London, in 1734, and so far as I know has never been reprinted.

There are two reasons for its being republished now. The first is that it's a damned interesting book, full of fascinating material and admirably written. The second is that the success of "Trader Horn"[48] has revived some interest in African travel, and gives an angle from which to approach advertising and sales.

Snelgrave won't suffer from comparison with the other book. I found it about *n* times as interesting.

His book tells of adventures on the Gold Coast between 1715 and 1727. He was captain of a slaver, and it was his fortune to be the second white man who visited the capital of Dahomey. His book opens with a description of the amazing rites of human sacrifice and cannibalism which prevailed in that country. At meal times he was troubled by the flies "bred by a great number of dead Mens Heads, which were piled on Stages, not far from our Tent. . . . The King's Heroes wore strings of dead Mens Teeth reaching as low as their middle both behind and before."

There follows an account of his experiences in the slave trade, and [it] includes magnificent descriptions of two slave mutinies. Finally he tells of being captured by the pirates who infested the Slave Coast. Here for the first time I got some insight into a neglected aspect of piracy—that it was a sort of popular revolt, like the jacqueries of the Middle Ages, against "base Merchants and cruel Commanders of Ships." Having revolted against all governments, they thought they had revolted against God as well, from which resulted a picturesque Satanism and a thirst for destruction. [. . .]

Snelgrave comes under my own special field of research. I should like to write a rather long introduction, dealing with the Guinea Coast in

Snelgrave's day, from material which I have already. I might also write a few notes on the Dahomey Amazons, on communist pirates, etc. The text will require a certain amount of editing, but all this work could be finished within a month, and the book itself could be published in the spring.

I've already talked to [Isidor] Schneider about the book, and he could give you further information.[. . .]

Sincerely yours,
Malcolm Cowley

[NL TL/CC-3]
[TO: BELLAMY PARTRIDGE, EDITOR, *BRENTANO'S BOOK CHAT*]
R.F.D. Gaylordsville, Conn.,
October 6, 1927

Dear Bellamy,

The time has come, said Mr. Walrus, twirling his moustache, to speak of many things, including our plans for the coming year. First, as regards a piece for the Christmas issue, I don't see why I shouldn't come right down to the brass tacks of the rock bottom, and write an essay "On Giving Books."[49] These three years I've been advising the readers of *Charm* what books to give for Christmas presents. I've had some amusing experiences, and received some funny letters, and come to some conclusions as to which books are suitable for gifts. I could use this experience as basis for an essay that would be not too heavy. [. . .]

[. . .]

During the course of next year, there are two general articles I should like to write:

(1) "Your First Book." It occurred to me, in thinking about your readers, that a great many of them are not only buyers of books, but hope to write books themselves. Now, for these people, I should like to write an informative article on the mechanics of publishing—what happens to their manuscript when it comes into a publisher's hands; who passes on it; why it is accepted or rejected; royalties, advance sales, reviewers' copies; why first books are generally not very successful, etc. I'll bet that such an article would arouse as much interest as any which you have published during the past year.

(2) "Love in the English Novel." English *and* American novel, that is. [...] It would mention that love *per se* is very rarely the theme of our novels, or even our short stories. The general subject of our novels is either success, or else the formulating of an attitude to, a philosophy of, life. Love is incidental. The essay would take up examples to prove the point, would mention other novels in which love is the dominating theme, and would end by suggesting that a real novel of love might be enormously successful. It would be a good article for your midsummer issue.

[...]

Now for the literary portraits. It impresses me that if the series is to continue, I'll have to go off on two slightly different tacks. The first is that of stating my frank reactions to authors whom I like, read, but do not approve of entirely. Last fall the article on Mencken seemed to prove that this method of writing arouses more interest than does an essay of unmixed praise. The stunt is not to leave people in a mood of dumb acquiescence, as if they were sitting in church, but to get them in a state of mind in which they approve, disapprove, shout, and get generally excited. In writing about Sandburg I tried something of this method; I'll be interested to learn whether it brings any reactions.

Now, the second tack is to write about authors who are not yet quite famous enough to deserve a portrait of their own, but who represent important tendencies. To write about authors, that is, about whom other authors can be grouped, and thus to treat five or six men in a single article.

Here are the portraits that I thought of doing in the course of the next year or so:

Theodore Dreiser.

Booth Tarkington.

Sherwood Anderson.

Maurice Werner—and American biography. This portrait should appear about the same time as Werner's new book on Tammany Hall.

Amy Lowell—Marching on. I was a very good friend of this extraordinary woman.[50] I know a dozen marvelous anecdotes about her, and I realize her influence on American letters. I'd also like to attack, though not by name, some of the ghouls that praised her when she was living, then gathered round to belabor her corpse. I think I could make this one of my best articles, though it shouldn't appear till some months after the article on Sandburg.

Ernest Hemingway. His style and method have had a tremendous influence on the younger writers, some of whom I could mention at the same time. I think that most of your readers are curious as to what the younger men are doing—which justifies this essay and the two which follow.

The Younger Dramatists. Especially those of the Dramatists Theatre, whose works are being published by Macaulay. John Dos Passos, John Lawson, Em Jo Basshe and others, who are trying to create a revolutionary theatre in this country. Also Sidney Howard, who doesn't belong to their group.

The Expatriates—The two sorts of expatriates; those who become completely denationalized and write about Europe or the past (Eliot and Pound); and those who turn nostalgically toward America (Bromfield,[51] Glenway Wescott, Hemingway, etc.)

If I wrote the eight portraits listed above, or most of them, my series in *Book Chat* would develop into a pretty complete survey of American literature since the war. I think that Max Lieber[52] ought to consider it seriously for a book. It would, of course, require a good deal of rewriting, but I've got together all the material; and the book would have a sure sale, if not a very large one. Also, it would be the first that developed out of *Book Chat*. I've always thought that a publisher's house organ should have two functions—to encourage the sale of books, and to develop new ones. If we did manage to make a book out of the articles, we'd have some tangible result to show for our collaboration.

[…]

Yours,
[Malcolm Cowley]

[YUL TLS-2] [NL TL/CC-2]
[TO: AUTHORS' GUILD OF THE
AUTHORS' LEAGUE OF AMERICA, INC.]

501 East 55th Street,
New York City,
March 20, 1928

Gentlemen:

Please excuse me for writing a very long answer to your kind invitation to join the Authors' League. The length of the letter is justified, I think, because it describes not only my own situation but that of ten or twenty writers of my acquaintance, none of whom are members of the League.

I belong to what might be called the proletariat of letters. That is, I live entirely by literary work and live on somewhat less than three thousand dollars a year. A little more than half my income depends on magazine articles, book reviews, reports to publishers, revision of other people's manuscripts, and a lot of other etceteras in most of which the League could help me very little, the work being too specialized for general action. The rest comes from translating books, and in this field the League could be of very great service.

Translators at present are in a miserable situation. They are underpaid, under-recognized, and subjected to competition from American amateurs, anxious at all costs to have their name on a book, and from English hacks. There are publishers who pay as little as three or four dollars a thousand words for translations. If translators put the proper amount of time on their work, and received this price, they would be earning from $75 to $150 a month.

As a matter of fact, the publishers who pay such prices receive very bad work. Sometimes they give it to other translators, like myself, for revision, which is a laborious and needless process. Sometimes they publish it as it stands, and are surprised when the book is a failure. Meanwhile they tell the few capable translators—"What! You want a thousand dollars for an English version of this book! Why, we can have the work done for less than half that sum."

This situation also reacts unfavorably on American authors in general. As long as translations involve low prices, haggling, and even at times a shade of dishonesty, certain publishers will issue foreign biographies and general works in preference to having the same books written by our own authors.

It seems to me that this is a field in which the Authors' Guild could perform very great services. It could draw up a standard contract for translations (none exists at present) in which the translator would be guaranteed a share of the English and the serial rights, and perhaps a small royalty in addition to his fee. It could see that the foreign author was not cheated (as sometimes he is). It could impress on publishers the idea that they would gain by skilled work, and thus raise the professional level of the field.

I know a great many translators, and know that all of them are at a disadvantage when dealing with publishers. I know that there should be some organization to protect them. Some of them are talking of forming an organization of their own, but most of them would be glad to turn to the Authors' League if it could take some interest in their situation. Personally I can assure you that I should be eager to join in that case, even though the yearly dues are high for a very unprosperous writer.

Sincerely yours,
Malcolm Cowley
[. . .]

[DIAL TLS-1]
[TO: MARIANNE MOORE, *THE DIAL*]
501 East 55th Street,
New York City,
April 11, 1928

My dear Miss Moore:

Thank you for your letter, which just arrived. I have set to work on the Shelley essay,[53] and will endeavor to make its length four pages. Possibly, in one or two paragraphs, I may have to speak in the first person. I know that you dislike this usage of criticism, but it is not always the mark of a merely impressionistic method; it may, on the contrary, arise from a desire to be more exact, and to define the critic's point of view—that distorting lens—in order to give the reader a juster opinion of the object so distorted. In such cases, don't you think that the first person is not only admissible, but necessary?

I think the title of the essay will be "Alastor, or The Unfortunate Boat-man." Professor Peck seems always to be emphasizing the number of times that Shelley narrowly escaped death by drowning before his last cruise. Curiously enough, the image of floating down a stream into rapids, and of a voyage ending in death, is to be found more than once in Shelley's poems—so that one might actually say that his life was sacrificed to a symbol—very much as if William Jennings Bryan had really been crucified on a cross of gold.

Sincerely yours,
Malcolm Cowley

[COLUMBIA TLS-3]
[TO: RENÉ TAUPIN]
501 East 55th Street, New York City,
June 14, 1928

My dear Mr. Taupin:

[. . .] As it happens, the subject of your study[54] is one to which I have devoted considerable thought, but the more I reflect upon it, the more difficulty I find in tracing literary influences from one language to another. The effect of Laforgue, Rimbaud, and Mallarmé upon American poetry has been real, but nebulous, vague, and paradoxical. The American poet who most resembles Rimbaud—the American poet who at present shows the greatest promise and the most interesting use of figures—is Hart Crane, who can't read French. Yet I happen to know that he has puzzled through all the translations of Rimbaud which have appeared, and I am certain that they have affected his style. You might, in this connection, read a group of translations from Rimbaud by Dr. Blum (J. S. Watson), which appeared in *The Dial* about seven years ago. I found this group of translations clipped and preserved in one of Crane's notebooks.

Among a very large group of younger poets, the influence of T. S. Eliot is overwhelming. Now, Eliot was *lecteur* at the University of Rennes; he spent some time in Paris and met several French poets. Which ones? I personally suspect that he was influenced by the group of Salmon and Apollinaire; "La Maison du Veuf" and other poems in the same volume by Salmon[55] bear a strange

resemblance to Eliot's Sweeney poems, and he may also have learned something from Apollinaire's "Marizibill." The tangential ending of that poem:

> J'ai vu gens de toute sorte
> Ils n'égalent pas leur destin
> Indécis comme feuilles mortes
> Leurs coeurs bougent comme leurs portes
> Leurs yeux sont des feux mal éteints

which I have probably misquoted, is a technical device characteristic of
Eliot; he also changes the subject at the end of a poem. . . . Now, if Eliot really transmitted the influence of Salmon and Apollinaire, as well as that of
Laforgue, into English, these poets may be said to have a more vigorous life
in America than in France. Laforgue, of course, is obvious in Eliot's "La fi-
glia che piange" and in "Prufrock."

Les Chansons de Maldoror have affected the poems of Matthew Josephson. Try, if you can, to get hold of an issue of *The Little Review* devoted to "a
group of younger Americans." I think it was published in the spring of 1926
or late in 1925, and you can find it at the New York Public Library. There
you will find an interesting poem of Josephson's, as also a group of my poems which show some influence by Philippe Soupault.

And so we come round to myself. I can admit to the following French
influences, being a pretty conscious writer:

a) Laforgue in my college days, as well as Laurent Tailhade. Unfortunately, I wrote nothing good under their influence.

b) Rimbaud's "Bateau Ivre," which for a long time I intended to translate. Instead, I finally wrote a poem of my own called "Leander," which was
published last summer, I think, in *The Dial.* Here are a few lines which I
remember:

> Regal and tired, O corpse that mapped the countries
> of Ocean, saw pelagic meadows where
> the sea-cow grazes, traveller that skirts
> the unicellular gardens of the foam
>
> Southward you drift where archipelagoes
> of stars deflect the current and waters boil

with lava, through indefinite Marquesas
spinning in the typhoon, and off Cape Stiff

In westerly gales your eyes commemorate
still tropical the wax and wane of moons.

The "archipelagoes of stars" are taken directly from Rimbaud without apology; so also I think are the "indefinite Marquesas." And the whole atmosphere of the poem is of course like that of the "Bateau Ivre."

c) The third French influence which I have consciously undergone was that of Philippe Soupault, but as this is hardly symbolistic, it is rather outside the scope of your study.

I do hope that these few observations and confessions will be of some assistance. [...]

Sincerely yours,
Malcolm Cowley

[NL TLS-2] [SC 182–183]
[TO: KENNETH BURKE]
R.F.D. Patterson,
Putnam Cty., N.Y.,
October 17, 1928

Dear Kenneth:

[. . .] Temporarily, perhaps permanently, I have no soul. People that work pretty hard at a job that partly interests them are apt not to have a soul. Writers are especially apt not to have a soul. All the feeling that goes into what they write is subtracted from what they say, and they are left to cherish such simple emotions as vanity, cupidity and lust. It would be nice to be permanently adolescent. Still, I should not like to return to the sense of futility that brooded over our own adolescence. We had determined to be writers, and writers, in America, play no part in public affairs. They are specialists, in other words cripples. I should like to have the courage to proclaim that nothing human is alien to my interests. Perhaps it is true that if, like Leonardo, we discover a methodology, we can apply ourselves to everything. If some American writer would take a stand in favor of the widest interests possible—a stand like that of Zola in the Dreyfus case—he would improve the status and resolve the doubts of all of us. But to reach this point he would have to have a long training in pride, in the noblest conception of himself. The pride of a good writer is to be disinterested, to observe everything, to be able to predict economic and social movements, and yet to draw no profit from his powers of prediction. I stop before this chain of thought is lost in the higher altitudes of bombast.

Yours,

M.

The End of a Literary Apprenticeship, 1929

The winter months of 1929 were a time of exhilaration and discouragement. With the generous help of Hart Crane, Cowley made significant progress toward compiling his first book of poetry. At the same time, his marriage to Peggy was beginning to fall apart. There had been affairs on both sides, and Cowley found it difficult to contemplate the contrast between his own relationship, childless and unstable, and those of his friends, most of whom were by now the parents of steadily expanding families. As his conviction grew that the fate of the American writer was inescapably tied to the exigencies of the marketplace and the conditions of American society, the underside to American prosperity became an inescapable reality of life in New York City, and Cowley felt his social conscience stir at the early signals of an impending economic crisis.

The 1920s ended for Cowley on a note of promise and relief: *Blue Juniata* received very encouraging reviews, and in October 1929, three weeks before the Great Crash, Cowley was offered a position as junior editor on *The New Republic*. The new job put an end to his persistent financial uncertainties and ongoing worries about the "mechanics of living." Soon it would offer him an influential platform from which to speak out on the intellectual, literary, and political crosscurrents of the turbulent 1930s.

[POETRY TLS-1]
[TO: HARRIET MONROE, *POETRY*]
33 Avenue B, New York, N.Y.,
January 29, 1929

Dear Miss Monroe:

Finally I've got round to publishing a book of poems. I had really been convinced for five years previously that there was no use even sending the manuscript around, and it would still be resting in my drawer with its ten thousand corrections in pencil if Hart Crane hadn't helped me out, retyped some forty poems, and sent them out. And then, by a strange accident, the book was accepted by two publishers simultaneously.[56] I chose Harrison Smith, for his projects are interesting and attractive: he no longer intends to treat poetry as a weak sister in the family of books; he intends to publish it in such a form and with such advertising that it wins back its popularity and economic self-sufficiency.

I'm busy once more revising the interminably revised manuscript. And I want to thank you at this moment for all that you and your magazine have done for me. Nowhere else could I have seen enough of my poems printed together to think that they justified a book, and to feel what sort of a book they would justify. [. . .]

Very sincerely yours,
Malcolm Cowley

I'm becoming more and more convinced that the principal problem for an American writer is one of living. [. . .] The authors of intelligence who fail because of aesthetic shortcomings are rare in comparison with those who surrender either to the need for making more money or, in other instances, to the narrower vistas imposed by the effort to spend less.

Cowley to Kenneth Burke, December 30, 1928 [NL]

[EW TLS-1]
[TO: EDMUND WILSON][57]
33 Avenue B, New York, N.Y.,
February 13, 1929

Dear Edmund:

This is one of those letters that will or won't reach you, depending on whether or not I get your new address. I hope it's a quiet place, about nine thousand miles from this city where every one is so blandly engaged in cutting every one else's throat, and I hope you'll get a rest (the first, I believe, in ten years), and come back with a new store of malice to join in that battle of malice which is literature. . . . Think, you have a special distinction; you're the only writer I know who has been successfully leading a double life—that is, who has been earning a living out of literature and at the same time writing good books. I ought to know the difficulty of this double task, since it seems to me that I've rather failed in both sides of it.

I just ran into [Wallace] Meyer, of Scribner's, and of course talked about your novel.[58] It seems that he, and Perkins their big egg, and all the rest of the editorial department are "crazy about it"—I think I'm using his words. I also learned that they haven't got the manuscript. . . . Here's a serious piece of advice, though God knows what justification I have for advising you or anybody else. Call it a finished job, give them the manuscript, and forget about it. Every novel, every poem, every essay, merits just so much of its author's life, and no more. There's a time when everything ought to be published (that is, buried, for publishing a book is exactly equivalent to burying a part of one's past. And if it isn't published, well, it decays on one's hands; I know this from my own experience with some of my poems). [. . .]

I just got a letter from Hart. He's seeing high life in and out of Paris—absinthe, champagne, chateaux, countesses and counts, cocktail parties, dinner parties, midnight and morning parties, God! He was going to Mallorca to finish "The Bridge"; now he speaks of staying in Paris.

Yours,
Malcolm

I think that you are fundamentally, like me, a regionalist poet. Your years in New York—and my years also—are only an extended episode. Eventually I think we shall both retire, you to Tennessee, I to Cambria County, and continue a friendship in letters and visits.

Cowley to Allen Tate, August 28, 1928 [AT]

[AT TLS-2]
[TO: ALLEN TATE]
R.F.D. Patterson, N.Y.,
April 2, 1929

Dear Allen:

I'm in New York at present, in a comfortable apartment on the lower East Side, listening to the predominantly human noises of Avenue B, but the spring is coming north; the arbutus buds are pink, the crocuses have blossomed and disappeared, the long stems of the tulips are rising from the ground, and by the end of the week we'll probably be in Patterson. What a flurried winter! I've been a rounder; I've seen my old friends seldom and strange faces often; I've come home at seven in the morning to watch the bread lines stretching for three blocks along this Main Street of Jewry. That was on Good Friday; the men standing in line were impassive and averaged from forty-five to fifty years, the cast-offs of our industrial civilization, which hires no men over thirty-five; I had a rather drunken phantasmagoria of being Christ and of descending myself into something or other. But don't think that all my time has been spent in the backwash of the romantic movement; I've been working immoderately, working badly, trying to finish translations, to hurry off articles for which the figurative presses were waiting, and I've been thinking hardly at all. However, I have managed to prepare my book of poems for the publisher.

It has changed considerably from the manuscript you saw. Principally it has grown. Instead of thirty-seven poems, there are now fifty-four, and there are several prose notes [. . .]. I was impressed by the idea that, in reprinting only poems that reached a certain technical standard, I was giving a false and incomplete picture of the author. Moreover, if I restricted the book to the poems I approved of wholly, I should have not 37, but perhaps 16 or 20, and these 16 or 20 without any very definite unity. By including other poems, however; by correcting their worst faults and arranging them in sections, I could give some idea of the development of a poet and produce a book with a unity that a shorter volume would not possess. I think I succeeded to some extent, and I think that the book as a whole is better than any single poem in it. At any rate, it's not a scrapbook, a collection of unrelated poems by the same author.

I appreciated your review, and agreed wholly with the mild strictures you made in the earlier draft of it. I have not a wide range of emotional or intellectual interests; I have a wide range of factual interests and a considerable intensity of emotion that I don't often manage to express. I think you exaggerate the quality of my craftsmanship. Certainly, in revising my poems, I found much that grieved me, and I couldn't remedy a great deal of it. [. . .]

Wilson will see that your review is run in the NR.[59] He has spent a very bad winter. People spread the rumor that he was going insane, which wasn't true at all. He was having just a swell nervous breakdown. For ten years he'd been living immoderately, and he had to pay the price of his Babylonian and Alexandrian nights. The psycho-analyst diagnosed his trouble as an acute case of mother-fixation, but psycho-analysts have a habit of disregarding the purely physical aspects of a case. Wilson had terrible fits of depression, talked of suicide, thought nobody respected him, decided he was an evil influence in the lives of those he loved, but his mind was never functioning better, and after a month of regular living, he's coming back to normal emotionally. Unfortunately, at the same time, he's beginning to work immoderately once more, and Mary[60] is having her usual mix-ups, so maybe the recovery won't be permanent. I've heard a lot of the case, both from him and, over the telephone, from Mary.

McSorley—did you meet that shiftless, charming Irishman?—McSorley's wife gave birth today to twins. Lysl Asch gave birth to a little Nathan, and big Nathan is proud of the resemblance, which every one else deplores. Hannah is about to give birth. Ah, this bloody everlasting talk of gestation and parturition, abortions and diapers. I don't know what to say when I hear it. I sneak off and get tight.

[. . .]

Yours,
Malcolm

[AT TLS-2]
[TO: ALLEN TATE]
R.F.D. Patterson,
Putnam Co., N.Y.,
June 3, 1929

Dear Allen:

I certainly haven't time to write you a letter this morning, but it occurred to me that my silence was becoming so protracted that you might begin to take the silence itself as the answer to your letter, even though Peggy had written you separately. Her answer, as she explicitly stated was her own. She is anti-nationalistic. I myself, [. . .] as you know very well, am a firm believer in regionalism, but I think there is this much truth in her criticism: namely that your regionalism, since it extends to eleven states and a whole civilization, is almost a form of nationalism, and that I myself should approve of it more completely if it were confined to a county or a township. The culture of the old South, like the culture of Athens, was confined to a very small ruling class. It was surprisingly high (as I discovered independently by reading some old reviews published in New Orleans) and at the same time it was somewhat sterile; only in Poe, an outcast from the ruling class, did it find a satisfactory expression. Since Kant's *Critique of Practical Reason,* most of us have been obsessed with an idea of social justice—not to employ human beings as instruments—and I doubt that a purely aristocratic society will ever again be possible. (Some one else might argue that geographical distance and not leisure was the cause of the comparative sterility of the Old South; it prevented the friction of minds which produces the brightest sparks; Poe moved to New York where at least he could talk to N. P. Willis and be irritated by the New England

school; personally I think that both leisure and distance were contribu-
tory causes. Had you lived in 1850, you would have written a very well
thought-out—but insufficiently documented, because of the lack of
libraries—essay perhaps on Sophocles and a volume of poems to ladies; then
you would have dozed in the shade before dying magnificently and quite
uselessly in a cavalry charge against the damned German factory hands
from Pittsburgh.)

As an article of unreasoned faith, faith in the present is pragmatically
effective.

[. . .]

Yours,
Malcolm

[NL TLS-2] [PARTLY *SC* 185–186]
[TO: KENNETH BURKE]
RFD Patterson,
Putnam Col, N.Y,
June 23, 1929

Dear Kenneth:

I've just finished the second of two leading essays for Mrs. Van Doren.[61]
One of them appeared last Sunday; the other appears next Sunday; they
deal, one with "Our Own Generation," the other with "The New Primitives." They speak in generalities, half of which are commonplaces, the other
half questionable. I hope you read them, and I'm anxious to get hold of the
essay you wrote for *The Bookman*.[62] Our judgments must have coincided
except on Hemingway, whose work I enjoy on the whole; out of malice I
listed "some of Kenneth Burke's short stories and the long description of
the fiesta in *The Sun Also Rises*" side by side in a brief catalogue of what I
thought were the permanent achievements of our own generation. My other
listings were *The Enormous Room*, the introductory essay to *Goodbye, Wisconsin* (and I should have added *The Apple of the Eye* if I had read it in
time),[63] *Orient Express*, "The Bridge," *My Heart and My Flesh*,[64] and did I
give others? I forget. Callaghan[65] is entirely trivial, so I did not mention
him anywhere.

You never read anything, you son of a bitch. For God's sake read *Variety* and *The Sacred Hill*.[66] They are both books from which one can learn— from Valéry, a method of thought, from Barrès, how a man who is not a novelist can write a novel that is like a big chunk of lyric granite.

I'm thinking of assembling a book of essays. Being visiting critic for *Books* next winter would give me a chance to write four of them in the same direction, and thus give a certain unity to the book. It could be either about French or American literature; personally I should like to make it American and to deal with the problems that are confronting ourselves. For example, an essay on "The Literary Life" in which I described the opportunities afforded by a career of letters, distinguished between men of letters and writers pure and simple, pointed out that very few Americans have achieved a literary career, demanded a higher code of literary ethics, etc. . . . Some of my pressing financial problems being solved, I feel a little more confident. And incidentally, I've been working like hell this spring; I never turned out so much in an equal space of time.

[. . .]

Yours,
Malcolm

[AT TLS-1]
[TO: ALLEN TATE]
R.F.D. Patterson,
Putnam Co., N.Y.,
September 9, 1929

Dear Allen:

Thanks in the first place for having written a review of *Blue Juniata;* thanks in the second place for having taken such extraordinary pains in the revision of it; thanks in the third place for what you said, and for having said it so well. [. . .] But I must say at this point that I can only agree with your flattering judgment when I am in my most sanguine moods. Then I arch my back and purr. If I were a lady poetess, I should know how to reward you concretely.

What next? The essays? They aren't a book. In collecting them, I shall have to find some such device as the notes in *Blue Juniata*. I should let them wait, if it weren't for a desire to clear decks and get to work on something new. One can drop things in a wastebasket or put them in a book. . . . Poems? I feel that I'm the sort of poet who writes one book, then tries to perfect it. Baudelaire is the archetype of the class. My next book of poems, when written, will probably be an expansion of the New York section of *Blue Juniata;* then I shall perhaps try to expand the country poems; then finally to revise and reissue the whole book.[67] A nice program, but what are programs worth?

Yesterday Hart suddenly appeared, driven from his comfortable New York apartment by emotional troubles and the desire to work on "The Bridge" in . . . peace. I can hardly use the word in connection with him. Like certain mountains, he has his own storms, his local weather. The phonograph is playing, the alcohol bottle uncorked; Hart is writing on the Cape Hatteras section, and writing well, which is news of interest to the world. The spell laid on him for the past two years by Malicious Animal Magnetism (in which he believes devoutly, as he believes in his own star) has been broken. All the perturbations of the last two years are justified in his eyes by the result. This is bad logic, I think, but how can it be disproved?

And when are you coming home?[68] [. . .]

As ever,
Malcolm

The Depression Years—Literature and Politics, 1930–1940

The Red Romance, 1930–1934

Even before the Crash of 1929 Cowley was persuaded that American consumerist capitalism had gone bankrupt and a new ideological and economic foundation was necessary. As the Depression deepened, he translated such beliefs into public political action. In 1931 he circulated a letter of protest against the torture and killing of twenty-four young Chinese Communist writers and joined the National Committee for the Defense of Political Prisoners. In 1932 he supported the Communist candidates for the presidency, William Z. Foster and James W. Ford, marched in the May Day Parade, and parceled out food to striking miners in Harlan County, Kentucky. He was drawn into the orbit of Marxian criticism, debated its pros and cons with Burke, and argued with Tate about the feasibility of Southern Agrarianism and anti-industrialism as solutions to the current crisis. Though his commitment to radicalism was hedged with reservations—he never joined the Communist Party—he became a fervent fellow traveler and de facto supporter of the Party line.

When in 1930 Edmund Wilson took a leave of absence from *The New Republic* to report on the social, economic, and human malaise of a depression-ridden nation (*The American Jitters*, 1931), Cowley assumed fuller responsibilities as literary editor. From his new authoritative platform he spoke out on matters of literature and politics, acting out his conviction, as he wrote in *Exile's Return: A Narrative of Ideas* (Norton, 1934), that the man of letters must be concerned with "every department of human activity, including science, sociology and revolution" (169). He became one of the magazine's more radical voices, with "almost complete authority" in the book section, although editorial decisions were taken in colloquy with his fellow editors, Bruce Bliven and George Soule. From his network of friends and acquaintance

Cowley enlisted contributors who combined literary sensitivity and critical acumen with a commitment to radical politics: Josephson, Burke, Coates, Brown, as well as Newton Arvin, R. P. Blackmur, Granville Hicks, Sidney Hook, and (later in the decade) Alfred Kazin, F. O. Matthiessen, and Lionel Trilling. He courted independent minds like Hamilton Basso and Nathan Asch and invited southerners of opposite persuasions—Allen Tate, Stark Young, Robert Penn Warren—to render their literary verdicts in the magazine. Last but not least, as early as 1930 he launched John Cheever on his writing career by publishing his first short story.

Often dictated from the offices of *The New Republic,* Cowley's correspondence was circumscribed by the pressures of an editor's job: soliciting reviews, suggesting articles, arguing with contributors, proposing cuts and revisions. Keeping his personal thoughts and ideas separate from his business correspondence, he reserved his more intimate and substantial letters for the scant moments of quietude in Sherman—or for the relative calm at Yaddo, the artists' colony at Saratoga Springs. Beginning in 1930 he served as an advisor to Yaddo's director, Elizabeth Ames, and would help shape admissions and policies for many years to come.

Yaddo also saw the beginning of *Exile's Return,* as—at the suggestion of Josephson—Cowley and a group of friends gathered there in the spring of 1931 to retrospect and compose "a collective book of memoirs" on the 1920s. It was at Yaddo that Cowley produced the first chapters of *Exile's Return* (1934). Part of a widespread Depression-inspired effort at stock-taking, the book offered a backward glance at the misguided aesthetics and political courses of the 1920s and, like Robert Coates's 1933 novel *Yesterday's Burdens,* suggested how a generation sought to shed the burdens of the past while looking toward a new, responsible beginning. In a long letter to Blackmur, Cowley articulated his own ideas on the social responsibilities of the American writer that would become the book's epilogue, a personal credo that Cowley remembered as the "high summit" of his "revolutionary enthusiasm" (*DGM,* 224).

Cowley believed the crisis required nothing less than a dramatic reorientation of literary and political as well as personal life. As he told Burke, not only had "a whole scheme of life collapsed," he had at last made the painful decision to separate from his first wife. In July 1931 Peggy traveled to Mexico to seek a divorce. In Mexico she was later joined by Hart Crane; over the winter of 1931–1932 they became lovers. It was during their homeward voyage in April 1932 that Crane committed suicide by leaping off the ship. Cowley's letters testify to the profound impact of Crane's early death and show him searching for a proper mode to memorialize his friend's demise: he composed an editorial on his death, published Crane's poem "The Broken Tower" in *The New Republic,* and (with Tate and others) sought to protect Crane's legacy and reputation. It was the start of a lifelong role as guardian of Crane's—and by extension his generation's—achievement.

On June 18, 1932, Cowley married Muriel Maurer, a beautiful New York fashion editor he had met a year earlier. Over the next two years he completed the writing of *Exile's Return.* At Yaddo Cowley found a welcome reprieve from the pressures of office life in the rural quietude and the camaraderie of fellow writers. An extended visit to Allen Tate and Caroline Gordon in the spring of 1933 at their home in Cloverlands, Tennessee, provided another respite and opportunity for writing. On the way down, toting his early letters to Burke, Cowley paid a memorable visit to Scott and Zelda Fitzgerald in Baltimore. In March 1934 he borrowed Harry Crosby's diaries from Caresse Crosby and spent two lonely weeks at an inn in Riverton, Connecticut, writing "Echoes of a Suicide," the symbolic account of the end of an era. When *Exile's Return* appeared in 1934 it met with a devastating reception, with many old-guard reviewers challenging Cowley's claim that his generation's story of exile and return was worth telling at all.

[EW TLS-1]
[TO: EDMUND WILSON]
[NR]¹ *August 27, 1930*

Dear Edmund:

[...]

Here in the office there aren't many books which would interest you. But *Flowering Judas,* by Katherine Anne Porter has just come in, and you might want to write about it. If you don't, my second choice would be Louise Bogan,² even though she keeps protesting that she wants to review a book by a man. Also in the office for review are Santayana's *The Realm of Matter* and Lizette Woodworth Reese's *White April*. I hardly think, though, that you would care to write about them.

This series on individualism[3] has been on my mind for a long time. I know you are sour on it, but isn't that chiefly because of its relation to dear old John Doughy?[4] It seems to me that dear John hasn't a monopoly on the subject, and that the problem of the individual in a world of mass movements and mass amusements—how he can preserve his individuality, and whether his individuality is worth preserving—is one of the two or three most important subjects of the present decade. I even think that it would be possible to sell the idea of a symposium on the subject to some obliging publisher, and thereby make the series financially profitable to the writers invited to contribute to it.

More later. It is hard to write a letter from the office.

Sincerely,
Malcolm

———————

[ARVIN TLS-I]
[TO: NEWTON ARVIN][5]
[NR] September 18, 1930

Dear Arvin:

[. . .] Didn't I hear that you had set out on the magnificent task of reading *Das Kapital?* Would you like to write a 1200 to 1500 word review of it, a purely personal review, giving the critical reactions of a literary man to the book nobody knows—this book which influences people only at second hand? "The Book Nobody Knows" might even be a pretty fair title for such a review. And also it would gratify me to see you try your hand at something outside the field of literature and literary criticism.

[. . .]

Sincerely yours,
Malcolm Cowley

I take the *New Republic* view of anti-industrialism, and believe that we can no more defeat present tendencies than we can make water run up hill—we can merely deflect them.

Cowley to Allen Tate, August 15, 1930 [AT]

[AT TLS-2]
[TO: ALLEN TATE]
c/o The New Republic,
421 West 21st Street,
New York City,
December 15, 1930

Dear Allen:

I've been so insanely busy since getting back to New York[6] that I haven't had time to write and tell you and Caroline what a swell time I had in Clarksville and what marvelous hosts you are. In some ways I got more out of Dixie than out of Mexico; Mexico was too entirely foreign; Tennessee was just enough different from my own country so that I could appreciate the differences beside the resemblances—and in what a fine background!

I had intended to review *I'll Take My Stand*[7] myself. I couldn't give the book out to the average Northern reviewer; his city background would make him unable to treat it justly; I couldn't give it out to a Southerner who held to the industrial system, and as for Southerners who don't, I'm afraid that most of the writing chaps were contributors to the symposium. I have a lot to say about it; Andrew Lytle[8] is going to come out very well in my review, better than the college professors, who, I think, are working the educational factories themselves and suffering all the handicaps of the industrial system. A professor who teaches four or five courses is a sort of moderately well paid and terribly overworked factory foreman. My own answer to the Southern agrarian dilemma is localized machines, operated by electricity, which can change the small plantation once more into an economic unit and fight the factory system with some chance for success. Borsodi,[9] crank as he is, should give a hint of possibilities. But the machines would have to be introduced cautiously, without draining the country of money as tractors have done; tractors don't have colts and don't make manure. . . . Now, by the way, is a good time for your agitation, when the rest of the country is beginning to be worse off than the South.

[. . .]

Matty lost several thousand dollars in the crash of Bank of United States—it was the bank which absorbed his father's bank in Brooklyn, and Matty had inherited some stock, most of which, fortunately, he had disposed of. New York has more bread lines than subways, and the financial situation here can really be described as panic—not like 1907, but like 1873 and 1837.

Kenneth, having no job, is writing a treatise on esthetics for a book of essays he hopes to finish by fall.

Bob Coates, fat and prosperous, is the literary editor of *The New Yorker*. Wilson believes the capitalist system is doomed, and has written a manifesto[10] to which George Soule will reply. [. . .] Dorothy Day, whom I haven't seen, is working at Wanamaker's. There are no publishers' teas this year, to give a free jag to everybody. Harold Loeb has sailed for Europe, with Ford, who says he is going to Clarksville in the spring.

[. . .]

Well, Allen, that's that. I thought the Shenandoah Valley was fine, a curious mixture of Virginia mansions, Pennsylvania barns and the landscapes of paradise—paradise after the longest drought on record. Washington and Lee University was indeed splendid in architecture. Gettysburg is the biggest museum of primitive sculpture this side of Carnac in Brittany. I made the trip in three days flat, arriving at 7:30 on Sunday evening.

How is Red Warren; I hope he's better. [. . .]

Who are Owsley, Lyle H. Lanier, Herman Clarence Nixon?[11] Where is John Gould Fletcher now? Was it a brave jester who put "the hind tit" as an answer to "whither Southern economy?"?

Yrs.
Malcolm

[KAP TLS-2]
[TO: KATHERINE ANNE PORTER]
336 West 19th Street,
New York City,
January 14, 1931

Dear Katherine Anne:

Sam Ornitz,[12] the ugliest man in New York, was here to dinner last night. So were Raymond Holden,[13] Louise Bogan and Léonie Adams,[14] but that isn't the story. The story is about Sam Ornitz and Humanism. Sam, on a vacation from Hollywood, first heard about Humanism when he sat in a whorehouse in Mexicali and opened a copy of *The Saturday Review of Literature.* He read gravely, then turned to the Irish whore sitting beside him and asked, "What do you think about this Humanism business." "—Humanism? The best day I ever had was last Fourth of July, when I turned ninety-four tricks and not one of them a Chinaman." Tell that to Irving Babbitt.[15]

Another nice story is about Luis Angel Firpo,[16] the Wild Bull of the Pampas, and how he appeared in a fairy café in Hollywood. "The Wild Bull of the Pampas," the pansies whispered one to another. "Isn't he just magnificent!" Till one of them became so excited that he sat beside Luis Angel and said beseechingly, "Moo—oo."

Sam Ornitz came sober to dinner. Louise and Léonie, after drinking together all afternoon, arrived here separately, each in a dudgeon. Raymond came in a dudgeon at Louise. I would have come sober, but I brought Edmund Wilson and John Chamberlain[17] here beforehand, lapped up some alcohol with them, and then wondered with Peggy how we could get Edmund out before Léonie arrived. That was done successfully. Then, with Sam Ornitz, I rushed up to 26th Street for a bottle of wine. We met there Peggy Robson and Bill Adams, her new boy friend, and had a drink with them. I'm trying to picture the complete disorganization of a dinner party over which Peggy had worked all afternoon. It was eaten, conversation was made, people sobered up, and at half past ten our guests went home. Peggy cried over the spoiled dinner. I walked down to Lee Chumley's, ordered a cup of cocoa, and sat there while Dr. Mary Halton talked to me about Art and asked me to write a 50-word essay on Love. Lee was drunk, as he often is these days. He wanted to buy me another cup of cocoa and put me under the table. I walked home, went to bed, couldn't sleep, and got up to read Gerald Manley Hopkins, who, I decided, would have been a fairy if he hadn't joined the Jesuits.

I wish to God an earthquake would destroy New York and everybody in it. I envy you in Mexico (and maybe next year in Europe, for if you don't get a Guggenheim Fellowship, it won't be for lack of strong recommendations). Wilson didn't make up his mind about you till two weeks ago, when he finally read *Flowering Judas;* then he became wildly enthusiastic and, as his custom is, began to look for the inner intellectual meaning of your stories. I myself, in a mild sort of treachery to the two candidates for whom I was sponsor, wrote Mr. Moe[18] that you were the most deserving of all this year's candidates (no, "deserving" wasn't the word; "gifted" I think it was). John Chamberlain, writing about other short-story writers in *The New Republic,* took occasion to talk about you; he thinks you have solved the short-story writer's philosophical dilemma by deserting both Behaviorism and Psychoanalysis and stressing Volition. Yes, really, that's what he said. Howdy-do Miss Katherine Anne Hegel, Mrs. Friedrich Nietzsche Porter.

The New Republic has had some pretty good issues of late. Edmund Wilson came out with a sort of Communist Manifesto which has set litry New York to worrying about its political philosophy. Everybody is planning to write his own answer to it, everybody but me, that is. I did a piece on Rosalie Evans[19] finally; it will appear in two or three weeks. [. . .]

After long discussions, we have about decided to print some straight short-stories in *The New Republic.* Edmund is bludgeoning the other editors into accepting a couple of not very good ones. Everybody is favorable to the idea of printing a story by you. What about writing us a short story as your next chore—that is, after you finish writing about Kay Boyle.[20] People are writing in and asking us why we haven't said anything about the short stories of the American woman writer who ranks with Katherine Anne Porter. [. . .]

Did I say that your long Christmas letter arrived yesterday? We spent Christmas in Gaylordsville, in Matty's house; it is being occupied for the winter by Peter Blume.[21] Peter has a new girl friend, Ebie Creighton; she isn't very pretty but is awfully nice and tender and in love with him; she's getting a divorce within two weeks and I shouldn't be at all surprised if Peter married. Matty has finished the first draft of his Rousseau and has gone to Boston for a short vacation. Bill, after spending 1400 hours on the wagon, has fallen into the Green River. [...]

I'm going to give you a subscription to *The New Republic*. It's 10 A.M. and I have to go there to work.

Love and kisses,
Malcolm

――――――

[NL TLS-2] [SC 190–192]
[TO: KENNETH BURKE]
Sunday morning. [February 16, 1931]

Dear Kenneth:

Until Tuesday morning I'll be here in Riverton, at an inn, designed primarily as a house of sin. There's a bar, there's a quarter slot machine, there's a hard-boiled proprietor who used to be a gangster in Hartford and now collects Hitchcock chairs, there's a disposition to ask no questions of the couples who rent a room for an hour or two—that is, if they have baggage. But sin lies dormant in Connecticut during the winter, and virtue is cheaper in hard times. There are no couples coming upstairs baby for an hour or two, no drinkers at the bar; there is nobody, in fact, except the town philosopher, a huge man of sixty-five with a drooping left eye, who grandiloquently repeats the news in the daily papers, then goes home at eleven o'clock to study spiritualism until dawn.

[...] I try to reconstruct a philosophy that will work in periods like this. When you're satisfied with things you don't need a philosophy.

One of my worries, not the chief one, I admit, but real for all of that, is the way you've been acting toward me for the last two months. I suppose it's chiefly on account of *The New Republic*[22] and partly, too, because you're bothered by my habit of loading my troubles on you and by the nature of those troubles. About *The New Republic,* there isn't much more to say. It's a magazine rendered wooden by the fact that everything printed has to be passed upon by four editors of different tastes (or very strongly endorsed by two or three). It has a sort of group personality, which isn't that of any single editor. If what a man writes agrees with that group personality, and is short enough, it is almost certain be printed. If it's 3500 words or over, it's almost certain to be cut, and the cutting job, if it's delicate, comes to me; in case of articles which are straight reporting, Bill Brown does the editing. Bliven, with his newspaper training, has cutomania, but most people write so diffusely that the cuts he orders usually improve the paper. I'm trying to restrain him, however, and have him consult with authors before taking action. In the book department I have almost complete authority; it's limited by space requirements, by the necessity for mentioning certain books, and by the judgment of the other editors on the reviews as printed. I'm anxious, damned anxious, for you to do as much writing as possible for the book department. As for the rest of the paper, if you'll talk over articles in advance with Bliven or Soule, there won't be any difficulty.

What you write, as I told you at Matty's, is always on the margins of journalism. That's what makes it good; it's also what makes it difficult to steer through an editorial board with strong individual prejudices. For God's sake don't put the blame on the least influential of the four editors.

The second matter is even more difficult to talk about. I'm in a hole; I've been in one for six weeks and I may be in one for the next six months. It isn't merely the bust-up of one affair, and being kept in doubt about what's going to happen next; it's the fact that a whole scheme of life collapsed at the same time, that I've got to find a new one and find it for myself. I haven't been putting enough into my work—with the result that when I needed it, my work hadn't enough to give me. I feel as hollow as a sucked egg. I feel as one has a right to feel at twenty. If I could drop everything, go to Europe, write an ambitious book, I'd be cured quickly; but I don't want to drop *The New Republic,* which seems to me the only paper with signs of life and the only one which gives scope to its editors. [. . .] What's the answer? I'll have to go muddling along in this direction, writing myself out of a hole as well as possible, until next October; then I'll take a two-months' vacation in France or Russia and hope that it gives me a chance to get readjusted.

I'll spend long week ends in the country till May 1; in the city I'll trot about. It's a bleak prospect; don't make it bleaker. I don't think my troubles are peculiar to myself. A lot of people I know have been moving in what now seems to be the wrong direction; they too will have to change or go bust. It's pretty late to change now, but not so late as it will be next year, or the next. But we can talk about that some other time.

Yours,
Malcolm

———

[YADDO TLS-1]
[TO: ELIZABETH AMES, DIRECTOR OF YADDO]
c/o *The New Republic*,
421 West 21st Street,
New York City,
March 15, 1931

Dear Mrs. Ames:

[. . .] The proposal for a conference at Yaddo has taken different shape since I wrote you last. In the first place, the idea of having a symposium on the future of individualism was laid aside by the editors of *The New Republic*, under pressure of events in the political world. Next, Mr. Matthew Josephson came forward with an exciting idea, that of writing a cooperative volume of literary memoirs in order to illuminate the intellectual and social background of the present generation of writers. Here is a project which would allow several people to unite in producing in what could hardly fail to be a very interesting book. If arrangements could be made, we thought of gathering five or six of the contributors to the volume and of visiting Yaddo the first week it opens, before the regular guests arrive. Would this idea be feasible? Matthew Josephson, Kenneth Burke, Robert M. Coates and myself could come, and we should like to invite two others,[23] but not more—for, with more than six present, it would be harder to preserve an atmosphere of work. [. . .]

Very sincerely yours,
Malcolm Cowley

[YADDO TLS-2]
[TO: ELIZABETH AMES]
421 West 21st Street,
New York City,
March 28, 1931

Dear Mrs. Ames:

[. . .] Sidney Hook[24] you will probably wish to invite to Yaddo on the strength of his learning and promise as a philosopher, which are really considerable. I should add, though I may be wrong, that you should make the invitation limited, for you might find him an irritating guest to have all summer. He is a young Jewish professor, dogmatic and opinionated, determined to make his way. That he should be a professor at New York University in spite of the anti-Semitic prejudice of the faculty—that he should be sponsored by both Morris Cohen[25] and John Dewey—all this speaks worlds for his ability, which in fact is so far above the average that it would be an injustice to refuse him your hospitality. He probably won't be the most popular of your guests, though I may be wrong in saying this.

[. . .]

Meanwhile my very best wishes for a successful season.

[Malcolm Cowley]

[YADDO TLS-1]
[TO: ELIZABETH AMES]
[NR] April 8, 1931

Dear Mrs. Ames:

[. . .] I should like to recommend another name to your attention, that of Robert Cantwell[26] who, I think, has written you already. His story, "Hanging by My Thumbs," was about the best contribution to the third issue of *The American Caravan,* and his story in the present issue is a good one, though not so distinguished as the other. He has finished a novel which will be published next fall and is anxious to work at other projects, but at present he is finding it almost impossible to get along in New York. Book reviewing, something he does well but slowly, is not at all a financial solution, and I shouldn't be surprised if a few vitamines and calories wouldn't have the effect of reviving his literary style. He has about as much promise as any young writer I know.

[. . .]

Sincerely yours,
Malcolm Cowley

[YADDO TLS-I]
[TO: ELIZABETH AMES]
421 West 21st Street,
New York City,
June 10, 1931

Dear Mrs. Ames:

This week I'm staying at home from the office to continue working on my memories from the year 1923, on which I made such a good beginning at Yaddo. I wrote a paragraph which suddenly reminded me of your own difficult task. "In the midst of the most unified civilization existing in the world today," I said "American writers are, by reaction, ferocious individualists. They fear collective action of any sort: it reminds them of the Y.M.C.A, the Elks, the Shriners, the Rotarians; they will neither lead nor follow, and 'the only club I belong to,' they often say, 'is the ancient society of non-joiners.' . . . They are bent on preserving the anarchy of their individual lives," etc., etc. It's all true, and it reminded me of the astounding success you've had in imposing order on these essential anarchists—not too much of it, but enough so that a dozen of them can live together in the collectivity of one household, and work there.

We all had a glorious time at Yaddo, and a fruitful one, too: I think enough has been done to guarantee that a book will come of it eventually—I hope next spring. [. . .]

Sincerely,
Malcolm Cowley

[NL TLS-1]
[TO: CARL SANDBURG]
[New York]
July 9, 1931

Dear Mr. Sandburg:

Have you read about the campaign of extermination waged by the Chinese government against the young writers of the country? The Chinese have an extremely able and vigorous younger generation of novelists, essayists and poets. They are engaged in the exciting task of creating a new literature in the vernacular. Most of them are radicals, for the simple reason that the whole trend of the intellectual world in China is toward Communism. The result is that the government is murdering them wholesale. Poets of twenty-four, novelists of twenty-nine, feminist pamphleteers of twenty-seven, they are first tortured and then led out to face a firing squad.

The Chinese government is weak enough and sufficiently in need of foreign loans to be very sensitive to public opinion in this country. A general protest of American writers against these executions might prove very effective. We'd like to organize something of this nature. May we use your name in requesting other signatures?[27]

Sincerely,
Malcolm Cowley

[NL TLS-1]
[TO: KENNETH BURKE]
Yaddo, August 6, 1931

Dear Kenneth:

The long chapter of memoirs has just been finished and revised; 15,000 words, no more, is the length of it. I couldn't have chosen a more difficult period to write about. It was easy enough to tell how I punched a café proprietor in the jaw, but telling about the [Ernest] Boyd affair[28] was a different matter; here I had to continue my frankness more as a pose than sincerely. I kept saying, what a damn fool I was, but also kept telling what Boyd did, letting the events themselves prove that he was cowardly and untruthful. Moreover, I subordinated the Boyd affair to the suppression of *Broom*. You'll be able to judge how well I succeeded when you see the episode in print, for I think *The New Republic* will use the whole business. It makes a little novel, somewhat in the Thomas Mann tradition, though in trying to be true to events, I found that fate didn't announce itself in advance as it does in a Thomas Mann novel; the door didn't slam before Claudia was seen; on the other hand, life furnished a good novelistic structure—statement, events that prove it, catastrophe, tangential episode, readjustment . . . [. . .]

Racing starts this afternoon;[29] I'll be there to cheer on my alma mater, dear old Vanderbilt Stables. Otherwise labor in the mornings, swimming or fishing in the afternoon, ping pong and reading in the evenings, to say nothing of the very fattening meals: I weigh a ton. [. . .]

Your'n

Malcolm

[ASCH TLS-1]

[TO: NATHAN ASCH][30]

Yaddo, Saratoga Springs, N.Y.,

August 7, 1931

Dear Nathan:

[. . .] Perhaps you've heard it from other sources. [. . .] Last winter I broke with Peggy, not theatrically, but painfully and slowly. I saw before me a long perspective of years in which I'd deceive her and fall in love with somebody else and get ditched in turn because the other woman demanded a man who was one hundred percent hers, even if he was only a passable specimen [. . .] and being broken hearted and sleepless and cruel as broken hearted people are, I separated, giving Peggy the farm. After some weeks I went to live with Muriel Maurer, who is an incredibly decent person with more virtues than I can hope to catalogue or equal; we'll probably end by getting married when Peggy divorces me sometime in the future. Peggy herself has been very decent and unhappy and I feel like hell about the whole business, but have no intention of changing my mind.

[. . .]

Malcolm

[NL TLS-3] [SC 196–198]
[TO: KENNETH BURKE]
Yaddo, Saratoga Springs, New York,
October 20, 1931

Dear Kenneth:

A man with less intelligence than Hoover—a man, God save us, with less character than Hoover—could end the present crisis (not restore prosperity, but stop the panic, the hoarding, the runs on banks) if the proper social machinery existed. Under the present system, however, only a man of superhuman ability could do so. This is the answer to several pages of your Program—but of this more later.

[...]

Returning with relief to your book[31]—[. . .] I think that in defining form as "the creation of an appetite in the mind of the auditor and the adequate satisfaction of that appetite" you discovered an important principle, and a true one—and one which in itself negates a good deal of what you say in other parts of the book. Your standards elsewhere tend to be Crocean by virtue of your emphasis on technique, on judging how far the author accomplished what he set out to accomplish. But if art is the satisfaction of an appetite created by the artist, we are driven inevitably to consider the nature of the appetite, to criticize the ends instead of means. Art is a form of propaganda—for what? And the lamest part of the book, to my mind, is your consideration of the "what," your program. (Before continuing, I'll stop to render tribute to your illuminating asides, to all the aphorisms scattered about so lavishly.)

I'll try also to define my own position. I'm being driven toward what is known as Marxian criticism by a mental process somewhat akin to your praise of inefficiency, or rather of the situations in which society can flourish even with lazy and vicious leaders. In running a book department, I've noticed that even unintelligent reviewers can write firm reviews, hard, organized, effective reviews, if they have a Marxian slant. There must be something to it, I conclude. It doesn't attempt to reduce all art to its economic, or rather its social, causes but it does consider art as organically related with its social background, and functionally affecting it. Technique it discusses too, without giving it first place. I can't achieve your overmastering interest in How; the field of discussion seems limited and, in the end, barren. I tend to judge your critical writing by the Marxian elements in it, which are so important that one would almost say you were being pushed into [it] backwards. Certain pages of your discussion—especially when you are discussing the relation of a book to its age, or the value of art as propaganda—are written as if you were continuing a discussion with some Communist critic, arguing against some of his conclusions from his own premises. A moment later you jump into paradox, shoot off at a tangent . . .

Granville Hicks[32] has reviewed your book for *The New Republic,* not very satisfactorily. He differs with most of what you say, understands most of it, but simply misses the significance of your central definition of form. (By the way, I think that definition, by its logical implications, is responsible for what I have just called the Marxian elements in *Counter-Statement.*) I'm going to see Hicks on Saturday and argue with him.

[. . .]

Yours,

M.

———

[AT TLS-1]
[TO: ALLEN TATE]
[NR] February 3, 1932

Dear Allen:

It looks as if I will be in Tennessee and Kentucky next week but, unfortunately, nowhere near Clarksville. Here's the story:

In the bloody and much-publicized Harlan County coal fields the latest development is that the operators, through the county authorities, are refusing to allow food to be distributed to the miners on strike. They have been stopping trucks at the county line, closing relief kitchens and arresting relief workers for criminal syndicalism. The idea now is to have a group of writers go down to Knoxville, leaving New York this Sunday, and on Tuesday morning ride north with three truckloads of provisions, on the assumption that the Harlan County authorities will be afraid of the publicity involved and let the trucks get through. Edmund Wilson, Waldo Frank, Leslie

Howard, Quincy Howe and several others are going and I've about decided to go with them. Why don't you come along yourself, meeting us Monday night at Knoxville?

[...]

As ever,
Malcolm

[AT TLS-I]
[TO: ALLEN TATE]
[NR] February 16, 1932

Dear Allen:

[...] You really should have been along on the Kentucky expedition. We didn't go in as Communists; we went as Jeffersonian Democrats to test whether relief could be distributed to the miners and whether anybody except coal operators had any constitutional rights in southeastern Kentucky. We proved pretty conclusively that nobody had. A good time was had by all—that is, except the miners and Waldo Frank, who was really pretty badly beaten.

As ever,
Malcolm

[CPS TLS-I]
[TO: CHARD POWERS SMITH]³³
[NR] March 2, 1932

Dear Mr. Smith:

A long poem has to be very good indeed if it is to be accepted for publication in *The New Republic*. The least objection is enough to blight its chances. Your own poem is vigorous, in places very amusing, in others provocative; but I disagree whole-heartedly with the ideas you express. On this subject I could say a great deal, but I'll limit myself to one remark: you praise the ivory tower attitude toward literature as producing individuals. Show me one. Show me any poet, any novelist, any dramatist in present-day America who is worth admiring for his career and character, who can be called, not a happy man, but a complete man—and I'll believe everything you say. The real trouble with ivory towers is that people go cockoo in them.

Sincerely yours,
Malcolm Cowley

————

[ASCH TLS-1]
[TO: NATHAN ASCH]
[NR] April 29, 1932

Dear Nathan:

After sliding down what drain pipes, floating down what sewers, bobbing in what tidal rivers among rotten bananas and grape fruit rinds, climbing out among what refuse heaps—then leaving the city behind you, strolling among suburban factories, looking at dull faces—in short, after what literary peregrinations did you arrive at the point of writing an idyll about a valley?[34] It's a swell piece, really. It's got faults, chief of which is your illusion that Warren Davis is a great artist when, to take your words at their face value, he's only a big, dumb fool: great artists aren't like that. But your style—or rather, your rhythm, which in your case is the same thing—is getting to a fine state of musical complexity; and the wedding that ends the story is as good a piece of writing as you've ever done.

As ever,
Malcolm

{ ——— }

Hart Crane † 1932

Hart committed suicide meet me

Radiogram wired from *SS Orizaba* by Peggy to Cowley at
The New Republic, April 27, 1932 [NL]

————

[AT TLS-2]
[TO: ALLEN TATE]
[NR] May 2, 1932

Dear Allen:

I'm going home at this moment to write something about Hart, a short editorial.[35] Whether we're going to carry anything else about him I don't know; I should be in favor of doing so but will have to talk about it in conference tomorrow. I'd give anything to be able to publish some new poems of Hart's. So far as I know only one poem of his remains unpublished and it's one of his best; he sent it to *Poetry* just a week before his death. His bitch mother has taken possession of everything he left, including all his papers; it may be a terrible job to get them away from her. I think there are enough poems for a small book, if we can get hold of them. He wanted Peggy to be his literary executor. Here is the story of his death as she told it to me and as I heard it from other witnesses:

About two weeks ago he got a letter from Cleveland telling him that the business was in a terrible shape and that no more money could be sent him for some time. That was enough to set him off on a mad fit of drinking. He attempted suicide once, but it was merchurochrome he swallowed, not iodine, and the doctor just laughed at him. Drunk or sober, he would throw up his hands and cry "There's no place for a poet in this world. All they need is men of action. Where's the place for a poet?" Peggy thought that if she could get him to his relatives in Cleveland he would have to straighten up. They started back together on the Orizaba. At Havana she got separated from him in the crowd. When she went back to the boat, a box of matches exploded in her hand and gave her such a serious burn that the doctor thought she was going to lose her finger.

That burned hand really signed Hart's death warrant, for if Peggy hadn't been under the doctor's care she would have stopped Hart's drinking that night and the next morning. He was put to bed forcibly by the steward three times during the night. The next morning Peggy knocked at his door and found him opening a bottle of rum. She suggested that he'd better have breakfast before he started drinking and then returned to her own room to have her finger dressed again. At 12 o'clock Hart burst into her room, said "good-bye" and rushed out again. Peggy hastily got up and went to look for him. He was not in his state-room. At that she heard cries from the deck and the sound of the engines being reversed. Hart, in pajamas and a bathrobe, had walked through the smoking-room and down the full length of the deck to the stern and then dived overboard. The sea was calm—not oily—but with hardly a wave. The people in the stern threw him a life preserver, to which he paid no attention. He came up, waved his hand to the vessel and began swimming away from it. By the time a boat was lowered he had disappeared entirely. The Orizaba continued the search for 35 minutes and then went on her course. To the very end bathos and tragedy were mixed. The Norwegian captain called Peggy up to the bridge while the search was still continuing. He threw his arms in the air and shouted, "If it wasn't for prohibition and the high tariff, this never would have happened." The effect of Hart's death on me has grown from day to day; at first I felt it deeply only on account of Peggy. Just before beginning this letter I read his last poem, called "The Broken Tower"; it's a love poem and it is really tremendous.[36]

As ever,
Malcolm

[ZABEL TLS-2]
[TO: MORTON DAUWEN ZABEL, POETRY]
Yaddo, Saratoga Springs, N.Y.,
May 19, 1932

Dear Mr. Zabel:

If you drop in to see me the next time you come to New York, I'll try to tell you the whole Crane story, or as much as I know about it. There's a lot of it that doesn't bear setting down on paper: it would seem like the mere retailing of scandal when, as a matter of fact, it's poignant and tragic.

Here's a little of it: Hart's mother and father separated when he was in his teens. He didn't have much formal education; I think he never finished high school. Sometimes he blamed his mother for this, sometimes his father. He took her side at first in the quarrel, but three years ago he broke with her absolutely, stole out of the house where she was staying in Los Angeles, and came back to New York uttering dreadful things about her: he was almost insane in his animosity. One of his poems, "Quaker Hill," has a passage about her that is a pure example of persecution mania. He was on excellent terms with his father, who died last summer, his stepmother, and his mother's sister, Mrs. Deming of Warren, Ohio, and in fact most of the baggage which his mother seized contained presents for these people. There isn't much doubt that his mother was ultimately responsible for the emotional difficulties that ruined his life: I say this advisedly on the strength of what I heard directly from Hart and at second-hand from his relatives. It seems to me a calamity that his mother should have possession of his papers. Yes, she has them all, so far as I know; I doubt that there were any manuscript poems except "The Broken Tower." There are naturally lots of letters, but his mother is right on that point: they can't be published without her permission. Everybody Hart knew must have a few of them.

He died without a will, and his mother is his sole blood relative in the direct line. He had made a will a few days before his death, but was dissatisfied with some of its provisions and tore it up. He had, as I told you, asked Mrs. Cowley to be his literary executor, but naturally his spoken instructions haven't the force of law. Mrs. Cowley and I had been separated since early last spring—I'm setting down these private details so you can judge the matter. Since July she had been in Mexico; since October she had been living in Hart's house. He began to drink and show signs of suicidal mania about ten days before they left Mexico; she was taking him back to his relatives in Cleveland, thinking that he would straighten up in that good middle-class atmosphere. "The Broken Tower" is written to her.

The day the Orizaba landed, I got permission to meet the boat at quarantine, with the ship-news reporters. I could picture a ghoulish scene on board, but fortunately most of them swarmed on board the Berengaria with their cameras and dull whimsical faces, to meet "little Alice" Hargreaves, come to New York to observe the Lewis Carroll centennial. That was luck. But when I got to the Orizaba, I found Mrs. Cowley in a frightful state; she had stayed for three days locked in her cabin, crying. Hart's relatives met her at the dock, where also there arrived this telegram from Hart's mother, ordering his baggage to be sealed and shipped to Chicago. It was all a nightmare.

From this fragmentary account, I think you can understand the personal reasons why I wanted Hart's last poem to be published in the magazine for which I work. [. . .] At present I deeply regret that I yielded to my personal feelings in the matter: the whole business of arguing over a dead poet's effects seems like ghoul's work.

[. . .] I think I told you that we have in type a fine poem on Hart by Jack Wheelwright.[37] The editorial about him I wrote myself, but don't tell this to Mrs. Crane. What I said is true so far as it goes, though nobody could write a completely frank piece on Hart while his mother is alive.

In this letter I have set down a good deal more than I intended to write when I began. There's more to the story, of course, but that can wait until I see you, if you are still curious. In any case, I hope you will treat all this information as wholly confidential.

My best regards to Miss Monroe.

Sincerely yours,
Malcolm Cowley

[AT TLS-2]
[TO: ALLEN TATE]
[NR] June 28, 1932

Dear Allen:

[. . .]

I read and liked your piece in *Poetry* on Hart's death. It's as if he asked a question which all of us tried to answer in our own terms. Perhaps the mistake that all of us make is being too inhibited by respect for the dead, so that none of us speaks fully enough of the effect which his life itself had on the drying up of his talent. There are a couple of points on which I disagree with your analysis and a couple of others which I cannot understand. For example, *The Bridge* is undoubtedly a failure as a whole, but it seems to me that three or four of the individual poems, considered in themselves, are the finest things he ever wrote; especially I admire "The River." When you speak of him as trying to substitute the will for the intellect, I can't follow you, since it seems to me that Hart's career is in some respects a magnificent example of willlessness. What he tried to substitute for the intellect was emotion, ecstasy. Perhaps the idea in which I follow you least is the one about Americanism. It seems to me meaningless to contrast America with Europe, for the simple reason that it is culturally a European nation. It could be contrasted with England, or France, or Germany, but not with Europe as a whole, since in most respects it stands among the European nations—more highly industrialized than England but less so than Germany, more provincial than France but less so than Denmark, younger than England but essentially older than Russia, or even Prussia.

As ever,
Malcolm

{ ——— }

[NL TLS-2] [PARTY SC 201–202]
[TO: KENNETH BURKE]
Yaddo, Saratoga Springs, N.Y.
June 2, 1932.

Dear Kenneth:

You remember the story told, I think it was by your mother, about the first time we met—I was three and you were four; I walked around your parlor touching things, and you walked after me saying, Don't touch. Mustn't. Anyone looking at us today or reading your letters to me would think that the same situation was being repeated, that I was plunging into Communism while you were saying, Don't touch, be careful, mustn't. But that's only an appearance. I suspect that you're not really a hell of a lot concerned over my adventures with our comrades of the Left—except in so far as they seem to reflect on your own beliefs. If you are concerned, you've got no right to be: I'm not plunging blindly ahead into anything, I'm sort of feeling my way and trying to fit things into a system that will make it possible for me to define my own attitude toward the world and guess what's coming next.[. . .]

[. . .]

I'm not saying, either, Come on over into our nice Red pasture and play with all us Communist boys. That would be swell, but you're not going to do it, so what's the use of arguing about it. [. . .] In the meantime, I want to reregister a couple of remarks, because you're always disposed to forget them. (a) I think more of you than of any other living person (read "man" for the sake of strict accuracy). (b) For that reason you can hurt me more than anybody else, when you're so minded. (c) I've got a vast respect for what you write, even when I think you're dead wrong... But of this no more.

[...] You're right about my prose lacking edges (or salt). I must have been trying unconsciously for years to reduce it to a transparent medium, and now I've got it too damned transparent. But I don't think this is a barren period for me, so far as prose goes; it's barren merely in style; thank God I've got something to say. [...]

Yours,
Malcolm

[JBW TLS-1]
[TO: JOHN BROOKS WHEELWRIGHT]
[NR] June 16, 1932

Dear Jack:

[...]

Well, Comrade Wheelwright, I congratulate you on your adhesion to the pink Socialists. Now it's up to you to buy a copy of *Capital* and at least read up to the place where I left off—page 295, at last reports. But get this straight: *The New Republic* isn't communist and never will be—Comrade Wheelwright has gone farther left than Comrade Cowley by joining the John Reed club.

More or less Comradely or Fraternally greetings,

Malcolm

Serialized in *The New Republic*, Cowley's installments of *Exile's Return* inadvertently resuscitated the animosities of a previous decade, with Gorham Munson taking to arms in articles for *Contempo* and *The Sewanee Review* and Cowley retaliating in kind. In the summer of 1932 Samuel Putnam challenged Cowley's contention that he and his friends had brought Dada to America and presented a urinating incident in Cowley's studio in Giverny (as told to him by Aragon) as "the Secessionists' culminating achievement." Cowley responded with the following letter to Milton A. Abernethy, one of the editors of *Contempo* ("not to be printed").

[CONTEMPO TLS-1]
[TO: M. A. ABERNATHY]
360 West 22d Street,
New York City,
July 29, 1932

Dear Abernethy,

In the last, European, issue of *Contempo*,[38] Samuel Putnam devoted a paragraph to me.[39] In the course of that paragraph, he makes, grievous, not to say egregious, errors, which ought to be more or less corrected, tho[ugh] not in print. I mean:

(1) My edition of Racine was not expensively bound. (2) I still have it, and it shows no stains of piss, and smells of nothing but old leather. (3) Then or now I wouldn't piss on Racine. At the time in question I was engaged in writing a long and I still think a very good essay in praise of his work. (4) I didn't do the pissing anyhow—that was E. E. Cummings.

The story is worth telling. Scene: Giverny (par Vernon, Eure). Persons (besides myself): Louis Aragon, Harold Loeb, E. E. Cummings, John Dos Passos. Much argued, much drunk. Finally, in the dim lamplight, I feel urged to make an oration on bad books. And the oration, in substance, is as follows:

Here I was in Giverny (par Vernon, Eure) and books were being sent me for review from New York (N.Y., États-Unis), and if they were good books, that was all right. But if they were bad books, what the hell could I do with them? A bad book in New York is something to give to your aunts by marriage or sell to the Fourth Avenue book dealers, something you don't think about, but here in Giverny (par Vernon, Eure) bad books were hung about your neck like so many dead albatrosses, pardon me, turkey buzzards. You couldn't give them away, you couldn't sell them in France, they cluttered your shelves, they were no good for anything in the world—why, I'd tried to wipe myself with one of them, being out of toilet paper, and it was stiffer than a January corn cob.

I selected half a dozen bad books from my shelves—they weren't classics, just irritating modern poetry and prose like Elinor Wylie's *Black Armor* and something by Jean Cocteau—and heaped them on the sheet of tin in front of the little coal stove and tried to set them afire—Jesus, they wouldn't even burn. I poured oil on them, and tried again—and at that moment Cummings pissed on the fire.

It was a tumultuous evening. About three o'clock we marched with Cummings and Dos into Vernon (Eure) so they could catch the last train for Paris; they missed it and had to sleep in a hotel; Louis and I walked back to Giverny in the dawn, Louis reciting poems. The next morning I woke and wondered what the sour-smoky smell was in the room. My landlady, Mère Teller, picked up the pile of books and saved them for years and left them as a legacy to her nephew. She didn't know how bad they were, not being able to read and having a cold in the head.

So that's the story, not to be printed. You might forward the note to Putman, for if he tells the thing again, he might tell it straight. As for the question WHO BROUGHT DADA TO NEW YORK? the answer is WHO THE HELL CARES?

Faithfully yours,
Malcolm Cowley

[GH TLS-1]
[TO: GRANVILLE HICKS]
[NR] September 26, 1932

Dear Hicks:

George Soule and I think that the last paragraph of this review [of Sherwood Anderson's *Beyond Desire*] carries more of an implication than is justified by the facts. The reader might argue as follows: Anderson is the author closest to the American people; Anderson feels and participates in a drift toward communism; therefore the American people is moving toward communism. But since the reader could also identify himself by personal observation that the American people is not, as yet, moving towards communism, he would be likely to conclude that your last paragraph is a pep talk.

The most one can safely assert about the movement of the American working classes, as distinguished from the diverse movements of intellectuals, business men and agitators in New York City, is that they have abandoned the half-hopeful, half-despondent waiting for something to turn up which characterized the first two years of the depression. Now they seem to be asking, where do we go from here?—but as far as they have gone is to vote for Roosevelt instead of Hoover. Any conclusions to be drawn from Anderson's novel must be tentatively raised. The book might indicate a future change, just as *Winesburg, Ohio* indicated such a change before it actually took place.

Personally I choke at such a sentence as, " 'Beyond Desire' adds to our hope—for Sherwood Anderson and for America." [. . .]

Sincerely,

Malcolm Cowley

———

[FSF TLS-1]

[TO: F. SCOTT FITZGERALD]

% H. T. Meriweather

"Cloverlands," Trenton, Ky.,

May 22, 1933

Dear Scott:

I copied out a lot of this piece,[40] a long passage beginning with your remarks on life at Cap d'Antibes; it will fit into a chapter I'm planning and will appear there with jue acjolliment. In writing some of this stuff I feel like a trespasser into posted land. You are the real historian of the jazz age: I saw it only from beneath, as a member of the typewriting proletariat. But I've got a hell of a lot of things to say about it if I can get them said.

I read almost simultaneously *This Side of Paradise* and *Not to Eat, Not for Love*. George Weller[41] graduated from Harvard in the class of 1919: he is thus a little older than you were when you wrote *This Side*. At that age, a few years are very important. Weller is immensely more slick and sophisticated than you were then. His book is more complex than yours was, and better, too. Except there is this remark to make: Weller had his literary models (Dos Passos and Thomas Wolfe); all he had to do was copy them, fill out the application blank to Parnassus with which they furnished him. He filled it out damned well. You didn't have a blank. You were trying to say something that hadn't been said. Weller is good, but isn't making history. (Addendum: I suspect that Harvard is a more complicated social mechanism than Princeton. There must be more shades of social ambition, just as there are more clubs of different sorts (including national fraternities) and more people outside the whole club system. Nobody at Harvard ever says, "Now I've made my club and I can take a rest." There's always one more club to make, one more necktie, on[e] more medal to hang on the mirror of the chiffonnier. And studies, too, are more important there than they were at Princeton in 1917.)

I read *The Great Gatsby,* expected to like it, and did.

I have started now to read Zelda's book. It moves me a lot: she has something there that nobody got into words before. The women who write novels are usually the sort who live spiritually in Beloit, Wis., even when they are getting drunk at the Select. Zelda has a different story to tell.

I'm living (for $25 per month) in high luxury two miles from a telephone and eight miles from a railroad. Two large rooms, private bath, pond with bass in it, coffee in bed. The Tates, who send you their best, are a mile away through a lane that is two red-clay banks in a tobacco field. Allen comes over to go fishing and sometimes we drive into town to drink a bottle of beer. In the mornings, which last from seven till one, I work at the god damned book, which isn't going ahead very fast.

I had a great good time in Baltimore. Couldn't you and Zelda manage to come and see us in New York?

Sincerely,
Malcolm Cowley

I think it is always wise to distrust either conservatives or radicals as soon as they reach a point at which they disregard human beings.

Cowley to Allen Tate, August 8, 1933 [AT]

[RPB TLS-5]
[TO: RICHARD P. BLACKMUR]
360 West 22d Street, New York City,
April 28, 1934

Dear Blackmur:

I'll answer your noble letter[42] in the same mood that it was written in. That is, I'll sit down at the typewriter—damn it, I've done so already—and without thinking in advance what I'm going to say, but letting the ideas gush forth like fountains or travail forth like the little round turds of the constipated, I'll tell you what I think in my almost inmost if any soul about Life and Art. I feel in a fit state for such an effort, having just been chewing the fat with Conrad Aiken while we lightly imbibed. Anyway—

Let's make up a questionnaire.

(1) What should an artist do about the class struggle?
(2) Should he write art or propaganda?
(3) What is the function of art?
(4) Why didn't I say so?

(1) I don't lay it down as a categorical imperative that artists should take part in the class struggle. Not being God or Allen Tate, I don't feel qualified to deliver categorical imperatives. But simply as an observer of how people act, I am qualified to say that artists *will* take part in the class struggle. They will do so because they are men before being artists, and because their human interests are involved, and because they can't stay out of it without deliberately blinding and benumbing themselves and making themselves less human—in other words, lesser artists. They are taking part in the class struggle already, and as it inevitably grows sharper, more and more of them will either choose their sides or else unconsciously support the side on which they were born. I hope that lots of them take the side of the proletariat. I think they will be better artists for having done so, although I do not think that the art of the ruling class is anywhere near dead.

(2) The choice between art and propaganda is a deceptive choice, because art is good and propaganda is bad and naturally hurrah for art (whatever that is) and to hell with propaganda (whatever that is).

Let's see what the question means in philosophical terms.

The whole thing goes back to Kantian esthetics and later to Schopenhauer's esthetics. Kant's idea was that esthetic activity and practical activity are forever separate; art for him was *Zweckmaessigkeit ohne Zweck*, purposiveness without purpose. Schopenhauer's idea was that the world was "will" (or change) and was evil, and that art was willless and permanent. Out of all this we get a whole series of antinomies, art against the world, artists against philistines, vision or imagination against will or purpose, esthetic activity against

practical activity, and finally art against propaganda. The whole series depends fundamentally on the idea that the outside world is *a completed system
of relationships*—that attempting to *change* this system is evil and impious—
that the artist's duty is *imaginatively to contemplate the unchanging world*.
But researches in psychology have shown—as much as such things can ever
be shown—that the whole idea of separate "functions" or separate compartments into which human activities are forever divided is blooey and phooey
and hooey. And philosophers since Marx—can one speak of philosophers
since the anti-philosopher? I'm going to anyway—have returned toward the
Heracleitean metaphysics and have tended to conceive the world as *process*,
as a system that won't be complete until it's dead.

The whole series of antinomies has to be recast in order to have any
value whatever, except the minus value of confusing the argument.

Yet there is a real distinction that covers the same territory as the dangerous art-propaganda distinction. I think that the real distinction is psychological and depends on the level of the mind from which one writes. I
think that if one writes only from the top level of the mind, from the beliefs
that one has only recently acquired, one is almost certain to write badly, to
neglect or distort things that exist on a deeper level of consciousness, to
write what is emotionally false and will be called propaganda. That is obviously a very foolish thing to do. But if one has fully absorbed the same beliefs, one might treat them in a way that was emotionally effective—that
was in other words "art."

(3) Yes, what is the function of art anyway? Is it a "purging," a "refinement
of gross experience," is it "relief," "amusement," or is it a useful means of incit-
ing people to good actions? I don't know. But I do know this: that there is no
single theory of the function of art that has not narrowed and confined and
impoverished art, whether that theory was Platonic, Aristotelian, Kantian,
Schopenhauerian, Marxian, Flaubertian, I don't care what. It is obvious that
the aspect of human activity usually called "art" is richer than any of the
theories that have been applied to it. I should hesitate to deny any of these
functions and should be sorrier still to have any one of them dominate the
field. There is one function of art that impresses me, however, as being the
principal one—it is the function of art as a humanizer. "All good works of
art," I said once, "have a thesis, namely, that life is bigger than life—that

life as portrayed by the creative imagination is more intense, more varied, more purposeful or futile, more tragic or comic, more crowded with incidents, than is the life we have [been] leading day by day. Sometimes we are discouraged by the contrast; we merely try to escape into the better world of art. Sometimes, however, we try to reinterpret our daily lives in the light of the artist's vision. The new values we derive from his work, when projected into our own experience, make it seem more poetic, tragic, or novelistic, more sharply distinguished from the world of nature, in other words, more human."

I am quoting from the end of an old essay on the Humanists,[43] but I haven't had occasion to change these ideas. "And art," I continued, "has another humanizing function perhaps no less important: it is the humanization of nature itself. The world about us was alien and terrifying to its earliest inhabitants in the beginning; vast portions of it are alien to us today. Before man can feel at ease in any milieu, whether that of forest, plain or factory, he must transform the dead shapes about him by transfusing them with myth. . . . This creation of myth, by whatever word we call it, has continued since the earliest of times: it is a necessity of the human mind. It is a sort of digestive process, one that transforms the inanimate world about us into food without which the imagination would starve."

Sometimes the world changes faster than our ability to digest it and I think that such a thing—I know that such a thing—has happened today. We see artists plucking in a careful way at little sections of the world, like a baby's fingers touching one or two keys of a piano, without having any knowledge of the whole keyboard. That is a bum simile—what I'm trying to say is that the conception of the class struggle is one that renders the world intelligible and tragic, makes it a world possible to write about once more in the grand manner—and that artists have greater days in front of them if they can succeed in living up to the stature of their times.

(4) Why the hell haven't I said this in my book? I've tried to say part of it here and there. The trouble is that my book is a history, and demands a historical method, and striking off into straight philosophy or esthetics is not only difficult but might destroy the structure of it. I'm now writing a piece to go at the end of the book in which I'll say some of these things. [. . .] Within the limits of the historical method, I think I showed plainly enough that the

religion of art led to futility for the people who practised it—to loneliness and hypochondria for the men of genius like Joyce, and to suicide or insanity for the little fellows like Harry Crosby and Scofield Thayer. That path I think is closed. There are many paths still open.

And that's all for this time, and a lot more than I expected to write. It's of course a compliment of one sort or another to have *Exile's Return* reviewed with a book by Eliot—my only kick would be that my own book is vastly different, is one in which the esthetic ideas are introduced only as they happen to cast light on a story I'm telling—and here I have to be writing you this long letter to tell you what my ideas really are.

[...]

Cordially,
Malcolm Cowley

[FSF TLS-1] [CFSF 350]
[TO: F. SCOTT FITZGERALD]
[NR] *April 13, 1934*

Dear Scott,

I am reading snatches of *Tender Is the Night*—one chapter here, one chapter there, as I usually do with novels before I can bring myself to sit down ambitiously and read them straight through. All I can say so far is that there are some swell side-shows in it. The one very near the end, of the English Countess and Mary North and the kick in the sailor pants, is absolutely immense. In spite of what you say,[44] I think I ought to review the book myself rather than pass it along to one of the young guys who would ask why you weren't a proletarian novelist. I am sure to be late with it, because I am just finishing up the last six pages of my own book. The hungry linotype machines are now eating the rest of it.

Thanks a lot for your list of neglected novels.[45] The next time you jump into New York, U.S.A., let me know you are in town instead of sitting mournfully at Tony's.

As ever,
Malcolm

[FSF TLS-1] [CFSF 366–367]
[TO: F. SCOTT FITZGERALD]
[NR] [date cut off; late May 1934]

Dear Scott:

Here is the review.[46] I'm not especially proud of it. After waiting all this time, and writing it against your wishes, I should have given you something better. I wanted to write you a long letter about the book, which I liked more and was more deeply impressed by than the review seems to say. Outside of all I said here, I think the double introduction interfered with the novel more than anything else—I mean the presenting of all the characters through Rosemary's eyes and then the going back to tell the story from 1917 to 1924; there is a confusion of time here that bothers most of the readers with whom I have talked. Wouldn't it have been better to have the story develop directly from Rosemary's meeting with the Divers? As soon as Dick fell in love with Rosemary his first instinct would be to tell her all about himself, even at the risk of a spiritual infidelity to his wife—that would have obviated the second introduction. You were certainly right in saying that the sideshows were fine—some of them are unforgettable.

My own book is out today, and I'm getting a swell run-around from the critics. I wish some of them had read it.

If I pass through Baltimore around the first of July, is there any chance of my seeing you?

As ever,
Malcolm

———

[JBW TLS-1]
[TO: JOHN BROOKS WHEELWRIGHT]
[NR] June 1, 1934

Dear Jack:

[...]

What a ton of brickbats my own book has been receiving this week. Often books are more severely reviewed, but never in my experience have they been severely reviewed at such great length. The book was assigned almost entirely to White Guard critics and editors, including our old friend Bernard DeVoto, who wrote the worst review of all.[47] I'm beginning to think that the class war really extends to the literary business.

[...]

As ever,
Malcolm

———————

[CC TLS-2]
[TO: CARESSE CROSBY]
[NR] September 7, 1934

Dear Mrs. Crosby:[48]

[...]

Ever since Hart Crane first told me about him, I have been very much interested in Harry's story, and I always wanted to write about him. I suppose you know that Harry's death deeply affected Hart, who was one of my best friends. I wish I could write about Hart too, but I am afraid it would not be possible to do so with complete honesty while Hart's mother is living, she being so much responsible for many of the defects in his character. But I felt that when I was writing about Harry I was also, in a sense, writing about this old friend of mine whose work I admire so much.

I thought I explained to you that I was going to write about Harry when I borrowed the three volumes of the diary. It seems to me that I told you a good deal of what I was going to say, especially about Harry's experience in the Ambulance Corps, and how I thought it colored his attitude.

At any rate, you will soon be reading what I wrote. It does include "big chunks" of the diary, but not consecutive chunks. The longest passage quoted is less than a page; it is one of those descriptions of the Quartz' Arts that Harry did so well. I was trying to pick out, not the personal passages, but just the ones that helped to interpret Harry's character. Very likely you won't agree with the interpretation, but I think you will sympathize with what I was trying to do. Harry was an extraordinary person,

and I don't think the world ought to forget him. And I like to think that
I have done something toward keeping the memory of him alive in people
who never met him.

   [...]

Cordially,
Malcolm Cowley

The High 1930s: Unity and Discord on the Left, 1934–1937

In the middle years of the 1930s Cowley's radical fervor ran high. He chose
sides, often quite vociferously, but usually with more ambivalence than was
publicly apparent. For Cowley good writing came first, but he was not always successful at separating his political preferences from his literary judgments; often his literary verdicts displayed a Marxist slant. At their best his
reviews and articles demonstrate a fine critical sensibility struggling against
ideological rigidity. As he observed in 1937, in his own practice he sought to
bring together "esthetic and social criticism."

   To the degree his *New Republic* duties allowed, he immersed himself in
public action. In April 1935 he read a paper at the First American Writers'
Congress, and he took on an active role in the League of American Writers—a
collective of writers containing Party members as well as "fellow travelers"—by
helping to organize its lecture series, chairing talks, or convening discussion
meetings on proletarian literature. Though he was a fervent supporter of the
Popular Front, he was less than happy about the Communist predominance
at the Congress and in the League, yet he allowed himself to be used as front
man for Communist activities. His correspondence radiates the exhilaration
of convictions put into action. He was convinced that the Communists offered the most effective opposition to fascism and actively campaigned for
their initiatives from within the League, insisting on the need for left-wing
unity; as he told Dos Passos, "We have all got to hang together or we'll hang
separately."

   Eager as he was to steer clear of sectarianism, Cowley could not avoid
becoming embroiled in factionalism on the left, and often personally
fanned the embers of political discord. Sometimes his fervor led to impetu-
ous action, as when he fell out with Dos Passos over the best way to help the

Spanish artist Luis Quintanilla. More seriously, he faced virulent criticism about his supposed use of his literary editorship of *The New Republic* to promote and defend a Stalinist party line. Disturbing reproaches came from close friends like Tate, who charged that Cowley's political views had led to a lowering of literary standards on the magazine. Political disagreements put a strain on their friendship through the 1930s, even as they were united in their passion for modern poetry and their efforts to protect the legacy of their friend Hart Crane.

Cowley admitted into *The New Republic*'s book pages a broad assortment of young poets and reviewers—among them John Berryman, Louise Bogan, Tillie Lerner (Olsen), Josephine Miles, Theodore Roethke, Muriel Rukeyser, James Stuart, Richard Wright, and Marya Zaturenska. But he also printed work by more established poets such as Cummings, Horace Gregory, Marianne Moore, Wallace Stevens, and William Carlos Williams—often appearing for the first time in *The New Republic*. He was eager to continue to publish contributions by Edmund Wilson, who could be difficult and peremptory, and it took tact and effort to keep this preeminent critic on board. He invited the Italian writer Ignazio Silone, whose novel *Fontamara* was cherished by those on the left, to write for the magazine. In private he carried on a lively correspondence with Chicago novelist Robert Herrick on the literary and social divide between generations. He wrote an introduction to Agnes Smedley's autobiography *Daughter of Earth* (1935) and launched a series of "revaluations" of American writers. The series was intended to stand as a collective statement of criticism on the left, and laid the groundwork for *After the Genteel Tradition: American Writers since 1910* (1937), edited and co-authored by Cowley.

In the heyday of the Popular Front Cowley gave the Communist Party the benefits of his doubts and allowed himself to be courted as a person of status and influence. Though he had private misgivings, he was widely perceived as towing the Stalinist line. In the *New Militant* of April 18, 1936 Felix Morrow published a blistering diatribe entitled "Malcolm Cowley: Portrait of a Stalinist Intellectual," in which he characterized Cowley as "the literary cop who patrols the *New Republic* beat for Stalin." A year later, John Dewey wrote to *The New Republic* to complain about the overtly anti-Trotskyite slant of the magazine's book section and resigned as contributing editor. In a long letter of explanation, Cowley confessed to a personal dislike of Trotsky and to unease about internal developments in the Soviet Union but balked at the suggestion that he was "a slave of Stalin and the Comintern" and renewed his plea for cooperation on the left.

As his letters and reviews make clear, Cowley had difficulty acknowledging the real nature of Stalinist oppression. His defense of Stalin's infamous Moscow Trials is a case in point. Convinced that unwavering support of Russia was the prerequisite of an effective fight against international fascism, he hesitated to accept the insights of more percipient critics like Wilson and shied away from overt and unambiguous criticism of the official Soviet report of the trials.

Cowley's hesitation was due in part to Russia's role in the Spanish Civil War, in which the Soviet Union seemed the only effective supporter of the Republican democratic side against the fascist Loyalists under Franco. Concerned that factionalism might damage the effectiveness of help to Spain, Cowley was eager to bear personal witness. In July 1937 he traveled to Europe on assignment for *The New Republic*. From Paris he traveled to Valencia, where as representative of the League of American Writers he attended the Second International Writers' Congress, and from there to Madrid. During his three-week trip he kept a separate notebook and wrote up his impressions of the civil war in Spain in five articles for *The New Republic* and one for *The New Masses*. In Cowley's absence at *The New Republic* Edmund Wilson filled in as literary editor. On February 15, 1938, Cowley donated the manuscript of *Exile's Return* to the League of American Writers, to help raise money for hospitals in Spain: "May it buy its weight in X-ray negatives! Even if it merely buys its weight in cotton bandages, it will have done something." His surviving correspondence makes scant reference to his journey. On his return trip, by boat, he wrote a first draft of "The Long Voyage."

On December 16, 1934, Malcolm and Muriel Cowley became the parents of a son, Robert William Cowley. In the spring of 1936 the Cowleys moved to Sherman, Connecticut, where they had bought a farm and seven acres of land. In Sherman they enjoyed the proximity of friends: Peter and Ebie Blume lived across the road, and Robert and Elsa Coates and Matthew and Hannah Josephson lived within walking distance. The remodeled Sherman barn would be the Cowleys' lifelong home and the rural base for Cowley's literary operations and excursions into New York City.

———

[LG TLS-3]

[TO: LEWIS GANNETT, *NEW YORK HERALD TRIBUNE*]⁴⁹

360 West 22d Street,
New York City,
May 14, 1934

Dear Lewis:

In recent issues of *The New Republic* we have been printing lists, contributed by various novelists and critics, of "Good Books That Almost Nobody Has Read." To judge by these lists, there are a lot of good books that instead of being sent out to reviewers and distributed to the bookstores might just as well have been loaded on a garbage scow and dumped overboard in New York Harbor. But there is another side to the picture, too. The public and the critics aren't always neglectful.

I'd like to make out a complementary list, of good books that almost everybody liked—of books that were generously praised, widely read, and deserved all their success, and more. All of them are books that I have reread during the past year, with the feeling that they are just as living and valuable now as when they first appeared.

In order not to make the list too long, I'll confine it to books by American authors now between thirty-five and forty:

The Enormous Room, by E. E. Cummings. This was almost a total flop when it first appeared, but it has been reprinted half a dozen times by different publishers. It is still the best American novel about the War.

The Time of Man, by Elizabeth Madox Roberts. This is a good book to reread in the light of recent arguments about proletarian fiction. It is a class-conscious novel, dealing with a countryside where the class distinction between owners and tenants is drawn more rigidly than anywhere else in America. It shows that a member of one class can write warmly, understandingly and without patronage about the members of another.

The Great Gatsby, by F. Scott Fitzgerald. This isn't quite such a masterpiece as it is thought to be by T. S. Eliot, Rebecca West and its author, but it's a fine novel all the same. Fitzgerald is the poet of the American upper bourgeoisie, the only writer who ever succeeded in surrounding it with glamor.

The Sun Also Rises, by Ernest Hemingway. Now if I were a first-class literary snob, I'd say that the best things Hemingway ever wrote were the early short stories of *In Our Time,* but that doesn't happen to be true. His first novel is just as new and fresh as the stories and more compelling. In retrospect it seems much better than *A Farewell to Arms,* which has a faint air of being fabricated. Incidentally, Hemingway's second-best book is *Death in the Afternoon.*

Zola and His Time, by Matthew Josephson. This was the first book in which Josephson revealed his special talent for organization. Nobody else that I know has the same gift for fitting details into a logical scheme and for seeing careers and movements in their simple outlines. Another reason why this biography is worth rereading is that, although there are many novelists greater than Zola, there is none whose problems and methods of solving them are more pertinent to writers today.

Axel's Castle, by Edmund Wilson. It wasn't until I began working with some of the same material that I realized what an absolutely first-class job Wilson had done with the symbolist novelists and poets. His special gift is for interpretation, for making difficult things seem clear, but he also has the ability to set ideas into their social context.

All of these books were warmly received, all of them had at least a fair sale—most of them a very good sale—and I think they prove that critics and the public have some right for self-congratulation.[50]

As ever,
Malcolm Cowley

———————

It is hard to understand a cry like yours for political fair play in the columns of *The New Republic,* which is not a call for fair argument but rather for an above-the-battle attitude like that of a baseball game in which nobody except the professional gamblers cares very much who wins.

Cowley to Maurice Zolotow, August 2, 1934 [Maryland]

[MARYLAND TLS-1]
[TO: MAURICE ZOLOTOW]⁵¹
[NR] August 10, 1934

Dear Mr. Zolotow:

Aristotle is still the best critic, and St. Thomas was great in his day, but I want to say frankly that the Thomists of the twentieth century strike me as a lot of grandmothers trying to take the monkey gland treatment. I would have more respect for the movement if more of its members could write six lines of decent poetry. Eliot can do so, but even he doesn't write half so well as he did fifteen years ago, when he saw the souls of housemaids sprouting despondently at Area gates.⁵²

Everybody writes political criticism today; it's absolutely impossible to keep it out of the book section without having said section go dead on your hands. The only people still living in their ivory towers are those so lacking in curiosity and sensitivity that they don't write well. I wish you would give the Communist Cabal a rest for a while⁵³ and start out to attack the White Russian Cabal that dictates book reviewing in the *New York Sunday Times*. There you will find real political reviewing, if you are looking for it and not simply out Red hunting.

I never said that Hart Crane's suicide was due to the capitalist system; it had a great many complicated motives but was mostly caused by a mother fixation. Harry Crosby's suicide was a different story. Crosby couldn't very well do anything that wasn't more or less connected with the capitalist system, considering the part that his family played in it. As for Proust's asthma and Joyce's blindness, I wish you had read more carefully what I said. The interesting point about them is that the doctors have never been able to discover any organic cause for Joyce's blindness, and that Proust's asthma was partly imaginary. What I said—and what can easily be proved by the evidence—is that writers in the Symbolist tradition are likely to be subject to hypochondria; it's an occupational disease with them.

Sincerely,
Malcolm Cowley

[YADDO TLS-1]
[TO: ELIZABETH AMES]
[NR] May 25, 1934

Dear Mrs. Ames:

[...]

Recently I received a letter from my young friend Jon Cheever, who doesn't seem such a young friend any longer because I have now known him for four years, ever since we published his first piece in *The New Republic*.[54] During the last year he hasn't appeared so frequently in print, but he hasn't ceased to develop, and I feel sure now that he will fulfill the remarkable promise that was held out by his first sketches. Newton Arvin knows him and I think will back up what I say about him. I know that it's very much too late now to write about asking guests to Yaddo. Still, from time to time there is someone who finds himself unable to come, and if such a vacancy should occur it might be very nice to have Jon Cheever come. I think you would like him.

[...]

Cordially[,]
Malcolm Cowley

[YADDO TLS-1]
[TO: ELIZABETH AMES]
[NR] October 8, 1934

Dear Mrs. Ames:

Now that the Mansion is closing for the fall, I begin to see the people who worked at Yaddo this last summer, and I can tell you that they are all very sorry to be back in New York. Robert Coates is in New York for a short visit to get some work cleared up. He is probably the most bitter individualist that I know of; on principle he hates all communities; and he keeps being surprised at himself for enjoying his visit to Yaddo so much.

I am writing you now about Kenneth Patchen, who was in correspondence with you early last summer. Several people think that he has a very fine talent as a poet; Archibald MacLeish, Lewis Mumford, are inclined to set a higher value on the poems he has written already than I am; my personal judgment is that he has so far shown more promise than fulfillment. One thing is certain in any case: he is now about as desperately hard up as anyone could be. Last summer he married a very nice girl and tried to make a home for her in New York but, after they had starved here for a while, there was nothing to do but take her back with him to his family in Warren, Ohio. The family strongly disapproved of his wife because they are full of native-American prejudice, and his wife is Finnish. So the Patchens had to separate again, Mrs. Patchen going back to her family in Boston (which can't support her) and Kenneth coming to New York to see what he can do. He has the manuscript of a book of poems with Farrar and Rinehart, and there is just a chance that they might take it, but not much of a chance.

I suppose the odds are 1000 to 1 that any openings you may have at Yaddo for guests during the winter have already been filled. I wouldn't bother you at all about this matter if Patchen's plight weren't so desperate. Perhaps you will have some suggestion as to where he might turn. (Another friend of ours whom you did a great deal for two years ago, Edwin Seaver, is now more or less fixed; he is editing *Soviet Russia Today*. That doesn't mean that he gets more than perhaps $25 a week, but at least it means that he eats.)

Mrs. Cowley, who sends you her best regards and wants to meet you, is looking better than she ever looked before.[55]

Cordially,
Malcolm Cowley

———

[EW TLS-2]
[TO: EDMUND WILSON]
[NR] October 30, 1934

Dear Edmund:

[...]

Make a point of reading H. G. Wells's *Experiment in Autobiography*.

I don't know whether or not it would fit into the plan of your book,[56] but if it doesn't you ought to do a separate piece on Wells. His autobiography is really a first-class job, and is of tremendous significance. The thing he does in it is to recreate the busy, hopeful intellectual atmosphere of England before the War, and then unconsciously to show the complete ineffectuality of the liberal ideas of that period in the new post-war world. When writing about Stalin and Roosevelt, the man's fatuousness is enormous—and yet somehow, in my eyes at least, it doesn't cause him to lose any stature. He reminds me of some prehistoric monster surviving into an age of smaller mammals, utterly unadapted to the new conditions, utterly incapable of recognizing the new conditions, but at the same time bigger and more generous than the new race of creatures pollulating on the earth.

The funniest and most persistent thing in Wells's intellectual history is his hatred of Marx and his complete inability to understand what Marx was driving at. [. . .]

As ever,

Malcolm

――――――

[NL TL/CC-2]
[TO: WALDO FRANK]
[NR] [no date, November 1934]

Dear Waldo:

I had a hard time reviewing your book,[57] because I was groping for the causes of a disharmony in it that is difficult to explain. Perhaps the definition was faulty, but the disharmony is there, in the novel, and I was not the only reviewer to be impressed by it. I said that it came out most clearly in the climax of the story, when Markand finds his new faith. It was also evident, however, in the alternation between naturalistic passages telling how people acted and rhapsodic passages that point the symbolic nature of their actions. The naturalism makes the symbolism seem strained, and the symbolism makes the naturalism seem less natural. Again, the same conflict appears in the characters, some of whom are copied from nature, and others introduced for their symbolic value. The novel would have had more force, I think, if all the characters and all the style had been conceived on the same plane.

It is hard to touch on fundamental ways of looking at the world in a short review, it is still harder to do so in answering a letter of reproof. But if you don't believe that a good deal of your past writing has not only been non-Marxian but anti-Marxian, you might consult the extracts from Marx's philosophical writings collected in *Marx: Pages Choisies* (Gallimard, 1934). [. . .] [P]recisely the greatest difference between your picture of the world and that of the Marxists lies in your insistence that "certain inward problems" must be solved before a man like David Markand can be released into social action. The Marxist point of view here is that action and theory are not divided into two compartments, but proceed along with each other step by step, the theory being expressed in action, which in turn develops the theory further, which in turn leads to new action. This is neither dualism nor is it mechanism and behaviourism—it is the only sound and practical way of unifying the different sides of a man's life. I think your own interests in the cause of the workers actually proceeded in somewhat this fashion: you were interested enough to go into Kentucky to bring food to striking miners; then, what you saw there and the actions you were called upon to perform, stimulated the growth of a new attitude. David Markand didn't proceed in that fashion: his pilgrimage would have been more likely to end either in sainthood or suicide.

But I didn't want to turn the review into a discussion of Marxism—a branch of knowledge in which I am not very well trained; I know enough about it, however, to see that the two sides of your philosophy have not been fitted together in *David Markand,* and that this intellectual disharmony prevents the book from having the great force you could have given it.

Malcolm Cowley

[RH TLS-2]

[TO: ROBERT HERRICK][58]

[NR] 22 November, 1934

Dear Mr. Herrick:

George Soule and I have read your article on the younger generation. We both like it and want to print it. But there is one aspect of it which we think is based on a misconception that ought to be cleared up.

You are casting up accounts between Youth 1890–1910 and Youth 1913–34. Now, from your own perspective, it may seem that youth from 1913 to

1934 is fairly unified, but I have to report with sorrow that said youth is divided into two hostile sections—at least two—and that I myself now belong to the older of these sections. Since about 1930 there has been an obvious change of direction and a stiff reaction against the ideals of the post-war generation.

The War was a real dividing line. One can't fail to notice the difference in ideals between the authors who began publishing their work before 1914 and those who began publishing, say in 1920. The reaction against patriotism in four-minute speeches and the belief that the world could actually be improved by beating Kaiser Bill, that was a cause, perhaps the principal cause, of the sentimentally hard-boiled attitude that you object to. But there was another element that entered into the change. Before the War there were two trains of literary thought going on simultaneously, that of the Art for Art's Sake writers and that of the socially-minded writers like Wells, Shaw and yourself. The disillusionment after the War caused the socially-minded writers to be held in very low esteem, and at the same time raised the reputation of the Art for Art's Sake writers. Joyce, for example, did not belong to the post-war generation; he began publishing several years before 1914. What happened after the War was that Joyce became a fad, a craze, a religion. But since the depression, things have changed again. A new generation of socially-minded writers has arisen and, simultaneously, the quotations of the socially-minded writers of the pre-war years are beginning to rise on the intellectual stock exchange. One example that touches you personally is that Newton Arvin in 1929 would scarcely have thought about writing an essay to be entitled "Homage to Robert Herrick."[59]

I have gone into this matter at such length on account of its bearing on your essay. It seems to me that if you were writing about the post-war generation—which you are, almost everywhere in your essay—then Joyce is out of place there, although the Joyce craze is not. And it also seems to me that you ought to take some account of the definite change in direction since 1930. The very youngest writers have bad manners and write about sex. On the other hand, they are not lacking in political conviction—quite on the contrary—and have quit drinking heavily. But since these various remarks may seem too nebulous here, there is a definite suggestion that would be easy enough to carry out. Wouldn't it be possible for you to recast your present introductory section [...]?

[...]

Cordially,
Malcolm Cowley

On November 20 an exhibition of the etchings of the Spanish artist Luis Quintanilla opened at the Pierre Matisse Gallery in New York. Quintanilla, a friend of Dos Passos, had been imprisoned as a member of the Madrid revolutionary committee, and Dos Passos had written a personal note to Cowley on the exhibit from Key West, hoping that publicity in the United States might foster Quintanilla's release and lead to a general protest against the brutal repression of rebellion by the Spanish government. Rushing into action, Cowley fashioned from Dos Passos's personal note a "letter to the editor" that he then printed in *The New Republic* November 28 issue. Cowley's unsanctioned act triggered the fury of Dos Passos, who feared the publicity might hurt rather than help Quintanilla's case.[60]

[POETRY BUFFALO TLS-2]
[TO: JOHN DOS PASSOS]
[NR] December 7, 1934

Dear Dos:

[...]

Naturally your letter of reproach—reproach is about the mildest word that could be used for it—has been bothering me ever since. After reading Hemingway's piece in the catalogue—it also mentioned the sixteen years sentence that was being demanded by the *Fiscal*—I think the only extra damage that could possibly have been done by printing the letter lay in the sentence about the possibility of getting better treatment for Quintanilla by organizing a protest in this country. On that subject you are a better judge than I am, but I don't think the Spanish government reads *The New Republic*. In the meantime, printing your note in the paper may help to get the signature you want.

Hemingway is a fine writer and I have said so several times and at great length. But I wish to God that he would save his ammunition for the real game. Every time he goes out hunting he gets buck fever and begins shooting both barrels at every lark and robin and catbird in the grass. He has done some damned irresponsible things and I know that I was the victim of one of them—I am thinking of the time he went to *The Dial* when a good deal of my income came from writing reviews for that magazine, and said, "Miss Moore, Malcolm Cowley says that you won't print my stories because I like bull fights." The truth was that she didn't, and didn't print his stories for that reason, but the information had come to me from Kenneth Burke, who was working for the paper, and I had passed it on confidentially to Isidor Schneider, and Schneider had told it to Hemingway, and Hemingway got us all in bad. Now he is turning on Isidor Schneider, who is the most simple and self-sacrificing person I know, and who won't hit back. Why doesn't Hemingway take a crack at Max Eastman[61] instead, who has it coming to him?

All this is a long subject for discussion in which politics and personalities are mixed up, as they always are in critical judgments. I think the crisis is going to be fatal to Hemingway unless he does get a clearer idea of what it is all about. For the *Cosmopolitan* he wrote a really lousy and disgraceful story last spring about fishing and smuggling Chinamen and the Cuban revolution. The point of it was, to this observer, that when a Hemingway hero got mixed up with a real revolution, he played the part of a gangster. But all this isn't any reason for losing one's admiration for the books that Hemingway did well. I think *The Sun Also Rises* is the best of all—then *Death in the Afternoon,* then *A Farewell to Arms*—or maybe this arrangement is all cock-eyed because I am leaving out the best of the short stories.

Considering that the inkspitters[62]—that isn't the word you need but it will do for a dictated letter—don't amount to anything anyway, why bother about them?

[...]

As ever,
Malcolm

[AT TLS-4]
[TO: ALLEN TATE]
360 West 22d Street,
New York City,
December 14, 1934

Dear Allen:

Cleanth Brooks's essay[63] isn't the last word on the subject, but it certainly casts some new illumination on it, and I'll pass the ms. on to the other editors with my recommendation. The point I like best was his development of [I. A.] Richards' point about irony. Incidentally I don't think this point is really equivalent to Eliot's use of "maturity" as a standard. Irony is a point *within* the poem, whereas "maturity" is a standard of reference applied from *without*, by the critic, and a very dangerous standard to boot, since it is easy to disparage anything with which we don't agree by saying that it is immature. It is one of those weasel or chameleon words that conceal subjectivity under an appearance of objectiveness. . . . I'd like to argue with Brooks about his use of the word "Marxist." He writes from a position so far to the right that Max Eastman appears to him as a Marxist critic, which he is anything else but.

The rest of your letter[64] bore on more difficult matters—namely criticisms of me as editor, of the NR book department as edited, and queries about your own relation to the paper.

Allen, we never know what sins we commit unbeknownst to ourselves, but the accusation that I keep writers out of *The New Republic* for fear of their talent seems to me pretty God damned far from the truth. I have too much interest in putting out a good paper. Nobody has to try to keep writers out of the paper. Limited space does that, and timely articles on politics and economics. My job is to go downstairs and fight to get writers into the paper. I do that a good deal and ought to do it more.

For the next year I'll be writing the lead review every week. Automatically that bars out the other writers, some of them very good, who might be doing the lead review. But that job was wished on me and I fought against it and finally had to be bribed to take it by a raise that I badly needed on account of the (probably day after tomorrow) forthcoming and forthyowling baby.[65] I hate writing on schedule, hate reading so many books and will duck out of the job as soon as I safely can.

I am not solely responsible for the book department. I edit it, but at certain times the editorial department or the business department or both together, or the subscribers or who-not, descend on me and howl for my head and why did you publish this and why didn't you have such-and-such a book reviewed by so-and-so. I keep favoritism out of the department, sometimes at the cost of leaning over backward, but have to compromise on questions of personality and policy. One error I make consistently is that of having too many books reviewed, especially books that don't really matter a damn but seem important during the week after publication. But also—

I'm trying to put these things candidly, and it's pretty hard doing so, and we're getting near the core of the question.—But also I have my own political convictions, and if I ever (and I guess I sometimes do) give insufficient space in the book department to writers whose ability I respect, it is because their convictions clash too strongly with mine. I believe that the present financial ruling class in America and in the world is going to crash because it can't run the world effectively, and I believe that it can be replaced permanently only by the working class, and I believe that before it crashes it is going to try to impose a capitalist dictatorship. With the forms of thought that seem to be preparing for that capitalist dictatorship I have no sympathy whatever. I'll never be a proletarian writer because by education I'm not a proletarian, but my instincts are all in favor of democracy and egalitarianism even, and I feel a deep aversion toward what I think are the cockeyed attempts to restore Authority, Tradition, the Church, Aristocracy and what-not. I don't want to lend my influence as writer or editor toward doing anything else than fighting them.

I'm trying to be candid at the risk of being tiresome. In a time of ferment like this, political lines get drawn on more and more questions and there is less neutral ground. On a lot of questions you and I have diverged pretty damned far. But, except in this letter written only because you roused the rabbit and I had to run after him, I don't want to emphasize this divergence, because there are so many questions on which we continue to see eye-to-eye. [. . .]

As ever,
Malcolm

Addendum—addenda

I don't think the book department has deteriorated. The judgment here is subjective on both sides. I think we could have fewer reviews and have them better written and not try to cover so many books.

You're right in saying that casual and frank criticism doesn't reach me as it used to ten years ago. There's malice and there's bootlicking and there's empty politeness, and you must have found that out also. Say what you think. I can take it and feel grateful to you.

———

[JM TLS-1]
[TO: JOSEPHINE MILES]
[NR] January 16, 1935

Dear Miss Miles:

All three of your poems are being printed in this week's issue of The New Republic. [...]

There is not a doubt in my mind that your work will be quickly recognized. It has all sorts of fine qualities. Early success, if that is really what you are destined to have, is something that may do incalculable good or harm—it works both ways on a writer, depending on how he reacts to it and whether his attention is focused on the work he is doing or on the reputation he is making. I hope you get the success and I hope you take it in a humble spirit and work like the devil.

Cordially,
Malcolm Cowley

———

[NL TLS-2]
[TO: IGNAZIO SILONE,[66] ZURICH, SWITZERLAND]
[NR] February 18, 1935

Dear Mr. Silone:

In our letter inviting you to contribute to The New Republic, we certainly should have gone to more trouble to explain the nature of the magazine and the sort of public it has. [...]

The New Republic is a weekly journal of opinion. It is not connected with any political party, but its general line of attack is left-liberal—something like the policy of *Die Neue Welt Bühne* or of the French magazine *Europe*. It stands definitely to the left of the English weeklies like the *New Statesman*. Since it appears every week and has to cover many subjects in each issue, it is under the handicap of not being able to publish many long expositive or historical articles. For the most part, it has to deal directly with what is going on about us.

The article you sent us has several great disadvantages from our point of view. In the first place, it is longer than most of the articles we are able to print. In the second place, its treatment is chiefly historical. In the third place, being an attack on the Church, it stirs up a controversy that we are not very eager to touch. The Catholic Church in this country plays a different role from the one it plays in the Catholic countries of southern Europe, and even from the one it plays in Germany. In the United States there is no single district that is definitely under Catholic rule (though the three states of New York, Massachusetts and Rhode Island come pretty close to being dominated by the Church). The division between Catholics and non-Catholics is often a class difference; this is especially true in the states of the East. Most of the Catholic support is drawn from the poorer layers of the population, and the result has been that the Catholic politicians, mostly Democratic, have been somewhat more pro-labor than the Republican politicians. Most of the strongly reactionary movements in this country have also been anti-Catholic. All these circumstances make it inadvisable for magazines like *The New Republic* to attack the Church.

There is a whole multitude of things that we should be eager to have you write about for us. One subject suggested by *Fontamara* would be an account of the peasant revolts and the small strikes that have been taking place in Italy during the past two years, and the tactics that the government has used in suppressing them. Another subject would be "How People Live Under Italian Fascism." Still another subject would be "The Prospects for Fascism in Italy"—whether there is any chance of its being overthrown without the outbreak of another world war. A fourth subject would be "Mussolini's Policy Toward Abyssinia."

I can't tell you how much I liked *Fontamara*—but maybe the review I wrote of it, which is enclosed in this letter, will give you some idea of the enthusiasm I felt for it.[67]

I deeply regret that we cannot use this first piece you sent us, for we should be proud to have you as a contributor to *The New Republic* and I think that your writing for us might do a great deal of good here.

Cordially,
Malcolm Cowley

[POETRY BUFFALO TLS-1]
[TO: JOHN DOS PASSOS]
[NR] April 30, 1935

Dear Dos:

The American Writers' Congress[68] went off much better than I expected. It always gives me tremors and trepidations to see a bunch of writers gathered in one room and talking about theories. This time there were more writers than ever before, and a greater number of theoretical discussions. The Congress had more political color than I would have liked. That is really a mechanical difficulty. It arises from the fact that Communists are more used to talking to an audience than non-Communists, with the result that more of them have speeches to make. But the papers read at this conference were carefully prepared, and some of them turned out to be extremely interesting. I think Waldo Frank was an excellent choice for secretary of the League of American Writers that grew out of the Congress. He will help it to broaden out its activities and keep it from being sectarian.

[...]

But this letter is written about another matter entirely. On June 3, in Paris, there is going to be an International Congress of Writers for the Defense of Culture. The subject has a somewhat flossy sound—but it is, after all, the subject that we are all beginning to worry about a great deal. For my own part, I am beginning to think that culture is already declining in most of the world. It seems to me that the tortures and beatings and assassinations that are now a daily matter in Germany and China could not have gone on when we were boys without a real upsurge in world opinion. Now people read about them apathetically—it is as if our sympathies were suffering from sclerosis. We are even becoming apathetic about another war.

The Congress in Paris has a darned good outline for discussion. It is going to have no special political color, except that no writers are being invited who have openly espoused fascism or who are living at peace with a fascist government. For the rest, they are asking most of the distinguished European men of letters—[G. B.] Shaw, [Bertrand] Russell, Virginia Woolf, Aldous Huxley, E. M. Forster, Selma Lagerlöf, Paul Valéry, Thomas Mann, Pío Baroja—and I understand that the majority of them are going to be present.

They are very anxious to have you come. They are so anxious, in fact, that they are willing to pay your passage. If you consider going, would you telegraph me immediately?[69]

[...]

As ever,
Malcolm

[LB TLS-1]
[TO: LOUISE BOGAN]
[NR] May 3, 1935

Dear Louise:

I suppose that you have seen the various anthologies printed in *The New Republic* during the last few months.[70] There have been damned few female poets represented among them. I am against the idea of setting the ladies apart, but when gents edit anthologies they seem to leave the ladies out, except for a few personal friends & sleeping companions. The result is that if we want our series of anthologies to be at all representative, we shall have to include a harem or seraglio of poets.

I suppose that this is a job that you wouldn't like to undertake. You can have it if you want it. But if you don't want it, will you write and suggest what lady is best qualified to do the work?

[...]

As ever,
Malcolm

[ARVIN TLS-1]
[TO: NEWTON ARVIN]
[NR] May 6, 1935

Dear Newton:

[. . .] I wonder what you thought about the affair?[71] The great mistake, it seemed to me, was the result of a political-personal difficulty. The Communist party wants to create a broad united front against Fascism. In order to do so it has to arouse interest among the intellectual classes and let them work in their own way as long as they aren't working toward any reactionary ends. The individual Communists are trained to talk, and exercise their training—with the result that any united front meeting, against the wishes of its sponsors, is likely to take on the aspects of a Communist meeting. The great defect in organizing the Writers' Congress was that insufficient provision was made for getting expression of opinion from unorganized elements and from the youngest writers. [. . .]

[. . .]

As ever,
Malcolm

I hope we can get to a point where most of these factional arguments can be disregarded and where a united front can be formed among writers as among other classes of the population, solely on the basis of opposition to fascism and of the struggle for a more rational way of living.

Cowley to Newton Arvin, May 16, 1935 [Arvin]

[POETRY BUFFALO TLS-1]
[TO: JOHN DOS PASSOS]
[NR] May 16, 1935

Dear Dos:

I saw Henry Hart at lunch today, and he showed me the revised version of your paper.[72] The plan is to print it along with the other papers in a long pamphlet that should appear within the next three weeks. Henry Hart, Joe Freeman[73] and Kenneth Burke are the editorial committee.

But that isn't why I am writing you. I wanted to make one comment on your worries about the free speech during a revolutionary period. It seems to me that the difficulty is absolutely insoluble if you look at it from the standpoint of an ideal—and therefore static—society. In practice, a solution is reached by an adjustment between conflicting forces. The political leaders want certain aims and are willing to suppress free speech, and ought to fight hard for it. In a revolutionary society not all the advantage is on the side of the politicians, because they have to depend on the support of the writers. Therefore, through a conflict of purposes, an adjustment can be reached—a dynamic adjustment. When the writers are terrified or don't fight hard enough for their art, you get a situation such as prevailed in Russia from 1930 to 1932. But you notice that the situation is already improving, that the writers are fighting harder and that the politicians are making concessions to them.

[...]

As ever,
Malcolm

[POETRY BUFFALO TLS-1]
[TO: JOHN DOS PASSOS]
[NR] June 3, 1935

Dear Dos:

No, I think you are wrong about the Communists not being able to do anything except call down repression on themselves and others. That seemed to be the lesson of the German situation—if looked at from one point of view—but I think the real lesson there was that it is insane for the parties of the left to remain divided. We have all got to hang together or we will hang separately. And as for repression, what you are saying in effect is that if we accept repression then we won't have it imposed upon us. In France, where they have conducted a united front against it, there would have been fascism a year ago without the fight. The only check on the anti-Red campaign at present raging in the United States is opposition by liberals who would not have taken any action at all if the Communists had not inspired them to do so.

I can't get all these things into a dictated letter. If you could spend some time in New York and get around here a good deal, you would find that things are surprisingly active. There is a surprising move toward organization among the white-collar classes, much of it inspired by the office-workers union. The C.P. is active and growing; people who have been in it for two years are regarded as old-timers. It's a general rule that you have to be in the middle of these things to get the feel of them—mass movements seem alien from the outside. You will never guess it from reading the newspapers, but a lot of things are much more encouraging now than they have been since the War. There is something of the feeling of the old Wobbly days. I'm sorry you're missing it.

As ever,
Malcolm

I am writing to hear your impressions of the Soviet Union. People are arguing on street-corners, bets are being laid, the big book-makers are taking it up.

Cowley to Edmund Wilson, June 3, 1935 [EW]

[EW TLS-1]
[TO: EDMUND WILSON]
[NR] July 15, 1935

Dear Edmund:

[...]

I was very much interested by what you say about Moscow. Possibly the change that not only America but England and France will introduce into Communism is a softening of outlines. The truth is that the class struggle here is both more violent at times and more sporadic than it was in Russia before the Revolution. There is more opportunity for persuasion among the middle classes. You can see that tendency already being acted out in France.

Here is one useful job you could do for the N.R. if you have any time. Fred Beal[74] is now writing a muck-raking series for Hearst to the effect that life in the Soviets is terrible, is slavery, is starvation, and all that. It would be interesting to find out exactly what Beal's experiences were in the Soviet Union and what is the story behind his writing these pieces for William Randolph Hitler. Many of the people you know must have met Beal in Moscow.[75]

As ever,
Malcolm

[CA TLS-3]
[TO: CONRAD AIKEN][76]
[NR] December 3, 1935

Dear Conrad:

To continue that debate we started in *The New Republic*[77] would require a book, and a book based on wide researches in psychology, esthetics and anthropology. I wasn't really trying to answer you—it couldn't be done in 1135 words—but merely to state the opposite point of view, for the record.

There are two points that I could clear up a little more in this letter. First, I have been interested for a long time in the direct effect of certain types of literature, and I began to see that this effect was clearly visible in diaries, if nowhere else. For example, Harry Crosby noted in his diary for July 19, 1924, that he had just finished reading *The Picture of Dorian Gray*. He quoted, "The only way to get rid of a temptation is to yield to it" and added, "tempest of applause." On July 21 he wrote:

> The sun is streaming through the bedroom window, it is eleven o'clock and I know by my dirty hands, by the torn banknotes on the dressing table, by the clothes and matches and small change scattered over the floor that last night I was drunk. . . . This is the result of reading Wilde. Blanche. Rhymes with Avalanche.

Now, Harry Crosby was an extraordinarily naïve young man, but the same sort of stimulus-response pattern can be noted in a good many other diarists who recorded their reading. From Kenneth Burke I have heard a good deal about the effect on him of Dostoevsky; and I have watched a whole bloody generation of young people trying to be Ernest Hemingway. And the one moral I have to draw from it is that the best literature sometimes produces the rattiest psychological effects. Given time and space, I could expand on this topic, which might irritate Communists and Catholics alike.

The other topic is that of psychological constants. There must be some of them; otherwise we couldn't enjoy *The Tale of Genji* or the Bible, for that matter, if we do enjoy the Bible. But they aren't the constants that we generally think of—they aren't the father-son relationship or the lover-mistress relationship (which the Greeks would shrug their shoulders at) or the individual-and-the-state relationship. Novelists ought to realize that a good deal of the material with which they deal is impermanent, is characteristic only of one period of one culture. That wouldn't necessarily lead them into choosing new subjects, but it would lead them into recasting the subjects with which they are accustomed to deal.

Psychologists, of course, would be helped by the same realization, if they haven't arrived at it already. For example, most of the psychoses that Freud describes are bourgeois psychoses that couldn't be understood by people living in a different society, who would presumably develop psychoses of their own. (Isn't the famous Oedipus complex a result of loveless marriages that were contracted for property reasons? How else could one explain the prevalence of this psychosis among French literary men, for example? The mother attaches the son to herself as a compensation for not receiving the love of the husband—that's the pattern you'll find in the lives of Baudelaire, Gide and how many others.)

[. . .]

And meanwhile, what about doing something else for *The New Republic*? [. . .]

Muriel and little Robbie are well—Robbie blooming, Muriel a little bent with the tasks of motherhood. They send you their love, or rather Muriel does, since Robbie hasn't even learned to wave by-by. Have you seen Foster Damon's life of Amy Lowell? It's an official sort of book, and Foster still seems to believe that Amy was a great poet, but I liked to read about those Boston days again. Think I'll review it in free verse.[78]

As ever,
Malcolm

———

[ARVIN TLS-1]
[TO: NEWTON ARVIN]
[NR] January 13, 1936

Dear Newton:

[...]

When Cantwell suggested this series[79] and I argued about it with him, two or three definite conceptions rose out of our discussion. One was that the change in literary standards during the last few years had also changed our ideas of the writers that were and were not important. One idea was that the value or non-value of a writer could be shown objectively in talking about his life and work. That is, a conscientious critic, by reading a man's books, by carefully reaching an idea of his purposes and standards, by also collecting some material about his life—insofar as it was not strictly private or scandalous—could present a picture of a writer that would be the basis for a sort of objective judgment infinitely more valuable than the opinions generally bandied about in book reviews. Cantwell also thought that we ought to choose the sort of writers who are important in any effort toward a united front. I haven't discussed that particular problem with you, but the effort to form a united front has vastly changed criticism on the left and ought to result in making it more human and less dogmatic.

Well, there is a weak statement of what we are trying to do. [...]

As ever,
Malcolm

———

[GH TLS-1]
[TO: GRANVILLE HICKS]
73 West 11th St., New York City,
January 26, 1936

Dear Granville:

Preparations for your lecture are now under way.[80] [. . .]

You'll laugh, you'll weep, you'll cry when you hear who is going to be chairman. Lewis Gannett, none other. Gannett did dirt to your book and dirt, more dirt, to mine, but this is the year of the united front, and united front we're having. By the way, you'll be surprised when you see for yourself how far the united front is going in literary circles. Trachtenberg[81] beaming on Dreiser. No fights at present, except with Hearst and the Trotskyites. Much good feeling. With this foundation we ought to be able soon to launch the League into an effective anti-fascist campaign.

The subject, as you remember, is "Our Revolutionary Heritage." That ought to be ideal for you, combining Jack Reed with the great tradition.[82] We'll have some critics around to start arguments.

[. . .]

As ever,
Malcolm

Don't get snowed in!

[AT TLS-1]
[TO: ALLEN TATE]
[NR] April 23, 1936

Dear Allen:

Here is my review of *Reactionary Essays*,[83] in case you haven't already received it. You can see that I fell into pretty violent disagreement with the political section of the book; I guess you were expecting that. But, as I said in perhaps not quite warm enough language, I thought the essays on contemporary poetry were splendid. The only one I disagreed with was the one on T. S. Eliot—I think you overestimate the quality of "Ash Wednesday," which is full of mechanical repetitions, poor in images and, to me at least, gives evidence of being what you in another place refer to as "poetry written from the will." Incidentally, I don't think that the poverty in Eliot's "Ash Wednesday" is inherent in his Anglo-Catholicism—some passages in "Murder in the Cathedral" show that he can write much more richly about the same material. "Ash Wednesday" is a transition poem, and to me there isn't much of it that seems worthy of Eliot's best work. But, as I said, this was my only serious disagreement with you in the essays dealing with modern poetry, and I found an enormous lot to admire—the piece on Crane especially, in which I would subscribe to almost every word, but your judgments of MacLeish, Millay, Robinson, Pound, were almost as good. I have never liked your "Emily Dickinson" quite so well as the others, but that is good too. And one thing that strikes me in all these essays was that, writing from an apparently opposite point of view, you arrived at the same sort of social judgments that a good radical critic might reach. That lent point to my feeling that in your political essays you were quite unjust to the standard of values that can be furnished by a more or less Marxist interpretation of the world. In some recent novels, especially Malraux's *Man's Fate,* one gets exactly the "epos, myth or code" that you say is lacking in Robinson—and, as a result of it, one also gets real tragedy. Perhaps in my review I should have dilated more on this point instead of arguing with your political essays, in which I think that you are handicapped by the contradictions in your position.

[...]

Is there any more news about the book of Hart's letters? I see that Philip Horton[84] reviewed your book in *The New Masses!*

As ever,
Malcolm

The topic most interesting now in the world of letters is people's reaction to the Spanish civil war.

Cowley to Edmund Wilson, November 23, 1936 [EW]

[EEC TLS-1]
[TO: E. E. CUMMINGS]
[NR] December 18, 1936

Dear E. E.:

They are trying to get up an ambulance service for the Madrid front—and God knows that such a service is needed. The sponsors of it—the Medical Bureau of the American Friends of Spanish Democracy—thought it would be an excellent idea to have the new ambulance service sponsored by people who had been with the American ambulance service on Norton-Harjes during the war. Dos Passos and Bill Brown and a lot of other people have come in on the idea, and Hemingway sent both his name and his check for fifty berries. Couldn't you let your name be used in memory of the enormous room? [. . .]

The papers are scared to death of handling honest news from Spain. Yesterday the British Parliamentary Committee that had been in Madrid made its report before Parliament. They charged that the Rebels were using poison gas and that the whole city was in danger of being wiped out. They begged the government to permit the shipment of gas masks to Madrid. Anthony Eden[85] agreed to relax the embargo to this extent. There was great excitement in London—but except for very brief items in the *New York Post* and the *Philadelphia Ledger*, we don't know of any paper that carried a line of it.

As ever,
Malcolm

———

[LT TLS-2]
[TO: LIONEL TRILLING]
RFD Gaylordsville, Conn.,
January 11, 1936 [1937]

Dear Lionel:

This is very good.[86] Objectively I wouldn't quite rank it with your piece on O'Neill, but subjectively I might rank it even higher, because the subject hadn't so much juice in it or her, and because you squeezed every last drop out of her or it. [. . .] For a title I suggest "Miss Cather Démeublé" in the magazine. In the book, "Willa Cather: A Return to Gentility" might be better, less flip.

[. . .] I might disagree with you about [the absence in American literature of] "completely satisfying single books." What about *Moby Dick, The House of [the] Seven Gables, The Conquest of Mexico, The Red Badge of Courage, Ethan Frome, The Ambassadors*—not to mention books like *Huckleberry Finn* and *Leaves of Grass* and Poe's poems that are great but flawed? It seems to me that American writers have produced lots of single books as completely satisfying as anything we could reasonably demand. What they have not produced is integrated careers—or simply careers that make sense (think of Melville's last years, or Hawthorne's, or Sinclair Lewis as a drunken buffoon writing a letter to "Dear David" the King of England). The curious thing about Willa Cather and Eugene O'Neill is that their careers do make sense, do move in a logical direction, but in the wrong direction.

[. . .]

I hope that you can send me the draft of your O'Neill piece [. . .]. And will the magazine draft of this Cather piece be okay for the book, or do you think that the old lady should be further catheterized? Cather ye rosebuds while ye may. Knock, knock, it's Willa Cather.—Willa Cather who?— Willa Cather rosebuds or Willa Cather thorns?

[. . .]

As ever,
Malcolm

[VFC TLS-1]
[TO: V. F. CALVERTON,[87] *THE MODERN MONTHLY*]
[NR] *February 19, 1937*

Dear Calverton:

I have been meaning for a long time to drop you a note about your piece on Mencken in *The Modern Monthly*. It was generally a keen job. But you made one factual mistake and, I think, one error of interpretation.

The factual mistake was your saying that the esthetes of the 1920s admired Mencken. They didn't. They were engaged in a long feud with him—one-sided, as it happened, because the esthetes had very few magazines in which to attack him. (Ernest Boyd's article, "Esthete: Model 1924," in the first issue of *The American Mercury,* and the magazine, *Esthete: 1925,* which appeared a year later, will give you some picture of the quarrel.)

Mencken was always a conservative in literary matters. But in those years he was fond of realistic books, and he was very good about printing the early work of people like Mike Gold[88] and Josephine Herbst.[89] He hated any sort of experimental writing, even Hemingway's.

What I think is your error in interpretation is partly concerned with your statement that Mencken was always a conservative politically and thus hasn't changed at all in this respect. That is partly true. But during the early 1920s his emphasis was on moral questions: he was fighting the censors and snoopers, who were also conservatives but in a different fashion—so that the general effect of his writing was to some extent progressive. At present he has quit fighting anybody on the conservative side.

But there is another change here that is a little more tenuous and hard to discuss. The fact that Mencken used to help young writers and now helps them not at all points to a change in his social psychology. I think he used to regard himself as one of the middle-class intellectuals—though he wouldn't have used that particular term. Now the controlling ideal of the middle-class intellectuals is "the ladder to success," "the career open to talent." They are trying to get ahead and they like to see other people get ahead also; they think there is always room at the top. But the controlling ideal of the ruling class is security. They have what they want, and they are afraid of losing it. They do not particularly welcome new people into their class; they feel subconsciously that every ambitious young man is a potential enemy. It seems to me that Mencken since 1930 has developed this ruling-class psychology. If so, we would have an explanation of why he no longer helps or even reads the books of the younger writers.

Sincerely,
Malcolm Cowley

I'd never sacrifice a literary admiration to a political opinion. It would much more likely be the other way around.

Cowley to Harry Hansen, May 28, 1937 [NL]

[FBM TLS-1] [PMC 473]
[TO: FRED B. MILLETT][90]
[NR] April 1, 1937

Dear Mr. Millett:

At present I am interested particularly in one critical problem, that of bringing together esthetic and social criticism. An error made by most of the critics who are politically radical has been to put the two into separate bins. They will say that such and such an author is admirable for his "form" or his "expression," but that his social ideas are deplorable. For my own part, I believe that form and matter can't be separated in this fashion, and that the really good authors are likely to be good from whichever point of view you approach them—whereas many authors whose social ideas are apparently quite virtuous are in reality bad and harmful to both literature and society because they lack any sense of living people. In other words, there must be some unifying principle that comprehends both esthetic and social criticism, and my present interest lies in finding and stating it. But I should also like to get back to writing poetry and get a rest from reviewing books.

[...]

Nobody has done an oil portrait of me, but the figure in Peter Blume's picture, "Parade," at the Modern Museum of Art, was done with me as the unfortunate model.

Sincerely,
Malcolm Cowley

In "The Record of a Trial" (*The New Republic*, April 7, 1937) Cowley reviewed the official report of the Soviet authorities on the Moscow Trials of the Trotskyite rebels against Stalin. Admitting to sympathy for the aims of the Soviet Union and a "bias" against Trotsky, he found it hard to believe the defendants had been forced into making completely false confessions and thought "the major part of the indictment was proved beyond much possibility of doubting it." But even on that assumption, he acknowledged, the trials revealed disturbing conditions inside Russia that cast doubt on "the scrupulousness and good faith of the Soviet authorities."

On April 15, 1937, Edmund Wilson took Cowley to task: "I believe you are mistaken about the trials. [. . .] [Y]ou sound as if you had read nothing but the official report. You ought to read the Trotskyist and socialist stuff too[. . .]. In the case of these recent trials, I imagine that not a word of these confessions was true. The victims had, I suppose, been guilty of some kind of opposition to the regime; and the technique evidently is to tell them that they can only vindicate themselves by putting on acts which will be helpful to the U.S.S.R. [. . .] The procedure is totally undemocratic."[91]

[EW TLS-2] [NL TL/CC-2]
[TO: EDMUND WILSON]
[NR] May 14, 1937

Dear Edmund:

[. . .] I went so dead on the Moscow trials that I can't get around to answering your letter. One weakness of your point of view is that it doesn't visualize just what sort of "opposition to the regime" the defendants in these last trials have been guilty of. I think that their confessions can be explained only on the hypothesis that most of them were guilty almost exactly as charged. With that guilt as a start, they could be made to confess still other things if that seemed desirable. But I have noticed that Trotsky himself walks on eggs when it comes to discussing the guilt of the accused. To the best of my knowledge, he has never said that they were innocent. He leaves that to his followers.

As ever,
Malcolm

[EW TLS-2] [NL TL/CC-2]
[TO: EDMUND WILSON]
[NR] May 19, 1937

Dear Edmund:

[. . .] I'm against any more articles on Trotsky or the Moscow trials until new material turns up. One thing certain is that the investigation in Mexico City didn't turn up any new material. One of the difficulties is that Trotsky can't afford to be candid for fear of compromising his own aims and getting more of his Russian followers arrested. He did some lying to the investigators in Mexico City—about Borodin and about Romm—in specific matters about which a good many people knew he was lying. But the chief trouble with writing more on this subject is that we have printed so damned much about it and still have more to print. Everybody except the sectarians is getting sick and tired of reading about it. [. . .]

As ever,
Malcolm

In March 1937 John Dewey became chairman of the "Commission of Inquiry into the Charges Made against Leon Trotsky in the Moscow Trials" (known as the Dewey Commission), initiated by the American Committee for the Defense of Leon Trotsky. Among the members of the latter Committee were Edmund Wilson, John Dos Passos, and Sidney Hook. In its final report, issued in September 1937, the Dewey Commission cleared Trotsky of all charges brought against him by the Soviet authorities and offered conclusive evidence that the defendants' confessions had been false and the trials frame-ups. *The New Republic,* a firm supporter of the Popular Front, had decried the Dewey Commission investigations. Shortly after, Dewey criticized the magazine, in particular its literary section, for its anti-Trotskyite slant, and resigned as contributing editor from *The New Republic.*

[HOOK TLS-3]
[TO: JOHN DEWEY]
[NR] June 4, 1937

Dear Dr. Dewey:

Bruce [Bliven] showed me your last letter with its various criticisms of *The New Republic*. Some of them are of course justified—it would be nice to think that for the last few years we had been editing a magazine that was above criticism, but I'm afraid that we have no right to hold that idea. Still more of the criticisms fall outside my own field. But since some of them apply to the book department particularly, I thought that I might save Bruce the trouble of answering criticisms which he had no share in calling forth. So, with his consent, I will proceed—

I certainly don't think it is true that *New Republic* reviews, including those in the field of economics and politics, have ever been in the hands of a clique. I wish that you had gone ahead to quote names as you said you could do. Among the more frequent economic and political reviewers of the period from 1934 to 1936 were Jonathan Mitchell, Lindsay Rogers, Horace Taylor, Frederick Schuman, Robert Morss Lovett, Walton Hamilton, Joshua Kunitz, Thurman Arnold, Norbert Guterman. Any clique that included all these people would have to be a pretty broad one. There hasn't been any great change in reviewing policy during the last year. Already in 1934 I began to feel that the younger Marxists were carrying their formula a great deal too far. If you have read many of my own reviews during the last two years, you will notice that fewer of them have been devoted to political subjects. I was of course very glad when the Third International introduced its united front tactics. That was what we had been doing all along, and it was nice to think that the Comintern now agreed with us.

The treatment of the Moscow Trials in the correspondence section does not fall within my department, but I happen to know about it. After my own article on the trials, I was shown all the correspondence that came in. Roughly about 10 percent of the anti-Trotsky letters were published and about 30 percent of the pro-Trotsky letters. The percentages aren't accurate, but it is an undoubted fact that letters supporting Trotsky got more than an even break in the correspondence department. Since we had gone the other way in the editorial section, we leaned over backwards in the correspondence.

But a good deal of the dispute over *The New Republic*—and evidently a good deal of the gossip you have heard—goes back to an older incident. In the summer of 1932 there was organized a League of Professional Groups for Foster and Ford, of which I was a member. The League did some pretty effective work at the time of the election. It decided to continue its activities. But that winter a great fight developed in its ranks. About a dozen of its members suddenly became Trotskyites. The fight over Trotsky paralyzed the activities of the League. For that reason I opposed the Trotskyites; I said it was better to do our limited best in this country rather than to quarrel over the policy of the Comintern in China and Germany. The fight got pretty hot, the League accomplished nothing and finally perished of internal friction. But the Trotsky faction never forgave me for the part I had played in opposing them at that time. They have published some bitter attacks on me, including one by Felix Morrow that was really an encyclopedia of abuse.[92] The general thesis seemed to be that because I didn't like Trotsky (which is certainly true) I was also a slave of Stalin and the Comintern (which certainly has very little to do with what I have written).

I want to make this letter an entirely candid statement, because I have the feeling that without candor we are never going to come out of the differences of opinion that have been impeding action among radicals and progressives. I personally think that Trotsky's policies have had a terribly bad effect. I think that he is now so egocentric that he lets his followers die for him. I wouldn't ever say it in print, but my personal conviction is that he is touched with paranoia, with delusions of persecution and grandeur. As for the Soviet Union, I certainly would not defend, and have not defended, everything that has been done there. There is too much repression and too much mass worship of one leader. But I also feel that in general the Soviet Union has been moving in the right direction and that it has to be defended against the fascist nations.

On these subjects I know that we disagree. But I don't feel that estimates of one country or of one man should be allowed to divide people who agree on so many other subjects.

And I know that one of the differences mentioned in your letter has already settled itself these many years. Today it seems to me that people in a democratic country who advocate a violent revolution are talking through their hats. And it also seems to me that people who advocate non-resistance are talking through their hats. The process of social change in the democracies seems to be that—finally—the people get control of the government and pass laws benefiting themselves. Then the reactionaries rise against them by force and violence. The force has to be combated when it is exercised. Preparation for combating it has to be made in advance. But for the popular forces to talk of "seizing" the government under present circumstances, with the present alignment of forces, is simple madness. I am glad to report that not many of them are now talking in that fashion.

This is a long letter and it hasn't said half or a third of the things that I have been wanting to say. Perhaps it all comes down to two points—first, that I think American progressives of all shades of opinion should be working together (they will have to hang together or hang some other way) and, second, that I feel a deep respect for your own work and for its spirit of inquiry and fair-mindedness and should feel deeply hurt if it ceased to appear in *The New Republic*.

Sincerely,
Malcolm Cowley

[EW TLS-1]
[TO: EDMUND WILSON]
[NR] August 16, 1937

Dear Edmund:

[. . .] Just now I am trying hard to write a bunch of stuff on Spain. The political situation there is very interesting, but I think that I'll confine myself simply to the things that I saw and heard. And in any case it is disheartening to find that there are any politics at all in Spain. What they ought to be doing now is winning the war. But before they win the war they have to create an army out of nothing but men—and that's a job more difficult than anybody realizes.

As ever,
Malcolm

[EW TLS-2]
[TO: EDMUND WILSON]
[NR] *December 9, 1937*

Dear Edmund:

[. . .] The piece on Edith Wharton is fine—one of the best that you have done for us for a long time. [. . .]

I liked your piece on Flaubert in the *Partisan Review*. But I think you give a great deal too much credit to his social and political ideas. In *L'Éducation Sentimentale* they are clear and impressive, but by 1871 they seemed to be no more than Liberty League thinking. The point to me is that all the French writers were tremendously stirred up by the long period of preparation that preceded the revolution of 1848 and by the utter discouragement that followed. Many writers of that generation did their best work between 1848 and 1860. Once they had really sunk back into hopelessness about politics, they lost their drive. There seem to be a lot of parallels between the situation today and that in 1848, even though the political set-up is quite different.

[. . .]

About my mother's death and funeral[93] I find it hard to say anything at all—it was a great deal worse than I expected. If my grandmother had given her a decent break when she was a little girl in Quincy, Illinois, she would have been a remarkable woman. She was a remarkable woman anyhow, in spite of the fact that during her whole life she never read a book. My father is holding up much better than I expected. I tried to get him to come back to Connecticut with us, but he refused to leave his patients.

As ever,
Malcolm

The Fading of a Dream, 1938–1940

In the late 1930s, Cowley's radical engagement more and more resembled a cautious advance through a moral and political minefield. Increasingly, he saw his hopes for a united endeavor on the left thwarted by factional quarrels between Stalinists and Trotskyites, in which he himself fired (and received) hurtful shots. He continued to cling to a Stalinist line in public long after more perceptive fellow travelers had seen through its fallacies and trusted friends such as Basso, Tate, and Wilson had tried to bring him to his senses.

As his earlier political idealism diminished, Cowley retreated behind a façade of political sophistication and editorial bureaucracy, allowing himself to be used as a Communist front man while attempting to maintain "a shopkeeper's honesty" (*WT* 139) about his beliefs. He had inadvertently drifted into a position of duplicity, as he failed to publicize the doubts and reservations he had confided in his notebooks (and, less frequently, in letters to friends) since 1937. Edmund Wilson challenged him, in an angry letter of October 1938, to clarify the inconsistencies of his stance on the Moscow Trials and to stop "plugging the damned old Stalinist line."

How deeply hesitant Cowley was to surrender his illusions about Communism and the Soviet Union is evident in a letter of July 11, 1939, to Hamilton Basso, written barely six weeks before Hitler and Stalin entered their non-aggression pact. Here we see his defense of Communism and the Soviet Union becoming strained, and his doubts are subsumed in a near-perfunctory, vociferous justification of allegiance to the Party line. As he later acknowledged, cumulatively his "sins of silence, self-protectiveness, inadequacy, and something close to moral cowardice" left him with an enduring "sense of guilt" (*WT* 139).

Even as his radical dream was fading, he remained active in the League, seeking to temper the influence of Communist members, working for its Exiled Writers' Committee, and following the fate of writers who fled the European terror to take refuge in New York. As an antidote to the political turmoil there, he sought relief in Sherman country living and resumed writing poetry, composing notable poems like "The Last International" and "The Long Voyage" (the latter begun on his journey back from Spain). In October 1938 *Poetry* published a group of his poems under the title of his future book "The Dry Season" and in 1939 awarded him its Harriet Monroe Memorial Prize. In December 1939, two years after his mother's death, Cowley's father passed away, having spent the last months of his life in Sherman.

The Nazi-Soviet Pact of August 23, 1939, served to bring Cowley's political reservations into focus but did not immediately lead to a break with

Communism. Instead it initiated a period of dismay and self-questioning, a rethinking of his radical commitments and his stance on U.S. and Russian foreign policy. On November 4, 1939, writing at length to Van Wyck Brooks, he asserted the need for "a new personal philosophy" and painfully and cautiously moved toward a disaffiliation with Communism. His prevarications brought him into conflict, one last time, with Edmund Wilson, whose reproaches triggered a long anguished letter in early February 1940, in which Cowley honestly probes the failure of his radical dream.

Events in the spring of 1940, however, changed everything. The short-lived Battle of France came to its unhappy conclusion on June 22, 1940, when France and Germany entered an armistice that divided France into occupied and unoccupied zones. This was a deeply shocking event for a writer who had come to love French culture as his own. It was not the Nazi-Soviet Pact, then, but the capitulation of France—and the mysterious disappearance of friends such as Louis Aragon—that finally forced Cowley to surrender the last vestiges of his radical commitments and confirmed his persuasion of the need for interventionism. On July 29, 1940, following the example of his friends Hicks and Arvin, he took the public stand toward which his private reservations had been pushing him and submitted his letter of resignation as vice president of the League of American Writers. Printed in *The New Republic,* it marked his public break with Communism.

Now, in advance of his fellow editors at *The New Republic,* Cowley committed himself firmly to the war policy of the Roosevelt administration. As a consequence, he was denounced as a traitor by his former Communist allies: *The New Masses* labeled him (along with Frank, MacLeish, and Mumford) one of the "laureates of betrayal," while a William Gropper cartoon excoriated him as a capitalist lackey: it depicted Cowley with a cracked chamber pot on his head and a flask of whiskey in his pocket, giving the fascist salute to a war-hungry capitalist.[94] Before long, these attacks from the Communist left, coming in the wake of Trotskyite attacks and the reprimands of friends, were matched in their ugliness by vilifications from the right, leaving Cowley buffeted on all sides.

In May 1940 Wilson offered to step in as literary editor of *The New Republic* so Cowley could take needed time off to write a projected book on the 1930s. Cowley jumped at the offer. In late September 1940 he took a

three-month leave of absence from *The New Republic*. Though he had come
to feel stale and "institutionalized" in his role at the magazine, he could not
foresee that he would not return to his editorial duties. For now, he reported
with relief to Wilson on August 23, 1940: "Today I went to see [W. W.]
Walter Norton and we drew up a contract for the new book."

[EW TLS-I]

[TO: EDMUND WILSON]

[NR] *February 21, 1938*

Dear Edmund:

Would you like to review a book called *The Seven Soviet Arts* by Kurt
London? The author's general thesis is that art does not flourish when it has
to follow the party line. I understand that he has a lot of very interesting
information about the actual status of art and artists in Russia.

I like most of your political piece on Russia a lot. But I think you have
got into the habit of writing mystery novels yourself about that country.
History sometimes catches up with you—it's been taking to the mystery-
novel phase these last two or three years—but not always. The very best reports that we get here in the office about Russia come from an American
kid who's working in one of the big tractor factories; he makes three carbons of his stuff and mails them from different postoffice boxes. They aren't
very sensational when they get here, but they seem to be very candid. The last
one told a wonderful story about sabotage and inefficiency in a plan[t] where
he was working. But, like most other observers on the ground, he sees that
people in general are eating and dressing better than they did two years ago.

Malraux's new book on Spain[95] is wonderful—not as a novel, but as a
picture of the Spanish war and as a discussion of the way Communists
think. I can recognize a lot of the characters in it, including Malraux himself, who splits himself in two and appears as Major Garcia and Colonel
Magnin. One of the characters is an Italian aviator who seems to present
the point of view of Silone, and Garcia-Malraux makes a very effective answer to him.

Congratulations on your marriage.[96] I didn't know anything about it
until Betty told me last week, on the very day that the news appeared in the

World-Telegram. No, Muriel didn't suspect a thing when she met you at the station—she saw Mary later on the train but didn't connect the two events.

As ever,

Malcolm

[NL ALS-2] [SC 222–223]
[TO: KENNETH BURKE]
RFD Gaylordsville, Conn.,
October 7, 1938

Dear Kenneth:

[…]

I wonder what is going to be the, call it spiritual effect, of the big sell-out in Munich.[97] To me the world situation resembles more and more the civil wars in the classical world that lasted from 300 BC till the reign of Augustus, with an aristocratic and a popular party in every state and the aristocrats always ready to sell out to the Persians, the Macedonians or the Romans. Then the popular party too is driven to extremes, as under Marius in Rome and Stalin in Russia; and the philosophers retire to Tusculum, till they are interrupted there by soldiers and politely asked to cut their throats. I can't set it all down in an orderly manner. We were betrayed, we were sold behind our backs. I almost feel like going into the service of the Comintern, like the hero of Hemingway's play (not a very good play) on the theory that it's better to fight for something half right than to lie down and let the bastards walk over us. I wish I knew how to fly or to operate a machine gun.

[…]

As ever,

M.

What in God's name has happened to you? I was told some time ago that you were circulating a letter asking endorsements of the last batch of Moscow trials—though you had just published articles in which, so far as I could tell, you were trying to express a certain amount of skepticism. I don't suppose you're a member of the C.P.; and I can't imagine any other inducement short of bribery or blackmail [. . .] to justify and imitate their practices at this time. You're a great guy to talk about the value of a non-partisan literary review after the way you've been plugging the damned old Stalinist line, which gets more and more cockeyed by the minute [. . .]—at the expense of the interests of literature and to the detriment of critical standards in general! [. . .] I wish you would purge your head of politics—revolutionary and literary alike—and do the kind of valuable work of which you're capable. I think politics is bad for you because it's not real to you: because what you're really practicing is not politics but literature; and it only messes up a job like yours to pretend it's something else and try to use it like something else.

Edmund Wilson to Cowley, October 20, 1938[98]

[EW TLS-6] [PARTLY *PMC* 473–475]
[TO: EDMUND WILSON]
RFD Gaylordsville, Conn.,
October 31, 1938

Dear Edmund:

I hate letters and would much rather do my explaining or berating face to face—that's why I wrote a couple of months ago that I was anxious to talk things out with you. But once I set out to write a letter, it will have to be a long one, because there are other things to talk about besides my piece on the *Partisan Review*.[99]

But anyhow let's start with that. I'm sorry I made the crack about *The American Mercury*, because I was trying to write a piece that would persuade as well as condemn, and it was a mistake to include a remark that would give the Partisans an excuse to jump up and howl. Actually there was a lot of truth in it. Both magazines are embarked on an anti-Communist crusade that has become a fixation. And a lot of pieces printed in the *Partisan Review* have had that cold supercilious sneer one associates with *The American Mercury*. Read anything by Dwight Macdonald,[100] not only when he is attacking the Soviet culture, but even when he is doing a piece on *The New Yorker*. Dupee's piece on Malraux[101] was disgraceful, especially when you consider that Dupee at other times has shown literary feeling. Incidentally, when he wanted to quote a French critic for confirmation, he chose Drieu La Rochelle, one of the Fascist politicians.

Isn't it self-deception when the Partisans call themselves Marxists and revolutionists? I always thought that Marxism called for a union of theory and practice, and the only thing I see the Partisans practicing is the book reviewer's trade. And I have read their magazine pretty carefully without finding anything of a revolutionary nature, or even anything dealing with the American working class, except for a story by Dos Passos and an innocuous little sketch by Rose M. Stein. It is true that they call for a revolution against the Kremlin, but it is pretty safe making faces at Stalin at a distance of five thousand miles. All the same things about Stalin could be said at an American Legion convention or a Holy Name breakfast attended by the New York police force in full uniform. I haven't much faith in revolutionists who run no risks, who agree with *The New York Times* and Cardinal Pacelli.[102] That's the theory of bedfellows again. There's a lot in it when you come down to the realm of practical politics. One crowd of politicians says to another, "You want to overthrow—Napoleon, let's say—so as to restore the republic and we want to overthrow him so as to restore the monarchy, but we both want to overthrow him, don't we? Let's work together, up to a certain point." Very often they do.

Of course the truth is that many of the literary Trotskyites have utterly lost faith in the revolution—not only in Stalin but in Lenin, Engels, Marx, *The Communist Manifesto,* the whole business. They have been disillusioned by hard work or defeats or dirty politics, and God knows and we know that there is plenty of reason for disillusionment. But they have formed a picture of themselves as revolutionists, and the picture has been widely published, and now they don't like to spoil it. The psychological conflict is serious and sometimes tragic. But there is an easy solution for people who are not too self-critical. They can become such extreme and uncompromising revolutionaries that they don't have to work with other people, and in fact don't have to work at all, except for writing just enough to prove their moral superiority. There are a lot of people like that. I'd be willing to respect them if they got straight with themselves and admitted that they had turned conservative. A great deal can be said for conservatism, so long as it sails under its own colors.

What is my own position? Generally pro-Russian, pro-Communist, but with important reservations. I think that the Communists have done marvelous work for the American labor unions, but sometimes they spoil it by getting their unions mixed up in international politics. I think that Russia is still the great hope for socialism. If it is attacked by Germany and Japan, and beaten with financial help from England, there won't be any socialism in our time. But I don't like a lot of things that are happening in Russia, for example in the arts. The Moscow trials revealed a widespread hatred of Stalin, especially among the old Bolsheviks. I think that the plot against him grew out of the industrial mess in 1930 and the famine in 1932, when it seemed as if the whole system might go to smash. Bukharin's policy at that time might have been wiser than either Stalin's or Trotsky's. What Stalin did was largely determined by the fear of foreign attack; he thought that a huge war industry had to be built up at all costs. The foreign situation is something that you tend to forget when discussing Russian affairs. But nobody can say that life is perfect in a country that let two or three million of its own citizens starve to death.

I did sign (with others) a letter about the Moscow trials, because I believe that they were about three-quarters straight. I didn't agree with everything the letter said, but I was writing two articles about the trials in which I proposed to say exactly what I thought.[103] Have I been bribed by the CP? I had cocktails once at the Russian consulate. You ought to know better than to talk like that. And you ought to know better than to base any sort of opinions on a so-called interview with Stalin published in *Liberty* and written by a woman who never saw Stalin. The last interview he gave to a foreigner was to Lion Feuchtwanger in 1937.

I agree with you that I ought to get out of politics and back to literature. We ought to all do that—and it's a course I want to urge on you very seriously. I don't lay claim to much political talent. But yours—my God—is a minus quantity, for the simple reason that politics is based on the activities of groups, and you have always congenitally mistrusted and at times completely misunderstood group activities. And when political convictions lead you to accusing me of being bribed or blackmailed by the CP—well, it's time to stop and think whether the whole business shouldn't be chucked overboard.

Did you read the piece I wrote about *To Have and Have Not*[104] or did you read Margaret Marshall's attack on the piece in *The Nation?* I'm asking because I don't think you'd disagree with most of what I said. The piece began with a general tribute to Hemingway, written because I heard that he thought that I had always treated him unfairly, and because I wanted to set the record straight. For God's sake, if I had wanted to praise him for helping the revolution, I'd have done it when he wrote *Green Hills of Africa,* because I knew then that he was doing a lot for the revolutionists both in Spain and Cuba. But after this general tribute, I said that *To Have and Have Not* was the weakest of his books (except GHOA [*Green Hills of Africa*]). The one part of my piece with which you'd seriously disagree was the end, where I said that *To Have and Have Not* sounded, with all its faults, as if he were about to begin a new career. It's still too early to decide whether I was wrong. He may crack up after all—there are dangerous signs of self-loathing and self-pity in "The Snows of Kilimanjaro," written about the same time. And his new play is only fair.

I told you that this would be a long letter, once I got started. There are two other things on my mind, both concerning the NR. For God's sake come down to earth in your dealings with the editors—or with this editor, at any rate. Some of your letters to me about the NR have been so curt and peremptory that I felt like a medieval tradesman being approached by a noble lord. I'm thinking of a couple of years ago when I was still writing you about business transactions. The result was that I ducked out of the job of writing you about business transactions, just as Bruce had done before. A few weeks ago I was reading your general summary article on Marx, the long chapter in which you discuss the labor theory of value, and was thinking how good it was. That happened to be just the moment when you phoned to bawl me out about sending you proof of the piece on the Greek tragedies instead of sending you the typescript. I felt as if I had been slapped in the face.

And one other point, this time about your Marx series. I had the feeling that although the biographical chapters will be very effective in your book, they weren't much good in or for the magazine. You seemed to be trying a good stunt—to bring the discussion of Marx down to earth, to write about him without awe or fireworks, as if he were a great literary figure—but the result in the magazine sounded like a combination of Mehring and Rühle, with the good points of both but without much added to either. [...] Meanwhile your two long essays in *Partisan Review*—on Flaubert and James—would have been fine for the NR, because we are terribly in need of good literary material. I don't think that any arrangement with the paper will be satisfactory on both sides unless you can talk or write to us in advance and tell us what you are planning to do.

In the middle of this letter I heard a loud barking outside the window. Rowdy the spaniel had found a cock pheasant in the alfalfa field and pheasant had flown down into swamp. I grabbed the shotgun and went out. Pheasant had disappeared. I walked on into a weed field. There I stopped and began thinking about your letter and suddenly pheasant flew up under my feet and I was so abstracted that I didn't shoot. So I'll blame you now for making me miss a pheasant. . . . Let's *actually* forget this political stuff, Stalin hiding under your bed and Trotsky in my hair, and talk about books for a change. There are three young poets, no four, who I think are pretty good. One is Winfield Townley Scott, who works on the *Providence Journal*. One is Howard Nutt of Peoria, Illinois; we're printing some of his stuff. One is Nelson Algren of Chicago, author of a proletarian novel; he is now writing a series of free-verse rhapsodic poems on the destruction of Mayor Kelly's Chicago at twenty minutes to two in the morning. One is an ex-Objectivist named Kenneth Rexroth, of San Francisco; he does very nice pedestrian poems, like translations from the Chinese, on his girl and his boyhood. Be watching out for all of them. The last three are or were on WPA. Another WPAyer named Sterling Brown, a Negro, is also very good, though I think you've heard about him.

I find it harder and harder to read novels. And I still want a chance to talk things out with you.

As ever,
Malcolm

[HB TLS-2]
[TO: HAMILTON BASSO][105]
RFD Gaylordsville, Conn., January 6, 1939

Dear Ham:

[...]

My complaint about the letters printed in "Books That Changed Our Minds"[106] was that most of our correspondents were choosing what they thought were *good,* i.e., uplifting books. The truth is that our society has been breaking up about as fast as it has been drawing together, and the books with a destructive influence should also have been mentioned. *Mein Kampf* hasn't directly affected American intellectuals, but—well, yes, it *has* affected them, and it stands as a symbol for a whole type of *bad* pamphlets which didn't in themselves *produce* the disorganization of modern society but which at least expressed it.

Note that I didn't contribute a list of my own. It would sound funny— the minor Elizabethan drama, Shelley's *Defense of Poetry,* the Dada Manifestoes, "The Love Song of J. Alfred Prufrock," the teaching of William Ernest Hocking, Emile Durkheim's idea that God is the image of society, the *Spoon River Anthology* and God knows what hodge-podge of plays, poems, novels and, as you say, personal friendships (not to forget *Of Human Bondage,* which poisoned my youth, and *The Sacred Hill,* of liking which I am ashamed, and *The Communist Manifesto,* as well as the War, Louis Aragon, Paul Valéry's *Introduction to the Method of Leonardo da Vinci* and Burpee's seed catalogue). To explain all these currents is the task of a novelist or an autobiographer. For a series of articles in the NR you need a neat pattern— ergo, "Books That Changed Our Minds."

One point you made in your letter worries hell out of me. That point about intellectuals talking to other intellectuals and generally taking in their own washing. Tis true, tis true. I used to know all sorts of people, but since working for the NR—nine years now—I have had to consort with my own kind, most of whom aren't really my own kind, but who have to be seen, encouraged, listened to, got drunk with, praised up, argued down, all in order that they may contribute good articles to the mag that carries our names on the masthead. I don't any longer know farmers, lumbermen, trainmen, not to speak of business men or ward bosses. Well, baby, I wish I had your genius for getting acquainted with all sorts of people, and I wish I had a little more time. Maybe in a few years I'll have some roots down in this town of Sherman, which is an interesting place abounding in civic spirit and private jealousy. But I could never learn to be a New Englander.

[...]

As ever,
Malcolm

[HB TLS-6] [NL TL/CC-6]
[TO: HAMILTON BASSO]
RFD Gaylordsville, Conn.,
Tuesday, July 11. [1939]

Dear Ham:

I read *Days Before Lent* on Sunday night. I read every last word of it before going to bed. To anyone who knows my desultory habits of reading, that is high praise, biological praise. If you had been writing just an ordinary novel, you wouldn't have taken so much trouble to make it interesting. But this time, knowing that you had ideas you wanted to express, you went to special pains to build suspense. And you built it.

I'll bet you never thought of it as a movie before the movies bought it. Yet for Hollywood it has damned near Everything. I hope if they offer you a good salary this time to come out and supervise the script, you'll accept it and go out and fight to get ideas into it and keep them from filming just another *Grand Hotel*.[107]

The background is really fine—because you were conscious of it at every moment. You didn't have to shove it into the reader's face, but he keeps getting glimpses of it around the corners of your mind. You did a fine story of the bayou country—much better than Sinclair Lewis's story of the plague, in *Arrowsmith*. You make New Orleans real. [...]

[...]

So far I've been talking about your story, not your ideas. My reactions there are mixed, as you knew they would be, but generally favorable. Let's start by saying that this is the best & biggest of your novels—and gives that impression too, which is all to the good. You seem almost to be working in another dimension than you were working in before. Yet at the same time you give the feeling of warmth, of being and giving yourself, that I liked so much in *Cinnamon Seed*.[108] [. . .] Your proof that man has an instinct for liberty (and later your proof that man has an instinct for religion) seem to me to belong in the same class as the various proofs of the existence of God that were so popular in the seventeenth century. The important questions to me are liberty of whom to do what? and what kind of church to express the religious instinct? [. . .]

There is one of your ideas, expressed through Dr. Gomez, that I want to argue about, because a lot of other people share it with you and because it is doing a lot of damage.[109] You've guessed it—it's the idea that fascism and communism are two wolves from the same litter and are the great enemies of human liberty. Of course the fascists are unspeakable, you would say, but let's not forget the communists, who let several million peasants starve to death and believe that the end justifies the means. You don't take the next step, but many others do. It consists in breaking off relations with all communists, and anybody suspected of being friendly with communists, in order to strengthen one's own position (the usual result being to strengthen Tom Girdler's[110] position and Adolph Hitler's).

There is nothing in communist doctrine—pardon me, ideology—from Marx in 1848 to Stalin in 1939 which says that the end justifies the means. There is nothing about the subject at all. On ends and means, communists agree in general with other people—in the abstract—though they have different ends in view, which require different means to achieve them. That's the real quarrel. Everybody, even Aldous Huxley, really believes that means are justified by ends. What else could justify them? Why else would we consent to appendectomies or use contraceptives or smear ourselves with bacon fat to kill chiggers? We suffer evil, and sometimes make others suffer evil, that good may come of it. The question is how much good and how much evil.

Do communists tell more lies than other people? Most of them, in my experience, tell less. Some tell more, and I think they're very wrong. They are people I don't admire as people.

But what about the 1932 famine? That's a different question and I have worried a lot about it. Obviously five million people didn't die or the fact would have been revealed in population statistics.[111] Russia's population is and has been growing faster than ever before. But many hundreds of thousands did die and no effort was made to save them by importing food. (There wasn't food for them inside the country; there was just enough to keep the workers from starving too.) A huge mistake had been made in the collectivization program, and the Soviets nearly went smash, and they kept their troubles secret for more than a year, thinking that if they made them public the country might be attacked when it was unable to resist. Now they can excuse themselves by saying that the country is more powerful than ever before[112] and that agriculture has been reorganized in such a way that there need be no famine ever. But that end—even that end—does not justify the human suffering that was necessary to achieve it. The Party made the worst blunder in its history and one of the worst in modern history. Still, to me it does not prove that communism is wrong or is the same as fascism.

There are three points I want to make about communism in 1939. The first is that it has come to embody the idea of progress—of progress by man's conscious efforts—that was first developed in the eighteenth century. It is the direct heir of the Enlightenment, of the faith in science, organization, justice, equality, intelligence, at a time when that faith elsewhere is growing weak.[113] (And notice that the faith itself is what the fascists are attacking.) The communists are really the intellectuals, and the Communist Party is the party of the intellectuals, for all its pretensions to being the party of the working class. Its weaknesses—for example its want of human consideration—are the weaknesses of the intellectuals. They aren't part of communist doctrine and a great deal might be done to remedy them.

A distinction must be made between communist theories as derived from Marx and communism in practice. I'm talking about communism in practice. It is government by committees—you have to understand that if you want to understand Russia—and it is government by a party. And the party is the second of the points I wanted to make. I am convinced of the need for a party if anything is to be achieved.[114] Comradeship within a party—decisions arrived at democratically but then obeyed—a strengthening of one's individual purpose by the feeling that it is shared—all this is the necessary social instrument in these times of crisis. I almost convince myself that I ought to join the Party, but it isn't my nature to do that; I'd have to sacrifice my freedom to criticize, which as a writer I want to retain. What I wanted to point out was that the communists of 1939 are the Freemasons of 1776—the Freemasons of 1939 having forsaken their own revolutionary traditions.

And a third point. There really is a process of polarity in the world today. People are attracted toward the extreme positions—those in between seem unstable, impermanent, a poor basis for acting or writing. People who turn violently away from communism move either toward fascism or toward Catholicism (while the Church, under the present Pope, is trying to make its peace with fascism on condition that it abandon its racial heresy). I'm sort of worried about you, Ham, because some things in the last book sound as if you were ripe for reconversion—now that Broun[115] is a Catholic God knows who'll go next, and I'd be worried about your soul if Mgr. Sheen, the demon converter, ever got hold of you. As a religion, Catholicism is wonderful, because after all it is Christian, but as a church under the present hierarchy it's out to smash not only atheistic communism but also American democracy (which, under the name of liberalism, has been condemned since 1870). If I have to kiss somebody's toe, I'd rather kiss Stalin's than Pacelli's.[116]

Humanism is my religion—not Babbitt's kind, but the simple belief in living people.

[...]

As for your book, it's damned fine and if it gets a fair break it may be very successful—I've got my fingers crossed.

As ever,
Malcolm

On August 23, 1939 Hitler and Stalin signed their non-aggression pact. On 1 September 1939, Nazi Germany invaded Poland, and a second world war seemed inevitable. Like many, Cowley found himself uneasily jockeying for position. After the Soviet Union invaded Poland on September 17, he found it increasingly difficult to defend the Soviet line yet shrank from an outright rejection and groped for a new radical stance and philosophy, independent of Soviet guidance, still hoping to maintain unity on the left.

What I think of the new Russian foreign policy is not very complimentary. I guess it's time for me to make another public statement.

Cowley to Edmund Wilson, September 8, 1939 [EW]

[ARVIN TLS-1]
[TO: NEWTON ARVIN]
[NR] September 22, 1939

Dear Newton:

[. . .] As time goes on, two things stand out more and more clearly. The first is that from the point of view of national Russian policy, and power politics in general, Stalin's course has been admirably calculated. The howls over the Russian invasion of Poland seem to me as silly as anything could be, considering that the Russian troops were marching into what had always been Russian territory and were keeping the Germans from seizing it. But the other thing that stands out is that Stalin is throwing the Comintern overboard—it will have to go underground very soon in Britain and France—and that the American Party discredited itself even without Stalin's assistance. We have now got to salvage anything that is salvageable, and in addition develop a new philosophy for ourselves without the disadvantage of Russo-Marxism.

As ever,
Malcolm

[KB TLS-2] [SC 224–225]
[TO: KENNETH BURKE]
Gaylordsville, October 14. [1939]

Dear Kenneth:

[. . .] The effect on me of the Russo-German pact was not to make me think any the less of Stalin—nothing succeeds like success—but to make me feel that I and all the other western liberals had been thrown overboard; in other words it was a phenomenon of alienation, of feeling that Russia is pretty damned good but isn't our country. For that matter, Russian communism has gone pretty far beyond Marx and I never liked a lot of the developments, especially those in the field of art, which ought to be an index to a lot of other fields.

The League of American Writers, prompted by me, is about to issue a statement to its members stating that it won't make a statement on the Russo-German Pact but feels that we had better get busy at home. The idea is to hold the League together and offer a common basis for its liberal and communist members.

[...]

As ever,
Malcolm.

———

[VWB TLS-3] [NL TLS-3]
[TO: VAN WYCK BROOKS]
RFD Gaylordsville, Conn.,
November 4, 1939

Dear Brooks:

I'm forwarding your letter to Folsom and letting him decide what to do next.[117] My own feeling is that on this particular matter there isn't anything to do next. That is, there are a lot of practical things for the League to do, about which everybody will agree—in particular we have got to get busy on civil liberties, now in a desperate situation, and on helping some of our friends abroad, especially in France, where the situation seems to be worse than anybody imagines. My best friend there, Louis Aragon, has simply disappeared—not even his wife knows his whereabouts, except that she gathers he was arrested while in uniform and carted off to prison. Jean Giono[118] has been in jail for two months now, and God knows how many others. The forty-hour week has given way to the seventy-two hour week, at about the same wages. England is still a free country, relatively—but as far as I can gather the English war aims as conceived by Chamberlain *et al* are simply to replace Hitler by Goering or the Kaiser. You read about what happened to the antifascist German refugees in France. And this country is going to adopt some of the same tactics unless the progressives get busy and get united....
Meanwhile, in the midst of other activities, we all have to work to get our

own minds straightened out. We have a labor of self-clarification that is going to take a long time.

And since each of us has to begin with himself, I'm going to try to set down some of my own ideas about Russia, communism and the USA instead of answering your letter. [. . .] [T]he immense moral prestige that communism—and through communism, Russia—has enjoyed in the western countries [. . .] resulted partly from the fact that gradually communism began to embody in itself all the hopes of *progress through intelligence* that survived in the West. Middle positions were becoming increasingly difficult to hold. One was either sympathetic to communism or sympathetic to the Catholic Church (which in turn was conducting what seemed to be merely a lover's quarrel with German fascism, and no quarrel at all with Italian fascism). If one did not believe in a revealed and immutable system of ethics, if one thought that the aims of life were fixed by life itself and not by divine intervention, then one was almost inevitably involved in the communist effort to remake the world. But meanwhile the one communist state was evolving in a different direction, and sooner or later the contradiction between the communist state in Russia and the hope of a new order in the rest of the world became too obvious for anyone but a blind party member to conceal from his own eyes.

Let me go on thinking to myself and plaguing you with my thoughts. . . . Hundreds of people have said that Russian communism has become more Russian than communistic, and obviously there is some truth in that remark. But is there anything in Marx's own ideas that would explain what we don't like about the Russian system? I think there are at least two features. One is Marx's dogmatism and inveterate quarrelsomeness, partly growing out of his sufferings after 1848. The worst qualities of his character became stamped upon his followers and have persisted until today. But the other feature is much more important. The force of Marxism was largely in its moral prestige, yet Marx paid no attention to ethical problems. Marx said that religion was the opium of the people, yet Marxism became a church, essentially, in competition with other great churches—it had its pope, its hierarchy of saints, its mythology, its rites, its great religious order. Quite obviously any faith that moves men strongly is going to develop into a church. Yet growths of this kind, if not controlled, if allowed to be spontaneous, are going to embody the weaker sides of human nature. And that is what has happened with communism as a *church*—it has proved in many respects to be a bad church, with bad rituals and with ethical standards that encourage certain vices, notably pride and self-righteousness and in some cases deceit. (Incidentally, deceit is the usual charge made against communists, and is in large part unjustified. There is, on the other hand, a dangerous opposition between Russia's declared aims and her actual aims, and between the ideas of the inner circle and those passed on to outsiders or the public at large.)

But this general matter of religion is one of the most dangerous of topics, because as soon as people begin talking about religion they get fuzzyminded. Another way to approach it would be to say that some of the most significant researches since Marx's death have been in the two fields of psychology and anthropology. Both of these would lead to a somewhat more complicated picture of the human animal than the Marxists present. For example, anthropology would seem to indicate that people need not only bread and love—the two staples—but also a reason for living and rituals to dignify their most significant actions. This reason and these rituals Marxism has failed to furnish. Moreover, after saying that it is weak in psychology and anthropology, we have to go beyond that and admit that most of the advances in thought during the last fifty years have been made by non-Marxists—partly because they were in the vast majority but also because Marxism has fallen into dogmatic patterns that Marx himself would have been the last to admire.

What then, should we reject Marxism? I think on the contrary that we might go back to the spirit of Marx himself, which apart from the faults of character I mentioned was one of the grandest that ever existed, but amplify and correct it with all the other knowledge that has been gained since his death. In other words, there is a vast labor of rethinking in front of us, and a labor that has been neglected completely. We have been great collectors of facts in this age, but we have shrunk from fitting the facts together.

And what about the communists here, should we cast them out of any organization? We ought to hesitate a long time before doing anything of the sort. Remember that the famous United Front, now broken, was not the sole work of the communists. In part, in large part, it grew out of an uneasy feeling among non-communists that it was necessary to reestablish unity among the progressive forces in western culture. I have not in the least abandoned that feeling, especially now when an attack on the communists is being used as an excuse to weaken all progressive movements. I'll be damned if I'll cooperate with the Dies Committee.[119] Furthermore, knowing a good many communists, I know that they are honest and hard-working, for the most part—resistant to abuse but not resistant to reason. I don't want to see them cut off from the society of their colleagues—their colleagues would lose too much.

One more subject you raised is that of the League's being "in the American grain." That suggests two thoughts to me. One is that quite deliberately I have never worried over Americanism, not my own at least. Born in Blacklick Township, educated in the Pittsburgh public schools, resident in Sherman, Connecticut, fond of hunting, fishing, gardening and cracker-box philosophy, I feel that if you scratch me anywhere, you'll find an American. I'd have to work very hard to be English, French, Spanish or Russian, but I can be American just by following my own drift. And it's that way with almost all of us. But not quite all. There is one non-American culture that is also established here permanently—the Jewish culture. It will always seem alien to me, and yet we should be much poorer without it. Now the trouble with too much talk about Americanism is that it is likely to get confused with the latent anti-semitism that exists in all of us. But don't for God's sake think that I'm saying this as a warning to you, knowing how scrupulous you are about such matters. It's just the danger that all of us have to face.

[...]

Excuse me for afflicting you with all these random reflections, some of them badly expressed and none of them carried so deep as I should like to carry them. What I'm actually worried about now is finding a new basis for my thinking, a new personal philosophy. The lines along which I'm working are those I suggested above—namely the search for a conception of the human species somewhat more complicated than that which one finds in practical and applied Marxism, with more stress laid on anthropology and psychology—especially the first—than on pure economics. Max Lerner[120] seems to have somewhat the same preoccupations. Meanwhile I'm going to stick to the League and support it in its practical efforts, which in these days will be very valuable.

As ever,
Malcolm

I was very, very grateful for what you said about *Exile's Return*.[121]

———————

[ARVIN TLS-1]
[TO: NEWTON ARVIN]
RFD Gaylordsville, Conn.,
December 11, 1939

Dear Newton:

I haven't written you for a long time, but that doesn't mean you have been absent from my mind. Here in the country, with a free hour, I thought I'd tell you more about the League. I went to a council meeting last week, and came away very disheartened. The argument was over the statement of policy, which I helped to write and endorsed fully at the time it was written. I said that the invasion of Finland had changed the situation, that considering that we had always condemned aggression and the bombing of open cities, we should now condemn the USSR. And furthermore, I said, even if this was not a moral duty it was a practical necessity if we hoped to hold the League together. We had to show that we were not dominated by our Communist members. There were three or four of them at the council meeting and they disagreed with me. Joe North[122] asked me definitely what I proposed. I answered that the League should issue a statement condemning the Finnish invasion, that the Communist members should vote against it (but would be outvoted by the League membership as a whole) and that they should stay in the League. But the Communist members said they would resign if any such statement was adopted. It was not adopted. I think the League is going to melt away, partly by resignations, partly by non-activity on the part of its members, and I think the Communists are to blame for killing it, once the issue has been so baldly stated. I am tempted to resign myself[123]—though not to publish a letter of resignation, considering the Dies Committee. But I am not going to do anything in a hurry. [. . .]

As ever,
Malcolm

[JB TLS-I]
[TO: JOHN BERRYMAN]
[NR] January 10, 1940

Dear Berryman:

I like the poem you call "Winter Landscape." But doesn't it deal with a famous picture of Breughel's? And, in that case, wouldn't it be better to call it "Landscape by Breughel" in order to give the reader a key to it? When I first read the poem I thought your remark that the three men were not aware that "they will be seen upon the brow of that same hill when all their company will have been irrecoverably lost" was a boast of the poet's, saying that his words would last through the evil waste of history, and not a comment on the picture. Anyhow, I'd like to know what you think about the title.[124]

Cordially[,]
Malcolm Cowley

[RW TLS-I]
[TO: RICHARD WRIGHT]
[NR] February 2, 1940

Dear Dick:

Erskine Caldwell's new novel [*Trouble in July*] is about a lynching in Georgia. Could you review it for us in not more than 600 words? [. . .]

Incidentally, we haven't yet received a review copy of your own book [*Native Son*].[125]

As ever,
Malcolm Cowley

I get more and more puzzled and disturbed by your political position as time goes on. The literary editor of the N.R. ought to be in a situation to be independent of entanglements with movements, parties and groups if anybody is in New York, but you seem to have given hostages to the Stalinists in some terrible incomprehensible way. Just at the time when it seems to me that the normal thing would be frankly to discard your illusions, you have been carrying on in a way that matches *The New Masses* at its worst. [. . .] You write better than the people on the regular Stalinist press, but what you are writing is simply Stalinist character assassination of the most reckless and libelous sort.

Edmund Wilson to Cowley, January 26, 1940[126]

[EW TLS-8]
[TO: EDMUND WILSON]
RFD Gaylordsville, Conn.,
February 2, 1940

Dear Edmund:

I'm back at home after three days in the office and have time to write you a pretty long letter, which at this time it seems important to do. Let's start with Robles and Krivitsky, the two instances where you accused me of "Stalinist character assassination of the most reckless and libelous sort." Those are pretty big words and I wish you would stop and think about them. In these days character assassination is not a peculiarly Stalinist phenomenon. You can find it in its full flower and rankest perfume in *The New Leader,* organ of the Social Democratic Federation, and again in *The Saturday Evening Post* or *Liberty* or *Collier's* when Stolberg[127] or Eugene Lyons[128] or any of the boys does a job on the American reds. It's a bad thing, even worse than you say it is, and I'm willing to speak out against it when anybody does it for any side, and apologize for it deeply if I think I have been guilty of it.

Do you really think I was in the Robles[129] case? I wish you would read the review over again and see what I actually said. I haven't a copy of it here, but I remember that I didn't even mention his name—the sentence bearing on him was something like this: "People who ought to know tell me that his guilt was fully established." The information actually came from Alvarez del Vayo,[130] through a couple of people who had talked to him. They may, of course, have been lying or trying to cover something up. But I mentioned Robles—without using his name—because the death of this man I had never met, and knew nothing of, beyond the fact that he was Dos Passos's translator, had deeply affected Dos Passos and had changed the nature of the book I was reviewing—of that I don't think there can be any doubt.

After Dos wrote his letter, we tried to gather information on the Robles case. What we wanted was a statement from Negrín[131] or Del Vayo, and we approached both of them without success. [. . .] The upshot was that in spite of writing a bunch of letters, we got no more information to print. I should think that printing Dos Passos's communication would absolve the magazine from the charge of trying to smear Robles.

If there's anything more I can do in this case—except say that *Adventures of a Young Man* is a good novel—I'll be glad to do it.

Krivitsky is a shady character on the basis of his own book.[132] Leaving to one side his exploits in the Russian secret service, about which it would seem that he told some lies, he acted the role of what the underworld calls a rat. [. . .] Read the last two chapters for the pay-off, where he begins giving names, addresses and aliases. My hunch is that a good many people are now in the prisons of the Gestapo, the Ogpu and the Deuxième Bureau as the result of information furnished by Krivitsky. That is why we couldn't get a review of his book signed by anyone who knew the facts. The obvious people to turn to were European ex-Communists, and I approached several of them, but they would not speak out for fear of being deported. The result was that I had to take the rap and rewrite two long memoranda furnished by these people into a review signed by myself. I had to swear up and down to keep their names secret, and after reading about the Dozenberg[133] case, I think their fears were justified.

But there's more to all this than Robles and Krivitsky (who shouldn't be mentioned in the same sentence, Krivitsky being the sort of bastard he is). There's this idea mentioned or shadowed forth in your letter for publication that mysterious forces, probably centered in the literary department, are at work to make *The New Republic* a Stalinist magazine. You've been listening to gossip that probably comes from the same sources as those extraordinary articles in *The New Leader*. About the sweetest-tempered thing I can say about it is that it's a lot of God damned poppycock and horse feathers.

Talk about character assassination. Beginning with a ten-column piece by Felix Morrow published around 1936 in the *New International*,[134] my character has been assassinated almost every week; it's a wonder there's anything left of it. Pretty nearly every imaginable type of lie has been told about me (and one type of lie has begun to get under my skin; but I'll talk about that later). And I wonder why so much attention is being paid, in the midst of class struggles, civil wars, imperialist wars and wars of annihilation, to a figure of minor importance not even involved in most of the world struggles.

There may be an explanation in terms of personalities. Back in 1932, when Hook, Morrow, Rorty *et al* were going Trotskyist—long before Hook had heard about democracy—there was a terrific row in an organization to which we both belonged, the League of Professional Groups for Foster and Ford. One week the League was doing a lot of interesting work; the next week and the week that followed it did nothing but argue about the Chinese revolution of 1927. I got sore because it seemed to me that one faction was deliberately hindering the League from getting anything done. I made a hot speech that must have been instrumental in getting them to resign from the League. I don't think they have ever forgiven me, Hook in particular, and I have written some things that kept the fight alive—some things that were partly answers to attacks, though I try not to answer attacks directly.

These personal quarrels have come to play a major part in one sector of left-wing politics. It is curious that many people trained by Marx to interpret history in terms of class conflicts and mass movements nevertheless interpret current politics in terms of personal devils. Old Karl himself yielded to that weakness sometimes. Trotsky, who wrote superbly about the 1917 revolution, called on a different type of explanation when describing his conflict with Stalin, implying that it was a continuation of his troubles at the Gymnasium, where the stupid but sly boys banded together against the bright boy. And when you take a very long downward step from Trotsky to *The New Leader,* you find that its contributors minify almost all political issues into conflicts of personalities, with bright boys bedevilled by stupid but somehow terribly sly and potent Stalinists—stage devils pulling wires behind the scenes. But that isn't to say that their attacks on the so-called Stalinists (a word which they use in the same fashion as Hitler uses the word "Jews") have no political purpose. I suppose they calculate that they can weaken the opposition by discrediting those whom they regard as its leaders.

And there's where I come in. They figure, probably, that if they could force me off the *New Republic* staff, the paper would go over to their side. If you ever talk to them, I wish that you would disabuse them of that idea. Ever since moving to the country three years ago, I have played a comparatively small part in shaping the political policies of the NR (not that my part was ever great). I'm in town only three days a week, working like hell on detail jobs largely connected with the style in which the paper is written. I rarely attend the Friday conferences where editorials are planned for the next issue. I don't choose the correspondence. I write something less than 2,000 words of editorial copy during the course of a whole year. I edit most of the copy written by others, but for style and effectiveness, not for sense— sometimes my own opinions are miles away from those expressed in the paper. Dig me down to bed rock and you'd find there was just one thing I was really fanatical about—clear writing of the English language, that and saying exactly what I think when writing over my own signature. And the type of lie that gets under my skin is the lie that I twist my literary opinions to achieve political ends.

As for the editorial policy of the paper, it is no great mystery. The NR was generally pro-Russian until August 23 of last year—partly because so many hopes were centered on a country laboring under such difficulties that it seemed only fair to give it the benefit of the doubt; partly because fascism seemed the immediate danger and the Russians were anti-fascist; partly because the paper believed in an alliance of liberals, socialists and communists to support progressive measures, and that was the line the Russians were taking. It is anti-Russian now, and sometimes much too pro-English, because the Russians have broken the people's front—not to speak of starting the war by their pact with Hitler and giving evidence of hypocrisy in their former statements by invading Finland. A few weeks ago there was an editorial, "Russia and America," that stated the case very well. It isn't on account of Russia that the paper has failed to accept Lyons, Stolberg, Hook *et al* at their own estimate. The difference with them is over domestic politics and the CIO. Note that the *New Republic* staff belongs to the United Office and Professional Workers of America—UOPWA—one of the unions that Stolberg has accused of being dominated and mismanaged by Communists. That doesn't make him popular with the assistant editors in particular, who are hard-working union members. And note also that all these people have been denouncing the paper in terms that make the NR editorials about them seem very mild indeed. I didn't write a damned one of those editorials. In fact, if you subtracted me from the paper its policies would probably be changed very little. You ought to tell those boys when you see them that by centering their fire on me they are wasting most of their ammunition.

As for my own attitude toward Russia, communism and all the etceteras, it is a little hard to define as of February 4, 1940.[135] We have a little time now for thinking, and I don't want to rush into any position that I will have to desert in a few months. I am profoundly disturbed by what has happened in the Soviet Union—as who isn't? I think that the Communists here are tied to the apron strings of Russian foreign policy. They have ceased to play the vitalizing part in the American labor movement that they played in 1937 and they are at this moment willing to destroy the united-front organizations they founded rather than lose control of them. You think that I should now frankly discard my illusions—but granting for the sake of argument that they are illusions, what is the good of discarding them if I have to adopt another set of illusions to the effect that Krivitsky, for example, is really a sterling character and Ben Stolberg a pure-hearted defender of labor unionism? And must I believe that Communists I saw working hard and sacrificing themselves are really without a single exception unprincipled careerists?

What I think as of February 4 is that the situation makes necessary a much more fundamental change in attitude than simply deciding that what used to be white is now black and vice versa. *Why* did the Russian revolution get into its present situation? Is it Stalinism or Leninism or Marxism that is essentially at fault? What is the essential element that was left out of all these directions for making a better society? Was it democracy that was omitted? This seems to me a rather simple-minded answer—since it involves the further question why democracy had to be omitted—and I am inclined to look for another. The Marxist theories are based on history and economics, among the social studies. Would anthropology give us a clue to their misreading of the human animal? What are the faults of communism as a religion? That it has become a religion in fact, there isn't much doubt, considering that all these heresies and inquisitions and excommunications remind one of nothing so much as the history of the Christian church during the first three centuries.

I am left standing pretty much alone, in the air, unsupported, a situation that is much more uncomfortable for me than it would be for you, since my normal instinct is toward cooperation. For the moment I want to get out of every God damned thing. These quarrels leave me with a sense of having touched something unclean. They remind me of a night a dozen years ago when I went on a bat with a lot of noisy and lecherous people I thoroughly despised, while realizing that I was one of them. We stayed a long time in a Harlem speakeasy, down in the cellar. When I came up the stairs at last, I saw the Negro doorman standing in the light of morning with his hands the color of cold ashes, and that is how I felt I was inside. Sometimes I feel a little like that today. Getting involved in these feuds and vendettas of the intelligentsia is like being an unwilling participant in a Harlem orgy.

It makes me wonder what the world would be like if it were ruled by the intellectuals. Some of them we know are admirable people, humble and conscientious, but intellectuals in the mass are not like that. A world run by them would be a very unpleasant place, considering all the naked egos that would be continually wounding and getting wounded, all the gossip, the spies at cocktail parties, the informers, the careerists, the turncoats. Remember too that the character assassinations now so much in vogue (and even you are succumbing to the fashion, with your open letters to the NR) are nothing less than symbolic murders. They would be real if the intellectuals controlled the state apparatus. Maybe that is part of the trouble in Russia.

(Note that nothing I said about the intellectuals is to be construed as an attack on the *intelligence*, which remains our best and almost our only tool for making this country a better place to live in. I am thinking about the customs and folkways of the intellectuals as a class—which compare pretty unfavorably with the folkways of coal miners and dairy farmers.)

Meanwhile I can't forget that all this business started with high purposes and dreams of a better society. Not many people, intellectuals or workers, go into the radical movement to make a career for themselves—some do, I suppose, but they are damned fools because there are much brighter and easier careers to be found elsewhere. No, the best of the radicals start out with a willingness to sacrifice themselves—and even when they betray their ideals I tend to forgive them in their bastardy. Once I wrote in a poem addressed to the people of tomorrow:

> Think back on us, the martyrs and the traitors,
> The cowards, swept by the same flood
> Of passion toward the morning that is yours:
> O children born from, nourished with our blood.

Well, we're all in a pretty pickle now, and I wonder how it happened. As a sequel to your present book describing the evolution of an idea to the moment of Lenin's arrival in the Finland Station, you ought to write another describing the devolution of an idea from Marx to *The New Leader* and from Lenin to the latest editorial in *Pravda* on exterminating the Finnish bandits.

I've gone on for longer than I intended when starting this letter; I've said more than I meant to, but also have left out a lot of things I wanted to say. That's all over now; there's just one point I have to make. It is that all this isn't written merely as a plea for you to understand my point of view. Understanding is all very well, but the situation is bad enough so that something more is needed. You ought to try to exert your very great influence toward ending these senseless and suicidal bickerings—I mean on all sides. No, I don't want everybody to kiss and be happy. There are going to be plenty of fights around us, and given the different intellectual directions that you and I have taken there are going to be plenty of matters on which we will oppose each other. But for God's sake let's keep these oppositions on a somewhat higher level, not finding foul motives or mysterious and incomprehensible forces at work, but arguing questions more impersonally and taking each other's good motives for granted. And let's try to see that others do the same thing.

As ever,
Malcolm

[CR TLS-1]
[TO: JOHN CROWE RANSOM, *THE KENYON REVIEW*]
[NR] *March 5, 1940*

Dear Ransom:

I have just read a rather brilliant essay—in French—by an art critic now in this country. His name is George Duthuit; he is Matisse's son-in-law and the author of several books on painting and esthetics. The essay, about nine thousand words long, is called "Towards a Sacred Art." It is an attempt to explain what the artists are thinking and trying to do in relation to the European crisis (which is most certainly an intellectual as well as a political crisis). He deals with the older abstract painters in their relation to society, then with the Thomists and the Surrealists, and finally describes a new tendency among the younger artists, one that appears to be a religious art without being Christian.

Though I don't follow Duthuit to his conclusions, I found the essay quite valuable in defining recent tendencies, deeply felt and eloquently written. It is unfortunately much too long for a weekly. [. . .]

Speaking of these matters reminded me that New York (with Buenos Aires) is almost the last refuge of the international culture that used to flourish in Paris, Munich, Vienna, Berlin, Madrid, Petersburg, even Bucharest. Strange that your magazine and *The Southern Review,* both founded by Tennesseeans, should give a refuge to ideas that aren't being expressed any longer in Europe, since the whole continent is absorbed in war. Well, in these times we have a duty to perform.

Cordially[,]
Malcolm Cowley

[EW ALS-2]
[TO: EDMUND WILSON]
*RFD Gaylordsville, Conn.,
May 1, 1940*

Dear Edmund:

[...]

I have just been reading Eliot's *Idea of a Christian Society* and found to my amazement that I liked it—for being humble (humility is a Christian virtue that most authors lack) and charitable and (once you have granted his crazy premise that a Christian society is possible) full of worldly wisdom. He has a wonderful passage on the Buchmanites & a most moving paragraph on himself that stands out from his impersonal narrative like the only tree on a prairie.

As ever,
Malcolm

[EW TLS-2]
[TO: EDMUND WILSON]
[NR] June 14, 1940

Dear Edmund:

[...] The MacLeish piece[136] is the answer that was waiting to be written. Muriel will be delighted to see it, because she has been frothing since she first read the MacLeish. [...] Hemingway, Dos Passos *et al.* were not to blame—nobody who writes literature, or writes honestly which is the same thing, was to blame. But there was certainly a destruction of faith in the word during the 1920s and 1930s. Most of the blame goes to the governments that lied and to the official spokesmen who repeated the lies. But especially during the period when disillusionment became profitable a lot of blame attaches to the second-line journalists who made capital out of disillusionment and attacked not lies but words and literature. Instead of writing against Hemingway and Dos Passos MacLeish should have attacked Stuart Chase[137] and his watered-down version of semantics. He should have attacked the Institute for Propaganda Analysis, C. Hartley Grattan,[138] and a host of people who have played a big part in American journalism. Then he would have had a real case.

[...] I should be grateful if you could tone down a couple of the passages where you attack MacLeish personally. I have been personally attacked so often that personal attacks on other people make me uncomfortable. Besides, your poem against MacLeish in *The New Yorker*[139] will be cited by a lot of people who will try to turn this into a personal quarrel instead of an attack on some dangerous ideas. I have always felt that MacLeish was all right emotionally but a very sloppy thinker, with the result that he lets his emotions carry him into a succession of weak positions. But I'm just putting this up to you as a plea.

I can foresee the day when *The New Republic,* through giving free speech to everybody will have offended absolutely everybody and will have to shut down for want of contributors.

As ever,

Malcolm

At the end of July 1940, following the earlier examples by Van Wyck Brooks and Newton Arvin, Cowley resigned from the League of American Writers.

[LAW TLS-3] [NL TL/CC-3]
[TO: FRANKLIN FOLSOM, EXECUTIVE SECRETARY,
LEAGUE OF AMERICAN WRITERS]
RFD Gaylordsville, Conn.,
July 29, 1940

Dear Franklin:

During the past few months the League of American Writers has issued two statements of policy, or rather of international politics, and each of them has led to the resignation of several active members. I have disagreed rather violently with both statements, as you know, and have been deeply disturbed by the resignations. The latest group of six or seven might be regarded simply as a defeated and disgruntled minority. But taken together with other members of the executive board who have resigned since last September—including the honorary president and three vice-presidents— they are close to being an actual majority. About the situation in the membership at large I am less accurately informed, but there is evidence that the League has lost the adherence of many distinguished writers. Everybody knows that for the past few months it has been unable to print names on its letterhead, because its officers were changing so rapidly.

Whatever else might be said about the policy of the League, one thing is certain. No policy should have been adopted that would lead so many active members to resign. They clearly belonged in the League, considering how many points they had in common with the members who remained, and how much they might have offered in carrying out the League's proper aims, such as finding refuge for authors exiled from fascist countries and defending democracy and good writing at home. The fight for both these aims was weakened when the League insisted on taking a controversial stand about the war in Europe.

But there is a great deal more to be said about the specific issue involved in the recent resignations. That issue has been misunderstood and sometimes misstated by many, simply because it cuts so deep. It is not a mere question of personalities; on that score there have been quarrels late at night, when everyone was tired, but no real complaints; we can take for granted the good intentions of everyone involved. It is not a question of what exiled writers should be helped and how. It is partly but not fundamentally a question of party domination; all the resigning members had proved their willingness to cooperate with any political group, as long as it was clearly working toward the same immediate aims; and as for Red-baiting, no—they all resigned privately, without sending angry letters to *The New York Times*. Nor is it even a question of whether this country should keep out of the European war; in the League nobody has been calling for an American Expeditionary Force. The real question is what the war means in the light of yesterday and tomorrow, and what steps this country should take to defend itself.

One theory is that the war in Europe is merely a struggle for plunder, another conflict "between rival imperialisms." According to this theory, Chamberlain and Daladier were as bad as Hitler; Churchill is almost as bad, and we should therefore stay neutral not only in deed but also in thought. We should not spend another penny for defense. Even if Hitler wins a quick and clear-cut victory, the United States will not be threatened unless it chooses to struggle for imperialistic—i.e., unworthy—aims, and in that case it deserves to be beaten. This is the general Communist Party line, though it has also been accepted by many non-Communists. It is the line that the League has chosen to follow. The key to it is not opposition to our going into the war, but opposition to (or deliberate ambiguity about) the need for national defense.

The other theory, held by most of those who have resigned from the League, is that the war in Europe is essentially a civil war, fought to decide what class will rule the world, under what forms of government. According to this theory, the United States is morally in the war—indeed, has been in it since it began nine years ago with the invasion of Manchuria, or four years ago with the revolt in Spain. The question whether we should now oppose Germany with our armed forces is therefore strategical rather than moral. The best strategical arguments, as of August, 1940, seem to be in favor of keeping our armed forces at home. But the ultimate issue of war or peace cannot be decided by the American pubic—even after it has listened to hundreds of pacifist speeches delivered by intellectuals trying to act as if they were at home on the soap-box. Hitler is the man who will make the decision, and if we want him to decide for peace we had better prove to him that war against us would be a costly undertaking.

This is the theory that I think comes nearer to the real situation, which of course is complicated by a thousand factors and almost impossible to reduce to any simple formulation. Everything about this war has been vastly and deliberately confused, and for an obvious reason, namely, that one of the best ways to attack any democracy is to spread confusion. Yet no one could read Hitler's or Mussolini's speeches, which mean a great deal of what they say—no one could reflect on the maneuvers that led to the defeat of France—without realizing that this is both a civil war and a struggle for something more than colonies and markets. The minds of men are being seized as well as their possessions. Marshal Pétain wants to abolish the French Revolution, that is, the whole nineteenth century. Hitler says that he wants to revoke the Peace of Westphalia, that is, the treaties recognizing the Protestant Reformation. This country was born out of reformation and revolution; even more than the British Empire, it is the conquest at which the fascists are ultimately aiming.

The present policy of the League seems calculated to weaken this country's power of resistance. For that policy there might be effective arguments, from the point of view of those who believe that a world proletarian revolution is just around the corner. Apparently some theorists of the Communist International are convinced that fascism is really a step in advance, the next step on the road toward world socialism, and that the sooner the "plutocratic democracies" are overthrown, the sooner all nations can be reorganized into world soviets. If that is what they think, they ought to say so publicly. Instead they have been preaching the sort of illogical pacifism they have always despised, as Bolsheviks. What they are now saying about "the imperialist war" is plausible enough to convince women's peace societies, small-town preachers, pulp-paper writers and other political innocents, but it has little relation to what is actually happening in Europe. And in any case, the League is not supposed to be an organization dedicated to the world proletarian revolution.

By following the Communist line on war and national defense, it has lately acquired some curious fellow travelers. Back in the days when the League was fighting fascism, I thought I knew its friends and its enemies; the latter were all those who favored appeasement abroad and reaction at home. Now it has joined company with the appeasers and even with the reactionaries. The political statements it has issued during the past few months—statements it had no call or capacity for making—could be read by Father Coughlin over the radio. They could be quoted by Henry Ford as an excuse for not making airplane engines. They are essentially the same statements that are being made by Colonel Lindbergh and the Cardinal Archbishop of Philadelphia. With the change of a few words, they could appear on the editorial page of the *Chicago Tribune,* the *New York American, Social Justice* or the *Brooklyn Tablet.* The League never agreed with these men or these papers before. If it wants to agree with them now, I can no longer agree with the League.

It has been very hard for me to write this letter. I have been a vice-president of the League since the day it was formed; as a matter of fact I was an active member of the committee that organized the first American Writers' Congress in 1935. During the following winter, when the League had to discharge its paid secretary and was in danger of disappearing for lack of funds, it was kept alive by a lecture series that provided its only income and activity. Isidor Schneider, Marjorie Fischer and I were the lecture committee and, in effect, the working staff of the League. I wrote most of the call to the second Writers' Congress, in 1937, and went to Madrid that same month as the League representative. All this is pretty ancient and personal history, but it explains why I have so far stayed in the League in spite of many disagreements over policy. Today those disagreements have become too deep to be smoothed over. Today it seems to me that the League is doing more to confuse American democracy than to defend it, and I hereby submit my resignation.[140]

Sincerely,
Malcolm Cowley

————————

[RW TLS-1]
[TO: RICHARD WRIGHT]
[NR] July 30, 1940

Dear Dick:

A couple of years ago I told you I never intended to give you books by negros for review, but I think you'd be interested in doing Langston Hughes' autobiography *The Big Sea*. Do let me know right away whether to send it to you.

Your review of *The Heart Is a Lonely Hunter* even if late was a very nice job indeed.

As ever,
Malcolm

————————

[NL TL/CC-2] [SC 228–229]
[TO: KENNETH BURKE]
RFD Gaylordsville, Conn.,
August 23, 1940

Dear Kenneth:

Being at home, though not on that famous leave of absence, I'll sit down to write you a not dictated letter. [. . .] During the last few years I have learned a lot about the institutionalization of human relations, and although all knowledge is supposed to be admirable in itself, I'd just as soon not have acquired that particular knowledge. An editor of a liberal weekly, and particularly a book-review editor, is not a man but an institution, a name to be signed to petitions, a possible speaker at meetings, a leg-up in other writers' careers, a sinister Stalinist or reactionary influence, a whole list of abstractions. He may end finding himself dehumanized by other people's attitudes toward him. Even his wife gets to judging his actions as those of a public figure. He is loved as a human being by his child and his dog, being lucky enough to have a child and a dog. . . . That's how I feel when I feel low. I begin to have a great pity for politicians and movie actors and other people whose lives are even more public. I understand why a lot of institutionalized people take to drinking a great deal, so they'll have an excuse for confiding in people, and why others are capable of totally false remarks like, "You know I like you," said with an assumption of simplicity—they're just trying by fraud to reestablish human relations. . . . All this might sound as if I were getting an exaggerated idea of my importance. Nothing of the kind. The editor of a liberal weekly is worth damned little except in a restricted world of radical politics and literary politics. But he's certainly institutionalized. Practically everyone who comes to see him wants to get something out of him. Social-service workers must have the same experience. What do they do when they're at home, away from their clients?

It will be nice to take that three-months' leave of absence. It is going to begin on September 15. Edmund Wilson will take my place, Oct. 1 to Dec. 1, then I'll be back again December 15, if the book is finished.[. . .]

Wilson by the way is tremendously acute in some ways, dumb and thick skinned in others, which is lucky for him. My theory is that it takes an area of insensitivity to keep writers going and keep them from being corrupted. If I had realized at the time the meaning of some opportunities I had in the 1920s I would have taken them and might have been finally corrupted. [. . .] And don't I realize the delicate infringements of honesty that are now involved in working for the NR, never any big choices, but so many little compromises? It's really easier to give your life for a cause than to hold out for a particular sentence that embodies your way of looking at life—yet if you surrender on the wording of a sentence, and another sentence, pretty soon you find yourself living for the opposite cause to the one you had intended to die for.

[. . .]

About my resignation from the League: it was connected with this process of being institutionalized. On account of the NR and the use of my name in the League, I couldn't just resign; I had to make it public. And I tried to resign on an issue, not just a squabble. The present CP line, which the League is following, seems to me not merely mistaken but crooked.

[. . .]

Too much of this yammering. It sounds as if I were sitting in my study weeping on this 23d day of August, 1940, the eve of my forty-second birthday, the anniversary of the two heaviest blows that American liberalism has suffered, I mean the execution of Sacco and Vanzetti and the Russo-German pact. As a matter of fact I'm feeling lustier than I have felt all summer, and quite eager to get down to work. And hope you're feeling the same. [. . .]

As ever,

[M]

PART V

The War Years, 1940–1944

War and Washington, 1940–1942

In October 1940 Cowley began his leave of absence from *The New Republic* with three weeks of self-imposed solitude on Prince Edward Island. In long letters to Burke, he outlined his new book on the 1930s, a "more impersonal" sequel to *Exile's Return.* As he revaluated his radical commitments and sought to own up to his own part in the factional quarrels of the decade, he experienced a typical "double drive" of self-justification and self-incrimination. Many letters reflect his ongoing struggle, as he fine-tuned his interpretation of Communism as a (faulty) religion and reappraised Marxism as a deficient philosophy of life. The book was difficult—and, at this early stage, perhaps impossible—to write. Over the next four decades it moved forward by fits and starts. It was not until 1980 that Cowley published his memoirs of the years 1930–1936, *The Dream of the Golden Mountains*; his treatment of the late 1930s would remain unfinished at his death.

Dramatic turns in Cowley's personal and professional life disrupted his leave of absence. Muriel had to undergo a mastectomy in New York, causing weeks of intense family anxiety. And on December 13, 1940, Cowley made an entry in his notebook about a lunch he had had with the ex-Communist Whittaker Chambers, one that would come to haunt him in the postwar anticommunist backlash. In their lunch meeting Chambers spoke freely about his time in the Communist Party and "ominously" predicted: "The counterrevolutionary purge is still to come." It would come sooner than Cowley could imagine.

That same month a shake-up took place at *The New Republic:* the magazine's British owners, Leonard and Dorothy Elmhirst, were unhappy with the magazine's stand on the war (which they deemed too isolationist) and objected to the leftist leanings of its editors, in particular Cowley and George Soule. Ironically, it was Cowley (for some time the only interventionist on the staff) who was now relieved of editorial responsibilities and demoted to the writing of a weekly book page. Coinciding as it did with his personal struggle to come to terms with his disaffiliation from radicalism and the writing of his book, this "coup" at *The New Republic* hit hard.

Disillusioned by "the bankruptcy of the intellectuals as a class and an order—*la faillite des clercs*," as he wrote to James Laughlin on January 29, 1941, Cowley turned again to poetry, preparing *The Dry Season* (1941) for New Directions. He continued to follow the latest developments in literature, greeting new magazines like *Vice Versa* and chronicling the changing directions of a literature no longer tied to radical ideology. In his weekly book page for *The New Republic* he covered an impressively wide range of literary, political, and historical topics, supplementing his (now reduced) income with freelance lecturing. "Poets as Reviewers," published in February 1941, offered scathing reflections on the current state of poetry reviewing, embroiling Conrad Aiken, Louise Bogan, and Randall Jarrell in public controversy.

Reestablished in the Connecticut countryside and beginning to feel "strictly human" again, Cowley confessed to Allen Tate and Louise Bogan (as he earlier had to Burke) how during his last years on *The New Republic* he had come to feel less a human being than an official in a bureaucracy. Taking the fate of ex-Communists to heart, he asked Archibald MacLeish to help Joseph Freeman find employment as a freelance writer and worked on behalf of European intellectuals who had fled the Nazis to seek refuge in the United States. But mostly, nursing a sense of personal failure and wounded pride, Cowley withdrew into a quiet country life to find compensatory rewards in the cultivation of his Connecticut garden.

By now he was firmly committed to the American war effort. In correspondence with MacLeish, now Librarian of Congress, he emphasized the need to make the public fully aware of the "terrible nearness" of the international crisis and the aims for which a war was to be fought. Writing to MacLeish in September 1941, he admitted to "a terrible feeling of not doing enough"; "I itch to do more work."

Cowley's plea did not fall on deaf men's ears. On November 16, 1941, three weeks before Pearl Harbor, he accepted an urgent invitation from MacLeish to come to Washington, D.C., to join the newly launched Office of

Facts and Figures. On November 24 Cowley was established in Washington as a chief information analyst, at $8,000 a year. Working among Washington bureaucrats was a new experience, and in early January 1942, awaiting the arrival of his wife and son from Sherman, and knowing himself to be under surveillance by the FBI, Cowley reported his first impressions of Washington to Burke. For all the bureaucracy and government inefficiency he witnessed, he felt encouraged "to be near the center of things."

But Cowley would not serve the national defense effort usefully for long. He managed to help write a number of speeches and statements for President Roosevelt—including his 1941 Christmas message and the "freedom of want" section of the pamphlet "The Four Freedoms"—but soon the Office of Facts and Figures fell under the scrutinizing glance of Martin Dies: on January 15, 1942, speaking on the floor of Congress, he singled Cowley out as "one of the chief Communist intellectuals" on the staff of the Office and denounced this "high-salaried government employee" for having had seventy-two separate connections with "the Communist party and its front organizations" (*Congressional Record* 88, 1 [77th Congress, 2nd session], 407–411). The charges were taken up and brought before the public, first by Westbrook Pegler in his syndicated newspaper column and then, in February 1942, by *Time,* which lifted lines from *The Dry Season* out of context to buttress Dies's charges. Cowley wrote an open letter to *Time* and fought hard to clear himself of the charges. Knowing he was under examination, he drew up a statement for MacLeish, reaffirming his break with Communism, his ongoing efforts to resist the advance of Hitler, and his loyalty to the U.S. democratic system and American values. He wrote letters of testimony and explanation to MacLeish (who privately intervened on his behalf with Henry Luce of *Time*) and to George J. Gould, chief of the Office of Emergency Management, who had examined him on February 5, 1942. Persuaded that his case had implications far beyond himself but also worried about injury to his reputation and ongoing ability to earn an independent income as a public writer, he sought legal advice from Louis S. Weiss and appealed to Roger Baldwin of the American Civil Liberties Union for help, noting on March 14: "we are being threatened with a Red Hunt that will dwarf the Palmer Raids of 1919–20." Hoping to expunge material from his FBI record that he knew to be false and misleading, he wrote to the office of the attorney general, Francis Biddle—but all in vain. In March 1942, finding that the efforts to clear his record consumed more time and energy than his position at the Office of Facts and Figures allowed, he wrote his letter of resignation to MacLeish and withdrew from public political activity, preparing to survive the expected counterpurge in silence and with self-respect.

[NL TLS-3] [PARTLY *SC* 229–231]
[TO: KENNETH BURKE]
Prince Edward Island, Monday, Oct. 14, 1940

Dear Kenneth:

I've been here on the island for two weeks and I'm leaving on Saturday. On the whole, the experiment hasn't worked out too badly. What one always forgets about Canada is that, compared to the U.S., it is a pioneer country. At present it is roughly in the same stage as the U.S. in 1917, both as regards the war and as regards its general social development. That involves one thing disappointing to the visitor: Canadian cooking is like American cooking in 1917—in other words, greasy, rich and indigestible—and my stomach isn't cast-iron as it was in 1917. [. . .]

Lower Montague, where I'm staying, is at the eastern end of the island, almost at the jumping-off place. The funny little newspaper from Charlottetown gets here a day late, the Halifax papers are two or three days late, the *New York Sunday News* arrives on Thursday morning (the bulldog edition at that) and letters from Connecticut take five days. With the island emptied of all its summer visitors, I am as undisturbed as I can possibly be. And here I came to start work on a new book.

Definition of it: I'm trying to do a sort of *Exile's Return* of the 1930s, but more impersonal, in no sense an autobiography this time. I suppose the old wish to kill one's past and be reborn is working obscurely once more, but I haven't been able to bring it to light, because I haven't been baptized into any new existence. The result is that the narrative will be somewhat more pedestrian. A good deal of it will use pieces I did for the NR, which were pretty good running commentary on how things looked from the left, and most of which seem to me to have stood up pretty well. My ticklish point will be dealing with all the quarrels of the decade. I simply can't leave them out, because I'm telling the story of a movement that was badly weakened by internal differences before it got slaughtered by external events. On the other hand, I'll be touching some sore spots on my own skin, and had better watch out.

In the case of this book, I'm doing something that I never tried before. [. . .] My main idea was that the writers' crusade of the 1930s (which is my subject, although I think Norton will try to sell the book as a literary history) was divided into three stages, and that these stages can best be understood by a religious metaphor, since the experience itself was fundamentally religious. The first stage was conversion to what was, in effect, a primitive church. In the second stage, the church broadened and softened its doctrines in the effort to become universal; that was the period of the People's Front, from 1935 to 1938. In the third stage, the church was weakened by internal schisms and external disasters, so that all but its most stalwart members and most honored priests were alienated. And the whole experience was closed by the Russo-German pact and the war. It makes a neat pattern. Any suggestions here?

I reread a good deal of *Exile's Return,* admiring the writing of it and feeling sore again at the treatment it got. That certainly was a bitter experience for me, getting generally hammered at with no one coming to my defense. This new book will get another hammering, but I'll be expecting it this time and can take measures. [. . .] Your analysis of the book has a big hole in it. The death-and-rebirth pattern is there, all right, but is complicated by the fact that the book was written at different times and tempos. Up to page 214, I was telling the story of my own adventures in ideas, writing a sort of autobiographical *Bildungsroman,* in which you play a great part, the last reference to you being on page 211. All this section, complete in itself, was written by July, 1933. But I had to do a longer book and I had to bring the story up to date. So, in the winter and spring of 1934, I wrote another hundred pages, in which you are not mentioned once—but neither am I. The author disappeared from his own story. He was now trying to do an objective narrative on the end of the 1920s, in which the chief characters are Scott Fitzgerald, Harry Crosby (two men he knew hardly at all) and Hart Crane, whose figure is in the background, Crosby being a mere surrogate for Crane. The Harry Crosby stuff is some of the best I ever did. One thing that reviewers went wrong on was this lack of connection between the two parts, and that was my own fault. I should have inserted a couple of auto-biographical passages into the objective stuff to give the book unity, and I should have explained why I omitted myself from my own story, the reason being that my life after 1923 was indeed quite interesting to me, but not especially significant—or at least I hadn't as yet digested its significance. In the new book, I'll appear only in scattered passages.

Well, that will do for this evening. It's after ten o'clock, and on Prince Edward Island ten o'clock is bedtime. [. . .] Prince Edward Island is dry, by the way—my last bottle of ale will be finished tomorrow, and then I'll drink nothing at all until reaching the states.

Bedtime positively.

As ever,
Malcolm

[NL TL/CC-2]
[TO: FELIX FRANKFURTER]
November 18, 1940[1]

Dear Felix:

I am overcome with the impropriety of addressing a Justice of the Supreme Court by his first name. But I would hardly know how else to address you, especially when writing about matters concerned with *The New Republic.*

A couple of weeks ago, Bruce told me that you hadn't at all liked a long review I wrote last spring, the one about Neville Henderson.[2] You said, so he reported, that it sounded as if I thought that Henderson and Chamberlain were as bad as Hitler. I am deeply sorry if I gave that impression to anyone who read the review, and yourself in particular, for it isn't the least what I think. A world populated by Neville Hendersons could remain at peace, and be not a bad world to live in, whereas a world populated by Hitlers—good God, I wouldn't like to think of it. No, my point against Henderson and Chamberlain (and Simon and Hoare and many others of their caste in England) was that by their own confession they were willing to cooperate with Hitler, having been blind to what he represents as well [as] to almost everything else in the world since 1930. They led England to the brink of the abyss and almost pushed her over.

Incidentally, that review produced some curious reactions. The only protests against it came from Americans. I know a great many Englishmen— liberals, naturally—and without exception they liked it. The English papers picked it up and reprinted it in extenso. It was even cabled to Auckland and Sidney and Melbourne. Perhaps it helped just a little to hasten Chamberlain's resignation, and if it did I am proud of having made a contribution to England, not being in the least an isolationist. Nor do I believe, as the Communists keep repeating, that this is a war "between rival imperialisms"— what hypocritical nonsense.

But it wasn't so much for myself that I was disturbed by your unfavorable reaction to this and other articles in *The New Republic*. I have been thinking for a long time about the need for unity among liberals or progressives or democrats with a small "d" or whatever one chooses to call them. Before the invasion of France, I differed with the policy of the paper, thinking that it was much too aloof and complacent about the war. But I felt that it would come round to a more realistic position, and that when it did it would produce all the greater effect on its readers for having waited so long. And that is about what happened last June, when the paper changed its position. I am hoping that it can hold its readers and its friends together.

The liberals and progressives have suffered a very great defeat these last two years, everywhere in the world except in England. In part the defeat was due to their tragic inability to agree among themselves. I have lately begun working on a book about the history of the American intellectuals during the last ten years, and one of the points that impresses me most as I go over the story is the amount of bickering among them and how it weakened all parties and opinions and factions. Unfortunately the catastrophe doesn't seem to have drawn the liberals any closer together, except in England where they are faced by immediate danger. Everywhere else they have become even more disunited, like the fragments of a beaten army, and the result may be that they will play a very small part in the building of a new world. That world is coming, no matter what we say or do, and perhaps it may prove to be a disagreeable world indeed. Though our own world seems marvelously desirable now that it is threatened, we cannot prevent its passing. But by closing our ranks we have a chance—just a chance, but that is enough—to guide the inevitable changes into a desirable direction.

All this of course is no answer to your reproof, which I will take to heart. I would have written you two weeks ago, but suddenly Muriel found that she had to undergo a very serious operation and it was hard for me to think of anything else. That is over now, and Wednesday she is getting out of the hospital.

Fifty-eight congratulations on your birthday, which was duly reported in the papers.

As ever,
Malcolm

————————

[NL TL/CC-2]
[TO: DUNSTAN THOMPSON & HARRY BROWN]
November 24, 1940

Dear D.T. and H.B.

Was pleased and excited by the first issue of *Vice Versa*.[3] Liked the poems better than the prose, though some of the prose was damned good too. In the opening Encyclical, your "first of all," "secondly," and "in the third place" should have been inverted, since the "first of all" of your magazine is publishing good poetry. Unless you do that, you can't slaughter the publishing fakes or the writing fakes; you can merely conduct guerilla warfare, not having any base to attack from. This business of the new men slaughtering the old men is repeated every five years or so, and now that I'm getting imperceptibly but unavoidably pushed into the camp of the old men, I'm beginning to think that geronticide can be carried too far. Anyhow the massacre only means something when the new men are really new and prove it by writing their own verse. That's why the front part of *Vice Versa* is the important part.

Wish you hadn't been so hard on Sandburg. He and Eliot are like the west and east sides of the same house, that house being American poetry in the 1920s. If it didn't have a west side or an east side, it wouldn't be a house but only a billboard. Or to put it in a different way and to borrow a distinction from Philip Rahv,[4] there have always been the Redskins and the Palefaces in American literature. You are lining up with the Palefaces, and that's where I belong too, by training, but don't forget that the Redskins, including Sandburg, have had a great deal to say, and some day the synthesis is going to be made. Marriage of the librarian of Harvard University with an Indian squaw, producing the perfect child.

[...]

One more point. Your program for publishing good poetry is too damned simple and negative. It's all right to say that it won't be poetry about the war or about the Worker, that it will just be *good*, but what the hell does that mean? Actually there is for some reason more good poetry being written just now than for many years in the past. I've had that impression for some time now, and have confirmed it by talking to other people who have to read a lot of manuscripts. The reason may be that people are more stirred by what is happening (even though they don't write Odes to a Spitfire). Also the reason may be that poets were embarrassed and confused for a long time by the doctrine that they ought to write poems that could be read by workers and that would hasten the proletarian revolution—now it is as if a load were taken off their minds and put on their emotions instead, with the result that new poems are squeezed out. But this isn't the time to embarrass and confuse them again with a new set of negatives. Who knows, maybe they *can* write good odes to a Spitfire or to a Worker? Let 'em try anything so long as that is what they feel.

So I have some reservations, but add them all up and cancel them out and what is left is a damned good magazine, for which my heartiest thanks.

Yours,
Malcolm Cowley

———

[NL TLS-3] [PARTLY SC 234–236]
[TO: KENNETH BURKE]
December 17, 1940

Dear Kenneth:

After Muriel got out of the hospital on November 20, we moved back to the country, and that's where we've been ever since. The Blumes had moved into the house and had taken care of Robbie. They had taken very good care of him too, but he is tremendously attached to his parents, as I suppose most children are, and he was terribly worried about his mother's illness, so that for the first two weeks after our return he looked sickly and nervous and used to have a nightmare regularly at ten o'clock every evening. Now he's back in shape again. Yesterday he had his birthday party, and I asked him whether he was any bigger now he was six years old. He said that he was the biggest boy in the first grade or the second grade, but there were some children in the upper grades who were taller than he was. And it's true that he's enormous. Muriel has been getting better too, at a fairly rapid rate, considering the nature of the operation. She still has to go into New York twice a week to have a dressing, but that will be over soon.

While she was in the hospital I took a room in New York, on East 71st Street, not far away, and tried to go ahead with the book. I made a little progress, not much. For that was just the time chosen by *The New Republic* to have a great shake-up and shakedown. For a time the atmosphere around the office was like Moscow during the purges. Our backers had got tough with us, that was the root of it, and they decided to put Bruce in absolute command and get George and me out of the office. The net result for me wasn't as bad as it might have been. My job from now on is to stay home and write a weekly book page at a decline in salary of $50 a week—but then it cost me about $25 a week to spend three days in New York, if you include city clothes and laundry and hotel bill and general disorganization. The real trouble—I'm telling all this to you in strict confidence—is that a man outside of the office is in a much less secure position than a man inside. For the moment, however, I'm content—I'll be able to go ahead working on the book, taking off two days a week to earn my beans and bread.

So the book becomes even more important than it was before. So I'm even more disturbed by the imperfections of it. Let's take up your yammer and consider all sides of it.[5]

Anyone who was as close to the radical movement as I was is going to be deeply shaken by breaking his connections with it. At that point the religious metaphor is absolutely accurate. You leave a church, and like a defrocked priest you can't think about anything else for a while. You want to justify yourself while blaming yourself—the double drive that one finds in all books by ex-radicals. And at that point you ask, why be an ex-radical? Here it isn't a question of the religion, which may be good or bad, I haven't decided yet, but of the church, the religion as institutionalized. The church is bad in its effect on people. There's no getting around that point.

And so I write a book intended to deal with the literature of the last ten years, and the CP keeps working into it—and especially into the outline for it. I'll have to bounce it out again. But I can't bounce all of it out, because the party did play a central role, not by giving all the answers but by stating the problems that people argued about. A difficult job here, to be solved only in the writing.

Meanwhile I adopted one simple formula that may answer some of your objections. No names! No inside revelations! If I want to document a point, I quote from somebody's novel or essay or poem, which is easy and hurts no feelings. If I want to tell a story that might reflect on somebody, friend or enemy, the story's hero is anonymous and some of the details are changed.

And I'm trying to get at something which is the essence of the decade but which has an application beyond immediate timelines. I want not a series of events or actions but the motives and moods behind them. I want as far as possible to open doors, to let people see that a whole lifetime and very deep feelings are necessary to explain a single speech. What I am really trying to write is a collective novel. The last decade lends itself to just that—having a beginning, a middle and an end, and having an inner logic that was timed to coincide with external events. In that sense, it's a damned ambitious project, more ambitious than I can carry out with my terrible habit of writing a page or two a day.

[. . .]

It's my sort of book, not yours, because I'll be sticking atmosphere into it—that's what I do easily and do well—but I hope and pray that there won't be anything cheap about it, or journalistic. It's in the later sections that I run into those dangers, and, boy, won't I have to be careful. Maybe the trouble is that once more I am trying to combine literary history with autobiography, and perhaps not making myself clear. But I'll play a much less important part in my story than in *Exile's Return*. [. . .]

What I'd be grateful for from you is not only comments on the project but also memories of how you felt and thought at different stages of the 1930s, documentation in other words. I can use it all without incriminating you. In the course of conversations lately I have run into some very strange people—none stranger than Bob Cantwell's friend Whittaker Chambers, who used to work for the GPU,[6] and who now proclaims himself as an agent of the counter-revolution, "Christian and democratic," he says, but mostly counter-revolutionary.[7]

Muriel has been wrapping up Christmas presents, all for the kiddies. Time for me to knock off and listen to the late evening news.

As ever,
Malcolm

[NL TLS-5] [PARTLY SC 238–241]
[TO: KENNETH BURKE]
January 9, 1941

Dear Kenneth:

No further progress to report on the book. I began writing the weekly *New Republic* pieces on December 29, twelve days ago; I have done two of them so far and nothing else, except a little woodchopping and whittling and a trip to New York. Damn me for [being] a painfully slow writer, always carrying water uphill in a leaky bucket, always feeling that my next piece has to be "better" and therefore getting an attack of stagefright before starting it. Then after starting it, the continual necessity to change, and change again, and go back and start over.

The first book I reviewed was Hallie Flanagan's *Arena,* the story of the Federal Theatre Project. She seems to be quite a woman, and she certainly did a marvelous job, and the glory and failure of her project had the quality of a morality play. Almost everything now seems to me to have the quality of a morality play, moving in accordance with foreordained patterns of social behavior. Everything is a fairy tale and a myth, except that the Youngest Son gets pushed down a well and drowned by the Wicked Stepmother before the action really starts. The other book I read, and wrote a belated comment on, was Hemingway's latest novel [*For Whom the Bell Tolls*], which I strongly recommend to your attention.[8] That too is a morality play and a myth [. . .].

You asked what sort of book I planned to write, saying that it still wasn't clear in your mind. Well, I want to write a story of the writers' crusade of the

1930s. Almost every word in that statement is important to me. "Story" in particular is important, because it places the emphasis on movement and sequence and the reasons for both. "Crusade" is important, though slightly inaccurate, because it brings in the religious element that I have been talking about. "1930s" is important—this answers another of your questions or complaints—I personally can only get at permanent and eternal truths in their temporal manifestations. Actually almost the whole experience of the 1930s happened before—notably in France from 1830 to 1848, though large parts of it also parallel the experience of the early Christians, of Milton, of the English Romantic poets, and of the little American renaissance from 1910 to 1919. But I don't want to touch the permanent motives till I have the whole thing situated in its own time. I can't. I don't think that way.

The writers' crusade of the 1930s is again a morality play to me, or at any rate a story with a beginning, a middle and an end. Beginning: the depression. Middle: the People's Front era. End: 1939–1940, when everything ended—the Spanish Republic (February), Czechoslovakia (March), the Federal Theatre (June), the People's Front (August), the long armistice (September)—then Poland (October), the illusion of Russia as a non-imperialist power (November), free Norway and Denmark (April), the French Republic (May and June)—did you ever stop to think how all our world crashed in those few months?

[...]

About your, what did you do in the Great War, Daddy? question—well, I didn't do enough, not nearly enough. I tried pretty hard to introduce an atmosphere of tolerance and humanity into the actions of the left-wing writers with whom I was associated; I tried to keep them back from reducing everything to politics, though I found myself falling into the vices I was trying to get others to avoid. During the last few years I found myself handicapped by a lassitude that I don't know how to explain—was it physical or moral; was I in bad health or discouraged—at any rate I found that I wasn't doing very much outside my job, which was becoming a bureaucratic job. And since I was doing so very little and saying so very little, I was in a false position—it was taken for granted that I was a Stalinist when, Jesus, you ought to know that I was a long way from that.

I knew that I wasn't getting any too damned popular. But since you started that topic, I wish you'd carry it a lot farther. I had some damned persistent enemies, notably Sidney Hook and Jim Farrell. There is reason to believe that one or the other of them helped to make trouble for me at the NR by writing to the Elmhirsts. But of course even very faithful enemies like that can't make really bad trouble for you unless other people agree with what they say—and evidently that was my point of weakness. But it's pretty damned important for me to know as much as possible of what was being said, in order that I can mend matters as far as possible and avoid similar mistakes in the future. So keep talking, kid, I'm listening and learning.

[...]

As ever,
Malcolm

Would it interest you to know that it's snowing?

———

[NL TL/CC-2]
[TO: LEWIS MUMFORD]⁹
February 13, 1941

Dear Lewis:

A good deal of the difficulty between us lies in the fact that we attach a different value to certain words, and notably to the word "fascism." It seemed to me in reading *Faith for Living* that each time you said "fascism" you really meant "evil." That of course isn't quite a fair statement—you did define the word, I know, but the definition impressed me as being too vague and inclusive, and didn't cast sufficient light on your own position.

Now to me "fascism" is the application of certain doctrines about the nature of society. It didn't start out that way, I know. It started out with Mussolini's gangsters and only later acquired the theories, but it most certainly has them now. Where did it get the theories? Well, it went to the fountainhead of anti-liberalism, namely, to the Jesuits of the Counter Reformation and to other Catholic thinkers of the nineteenth-century Counter Revolution. It is no accident that all the fascist leaders of western

Europe—Mussolini, Hitler, Franco, Pétain—were deeply influenced by Catholic thought. It is no accident that liberal Catholics—Don Sturzo, the Benedictines, the German Centrists, the followers of Mercier in Belgium—have always been among the first victims of fascism.

The concepts at the basis of fascism are status, authority, tradition—as against the liberal concepts of progress, individualism, logic.

But "fascism," as I said in writing about Schuman,[10] is a much too general word, applying to many different schemes. We had Italian fascism, which was a mixture of tyranny and bombast, with only the façade of fascist ideas. We had the Catholic fascism of Schuschnigg, of the Church in Quebec and also of Pétain [. . .]. We had Spanish fascism, a mixture of Jesuit ideas and purely Spanish elements with a good many borrowings from Mussolini and Hitler. Finally, we had and have German National Socialism, the fascism that I hate and fear, which itself is a mixture of Catholic and Bolshevist notions (I don't see Luther in it, but only in the German *acceptance* of it) with the romantic notion that the Germans are a master race destined to conquer the world or perish in the attempt—an explosive mixture rendered ten times more powerful by German method and logic and insanity.

It is German fascism that threatens us. And our chief duty in the face of it is to *survive*. That I think is the one imperative: everything else must be examined in relation to it. I would guess that in order to survive we have got to conquer, since this is the struggle for the mastery of the world. But in order to conquer we have got to have a faith strong enough to persuade other peoples.

It follows that to me the idea of a liberal and universal fascism is not wicked or insulting, but a course to be examined along with others, in relation to our survival. But I think it has got to be examined quite carefully, so that we know exactly what it means. For example, I would like to know whether the—to me—Catholic idea of status (family, land, work) should play a large part in it, or whether we can still depend on the Liberal ideas of logic and science, or whether we must work toward a synthesis. I would like to know what part religion is going to play in the new faith, and what sort of religion it will be, Catholic or Protestant or Jewish or positivistic.

If I sound a little confused here, it is because this whole group of ideas and this whole situation are new and difficult and I have to grope my way. But I think I have suggested why it seems to me that you have borrowed a good many elements that I would call fascist, and sometimes without your examining their implications. Of course there has to be a division of labor.— You are exhorting. I am a damned poor exhorter and I am trying to get the whole business straight in my mind. Exhortations are more useful just now than definitions, but they both are needed. And we are agreed on the dangers faced by the world and on the necessity for taking revolutionary steps to meet them.

Fred Schuman is perhaps more strictly logical than either of us. But I think he is getting to be as fascinated by National Socialism as a monkey about to be swallowed by a python—remember, in the *Jungle Book,* the story of Kaa's hunting?

As ever,
Malcolm

_____

[NL TL/CC-I]
[TO: LOUISE BOGAN]
February 27, 1941

Dear Louise:

Hey there, stop and think a minute. I wasn't trying to step on your toes in that Aiken piece[11]—in fact I was keeping strictly away from them. [. . .] The fact was that I didn't step on Jarrell's toes very hard either, he being a good writer if a very harsh critic. I was hot and bothered about the set-up in which a talented poet like Aiken can publish what he thinks is his best book, and then have it drop like a stone into an abandoned well, without even the echo being heard. Think of it—seventeen reviews in all, and only two of them in magazines of general circulation. And those two reviews like bricks on his head. Jarrell seemed to write under the misapprehension that he was opposing a whole body of favorable criticism—but the body was thin air.

In your own piece, I don't think it was accurate to say that Aiken and Millay sound just alike. Whatever you think of his sonnets they are damned well done, whereas Edna seems to be writing patriotic gush, damned awkwardly.

And think a minute—What if Aiken did or didn't include somebody's character in a novel that wasn't even reviewed, let alone being read?[12] And what if he tried to get your job on *The New Yorker* (it doesn't seem like him, but let it pass)? For that matter, what if he poisoned your dear old mother, after giving you knockout drops and setting fire to the curtains? What has all that got to do with his poems? Jesus, if somebody tried to review Byron or Baudelaire or Rimbaud on the basis of his personal relations, wouldn't it be a pretty mess?

Let's hold a be-kind-to-poets week. These days everybody seems to have joined a scalping party—the Romanticists scalping the Intellectualists, who are busy scalping the Surrealists, who are busy scalping the Moralists, who are busy scalping. The result is that no good poet has been getting a square deal, including yourself. Maybe poets aren't rivals, but schools of poets are, and they're beginning to talk just like merchants running down a rival merchant's stock. Why not light into the non-poets for a change?

I hope my chance will come when you publish a book of poems yourself. Not to knock you but to say you're a damned good poet. And a damned good critic too, except when you've got a chip on your shoulder.

As ever,
Malcolm

———

[AT TLS-2]
[TO: ALLEN TATE]
March 6, 1941

Dear Allen:

Jarrell, whom I haven't ever met, is a fascinating puzzle to me. I have been reading his poems in *Five Young American Poets,* the New Directions book, and they are much more tangible than the work of any of the other contributors, they are something to get your teeth into, but then you wonder just what you have got your teeth into. (By the way, I wouldn't go so far as you in saying that he was nearly the whole claim of his generation to recognition—Harry Brown has something to say and so has Weldon Kees, of whom I have so far seen only one poem and one story, but both were brilliant.) If Jarrell the critic were somebody else, he could write a wonderful snotty review of Jarrell the poet, quoting the phrases and the ideas coming directly from Auden without even being disguised by a Made in America stamp ("the shires," for example; what business has a Tennessee poet talking about the shires?), and the attempt to reproduce Dylan Thomas and the images borrowed from Wilfred Owen (better done than the Auden images because not so faithful to the original), and the professorial jargon creeping in where it doesn't belong, and the unwillingness to come out and say what he means, when usually it is simple enough, God knows. But Jarrell the critic is notoriously unfair, and it would take somebody else to praise Jarrell the poet for his visions of doom and for an intensity of emotion that seems heightened by a technique designed to express something else. You sense in him a simple man puzzled by the world in which we live and deeply hurt by a love affair, yet determined to make his hurt and puzzlement impersonal and bookish. Then, in his reviews, you get a picture of what other poets feel after they have read his comments on their work, the shivering in bed late at night, the feeling of utter aloneness, the salt taste in the mouth, the asking "Am I really so utterly null as he says I am?"—why, if he whipped them with a whip soaked in brine, kicked them in the kidneys, held lighted matches to their sexual organs, he could scarcely cause them more pain. It's not his saying that their work is bad—it's the way he bullies them and exults at their discomfiture. Remember that as Kenneth is always saying, a good deal of writing is symbolic action; and when a critic kills and tortures poets, he is symbolically killing and torturing their bodies.

Well, enough of him for this time. More will be heard about him, and in two or three years we'll have a clearer picture. He must as a person be better than his reviews. He certainly is as a poet.

I was very glad to get your letter because I had been meaning to write you for a long time. And to say what? Well, I don't know, except that as long as I was running the *New Republic* book section it seemed to be getting increasingly difficult for me to conduct normal human relationships. An editor, no matter what his intentions are, gets driven into the position of being a literary official, part of an institution, executor of a policy laid down by others. Besides, I was so busy I never had time to write for pleasure. This winter I'm living in the country, working on a book (rather sluggishly), reading other books that I hadn't got round to reading, writing a weekly page on which I have time to work, and responsible for no opinions except those that appear over my own signature. I feel as if I had taken off a pair of shoes that didn't fit. I see hardly anybody, but I get a chance to write letters to my friends, and I feel strictly human.

We certainly had a tough time during the fall. Muriel had been feeling tired and run down for a long time—and I wonder whether a malignant tumor is really "local," as the doctors say, or whether it isn't connected with a whole physical and moral set-up. At any rate, this one was discovered in good time, and Muriel had a not dangerous but drastic and terrifying operation, and in the middle of it came a great ruckus at *The New Republic*—I guess Edmund told you about it—and Robbie began to get nightmares and stop eating, and so on and so on. But once we were all back in Gaylordsville, Muriel began to mend and she now seems healthier and happier than for two years, and Robbie is fine and I'm not afraid any longer to look a typewriter in the face—so I guess we're ready to survive until one of these days our whole world crashes, and maybe we can even survive through that. [. . .]

As ever,
Malcolm

[LB TLS-2]
[TO: LOUISE BOGAN]
March 9, 1941

Dear Louise:

[. . .]

Perhaps I have a deeper grudge than yours against the intellectuals. Taken separately they may be very appealing, even the ones you would never suspect of being appealing. Joe Freeman,[13] for example. He's been cast out by the Party, and he's absolutely pitiful, no friends, no market for his writing, his wife as embittered as he is, and I don't pity him any the less because he once acted like a mug. And if Joe Freeman turns out to be a pitiable human being, devoted now to poetry (bad poetry) and scholarship, I guess all the intellectuals must be that underneath. But put ten of them together in a room, and they can be as disgustingly heartless as any Nazi official. Incident: my father died just before Christmas, 1939. Martha Dodd[14] gave a big party for all the radical intellectuals, and I decided to go to it with Muriel because I was feeling bad enough about my father's death so that I didn't have to throw any front of false mourning. I got there and the intellectuals were drunk and talking about the death of Heywood Broun and saying that maybe it was just as well he died because his usefulness was over—and he being in his way a sort of saint, though I suppose you'd never admit it—and I got so disgusted I never wanted to see any of them again. Muriel got disgusted too and we fought all the forty miles home. I'm not giving you the atmosphere of that party, because I'd have to mention the wolfing of turkey, the glouglou of highball glasses, the woman who came with her new lover, straight from a week-end with the new lover's ex-girl friend—and delivered her speech against Heywood Broun, then collapsed into the arms of her former lover, now living with her new lover's ex-girl friend—and this being the crowd that believed in the Revolution and the Working Class—and old Dr. Cowley (who somehow got identified in my mind with Heywood) lying on a hillside under the thin snow, after living for seventy-five years as an impoverished gentleman, a Swedenborgian and a Hahnemanian homeopath. The intellectuals, darling, you can have them. Their game is played out.

We will now speak about AMOR.[15] I believe in AMOR. Personally I love everybody, but I only love everybody when he is broken, desperate, proud, humble and trying to say exactly what he thinks.

As ever,
Malcolm

[KB TLS-2] [SC 246–247]
[TO: KENNETH BURKE]
May the what? 1941

Dear Kenneth:

Il faut cultiver son jardin. That's what I've been doing, cultivating my real garden to the neglect of my metaphorical garden. Escapism, of course. With the social world crashing around us, digging in the earth and moving plants gives a sense of power, that essential feeling of potency, which seems lacking elsewhere. The law of cause and effect can still be applied among plants, whereas among men it is only the Germans who can apply that law, having borrowed social levers from Ford and Lenin and combined them with Bismarck's army. So, after listening to the radioed accounts of twelve thousand parachutists landing on Crete, men from Mars in the land of the Minotaur, I move thirteen tomato plants into lily cups before setting the lily cups in the garden and feel very well satisfied, because I know the plants will grow safe from cutworms or sun-wilt. [. . .]

[. . .]

As per your remark about my hating the things I was destined to become—it's no news to me. [. . .] One might also say that my quarrels with the anti-Stalinists were prophetic, were made worse by doubts I was trying to repress—but in that case the judgment would be external, since I wasn't trying to repress the doubts and since there is a Trotskyist mentality that existed anterior to Trotskyism, and that is not my mentality at all—the quarrel was a renewal of my high-school and college quarrel with the grinds, the people who made no higher marks than I did, or not much higher marks (remember I was ninth in my class at Harvard) but hadn't cultivated the ironic attitude that study was unimportant, whereas I made my parade of drunkenness and did my studying in private.

The NR under Bliven's editorship seems to me a pretty sad mess, an emotional and propagandistic sheet directed toward people who have to be emotionalized and propagandized by logical arguments, a lowbrow sheet for highbrows.

As ever,
Malcolm

———————

[AM TLS-2]
[TO: ARCHIBALD MACLEISH][16]
May 10, 1941

Dear Archie:

Thanks a million for writing the letter about Joe Freeman.[17] I may need more than that service myself, some time.

I had the hardest time in the world reviewing your *Selected Prose*. [...]

A group that your criticism would fit like an old shoe is the advisory board for the Pulitzer awards. The prizes they gave for 1940–41 are the purest example of intellectual irresponsibility that I have come across for many years—timidity, ineptitude, scholarly escape from the issues of the present. No award to foreign correspondents because, I suppose, too many of them are now doing dangerous work. No award to a novel because *For Whom the Bell Tolls* was too vital a novel. On the other hand, a prize for a smoke-prevention campaign, another for an academic biography of Jonathan Edwards, another for a smug and pharisaical cartoon taking no sides, another to a labor-baiter, another to the most cockeyed editorial writer in the country—the whole business is sickening. If this is an example of democratic culture, what the devil are we defending?

But for the other intellectuals, those who did accept political duties, I think the fault and weakness of their course was personal instead of social irresponsibility. Too many of them talked about creating a more human world while acting in a completely inhuman fashion towards their families and associates, loving to attack and denigrate, becoming more and more spiteful, shallow and extraverted. Then, when their political ambitions failed, they had lost everything. I suppose I sound pretty discouraged about the intellectuals, but I have seen too much of them. About the world in general, I don't feel so hopeless as I did a few months ago. There are terrible things in store for us and it is not inconceivable that this country might go the way of France—not if you can help it and not if I can help it, but then people like us may not have the power to arrest the process or make people realize the terrible nearness of the crisis. But curiously there seem to be new forces for good released as well as forces for evil, and in the long run—maybe after we are all dead—something good will come of these troubles, if civilization is strong enough to live through them.

What I find writers lacking today is not the ability to create new faith, which I don't think they ever had, but the ability to see and imaginatively recreate the vast changes that are occurring before our eyes.

I wish that someone would convince FDR that he ought to make a straight-from-the-shoulder speech full of facts and more facts, telling what he thinks this country should do in face of what may be the impending crack-up of Great Britain. About sixty percent of Americans are willing to go to war if that is the only way to keep Britain from being defeated. Well, it is now the only way, and maybe it is time to say so. It *is* time.

As ever,
Malcolm

[GH TLS-1]
[TO: GRANVILLE HICKS]
June 24, 1941

Dear Granville:

Soskin promised a $50 advance and I signed the contract today.[18]

What a nice lot of crow the comrades are eating now. Well, I've been a war-monjer these many months, and today I am even more of a war-monjer, and I'll have company. Of course my fear is that the purges have so weakened Russian morale that the country won't fight as it would have fought in 1936. It's all nonsense to say that you can wipe out disloyalty by shooting not only the disloyalists but those suspected of possible sympathy with them. All you do is transform disloyalty into passive cynicism—and we may find a lot of that in Russia. On the other hand, the Red Army will surprise me if it doesn't pull a lot of surprises on Hitler. He is fighting somebody now who fights with his own weapons.

The pro-Nazis in this country are certainly revealing their hand—Wheeler, General Wood, Colonel McCormick and the rest of them. On the other hand, I thought that W. Churchill's Sunday speech was simple, honest and marvelous. [. . .] This time it is England that is coming through with clean hands—quite a contrast with 1937 and 1938. And now our future depends on the Red Army, and the Royal Air Force, and American help to the Royal Air Force (which the Party here tried so hard to sabotage). The Party comes out of this with not enough shreds of moral or intellectual respectability to hide the pimples on its bare bottom.

As ever,
Malcolm

[POETRY TLS-1]
[TO: GEORGE DILLON, *POETRY*]
October 28, 1941

Dear Mr. Dillon:

This afternoon I finished the manuscript of "The Dry Season" and mailed it to New Directions. I went out and shot three squirrels—that always gives me a bad conscience, but there isn't any other game around this year—I helped Peter Blume celebrate his thirty-fifth birthday, and now I'm sending you the unpublished poems from the book.[19] [. . .]

I don't know how you'll like these pieces—they are my mood as of this autumn, the break-up of a world that deserved to be broken up, but not by the people who are doing the breaking. In my mind, the four poems enclosed are more or less connected—that is, Roxane and the patrons who drink white wine and seltzer at Moscowitz's (the Original Moscowitz's) are the Lost People whose adventures I describe in the longest of these poems; and "Seven" is the dream they gave me. "Seven" is also the poem I like best, though I think "The Lost People" says a lot about that famous generation; I thought of dedicating it to F. Scott Fitzgerald, who told the same story at greater length in *Tender Is the Night* (but without mentioning the womb hunger that I think is so deeply involved in it).

[. . .] [I]f there's any chance of your using all or some of them in the December issue, why, God be with you.

Cordially,

Malcolm Cowley

I'm living here in Gaylordsville with my books, my garden and my bees—not to mention the radio—and I'm getting a terrible feeling of not doing enough, of being out of things. For the last year I haven't been working in the *New Republic* office, but just writing for it, and in these times writing doesn't seem to be enough; I itch to do more work.

Cowley to Archibald MacLeish, September 28, 1941 [NL]

[NL TL/CC-I]

[TO: ARCHIBALD MACLEISH]

November 16, 1941

Dear Archie:

If the need is urgent, I could come on very short notice[20]—as little as three or four days—provided that I could have some time off afterwards to settle my affairs. [. . .]

Once again a close vote in Congress[21] makes it evident how important your job is going to be. The figures on neutrality repeal would seem to show that the country was split into two almost equal factions, but that picture is wholly false. Talking to ordinary people, I get the impression that they are much more united in their attitude toward the war than almost anyone believes. But there is a great deal of confusion, caused by conflicting information or the lack of information, and there is a general *appearance* of disunity.

Just now, that appearance is almost as dangerous as real disunity would be. It weakens the effectiveness of our foreign policy, by weakening the belief of other countries in the power behind that policy. It is likely to plunge us into war at the wrong moment. That is, it might mislead the Germans or the Japanese—or might enable the Germans to mislead the Japanese—into believing that they were dealing with a divided nation and could win an easy victory. And the moral is that some of the people who are shouting loudest for peace are actually doing the most to push us backwards into war. . . . You certainly have a job cut out for you, almost the biggest and most vital there is at the moment.[22]

As ever,

Malcolm

[RPB TLS-2]

[TO: RICHARD P. BLACKMUR]

November 22, 1941

Dear Blackmur:

[. . .] I reviewed Van Wyck Brooks[23] for the NR serially—first instalment, saying how nice a book he has written; second instalment, saying that he attacks books & writers without stopping to find out what they mean. In this 2nd instalment, coming out next week, I had a chance to praise your technical criticism. But Brooks is right in saying that you and others don't pay enough attention to *what* an author is saying, in your concern with the *how*. Form & matter can be distinguished only for convenience' sake. A writer's emotions when writing determine his form—if he's bored, his sentences go flat; if he is deeply moved, his periods become longer (being partly determined by the length of his breaths), and if he is excited, his periods become short again, staccato. If they don't determine his form, he is saying things that he doesn't feel, he is being a hypocrite. Conversely, form determines matter—in the sense that only certain things can be said in the sonnet, the short story, etc. When Brooks judges writers by what they are saying, explicitly, he is surrendering his powers of detecting hypocrisy (the commonest vice of writers). Hypocrisy is always revealed by style. But when *you* pay all your attention to form, you are likely to miss the writer's whole purpose in doing a certain job, and are likely even to miss the *why* of his technical weakness. (But I didn't say this in the review.)

As ever,

Malcolm

[KB TLS-3] [PARTLY *SC* 247–248]
[TO: KENNETH BURKE]
621 East Capitol,
Washington, D.C.
January 11, 1942.

Dear Kenneth:

For a little more than a month, I have been staying in a tourist non-home—a medium-sized room with two double beds in it, two radiators but not enough heat, so that my fingers at the moment are pretty nearly frozen to the keys. $10 a week; worth fully $6 by the standards of other countries. Much loneliness, much looking forward to the day two weeks from now when Muriel and Robbie come down and we get established in what seems to be a comfortable apartment.

It's a strange place for me to be; I mean Washington, not the room. I'm a Chief Information Analyst (but my office is full of Chief Information Analysts); I get what seems to me the lordly salary of $8,000, which is too much for the work I'm doing; the FBI is of course trying to get me fired—you ought to read the long dossier they prepared on me—and I have to depend on A. MacLeish to save my job; the whole information set-up here is uncertain, so that our organization might be abolished or merged, and altogether it's a lot of sand on which to build a house where I don't want to build a house. Meanwhile it seems that every second writer in the country wants a job like mine to preserve the American Way of Life.

Outside of the office, I haven't written a word since coming here, and there is little prospect of my writing more than a couple of words as long as I stay. Night work and Sunday work are commonplaces. And yet it's a hell of a sight better to be here than to assist in the agony of the NR, where people tell me that "all hell has broken loose," without explaining what they mean by "all hell." On the credit side, it's comforting to be near the center of things, even if I don't know much more about them than I learn by reading the papers.

[...]

On the whole, it's better than I thought it would be. The worst feature of a bureaucracy is the struggle for power that has taken the place of a struggle for money. Bureaucrats here can't draw down more than $10,000 a year, because that's how much the congressmen get, and congressmen hate to see anyone else getting more. But they can, like Russian bureaucrats, find other satisfactions, in terms of long-distance phone calls, admiring subordinates, orders obeyed in Honolulu, decisions reflected in victories or defeats in Asia. They can get to feeling pretty good about themselves.

You can get a vague picture of a government agency by imagining the business of General Motors being run by the faculty of the University of Chicago, or better of Columbia—which has now contributed 95 of its faculty members to Washington.

[...]

We rented our house for the summer. It's a dreadful thing for the whole family to leave it. For the first time in my life, I look forward to the future with dismay.

As ever,
Malcolm

[NL TLS-1]
[TO: ARCHIBALD MACLEISH]
Office of Facts and Figures, Washington
January 21, 1942

Dear Archie:

Here is a brief statement that I would like to get on the record, if the defendant has any right to be heard.

I am not and have never been a Communist. I do not believe in the Russian system of government, or in any other system except our own. I have no connection with any organization whatsoever in which there are Communist members. I have been frequently and bitterly attacked in the Communist press.

Since Hitler came to power in 1933, I have felt that a clash was inevitable between the Nazi system and the democratic system. Almost everything I have written about politics since then—and a great deal of what I have written about books, as a literary editor—has been devoted to warning the American public about the need for resisting Hitler's plans. Most of the prophecies I made have come true.

As long as the Communists seemed to be Hitler's most active enemies, I was willing to cooperate with them. This cooperation ceased immediately after the Russo-German Pact of August, 1939. It has not been and will not be renewed.

By politics I am a democrat with a small "d" and an American with a big "A." There is no use being afraid of words in times like these, so let me use some plain ones. I was born in this country, I love this country, and I will do anything that one man can do to defend it. I would like to serve in the army, as I did in the last war. But since the doctors wouldn't pass me any longer, I want to serve this country by any means within my power. That is the one reason I am here.

As ever,
Malcolm

Dear Archie:

The story about me in the February 16 issue of *Time* starts out with a misstatement of fact in the first line. "Most inopportune book of the month is *The Dry Season* . . ." *The Dry Season* is not a book of the month or even a book of the year; it was published on December 10, 1941. *Time* used to have an ironclad rule against reviewing books more than a week old, but the rule has either been abolished or else it can be broken when it is a question of making a political or personal attack.

To call me "chief information analyst" is not a misstatement of fact, but it certainly leads to a misapprehension. "Chief information analyst" is—as you know better than I—merely a civil-service rating. My job here is exactly the sort of work I have always done—writing, rewriting, handling copy. I ought to know how to do it. I've been at it for twenty-three years.

The *Time* story deals with two poems, one written in 1935 and the other in 1937. By shamelessly taking lines out of their context, it makes both poems mean exactly what they do not mean when read as a whole.

Thus, "The Last International" (1935) is a poem about all the millions of people who died in the unsuccessful revolutions that followed the First World War. It describes a nightmare, a fantastic parade of the dead of all nations—some of whom had been beheaded, some bayoneted, some burned at the stake, while others had been—

> Shot down in Florisdorf or Chapei Road
> And now released from prison graveyards piled
> So high with sorrows that they overflowed.

The scene of the poem might be Paris, with its boulevards and iron-shuttered windows; it might be Berlin or Vienna, Budapest or Shanghai (the fact happens to be that I wrote the poem after reading Malraux's novel, *Man's Fate,* about the Shanghai rebellion of 1927). The scene could not be the United States. Thank God, there hasn't been a revolution here, or the sacrifice of millions of lives. No blood has flowed, only printer's ink.

"Tomorrow Morning" is obviously a poem about the civil war in Spain—that explains "the Central Committee" and "the labor unions." But in terms of the Spanish civil war I was trying to say something about the frantic and fanatical preoccupation with the future that has cost so many thousands of lives all over the world. "Remember us," the poem says—and the "us" obviously does not apply to Americans—

> ... remember us who died
> At Badajoz, like beasts in the arena,
> At Canton, cornered in an alleyway.

"Tomorrow Morning" is not even a political poem, let alone being a revolutionary poem. It is a lament for those who died in vain.

That is the truth of the matter. It is only by desperate juggling on the part of *Time's* editors that two poems can be torn from a book, that half a dozen lines can be torn from their context in the two poems and given a political meaning they do not possess, and that the whole discussion can be moved seventy-five pages forward in the magazine from the book-review section, where it belongs, to the Washington section—where, presumably, it must be proved that the country is in danger of being overthrown by a rabble of poets and literary editors.[24]

The country is in the gravest danger but from without. Its greatest internal danger is from the people of any political party who want to make it less united and therefore less able to defeat the Axis.[25]

As ever,
Malcolm

[NL TL/CC-3]
[TO: GEORGE J. GOULD, CHIEF OF INVESTIGATIONS,
OFFICE OF EMERGENCY MANAGEMENT]
2116 Kalorama Road, NW.,
Washington, D.C.,
February 18, 1942

Dear Mr. Gould:

I am very glad to follow your suggestion and write you a letter about the points that were not cleared up in a very long and fair examination.[26] The record ought to be complete.

For twelve years before last December, I worked for *The New Republic,* during most of that time as literary editor and chief book reviewer. That is not a position of great prestige in the world at large, but it carries weight in the smaller world of writers and English teachers. A literary editor, if he says what he thinks—and that is his job, after all—makes friends and enemies. He is likely to get involved in literary quarrels which, during the 1930s, were no less bitter than political quarrels. I tried to steer clear of them, and usually with success, but not always.

And *The New Republic,* too, was a journal of opinion that had its enemies. In the editorial section, with which I had very little to do, it attacked at various times the conservatives in Congress, the Dies Committee, J. Edgar Hoover, the isolationists, Hearst, the *Chicago Tribune;* it supported the New Deal. My appointment was a convenient occasion for getting back at it.

Mr. J. B. Matthews, chief investigator for the Dies Committee, has been severely condemned in *The New Republic* and has answered by making violent and unjustified attacks on the magazine; I remember that in 1936 or 1937 we were on the point of bringing a libel suit against him as a result of the false statements he was making in speeches. I had known Matthews some years before, in the days when he called himself a Revolutionary Socialist and was making wild speeches calling for the overthrow of capitalism, to one of which speeches I listened with disapproval. Matthews is said to bear a special grudge against anyone who knew him in those days. Considering the number of charges he has brought against government officials, and the amount of generally useless work he has forced government investigatory agencies to undertake, he might himself be the subject of an investigation. A good way to begin it would be by reading his book, *The Odyssey of a Fellow Traveler,* which does not leave the impression that he is a man of judgment or emotional balance.

Internal evidence—and some external evidence as well—makes it clear that Westbrook Pegler's attacks on me were written on the basis of material furnished to him by the Dies Committee, and presumably by Matthews. Much of this material was inaccurate—for example the statement that I had been on the staff of the *Daily Worker*—and some of it was clearly libelous.[27]

I mention these personal matters only because you asked about them; I have never liked to deal in personalities, and this is a time when they should be put wholly aside. The Cowley affair has already consumed far too much of the government's time, and too much of my time as a government employee. But in one sense it is becoming a question of more than personal interest.

By now the issues involved should be clear enough. The character investigation has not, to the best of my knowledge, revealed anything damaging to my character. Neither has it revealed that I ever called or hoped for the overthrow of the United States Government, or ever belonged to the Communist Party, or ever permitted it to do my thinking for me. It has revealed, on the other hand, that I belonged at various times in the 1930s to a number of organizations that had Communist members, and that I allowed my name to be used by many others to which I did not belong. It has also revealed that I resigned or dropped out of all such organizations, that I stopped allowing them to use my name in any way, and that ever since the war began in Europe I have been violently condemned by the Communists as an American patriot, something I had never ceased to be.

All these facts should by now be beyond dispute. A writer for a weekly magazine doesn't lead much of a private life; all the information about him is on record. An investigation of Malcolm Cowley yields about as startling results as the investigation of a billboard.

The question that remains is whether a man devoted to this nation should be judged unfit—by character—to serve the government because he once belonged to certain organizations and signed certain documents expressing views more radical than those of the two principal political parties. It is a question that goes far beyond my own case, since there are thousands of people, many of them able, distinguished and patriotic, who once belonged to the same organizations and signed the same documents. Should they be barred from government service on account of their past opinions?

Two more points might be mentioned. *The New Republic* for the last twenty months has been one of the strongest and most consistent supporters of the President's foreign policies. Among the editors, I was the first to support that policy; I have argued for it ever since the President's Chicago speech in 1937, and even before then. During the first six months of the war, I had a good many disputes with the other editors, until they swung round to my position after the fall of France. At present, considering the source and the nature of the attacks on me, I feel that I am being heavily penalized for having shown too much foresight and too much concern for the fate of my country.

The final point is one that I hesitate to bring up, because it is personal, but nevertheless it had better go into the record. For the last six weeks, I have been the subject of several unfair and vicious attacks, and my position has made it impossible for me to answer them. I have been accused of being a Communist, a Godless revolutionist, and of seeking to undermine the government and nation I hope to serve. As a writer, an editor and a lecturer, I have always had to depend on my relations with the public to earn a living. If it were now decided that my record made me unfit to be a government employee, the decision would have the effect of confirming—by implication—these false and unjustified attacks against me. It would make it very difficult for me to sell articles, get lecture dates or find an editorial job. It would mean that I and my family were paying a heavy price indeed for wishing to serve the government during its worst emergency.

I hope that all these matters will be taken into account.

Sincerely,
Malcolm Cowley

[NL TL/CC-3]
[TO: LOUIS S. WEISS][28]
2116 Kalorama Road, NW.,
Washington, D.C.,
February 22, 1942

Dear Mr. Weiss:

I am writing you at the urgent suggestion of our friend Max Lowen-thal,[29] who thought you would be interested in my story.

On November 24, I went to work in Washington for Archibald Mac-Leish, in his new Office of Facts and Figures. I was leaving the very good job that I had held for twelve years as associate editor of *The New Republic*, but I was eager to work for my country in what I already foresaw would be its worst crisis. I hadn't asked for a place with MacLeish; the offer came from him. I didn't know what my new salary would be until I received my first pay check on December 30; then I found that I was to get $8,000 a year, which seemed very generous, but not out of line with what I had been receiving in New York.

I foresaw that there would be opposition to my appointment, on account of the fact that I had joined many United Front organizations during the 1930s. MacLeish knew my record and was prepared to back me up, for he also knew that I had supported the President in his foreign policies and had been violently attacked by the Communists.

Everything went well enough at first. The work was the sort of work I had always been used to doing; I was enthusiastic about it, even if I didn't like living in what is now the most uncomfortable city in the western world. About December 20, the FBI started the investigation that it makes in the case of every new government employee. I knew I would be subject to special attention, but I wasn't greatly worried.

Then on January 13 the storm broke. Representatives Ford of California and Hoffman of Michigan attacked me in the House. First the *Journal-American* carried a long story about me, then the other New York papers followed. On Wednesday the *Journal-American* carried an account of a speech against me by Martin Dies, which actually wasn't delivered until Thursday the 15. It was full of false implications. Shortly afterwards Westbrook Pegler chimed in, making statements that by this time were clearly libelous—but my position made it impossible for me to answer them, let alone bringing suit against him.

And now the FBI redoubled its efforts; it really went to town on me. They visited everyone who they thought would know me, including many people who knew me only slightly or not at all. I should hesitate to compute the cost of this investigation in terms of man-hours, money, tires and type-writer ribbons. One of their great achievements was to track down, after an intensive search lasting for three weeks, my first wife, from whom I was divorced in 1931.

By the many accounts that have reached me, the FBI agents were unfailingly polite and completely uninformed about all the matters they were supposed to be investigating. One of them, on being told that I had supported collective security, revealed by his remarks that he believed it was a form of collectivism, and hence next door to revolutionary communism. People who didn't know me must have been left with the impression that I was some sort of dangerous criminal who was being tracked to earth by a manhunt scarcely smaller than that for John Dillinger. This was especially true in Sherman, Conn., the farming village where I have spent the last five years; my neighbors there were disturbed and astounded.

I realize fully that in peacetime and above all in wartime, every employee of the United States Government must be entirely loyal. I realize that investigations are necessary in any doubtful cases. What disturbs me is the nature and the extent of this investigation, carried on at a time when our ships and warehouses are insufficiently protected against sabotage;—and carried on not only in the case of Malcolm Cowley, but in hundreds of others. The agents seem to have curious misconceptions about whom we are fighting.

My own record is public. The editor of a weekly magazine has very little private life; everything he believes is written and printed. All the pertinent facts about me could be discovered in the course of two visits to the Library of Congress. [...]

Yet for two months, I have been the subject [of] an opinion hunt carried on like the search for a desperate criminal. My reputation has been damaged, and since a writer has to depend on his reputation for earning a livelihood, my whole future has been compromised. My work for the government has been interfered with and my efficiency lowered. I have spent many sleepless nights worrying not about myself—I can take it—but about my wife and child; how I will provide for them if I lose my job here and what sort of slurs and insults they will have to suffer. This is a high price to pay for wishing to serve my country in its greatest emergency.

Of course the attack and the investigation are part of a general campaign against liberals in the government. The more I can be made to suffer, the more embarrassing the situation will be for MacLeish and eventually for the President. Already most of the government agencies are afraid to hire the people they want and need—either they would refuse to come, or else Mr. Dies and the FBI would get on their trail. And if I get forced out, the situation will be still worse.

[. . .] Anything you can do will be deeply appreciated.[30]

Sincerely yours,
Malcolm Cowley

[NL TL/CC-3]
[TO: GEORGE J. GOULD]
2116 Kalorama Road, NW.,
Washington, D.C.,
March 3, 1942

Dear Mr. Gould:

It isn't any wonder that the reports about me were conflicting. As I tried to explain, my job as literary editor of *The New Republic* was one that involved me in several quarrels, literary and political, even though I tried hard to keep out of them. You have now heard the two sides of these quarrels. I think you will find that, without exception, the favorable reports on me were made by people who knew me and had worked with me. The unfavorable reports were made by people who knew me slightly or not at all, and I do not think it fair to accept their judgment.

As for the quarrels themselves, they go back to that crazy winter of 1932–33, when the country was at the bottom of the depression, when the nation as a whole was deeply disturbed and when all sorts of movements were under way—Technocracy, the hunger-march, self-liquidating money, the Townsend Plan, to mention only a few. The League of Professional Groups was one of these.

I belonged to it; so did Sidney Hook, Herbert Solow, Felix Morrow, James Rorty and others. These gentlemen were just on the point of being converted to Trotskyism, this being a long time before any of them had heard about democracy. Politically naïve at the time, I didn't know what was happening to them, but I did know that something strange was happening to the League—one week it was doing interesting work; the next week, and all the weeks that followed, its meetings were devoted to wrangling over abstruse and distant subjects like the failure of the 1927 revolution in China. I became angry and made a hot speech that kept the Trotskyites from getting control of the League. A short time afterwards the organization was disbanded—but it seems to live on in their memories. They had every right to be angry with me, but no right at all to invent slanders. To say that I transmitted or acted on orders from the Communist Party is a malicious falsehood.

A second item in their story has to do with the League of American Writers, founded in 1935. Here again they have me acting on Communist instructions—but at this point the whole business begins to be fantastic. How I ever got time to receive Communist instructions, let alone act on them, is a puzzle I am completely unable to solve.

In September, 1936, I had moved to the country, being tired of New York literary life and glad to get out of it. My job meant that I was in the city three days a week. [. . .] When in the name of all that is reasonable would I have gotten time to consult with Communists? At the office, under Bruce Bliven's eagle eye? It's preposterous. Back in the country for four days, I read the week's books, I wrote a review, sweating over it, I gardened, I fished in the spring and hunted in the fall, I occasionally spent an evening with my neighbors. I saw nobody who talked radical politics. I was thoroughly disillusioned with politics.

No, at the time I did not publicly condemn the Communists. I was very skeptical about them—as I find once more by reading old entries in my notebooks—but on the other hand I was desperately worried about the rise of fascism in Europe. It seemed to me that the democratic powers would have no chance of defeating Hitler in the war that was already inevitable unless they rallied all the available forces on their side—and all the available forces included Soviet Russia. Therefore I did not attack Soviet Russia, as Hook, Stolberg and Eugene Lyons were doing; I wanted this country to be on good terms with it. But when occasion offered, in the *New Republic* book department, I tried to say exactly what I thought about it, good and bad.

The bad thoughts definitely outweighed the good ones after the Russo-German Pact of 1939 (though even then I continued to believe that Russia and Germany would eventually fight each other). I didn't rush into print saying, oh, how terrible. By that time I was convinced that professional literary men had done a great deal too much rushing into print and saying, oh, how terrible. It was time for me to stick to my own job of writing about books; time to do a lot of thinking and not make solemn pronouncements. Nevertheless I tried to make my position absolutely clear, as is abundantly shown in some of the attached clippings and quotations.

One of the most outrageous slanders I now have a faint chance to answer is that I merely played along with the other editors of *The New Republic* because I was afraid of my economic position. The truth is absolutely the opposite. The other editors of *The New Republic* were at that time mildly isolationist. I argued with and opposed them. I told them that if Great Britain was defeated, the United States would be exposed to attack, and would have no allies. I told them that the Atlantic Ocean, if we ceased to control it, would not be a bulwark but merely a highway for invasion. I was only the literary editor, and I was overruled. But after the fall of France, the other editors came round to my position.

I was the war-monger on *The New Republic* in those days when the Communists were calling for peace at any price. That is why they attacked me so bitterly. As for defending my economic position, by now you should have discovered that I have a positive genius for acting against my own economic interests. I have always tried to say exactly what I thought, no matter what it cost me. And my one purpose during the course of these examinations has been to make the record clear.

[. . .] For the rest, let me close this letter by saying as simply as possible what I believe—what the political convictions have been at the basis of my writing:

I believe in rule by the people, under the American system of government.

I believe that our system has its faults, like everything devised by men, but I do not believe that it has any deep defects which cannot be remedied peaceably, by action under the law.

I believe—at the risk of sounding old-fashioned—that Christ's teachings are more profound than Lenin's or Hitler's.

I believe that democracy and Christianity are now more gravely threatened than ever before in our history.

I believe that in order to defend our democracy, we shall have to call on all our resources as a nation—all our materials, all our money, all our men and women of all political parties, liberal or conservative, so long as they are good Americans.

I believe that in this crisis we have to be a united nation. We have to stop wrangling; we have to obey orders, and I stand ready to obey them, at any cost to myself.

Sincerely yours,
Malcolm Cowley

[NL TL/CC-2]
[TO: ARCHIBALD MACLEISH]
[Washington] March 12, 1942

Dear Archie:

With deep regret, I am submitting my resignation from the Office of Facts and Figures, but first I should like to tell you the whole story.

As you know, I accepted your very kind offer of a position here for one reason and one reason only—because I wanted to do what I could for my country in the crisis. I wasn't looking for a job; I had a good one already. I wasn't seeking to advance any political ideas whatever, except the simple idea that this nation has to stand united to win the war, and has to defeat Hitler and Hitlerism in order to survive.

For the first six weeks, I was able to work without interruptions. Since the middle of January, however, I have been subjected to one of those campaigns of abuse that are frequently waged against government employees.

During the course of it, I learned things about my past that nobody had ever known, and least of all myself. I learned that I had belonged to organizations whose names I had forgotten or had never heard. I learned that I had been on the staff of the *Daily Worker* and the *Sunday Worker,* which must have been news to both those publications. I even learned that I was charged with being disloyal to the nation and the government for which I had fought a war and which I had always served to the best of my powers.

Every new government employee is thoroughly investigated, a necessary precaution in wartime. Until these attacks began, the investigation of my own case had proceeded along the normal lines, but I now learned by reports from friends that it was assuming fantastic proportions. Everybody who knew me well and dozens of people who knew me slightly or not at all were asked whether they were sure I wasn't subversive. Strangers must have received the impression that I was a dangerous criminal who was being tracked down by a manhunt scarcely less intensive or expensive than the search for John Dillinger.

It would be hard to estimate the amount of rubber and gasoline, of money and precious man-hours, that was consumed in this search for past opinions, carried on at a time when the country was in real danger from other people than literary editors. The truth is that all the pertinent facts about me could have been found by reading the files of *The New Republic.* A writer for a weekly magazine hasn't much chance to lead a private life; all his opinions go on record. An investigation of his career will yield—and in my case has yielded—about the same sensational results as investigating a billboard.

I apologize for talking about personal affairs when the country has bigger problems. But my story is only an extreme example of what has happened already to hundreds of government employees. They are exposed not only to criticisms of their official conduct, which are always justifiable, but also to irresponsible attacks on their personal lives, which they have no fair opportunity to answer. Often they are investigated in a fashion that interferes with their work and inflicts lasting damage on their reputations, even if they are innocent of any offense. Their whole careers may be compromised, and under the present arrangements they have no redress whatever.

In ordinary times, I should insist on staying here until the truth of my own case was established and put before the public—the simple truth that I have acted and written at all times as an American devoted to the interests of his country; that I foresaw the conflict in which we are now engaged and warned people to prepare for it; that for this reason I was roundly abused by the Communists as a war-monger, an imperialist, an agent for Wall Street interests and a tool of J. P. Morgan. All this would be easy to prove from the records.

But in times like these, no personal aims or interests or sense of having suffered injustice can be set in the balance for one moment against the possibility that these attacks on one member of your organization might embarrass or impede the Office of Facts and Figures in the wartime work it has been called to do. Nothing that happens to private individuals is of great importance in these times. Nothing matters to all of us but winning the war.

With the highest respect for yourself and the work you are doing for the government, and with deep regret that I cannot continue to serve under you, I am therefore taking this opportunity to withdraw.

Sincerely,
Malcolm Cowley

Retrenchment and Rehabilitation, 1942–1944

For a time Cowley fought on to clear his name and record, but on April 1, 1942, he was back on *The New Republic,* not in his former editorial capacity, but as the writer of a weekly book page. By May 1942 he was preoccupied with literary matters and taking pleasures in the distractions of country life—planting trees, growing melons. In his correspondence he now frankly owned up to his failure to publicly acknowledge the doubts and reservations about Communism he had had since 1938, but he remained convinced that "honest love of literature still exists and can still be honestly expressed."

Through the war Cowley remained deeply concerned with the fate of European writers in exile and with French writers under German occupation. For *Life* he translated an anonymous manuscript (written, he later learned, by his friend Louis Aragon) on the execution of twenty-seven hostages in a camp for political prisoners in Brittany ("They Died for France" appeared in *Life* on May 25, 1942). Cowley donated half of the money he received ($200) to the Exiled Writers' Committee. On the home front, he took to heart the case of James Thurber, sunk in despondency over his advancing blindness, and asked Elmer Davis, the new head of the Office of War Information, to buck Thurber up by enlisting Thurber's advice. Cowley recurrently sought reprieve at Yaddo, where, among other tasks, he worked on translating the wartime poems of Louis Aragon. In the fall and winter of 1943 at Yaddo, he associated with Newton Arvin, Katherine Anne Porter, and Carson McCullers and met with an assortment of European and American writers— among them Agnes Smedley, Langston Hughes, and Alfred Kantorowicz, a German writer-in-exile whose work he subsequently brought to the attention of the Scribner's editor Maxwell Perkins. He also corresponded with Weldon Kees, whom he regarded as one of the most promising younger poets, and Randall Jarrell, who (like Nathan Asch) was soon to serve in the U.S. air force, where he would write some of his most memorable poems.

Hidden away in his "Hermit Kingdom" in Sherman, Cowley slowly became reconciled to having largely abandoned public life. In the newspapers he closely followed the tragedy of war in Europe and Asia, but literature was now his principal concern. He took an active role in the large-scale revaluation of the 1920s that gained momentum in the 1940s, but he also looked forward to the arrival on the postwar scene of a new literary generation. In April 1944 he published in *The New Yorker* a two-part profile of Maxwell Perkins, and he used his connection to Perkins to promote the stories of John Cheever. He consulted Perkins about William Faulkner, whom Perkins believed to have "fallen into a certain position which is not nearly as high as it should be." And, Perkins thought, "once that happens to a writer, it is extremely difficult to change the public's opinion" (Perkins to Cowley, January 31, 1944 [NL]). It was the spark that set Cowley on his quest to bring Faulkner's reputation in line with his achievements, a critical endeavor that culminated in *The Portable Faulkner* (1946).

The Cowleys spent the winter of 1943–1944 in New York City, sharing an apartment with Bob and Elsa Coates at 255 East Seventy-Second Street, directly above Alexander and Louisa Calder. During this period Cowley often did his writing at the New York Society Library on Seventy-Ninth

Street. It was a productive time, and he wrote on a wide variety of topics, but his weekly book page for *The New Republic* left little time and energy for the bigger project he was now eager to undertake. In March 1944 he signed a contract with Doubleday, Doran for a one-volume history of American literature. "There is so much that can be done that I begin to feel like Dan'l Boone crossing Cumberland Gap."

[NL TL/CC-4]

[TO: DOROTHY DUDLEY HARVEY][31]

May 29, 1942

Dear Miss Dudley:

I was very sorry when you stopped reviewing for *The New Republic,* on account of what I think was a misapprehension. [. . .]

I have heard several echoes of your fulminations against me in those days, and I'd like to set the record straight. My feelings about Russia in 1938 were almost the same as they are today (which isn't to say that they didn't change in the interim). By 1938 I had lost whatever faith I once had in Communism as a church—"church" being the key word here, for it is the religious attitude inspired by Communism that explains the strength of the sympathies and antipathies it arouses. My faith in it could never have been very strong, or I would have joined the church—but no, that isn't the way to put it; let's say that the faith was strong and the doubt was strong too, so that I preferred to stay outside. The doubts were stronger and the faith weaker in 1938, for the obvious reasons. But still, I had been involved in so many battles with the Trotskyites and disturbed some of them so much that I couldn't follow their example. Accordingly what I did was nothing at all. I worked for *The New Republic* three days a week. In the country I tended my garden—I mean literally, not metaphorically; if you ever saw our place here you'd know what I had been doing for the last five years.

Well, doing nothing was my mistake. Instead of waiting, I should have made a clean break. I didn't realize that as long as I said nothing, the Communists would continue using me as a name, a front, a symbol, or that anti-Communists would think there was some reality behind the symbol. One of the ex-Trotskyists later told the FBI, as I learned in Washington, that I had been "the chief representative of Stalinism among American writers" and "the sinister force behind the League of American Writers."[32] All this time the "sinister force," the "chief representative" was hoeing potatoes and thinking he was well out of it all. I didn't discover until a long time afterwards that it wasn't so easy to get out of it all.

There was, of course, another reason why I didn't speak up at the time. In 1938 I already felt strongly that as a military power the USSR was indispensable to the Western world; that without it we were certain to be licked by Hitler. It seems to me now—though maybe I'm flattering myself—that I had a foresight or forefeeling of Munich and the Russo-German pact. No matter how much I disapproved of what was going on in Russia, I didn't want to launch out into any attacks when I felt that Hitler was the enemy and that we would be needing Stalin's help. And I did manage to say what I thought in reviewing the last big Moscow trials, but apparently nobody paid any attention to my qualifications. I wrote two articles on those third trials; in one I said that I thought the defendants were probably guilty; in the second article, I said that their guilt made it seem that things must be pretty bad in Russia. Months later Eugene Lyons printed a violent attack on me for the first article; he said or implied that I was a paid and dishonest apologist. He never even mentioned the second article.

That's the story, or part of the story. The question is how all of us who started out from the same point and had for a long time pretty much the same judgment of events, managed to reach such different destinations. Personally I felt from 1937 or 38 that something very deep had gone wrong—that the Russian Party was probably right in all its minor decisions but wrong in its fundamental picture of human life—that the Trotskyites were even more mistaken and would have made a worse mess of things if they had been in power. The mistake lay partly in intellectual pride, which made the Communist leaders blind to their own faults and capable of finding texts in Lenin and Marx to justify their self-interest; and partly it lay in the willingness to sacrifice people to principles (and principles to tactics—"the end justifies"). Communism as a system of ethics led straight to the trials, the purges, the lies about people who had fallen out of favor. But the anti-Stalinists were no better—they had their own lies and purges and their intellectual pride towering far above that of the Stalinists. (And my feeling of 1938 was confirmed later, when I found that two or three of the anti-Stalinists were cooperating with the Dies Committee and telling outrageous lies about me to the FBI. I feel as if I'd been a victim of the Moscow trials without ever having seen Moscow.)

Something has happened that we haven't yet had the imagination to comprehend, some vast defeat for an ideal of life, something that has to be expressed in terms of drama rather than logic. The best book I ever read on it was Arthur Koestler's *Darkness at Noon,* though there are hints of it in several autobiographies I have been reading, and in the strange story of General Krivitsky, who started as an honest revolutionist, who found himself being ordered to do more and more things that he revolted against, but justified himself by the doctrine of "state responsibility," who finally lost faith in the state for which he had sacrificed his integrity, and was left with nothing at all; and who in his last letter to his wife counseled her not to trust the enemies of the Soviet Union, "they won't do anything for you." Again, I think it was all summed up by a refugee,[33] an ex-Communist who had been telling me the story of his life, and then said after a long silence, "We are broken men; the best of our generation are dead. *Nous sommes des survivants.*"

All this, written for myself as much as for you, is a long way from our disagreement of—was it?—1938 at *The New Republic.* I liked your writing and thought you had something fresh to say, but I thought you were getting a fixation against Stalin, so that if you had at that time been reviewing "The House That Jack Built," you might have started out by proving that Stalin was the rat that ate the malt that lay in the house that Jack built. I wanted you to write for us, but write about something else (just as I had gotten sick and tired of the opposite sort of reviews—or rather the opposite side of the same sort—which proved that Trotsky was the rat). Well, that's a long time ago now, and I hope you'll write for the NR and prove that anybody is a rat, but preferably that honest love of literature still exists and can still be honestly expressed.

Sincerely yours,
Malcolm Cowley

[NL TL/CC-1]
[TO: ELMER DAVIS, OFFICE OF WAR INFORMATION]
June 16, 1942

Dear Mr. Davis:

I hope you can find or seize or invent time in the midst of your new job to write a letter that would do a lot of good.

Jim Thurber, as you know, is now practically blind and there is very little hope that he will ever recover his sight. He is becoming more and more despondent and has begun to talk a lot about suicide. The real trouble is that he hasn't enough to occupy his mind.

Could you write him—without saying that the suggestion came from me or anybody else—and ask him whether he has any suggestions about the sort of propaganda we ought to be feeding the French and the Germans?

That would help to restore his self-importance and keep his mind busy. But I wouldn't be suggesting it unless I thought that he would have some valuable ideas to offer. He has a damned good head on him, besides being a better writer than most people realize when they set him down as a humorist. [...]

Everybody was delighted to hear about your appointment. But nobody envies you—realizing what a tough job you are going to have.[34]

Sincerely yours,
Malcolm Cowley

[ARVIN TLS-1]
[TO: NEWTON ARVIN]
February 6, 1943

Dear Newton:

[...]

Sherman, Connecticut, is empty this winter—the Josephsons, the Coateses and the Blumes all in New York; in fact there has been a great movement into New York of all the people who are accustomed to work in the country during the winter, with the result that New York seems, during my brief visits there, much gayer than it has been since the 1920s; lunches and cocktails and dinners and gossip. I come back here, write my piece for *The New Republic,* sweating it out word by word, and listen to the radio, which these days seems equally divided between marvelous news from the Russian front and utterly dispiriting news from Washington. We are in the middle of a vast reaction here (or are we only at the beginning?) and I don't know how far it will carry us. Congress is bent on wiping out the New Deal, the executive agencies are threatened, and like willow trees (for there is no hickory in the executive forest) they are bending before the storm; and Congressman Martin Dies of Orange, Texas, is being used by Congress in the same spirit that a respectable business man hires a goon squad. The only hope, of course, is that the Russian successes will provoke a reaction against reaction, but that is a faint hope, considering that liberal periods almost always fail to coincide from nation to nation (note how the French Popular Front was dead and gone before the English began to be liberal) and what we might have is a great international rivalry, leading eventually to war, between U.S. and USSR.

The German refugees are bitter and disconsolate. [. . .] I talked to Paul Massing,[35] one of the most intelligent. He said, "we have lost the war. I wanted to become an American citizen, but I have changed my mind about that, and as soon as Hitler falls I'm going back to Germany, because there is more hope there."

[. . .]

As ever,
Malcolm

———

[WK TLS-1]
[TO: WELDON KEES][36]
February 6, 1943

Dear Weldon:

I'm tickled to death with the dedication of the poem ["Girl at Midnight"], which I like very much, except for one line, "Upon my breasts, again, again, again, again," which sounds like putting four loaves of bread into the oven; maybe I merely envy the lustiness of that feat. But the whole atmosphere of the poem is fine and true. [. . .]

I had a sweet time at Yaddo, mostly long talks with Newton Arvin, Katherine Anne and Carson McCullers. Nathan Asch is now in Miami at an air force school and loving it. He says that the tough guys who liked the army during the last war, or rather their sons, hate the army now, whereas all the Greenwich Village bums are enthusiastic about it. In fact, the army is now the only refuge from the disappointments of civilian life, where everything is moving faster and faster toward utter reaction that may go God knows how far. When Mr. Hitler came into power, he had to fire only three percent of the German bureaucrats; the others went along with him. An American Hitler might have to fire as many as five percent of the bureaucrats in Washington, and might have to put as many as thirty congressmen in a concentration camp. [...]

As ever,
Malcolm

[NL TL/CC-I]
[TO: ARCHIBALD MACLEISH]
February 17, 1943

Dear Archie:

Your plans for the Jefferson Bicentennial sound extremely interesting, and I feel honored by the invitation to join in the morning discussion.[37] [...]

Everything is very quiet on the Connecticut front; in fact we are snowed in, if that isn't a military secret. . . . I took a pretty bad financial licking in Washington, and somewhat of a moral licking too, so that I retired into a state of estivation last summer, something like a bear's hibernation—but then in the fall I got back to work. Maybe it's very fortunate for literature that writers as a class are kept out of official life and maintained as another oppressed minority. Literature has to keep retiring into the catacombs to rediscover itself. If only human liberty isn't sent to the catacombs too.

As ever,
Malcolm

[NY TLS-I]
[TO: WILLIAM SHAWN, *THE NEW YORKER*]
April 8, 1943

Dear Mr. Shawn:

I just finished a pretty careful first draft of the Perkins piece. [. . .] Perkins, I discovered, is the nearest thing to a great man now existing in the literary world. Legends are clustered around him like truffles round an oak tree in Gascony. Scribner's when he went to work there was a fantastic publishing house, with an atmosphere like Queen Victoria's parlor. The story of Perkins and Wolfe is pretty touching. And when I put all this into the piece, it turned into a regular behemoth, yes'm. About twelve thousand words in the first draft. I'm going to pare about three thousand words out of it—howling with pain like Thomas Wolfe when Perkins amputated one of his chapters—and then send you the remaining nine-thousand odd, with the prayer that maybe it could be turned into a double-decker profile. If not, we can sharpen up our blue pencils and go to work—but Perkins is really a very important guy, even if he likes to stay in the background like a gray eminence.

Sincerely,
Malcolm Cowley

[RJ TLS-I]
[TO: RANDALL JARRELL]
June 15, 1943

Dear Mr. Jarrell,

I like these poems, though I don't agree by a damned sight with their sentiments. They sound too much as if they were striking the simple equation, we equal they—or, there, but for the accident of birth, go all of us. This war isn't being fought for marbles or foreign trade, though there are plenty of people here who would like to make it that kind of war.[38] But I'm not inclined to worry about the ideology of poems, and I'd take both of these if I were buying verse for *The New Republic*. I'm not, as you could see by a lot of the verse we've been printing. And the verse buyers are more worried about ideology than I am, and wouldn't take them. Regrets.

It looks as if you were in the air service. [...] There seem to be hardly any young men in New York, except fairies, who are now exempt from service— homosexuality being treated as a disease on exactly the same level as asthma, stomach ulcers, nervous breakdown and severe sinus trouble. That provides a simple method of keeping out of uniform, and I wonder that more people haven't taken it. Back in the last war, Hans Arp[39] got himself exempted from the German army by writing his age, height, weight and date of birth, and then adding up the column of figures. The doctors diagnosed dementia precox. But it's easier in New York this time—all the prospective soldier has to do is to wave a loose wrist. I think I'd prefer army to civilian life these days, considering the vast muddle of civilian affairs—but 45 years and partial deafness keep me at home cultivating the garden.

Cordially,
Malcolm Cowley

[KB TLS-2] [SC 257–258]
[TO: KENNETH BURKE]
September 5, 1943

Dear Kenneth:

[...]

I listen to the radio and read the *Times* all the way through as usual, and get bluer and blacker about the next few years. We're certainly fixing to have a nice little war with Russia, besides planning to restore capitalism in Europe. Some things were mighty funny when I was in Washington last year, and one of them was that although most people in government service agreed that we ought to state our war aims, any suggestions to the Chief were disregarded by the Chief. Once, for example, I wrote a radio address that Mr. Big was to deliver by shortwave to the common people of Germany and Italy, but nothing came of it. We also did a pamphlet on the Four Freedoms, and there seemed to be one objection after another to having it published. Finally it came out, in a very innocuous form, eight months after it had been written. I feel now that the war in Europe could be over by Christmas if we laid down a sensible political program, and I sometimes feel that the big people know it could be over by Christmas and don't want it to end—not while the Red Army is still a going concern. Of course their big nightmare is that the Red Army will lick the Germans all by itself. If it crosses the Dnieper line, we'll have a second front PDQ, but not to help the Russians; just to keep them out of Berlin.

[...]

As ever,
Malcolm

[SCRIBNER'S TLS-2]
[TO: MAXWELL PERKINS]
January 26, 1944

Dear Mr. Perkins:

[...]

About Tom Wolfe—When I said that the separation weighed on his conscience, I was referring to public evidence, i.e., the letter at the end of *You Can't Go Home Again,* which I understand was a revised version of the 130-page letter he sent you (but of course had nothing to do with that absolutely heartbreaking note he sent you from Seattle, which, when you showed it to me, left me speechless for several moments). It doesn't seem to me that that particular paragraph requires changes, but I'm taking care of your other suggestions in one way or another, and thank you very much for making them.

I have greatly enjoyed writing this piece about you,[40] since it gave me the opportunity of meeting you and finding that you were a man with more devoted and admiring friends, all nice people, too, than anybody else I have known. But since I'm a critic (though not in this profile) I could wish that you now had more authors of the stature of Hemingway and Wolfe and Fitzgerald, if they now exist or are coming up. Faulkner is one, and he isn't being well published at present. I also mentioned John Cheever, a younger man who is a natural writer, though I fear his ambitions are limited; he is another man who isn't being well published, and if you are interested at all in his work (especially his army stories and the possibility of a novel) I should be glad to talk to him again. . . . *The New Yorker* is getting my piece ready for the printer; I hope they're not cutting it all to hell or writing in cracks to make it a *New*

Yorker piece; fortunately they like you too, so there's not much to worry about.

Faithfully,
Malcolm Cowley

My ambition is to write a piece so smooth that reading it is like being launched in a canoe and floating down a mill race.

Cowley to William Shawn, February 28, 1944 [Scribner's]

[NL TL/CC-1]
[TO: WILLIAM SHAWN, *THE NEW YORKER*]
April 7, 1944

Dear Mr. Shawn:

I don't feel the Perkins profile is finished until I've written you a letter about it—a sort of love letter to *The New Yorker,* in a mild way.

[. . .] [T]he whole business of writing the profile was an education, especially in the value of first-hand facts. I had been getting into a rut, and sometimes into bad habits of writing, with my weekly *New Republic* pieces, and this was the biggest change possible. I think you sometimes went too far in editing the manuscript; there are places where I feel my original wording would have been better. But, God, I was glad to find an editor who thinks that words are worth fighting about and getting right. I'd rather argue about them, and get licked in the argument, than work for a paper where they simply don't care.

I've kicked around magazines for a long time, writing and editing, and though I have no complaints for myself, I have seen a lot of writers tromped on and their manuscripts treated like rough lumber in a glutted market. *The New Yorker* is only the second magazine I worked for where writers were given better than an even break. The other, you might be interested to know, was the old *Dial* when it was run in succession by Stuart Mitchell, Gilbert Seldes and Kenneth Burke. Marianne Moore would have liked to be good to writers too, but she didn't know how. It's interesting to me that these two magazines, so different in other respects—but both the best of their separate kinds—should have had this point in common.

Perkins' friends say that he mumbles about the profile, "Do I really dress in shabby and inconspicuous grays?" but is actually tickled to death. I felt like telling him that if *The New Yorker* said he dressed in shabby and inconspicuous grays, by God he dressed in shabby and inconspicuous grays, and no two ways about it. *Life* phoned in excitement and wanted me to do a profile for them. I don't know that I'll have time, and anyway Moe[41] comes first; I saw him last week, for a starter.

Just forget what I've said in this letter, but I'd feel bad if I hadn't said it.

Cordially,
Malcolm Cowley

[NL TL/CC-2]
[TO: FREDERICK J. HOFFMAN]
March 3, 1944

Dear Mr. Hoffman:

The questions you ask in your letter of January 25[42] are hard for me to answer, for the simple reason that the literary world has always been divided into groups and generations, which had different attitudes toward Freud as toward almost everything else.

In this country, the group or generation that read Freud with a sense of discovery was composed of the people who began publishing about 1910–11, during the so-called American renaissance and the revolt against the genteel tradition. His influence was very strong in the work of Sherwood Anderson, Waldo Frank, Floyd Dell, Susan Glaspell ("Suppressed Desires") and other writers born between 1880, let us say, and 1895. On the other hand, Freud's influence on the post-war or inter-war generation of writers (Hemingway, Dos Passos, Fitzgerald, Crane, etc.) was not strong at all. I remember that we used to call Floyd Dell "Freud Dell." For my own part, I didn't begin reading Freud until the late 1930s, and then it was his studies in religion that interested me, not the studies in sex.

Eugene O'Neill, born in 1888, is the archetype among the American creative writers influenced by Freud.

I remember that we younger people used to think that our Freud-obsessed elders were simply funny. They were obviously trying to get rid of inhibitions; they were puritans trying not to be puritan. We didn't have many inhibitions to start out with. We talked about psychoanalysts who were obvious fakes and mischief-makers—I remember one lady who made a specialty of breaking up marriages.

There was a second wave of interest in Freud beginning about 1930 and having several causes. First cause, there was an epidemic of nervous breakdowns about that time, and a lot of writers had to go to psychoanalysts—some of whom, they discovered, were serious, scholarly and able to effect cures. Second cause, the experiments of the Surrealists with unconscious or automatic writing. Third cause, the interest of some writers (notably Kenneth Burke) in symbolic criticism—to be more exact, the study of the symbols used by creative writers. Fourth cause or influence, the new English poets, notably Auden. This interest was kept in the background by the interest in Marx, but came to the front during the period of discouragement that followed the defeat of the Spanish republic.

In literature one can trace many indirect results of Freudianism in general. Perhaps the biggest result was the substitution, in fiction, of the interior monologue for direct comments by the author (compare *The Sound and the Fury* with *Barchester Towers* for the two extremes). Another result was the fantastic story or poem that is essentially a dream—Kafka being the archetype here. The opposite tendency to Freud was behaviorism, which was actually much stronger in most writers of the inter-war generation; there are few interior monologues and little fantasy in Hemingway, for example; he tells what people said and did and leaves us to infer their secret thoughts.

[...]

Sincerely yours,
Malcolm Cowley
[...]

[IS TLS-I] [NL TL/CC-I]
[TO: ISIDOR SCHNEIDER][43]
March 5, 1944

Dear Isidor:

If anyone should ride up on a bicycle and ask me, "Mr. Cowley, what do you think is the funniest piece you ever read?" I would answer just like a shot, "Joe Mitchell's piece, 'Fascism Comes to Black Ankle County,' published originally in *The New Yorker* and then in his book, *McSorley's Wonderful Saloon.*"

The second piece I'd mention is a long story by William Faulkner, who, when he isn't hypertragic, is a humorist such as hasn't lived since Mark Twain. It is "Spotted Ponies," originally printed in *Scribner's,* then used, with a few changes, as part of his last novel, *The Hamlet.* (Perhaps even funnier, though, is the scene of Uncle Bud and the three madams, in *Sanctuary.*)

The third piece I'd mention is by Erskine Caldwell and I forget the exact title, though I think you would find it in *Jackpot*; it may be called "Jasper and the Billygoat." There are other very funny pieces in that book, and very funny passages in *Tobacco Road.* . . . Note that all these three writers are Southerners. Backwoods humor, the sort I most enjoy, survives best in the South.

Sid Perelman is very good sometimes—best, I think, in the piece on remodeling a farmhouse, with two characters called Mibs (of the super-dirndl) and Evan (who polished his briar pipe against his nose). Again I forget the exact title. Otis Ferguson's[44] piece on the radio, "Nertz to Hertz," is very good in spots.

All these are contemporary pieces. I never found myself laughing very hard at our elder humorists (except sometimes Mark Twain), because humor changes from one generation to another. Jim Thurber on the dam that didn't burst (in *My Life and Hard Times*) seems infinitely funnier to me than the famous jumping frog. You're a pretty funny man yourself, when you talk or write about the old days in East Harlem. Wilson on the Three Limperary Cripples is the best piece of literary humor I remember.

[. . .]

As ever,
Malcolm

[NL TL/CC-3]

[TO: THOMAS B. COSTAIN, DOUBLEDAY, DORAN AND COMPANY]

March 17, 1944

Dear Mr. Costain:

Well, I have definitely decided to accept your proposal [. . .] and set to work on a short history of American literature. Before making up my mind, I talked at length to Van Wyck Brooks, who was enthusiastic and helpful, and to Matty Josephson, who gave me some sound advice. Then I went to the New York Public Library, where histories of American literature are grouped together on the open shelves. I found that there is a crying need for such a book as you suggested; all the existing one-volume histories are out of date— including Lewisohn's *Expression in America,* published in 1932, which was out of date before it was written; nevertheless it has had a pretty impressive sale. The two projects now under way are in many volumes—Brooks will be complete in six, about 1954; the Spiller-Thorp project, *Literary History of the United States* [. . .] will consist of ten books that would have to be printed in three or four volumes; it will be written chiefly by professors. Brooks does not contemplate writing a one-volume history. Kazin[45] is working on Blake. [. . .] In brief, we haven't any rivals to fear.

[. . .]

I would be writing a history of literature, not a *Kulturgeschichte,* like Parrington's or Curti's[46]—though I have great admiration for both these authors. Accordingly, I would emphasize the writers of *literary* importance, not the merely historical figures. I think that almost all our literary historians have failed to consider the importance of imagination as a literary quality, in their search for the representative; that's why they delight these days in running down Poe and Faulkner, to the profit of authors like Howells and Dos Passos, who have lots of representative ideas with which they can deal and thereby save themselves the difficult problem of talking about imaginative power, which can't be reduced to graphs and tables and tendencies.

I want to pay more attention than other critics to Continental influences on American literature. It seems to me that in our best periods and authors, the Continental influence was strongest; in our worst periods the English influence was strongest. That doesn't mean that English influence is bad in itself—by any means—but merely that a completely foreign leaven was needed to raise our bread; when we followed the English too closely, as in the Gilded Age, we were merely colonial, or provincial.

I'll have to be rigidly selective if I want to get the job done—but I can work a good many minor authors into chapters on leading figures; and I can have other chapters on groups (like the New England historians). Thank God I can carry the process of selection farther down toward 1940 than other literary historians; I have worked on this period long enough to know who are the leading figures and who can be pushed into the background (instead of writing chapters on "The Novel" that try to cover everybody and his valet).

I would have a good deal to say about political and philosophical writing, but would try to approach it from the literary point of view. For example, it seems to me now that Jefferson was not only a statesman but also the great writer of the period from 1776 to 1820, towering above such figures as Philip Freneau and Henry Hugh Brackenridge. Veblen, Dewey, Santayana, Beard all deserve attention from a literary historian—and I hope I have space for Roosevelt I and Wilson.

I don't want to forget the actual circumstances under which books were written—including the fees paid by magazines and the effect of the copyright laws. Conceiving the book largely as a *story*, I hope to make use of some fairly dramatic conflicts and contrasts—Franklin in France, Poe against the New England school, Whitman and Emerson, Maxim Gorky's visit, etc. There is so much that can be done that I begin to feel like Dan'l Boone crossing Cumberland Gap. [. . .]

Cordially yours,
Malcolm Cowley

[RPW TLS-1] [NL TL/CC-1]
[TO: ROBERT PENN WARREN]
March 29, 1944

Dear Red:

I was very sorry to miss you in New York, especially as I'd been thinking about you for a long time and even planning a long letter, which of course won't yet be written. I was greatly moved by *At Heaven's Gate* (and by the way, did the title come from Wallace Stevens' "Out of the tomb we bring Badroulbadour"?). It sometimes seems to me that you are a very different sort of writer from what anybody would expect from your Kentucky plus Vanderbilt plus faculty background. Maybe the pay-off was that your first poems were "Kentucky Mountain Farm," not merely two hundred miles from Guthrie, but depicting a different social background—no cavaliers, no Cloverlands or Waverly with their slave quarters and fishponds; more nervous, rebellious, sometimes more urban, full of sympathy for poor farmers and factory workers—Agrarian, yes, in one sense, but there's a lot of difference among agrarians, as to whether their sympathies are with the big house or the little houses. Then in *At Heaven's Gate,* there was something I didn't want to expand on in my own review[47] because it might have led to misunderstanding—but, Red, you were obsessed by a book that obsessed me too, because it was a failure and shouldn't have been—I mean [John O'Hara's] *Butterfield 8.* If I had talked much about it, people would have thought I meant that you admired it and were imitating it, but that wasn't the thing at all; I think you were puzzled by why it was so good and yet not so good as it should have been, and tried to give the explanation that O'Hara didn't, that he threw up his hands about and said, in effect, "Well, she died, didn't she, and isn't that the end of the novel?["] But there's a wonderful fight in *Butterfield 8,* in which the principal male character, the Yale man, gets himself bumped in the coccyx—what a word!—and you had that fight not once but twice: once in a speakeasy, for its moral values, and once where the labor leader tangles with the villain, for its physical description, the double punch and slap with the heel of the hand.[48]

No time to write more this morning before the mailman comes. I have to report that there is a golden pactolus descending on the heads of writers in wartime, and, after the gold was transmuted into copper and steel pennies, I even got a little of it—and a contract for a long book that I want to talk to you about when I get the chance, for you could give me valuable advice on it. A one-volume history of American literature. What would you do about that? What new emphasis would you give? Why don't you get a year's leave of absence and come to New York?

As ever,
Malcolm

❧ PART VI ❧

The Mellon Years, 1944–1949

In the spring of 1944 Cowley's literary career was given an unexpected boost when he received a five-year stipend from Mary Mellon (the Bollingen Foundation), which allowed him to focus, with unbroken concentration and without financial worries, on his projected one-volume history of American literature. In June 1944 Cowley resigned from *The New Republic.* That same month, he embarked on *The Portable Hemingway* (1944), the first of three such portables for Viking Press.

Literature now came first, yet his radical past continued to haunt him, occasioning bitter reflections in letters. "The whole experience left me with a thirst for such simple virtues as honesty, fairness, generosity, humility," he wrote to Hicks on July 15, 1944. "Good literature is written with the whole man, with what he believes and feels today, with what he remembers from yesterday, and even with what he has forgotten."

On the wave of such convictions, in July 1944 Cowley contacted William Faulkner to initiate a literary project of historical impact: *The Portable Faulkner* (1946). His aim was ambitious: to remedy critical misinterpretations and elevate Faulkner's standing in the literary world. It took some effort to persuade Viking Press, but, with Faulkner's cooperation, the project materialized over the next two years. At the urging of Allen Tate, now editor of *The Sewanee Review,* Cowley entered his essay "William Faulkner's Legend of the South" in a contest organized by the review—and won the John Peale Bishop Memorial Prize of $200. In mid-April 1946 bound copies of *The Portable Faulkner* reached Oxford, Mississippi, eliciting the compliments of Faulkner himself: "The job is splendid. [. . .] By God, I didn't know myself what I had tried to do, and how much I had succeeded" (*FCF* 90–91). Caroline Gordon's front-page review of *The Portable Faulkner* in *The New York Times Book Review* and Robert Penn Warren's long, two-part appreciation in *The New Republic* brought significant attention to the book and helped to lift Faulkner's reputation—and Cowley's own.

In the Mellon years almost all of Cowley's efforts were dedicated to American literature, preparatory to the writing of his literary history. Besides important revaluations of Hemingway and Faulkner, he published "a dissenting opinion" on Robert Frost and a reassessment of Henry James. A 1946 lecture at Princeton on American literary naturalism prompted a series of essays on Theodore Dreiser, Frank Norris, and Stephen Crane. He spoke up in defense of the writers of the 1920s against the nationalist critiques of Archibald MacLeish, Van Wyck Brooks, and Bernard DeVoto, who had charged Cowley's peers with having "irresponsibly" weakened American democracy, by cultivating disenchantment and alienation. In 1946 three long essays on Whitman, including a frank treatment of his homosexuality, formed the stepping stones to a new edition of Whitman's poetry and prose, published in 1947. The following year Viking published *The Portable Hawthorne*.

In late 1943 Cowley was invited by Robert E. Spiller to contribute to the *Literary History of the United States* (1948), a book that would retain its authority through the 1960s. Defining American literature as the aesthetic and moral expression of American values, the project legitimized the new international standing of the United States as bulwark of the free democratic West. In two chapters on the instruments of culture Cowley brought his knowledge of the "economics of authorship" to bear on the literature of his own times. He also wrote the book's final chapter on the reception and resonance of American literature abroad, a virtually uncharted field requiring pioneering research; working against the grain of academic opinion, he acknowledged the importance of popular literature not part of the "canon" of American writing.

Cowley's association with the magazine and publishing world thus helped him approach American literature and its history from a more inclusive and international perspective. It was one of his self-imposed tasks as a critic to consider developments in book publishing, the creation of a reading public, and the economics of authorship. In addition, he remained an active mediator of foreign, especially French, literature. He advised publishers on manuscripts for English-language publication, translated André Gide's *Imaginary Interviews* (1944), and defended his friend Louis Aragon against unwarranted charges of collaboration with the Vichy regime. With Hannah

Josephson, he edited and translated Aragon's wartime writings. As the war continued on the Pacific and European fronts, Cowley's letters evinced his anxieties over its outcome. On August 24, 1945, his forty-seventh birthday, he expressed horror at the recent bombing of Hiroshima and Nagasaki, envisioning a nightmarish postwar world slowly dying of leukemia, and governed by U.S. cultural and economic imperialism abroad and consumerism at home.

As he observed the Cold War reaction taking root in the postwar years, Cowley remained critical of the United States yet now only rarely entered the political fray. Writing presciently to Burke on July 14, 1945, he anticipated a backlash of conservatism and retrenchment: "We are probably entering another era of private lives; in other words, we are entering an era of political reaction. The political pendulum doesn't swing from left to right, from radical to conservative; what happens is more like the expansion and contraction of membrane, like the systole and diastole of the heart: when the membrane expands, when more people enter political life, we have a radical era; when the membrane and the governing class contract, when fewer people vote, attend meetings, write letters to the newspapers, we have a conservative era" (*SC* 266–267). He was disturbed to see American progressives not taking a strong public stance against red-baiting but took heart from a few voices that dared to speak out with "fine unself-protectiveness": F. O. Matthiessen in *From the Heart of Europe* (1948) and Dwight Macdonald in his newly launched magazine *Politics,* to which Cowley contributed—anonymously— the story of his FBI dossier.

In late 1947 Cowley contracted with Robert Coughlan of *Life* to write a pioneering biographical portrait of Hemingway. In March 1948—plane tickets courtesy of *Life*—he spent a long week with Hemingway in Havana. Writing to Hemingway, Cowley showed an intuitive understanding of his subject, rooted in a shared love of the land, trout fishing, and the standards of good writing. But he had to tread cautiously in broaching the sensitive topic of Hemingway's wounding in World War I. In August 1948, in the midst of his work on the Hemingway portrait, Cowley was shocked by the suicide of the Armenian-born artist Arshile Gorky (a distant cousin of the author Maxim Gorky), who lived in the Sherman area.

After a harrowing search, Cowley and Peter Blume discovered the body. Cowley conveyed painful and personal details about the suicide to Hemingway.

By the summer of 1948 Cowley could report to Faulkner that the *Portable* was having its intended effect: Faulkner's reputation was rising, and his work was being widely read and studied in American colleges. He also coached Faulkner on bearing up under the burdens of fame and publicity, holding up Hemingway as an exemplar. In October 1948 Cowley met Faulkner in person for the first time, at a dinner in New York. He managed to persuade Faulkner to spend a few days at Sherman, helping him to sober up, and (in vain) hoping to entice him into cooperation on a portrait for *Life*.

From a literary perspective, the Mellon years had been Cowley's most productive period to date. By 1949 he could rejoice in the knowledge that his work had grown in depth and complexity and that it was reaching a large general audience, even as it enjoyed recognition in the academic world. Though his projected history of American literature remained unfinished, he had made significant contributions to American literary history. In early 1949 Cowley was elected to the National Institute of Arts and Letters.

[NL TL/CC-3]
[TO: STANLEY YOUNG][1]
RFD Gaylordsville, Conn.,[2]
April 11, 1944

Dear Stanley:

When you first got in touch with me, I wasn't very excited, because it's always a good rule not to believe in miracles; but afterwards I began thinking about projects and possibilities until I couldn't sleep. There are so many things I had planned to do, so many books I had planned to write as soon as I had the time; and there is so little time when one is working for a weekly magazine. My fifteen years on *The New Republic* haven't been wasted by any means. I put almost excessive care into my book reviews, which were never intended to be read once and thrown away; and I learned the habit of writing day by day and week by week—"in sickness and in health," one might quote from the marriage service, for any good writer has to be married to his profession, and no infidelities. But today all this work seems nothing more than a preparation; nothing more than knowledge stored up, proficiency acquired and material assembled for the books I want to write in the next five years. It isn't any wonder that I couldn't sleep that night or the night after.

You asked for some record of what I have done so far. Well—I was born in a farmhouse—a "summer home," as people used to call it—in Cambria County, Pennsylvania, on the northern slope of Laurel Hill. The year was 1898. The family was from Pittsburgh, that world metropolis of the Scotch-Irish. Back in the 1840s, the Cowleys were next-door neighbors of the Carnegies over on Troy Hill, and my Great-uncle Will was one of the original Carnegie partners; but he went off to the Civil War and died of prison fever. His share in the Carnegie Iron Works was sold and my great-grandmother used the money for a trip to Belfast. His fiançee married my grandfather, who was a homeopathic physician, as was my father after him—an impractical, wholly lovable man.

I broke the family tradition; I wanted to be a writer from the time I entered Peabody High School and began contributing to the school paper. I earned myself a scholarship to Harvard because I had heard that other writers went there. When the war came, I went to France with the American Field Service to drive an ambulance, but I wound up driving a munitions truck for the French army. That was the beginning of my great interest in French literature and civilization. After the war (and some adventures in Greenwich Village) I was awarded an American Field Service Fellowship and studied for a year at the University of Montpellier, and later at the Sorbonne;[3] I met most of the younger French writers. Coming back to this country, I earned a living as a free-lance writer. Besides doing magazine articles and book reviews, I translated many books from the French, mostly by good authors: Valéry, Barrès, Delteil, Radiguet and others. In October, 1929, I went to work for *The New Republic*, and I have stayed there ever since, as associate editor, then literary editor, then staff critic writing a weekly book page.

[. . .][4]

The work mapped out for the next five years is much more ambitious. Here is what I propose to do:

1. I want to write a one-volume history of American literature from the beginning to the present day. There is a great need for such a book, and it is simply not supplied by any of the one-volume histories now existing. Either they are hopelessly out-of-date (like Barrett Wendell's book, published in 1900), or they are dully academic (like Boynton, 1919), or they try to support some wholly personal thesis (like Ludwig Lewisohn, who treated American literature chiefly as evidence of sexual starvation). I want to write about American literature *as literature,* not as evidence of any theory about sex or society; simply as books by greater and lesser artists forming a living continuity.

2. The Harvard University Press wants me to collect a volume of my essays on French literature. The essays are already written, but they will require a good deal of reworking.[5]

3. Another publisher, W. W. Norton, wants me to collect my essays on contemporary American writers. These too must be reworked.

4. I want to finish translating the poems of my friend Louis Aragon, who, it seems to me, is the one great poet to have come out of this war.[6]

5. And I want to complete and collect my own poems in one volume that would also serve as a history of one man's spirit in these times.

This is work enough for five years of reading and writing. The history of American literature should have three full years by itself to be the book I want to write. But beyond this, I have a long-time purpose, not flamboyant, but useful, I think, to the cause of letters. At the present time, almost all American critics fall into one of two classifications. Either they are academic critics who know the past but not the present; who have read the collected works of Jonathan Edwards and Charles Brockden Brown, but lack completely a sense of good writing in 1944; or else they are book reviewers who know what the publishers are bringing out next fall and what the public is buying, but lack any notion of literary history and of permanent standards in America or France or England. I would like to combine both types of knowledge; I would like to write about the books of today from the standpoint of the classics, and to write about the American classics as if they were books that had just appeared. Nobody else is doing that; hardly anybody can; and yet it is exactly what our literature needs and deserves—the sort of thing that Saintsbury could do, and Sainte-Beuve before him.

[. . .] I should think that $5,500 a year would carry me through safely. That sounds like a great deal of money, and I am tempted to ask for less—but on the other hand, if I did receive less, I might also be tempted to add to it by writing too much for the magazines. [. . .] All I'm concerned about now is to get the books written.

Cordially yours,
Malcolm Cowley

[NL TL/CC-2]
[TO: MARY MELLON]
May 5, 1944

Dear Mrs. Mellon:

Up here, spring is an explosion. For a week we'll shiver in a nor'easter, walk out into a cold drizzle and at night reach for an extra comforter; everything seems to stand still, but with a curious feeling of latency; then suddenly, crack, bang, boom, it's hot, it's spring, and all the trees have burst into blossom like incendiary bombs. The process that takes at least ten weeks in northern France—first the almond tree at the end of the garden has its pink blossoms in February; then one after another, like the successive acts of a drama, the peaches bloom, the apricots bloom, the plums bloom chalk white, the cherries with a very faint touch of pink, the pears, and finally after the middle of April the apples, in all shades from crimson to alabaster, great mounds of strawberry ice cream in the Norman orchards that last until May—that process here is finished in ten days or two weeks, then the blossoms are gone, the dust is on the grass and we are in the middle of summer. Maybe there is some of that vegetable violence in the American temper. And curiously our slow period of development, of new beauties from week to week, is autumn, when we are getting ready for death.

At this violent season (it must be nearly over in Fauquier County) I usually have to take myself by the scruff of the neck and drag myself to the typewriter. I want to plant the garden and then go fishing. If you asked me what I'd rather do or go fishing, than go fishing, I'd have a hard time to answer, and yet, God knows, it isn't the little trout that I want to catch—it's the little brook with a big name, the

NAROMIYOCKNOWHUSUNKATANKSHUNK

if you can pronounce all those letters, that comes down through my place very clean over the stones, and the bloodroot in flower under the alders, and the perfect movement in perfect loneliness, I standing so still at the head of a pool that sometimes a squirrel doesn't see me till he's three feet away, then runs up a tree horrified to tell his children. But this year the gardens look pretty neglected and I haven't caught enough trout for one really good breakfast; I've been typing away till late in the afternoon. It seems to me that I'm just now learning to work, after all these years. Oh, I used to work hard on occasions, up to twenty hours in a single day when it was a question of finishing an article that had to be mailed to the press at six in the morning; and once I was so tired coming home that I woke up at the wheel to find my car on a high bank with the two left wheels in midair. But the sort of work I love now is work day after day, coming to my desk in the morning to find page 110 of a manuscript in the typewriter and finishing a paragraph started the afternoon before; then going on to write three or four pages more while feeling all the time that the work will go a little farther tomorrow and tomorrow. That's what I'm doing and hoping to do from now on.

[. . .] Just now I'm working on a translation of André Gide's *Interviews Imaginaires,* a terrible job for me partly because of temperamental conflicts—I don't think in his words—but at the same time rewarding, because the whole past and present of French literature is or are present in his mind simultaneously. For one of the interviews, which became quite technical, I found that I had to write a 1500-word footnote on the laws of French poetry, a subject that isn't even discussed in the Britannica.[7] [. . .]

No more today. Back to Gide.

Sincerely,
Malcolm Cowley

[NL TL/CC-2]
[TO: BERNARD DEVOTO]
April 15, 1944

Dear DeVoto:

I wanted to write you about *The Literary Fallacy,* because, although I had a note on you in last week's *New Republic* and will have a very long review of the book in next week's issue,[8] there are still some things I didn't get said. First of all, I hope you notice that the note and the review, although very negative as regards the book and its thesis, are not in the least hostile. [. . .] [Y]our main argument was based on personal feelings, not on the objective world to which you are always appealing; and I think it right for arguments to be based on feelings inside us—where else, in God's name, are they to come from? Emerson said, if you insist on quoting Emerson, "He," the scholar, "learns that going down into the secrets of his own mind he has descended into the secrets of all minds. . . . The deeper he dives into the privatest, secretest presentiment, to his wonder he finds this is the most acceptable, most public and universally true." So I liked this feature of your book; I liked it when you said "the literature of my generation tried that path and found that the path ended in impotence and the courtship of death"—for, if I'm not mistaken, there is personal feeling in those words, an implied confession that you went wrong also, something in the same mood as the confessions made by MacLeish and others, including Brooks.[9] But the other half of the truth is that this personal feeling with which we start has to be checked by external events and observations till we find the true statement of it; and in *The Literary Fallacy* you didn't do enough checking—and you didn't sufficiently turn your anger on yourself as well; if there have been mistakes in the last twenty years, we have all been involved in them, in our varying degrees.

As for checking against external facts, if you want to attack a group of writers, you have to begin by being sure that they're a group. You can attack Hemingway, Faulkner, Fitzgerald, Dos Passos in the same words, for, in spite of all their differences, there was something that united them. In the same way you can attack Sherwood Anderson, Brooks and Waldo Frank—or you can even extend that attack to include Dreiser and Lewis in one direction,

Cabell and even Mencken in another. But you can't indict Hemingway and Brooks, Dreiser and Faulkner, Lewis and Eliot *et al* in the same words and hope to make the indictment stick. They represent too many different ages, theories and hostile attitudes.

I wish you would make a more careful study of the period from 1905 to 1925; it seems to me that you have made several mistakes about it in various essays. Maybe you were too late in joining the literary hurly-burly to catch the feel of that particular time—and having discovered that false statements were made about the eighties and nineties, you simply extended your findings about the so-called Gilded Age to cover the early nineteen-hundreds. I used to know the small fry of that period; I met them at Luke O'Connor's saloon in the village, where they hung out—and I can testify that the reason they accepted Brooks's *America's Coming-of-Age* as gospel, was that it corresponded to their own experience. His scholarship was weak, as you pointed out—he didn't succeed in analyzing the causes of the condition he described, but he was accurate about the condition itself, because he was describing it at first hand. Literature *was* in a very bad way; and the rebels of 1911 did a considerable work for which we owe them a debt. You ought to look into this period, say, from the files of the old *Masses, The Nation,* etc., before writing about it again.

[. . .]

Well, forgive me for writing at such length, and without saying half of what I wanted to. For example, I wanted to point out that American Civilization hasn't proved itself to be rugged, vital and adventurous during the war[. . .]. We're in for some bad times that might confirm the direst predictions of the 1920s[. . .].

Sincerely,
Malcolm Cowley

P.S. —I wonder if you know that Brooks had a complete breakdown during the 1920s. I don't know what the causes of it were, and they also must have been partly personal, but also in part they were connected with his feeling at the time that literature was going in the wrong direction. The manuscript of *Emerson and Others* had to be practically filched from him by Mrs. Brooks and Max Perkins before it could be published. Then slowly he recovered and went to work on *The Flowering* in an entirely different mood, much more scholarly, but also somewhat shallower, as if his own experience had made him afraid of depths. This is the sort of thing that can't be said in print as long as Brooks is alive, but it casts a light on his two periods that people wouldn't get from reading your attacks on him. He started out as a sort of prophetic Emerson; he's ending as a Prescott-cum-Holmes—and a terribly nice man through it all.

M.C.

————————

[NL TL/CC-3]
[TO: PAUL ROSENFELD][10]
May 3, 1944

Dear Paul:

I was greatly disturbed by your piece about Louis Aragon in the April 15 issue of the *Saturday Review*.[11] I think you will be disturbed too, when you hear the whole story, for I know you must feel that it is not fair to bring charges against a man who can't answer them, and whose friends can't answer them (owing to the special circumstances), especially when those charges happen to be based (although I'm sure you didn't know that fact) on utterly false and malicious charges spread by his enemies.

Aragon isn't pro-Vichy and never was. As far as I know he is still a Communist, though he rebelled strongly against the party line after the defeat of France and before the invasion of Russia. The feeling of French patriotism that was always latent in him became his ruling passion, after the experience that he describes in "Zone Libre." From that time his poems were rallying cries for the French resistance. Like everything else published in France at the time, they have a double meaning; they had to have a double meaning in order to say what he felt and at the same time pass the censorship. But the second meaning is not at all hidden: it is always France, liberty, revolt. [. . .]—always Aragon is invoking the French past to find strength for further resistance. One point worried me: the almost unmanly idolatry of his wife in poem after poem. Aragon would say that he meant it literally; but to most of his French readers, Elsa becomes identified with France; and Aragon makes the confusion deliberate in one of his finest poems, "Plus Belle que les Larmes," in which France assumes the body of a woman.

[. . .]

Aragon's brief war record was extremely distinguished. He was awarded not only the Croix de Guerre, with palms, but also the Médaille Militaire, a very high decoration. It was this fact that enabled him to survive under Vichy; this and the natural timidity of the Vichy regime, which wanted to be regarded as patriotic and was afraid at first to proceed against a war hero who wrote patriotic songs. Aragon permitted some of them to be read (not by him, I am pretty sure) over the Vichy radio; that was pardonable, considering that his book of poems, *Le Crève-Coeur,* had been suppressed by the Germans after 250 copies were printed. *Les Yeux d'Elsa* was printed in Switzerland, and only one copy was permitted to be imported into France, for the author himself. *Cantique à Elsa* was printed in Algiers, where the censorship was less strict, but couldn't be imported into France. Aragon himself was arrested by the Germans during the summer of 1941, but talked himself out of prison by claiming to be "Dr. Aragon" and no relation to the poet. I have been trying to find out what happened to him after the German occupation of what used to be the Free Zone. He was living near Nice in early November, 1942. After that he simply disappeared from sight. Gide heard the rumor that he had escaped to Switzerland and was living there in a sort of concentration camp; but the rumor was almost certainly false. Other Frenchmen more recently escaped say that they think he is living underground. His wife, Elsa Triolet, is a Jewess and, to make matters worse in German eyes, a Russian Jewess, the sister of Mayakovsky's widow. If the Germans got hold of her she would be sent to Poland and death: and that would mean Aragon's death too.

Meanwhile the pre-war political animosities continue. A French anticommunist paper published in London printed the news that Aragon had joined the Doriotistes;[12] I don't know who thought up that particular lie. If he had become a Doriotiste, his books would be sold openly and they would carry a very different message. *Pour la Victoire,* also concerned with attacking the Communists, reprinted the story, but retracted it when the facts were brought to the editor's attention. Dwight Macdonald, who is not very scrupulous in attacking people he regards as Stalinists, again printed the story in *Partisan Review,* copied from *Pour la Victoire,* and didn't bother to note the retraction. And the damned thing is that Aragon's friends can't do much about it. If I said what is the truth, that Aragon like Malraux is close to the Communists, active in the resistance movement and that his poems, now circulated in mimeographed copies, are rallying cries of the French patriots—if I said that, I would be starting a manhunt and might end by having his blood on my hands.

But, Paul, with your sense of fairness, couldn't you write a short note to the *Saturday Review* and say that it had been called to your attention that Aragon was not a collaborator and that, on the contrary, his books (including those under review) were not allowed to be circulated in any part of France—that being the simple truth—couldn't you do that and set your own record straight? It seems frightful to me that when a poet has to live in hiding, he should at the same time be abused as a traitor to everything he believes in; we must be very careful not to malign those who are unable to speak for themselves; who must live in silence and secrecy.[13]

As ever,
M.

[GH TLS-2][NL TL/CC-2]
[TO: GRANVILLE HICKS]
July 15, 1944

Dear Granville:

Raymond Postgate,[14] a very nice fellow, very intelligent and really the greatest authority on the history of revolutions, ancient and modern, sent me a manuscript with a covering letter, asking me to have it read around. [...]

I find myself less interested in the whole subject than I should have been a year ago. I feel almost like Rimbaud toward the end of his life, when they asked him about his friendship with Verlaine and he said, "All that was bad." It wasn't the revolution that was bad, but a lot of the revolutionists, especially the ex-conspirators like

J. B. Matthews	Eugene Lyons
Robert Cantwell	Sidney Hook
Whittaker Chambers	Felix Morrow

—and should I go on with the list, the Liston Oakeses, I won't list an oak, and, on the other side, the functionaries (with a silent "n"), the creatures like V. J. Jerome?[15] I still have a great deal of respect for rank-and-file Communists; they have discipline and self-sacrifice; but the leaders and theorists of the movement seem to lose their sense of human values. My God, what kind of a new world would V. J. Jerome manufacture, if he were God? Would you like to live there, or would you prefer a world inhabited by Sidney Hooks? Or would you like to live in a cage of hyenas? The whole experience left me with a thirst for such simple virtues as honesty, fairness, generosity, humility. You can't build a new world on their opposites.

And in literary criticism, which is my own field, I come to be more and more impressed by the need for depth. Good literature is written with the whole man, with what he believes and feels today, with what he remembers from yesterday, and even with what he has forgotten. You can't tell an author, "Your ideas are wrong. You are a pessimist. You must change and become an optimist"—for to change really he must develop not only new ideas but a new attitude toward his own past, a new interpretation of his experience, which must then be lived in turn, and remembered, before he can write good books about it. When the Russians wanted different books for the NEP,[16] the Five Year Plan and the Stalin Constitution, they were making sure that they would have bad books about all three, for their writers, at present, are about ready to write about the NEP with understanding. But I still feel that good literature is on the side of life, even when—as sometimes happens in Hemingway—it is dominated by suicidal impulses. [. . .]

As ever,
Malcolm

[WFC TLS-2] [FCF 8–12]
[TO: WILLIAM FAULKNER]
July 22, 1944

Dear Faulkner:

You can see that I'm pretty nearly as bad as you are about answering letters, and I haven't the excuse of a system either; it's just a mixture of indolence and busyness, one part of each, and life as a succession of dead-lines that I just fail to meet.

I want very much to write the article about you, and I want to meet you too, but it's quite possible to write the article without meeting you and without knowing very much about your biography, which wouldn't go into the article anyway—you're right about that point; but I ought to know something about it for the thinking that has to be done before the article is written, so that I wouldn't make too many bad guesses. [. . .]

[. . .]

Do you want to hear a New York market report on your standing as a literary figure?

It's about what I suggested in my other letter[17]—very funny, and a great credit to you, but bad for your pocketbook. First, in publishing circles your name is mud. They are all convinced your books won't ever sell, and it's a pity, isn't it? they say, with a sort of pleased look on their faces. (I haven't talked to [Bennett] Cerf [of Random House] or his new editor, Bob Linscott, about you; but I'm going to try Linscott, who really likes books, and see whether I can't get him to do a better job on your next one; if he's vague or regretful, I should advise your getting another publisher, but I have no idea who he would be.)[18] The [second rate][19] bright boys among the critics did a swell job of incomprehending and unselling you, Fadiman[20] especially. Now, when you talk to writers instead of publishers or publisher's pet critics about the *oeuvre* of William Faulkner, it's quite a different story; there you hear almost nothing but admiration, and the better the writer the greater the admiration is likely to be. Conrad Aiken, for example, puts you at the top of the heap. [. . .] The funny thing is the academic and near-academic critics and the way they misunderstand and misstate your work. You probably haven't read Maxwell Geismar's book, *Writers in Crisis,* but he's not so dumb for a professor[21] and does a very good job on Hemingway, but when he comes to Faulkner, you might as well have written your novels in Minoan or Hittite for all the sense he makes of them.

So, a good piece on your work has to be written, and[,] if my indolence doesn't get the best of me, I'll try hard to write it—and thank God, I'm too indolent to stop working once I get started.

Now, there's one question I wish to God you'd answer for me, not because I want to quote you, but so that I won't make a fool of myself when I come to write the piece. It's about the symbolism in your work. It's there, all right, and I don't see how anybody but a learned critic can miss it—I mean, of course, that Sutpen's Hundred, in *Absalom, Absalom!*, becomes, for the reader [at least], a symbol of the old South, with the manner of its building and its decay after the war, and its owner killed by a poor white, and the only survivor of the Sutpen family a mulatto; that's almost an allegory or legend and you repeat the legend explicitly in the fourth [*second*] part of "The Bear."

Once in *The Southern Review,* Cleanth Brooks, I think it was,[22] gave a whole allegorical scheme for *Sanctuary,* saying that the gal was the South, raped by modern industry (in the form of Popeye), except that modern industrial civilization is so sterile it didn't have strength to rape her and had to get a substitute. I thought that Brooks's scheme was a lot too definite and pat, but still Popeye does seem to have something of the quality you impute to the representatives of modern civilization, and the sterility pops up again in the reporter in *Pylon*—and that same book has the sex [*fucking*] in the airplane, a marvelous scene with no *double entendre* but with a double meaning, certainly. Well, the question is (speaking roughly) how much of the symbolism is intentional, deliberate? Or is that the sort of question I shouldn't ask, even for my own information?

(I found out when rereading Hemingway that there's a lot of symbolism in his work too, but the question of deliberateness didn't arise there; because the early symbolism was plainly unconscious, and some of the later symbolism—as in "The Snows of Kilimanjaro"—was plainly conscious; in either case the reader wasn't left in much doubt.)

Too much for one letter already. For God's sake don't throw it in the drawer till the drawer gets full.

Sincerely,

Malcolm Cowley

[...]

[FOM TLS-1][NL TL/CC-1]
[TO: F. O. MATTHIESSEN][23]
July 24, 1944

Dear Matthiessen:

I am just now reading your *American Renaissance* and I thought I ought to write and tell you how very good it is. Not for style: I wish to God you'd loosen up a little and write more conversationally (which doesn't mean at all writing carelessly); it seems to me that your paragraphs get a little involuted and occasionally have a faint suggestion of Blackmuresque. But for perceptions, which are vastly more important, there is absolutely no American critic who is doing fresher and more valuable work. Valuable to me, at any rate: I was doing a long piece on Hemingway, and I was impressed by the way your remarks about Hawthorne and Melville contained implicit comments on the writing of today. I even used one sentence of yours, and without quotation marks: the one about Hawthorne's writing, not as he would, but as he must. I repeated the same words about Hemingway, for they are true of him also: I said, "He is one of the novelists who write, not as they should or would, but as they must"—then I tried to give you credit, but it made the sentence so awkward and the paragraph so full of names that I decided to leave you out for the moment and give you credit some other time. But Hemingway is another of the hypnagogic writers, whose best stories seem to be based on the things that come to him while he has insomnia; your quotation from Poe in this connection was also highly illuminating. So thanks a million.

[...]

Why is it that most of the good American novelists and poets are "haunted" writers; and why is it that, even if they begin as naturalists, they end essentially as Symbolists?

As ever,
Malcolm Cowley

[NL TL/CC-2]
[TO: MARY MELLON]
August 18, 1944

Dear Mrs. Mellon:

There is no business to bother you with, but I'm writing to tell you how things are going, as if to continue our conversation—I wish it were over a very cold bottle of Pouilly Fumeux.

Yes, it's hot here, so hot that there have been many days when I wasn't able to work, even when I carried the typewriter down to the cellar. But unlike most of the East, we've had enough rain and the garden has flourished. This is the time of the year when it assumes a look of slatternly, sprawling abundance, like an unpainted farmhouse overflowing with children. The melons spill into the grass, the squash vines climb the cornstalks, the tomato vines loll among the zinnias with terrific clashes of color, the eggplants bend down the branches till they rest on the ground. Everything is rich and diseased, with the grapes suffering from mildew and the bugs crawling over everything [. . .] as if nature in this next-to-last month were trying to exhibit her inexhaustible fecundity. And I too in this month would like to have innumerable children, dirty and crying and laughing and fat as the pumpkins among the corn. Instead of that, I have one nice child and I'm squeezing out words with that American scrupulosity and straining for perfection.

I have finished one job that pleased me very much, a one-volume Hemingway for the Viking Press, with a long preface[24] and editorial notes. Rereading his books in rapid succession, I discovered that he was quite a different writer from what people had suspected: not a realist at heart, no matter how carefully he has tried to copy reality, but a tortured and haunted novelist with curious affinities to Hawthorne and Poe and Melville. His heroes always suffer from insomnia, and half their experiences are walking nightmares. He seems to have a natural feeling for legends, rituals, ceremonies, sacraments. And his four novels tell a sort of continued story dealing with the relations between one man and society and with his efforts to overcome the fear of death. The critics have always kept urging him to get rid of his obsession with death, as if he could perform that feat by an act of will. In reality, he has done something more admirable: that is, he has come to terms with death; he has accepted it for his hero (and thereby symbolically for himself).

Just now I'm reading Robert Frost for a different sort of piece.[25] I don't like Frost—or, to be more exact, I don't like the sort of veneration that surrounds this honest but rather minor poet. He is the Cal Coolidge of American literature, and I don't like to hear him mentioned in the same breath with Emerson and Thoreau and those other Yankees who really wrestled with their problems, instead of saying (in verse as lax as the sentiment it expresses, "Me for the hills where I don't have to choose.") He's a genuine Hitchcock chair, a saltbox cottage, a grandfather's clock, a well sweep carefully preserved after the electric pump system has been installed; he's everything nice in the antique shop, but he isn't the voice of America.

There is a long piece I'm anxious to write on Faulkner too; nobody has ever done a good job on him. All this is preparatory to the book on American literature. I had another talk with the publishers recently, and they agreed that it would be better for me to do a short book on contemporary writers before launching into the longer work on American literature from the beginning [...]. You can see that I'm being a very busy writer under the new dispensation, perhaps more fecund than I expected to be, and more like the garden in August, though not so slovenly.

And I'd better close before this letter gets too long to read in the August heat. Maybe by the time it reaches you, the American tanks will be rolling through Pouilly, and the tankmen will be learning to drink the smoky wine. I wish I were there.

As ever,
Malcolm Cowley

[FOM TLS-1] [PMC 475–76]
[TO: F. O. MATTHIESSEN]
November 22, 1944

Dear Matthiessen:

[...]

One idea has been on my mind, about the general subject of literature in the colleges. Why, for God's sake, doesn't some big university give a chair of prosody, or at least a year's professorship of prosody, to W. H. Auden?[26] I know the arguments that would be brought against such a proposal. But the facts are that Auden is one of the few great living poets; that his coming to this country was an important event, like Eliot's going to England; that he is now writing some of his best work, but meanwhile wasting his great talent for teaching on freshmen English students at Swarthmore; that he knows more about the forms of English verse, and of verse in general, than anybody else since Saintsbury (and unlike Saintsbury knows how to write them too); that one of his last long poems, the commentary on *The Tempest,* is almost a specimen book of verse forms—and that young poets learning to write ought to have the benefit of his knowledge. [. . .] The educated public in this country is so damned ignorant about the rules and conventions of English verse that it is hard even to write about them. The criticism of verse has no firm foundation because you can't refer to the rules, except at the risk of be-fuddling your ignorant readers. The poets themselves, in most cases, are so ignorant that they don't even know when they're being conventional, let alone when they're being experimental. Auden with a good course to give, and good students, might change a lot of that. Of course he's Christian, homo-sexual, and has been seen to blow his nose on his dirty socks—but he keeps his sexual proclivities under cover and is probably trying to change them; he'd buy handkerchiefs if he had a housekeeper, and the real professorial objection to him would probably be his Christianity.

Cordially,
Malcolm Cowley

[FOM TLS-1]
[TO: F. O. MATTHIESSEN]
January 4, 1945

Dear Matthiessen:

[. . .]

I'm going to review your James books after all,[27] but don't expect anything world-shaking, for I haven't studied James enough to reach conclusions, except that his later style was bad, flatly bad—short-breathed and long-winded and psychologically incapable of reaching conclusions, even afraid to reach the end of a sentence—and why not say so? His stories written at the same time as his great novels were also bad for the most part, at least those in *The Better Sort,* with the sole exception of "The Beast in the Jungle", and even that goes moving toward its fine conclusion like an elephant on tiptoes. I don't share your fondness for "The Story in It." I suspect that James, in his stories (not his novels) at that period was trying to do what Ray Limbert[28] tried to do, and that the product was neither a sow's ear nor a silk purse, but, in some cases at least, just a potboiler that didn't boil. Like most people, I'm getting more and more enthusiastic about the early and middle James stories, from "The Pension Beaurepas" to "Greville Fane." Is that a sign of undeveloped taste? [...]

Cordially,
Malcolm Cowley

[NL TL/CC-2]
[TO: MARY MELLON]
January 5, 1945

Dear Mary:

It's been a long, long time since I wrote you to report progress. Ça existe quand même. It's slow, but then it's always slow. I have just finished the second draft of a long essay on William Faulkner. It's so long that I'll have to split it into sections and print it in two or three magazines. Faulkner was a fascinating man to work with, because he's saying something, he has said it over and over, and still the critics refuse to understand what it is. In a dozen novels he's been writing a legend or epic of the South—not the conventional legend of the big white plantation house and the mocking bird singing in the magnolia tree while the banjoes go plunky-plunk and all the faithful retainers crowd round saying, "Yassuh, Massuh," but another legend full of crime and punishment, miscegenation, incest and corruption, with sexual symbols for social realities—It's funny how the contemporary American writers end up as symbolists. Take John Steinbeck, for example, who's not nearly so good as Faulkner. His stock symbol, his central situation, is a biological laboratory full of starfish, octopi, nudibranchs, rattlesnakes, sea anemones and alley cats, all anxious to kill each other, all emitting sperm and semen, and the whole collection presided over by a scientist named Doc Phillips, a sort of God with a face "half Christ and half Satyr." You gather eventually that Steinbeck regards human beings as animals, as turtles, rattlesnakes, tomcats or red ponies. And he treats them in his novels just as Doc Phillips treats his alley cats—that is, he pats and strokes them and puts them into a little airtight box where he asphyxiates them; then, making incisions on the corpses, he injects a red fluid into the arteries and a blue fluid in the veins; he simplifies them for his readers.

As I keep working on my literary history, I keep making generalities and discoveries that I don't know whether I'll be able to document and use. For example. Almost all French writers in the religion-of-art tradition, from Flaubert down, were examples of mother fixation. You can check it in the biographies of Flaubert, Baudelaire, Rimbaud, Proust, Gide and many others. I think it's a case where literature reflects society. French marriages being largely contractual arrangements, and French husbands finding their sentimental interests outside the home, the wife and mother turns to her son for an outpouring of emotion, and the son becomes incapable of loving other women (which doesn't necessarily mean that he becomes homosexual). Not all mothers, obviously, and not all sons, but a surprising number of those who figure in literature. American writers, as a group, are just the opposite. In their books you find the most unpleasant and hated mothers in all literature. The fathers presented in their books are usually weak but loveable creatures to whom the sons are deeply attached. There's a great deal of castration complex in American literature (openly in Faulkner and Hemingway; secretly in Henry James).

But enough of this shop talk from Dr. Cowley's psychological study. [...]

Still gratefully yours,
Malcolm Cowley

[KB TLS-2] [PARTLY *SC* 263–264]
[TO: KENNETH BURKE]
February 16, 1945

Dear Kenneth:

[...]

I find relief from myself in thinking about the sinister shape of things to come. Ah, Hitler and his SS leaders and the Japanese Imperial Rule Assistance Association thought they had discovered total war, simply by abolishing all moral limitations on actions directed toward winning the war: they could suppress, enslave, exterminate to their vast intoxication. But they never blundered into such a total concept as Unconditional Surrender: no, they defeated a country and occupied a country and enslaved a country, but always by means of military force plus negotiations with the country's government. But the moral Anglo-Saxon powers are bent on wiping out nations as nations by making no terms, by coming in to occupy them totally. And what's going to be the result in Germany, in Japan—a long period of guerilla warfare exactly like our occupation of the Philippines, but against people who die instead of giving up? How is the Japanese war in particular ever going to end? And (another worry) how much economic policy is there in our bombing of Germany and Japan, our two great commercial rivals? Waste, the Future of Prosperity. War is the great waster. Therefore wipe out the German industrial cities one after the other. Impose biological indemnities too, oh, not deliberately like Hitler, but what a pleasure to think that our actions are decimating the German and Japanese races (I mean reducing them by ten percent). Then what a scope for democratic capitalism, what a transfusion of vigor on account of these man-created wildernesses to be pioneered. General Motors climbs aboard the covered wagon.

I wish you didn't live at such a distance, multiplied by war. [...]

As ever,
Malcolm

[CO TLS-1]
[TO: CHARLES OLSON][29]
May 3, 1945

Dear Mr. Olson:

[. . .] I think if Pound is captured—if the Swiss didn't let him in—he ought to stand trial, to establish the principle that poets are responsible people. To have him pardoned as a poet—on the opposite principle that poets are all crazy—would seem to me an intolerable injury to poetry. On the other hand, I'd be in favor of giving him a very easy sentence, on the ground that he was foolish—not as a poet but as a person—and that his broadcasts didn't do any harm, because nobody listened to them.

Sincerely yours,
Malcolm Cowley

[WFC TLS-2] [*FCF* 21–24] [*PMC* 476–478]
[TO: WILLIAM FAULKNER]
August 9, 1945

Dear Faulkner:

It's gone through, there will be a Viking Portable Faulkner, and it seems a very good piece of news to me. [. . .]

It won't be a very big transaction from the financial point of view. The Viking Portables have only a moderate sale—the Hemingway I edited sold about 30,000 copies [in the first year] and they thought that was extra good. But the reason the book pleases me is that it gives me a chance to present your work as a whole, at a time when every one of your books except *Sanctuary*— and I'm not even sure about that—is out of print. The result should be a better sale for your new books and a bayonet prick in the ass of Random House to reprint the others.

And now comes the big question, what to include in the book. It will be 600 pages, or a shade more than 200,000 words. The introduction won't be hard; it will be based on what I have written already (bearing your comments in mind)—but what about the text?

I have an idea for that, and I don't know what you'll think about it. Instead of trying to collect the "best of Faulkner" in 600 pages, I thought of selecting the short and long stories, and passages from novels that are really separate stories, that form part of your Mississippi series—so that the reader will have a picture of Yocknapatawpha county [I misspelled the name in those days] from Indian times [*days*] down to World War II. That would mean starting with "Red Leaves" or "A Justice" from *These Thirteen*—then on to "Was" for plantation days—then one or two of the chapters from *The Unvanquished* for the Civil War, and maybe "Wash" for Reconstruction— you can see the general idea.

I'd like to include "Spotted Horses" (is there much difference between the magazine version and the chapter in *The Hamlet?*), "The Bear" certainly, "All the Dead Pilots" (that being part of the Sartoris cycle), "That Evening Sun" (anthologized till its bones are picked, like Nancy's in the ditch, but still part of the Compson story), "Old Man" (from *The Wild Palms*—it's not Yocknapatawpha, but it's Mississippi), "Delta Autumn" and a lot more.

The big objection to this scheme is that it has nothing from *The Sound and the Fury*, which is a unit in itself, and too big a unit for a 600-page book that tries to present your work as a whole; and nothing from *Absalom, Absalom* (except "Wash," a story with the same characters). If I include any complete novel it would have to be *As I Lay Dying,* because it is the shortest of them all; it's not my favorite. But in spite of this objection, I think that a better picture of your work as a whole could be given in this fashion. You know my theory, ex- pressed somewhere in the essay—that you are at your best on two levels, either in long stories that can be written in one burst of energy, like "The Bear" and "Spotted Horses" and "Old Man," or (and) in the Yocknapatawhpha cycle as a whole. The advantage of a book on the system I have in mind is that it would give you at both these levels, in the stories and in the big cycle.

[...] [T]he chief thing is that your Mississippi work hangs together beau- tifully as a whole—as an entire creation there is nothing like it in American literature.

For God's sake, send me an answer to this, because it will soon be time for me to get to work on the book, and I don't want to plan it in a way that would meet with fundamental objections from you.

Did I tell you what Jean-Paul Sartre said about your work? He's a little man with bad teeth, absolutely the best talker I ever met, not the most eloquent but the most understanding. He's the best of the new French dramatists: one of his plays has been running in Paris for more than a year, and he says that his work is based on qualities he learned from American literature. What he said about you was, "Pour les jeunes en France, Faulkner c'est un dieu." Roll that over on your tongue.

Cordially,
Cowley

[KB TLS-3] [PARTLY *SC* 268–269]
[TO: KENNETH BURKE]
August 24, 1945

Dear Kenneth:

It's my birthday and a slow cold rain is falling and in general it's a good day to write a letter, except that I haven't anything much to say. The atom bomb. We can't keep it out of our minds. It gets worse as time goes on and we learn about its effects. The Japanese say, of course they may be lying, as today's radio announcer piously suggests, but then again they may be telling the truth, and they say that people in the Hiroshima area continue to die from radioactivity—they lose their red corpuscles and peg out—and the Japanese say they can't afford to send their doctors to Hiroshima for fear of losing them too—and they say that people just a little burned by the bomb found the burns growing worse as time passed, and pegged out, so that the death toll (what a horrible phrase) was 30,000 in the first week and 30,000 more the second week—and you get a new picture of the way radioactivity will wipe out our world, not in a good healthy smash, as you pictured it, with a new sun appearing in this constellation, but rather in slow leukemia, the world simply made uninhabitable. Some people will certainly get so frightened by this picture that they'll go off into the jungle or the mountains and live by raising roots, in the hope that when the next war comes it won't be worth while wiping them out. Ninety-nine people out of a hundred will want never to use the atom bomb again, but there's always one bad apple in the barrel, always one mad scientist or mad dictator, and in the long run I don't see much hope—but in the short run we're living in the great imperial republic of the twentieth century, we'll be rich, we'll all have three automobiles, we'll have to have them, by law, whether or not we want to sleep with

Mae West, we'll have to sleep with her, we'll have to eat too much and then take expensive cures to be slenderized, we'll have to eat expensively denatured food expensively renatured with expensive vitamins, we'll have to have a good time, by God, so we might as well grit our teeth and eat, drink, and be expensively merry, for tomorrow we'll be blown sky high.

[. . .] About my only long-range planning is trying to establish myself as a high-price author with various magazines and publishers, so that when I have to go back to actually earning a living, I'll be able to do so.

But any flirtation with the Lucepapers has been all on their side. I told you that last spring they wanted me to be book editor of *Time*—nixy, I said. Then they asked me to do a story on Horatio Alger, and that time I consented, after jacking up their offer to the equivalent of 20 cents a word—I wanted to do something on Alger anyway and was glad to be paid for my trouble. But I fancy that's the end of it. I would as soon go to prison or the booby hatch as work on a salary for Luce—and if I ever write another article for any of his papers whatsoever, it will be because I want to write it anyway. [. . .]

I'm more disturbed by certain moral qualities in the American world at present than by the triumph of capitalism. I mean the sudden ending of Lend Lease, though it means breaking up the machinery by which Europe has been supplied with a little food, and I mean the curt words with which Truman dismissed the French newspaper men. There are a lot of other signs like that, all pointing to the want of sympathy and the want of imagination that are coming to distinguish this country. But we had god damn well better have sympathy and imagination, for now we're on the top of the heap and all the envy of an envious world is going to be directed toward us—and the world will whoop when the first atom bomb falls on New York. Ah, we have triumphed, we have given the Germans and the Japanese lessons in cold-blooded, abstract, self-righteous cruelty, in the name of freedom and democracy. But people who triumph in this world don't last long.

This is a pretty long letter for a guy who had nothing to say, but, hell, it's my birthday, and I decided not to do any writing. [. . .]

And me, as ever,
Malcolm.

[WFC TLS-2] [FCF 27–30]
[TO: WILLIAM FAULKNER]
September 17, 1945

Dear Faulkner:

I finally got down to working on selections for the book, and after the first day I began running into difficulties. [. . .][30]

I'll go on mulling over the material, feeling that something very good has to come out of it, because of all the extraordinary stories that are going into it. That's one thing about your work—the more one reads it, the better it seems. It's written, as Gide said of the writing he liked, to be reread. Did I tell you about the story I heard from Sartre, about Hemingway drunk in Paris insisting that Faulkner was better than he was? Hemingway wrote me a long, rambling, lonely letter complaining that writing was a lonely trade and there was no one to talk to about it. He said about you, "Faulkner has the most talent of anybody but hard to depend on because he goes on writing after he is tired and seems as though he never threw away the worthless. I would have been happy just to have managed him." Hemingway would be a good manager, too—he knows how to say exactly what he feels and set a high price on it. But just now he seems to be very lonely and unhappy [—*probably about the break-up with Martha Gellhorn, though he doesn't mention that in the letter*—] and if you're not corresponding with him already, it would be nice if you sat down some time and wrote him. [. . .] Also it would be wonderful if some time you put your Yocknapatawpha County cycle together yourself—not doing much rewriting, except to make the names agree where you had to change them, but making a lot of cuts in some books. I would say that *Absalom, Absalom* would be better if cut by about a third, maybe all the early parts of it omitted, leaving only Quentin's story to his roommate.

No more today—I don't feel very eloquent[. . .].

As ever,
Cowley

[NL TL/CC-2]
[TO: PETER DE VRIES, *POETRY*]
December 19, 1945

Dear De Vries:

An idea about *Poetry, a Magazine,* not *The New Yorker:*[31]

A little while ago I heard that Duell, Sloan and Pearce were planning to publish Conrad Aiken's collected poems next spring in two volumes. It seemed to me that something ought to be done about the occasion beyond the ordinary perfunctory gesture of printing a review. Aiken's first two important books (after *Earth Triumphant,* 1941) were *Turns and Movies* and *The Jig of Forslin,* both published in 1916, just thirty years before these collected volumes. During those thirty years he has devoted himself to poetry more single-heartedly than any other American (except Robinson, who was twenty years his senior). Even Frost has taught and lectured, but Aiken has never done anything but write, and has never been able to write anything but his best. He is by far the most neglected of our major poets; he simply doesn't take care of his own reputation; he is terrified of appearing in public, and has managed to antagonize the people who write most of our poetry criticisms, so that on occasions I have had the impression that he was almost the victim of a cabal. Nobody has bothered to explain what he was saying— for example in *The Coming Forth by Day of Osiris Jones,* the book that Joyce had read and lost and was trying to get hold of again when France fell in 1940; so that his inability to get hold of it came to symbolize in his tired mind the whole tragedy of Europe.

What I wondered was whether *Poetry* couldn't devote an issue to Aiken's work about the time that his book appears next spring—I mean, print a lot of his poetry with two or three articles about it, or a collection of opinions from various poets. Something like that is called for now. We ought to honor our older men who have given their lives to poetry, in order to encourage the young.[32]

I very much liked the issue of *Poetry* dedicated to the French resistance— everything came out very well; and I was delighted to be able to include the poems by [George] Dillon and [William Jay] Smith in the Aragon book.

I'd like to get another crack at that book now, so as to expand the poetry section with some new and good translations that I found out about too late to include them. But it's been a great pleasure to have it well reviewed, especially since Hannah Josephson and I did our work on it for nothing.

Cordially,
Malcolm Cowley

———

[NL TL/CC-2]
[TO: STOW PERSONS, PRINCETON UNIVERSITY]
February 1, 1946

Dear Mr. Persons:

I was very much pleased and flattered by your invitation to give a lecture at Princeton and contribute an essay to the Princeton Studies in American Civilization; but as yet I don't know how to answer you, with a yes or a no. [...] I had better warn you that I don't feel now, and probably will never feel, that naturalism is one of the most important movements in American literature. It runs counter to two deep-lying tendencies in the American spirit, toward optimism and toward seeking external objects and events as symbols of something else. With many of the American would-be naturalists, you can feel their instinctive high spirits, their faith in the goodness of people, bursting through their pessimistic doctrines. Parrington thought that pessimism would be a natural result of urbanization and industrialization; he had a point there. But even when American writers are fundamentally pessimists, they still retain the other tendency, toward symbolism. Even a writer like Hemingway, who started out to tell "just what happened," ends as a symbolist, and Faulkner was a symbolist from the beginning. At the present time, James T. Farrell is about the only naturalistic novelist of any standing.

I have been thinking what I could do in a lecture or essay. Dreiser would have to be the center of it. Germanic as he was in spirit, he got his early ideas from "Darwin and Huxley *et al*," that is, from English sources. Norris got his ideas from Zola; London got his from Nietzsche and Marx. That makes a fairly neat pattern: English, French, German. Crane's *Maggie* (they haven't found *his* sources) and Sinclair's *The Jungle* could be mentioned more briefly—then I would have to swing into my thesis that naturalism was never fully acclimated here; but that it did have a liberating effect. The question is whether you want me to do it, with my present lack of preparation, and whether someone else couldn't do it better[33] [. . .]. In this field, you have no lack of authorities, whereas Cowley, poor man, would have to make himself an authority with midnight kilowatts.

[. . .] To get back to naturalism: it was the eighteenth, not the nineteenth century that set the pattern of American thought; it is Progress, not the Struggle for Survival, that exists in the back of our minds. Nineteenth-century thought was merely accepted as something progressive, in the naïve spirit of Whitman's:

Hurrah for positive science! long live exact demonstration!

Now, with our eighteenth-century equipment, we have jumped, or rather have been pushed, into the center of the atomic age. But no more for today.[34]

Cordially yours,
Malcolm Cowley

{ ——— }

Literary History of the United States (1948)
1944–1946

In December 1943 Cowley had been invited to contribute to the *Literary History of the United States* (1948), recently initiated by Robert E. Spiller, its general editor, with Willard Thorp, Thomas H. Johnson, Henry Seidel Canby, and others. Though Cowley was uneasy with its nationalism and felt "a little out of place" among academic specialists, he contributed three chapters: "Creating an Audience" (with H. S. Canby), "How Writers Lived," and "American Books Abroad." The following four letters pertain to the project.

[NL TL/CC-1]
[TO: ROBERT E. SPILLER]
April 9, 1944

Dear Mr. Spiller:

[. . .]

I read the outline of the "Literary History" with care and with great admiration, too, especially for the earlier sections—the divisions of space, the choice of writers for "major-writer" treatment, the emphasis on the political writing of the revolutionary period, the relegation of Longfellow to part of a chapter; all this sounds full of promise. My criticisms (and my right for making criticisms) would deal chiefly with the contemporary period. Ten thousand words is not enough for contemporary fiction; it is the major form of our period and engaged the energies of most of the major writers. Hemingway, Dos Passos and Faulkner should all have major-writer treatment. On the other hand, 10,000 words is too much for contemporary drama, and I fear for contemporary poetry as well. You ought to put up a red signal, *Achtung*, over Zabel's chapter on contemporary criticism. If it follows the outline, it will continue his obsession against [Van Wyck] Brooks and erect the *Southern Review* critics into major figures, while the outline doesn't even mention Wilson, who, except for Brooks (and in one sense Kenneth Burke), has been the one major critic of our immediate time. And considering that Brooks is writing what in one sense is a rival history, isn't it untactful to give free rein to his second bitterest enemy (the first being DeVoto)? The three Epilogues sound to me very unpromising, almost like passing wind after a big dinner.

[. . .]

Cordially yours,
Malcolm Cowley

[RES TLS-2]
[TO: ROBERT E. SPILLER]
February 21, 1945

Dear Bob,

Now I think you're really talking about the final chapter of the History.[35] That's a subject on which something can be said—imagine, for example, the contrast in a few years between Eliot's going to England in 1914 and Auden's coming to America in 1938, both to find a milieu in which they could write. Or the fact that James and Twain, our two best writers of their time, were never seriously considered for the Nobel Prize, whereas Lewis and O'Neill and Pearl Buck all received the prize in a single decade. Or the religious study that young French writers devoted to Faulkner, young English writers to Hemingway, young German writers before the war to Thomas Wolfe, young Russian writers first to Dos Passos then to Hemingway. Or the printing of [John Steinbeck's] *The Moon Is Down* by the French underground, while *The Grapes of Wrath* was being published in Germany as anti-American propaganda. But I should think the chapter might be expanded, not in length but in subject, to a consideration of the interaction between European and American literature—American literature freed by Europe in the years after 1910 (see studies like Oscar Cargill's) and European literature looking for freedom to American literature in the years after 1933; the wave of American exiles to Europe being replaced by a wave of European literary exiles to America, with New York becoming for a time the center of free literature in the world. Or a comparison of American publishers' lists in 1914 (especially Macmillan's and George H. Doran's, the two largest), with English publishers' lists in 1938—the first full of English books, the second full of American books.

Who to write it? MacLeish knows the subject, and although his style seems to me inflated, he might do a very good job on this subject, especially if he'd put one of his Library of Congress assistants to work digging up new material. I'd try him first.[36]

[...]

As ever,
Malcolm

[NL TL/CC-2]
[TO: MRS. JOHN R. MARSH (MARGARET MITCHELL)]
August 7, 1945

Dear Mrs. Marsh:

The last chapter of "The Literary History of the United States," which I have the job of writing (I mean the chapter, not the history) is supposed to deal with the influence of American literature abroad since 1900. And a great deal of that influence is centered in *Gone with the Wind*.

"The Literary History of the United States" is a big symposium planned to take the place of *The Cambridge History of American Literature*. [...] The contributors will include most of the distinguished professors of American literature in American colleges. I don't know what I'm doing among all those long gray beards, but there I am, and I'll try to make the best of it. The contributors took me in, like an orphan on the doorstep, because they thought I knew more than they did about American books abroad. I do, but there's a lot of research to be done before I can write the chapter.

I am writing you now, with a cry for help, because it seems to me that the reception of *Gone with the Wind* is the biggest single phenomenon in the history of American literature in the rest of the world. I should guess that you would prefer not to have the subject discussed in the big magazines, or articles would have appeared already. But this scholarly symposium, this history of American literature, is a different matter—a matter of historical records that ought to be complete—and perhaps you could find a few minutes to answer some questions, from your own records.

What I should like to know is:

1. In how many foreign countries has *Gone with the Wind* been published?
2. Into how many foreign languages has it been translated?
3. What (if they aren't a secret) have been its approximate sales in Great Britain? In France? In Germany before the war? In Sweden? In Argentina?
4. (Less important)—when was it published in each of the six countries listed above?

[...]

I ran into some facts about *Gone with the Wind* in France that might interest you. Jean-Paul Sartre, the best of our new dramatists, explained to me its special wartime popularity. "The Germans allowed it to be read," he said, "because [they] thought it would make the French dislike the Yankees. But it didn't have that effect at all. The reason the French read it—devoured it, you might say"—I'm translating freely—"was that it gave a picture of another occupied country that resisted the invaders. They drew strength from it."—Jacques Schiffrin, who is André Gide's friend and publisher, gave the highbrow French verdict on *Gone with the Wind*. He said to me, "Now confess—it's better than Dos Passos, isn't it?" Dos Passos having a very high standing among the French highbrows. Peter Rhodes, a young man who works for the Office of War Information, reached Lyons with the first American forces. He found copies of *Gone with the Wind*—worn second-hand copies—selling on the semi-black or gray market at 3,500 to 4,000 francs per copy, depending on their conditions, from $70 to $80 at the official rate of exchange. I hear that new copies of the "limited" edition sold for $100.

Sincerely yours,
Malcolm Cowley

[NL TL/CC-2]
[TO: ROBERT E. SPILLER]
August 5, 1946

Dear Bob:

[...]

And one more point of difference: I think it's very hard to make a distinction between serious and best-selling literature. A highbrow French publisher once said to me, speaking of *Gone with the Wind,* "After all you'll have to admit that it's better than Dos Passos," and I thought about it and I'm not sure that he isn't right. I'm not sure that *Uncle Tom's Cabin* isn't better literature than Melville's *White-Jacket,* and I'm sure that it's better than *Maggie, a Girl of the Streets.* Without mentioning some of the popular authors, it's hard to get a true picture of the foreign reception of our books—especially since some of those authors are taken very seriously abroad (z.B. Jack London in Russia). [...]

As ever,
Malcolm

{ ————— }

July 4, 1946

Dear Newton:

[...]

Thanks for your remarks about the Whitman pieces, about which I wouldn't have been offended if you had spoken much less gently.[37] I had read a good deal of the writing about Whitman, and had gotten pretty impatient with it. Everybody except you and one or two others skirted delicately around his homosexuality (on this subject Canby, who knows better, made me feel like an attendant at a funeral service for the town drunkard, at which the deceased is praised without one reference to the bottle). Also I thought I really had a little illumination to offer, having known Hart Crane very well and noted some respects in which his pattern of action illuminated Whitman's pattern—but with a difference, for Hart was in many ways a repressed heterosexual, whereas old Walt physically couldn't bear women; maybe he visited a Brooklyn parlor house in his youth, for sometimes the "Children of Adam" poems seem to be documented from memory; but once he discovered the delights of another way of love, he was through with all that. I thought that all this had better be said for once and said flatly, without apologies or anything, just said—after which the discussion of Whitman could proceed with all the facts taken into account. The two pieces in the NR were part of a projected, much longer essay, in which I intended to try to fit the pieces together and make judgments; and I'm still going to write that essay some day; and if or when I do Whitman as part of a longer study of American literature, I'm going to cut down my discussion of his homosexuality, on the theory that once it has been said, it has been said.

[...]

As ever,
Malcolm

––––––––

[RPW TLS-2][PMC 479–480]
[TO: ROBERT PENN WARREN]
July 24, 1946

Dear Red:

I like very much the idea of a special number of *Kenyon* [*Review*] devoted to Faulkner, and I should like to contribute to it. Unfortunately I find myself in the state of being written out, practically, about Faulkner. There is just one point that I had to make and didn't develop in my series of pieces about him [...]. The one point was about Faulkner [...] as a Southern nationalist, and the South itself as a sort of incomplete or frustrated nation, belonging somewhere in a scale of more or less realized nations that might include, say, Scotland, Brittany, Provence, Catalonia, Croatia, Ukrainia, God knows how many other countries that aren't shown on most political maps. I sometimes think that the Southern attitude toward Negroes, which to Northerners is the sticking point, is maintained partly as a slogan or flag or emblem of something that is fundamentally quite other . . . Language is another flag or emblem which Southerners, in this case, have chosen not to wave, although they would have more justification for doing so than Norwegians or Croatians or Slovakians, each of which peoples has *invented* a language, simply by writing literary works in the dialect of a given district. [...]

[...]

I read your novel [*All the King's Men* (1946)] and was enthusiastic. Wrote a letter to Lambert Davis[38] about it, which he wanted to use as a blurb—now he tells me that he lost the letter [...] but the gist of my remarks was that one felt from the first page that here was a picture of how things were—that one was held from the first page—that your work as a novelist, always brilliant but sometimes dispersed, had this time come together, taken shape. . . . For your own ear, let me add that the Huey Long figure is more

interesting than the hero, that I think the structure does get a little loose beyond the middle of the book (until the drama of the end) through the divided
focus; that the women are fine, especially the Governor's wife and Sadie
Burke; that all together it's a damned impressive job, the best novel I have
read since God knows when.

I'm hoping you get the trip East so we can see you.

As ever,
Malcolm

[NL TL/CC-I]
[TO: ALLAN DOWLING]
[August 22, 1946]

Dear Mr. Dowling:

I was more than pleased, I was delighted to get your letter.[39] You can be
sure that everybody who wrote for *The Dial* and thousands of people who
merely read it would be glad to have the magazine revived. [. . .]

I think its policy might be to gather the best contributors to the old
Dial, including Burke, Marianne Moore, Cummings—then jump forward
a whole generation to discover the new writers now beginning to appear.
Like the old *Dial,* I think it should have European connections and print
some of the best of the new work from France, England, Scandinavia, the
Argentine; possibly from Russia if good work can be discovered there. I
think it should be dedicated (like the old *Dial,* but more explicitly) to the
ideal of a Republic of Letters existing in spite of national divisions. I am at
present an old-fashioned Unpolitical Man of the type existing in greater
numbers before the First World War, but I loathe and detest the sort of loud-
voiced nationalism from which we are beginning to suffer, and I should like
to do a little to counteract it by presenting the best literary work of other
countries.

[. . .] The magazine should try hard to maintain a tone of cultivated and
easy writing, not a *Dial* style, but just style. To my knowledge there are not
fifty men in the United States who write well enough so that one can send
their copy to the printer without correction. Those fifty (or not-fifty) should
be encouraged to write for *The Dial.*

[. . .]

Perhaps I sound dogmatic in setting down all these ideas, which may not fit in with your ideas at all. I simply thought that if you were interested in having me as an editor or consulting editor, you would want to know exactly how I felt about the sort of magazine for which there is a place. It is the one organ this country needs, the one lack that has existed (with a few admirable but unsuccessful attempts to fill it) since [James Sibley] Watson got tired of supporting *The Dial* in 1929, after poor [Scofield] Thayer had gone to the asylum. We have illustrated magazines, political magazines, story magazines, but we haven't any magazine—except the little ones—that tries to maintain literary and artistic standards, that tries to present, simply, the best work, without being frightened because it is new or disdainful because it isn't in the fashion—Eliot and Faulkner and Sartre and boys just out of the army and Van Wyck Brooks when he's writing instead of scolding, graybeards and pantywaists, so long as they are writers, so long as they have the métier, not just the profession.

[. . .]

Faithfully yours,
Malcolm Cowley

———————

[NL TL/CC-2]
[TO: MARY MELLON]
October 5, 1946

Dear Mary:

In spite of the address at the head of this letter, I'm writing from Yaddo, where I've been spending the last three weeks. Yaddo is wonderful, beginning with the name; I'll have to tell you something about it. The name was a little girl's pronunciation of "shadow." The little girl was the daughter of Spencer Trask, a real robber baron of the 1890s; his portrait hangs downstairs, that of a big, dignified man with a short, heavy beard and short velvet breeches, like the Laird of Skibo. The little girl died; so did her sister and her two brothers, and the Trasks were left childless by 1900. Mrs. Trask managed not to go crazy by developing an interest in poets and poetry; she used to hold court for the poetasters of the time, including the Episcopal Bishop of

Albany, who wrote sonnets to her and incised them on the lattice windows with his episcopal diamond ring.

Mr. Trask had six horses hitched to the coach and drove to the railroad station on Christmas day, 1904; he had to get back to Wall Street. But he missed the train, ordered up a special train in his baronial fashion, just as he might have told the doorman to whistle for a cab, and the special train was wrecked. Mrs. Trask married George Foster Peabody, her husband's former partner, who had loved her mutely for many years; she went on entertaining poets; and when she died about 1920, she left her estate as a refuge for creative artists.

That's where I've been for the last three weeks, refugeeing among the creative artists. The fact is that I'm an old refugee of the place, a member of the Corporation, no less. It really has done a lot for writers and painters and musicians who hadn't anywhere to work in quiet, and sometimes not enough money for baked beans. When the place is thick with artists, in summer, the atmosphere gets too rich for me; but I like to come here in late September, when Mrs. Ames, the director, has cleared out all but half a dozen, who live in a quiet way and work. No interruptions, no activities—you just eat breakfast, go to your room and write. In the late afternoon, you go downstairs and look over the furniture that the Trasks assembled—dark Jacobean oak, little mother-of-pearl inlaid gimcracks from India and a couple of Russian troikas scattered through a hall as big as a parade ground. Paintings by Elihu Vedder and imitators of Sargent. Enough silver plate to fit out a luxury hotel. You go into a dark hallway, stumble over what you think is a hatrack, and find that it isn't a hatrack at all, but a stray Chinese novelist named Lao Shaw.

Enough about Yaddo, though I could go on for a volume. [. . .] There's a man named Allan Dowling who wants to revive *The Dial*. I'm very much interested in his proposal because I thought *The Dial* was fine, and now there is absolutely no literary magazine of general circulation to take its place; there's nothing in the magazine world—not to mention *The Dial*—that's as good as *The Century* and *Scribner's* and *Harper's* were in the 1890s when they serialized Henry James; no American magazine would dare to serialize a writer as difficult as James today. Those literary magazines of the 1890s had quite large circulations—more than half a million for the three of them

together—and held the circulations until 1910. I think a good literary magazine today might have as many as 100,000 readers eventually; and if I decide that Dowling has the ability and the capital (that's a big question) to
revive *The Dial*, I'll give him all the help I can.[40]

But you must be getting bored with this too-long letter. Do tell me about
your trip to Switzerland; why, you may be there now for all I know, or you
may have run into difficulties that delayed you. I hope very much to see you
when you get to New York.

As ever,
Malcolm Cowley

―――――――

[NL TL/CC-1]
[TO: PAUL MELLON]
October 12, 1946

Dear Mr. Mellon:

I was startled and shocked and grieved more than I can tell you by the
news that I just now read in the morning paper.[41] The last time I saw Mary—
and you for a little while—in New York, she seemed not at all borne down by
all her illnesses, much more concerned by the troubles of her parents, and, as
always, the most vital and interested person I had ever known. She had a
genius for life; I think she lived more than people who survive to a hundred.
And yet she told me another time, when we were talking about Jung, that
one had to make oneself ready for death, like—I think she said—wheat
ripening for the harvest; it was a remark that always stuck in my mind when
I thought about her. Perhaps we could think of all her intense activities during the last few years as a sort of ripening and preparation for an event to
which I am sure she unconsciously looked forward without fear.

I owe such a great debt to her that I could never tell anybody except you.
It was after three or four bad years, when my head was unbowed but pretty
bloody, that I had a telephone call from Stanley Young, who explained her
plan for writers as well as he could over a party line. Soon afterwards I met
Mary, and we talked at a restaurant table for a whole afternoon, a little about
books, but mostly about our parents, our children and everybody's problem
of adjusting himself to life and death. That afternoon was a turning point in

my own life; after that I had time to do my own work, instead of just writing for magazines, and the work, I think, has been good—at any rate the critics have liked it; and every time a book or an essay of mine has been praised, I have felt like saying, "I could tell you who is really to be thanked and praised for it." And when I think how many other people Mary has helped, often with money, often, too, by merely talking to them and giving them a new direction, I believe that she was one of the great women of our time. The world is different for me and many others because of her.

Sincerely yours,
Malcolm Cowley

[DM TLS-2] [NL TL/CC-2]
[TO: DWIGHT MACDONALD, *POLITICS*]
March 6, 1947

Dear Macdonald:

Here is a letter, not for publication, that is costing me $3.50 to write, so I'll try to keep down my expenses to minus one cent per word. The point is that I've been reading a whole collection of non-commercial, chiefly literary magazines for an article in *The New Republic*.[42] *Politics* is the most interesting of the lot, maybe the only one I'd eagerly pick up to read, and I want a subscription. But also I'd like, not for publication, to state some differences and agreements with your policies.

On Russia first. You say often, and I'd echo you more loudly, that qualities like truth, freedom, courage, kindness (and why not say more often, humility?) are more important than immediate political aims. You think that Stalinism is at present the chief enemy of these qualities (I'd dissent only by saying "one of the chief enemies") and therefore (here's where my dissent comes in), you use less than your ordinary measure of truth, freedom, kindness, etc. when writing about the Stalinists. There's a great difference here, though, between *Politics* and *Partisan* (when it goes in for politics). *Partisan* when writing about Stalinism feels that it has an entire license to forget about truth, freedom, courage, kindness or humility; and thus makes itself an example of bolshevism turned upside down, bad means justified by no end whatsoever except (as you pointed out) defense of American policy.

Now, I may be even more impractical than you, but it seems to me the best weapons against the bad side of bolshevism are exactly truth, freedom, courage, kindness and humility.

[. . .]. The danger of a monolithic state is now so great that *any* opposition based on individual thinking is to be encouraged, even if the thinking is weak. But that same argument also applies to the American Communists, in so far as they aren't Russian agents, and very few of them are; the agents belong to another *Apparat*. They have the virtue now of being a dissident and persecuted minority, and I'll be damned if I howl with the mob against them. When there aren't any more political minorities in this country, we'll have gone the way of Sodom and Gomorrha.

Two suggestions that might give future articles in *Politics* a more practical base. (1) Why not a little Marxian analysis in the field where it is best, that of class economics? [. . .] And (2), what about setting somebody to work on the American secret police in its various branches, notably the FBI. As a result of my experiences in Washington five years ago, I'm one of the few Americans who have seen their own dossiers in the FBI files. Mine was immense and so full of unsupported falsehoods that it was terrifying. I went to Biddle[43] and demanded some sort of hearing so that I could set the record straight. Biddle wanted to give it to me, but there were administrative difficulties and he wasn't much of a fighter—and the result is that that enormous dossier full of lies still rests in the FBI files. If you could see your dossier, I'll bet it would be terrifying too—especially if the FBI has followed the system with you it did with me, of reading my articles to see whom I had differed with, then going to these persons to get their statements without any witness to check them. In the present economy wave, I'll also bet that FBI gets more money than ever, because American conservatives want to dismantle the state apparatus *all except its police system*. This is a subject that even the "progressive" magazines—or perhaps the progressive magazines most of all—are now afraid to discuss.[44]

Anyhow, here's my check, and I see that I have overrun my wordage again.

Sincerely yours,
Malcolm Cowley

Two lectures that Cowley gave at Syracuse University in June 1947 show that he fully shared in the attempt to establish a canon of American writing that was based on defining "the American character" and that could usefully serve in the growing institutionalization of literary study in the postwar years.

[NL TL/CC-1]
[TO: EDWIN H. CADY, SYRACUSE UNIVERSITY]
June 2, 1947[45]

Dear Mr. Cady:

[...]

For my first and rather more formal talk, I thought of the title "Why Teach American Literature? A Critic's Answer." The answer would be affirmative, of course; and I should discuss, among other things, the need for books that one can take for granted that almost everyone has read, and the reason why certain American books should be required reading in every American college. I wouldn't say that they were the world's best books, for that is literary chauvinism, as objectionable and almost as dangerous as other forms of chauvinism. What I would say is that they cast an absolutely necessary light on the American character.

For the second and more informal talk, on Tuesday, my title might be "Some Notes for Postwar Writers." I would make it a more personal, even autobiographical talk and would try to compare the situations facing two literary generations, in 1919 and 1947. And though I should be talking *for postwar writers*, not teachers, I don't see any harm in that, because my audience would consist of the men who will have to teach the writers; I should be trying a combination shot rather than a direct cut into the corner pocket.

[...]

Sincerely yours,
Malcolm Cowley

[NL TL/CC-1]
[TO: EDWIN H. CADY, SYRACUSE UNIVERSITY]
June 12, 1947

Dear Mr. Cady:

[...]

I promised to give you brief abstracts of my two talks; they are enclosed with this letter. Very brief and bad abstracts they are, but perhaps they will serve your purpose.

[...]

Cordially yours,
Malcolm Cowley

June 9 Lecture, "Why Teach American Literature?"

American literature deserves a more central position in the college curriculum than it has received during the last ten years, which in turn is vastly more central than the position it received at any previous time. The justification for giving it such position is not that it is the greatest of modern literatures; that American civilization is the greatest in the world; nor even that it furnishes an accurate copy of American civilization. These various doctrines are a danger at the present time because they lead to at least two heresies in the teaching of American literature: the first heresy is chauvinism; the second might be called representationalism, the doctrine that a book is to be judged as a copy of the external features of American life.

Literature has many functions, but one of its chief functions is to *humanize* society and nature by transforming both into concepts that can be seized by the human imagination. American literature has performed this function admirably by filling the once alien countryside with legends. A national literature also has the function of serving as a unifying element in the national culture. American literature can serve this function, too, but only if it is generally known. And because it *should* be more widely known, the critic recommends the compulsory study of those American books that can be generally recognized as classics.

A final point in the lecture was the continuity of certain national qualities in American literature. Once this country built up a literary tradition based on those qualities. The tradition was broken somewhere between 1890 and 1910, so that the revival of American literature was based on European instead of American models. Nevertheless, instinctively, the new writers returned to the mood of the old ones, so that in some measure Van Wyck Brooks in his early years repeated Emerson, Faulkner repeated Hawthorne, Wolfe and Hart Crane in their different fashions repeated Whitman, and Hemingway in his novels presented the same mixture of abnormal psychology and wild adventure (with Indians) that one finds in Charles Brockden Brown.

June 10 Lecture, "Some Notes for Postwar Writers"

The interwar generation of American writers—Hemingway, Faulkner, Dos Passos, Wolfe, Crane, Cummings and the others—has played an important part in the history of American literature. It established a new level of professional competence in American fiction. It wrote books with a new sort of depth and complexity and power. It dealt with aspects of its own country and revealed them under a new light. It developed a new prose style based on American as a spoken language. It managed to win for itself a place in world literature. Finally, it managed to make the writing of books a career, and one that is open to young Americans.

It was a lucky generation; and the generation that followed was not so lucky, since it had to face the disabilities forced on it by a long depression followed by a long war. The fact that it hasn't produced so many interesting books as the other generation had produced at the same age is not its fault, but still is a fact to be noted. The still younger generation, the one that came of age during World War II, has apparently more opportunities, and we look forward to the books it will produce, without being able as yet to prophesy their nature (except for already obvious tendencies like that toward the study of psychology and the interest in what has come to be known as "magic" in the Kafka manner).

There is a special need for good writers today because the world is suffering from lack of imagination that makes us too tired or torpid to picture the joys and suffering of other men. The writer—the good writer—has imagination and uses it as part of his technical equipment. He has the power to broaden our imaginative scope; to make us feel, for example, that Frenchmen are not merely Frogs, or Italians Wops, or colored persons niggers; that all of us are part of a brotherhood that is bigger than national or racial boundaries.

[NL TL/CC-2] [PMC 480–482]
[TO: SHEILA CUDAHY PELLEGRINI, PELLEGRINI & CUDAHY]
June 27, 1947

Dear Mrs. Pellegrini:

You could have knocked me over with a large humming-bird's feather when George Soule telephoned me to say that Pilot Press was disposing of its effects to Pellegrini & Cudahy. [. . .] But I was delighted to hear that the American Classics series[46] was falling into good hands, namely, yours.

[. . .]

I have a lot of new things to say about Whitman—good Lord, I could write a book about him instead of a simple essay. I used to hate his poetry for its inflatedness and catalogues of names and damp, sticky quality; he wrote more bad verse than any other American except Ella Wheeler Wilcox;[47] but when he was good he was, oh, so good, so full of fresh sights, sounds, phrases, as if he had waked at five in the morning in a totally new summer world. If you remember that he lied about his family—that actually it was poor, that one brother, a sailor, died of paresis, that another married a drunken prostitute and still another was a congenital idiot, then you understand what he meant when he said in one place that he spoke for inarticulate generations:

> Through me many long dumb voices,
> Voices of the interminable generations of prisoners and
>   slaves,
> Voices of the diseas'd and despairing and of thieves and
>   dwarfs,
> Voices of cycles of preparation and accretion,

And of the threads that connect the stars, and of wombs and
        of the father-stuff,
And of the rights of them the others are down upon,
Of the deform'd, trivial, flat, foolish, despised,
Fog in the air, beetles rolling balls of dung.

There—and elsewhere in his earliest poems—he struck down to something grand and elemental. "Song of Myself" is his longest poem, and his best, and it's more like Rimbaud's "A Season in Hell" than like anything written in America, and it comes before Rimbaud, and is actually better, and it has always been read by the wrong people. Whitman has to be taken away from the professors and the politicians; he's too good a poet to belong to them. [. . .]

As ever,
Malcolm Cowley

———————

[NL TL/COPY-3]
[TO: NATHAN ASCH]
December 31, 1947

Dear Nathan:

I would like to start the New Year by immediately getting to work on your novel which you have been painstakingly evolving for the past two years.[48] But I would not be doing justice to you nor to my own conscience if I did not let you have my honest reaction to it.

Let me say right off that the quality of your writing is, as I expected, enormously satisfying from the standpoint of craft. There are sections (such as the description of a day at Café [du] Dôme) which are brilliantly evocative. It is writing which flows with seeming effortlessness, arousing vivid pictorial images, evoking subtle nuances of feeling, and generally setting the stage in time and in emotional tone, and peopling it (if in fleeting, cinematic fashion) with credible personalities. What is disturbing to me is the absence of a unifying idea. This is a lack which is undoubtedly more real to me than it is to you; you have the advantage of having in your mind's eye a beginning, a middle and an end which may be fully realized when all of Kranz's life unfolds in the remaining books of your series.

[...]⁴⁹

To sum up my reaction in an undoubtedly inadequate way, I would say this: I am charmed, affected, and frequently dazzled by the excellence of your writing. I am also at a loss to discover in it any recognizable philosophic content. I say this fully realizing that this will never be the kind of book to be judged on the basis of "narrative drive," "story line," or any such standard yardstick. It may be that there will be a cohesion of idea when you finally have all of your series on paper. But as this particular book stands now, it carries no meaning for me, only the enjoyment of fine prose and the savoring of individual episode.

Well, I now bare my breast to the blasts which I know will blow in my direction from California. I am waiting for your comments on my possibly reckless ones; perhaps something will be said which will make me proceed more hopefully at this end.

My very best to you and Carol for the New Year,

Malcolm

[ASCH TLS-1]
[TO: NATHAN ASCH]
March 19, 1948

Dear Nathan:

[...]

The *famille Cowley* is just back from Havana.⁵⁰ The idea was that *Life* wanted a story on Hemingway, to be published when his novel appears. I learned that the novel won't appear until the fall of 1949, though the manuscript is now immensely long—apparently the project keeps growing as he works on it. I thought that Papa, as everybody calls him now, was an extremely nice person. He regards himself as a great man, which is irritating, but also he is willing to pay the high cost of greatness, which is admirable. By the high cost of greatness I mean not only the financial cost—and he lives continually beyond his means—but also the emotional cost, the sheer labor of being continually attentive to the people around him, of *giving* himself at much expense to his work. He spoke highly of you. He said, "Nathan can write," something that he says of very few people. He also said, "He doesn't think," which is not so true, but which is a comment on the behavioristic quality in your writing—it *is* your fault that you give the stream of sensation too purely. But in Hemingway's mind the ability to write outweighs every- thing else and he thinks that damned few people can do it.

If you have any time or energy outside of your toil over the manuscript, I'd be very grateful if you'd write me some notes about Hemingway. What I could use best would be specific information about H as a boxer (the Charles Francis affair, for example), as a big man among the young writers in Paris, and as a war correspondent at the Ritz.[51] Is the stuff in your book straight reporting that can be used, or did you change the facts in changing the names? I might end by writing a longer piece about him than *Life* could use, for I gathered a lot of dope during the trip.[52]

[. . .]

As ever,
Malcolm

————

[KB TLS-I] [SC 282–283]
[TO: KENNETH BURKE]
February 14, 1948

Dear Kenneth:

[. . .] I work on Hawthorne—find more of his deliciously narcissistic fig- ures of speech and symbols. Mirror equals fountain or pool or brook; snakes live in pool ("The Bosom Serpent"); brook winds like serpent; once Mr. Bull- frog thinks of marrying his own image in the mirror. Through self-absorption the outside world grows unreal (many passages at this point) and the heart itself grows chill, sluggish, torpid—he abounds in such adjectives. His wife ("The Birthmark") has a birthmark on her face in the shape of a little hand! My guess is that Hawthorne masturbated much less than the average college- level male interviewed for the Kinsey Report; he simply brooded more over the fact, had a sharper conscience, felt himself more utterly damned. Then he became *real* through marriage and tried to build himself a new factual life on the crust he formed above his quagmire—that failed him because he buried his Demon, finally. I shouldn't spend so much time on this bedroom peeping. The more important fact is that Hawthorne was really the first artist in American fiction—much more conscious of his own aims than Poe, who chiefly made a parade of consciousness.[53]

As ever,
Malcolm

———————————

[EH TLS-2] [PARTLY *PMC* 482–483]
[TO: ERNEST HEMINGWAY]
July 11, 1948

Dear Ernest:

I found your letter (July 5) waiting when we got back from a short trip into New Hampshire and Vermont. I had to give a lecture and also we had to deposit Rob at the Exeter summer school. It was his first separation from his parents. On the morning we left, he was ready before anyone else; he kissed the dog and then went outside to touch the trees. He spent a long time in the bathroom and when he came out his mother saw that there were streaks on his face. "Those look like tears," he said, "but they're just water where I splashed my face." On the trip he was unusually silent, and very nervous when we were delayed by a rainstorm; but we reached Exeter in time and he was caught up in the machinery. We left him in a big brick dormitory feeling a little consoled because his bicycle had arrived. [. . .]

[. . .]

[. . .] I feel honestly and humbly grateful that you should have offered a loan, but it isn't needed now, and I'll bet you're going to need it about the time that income-tax payments fall due. For me the problem is to get over the buck fever that I feel so often when sitting down at the typewriter. Trouble is that I always want to do better work than I'm capable of doing, with the result that often I don't do any work at all. I suspect that a great many serious authors suffer from that same complaint. I hear that Mark Twain had whole trunkfuls of unfinished books, and he wrote easily—comparatively speaking—whereas most of us write hard, and it keeps getting harder all the time. But it has to be done, and without shortcuts. I've known a lot of authors who were psychoanalyzed and cured, both of the complaints they wanted to have cured and also of that other complaint known as good writing. Maybe our faults are all we have to depend on.

Look, I'm still in a state of profound confusion about your wounds in Italy, after reading pretty near everything that was ever published about them. Here's the story that I've got pieced together: (1) Bad wound two weeks before your nineteenth birthday, when you were on that morale job. Trench-mortar burst; something between 180 and 257 fragments removed from legs; in hospitals all summer. (2) Wounded on two other occasions before Armistice Day. (3) One of these two occasions was at night on the Piave, when you carried the guy up the ditch away from the river, with the searchlight playing on you; that might have been when you got machine-gunned. At the time you were a lieutenant in the Arditi. (4) In hospitals for some time after Armistice.

[...] Tell me if I'm too far wrong, or don't tell me if you don't want to talk about it, what the hell.

My best regards to all your 209 ¾ pounds and hail and farewell to the poundage that has disappeared. Weight now sounds swell, and you sound as if you were keeping good watch on the pressure in the pipes. Hope the writing has gotten under way again.

As ever,
Malcolm

Over-compensation is probably the answer to a lot of things in [Hemingway's] character. [...] He wasn't a tough guy who taught himself how to write; he was a tender guy who painfully taught himself how to be tough.

Cowley to Otto McFeely, July 24, 1948 [NL]

[WFC TLS-3] [FCF 99–102]
[TO: WILLIAM FAULKNER]
July 20, 1948

Dear Brother Faulkner:

[...]

When you get North you'll find that you're not a neglected author any longer, that they're studying you in the colleges, including Yale, where lots of the kids think that "The Bear" is the greatest story ever written, and that you'll have to resign yourself to bearing the expense of greatness, which is a pretty high expense. Hemingway loves being a great man, it's something he needs and demands, and nobody begrudges it to him because he keeps paying for it at every moment in terms of kindness and attention and thoughtfulness to anyone around him. He lives like old Father Abraham in the midst of his flocks and herds of servants and wives and children and friends and dependents, watching out for them, teaching and advising them, writing them letters—and meanwhile screwing the big motion-picture people so that he can get money to maintain his retinue. He just sold an almost unfilmable short story, "The Snows of Kilimanjaro," to the movies for $125,000. It's a curious life for a writer (though Mark Twain lived something like that) and Hemingway is a curious and very likeable person and drinks enough to put almost anyone else in the alcoholic ward—then spends much of the night reading because he can't sleep and goes to work in the morning on the big novel he's had around for seven or eight years and doesn't know when he'll finish; I think he's got buck fever about that novel; it *has* to be good when it comes out, and either he'll keep working on it until it *is* good or else he'll somehow manage never to finish it. You would stifle and go crazy in the mob that surrounds him—and yet when you come North you're going to have your experience of being admired and flattered; and you might as well get ready to face it, because it's one of the things you bargained for, part of the stuff in fine print that was on the contract you signed when you became a writer, a hell of a long time since.

I went to a local party last week end and a drunk whom I like walled me off in a corner to talk about Faulkner. First he praised the *Portable* and then he became belligerent. "Why, you bastard," he said, "why did you say that 'Spotted Horses' was as good as Mark Twain? Couldn't you see that it was twice as funny as anything Mark Twain ever wrote?" Well, I ducked out of that one by mixing him another drink; but you can see how things are going. My uncalled-for advice: just keep away from big parties, from fools and old women, and everything will be swell.

[...]

Two questions meanwhile: what's the novel that's coming out this fall (I'll have to review it), and is the other novel, the one about World War I, finished yet?[54] And a mild speculation: why shouldn't the movies buy some of your old stories, the way they buy Hemingway's, so that you wouldn't have to work for the bastards any more?

As ever,

Malcolm

[EH TLS-2]

[TO: ERNEST HEMINGWAY]

August 5, 1948

Dear Ernest:

Long time I no write. I was going to write you on your birthday and then a painter named Arshile Gorky[55] went off and hanged himself and I was kept busy searching for the body, making statements to the police, etc. Gorky had been threatening to hang himself for a long time. Three years ago his studio burned down and he lost a lot of paintings. Right after that he was found to have cancer of the rectum and his big intestine was removed, so that he had to shit through a hole just below his navel—every other morning he would spend three hours flushing himself out till the water came through absolutely clean. On July 6 his dealer was driving him home through a rainstorm, went too fast, skidded and overturned the car. Gorky had two vertebrae fractured, was kept in traction at the hospital for ten days, and then was sent home with a sort of football harness, but bigger, like the one that Erich von Stroheim wore in *The Great Illusion*. He was afraid that his right arm was paralyzed and that he couldn't paint.

That's the story I told the police, every word of it true. But the reason he committed suicide was that he had a beautiful, charming and hyperthyroid young wife who was leaving him and taking the two little children, whom he adored. I think the operation had left him impotent or nearly so and wife just couldn't stand it, and he couldn't stand having her sleep around, so he beat her and she said it was over. She had taken the children and gone to her mother's in Virginia. On the morning of July 21 he telephoned friends in Connecticut and New York and told them that he was going to hang himself. The friends telephoned us and telephoned the Blumes and we went over to see what we could do. We found the house empty, though we kept opening closets expecting to find a body. In his studio the big canvas on the easel had a hole punched in it. Upstairs in his wife's sewing cabinet Muriel and Ebie Blume found his wallet with $200 in it. The wallet was in his wife's diary, next to the last entry, for June 18. She had written: "A day for life and love. I know that people are going to think I'm a bitch for what I'm going to do, but I have to do it."

Peter Blume and I made a search of the grounds. We found a rope lying on the ground at the door of an old barn and another rope inside, hanging from a rafter, and still another rope under an apple tree near his burned studio. We went to a waterfall on the property where he used to sit and sketch. That was a drive and then a walk through the woods, and when we got back from the walk I found that I had lost the key to the car and had to go look for it. By the time I found it and drove back to continue the search through a lot of outbuildings, it was nearly one o'clock. As Peter and I approached a shed near an abandoned stonecrusher, Gorky's dog came out and began nipping at our heels, so I was expecting to see what I did when I turned the corner. But I hadn't expected him to be so waxlike, with his neck stretched until his toes were only an inch from the ground and his eyes wide open and staring down at us contemptuously.

His wife came up next morning with her father, a retired naval officer, and arranged for the funeral. She stood by the grave and waited until the last shovelful was thrown in and tramped down and the sod smoothed over it, as if she wanted to be sure that was the last of him. And she told the Blumes what seems to me the strangest detail of the whole affair—he had phoned her in Virginia that morning, "I'm going to hang myself. I've washed my bowels this morning and I'm clean. I'm going out to the shed by the old stonecrusher. Goodbye." The wife said, "Goodbye, Gorky." If she had telephoned us then we could have gone to the stonecrusher and stopped him, but instead she went househunting with her mother and was very much relieved, she said, when she got back at one o'clock and heard that it was all over. Peter says that every suicide is a collaboration. But even if we had stopped Gorky that morning he would have killed himself later. If he couldn't have his beautiful wife he was going to make her feel guilty. That's what he said to one of his friends, "I'm going to hang myself and Agnes will feel a little guilty. I think it will be good for her to feel a little guilty."

I don't know why I'm telling you this anecdote except that it's been very much on my mind for the last two weeks, until at last I don't pity Gorky or condemn Agnes or feel that Gorky's death was anything but a formal spectacle, like a bullfight.

I've been writing about Papa Hemingway in my slow fashion and I've done ten thousand words so far, pretty pedestrian words, I'm afraid. Think I'd better cut loose soon and write some shit, as you call it—no, I'm getting your words wrong; you call it crap, and crap is what you want cut out of your manuscripts, but it's something that has to be written as a means of getting you (one) into the mood for writing good. Shit, in your vocabulary, is something else, it's dishonest writing, which should never be done at all. Well, I now propose to write some crap that I can cut out later. I never learned how to write, I only learned how to rewrite—but I'm trying your system of never stopping the day's work at the end of a section, so that I don't get left on dead center the following day.

I hope you've received Nathan Asch's manuscript—and remember that you asked for it.[56] [. . .] Sandy Calder and I are having a 50th birthday party next week, which is midway between his July 22 birthday and mine on August 24. Wish you could be there as a junior guest. You'd be amused by Sandy, who is 225-pound baby without brains in his head but a sort of genius in his fingers. At parties he usually goes to sleep right after dinner, then wakes at midnight when everybody else is dead tired and wants to start all over again. How's the slavery going? It had better be going good, because you haven't dedicated a book to Mary and I wouldn't blame her for getting impatient. [. . .]

As ever,
Malcolm

Yaddo, Saratoga Springs, N.Y.,
October 5, 1948

Dear Matty:

It was nice of you to write me about the review of *From the Heart of Europe.*[57] I'm not surprised that the book received unfair treatment in the press. These days the reviewers are falling over one another to prove that they detest the Russians and detest everybody who doesn't detest the Russians; and of course you left yourself open to their attacks with your fine unself-protectiveness. I think the book would have been more effective if you had kept your own opinions more in the background and had placed all the spotlights on the people you met in Europe; then the conclusions would have been implicit in the narrative. But it was fine of you to come out and say what you thought with disregard for the current hysteria.

[. . .]

These aren't very encouraging times in which to live, and I note at Yaddo that the seven guests don't rush for the morning paper as the guests always used to do—it lies there until I read it, not carefully, as I used to do, but just reading the first few paragraphs of each story. It's a sign of withdrawal and surrender by the intellectuals.

As ever,
Malcolm

November 17, 1948

Dear Granville and Dorothy:

[. . .] I've been pretty busy since I saw you. Faulkner was fine that Tuesday night at dinner, but they got him drinking and he went off the deep end. The following Sunday I drove to NY and brought him out here to sober up, which he did, by an effort of will that that made the sweat stand out on his forehead.[58] He'd have been a hopeless alcoholic years ago if he hadn't wanted to write novels more than anything else in the world. Anyhow he went back to NY and when I saw him at Random House two days later he was in fine shape, talking about his next two books—(1) a collected edition of his short stories—not including those in *Go Down, Moses,* which he wrote as a novel, just as I had suspected (and did you ever hear of any other author so casual about publishing that he allowed a novel to be published as a collection of short stories?) and (2) a very long allegorical novel, "The Cross: A Fable"— only it will just have a cross on the cover; it's the story of how Jesus appeared on the French front in 1918 and was executed; that sounds pretty bad, but he told me the story at length and some of it is going to be better than anything he has written. He's got 500 pages of it finished, with at least 500 more pages to come.

He's so much of a Southerner that he feels ill at ease in the North, like a German visiting in France. He's a small man (about 5 ft. 6 and weighing 140 pounds) who carries himself erect, almost like Napoleon; broad, low forehead, eagle beak—the face is classical, Mediterranean, though all his ancestry is Highland and Lowland Scots. He insisted that Gavin Stevens in *Intruder in the Dust* was not speaking for him, Faulkner, but for the best type of liberal Southerner; and when he read Wilson's review in the NYer he said, "I guess that was my fault for not making it clear that Stevens wasn't speaking for me." What I noticed in Faulkner was a bad conscience about the Negro—he can't do anything publicly without divorcing himself from his neighbors, so he keeps atoning for the Sin of the South by doing favors for individual Negroes. But he did cause a stink at the University of Mississippi by telling the students that Negroes should be admitted to the University.

[...]

As ever,
Malcolm

[NL TLS-2] [SC 285–286] [PMC 484–486]
[TO: KENNETH BURKE]
December 9, 1948

Dear Kenneth:

Here I am faced with the problem of writing a piece on Myths in American Literature[59] and the piece refuses to write itself and so I'm thinking aloud in a letter as if I were walking east along Ellsworth Avenue after the library had closed and telling you what I was vaguely planning to do.

Myths, I want to say, are permanent archetypes of human character and experience. Myths are the wise Ulysses, the dutiful Aeneas (is that the best reading for *pius*?), the courtly Lancelot and—leaping over a few centuries— Daniel Boone in the forest, Huckleberry Finn on the river and Buffalo Bill on the prairies. Myths provide a pattern for our emotions; they are variously shaped windows through which we look at the world.

A country without myths is a country naked of human associations in which we are intruders, not residents. A central concern of American writers from the very beginning has been to create or give a final form to myths that would make this new country our home. Many of them (Irving, Hawthorne, Poe) started by writing ghost stories. They were acting on the sound instinct that a house has to be a little haunted before we can feel at home in it.

In older countries the myths had a basis in folklore; they were repeated time after time at the fireside on winter evenings before they were copied into manuscripts. But this country was the first to be settled by men and women who were, in the majority, literate, so that they worked with printed words from the beginning. Oral traditions have played a great part in our myths, but they were quickly seized upon by professional writers, so that a figure like Paul Bunyan, for example, is one-tenth an invention of the lumbermen and nine-tenths a literary elaboration. Sometimes, yes, often, a figure invented by a man of letters—like Peter Rugg, invented by an obscure New England man of letters named William Austin—has passed into folklore and has been taken from folklore by other professional writers, as a subject myth; it seems to me that more of them—Leatherstocking, Evangeline, Captain Ahab, Huck Finn, the Connecticut Yankee, Babbitt, Daisy Miller and the Hemingway hero among others—come from literature than come from history

(Washington, Boone, Crockett, Lincoln) or from folklore like Mike Fink and Paul Bunyan. Indeed, it is the folklore heroes who have the dust of scholarship. Skipper Ireson (literature) is vivid where Captain Stormalong (folklore) seems academic.

Whitman was writing about the importance of myths in "Democratic Vistas." [. . .] And Whitman wrote the essay, not only to justify his own career, but to summon other "orbic bards, with unconditional, uncompromising sway," to create new myths for the nation.

I have a lot to say on the subject, and some fears that I might fall into nationalistic hurrah. I don't think most people realize how consciously our nineteenth-century writers set about the task of creating or transcribing American myths. They had found what they called romance in Europe and wanted to transport it to the American scene, so that it too would "serve to make our country dearer and more interesting to us," as Hawthorne said, "and afford fit soil for poetry to root itself in." By 1890 they had actually created a unified tissue of nationality—but then the country began changing from agricultural to industrial, rural to urban, and the new generation required new myths. The battle between idealism and realism that raged from 1886 to 1910 and after (to be revived in the Humanist controversy) was also a battle between two mythologies. Now the country has changed again and we are looking for new myths to express a new time.

And more and more to be said—but still I don't know how to begin or how to phrase my remarks, and I'm writing this letter chiefly in the effort to clarify my own muddy mind. But so far the mud refuses to settle. [. . .]

As ever,

Malcolm

[NHP TLS-1]
[TO: NORMAN HOLMES PEARSON][60]
December 19, 1948

Dear Norman:

[. . .] I'm impressed by the very complete mythology we had in 1890, in literature, and by the extent to which it was denied and even forgotten during the next thirty years, so that young American writers in 1920 started out like first settlers of an empty land. Of course the difficulty was that

Mythology I (Mythology I has Franklin; Mythology II has Jefferson, Jackson, Lincoln, Roosevelt) was built about an English (by derivation) and agricultural society, and was unsuited to an Irish-German-Norwegian-Lithuanian-Polish-Italian urbanized industrial society. The battle after 1890 was between two mythologies; the old one was rejected, but the new one has never been so well elaborated—even if, to set beside the Puritan, the Yankee Peddler, the Cavalier, the Frontiersman, the Roaring Boy (or hand-painted Crockett), the Self-Reliant Man, the Young Girl, the virtuous Self-Made Millionaire and other figures of Mythology I, it produced other stock figures—the Bad Titan or Robber Baron, the Little Man Oppressed by the Trusts, the Abysmal Brute, the Girl in the Green Hat (even if she started out by being English), the Mean Little Town, Babbitt, the Hemingway Hero, Tom Wolfe Himself, the Joads, the Decayed Plantation—and what others do you suggest? Lily Bart is pretty nearly a demigoddess in the pantheon; the last time I heard of her she was called Blanche DuBois, had been living in New Orleans near a streetcar line and was being led off to the loony bin. The mother with a silver apron string: she certainly belongs in the picture.

[. . .]

As ever,
Malcolm

———————

[WFC TLS-1] [FCF 122–124]
[TO: WILLIAM FAULKNER]
January 11, 1949

Dear Bill:

I understand how you feel, or rather I don't understand but merely accept it as a looming fact of nature.[61] Hadn't ever thought of doing a piece about you like the one on Hemingway, because I knew you didn't want that. The pictures & captions that go with the Hemingway piece are pretty God-awful—I hadn't anything to do with them—but my part of it, the text, is straight and I think it's what Ernest wanted, once he had decided to let himself be profiled. The story is what he told me and what I learned about him—except for the things that might have made trouble for him, which I was careful to omit. I'll hear how he feels about it very shortly, having just mailed him the piece to his Italian hide-out; he had refused to see it before publication.

About you I had thought of doing another sort of piece entirely, taking the focus off Mr. Faulkner and putting it on Yoknapatawpha County. Assembling the county from its scattered pieces. Pictures, but not of the author—pictures of a house like the Old Frenchman's place, and of a black man plowing, and of an old church in the pine hills, and of a crossroads store on Saturday afternoon. There would have to be something about you in the piece, but I thought I could confine myself to what has been printed by or about you and is therefore public property.

That's what I thought, anyway, but your letter makes me stop to think again. Maybe we can still work on this angle or find another that wouldn't infringe on your privacy. It would have to be something that would make a good piece or it wouldn't be worth doing—and by a good piece I mean something interesting to write and useful to readers of your books. But if we can't use this angle or plot out another, I'll have to let it drop and with a hell of a lot regret, because Messrs. Life & Co. would stake me to a trip to Mississippi and I would love to see you there, and they would pay a large round sum for the article, something I could use right now and feel happy about.

[...]

[...] I just finished reviewing Dos Passos' last novel [*The Grand Design*], which is terrible—disillusioned with everything he once admired and with everybody he used to like, and there have been great novels of disillusionment, like *The Possessed,* but it doesn't give Dos Passos an edge as it gave Dostoyevsky; it leaves him flat and trite and unable to feel anything about people except sometimes a dead pity and oftener a cold disgust.

As ever,

Malcolm

[AT TLS-2]
[TO: ALLEN TATE]
January 31, 1949

Dear Allen:

I was in NY yesterday for the annual dinner of the Poetry Society, the first time I had attended one of its august meetings for thirty-one years. Conrad Aiken beat my record; he hadn't been there since resigning from the society in 1917, thirty-two years. We were both charmed in to the occasion, a luncheon at Sherry's, by being invited as honorary guests, luncheons paid for and a bottle of Scotch circulating at the speakers' table, Conrad sitting between Marianne Moore and me and pretty happy till the meeting ended and he was assaulted by all the females in Queen Mary hats. On my other side was Emery Neff, whose work as a biographer of Robinson I had recently insulted by saying that he copied Hagedorn so closely that Hagedorn would have a good case against him under the copyright law.[62] But Neff, genial, didn't mention my review, and Marianne Moore said, "That was a good sentence of yours," as if in all my life I had written only one sentence. I was lucky—usually what she picks out to praise is one adjective. She has a mind like ten thousand sparrows, or a vision like them, and a cast-steel memory. Jim Putnam, that enormous ass, definitely rejected her translation of La Fontaine for Macmillans, so it is being published by Viking.[63] Leonora Speyer[64], dressed like a debutante, talked about something *Life* had done about the Sitwells and their choice of the world's greatest writers, which I hadn't heard about or seen. She said, "After *Life*'s Sitwell fever, I sleep well." Ridgeley Torrence[65] and Percy MacKaye[66] appeared from their respective mausolea, and I found that I felt a great admiration for them and liking for Torrence—not for their poems any more than before, but for their lives. Bob Hillyer was definitely on the wagon and crazy about Kenyon College, whither he had been brought, he said, as a counterpoise to Ransom. I never saw a man so dependent on his son. The meeting ended. Conrad and I took the remains of the bottle of Scotch and went over to the Harvard Club, where he was interviewed by a creature he calls the Star Spangled Bonner, now poetry critic for the *Christian Science Monitor*. He had enjoyed himself in Washington when good fellows got together and had been very much impressed by Cal Lowell.

Then I took the train back to Brewster.

[...]

As ever,
Malcolm

[NL TL/CC-I]
[TO: PAUL MELLON]
February 6, 1949

Dear Mr. Mellon:

I very much appreciated your note of thanks for the Whitman;[67] but I hope the sober appearance of those two green-backed volumes doesn't keep you from dipping into them. My introduction, printed in the Poetry volume, is what I'm especially anxious to have you read. It's one of the pieces of writing that I'm most satisfied with—if one can ever be satisfied; at any rate I found some new things to say about Whitman and his pretty extraordinary personality and his superb early poems, so much better than the later ones; and I like to think that you were responsible for the time I was able to devote to him.

Another result of the last five years was the rediscovery of William Faulkner. These days one finds his name everywhere in the critical reviews and it seems to be a commonplace to call him the greatest American novelist—at least if you venture to suggest that there are faults in his books you find a bunch of youngsters pummeling your neck. It amuses me to think that all this goes back to the Viking *Portable Faulkner* I did in 1946 when all his books were out of print and nobody read his work; then I told what he was doing, which nobody had bothered to find out, and gave a historical outline of his work, and suddenly everybody was reading him, and his publishers—who had allowed him to go out of print—suddenly made him a big advance and he set to work on what he thinks will be his great novel. He'd be surprised to find that the writing of it was really made possible by you, indirectly—that shows how effects spread out like ripples. [. . .]

This spring I was elected to the National Institute, along with Allen Tate, E. E. Cummings, Christopher Isherwood and two or three others. A few years ago I wouldn't have cared, but now the election pleases me, sort of, as proof that I haven't been wasting my time.

Cordially yours,
Malcolm Cowley

PART VII

Literature and Politics in Cold War America, 1949–1954

In 1949, freshly elected to the National Institute of Arts and Letters, Cowley embarked on a mix of professional literary activities that would mark his lifestyle for the next three to four decades. Working mostly from Sherman, Connecticut, he remained an independent, self-employed critic and historian of (mostly contemporary) American writing and began his long affiliation with Viking Press as advisory editor, which brought him from Sherman into Manhattan for weekly meetings. He recurrently taught and lectured across the country, served as judge for the National Book Award and the Bollingen Prize in poetry, wrote recommendations, and continued to serve as advisor and director at Yaddo. More immediately, he took a prominent part in the postwar revival of the 1920s: he compiled an edition of the short stories of F. Scott Fitzgerald, prepared a new "final" edition of Fitzgerald's *Tender Is the Night,* and revised and expanded *Exile's Return: A Literary Odyssey of the 1920s* (1951). Last but not least, he wrote substantial essays that would become part of a new book, *The Literary Situation* (1954).

As literary scout and publishing advisor, Cowley offered views on manuscripts and reflected on the changing dynamics of the book industry in the early 1950s (the growing market for criticism and nonfiction, the rise of paperbacks, the impact of the loyalty purge). He suggested revisions to Philip Young's pioneering critical study of Hemingway and against odds tried to persuade a recalcitrant Hemingway to cooperate on the project. He offered advice and encouragement to writers in whom he believed—William Goyen, Josephine Miles, Weldon Kees—recommended Nelson Algren for a Fulbright, and tried to engineer "a front-line reputation" for John Cheever. July 1953 saw the beginning of Cowley's efforts on behalf of Jack Kerouac, "the most interesting writer who is not being published today," as he told Allen Ginsberg.

Despite Cowley's growing reputation as a literary critic and historian, the role of his political past was far from played out. In effect, his endeavors on behalf of American literature took place in a sharply intensifying reactionary political climate of Cold War threat and anticommunist witchhunting. Several experiences in 1949, broadly publicized in the national press, served to place Cowley's radical past in the limelight once more: in the winter and early spring he was embroiled in the notorious "Lowell affair" at Yaddo; in June and December he was summoned to testify in the Alger Hiss trials; and in the winter of that year he became the unwanted subject of political controversy when his appointment as guest lecturer at the University of Washington in Seattle was challenged by local reactionaries.

Cowley's career in the late 1940s and early 1950s illuminates how difficult it was for him to simultaneously face his guilt-laden radical past, preserve his self-respect, and minimize professional damage. In a climate of political intolerance, suspicion, and intimidation, he worried about the passivity and the self-imposed silence of progressives like himself. Though time and experience had tempered Cowley's views, he held strong political opinions but felt himself effectively gagged. Like many, he resorted to an uneasy compromise, refusing to comment publicly but working behind the scenes to fan opposition to conformity, orthodoxy, and a hysterical pro-Americanism. Thus, in the wake of the first Hiss trial, he invited the *Washington Post* journalist Alan Barth to write an "honest and thoughtful" book on the loyalty crusade for Viking, which became *The Loyalty of Free Men* (1951). As a Viking editor he worked with Granville Hicks on *Where We Came Out* (1954), the story of Hicks's conversion to and disillusionment with Communism. With Carey McWilliams, Cowley pleaded for a civil liberties organization that would defend liberals unjustly accused of disloyalty or un-Americanism, yet (mindful of his experiences with Dies in 1942) declined an invitation to participate in an act of public protest on behalf of the Hollywood Ten. He urged Bruce Bliven to chart a course of liberal oppositional action in the pages of *The New Republic* and in letters to Hemingway and Alan Barth he diagnosed what he believed were affiliations between Catholics and McCarthyism (the "great Irish-American job hunt"). He criticized ugly Communist-style tactics to combat perceived modes of un-Americanism and advanced a nuanced verdict on the Rosenberg case. And he was shocked and saddened by the suicide of F. O. Matthiessen, which he believed was caused at least in part by the impossible political situation. The 1952 elections were hardly encouraging: though his hopes were set on Adlai Stevenson, he ominously saw McCarthy rising and Eisenhower "sailing to victory on his resemblance to Daddy Warbucks," as he wrote Burke on October 8.

In the field of literature, too, there was reason for concern. When in 1949 the Fellows of the Library of Congress decided to give the Bollingen Award for Poetry to Ezra Pound, then incarcerated in St. Elizabeths psychiatric hospital, Robert Hillyer (writing in the *Saturday Review*) thought he detected a fascist conspiracy that included the Bollingen Foundation and admirers of Eliot and Pound; and he imputed an anti-American agenda to the New Criticism, with its obsessive concern with form. Incensed at what he felt was Hillyer's betrayal of the Republic of Letters, Cowley flung himself into the controversy, challenging the award to Pound on literary, not political grounds. "Patriotism is the last refuge for paranoiacs," he observed to Willard Thorp.

Subterfuge, suspicion, paranoia, timidity—such qualities Cowley saw reflected in political life as in contemporary literature. In a letter to Hemingway he signaled a tendency among writers to focus on the moral problems of individuals ("evil is in the human heart") and to avoid the risk-taking big scene in favor of "fine jewelry work, as if they were carving cameos on the side of Stone Mountain." Timidity even seemed to have infected criticism: "Not sticking one's neck out is really becoming the American vice," he observed to Cleanth Brooks. "In politics it makes civil liberties meaningless [. . .]. In literature it is fatal." The New Critics, he adjured, neglected a chief responsibility of the critic—to discover new writers—and should move beyond their narrow circle of anointed, canonized writers. Moreover, by eliminating the social, biographical, political, historical, or psychological contexts of a work, they impoverished criticism. For Cowley, the relation between literature and life remained axiomatic. A humanist critic, he was deeply interested in writers both as human beings and as craftsmen in search of solutions to professional problems, including the economics of authorship.

For all his skepticism about the writer's ability to freely function in the Cold War context, Cowley accepted an invitation from James Laughlin to edit an issue of a new quarterly intended to promote American literature and culture abroad. Funded by the Ford Foundation, *Perspectives USA* (published in English, French, German, and Italian) aimed to correct European perceptions of American culture as imperialist and driven by crass commercialism and to show that the greatest achievements of American culture were equal to the best of what Europe had to offer. Though Cowley was doubtful of its Cold War jingoism, the project fitted his internationalist bent and gave him a chance to present the work of American writers and artists he felt were underappreciated both at home and abroad. The editorial essay he wrote for the issue, on American literature under conditions of Cold War anxiety and New Critical dominance, in effect formed the starting point for *The Literary Situation* (1954).

{ ——— }

Yaddo 1949

In the early months of 1949 Cowley, who with Granville Hicks and Newton Arvin had long served on Yaddo's board of directors, reluctantly became embroiled in what at the time was known as the "Yaddo affair," a sad precursor to the McCarthy trials. It erupted when the Yaddo resident Agnes Smedley, a longtime sympathizer of Chinese Communism, was publicly accused by General MacArthur of having been a Soviet spy. Though Cowley, who had personally known Smedley since 1934, did not believe the accusation, he was drawn into the affair when the FBI descended on Yaddo to conduct investigations. The affair took a grim turn when several guests, led by Robert Lowell, accused the director, Elizabeth Ames, of having been "somehow deeply and mysteriously involved" in subversive activities and demanded her dismissal. Though Ames was exonerated, the affair led to a reorganization of responsibilities and selection procedures at Yaddo. Cowley reported on the atmosphere of conspiracy and intrigue at Yaddo in letters to Tate, Hicks, and Hemingway.

I can take only one side in a civil liberties case, even if [. . .] it is going to be a costly side for me to take. But it would be worse if I acted against my convictions, because I'm going to have to live with myself for a long time.

Cowley to Granville Hicks, March 1, 1949 [GH]

[AT TLS-2]
[TO: ALLEN TATE]
RFD Gaylordsville, Conn.,
March 6, 1949

Dear Allen:

This time there's a lot to write you about [. . .]. Maybe I'd better start with the Yaddo story, which ought to be funny, but isn't. Agnes Smedley had spent four and a half years there, until Elizabeth Ames finally asked her to leave last spring. She is quite an impressive character and she had won Ames's gratitude by being nice to her when Ames's sister was dying. That's been a mistake at Yaddo, that Ames has let herself be influenced too much by personal friendships—people like John Cheever, Leonard Ehrlich,[1] Katherine Anne have stayed for years at Yaddo, each working on a novel which was never finished, because the atmosphere of that magic mountain seems very conducive to work during short visits, but not over the long haul.

But the Smedley business became more serious when General MacArthur issued his blast against her on February 10. At once the FBI descended on Yaddo and interviewed Ames, Edward Maisel and Elizabeth Hardwick. There were five guests at Yaddo at the time: besides Maisel and Elizabeth H. the others were Cal Lowell, Flannery O'Connor and James Ross, who had just arrived. The guests got very much disturbed, conferred with each other, conferred with directors separately and finally decided—or four of them did—that there was a great spy plot at Yaddo and that Ames was involved in it. James Ross left immediately, not wishing to get involved in a fight. A meeting of the directors was summoned on February 26, and the four remaining guests demanded that Ames be fired, that pending her dismissal she be suspended immediately—and furthermore declared that they were going to call a mass meeting in NY if the directors didn't accept their demands at once and in full.

It was pretty awful. There was a sort of trial of Elizabeth Ames, with Cal Lowell in the role of prosecuting attorney. He called the other guests and Ames's secretary as witnesses. Ames's secretary announced that she had been submitting the names of Yaddo guests who made questionable remarks to the FBI. The testimony was pretty trivial as far as Ames was concerned; in fact it began to sound silly. But it wasn't funny, because of the strained emotions; it wasn't even funny when Hannah Josephson—who was at Yaddo two weeks last fall to finish a book—was charged with having served Molotov cocktails at a party. The terrible thing is the suspicion and hysteria in this country as a result of all the spy stories. In the present case Agnes Smedley wasn't a spy, as far as I have been able to discover. Spies don't go around making speeches. To think of Ames being involved in a plot should set everybody laughing. But it doesn't, in these times, and when I defended Ames I saw Cal Lowell looking at me hostilely and realized that I'd got myself implicated, too. Atmosphere like Russia during a purge.

[...] My own instinct is to get to hell out of things like that. But as long as I'm in them I can't help acting on my feeling that persons are more important than opinions and culture, as Mr. Eliot would say, more important than politics.

No more of Yaddo for this letter [...]

As ever,
Malcolm

[AT TLS-2]
[TO: ALLEN TATE]^2
April 8 [6?] [1949]

I was shocked and amazed, but mostly shocked, to hear about Cal Lowell.^{3} I think he writes the best of all the younger poets and he was very good company, too, when I saw a lot of him at Yaddo last fall. There were no signs then of delusions and there were some signs of a reversion to Bostonism, so that I wondered whether he wouldn't finish up like his ancestors. Meanwhile he seemed to be developing practical judgment, a quality he hadn't possessed before, or hadn't exercised. Even at that grisly directors' meeting, where he was fanatical and Robespierrean (or Vishinskian), I still didn't think of the word paranoid.

Don't worry about having told me about him. I went to NY yesterday to see the dentist and heard the story from other sources half an hour after I left Grand Central. Apparently Peter Taylor had written it to Albert Erskine, who had told Bob Linscott, etc. The new detail I heard was that Cal had rolled up his sleeve and said, "See, I have stigmata." Of course the big question now is whether the condition is curable—a "catathymic crisis" in the psychoanalysts' jargon—or whether it is schizophrenia. It may well be the former. [. . .]

I don't think Lowell's misfortune will have much effect on the Yaddo situation, at least not permanently.[4] [. . .]

That's how matters stand at Yaddo. Yaddo, I hope I may never hear the name again. [. . .]

As ever,
Malcolm

———

[GH TLS-1]
[TO: GRANVILLE HICKS]
April 20 [1949]

Dear Granville:

[. . .] Did you happen to think that Cal's case in some ways suggests Bob Cantwell's? The whole world is in a paranoiac phase, and sensitive individuals become victims and representatives of a general condition. And now we're asked to prepare for twenty years of cold war, unless conditions are changed by the death of the Great Kahn. They will be black years for human freedom, and for literature, which depends so much on free minds. What is happening to the arts in Russia fills me with tears and nausea; and then I remember that statement attributed to Huey Long, that of course we'd have fascism, under the guise of anti-fascism. Now we're beginning to get some of the worst features of communism, under the guise of counter-communism. I do think that an assertion of individuality, not as a theory, but in one's own life and work, is perhaps the best that American writers can do now.

As ever,
Malcolm

[EH TLS-2] [*PMC* 487–488]
[TO: ERNEST HEMINGWAY]
May 3, 1949

Dear Ernest:

[. . .] I haven't written you for an age, or damned near ten weeks. [. . .] I got involved in a hell of a troublesome situation that kept me busy for a long time. It was about Yaddo, an old Robber Baron estate in Saratoga Springs endowed as a foundation to give free board and lodging to writers, artists and composers. I'm on the board of directors, worse luck. One of the writers who had spent a long time at Yaddo, more than four years, was Agnes Smedley. She is and has always been an enthusiastic supporter of the Chinese Communists. A year ago it began to look as if her political activities would make trouble for Yaddo, and Mrs. Elizabeth Ames, who runs the place, asked Agnes either to moderate those activities or else to leave. She left. On February 10 of this year General MacArthur's headquarters issued a big statement that accused Smedley of being a Russian spy. She isn't, of course, and Smedley forced the Army to apologize. But meanwhile the effbiyai had descended on Yaddo to ask questions of Mrs. Ames and the writer guests.

Does this sound complicated? It's only the beginning of a story that belongs in the history books. The guests, as it happened, were all of the type now described as "passionate anti-Stalinists." They became so disturbed at being questioned by the effbiyai that they got together, added two and two, squared the result, multiplied by pi squared, and reached the conclusion that Mrs. Ames was, in their words, "somehow deeply and mysteriously involved" in subversive activities. A meeting of the directors was called in Saratoga, and it turned out to be one of the grisliest days through which I have ever lived. All sorts of suspicions, dislikes, malice came to the surface. Charges were made, evidence was offered, and in the course of seven or eight hours the evidence slowly dissolved into nothing but unfounded gossip. The meeting was adjourned for a month to allow the directors to make further investigations.

The end was, as you might say, happy for these times. At a second meeting in New York Mrs. Ames was formally cleared of the charges. But then the guest who had been most active in bringing the charges, Robert Lowell—who is incidentally a fine poet—suddenly went out of his head, not at the meeting, but a few days later in Chicago, and had to be put in handcuffs by four sweating policemen and carried off for treatment. Paranoid psychosis was the doctor's verdict. What we had really been living through and sitting in grave judgment over was paranoia that had passed from mind to mind like measles running through a school. Not so long afterwards Drew Pearson gave his famous broadcast about Forrestal[5] and how he had been carried off to the loony bin shouting, "The Russians are after me." This great nation had been adopting its policies on the advice of a paranoiac as Secretary of Defense. Maybe this is the age of paranoia, of international delusions of persecution and grandeur. Maybe persons like Forrestal and Robert Lowell are the chosen representatives and suffering Christs of an era.

Anyhow my getting involved in this business is a principal explanation of why I didn't write. [...]

As ever,
Malcolm

[GH TLS-1]
[TO: GRANVILLE HICKS]
May 10, 1950

Dear Granville:

[...] So Agnes [Smedley] is dead.[6] The next time I see you I'd like to show you the long letter she wrote me in 1941, detailing her troubles with the Communists and her persecution (it was close to that) by the Communists. She had enjoined me to burn the letter; I kept it instead, but wouldn't show it to anybody as long as she lived. She had a burning faith in the Chinese peasants and a burning hatred for the Nationalist government. Because she thought the Communists were helping the peasants she did almost as much for them as any one of their secondary leaders, for example, Chou En-lai. But the Communists never trusted her, she was too independent, and in fact her sympathies lay with the middle faction in Chinese politics, the Southern group that fought on the Nationalist side but distrusted the Kuomintang. She fell in love with a Southern general, and the Kuomintang got rid of him and his whole army by ordering him into a hopeless battle. Then, when she came back to the US, the Communists kept her from telling her story in magazines and on the lecture platform. It was at that time that I wrote Elizabeth about her. Later she seems to have become reconciled with the Communists, but I never learned that part of the story. Her life would make a strange novel of our time. What a shame that she hadn't the fictional talent to write it herself. [. . .]

As ever,
Malcolm

{ ——— }

Testifying for Hiss in full knowledge of the cost I would have to pay was the boldest thing I ever did.

Cowley to Hans Bak, June 25, 1981

[CA TLS-2] [NL TL/CC-2]
[TO: CONRAD AIKEN]
July 3, 1949

Dear Conrad:

[. . .]

I have [. . .] been teaching frantically for the last six weeks[7] and earning what seemed to me a large sum of money—but at the end of those weeks I find only $175 in the bank, and I had more at the beginning. Good God, how are we going to live these days? And then this damned Hiss business[8] that dragged up my pro-communist past and probably made it much harder for me to get work. Thing was that I had had lunch with Whittaker Chambers in 1940 and he had told me his story and I had been so impressed and dismayed that I had gone home and written it all down in a notebook. Joe Liebling[9] was doing a piece on Chambers for *The New Yorker* and asked me whether I knew anything about him and I read him the notes I had made. Liebling—as I didn't know—was in touch with Hiss's lawyers and they asked me for the testimony; and if I had been wise I would have ducked out of giving it; but I don't know whether I could have gone on living with myself afterwards. There is so much cowardice and evasion these days that somebody has to say what he knows and damn the consequences—even if it means whispering among the neighbors and little silences when I enter the room and other damn fools coming up to me to talk with self-conscious nobility as if to say, "*I'm* above the herd, just see how brave I am." Maybe my right place is outside the pale. What made the matter worse was that Chambers issued a statement about me composed entirely of lies (and he knew damned well they were lies) and there was no hope of answering his statement in the papers that printed it, because they're embarked so gaily on their anti-Red crusade and to hell with the truth.

[. . .]

As ever,
Malcolm

———————

[NL TL/CC-2]
[TO: W. H. AUDEN]
c/o The Viking Press,
18 East 48th St., New York 17
July 27, 1949

Dear Auden,

I was impressed by one sentence among others in your general preface to the big anthology of poets of the English language.[10] "As to structure in any of its aspects, e.g. prosody," you said, "he will probably have to work that out for himself from the poems themselves, for, if there is any book on the subject as a whole which combines learning, an ear, and common sense, we have yet to read it."

Now, if "he" in your sentence referred to the young poet, you wouldn't be describing an ominous situation. Yes, the poet will have to work out a prosody for himself if he wants to *be* a poet; and working out a prosody is part of his job. But your "he" refers to the reader (and inferentially to the general critic), who simply hasn't time or knowledge to work out a prosody; and that leads to the situation we have today, in which poets can't find a dozen trained readers among non-poets to understand what they are doing with the music of the language. We need a book of prosody that combines learning, an ear and common sense.

Why don't you begin thinking of writing that book? [. . .]

[. . .]

You're lucky to be in Europe this summer; here it has been the hottest, muckiest summer in years, with the New England valleys as stifling as Washington. [. . .] I got dragged or subpoenaed into the Hiss trial in June; with the strange figure of Whittaker Chambers in the foreground, it's as crazy as any Renaissance intrigue. Paranoia is the disease of our times.

As ever,
Malcolm Cowley

[AB TLS-1]
[TO: ALAN BARTH, *THE WASHINGTON POST*]
July 29, 1949

Dear Alan:

Ever since the first Hiss trial ended with a hung jury, I have had the notion that someone should do an honest and thoughtful book about the whole case. It would be, if done right, a useful and almost indispensable book, because the case reflects a great deal of American life, now and in the 1930s, and because the court trial has concealed instead of revealed some of the most important issues, including the whole question of loyalty in the government service and how to best assure it; and that other question why some government servants—like Wadleigh[11]—thought they were doing their duty to the world by giving information to the Communists.

It strikes me that with your background and training you would be the right man to do such a book.[12] Writing it would be a public service—and a service to you, too, because after all these years of doing fine editorials it is time for you to publish a book of your own.

[. . .] Incidentally, the author of the book doesn't have to decide that really less than momentous question whether Hiss or Chambers is lying; he can simply present the facts. I know that Chambers lies, from personal experience; I don't know anything about Hiss. If you are interested and see a possibility of writing the book, I will immediately take up the question with the Viking editors, who have already [. . .] expressed their great interest.[13]

[. . .]

As ever,
Malcolm

I accept Eliot's ideal of plural loyalties and have a sort of horror of any society in which individuals are called upon to be false to family, church, region or profession in their devotion to the Great State. Hillyer was betraying the republic of letters in exactly the same fashion that Pound betrayed his own nation.[14]

Cowley to Allen Tate, September 19, 1949 [AT]

[NL TL/CC-I]
[TO: WILLARD THORP, PRINCETON UNIVERSITY]
August 10, 1949

Dear Willard:

[. . .]

I have been following with great interest the controversy over Mr. Pound and Mr. Hillyer:

> Oh, Mr. Hillyer, oh, Mr. Hillyer,
> You gave me such a patriotic fright—
> How you frighten little mags
> When you wave your starry flags!
> Our Christian dead are sleeping well tonight.

I thought you Fellas were pretty rash when you gave Pound the prize, and I never joined the chorus that confirmed his self-election as a great poet—

but Hillyer! What filth. I've written a piece about the controversy and think it is coming out in *The New Republic* and think that's a good place for it to appear, because Hillyer, that eager partisan of Franco's, was wrapping himself in the mantle of patriotic liberalism. Patriotism is the last refuge for paranoiacs.

[...]

As ever,

Malcolm

―――――――――

[LH TLS-1]
[TO: LILLIAN HELLMAN]
August 12, 1949

Dear Lillian:

Half the time I've been traveling round the country, to writers' conferences, and the other half I've spent at home prostrated by the heat. That's why I never found opportunity or energy to tell you what I have already told a dozen people—that you did a wonderful job with *Montserrat*,[15] that the English play is incomparably better than the French, that you played with it like Beethoven constructing a symphony with themes borrowed from the bandleader at the corner café.

[...]

I especially admired the first scene—all new, all yours (except for the names of the characters); it's better than any scene in the French version. I admired how you gave personalities to characters who in the French version were merely types. How you made the priest palatable to Catholic critics (partly by making Montserrat himself a Christian and a friend of the priest's). How you decreased the number of hostages and executions. How you made the Indian artist credible by making him a woodcarver. How you reduced the actor's last scene by shortening that ham speech. How you added drama to Montserrat's death by having him crawl wounded up the stairs. It's your play now, and a good one—not the French author's.

Conflict, hesitations, complexities, credibility: those are things you added.

[...]

I'm hoping to see it on the stage next fall. Good Lord, I always knew you were a playwright, but until I saw this example of revision and new creation I didn't know what the word meant.

As ever,

Malcolm

[EH TLS-1] [PMC 490–491]
[TO: ERNEST HEMINGWAY]
October 7, 1949

Dear Ernest:

[...]

Just now I'm doing a pretty hard critical job. I've got stacked in front of me ten novels by authors who appeared during or since the war—novels that have been favorably reviewed by the highbrow critics—and I'm trying to see whether they reveal negative tendencies: they aren't naturalistic, aren't experimental, aren't rebellious, aren't social, aren't behavioristic. On the positive side, they are concerned with the moral problems of individuals. About their most striking feature, outside of the conscious efforts at symbolism, is how they are preoccupied with evil—how they personify or objectify evil as an old fairy, a little girl, a professor, a hired man or a mountain lion.

I'm talking about authors like Lionel Trilling, Saul Bellow, Eudora Welty, Truman Capote, Jean Stafford, Robert Lowry. They write good prose, sometimes very good prose. They can tell you the shades of meaning conveyed by a look; you might say that was their specialty. But, God, how most of them flinch away from a big scene. And if they happen to run into a big theme (like Mary McCarthy in *The Oasis*), how they do insist on avoiding its implications and sticking to their fine jewelry work, as if they were carving cameos on the side of Stone Mountain . . . Thought I would contrast them with Nelson Algren, who, as far as subject goes, might still be writing in 1935, but who has recklessness and a real feeling for the language as it is not spoken at Vassar. Outside of writers like Algren, and there aren't many of them, we're getting back into an era of books by old maids—and they're still old maids even if they're pansies, lesbians or nymphomaniacs; the membrane over their minds has never been broken.

[...]

As ever,
Malcolm

[CB TLS-1] [NL TL/CC-1]
[TO: CLEANTH BROOKS]
October 21, 1949

Dear Brooks:

I was very glad to get your letter.[16] About the point under discussion, whether criticism is having any adverse effect on the new poets, I should say that it was a very legitimate subject for discussion. I know that some of those I have met are frightened almost to the point of falling silent, and I know that Jarrell himself, with his slashing and sometimes unjust reviews, has helped to frighten them—but perhaps we should blame the frightened people rather than Jarrell. Not sticking one's neck out is really becoming the American vice; perhaps one should call it the democratic and egalitarian vice. In politics it makes civil liberties meaningless, because even when they exist people are afraid to use them. In literature it is fatal.

My quarrel with many of the new critics—and I do have a quarrel with them—is that they haven't been taking one sort of risk. They have confined themselves to a single group of authors, whose names you know, whose names everybody knows by now, Kafka, Yeats, Proust, Joyce, Eliot, Faulkner and a few others—very great authors, but not the only ones. From time to time a new author is added to the list, as Fitzgerald's name has recently been appearing in the critical reviews, but the name is not added by the new critics, who have usually been content to work with and deepen our appreciation of the *given*. They often surrender that other function of the critic which consists in discovering new books to appreciate; and when they surrender that function it is performed by whom?—by the journalistic and historical critics whose work they contemn. Brooks, your homonym, at least plunged into American literature and came up with William De Forest and John Lloyd

Stephens, among others. Edmund Wilson in this country and Cyril Connolly[17] in London are always exploring. If I tried to write you an exhortation it would be to go on as you are going with criticism; what you are doing is illuminating and useful and I feel a lasting gratitude about your writings on Yeats, for example; but if I tried a second exhortation it would be to take more risks in appreciation and try to discover new writers, outside the circle of the anointed, to analyze by the same methods.

[. . .]

Yours,
Malcolm Cowley

In the fall of 1949 Cowley accepted an invitation from Robert B. Heilman to teach for a term in Seattle as Walker-Ames lecturer at the University of Washington. Because he knew that, locally, a campaign was being conducted against alleged Communist infiltration of the state university, Cowley openly discussed his former ties with left-wing organizations. Conservative opposition to Cowley's appointment flared up when his testimony in the Hiss trial in June 1949 brought his radical past again before a national audience. As Cowley had to testify a second time in December (just before the start of his lectureship), he had reason to expect trouble in Seattle, as right-wing conservatives believed that with Cowley's arrival the red menace would enter the gates.

[NL TL/CC-3] [RBH 189–192]
[TO: ROBERT B. HEILMAN, DEPARTMENT OF ENGLISH,
UNIVERSITY OF WASHINGTON]
November 21, 1949

Dear Heilman:

[. . .] [N]ow let's work on your paragraph about the possibility of newspaper headlines during my ten weeks at the university. One thing I must say immediately. If you think there are going to be attacks that will prove embarrassing to the university, it would be wisest to call off our arrangement now, and fast. I have plenty to do this winter without crossing the continent and I have absolutely no wish to be a victim or a martyr. I'd like to set a class working on the second flowering of American literature, and I wouldn't like to have them distracted by arguments about who belonged to what radical organization in the 1930s. I belonged to a lot of them and that is absolutely no secret.

I'd better set my record down, so that there won't be any surprises. During the period from 1932 to 1936 I was pretty crimson, or at least deep pink. I voted for William Z. Foster in 1932 and registered as a Communist in 1934 and 1936, though I didn't vote that way in '36. I never joined the party, thank goodness, for it seems to me that a lot of people who did join it had their minds permanently twisted. After 1936 I was a great deal more critical of Communist tactics, but I was also deeply disturbed by Hitler and Franco and thought that in the European conflict the Russians were generally on the right side. I continued to think that way until the Russo-German Pact of 1939; then I got out of politics as gracefully and completely as I could.

I was literary editor of *The New Republic* until 1940. The political editors of the NR made a great attack on the Dies Committee, and the Committee retaliated by getting up complete files on all the editors. When I went to Washington in the winter of 1941–42, to work for the Office of Facts and Figures, I learned from a speech on the floor of Congress that I had been a member of 72 subversive organizations. I think the count was wrong, because the organizations were named and many of them I had never heard of. The point was that when a new organization was started, some girl would be set to work finding sponsors, so-called, to list on the letterhead. The girl would phone me at the office and I would say, "Look, your organization sounds like a good thing and you can use my name—on one condition, that you never ask me to do any work and never phone me again." Ah, that was a grievous error, as I later discovered when all the letterheads were collected by the Dies Committee. There was one organization, later listed as subversive, to which I actually belonged, as one of the vice-presidents; it was the League of American Writers. It had a vast majority of non-Communist members and after the Russo-German Pact I thought it could be weaned away from following the party line; but my efforts failed and I wrote an open letter of resignation that was published in *The New Republic* in July 1940. Since then I haven't belonged to anything political except the Democratic town caucus of Sherman, Conn. (pop. 600, including 30 Democrats).

This letter is getting pretty long, but I am anxious for you and the university administration to know everything there is to be known. Last spring I was put into a situation where I had to testify at the Hiss trials. How that happened is a story too long to tell, but briefly Hiss's lawyers learned that I had kept a written record of a long conversation with Whittaker Chambers and either I had to consent to tell about it in court or else I had to scuttle for cover, and I don't like scuttling. They are going to subpoena me in the second trial, too, early in December and I'll arrive in Washington with this cloud hanging over me. In court Mr. Murphy will ask me, "Did you register as a Communist in 1934," and I will say, "Yes, Mr. Murphy, and I think in 1936."[18] That afternoon Chambers will unblushingly tell the newspapers that I gave false testimony. I look forward to the episode about as eagerly as a soldier looks forward to the next attack, after his company suffered casualties in the last one.

So, if all this adds up to trouble for the university, we can call off the arrangements as of today, before we are all too deeply committed. If you say go ahead, I'll lay my plans with some view toward handling the Seattle newspapers as well as possible. I'd want to ask the advice of the university press agent, who will know the local set-up; but my own notion would be to arrive in Seattle on January 2 and see the reporters that day if they want to see me. I wouldn't know how to tell them anything less or more than the complete truth. If they asked me whether I was a Communist I'd have to say that on the contrary I was a Christian, if not a very good one, and something of a social conservative. I believe in private initiative and a free press (not controlled by Hearst, I wouldn't add, except mentally). I haven't any opinions to offer on Russian or American foreign policy, which is out of my field, but I could speak about Russian policy in the arts, which I think is tyrannical and deadly to literature; may God grant that we don't follow it in this country. I believe that two of the Commandments are especially applicable to our present situation: "Thou shalt not bear false witness against thy neighbor," and "Don't be a heel."

Mightn't it be a good idea to show this letter to the administration?[19] I think it contains the gist of everything that might be urged against me, and

I'd like it to be known, because I abhor everything secret or underhand. And I'll wait to hear from you, while continuing to work on the prospective courses.

Sincerely,
Malcolm Cowley

––––––––––

The battle lines have been drawn on the issue whether a state university should blacklist a lecturer who is not accused of being a Communist or a sympathizer at present or of ever having been a Communist party member, but who freely states that he sympathized with the Communists fifteen years ago. The issue is out of my hands, but for the sake of others who might find themselves in the same situation, I'll fight it through to the end—or rather will try to make the issue clear, while otherwise confining myself to literature, which is my own topic.

Cowley to Robert Heilman, December 23, 1949 [NL][*RBH* 201]

[NL TL/CC-2]
[TO: HARRY POST, *NEW MILFORD TIMES*]
4111 36th Ave. NE,
Seattle, Wash.,
January 8, 1950

Dear Harry:

Out here in Seattle I'm embroiled in what is practically the damnedest row you ever heard about. I want to tell you the story, just in case it should break into the newspapers again. But what I'm writing you isn't for publication, since I have to protect my very responsible sources of information. In brief—

There is a man in Seattle named David E. Stuntz who is a former member of Pelley's disloyal outfit, the Silver Shirts. Since that time Stuntz has gone into politics and achieved some local prominence; he is a regent of the state university and an active though not a very popular member of the American Legion. Lately he has been feuding with President Allen of the

University of Washington; he wants to get Allen fired or force his resignation. He thought that my appointment as a Walker-Ames Visiting Lecturer, a fairly important university post, was a good occasion to bring his undercover war into the open.

First he attacked my appointment on political grounds. That was an easy thing to do because, as you know, I had belonged to many Communist-front organizations in the early 1930s and had even voted Communist in 1932 and 1934. Nevertheless the attack fell flat, for the simple reason that I made no secret of my past affiliations (or of anything else for that matter) and had been opposing the Communists ever since the Russo-German Pact of 1939. In the end Stuntz gained nothing by his researches into ancient history.

Then he found a new angle, and that was the one that broke into the Seattle papers. He got hold of two volumes of poetry, *Blue Juniata* and *The Dry Season,* which I had published in 1929 and 1941, respectively. Both books have been out of print for many years, but Stuntz read them carefully, hoping to find that I had expressed disloyal sentiments. He found nothing of the kind. What he did find were half a dozen lines that he thought were dirty. He took them out of their proper context (in which they weren't dirty at all) and quoted them in an anonymous document which he circulated among various patriotic and church organizations: the Legion, the VFW, the Council of Churches, the PTA, the DAR, etc. He thought he could get those organizations to do his work for him, make them condemn me and thus force out the president of the university, who had appointed me. In all this business he's been shooting at me in order to hit President Allen.

This second attack came very near being successful. The only way to answer the charge that I had written dirty poems was to have people read the poems—and that was impossible because the books were out of print and because Stuntz had cornered all the copies in Seattle, including those in the university library. Nevertheless the university sent off to Berkeley, Calif. for the poems and the head of the English Department [Robert Heilman] read and defended them before all the organizations to which Stuntz had mailed his anonymous attack. They withdrew their complaint. The Americanization Committee of the local American Legion went into the case at length and wrote a confidential report (which was shown me in confidence) giving me a clean bill of health. So, I'm here and my lectures are being given to audiences at least three times as large as they would have been without the newspaper publicity.

But Stuntz hasn't given up hope of winning his war against the university administration. The latest of his stunt(z) is to write a letter to the Sherman post of the American Legion, asking for a report on me which he hopes will be unfavorable, so that he can use it in the newspapers. Of course there is no Sherman post of the Legion, and the letter will undoubtedly be turned over to the New Milford post. [. . .] I'd hate to see the New Milford Legion involved in it. Incidentally I don't see how they could make any report on me except that I was a responsible citizen who paid his bills and minded his own business. I wouldn't worry about the report at all if the New Milford people knew me as well as my neighbors in Sherman.

Isn't it a pretty mess, all told? Actually it's not so bad as it sounds, because a lot of people here know the inside story. The university is behind me a hundred percent and I'm having a very pleasant time with my lectures and with my new friends on the faculty. [. . .]

As ever,
Malcolm

[NL TL/CC-1]
[TO: ELIZABETH AMES, YADDO]
4111 36th Ave. NE,
Seattle, Wash.,
Jan. 16, 1950

Dear Elizabeth:

Phoebe Pierce[20] didn't get the whole story, or got it all from Ted [Theodore Roethke], and the situation is a little more complicated than she thinks. He *was* a most brilliant teacher here at Washington, gave too much of himself to his students and his work and had a complete breakdown last October. It was something like Cal Lowell's, but more manic-depressive, with the paranoiac elements not so marked (although they were present). He was confined in a sanitarium, but persuaded his students to take him out every night and finally escaped with their help—but reaching a little town in Oregon he realized that he couldn't go farther and asked to come back. At present he is in a first-rate sanitarium (the Pinel Foundation), denied visitors, all his letters opened, and everything done to keep him in an atmosphere of tranquility and security. The doctors think (I get all this at second hand) that perhaps in two months he will be able to go back to Ann Arbor. They also think they can put him on his feet again without shock treatment, which they are trying to avoid.

I think he is a very fine poet and needs help. On the question whether he should be invited to Yaddo I should say, yes, provided you are warned that there might be difficulties—not serious ones, I think—and provided that he is on his feet again in time to come *before* the regular season (for the regular season I should say No). The point is that Yaddo might perform a service in his case beyond the usual line of duty, and he is worthy of help. Meanwhile I'm going to write to the doctor in charge of his case and see Ted himself if the doctor thinks it advisable, and I might have a further report for you. [...]

As ever,
Malcolm

[NL TL/CC-2]
[TO: WILLIAM COLE, CHAIRMAN
NATIONAL BOOK AWARD COMMITTEE]
4111 36th Ave. NE,
Seattle, Wash.,
February 28, 1950

Dear Mr. Cole:

Here is my ballot and here are my comments on the novels under consideration for the National Book Award:

50 points   *The Man with the Golden Arm,* by Nelson Algren—because it is one of the few, the very few, novels about life in the slums in which the author really loves his characters and portrays them as having their own kind of self-respect; and because Algren writes a sort of Chicago poetry, unexpected and authentic—but chiefly because he can write.

40 points	*The Golden Apples,* by Eudora Welty—because she gives an air of distance and mystery and eternity to a little Mississippi town (though I'm not always sure that I catch her implications) and because her prose is a pleasure to read.
10 points	*The Hunter's Horn,* by Harriet Arrow—because, though it lacks originality of form or vision, being too much based on Elizabeth Madox Roberts and William Faulkner, not to mention its revival of Moby Dick transformed into a fox and a female fox at that (those animal symbols are getting tiresome), still it is so full of fresh knowledge about the Kentucky hill people that it sticks pleasantly in my memory.

I also liked the following books in about the order mentioned:

4. *The Girl on the Via Flaminia,* by Alfred Hays—because of the terrific meaning it compresses into a few characters.

5. *The Christmas Tree,* by Isabel Bolton—because it is beautifully written, especially the first half of it, and, though it later becomes dispersed, manages to end in a piece of convincing melodrama.

6. *Point of No Return,* by John P. Marquand—because it is an even more terrifying picture of American business life than the author thought he was presenting; it is Marquand's best book since *The Late George Apley.*

7. *The Sheltering Sky,* by Paul Bowles—even if it has been overpraised.

8. *The Big Wheel,* by John Brooks—but at this point my enthusiasm is getting pretty tempered with doubts and with the feeling that Brooks doesn't get outside the prejudices of his own (Princeton) caste.

[. . .]

I would not vote under any circumstance for *The Track of the Cat,* because the Moby Dickolism is dragged in by the cat's tail; or for *The Brave Bulls,* because it ends with a bullfight to end bullfights; or for *Knight's Gambit,* which is third-rate Faulkner—let's wait till he writes another good book; or for *The Way West,* which might better be called "The Way to Write Superior Westerns." I could with difficulty be persuaded to consent to any novel not on my own top list of eight. [. . .]

Cordially,
Malcolm Cowley

[NL TL/CC-I]
[TO: CAREY MCWILLIAMS]²¹
April 3, 1950

Dear McWilliams:

I too think that the case of the Hollywood Ten is one of the crucial cases, one among many others, but after a good deal of reflection I decided that it would be unwise for me to join a national committee to act on the case. Why unwise? Because I begin to think that the whole method of organizing ad-hoc committees and writing letters to Congress has become ineffective and is serving as a booby trap and as a method of fattening dossiers in the FBI files. We have to hit the problem from some other angle. What we need is the help of respectable (and rich) conservatives; I begin to suspect that some of them are feeling that they ought to help. What we also need is some quiet organization, very respectable, that can supplement the work of the Civil Liberties Union in fields were the ACLU doesn't operate. The ACLU has been chiefly legalistic and has operated to keep the courts in *pretty* fair shape in the midst of the general hysteria. But the police-state methods that have developed during the last few years are extra-legal and their principal method is punishment by publicity, by blacklist, by segregation into a new radical ghetto. An organization that could give legal help to those falsely accused and that could hire a publicity man to shoe-horn favorable items into the newspapers in spite of their adverse policy—such an organization, a sort of Anti-Defamation League for liberals, is what is most needed at the present time. Have you ever thought of working to found such an organization? I'd work for it, for one; but I'd hesitate to work for any ad-hoc committee with a lot of names on the letterhead that simply go into the files of the FBI and the Committee on Un-American Activities—in Washington, years ago, I got a good sample of how that works.

Cordially yours,
Malcolm Cowley

I am one of many people who have been deeply disturbed as well as saddened by Matty's death.[22] We couldn't afford to lose him and now we can't afford to let his death stand as a surrender.

Cowley to Kenneth B. Murdock,[23] May 4, 1950 [NL]

[NL TL/CC-1]
[TO: BRUCE BLIVEN]
May 4, 1950

Dear Bruce,

[. . .] The general campaign against liberals, which is disguised as or deliberately confused with a campaign against communism, is just now the central fact in the political situation. *The New Republic* can do a lot of good in the situation by pointing out a course of action to liberals. I think the two slogans for the present should be Explain and Counterattack. Explain—it takes a long time, but eventually people can be made to see that general sympathy with Russia in the 1930s is a far cry from disloyalty in the cold war. [. . .] Since they are attacking liberals for what the liberals did in the 1930s, the intellectual history of the 1930s becomes an important topic of *this* day.

[. . .]

[. . .] [O]ne topic for counterattack that hasn't really been opened up is the suicide of F. O. Matthiessen. He had done such fine work in American literature and there is behind his suicide such a tangle of political persecution and faculty intrigue that his life and death should be discussed at greater length—perhaps two or three persons (MacLeish, Murdock among them) might contribute to a little symposium about him. Also he wrote a three-page letter to the Boston police that hasn't been published except in very short extracts; it should appear in full. [. . .]

As ever,
Malcolm

[NL TL/CC-I]
[TO: ALAN BARTH]
May 15, 1950

Dear Alan:

[. . .] Communism has come into American life by the back door; it has been introduced by these ex-Communists like Budenz[24] who can't get over the lessons they learned while they were members of the Party and who keep reproducing the atmosphere of the Moscow purge trials. Catholicism supported by Communist means is Communism in effect; means determine ends.

[. . .] I still think that Matthiessen's death was a political suicide. He was on the edge of a breakdown and it was the political situation that pushed him over (just as it pushed over Forrestal on the opposite side). The political situation is so paranoiac and depressive that it gives the last push to scores of sensitive persons who wouldn't otherwise succumb to their inherent paranoia or to a manic-depressive psychosis. That's a point I may write about some time. [. . .]

As ever,
Malcolm

———

[NLTLS-I][SC 297–298]
[TO: KENNETH BURKE]
August 30, 1950

Dear Kenneth:

Wrote a review of Hemingway's new one [. . .].[25] It probably means the end of a beautiful friendship, although I said as much for the book as I could find it in my conscience to say. What I'm afraid of is that the guy has been living for ten years in an alcoholic haze and can't write any longer except an occasional paragraph—while he's been earning close to a hundred thousand dollars a year as a writer. One quote I loved because it expresses something I feel about our situation:

"Now we are governed in some way, by the dregs. We are governed by what you find in the bottom of dead beer glasses that whores have dunked their cigarettes in. The place has not even been swept out yet and they have an amateur pianist beating on the box."

He's wonderful at making those sweeping remarks, as if in a bar late at night, but there are too many of them in his novel and there is no sustained episode—one chapter is of 300 words, and anybody knows that when you get to writing 300-word chapters the brain isn't working. After his breakdown Scott Fitzgerald could at least do the early chapters of *The Last Tycoon*—but then he'd got to the stage where he had to go on the wagon for months and had time to think.

[. . .] We are being governed in some way, by Cardinal Spellman and Henry Luce, and the dregs are pretty thick at the bottom of the dead beer glass. Pretty soon I won't dare to say such things in a letter, unless I mail it in some other town and sign it yrs, Fulton J. Sheen.[26]

As ever,
Malcolm

———

In the fall of 1950 a reprise of the Seattle affair threatened, when Cowley was invited by Theodore Hornberger, chair of the English Department at the University of Minnesota, to take over Robert Penn Warren's classes for the winter term of 1951. Cowley again carefully explained his radical commitments in the 1930s, the backlash in 1942, and the sequel in Seattle. Though the Minnesota department, which included Henry Nash Smith and Samuel H. Monk, unreservedly supported Cowley's appointment, the university president, James L. Morrill, refused to confirm it, fearing to stir up trouble in a time when state legislators were considering loyalty-oath bills.

[NL TL/CC-2]
[TO: SAMUEL H. MONK]
November 1, 1950

Dear Mr. Monk:

Thanks for your letter; I appreciate your writing it and it gives me the chance to answer by saying some things that have been on my mind.

On one level I'm just as glad that the appointment fell through. By not going to Minnesota I'll have a chance to stay home and finish some writing jobs that are now long overdue. President Morrill turned down the appointment in an awkward manner, so as to seriously compromise my chance of getting other university appointments—but perhaps that was a well disguised favor too, because I can get along without them and do more of my primary work; teaching would always be secondary.

On another, and less private level the rejected appointment was a blow to the university and to the whole cause of academic freedom. After all I was a sort of test case, in the midst of other test cases. I wasn't a Communist or accused of being a Communist or accused, for that matter, of being anything at all. I simply insisted on making it clear that I had belonged to Communist fronts during the 1930s and had voted for Communist candidates in two elections—the last in 1934. I wanted to make it clear that I *might* be attacked on those grounds. If attacked I would be vindicated—there wasn't any doubt of that or I wouldn't have accepted the appointment. The battle would be won if fought. The blow was the retreat before a battle was even threatened.

I'm pretty deeply worried, not by this experience, but by the whole situation that it helps to reveal. Call it "the advance of reaction" or "the erosion of our liberties" if we are willing to use old phrases. But the liberties are not being eroded; they are being atrophied by failure to exercise them; and reaction is not advancing except into territories that have already been abandoned and ceded to reaction.

The real catastrophe today is the self-defeat and fragmentation of the liberals. It's the result of some historic errors: the belief in automatic or almost automatic progress, a wrong conception of man (as a separate and reasoning animal who could make decisions independent of the tribe) and finally, and most disastrously, the notion that Soviet Communism, which was also based in the beginning on a belief in progress and a conception of the reasoning man, would therefore be an ally of liberalism in the West. But the Soviets abandoned the liberals after Munich—lost faith in them as allies—and revealed their own belief in survival and power as the two great aims to be followed above all questions of principle.

Then the liberals were left standing alone, exposed on all sides and attacked by their own sense of guilt. Worst of all they were separated, fragmented, partly by the attack of their enemies on all liberal organizations. They can be and are being picked off one by one.

I'm more or less thinking to myself in this letter and I won't go on to discuss the beliefs that I think liberals should hold at this time. They can't any longer believe in automatic progress or the omnipotent intellect—but certainly they ought to believe that progress can be encouraged by human efforts (Hawthorne was wrong on that point) and that the human intellect, weak as it has proved to be, is still our best hope for survival. They can use the conscious mind to illuminate tradition and the unconscious. And they can keep their freedom of speech to some extent, even in this era, by speaking freely.

These are points that would have to be developed at great length. What I wanted to say in this letter was two things. First, that I don't think the present case is the proper occasion for making a fight. Though President Morrill has deserted us in this instance, Minnesota still has a much better record than most universities. I think that if pressure can be brought on him to keep the record good, the pressure should be brought—but quietly, not in the press or by public actions.

The second point is about one long-term measure that should be of value, though it seems off the point at present. Since one of the great difficulties is the fragmentation of the liberals (using that term in a very broad way as applying to all those who believe, not in the existence of human freedom, but in the desirability of working toward it as an ideal), then one of the long-term answers is working toward the unification of the liberals, by keeping them informed and working together. At present they don't have such a thing as a press—*The Nation* comes nearest to being a liberal organ and there one has to make a lot of qualifications. I think we're actually down to the point where we have to write a lot of private letters, with carbon copies, and send around the carbons. Not on my case, I'm not thinking of that, but on the situation in general and on what is happening in specific localities and on dangerous points to be watched out for. We have to re-establish the community of minds.

[. . .]

Cordially,
Malcolm Cowley

[NL TL/CC-I] [RBH 234–235]
[TO: ROBERT B. HEILMAN]
December 14, 1950

Dear Bob:

[. . .] I'm not going to Minnesota this winter, as you must have heard. [. . .] These are very curious times in which we are living and make me think often of that story about Yeats in Dublin in 1916. Said an Englishman, "Why aren't you in uniform like us, fighting to preserve civilization?" Said Yeats, "I am the civilization you are fighting to preserve." The Minnesota business makes me think that I should change my name to Democratic Rights. [. . .]

As ever,
Malcolm

{ ———— }

The Revival of the 1920s
Exile's Return and F. Scott Fitzgerald

Riding the postwar wave of revived interest in the 1920s, in late 1949 Cowley decided to revise and expand the original 1934 edition of *Exile's Return: A Narrative of Ideas.* The new edition divested the book of its radical politics and placed the story in a more balanced and timeless, if more nostalgic, perspective. The 1951 edition, now subtitled *A Literary Odyssey of the 1920s,* was as critically acclaimed as its 1934 edition had been condescendingly dismissed.

[NL TLS-2]
[TO: MARSHALL A. BEST,[27] VIKING PRESS]
November 16, 1949

Dear Marshall:

Some time ago I promised to write you a memo about *Exile's Return* and the reasons why it should be put back into print. Well—

Long out of print, the book has a sort of subterranean public in the universities and outside of them. I keep running into people who recite stories out of it and get angry at me for having changed some of my ideas since I wrote it. There is a steady unsatisfied demand for it and several book dealers have told me that it sells at a premium when and if a copy can be found; they also say that it is one of the hardest titles to find. I have seen college-library copies rebound, mended and remended with Scotch tape and practically fingered to pieces. With this backlog of demand—and with enough new material to get it reviewed as a new book—I think the publishers of a new edition could count on a good advance sale for it and a continuing sale for many years. [. . .]

What I'd like to do is revise and slightly expand *Exile's Return* and bring it into permanent form before it is reissued. Most of the text I wouldn't touch, because it represents what I had to say in 1934 and has a right to be preserved.[28] The four principal changes I thought of making were:

1. A completely new introduction, written as of 1949–50, putting the whole story into its frame of reference.

2. A new transition between Chapter VI, "The City of Anger," and Chapter VII, "No Escape" (at pp. 214–5). At present the break between those two chapters is the weakest point in the book; for up to page 215 I had been telling my own story, and after that page I was talking about others, including Harry Crosby. I want to make clear in the text just why I dropped out of my own book; and also I'd like to talk more about Hart Crane and other important figures, to balance Crosby, who is wonderfully representative but not important in himself.

3. A new last chapter—as a matter of fact most of it is already written; but I'd like to make it balance the introduction and put the whole story into perspective. No politics this time, to outrage the reader. I'd talk about the return to favor of the 1920s.

4. I have various ideas for an appendix; but the best of them, I think, is to reprint the Literary Calendar which now occupies 16 pages at the end of *After the Genteel Tradition*. It makes good reading and good reference.

[. . .] [M]ore than anything else it would please me to see *Exile's Return* put into final shape and back in print. On its record, it would go on selling for a long time. It would please me a great deal to have it on the Viking list.

As ever,
Malcolm

[NL TL/CC-2]
[TO: JOHN W. ALDRIDGE]²⁹
January 21, 1951

Dear Jack:

I don't mean to be such a slow correspondent, but I've never been busier than this winter. It's trying to finish my revision of *Exile's Return*, which of course involves more changes than I had at first intended. I love the work and wish I could spend months instead of weeks on it; if you asked me what I was by trade I'd have to say that I was a revisionist. There is going to be a new introduction and a new epilogue, neither of which has been written. Some passages are going to be omitted, mostly those in which I talked too vehemently about politics, and instead there are going to be a great many more literary reminiscences. Well, not a great many more, but I introduced, for example, a couple of thousand words about a visit to Ezra Pound, put in my "Dedication Ode for the Battlefield of the War of Secession," put in another passage about the effect of the Sacco-Vanzetti case on the intellectual world, and another passage about winters in New York in the late twenties, and still another passage about Hart Crane on Tory Hill. I made little changes to identify characters when I spoke about them, and added several footnotes to give the subsequent careers of some people mentioned in the text. Then, by another change, I got the Harry Crosby chapter better integrated into the rest of the book—and all in all this new edition will be a better (and longer) story than the first edition—and I hope it will find more readers.

[. . .] I'm anxious to read *After the Lost Generation* and see what conclusions you come to. But now the postman is coming and I had better sign off.

As ever,
Malcolm

───────

In early 1950 Cowley prepared a new edition of Fitzgerald's short stories for Scribner's. The project was part of a wider revaluation of the 1920s, centering around Fitzgerald and involving critics such as Arthur Mizener, Henry Dan Piper, Edmund Wilson, and Alfred Kazin. Cowley wanted to correct the image of Fitzgerald as a tragic failure whose talents and career had been squandered. He emphasized the hardworking and disciplined writer in Fitzgerald.

When Scribner's asked him to edit *The Great Gatsby* and *Tender Is the Night* for a new omnibus edition of three of Fitzgerald's novels—Wilson was to edit *The Last Tycoon*—Cowley had to decide how he would present the text for *Tender Is the Night*. Reading Fitzgerald's papers in Princeton he discovered that Fitzgerald had had second thoughts about the novel and had been planning a restructured version that would restore the chronological order of events. He also found that Fitzgerald had been at work correcting errors of spelling and inconsistencies in the plot. Though Cowley had misgivings about altering the novel's structure, he took it upon himself to carry out what he felt were Fitzgerald's intentions, hoping to establish a correct and permanent text.

{ ——— }

[NL TL/CC-I]
[TO: FRANCES SCOTT FITZGERALD LANAHAN]
July 8, 1950

Dear Mrs. Lanahan:

I am having an interesting time working over your father's stories. What I like especially is reading them in bound volumes of *The Saturday Evening Post,* those dating from the pre-depression days when the *Post* was so big that four issues made a volume bigger and heavier than a volume of the *Encyclopedia Britannica.* A lot of the old and uncollected stories stand up very well indeed and some of them are better than most of those he put into *Taps at Reveille.* I'm planning now to put three or four of them into the book; my favorites are "Magnetism," "The Bridal Party," "A New Leaf" and "One Trip Abroad." If they go in, I can make space for them by omitting some of the early stories that I was never really fond of, like "The Cut-Glass Bowl" and "The Curious Case of Benjamin Button."

Yesterday I talked with Wallace Meyer of Scribner's and Harold Ober about the question of including stories written between 1936 and 1940. They felt strongly (and said you were of the same opinion) that the book should include what I thought were Scott's best stories of *all* periods. I think they are right and shall choose accordingly.[30] [. . .]

Not having seen you since that day in Baltimore in the spring of 1933 I simply can't picture you as the mother of two boys and a girl. Why, in a couple of winks and days and years (which are getting to seem as short as winks to me now) your oldest will be as old as you were when we went horseback riding and Zelda tried to teach me how to post. She wrote me a long letter from Montgomery in 1945, with religious adjurations at the end and with some really brilliant analysis of Scott. Last month at the Princeton library I looked at her scrapbook of dance programs and newspapers clippings and thought of all that beauty and wildness and courage and nearly bawled. There's a greater story there than your father ever wrote, though he wrote some very, very good ones.

Sincerely,
Malcolm Cowley

[NL TL/CC-2]
[TO: ARTHUR MIZENER][31]
January 21, 1951

Dear Arthur:

[...] Your profile [of Fitzgerald for *Life*] was fine—I thought it overemphasized Scott's drinking and Zelda's madness and underemphasized his efforts to straighten himself out; but I reflected that the choice of detail was either the result of editing or else the result of your accurate notion of what the bastards would and wouldn't print. On the other hand, you told the story very well indeed and showed once more your gift for choosing the right quotations and gave a wonderful picture of Fitzgerald. The editorial headings and choice of pictures and text under some of the pictures were pretty disgusting. *Life* treated Fitzgerald even worse than it had treated Hemingway, and I don't think I told you that Pauline H. and her two boys still haven't forgiven *me* for what *Life* did. You'll get the same reaction from Scottie, only more so—but eventually I think she'll realize that the magazine was to blame.

[...]

Now Scribner's are at last going to reissue *Gatsby* and *Tender* and that brings up the great question of text. Not on *Gatsby*—I went to Princeton last week and copied out the *Gatsby* corrections and that's the end of it. But *Tender* is a more complicated question and I went over Fitzgerald's revision without coming to a firm decision about it. On the whole I think his revision improves the novel; that's what I wanted to talk about, because you have been of a different opinion. They were more carefully considered than I think you believed. He didn't have many textual changes to make, but he had some—for example, the end of Nicole's soliloquy is changed so that it fits into the appearance of Rosemary, and the episode of the American newspaper vender (pp. 120–21) is omitted now. Also the novel is divided into five books instead of three, a change which helps to bring out the time element.

The changes meant that he lost the fine effect of leading into the story from outside, from Rosemary's angle; also he lost something else, because the present Book II, which becomes Book I in the revision, is less effectively written than the Rosemary story. On the other hand, with the changes we no longer feel that the novel falls apart; Rosemary takes her proper place in Dick's life, so that the revision leads to an architecturally sounder work. The revision also carries out Fitzgerald's original conception of *Tender* as the story of an idealist who goes to pieces as a result of marrying a rich woman and being introduced to the *haute bourgeoisie*. He had thought about the changes for a long time—at the very least from 1936 to 1938—and when he says, "This is the *final version*," perhaps we had better take him at his word . . . Those are some of my thoughts at present and I'm anxious to hear your reaction.[32] [. . .]

As ever,
Malcolm

[NL TL/CC-1]
[TO: GILBERT HARRISON, *THE NEW REPUBLIC*][33]
Sherman, Conn.,
January 25, 1951

Dear Hal:

This Fitzgerald business is blowing up like a balloon. [. . .] Poor Scottie is frantic about the "beset by drink, debt, a mad wife" line in *Life*. The fact is that it's Fitzgerald the alcoholic and Zelda the schizophrenic that everybody is writing or dreaming of making pictures about,[34] and they seem to forget that poor Scott was also a writer who produced a considerable body of work. Anybody can marry a mad wife, and Zelda's madness was a hell of a sight more tragic and dignified than anything written about her. Not everybody can write *Gatsby* or *Tender Is the Night* or "The Rich Boy" or "Babylon Revisited."

That's the point of this piece I'm sending you[35]—I thought that in all this hullabaloo it was time for somebody to publish something about Fitzgerald as a serious writer, which he was. [...]

As ever,
Malcolm

[NL TL/CC-2]
[TO: FRANCES SCOTT FITZGERALD LANAHAN]
May 21, 1951

Dear Scottie:

You must have learned by now that I'm an undiligent letter writer, without your excuse for delay of being a mother with small children. There's only one child in the Cowley family and he's not a child but a boy of sixteen in his third year of Exeter. He's a good boy generally speaking and a damned nice one, better than I deserve, but he has his shortcomings and his spiritual troubles and sometimes I address him in the tone that Scott sometimes addressed you. Incidentally Scott's letters should *certainly* be collected and published, but I'd rather think that this wasn't exactly the right time to do it. In a year or two the letters can be published in a perfectly dignified way, without reference to the hoopla that is only now dying down. I think we're about to subside into the trough of the Fitzgerald wave. First there was the unjust neglect in 1940, then the great hoorah that followed the Schulberg and Mizener books, with a lot of silly things being said, then the unfriendly critics will have their say (they're having it already)—down and up and down and up again go the quotations on the literary stock exchange and you'd think that people were actually changing their opinions about Fitzgerald, but the truth is that intelligent readers' opinions don't change; they know the truth is that Scott was a good writer and as such his reputation, his real reputation, not the quotations on the Big Board, will always be there and living. It's the permanent Fitzgerald that we ought to be concerned with in any question of publishing his books and papers.

What I'm trying to do with *Tender* is to establish a text that can always be read. Once we had decided on the big change, in accordance with Scott's wishes, there was still the job of proofreading the book. That was something that practically speaking had never been done—I think the book wasn't proofread at all, except by the proofreader at the Scribner Press, and of course by Scott himself—but it appeared when he was almost at his worst stage emotionally and he was a pretty terrible proofreader at his best, says this truthful critic. Anyhow I found some slight error in spelling or punctuation or French or German on almost every page of the book; and I suspect that carefully as I went over it I didn't find them all. [. . .] I'm going to make the introduction short, so that I won't be playing the part of a guide who takes the reader by the hand to point out the scenery, and points it out so insistently that he blocks the reader's view of the scenery. Anything more I have to say—and there will be more—can go into an appendix [. . .]. You know that Scott worked at the novel for nine years, off and on, and wrote a manuscript of 400,000 words, then cut it to a little more than one-fourth that length. Some of the cut things, now at Princeton, are very good, and I thought that a couple of the best might go into the appendix, both because they are interesting in themselves and because they show how ruthless Scott could be with his own writing and what good things he was willing to sacrifice for the sake of the whole effect. One passage I like particularly is the one that Mizener printed in *The Kenyon Review* under the title of "The World's Fair"—it's about Francis Melarky going home with a girl who turns out to be lesbian and tries to shoot herself with a revolver so old that the pearl handle of it comes off in her hand. It's one of the eeriest things that Scott ever wrote and it's marvelous as a picture of that life.[36]

[. . .]

Sincerely,
Malcolm Cowley

[NL TL/CC-1]
[TO: RAY B. WEST, EDITOR, *THE WESTERN REVIEW*]
March 23, 1953

Dear Ray:

I want to query you again about the piece on Fitzgerald and the romance of money.[37] [. . .] It was hard at this stage to say something new and definite about Fitzgerald, but I think I found it here. To simplify, most of Fitzgerald's stories and his two best novels are concerned with the conflict between two moneyed classes, the old moneyed class (the girl) which inherited its wealth and regards money as a solid profession, and the new moneyed class which regards money as liquid income. The plot of *Gatsby, Tender* and "The Diamond as Big as the Ritz" is that the man, representing the new moneyed class, gets the girl but is murdered by her wealth or her relatives (as if Lochinvar had been hunted down and destroyed by fair Ellen's kinsmen). Once given this clue, it's amusing how it is supported by quotations from one story after another. And the theme is socially and historically central, because the 1920s were exactly the period at which the old, solid, Freud called it excremental conception of wealth was replaced by the new liquid conception—saving money in 1910 was "piling up the rocks," but by 1925 money was more like the nourishing stream of mother's milk.

[. . .]

As ever,
Malcolm

{ ———— }

Ernest Hemingway, 1951–1952

In the early 1950s Cowley's epistolary friendship with Hemingway was strained, as a controversy erupted over a first biographical-critical study of Hemingway written by Philip Young. Mediating between Young, his publishers, and an ultra-sensitive Hemingway, Cowley maneuvered with tact and grace, but still became entangled in misunderstandings and finally cut off the correspondence.

[NL TL/CC-2]
[TO: PHILIP YOUNG]
April 20, 1951

Dear Mr. Young:

I haven't finished reading your manuscript, and I shall want to read it twice and mark it up before returning it to the publisher, but to save time I had better make you a private and interim report on it.

You are brilliantly on the right track, I think, but you have gone wrong in various places and have made too many judgments, moral judgments, that don't take all the circumstances into account. The secret of good criticism is to qualify, qualify—for it takes a lot of qualifications to arrive at the truth. I would strongly advise a month or two for thinking about what you have written and making further revisions.

I'll give you some background information that will help. It must not be quoted and must not be used except as a background for your own judgments. If it could have been used I would have used it myself.

You are right, Hemingway was shell-shocked by his wound in Italy. The wound was I think the central experience in his career. I did a lot of work on it and the account in *Life* was careful. Of course he couldn't have carried a dying soldier on his back if he had no knee—at that time, after the Minenwerfer blast, he was simply filled with little pieces of steel—but an Austrian searchlight caught him in its beam as he walked back to the Italian lines and a heavy-caliber machine gun opened up on him, hitting him twice, once in the foot and once in the knee. At the dressing station they thought he was dying and let him lie, till a British ambulance driver came up and insisted that he be attended to. Then he went back to the hospital and slowly recovered and I don't know what happened afterward—I'm pretty sure now that he never enlisted in the Arditi and he may have done something that he is ashamed of—anyhow he won't talk about his experiences after getting out of the hospital. He did get the Silver Medal for Valor, the second-highest decoration in the gift of the Italian government, about equivalent to the French Médaille Militaire; it's a big decoration.

In those days I think he told some lies about himself. Afterwards he picked himself up and became very careful to tell the truth. I tracked down a lot of his stories—and they were always confirmed, I mean the stories he tells now. Often you found that the story told by others was much more to his credit, much more dramatic, than the story he told himself. Hemingway the soldier and sportsman is a pretty incredible person, but true.

You're absolutely right about "Big Two Hearted-River"—it's about a man with shell shock going fishing. I would guess that the place the river narrows and goes into the swamp is a vagina. But most of the talk about Hemingway's being a repressed homosexual and woman hater is dreadfully unfair to him— isn't the world full of repressed homosexuals?—and do many of them make the repression so thorough and become as good men as Hemingway? —and are any of them as essentially honest in their writing?

The point is that for twenty years Hemingway was a frightened man—or so I gather—continually fighting his fear and continually seeking out danger to test himself again and again. I asked him when he got over his fear— for obviously he did get over it—and he said partly in Spain and partly in an airplane in China, circling round and round the Hongkong airport in a fog while the gas got lower and it seemed they must surely crash into a mountain— after that, he said, he was never frightened again. In World War II he was not only brave but seemed to be deliberately seeking death. There's a great story here, of a man who conquered fear by always walking into danger. But all this information is confidential and you can't mention China because Hemingway would know the story came from me.

You missed a trick on the story "The Doctor and the Doctor's Wife." Hemingway said, "It's a story about my finding out that my father was a coward"—with that key you can see how it fits into the rest of the pattern.

You take a lot of risks later on in identifying Hemingway with his heroes. There are at least three critical or psychological concepts to make use of: identification, projection, persona. Hemingway has created at least two personas, as you point out without using the word: the soldier living by the code and the Nick Adams persona, the frightened man. The point I wanted to make is that Nick is to some extent a persona too, not the "real" Ernest, whatever the real Ernest may be. Just be very careful in your language when extracting biography from stories. Hemingway makes a distinction between the "true" stories and the "made-up" stories. "Now I Lay Me" is a true story. So are I think all stories about Nick Adams in Michigan. But "Macomber" and "Kilimanjaro" are made-up stories. About Macomber you are two thirds wrong. Hemingway could never *identify* himself with a rich Bostonian and Harvard man like Macomber, never in the world. Mrs. Mac has nothing to do with Pauline and Hemingway, even in anger, wouldn't have accused Pauline of betraying him (as note his quite different accusations against the heroine of "Kilimanjaro"). The most he could do was *project* some of his fears into Macomber, or, let us say, understand Macomber better because of his own fears. I am certain that Hemingway never, never disgraced himself by running from a lion. On the other hand, he most certainly did *identify* himself with the hero of "Kilimanjaro" and ritually kill his dead self in the hero. He also undoubtedly identified Pauline with the heroine, at a time when his marriage was going badly, and maybe that was unforgivable, but Pauline has forgiven him and they are good friends (whereas he hates Martha, who treated him badly, who *used* him).

Why don't you document one of Hemingway's quarrels and revenges by quoting what Sinclair Lewis said about him, and then what Hemingway said about Lewis in "Across the River"—using the magazine version, before he had changed it to avoid, possibly, a suit for libel?—he wasn't talking about Pound when he mentioned the potato-faced poet; that may have been any one of several persons; I guessed Matty Josephson, whom Ernest doesn't like too well.[38] Alice Toklas doesn't like Hemingway and he thinks that lay behind the quarrel with Gertrude—they made up in Paris in 1945.... "My Old Man" was the only story saved from those stolen in the train at Lyon—it was my guess that the others were also in the Anderson manner.

I'll have more notes of this sort for you later on—but I thought I'd start with these so you could get to thinking about necessary changes. The chief point is never to forget the real courage and obstinacy and patience of this man—there are others with his psychological handicaps, there isn't any other who has grown so strong in the wounded and broken part. I want you to do your best for the book, because it is something new and needed on Hemingway, and you should make it right.[39]

Cordially,
Malcolm Cowley

[EH TLS-2]
[TO: ERNEST HEMINGWAY]
May 9, 1951

Dear Ernest:

About the Young book: Tom Bledsoe of Rinehart & Co. asked me whether I would do a long report on the ms. I debated with myself, thought about you, and decided to say yes. Now I am very glad that I did so. The book isn't anything to worry about, but on the whole, in its present form, it is not good. It starts well, with a pretty keen reading of the Nick Adams stories, and ends well too, with a long comparison between Nick Adams and Huckleberry Finn, but the middle chapters are flabby and show a deplorable tendency to confuse you as author with the various heroes of your novels and stories. I don't think there is anything you could or should do about it, since Young depends on printed sources and is writing a sort of biographical criticism, not straight biography. He is an instructor at Washington Square College of New York University, bright but not extremely bright, and I gather that he is well intentioned, and he admires your work. It wouldn't have helped for me to say to Bledsoe, "Don't publish this book," because he'd made up his mind to publish it anyway. If he didn't publish it somebody else would, because a book on your work is needed. I decided that the best thing I could do was try to make the book as good as possible—I suggested very extensive changes and told Bledsoe I didn't think he should publish it unless the changes were made. I am pretty sure that Young will now revise the ms. and if he makes the changes I suggested it still won't be a book you like, but it will make sense and help your permanent reputation as a writer. I'll try to get another look at the ms. in three months or so when he hands it back again.

I should have done the job myself. Every time a young professor like Mizener or Young goes to work on a writer of our generation it seems to me that he doesn't know what it was all about. I've always had a feeling of loyalty to all the writers of our generation, except to the stupid ones or those like Bromfield who sold out. We started from the same place, even if we have had very different experiences since we drove ambulances or camions in that other war that's so far away now. I think that as a generation of writers we have done a good job, one of the best, and if each man has had his individual failings that's something we can talk about among ourselves and let the twerps find out for themselves—but it seems to me that they always pick the wrong things as failings. They're shouting up Scott Fitzgerald now, but they don't know why he was good, let alone why he was bad. And there's your immense work for them to attack with their poisoned spitballs (though Young doesn't attack the work, I'll say that for him). Well, your work is big enough to stand a hundred times as many devastating attacks and still be there. [...]

The worst thing written about you was that *New Yorker* piece.[40] I think it was as bad as it could be—if it had been any worse it would have been better, because the malice of it would have been clearer. It was obvious that you were nice to Miss Ross and she showed her gratitude in a curious fashion.

[...] Wish I were sitting at your table now, arguing or just talking over the wine. Our love to both of you.

As ever,

Malcolm

―――――――――

[EH TLS-2]
[TO: ERNEST HEMINGWAY]
July 19, 1951

Dear Ernest:

This letter should have been started two or three days sooner, so as to reach you on July 21, but it counts as a birthday letter anyway—and my warmest and heartiest to you on having survived more than thirty years of the tough trade, the worst of it, I hope, and still being able to do your best work when so many of the boys have given up in one way or another—and now I think the best writing years are in front of you (and in front of me, too, because I'll be your senior by a year on August 24). At a party last Saturday I ran into the character Sammy Boals—I've known him for years, though I don't see him often—and he said that he'd spent a week in your neighborhood and you'd shown him a long story that was marvelous, that was such writing as nobody else could do. That's something to look forward to reading when it comes out in the prints.

At the same party was a very different character named Hede Massing,[41] who had testified against Hiss and then written a book about her life in the Communist underground. I had known her after she left the C.P. but before she embarked on her career of confession. She rushed up to me drunkenly and asked me what I thought of her book, which I hadn't read but promised to read; then I shied away. In half an hour she was back again talking about what we Americans (using the uvular "r" in the Berlin fashion)—what vee Amerrhicans should do to combat the Rrhussian enemy in our midst. People don't appreciate Senator McCarthy, she said—he has his faults, of course, but the difference between him and Molotov is that McCarthy is one of us.—One of you, perhaps, I said, but not one of me. Then she said, "When the Rrhussians are looking for tools among us Amerrhicans," looking at me and another character, "they will find that you are the sort of dupes they can use. Good night, gentlemen," and she flounced upstairs to bed. She had come in a new car, with her psychoanalyst, and it seemed to me that her new career of informant was profitable financially—but it left her with a sense of guilt that she kept thrusting into people's faces like a crippled beggar showing his stumps and asking us to observe that they had real maggots in them. . . . That's a fair sample of social life today in these United States—everyone shies away from talking politics except the pure bastards and they appear and talk very loud and dare you to disagree with them.

[. . .]

Did I tell you that I was doing a labor of piety for Scott Fitzgerald? Back in 1938 he decided that what was wrong with *Tender Is the Night* was that the real beginning—the young psychiatrist in Switzerland—was tucked away in the middle of the book. He rearranged the story in chronological order and wanted Perkins to reissue it that way, but by that time it wasn't having any sales at all and Perkins couldn't afford to reissue it. Now I'm doing a new edition for Scribner's based on Fitzgerald's changes and I'm taking the opportunity to correct his proofreading errors, for the novel is full of them. The book is being read again now and it might as well be read right. *Exile's Return* had fine reviews this time—it had terrible reviews when it first appeared—but reviews don't do much for the sale of a book like that and I doubt if it ever goes to 5,000 copies. It was fun, though, working over it again and now it's off my chest for good and I can go on to something else—and high time. I was interviewed by Johnny Hutchens[42] and Harvey Breit[43] and that was a new experience, because I hadn't been on the giving end of a literary interview before. When Harvey in his piece in *The New York Times* made me refer to Fitzgerald as "Fitz," not once but several times, it made me sound like a drunk who had come up to Fitzgerald in a barroom and slapped him on the back and insisted on calling him "Fitz, old man." It's a little point, but it helped me to appreciate your troubles with backslappers and interviewers. If they are fools, then everybody they write about sounds like a fool.

I was sorry to read about your mother's death. The obituary made her sound like a woman of very determined character, like someone who would try to impose her will on the family, but losing one's mother is always something heavy and sad, no matter how far away she has been in life—the parents stood there like buffers and bulwarks between us and the future and after they're gone we're left standing out in the bow and taking all the waves—not that we didn't take them before, but now there's not even an imaginary screen. I'm getting God damned solemn and I had better stop.

As ever,
Malcolm

[EH TLS-2] [PARTLY *PMC* 494]
[TO: ERNEST HEMINGWAY]
January 28, 1952

Dear Ernest:

Again I say, wish to God that I hadn't ever seen the philipyoung ms. Undertaking to read and report on it last spring, then telling you about it, has got me into the damnedest Hippocratic, hypocritic and hypercritical situation I never imagined [...].[44]

[...] I'm not writing [Bledsoe] these days because I really and truly want to get shut of the business completely [...]. This is my last will and testament on this subject signed malcolm cowley so help me god amen.

[...] Connecticut in the winter aint fitten for man nor beast. But Southern beasts and birds are beginning to invade the neighborhood: first came turkey buzzards (looking for the Confederate dead, I suppose), then possums (one farmer in the next town has shot 17 of them this winter), and now there's a pair of cardinals in town; I call them Cardinal and Mrs. Fulton J. Spellman. The great Irish-American job hunt, otherwise known as the loyalty purge, is reaching new heights. Every time a Jew, a Protestant or a free thinker gets bounced out of his job for the govt (or in radio, TV or the colleges), an Irish-American shows up to ask for it with a letter from his priest. Don't misread me; I have a great admiration for the Catholic faith, but I'm no friend of the American Irish bishops, who are up to their stoles in Power elections. This *Counter Attack-Red Channels* business[45] that you've been reading about is a racket run by two ex-FBI agents, Irish Catholics, who have the aid of the Catholic War Veterans—they print somebody's name, then the CWV's write letters about him, then the Jew or free thinker loses his job and an Irishman gets it. It would be nice if someone could convert those racketeers from Spellmanism to Catholicism (oh, little town of Bethlehem).

What's Dos been converted to? Pelmanism? I haven't read his last novel about the Chosen Country, but the reviews made it sound as exciting as cornmeal mush. Still, it seemed to have a lot about his family and early life in it, so that I'll have to pour milk on it and lick the bowl, sooner or later, but not in this dismal weather. Right now I couldn't stand his bracing sentiments. Dos did something truly remarkable in his early novels, especially *Manhattan Transfer* and *USA*. Here for a hundred years the world has been getting more and more crowded and collective, so that the real heroes of an action story are likely to be not a man (where are men these days?) but a squad, a platoon, a company, an army or a city or a nation. Dos discovered and evolved a technique for treating these collective heroes in a unified novel. That was something for the age, and hundreds of younger writers have been adapting his technique to their own subjects. Most of the World War II novelists did so (Mailer, Burns, for example), besides Sartre and many other Frenchmen—in fact the French still think that Dos is one of the world classics. After a man has done that sort of job it's a pity to see him conked or sapped or sandburged into conformity and hurrah for the American way of canned life. I love my country when it's in trouble but not when it's a chosen country throwing its platitudes around.

[...]

Our best to you and Mary in this year of our Luce 1952.

As ever,
Malcolm

――――――

[EH TLS-2] [PARTLY *PMC* 495–496]
[TO: ERNEST HEMINGWAY]
May 24, 1952

Dear Ernest:

It's very good news that you're bringing out a book [*The Old Man and the Sea*] in September, even if the book is only a section of the big job you've been working on. [...] From this distance I don't get the logic of publishing only one-quarter of the sea book, which in turn is only one-third (isn't it?) of the big job—but you have experience and wisdom in these publishing matters, and patience and independence, and bringing out the books as they are ready will probably prove to be the best course. Let the kids who are starting and have to impress readers with mere bulk, let them do the behemoths. (Of which the chief advantage is that 1. the daily reviewers haven't time to finish them, and 2. are too polite to say mean things about what they haven't read, and therefore 3. say nice things about them in spite of being bored from here to eternity.) A short, wonderful book will be a wonderful relief.

I didn't know Charlie Scribner very well, but he had character and I liked what I knew of him. His death coming not so long after Max Perkins' was tough for the house and for the literary world. I hear that young Charlie is taking hold of things in a good fashion. In general the publishing trade is in a pretty chaotic condition—readers are showing more hesitation about paying $3 or $4 for novels when they can wait and buy them for 25 or 35 cents. Brentano's took the books out of its gallery and is replacing them with a line of sea shells—I'm not making a joke, that's what they're doing. Maybe we should try inscribing little poems on sea shells. The great purge hasn't really hit the publishing trade (except at Little, Brown), but there are signs that the purgers are working in this direction and the publishers are scared enough so that they don't bring out some books that would probably have a large sale.

Hollywood has just made the big surrender to the American Legion, which henceforth will decide who is to be hired and fired. The motto everywhere is Play It Safe, and that explains why publishers' lists are so full of the trivial and inconsequential. Last year the movies tried to break over, since they were suffering from malnutrition in the box office; they produced several good films (*Streetcar, Place in the Sun, Death of a Salesman, Born Yesterday, The Marrying Kind*) and most of the good films were picketed by the American Legion and the Catholic War Veterans, so that the error is unlikely to be repeated.

The Fitzgerald boom is over. The Faulkner boom is still running strong, and it's encouraged by the fact that Faulkner is getting holy. These days nothing succeeds like a strong dose of piety. I don't blame Faulkner at all, since he doesn't give a damn for the public, but the Faulkner critics are becoming seriously silly. The young novelists are just crazy about symbols, symbol, symbol, who's got the symbol. They think that a good symbol takes the place of a story—lucky for them *if it does*, because most of them can't tell stories. Their characters are so damned symbolic you don't know what they mean. The two mottoes of the young novelists are, "Mother was to blame" and "Evil is in the human heart."

In these crazy days it is a great relief to get to work on our lawn and garden, where the only subversives are bugs and weeds. I work until I'm reduced to a state of narcotized insensibility. [. . .] Love to Mary in this time of personal and public trouble.

As ever,
Malcolm

{ ——— }

[NL TL/CC-I]
[TO: E. E. CUMMINGS]
April 27, 1951

Dear Estlin:

Since you're sailing early next week it doesn't look as if we could get together [. . .]. Here's the general question I wanted to ask, and step on me if you'd rather not talk about it. I'm putting together a book of which the real subject is the contributions to prose fiction of the new writers who appeared in the 1920s.[46] They were big and varied contributions, if you add them all together or even if you take them separately. You never wrote any prose fiction that I know of, but *The Enormous Room* comes into the story because it had a very great influence on other writers. It was something absolutely new when it appeared, as your poems in the first issue of the monthly *Dial* were absolutely new. There had been a big change since 1915, when you were a kid writing for the *Advocate,* and the question I wanted to ask was how the change came about. It isn't the old question of literary influence, as if I wanted to end by saying that Cummings "was influenced by" or "derives from" so and so. You found something that was new and your own—the real question is what started you to looking for it? Was it mostly your reading (and of whom?) or was it partly because you started painting and wanted to get some of the same immediate effects in words? And also when did you write *The Enormous Room?*—I know it was some time before the book was published, but was it in 1919? I want to be sure that when or if I do a piece on the very big room I'm not talking through my hat.[47] [. . .]

As ever,
Malcolm

[NL TL/CC-I]
[TO: WILLIAM GOYEN][48]
August 20, 1951

Dear Goyen:

"A Shape of Light" comes as close to being music as any prose work I have ever read. That other story I remember, without remembering the title, had the structure of an old ballad, with a many times repeated refrain; but the structure here in "The Shape of Light" is that of a tone poem—in three movements, though it isn't a symphony, with the themes stated, developed, disappearing and reappearing, and then, as you say, wafted away into the region where no sounds are. And it does contain, as you also say, the sort of writing that rises off the page—I remember especially the nausea of the city streets ("dogshit" is the right word there, to pin it down) and the trees full of dead children. But that other side of your ambition—"to be clear, to tell

clearly and passionately so that I may be listened to"—isn't always realized
in the story. I don't know whether you think about reworking it—some
things reach a state where they can't be reworked—but if you *do* make
changes in it, I would, if I were you, work on the confusion of voices at the
beginning of the story— [. . .] the reader is a little stunned, as if he came
into a room where many people were talking at once—only here he is coming into different rooms, in different decades. What I'd think about is
omitting some passages, so that the musical outline of the story would become clearer. [. . .]

You've surrendered yourself to the material and that's something that
writers without talent never learn to do. You've surrendered yourself and the
story has taught you—but I feel, old classicist that I am, that now you should
reassert your control of it by saying at one point or another, "You, this voice
in the story, spoke to me and I wrote down what you said, but now I find
that I don't need you for my general effect and so I'm going to silence and
expunge you." Leaving the story shorter and better articulated, but still with
that soaring quality and that other quality of dying away at the end into that
region where no words are.

By the way, one long poem you have perhaps read you should certainly
read again, because the author, like you, was letting the voice speak for him;
it's Whitman's "Song of Myself"—and if you can find it at the library in the
facsimile reprint of the 1855 edition, it's still more interesting than it became
after Whitman made his much later revisions. That would seem to deny
what I said above on the subject of revisions—but Whitman had made
plenty of them before he published the poem in 1855, and in his later revisions he wasn't able to recapture the original mood and idiom.

As ever,

Malcolm Cowley

[EW TLS-1]

[TO: EDMUND WILSON]

August 20, 1951

Dear Edmund:

[. . .] I've been reading some new stories by William Goyen. If I were a
psychiatrist I'd say that the prognostic in his case was very bad; he may be

headed straight for the nuthouse, but he's one of the few younger writers who take risks—there's a sort of early-Whitman quality in his work that reminds me of the "Song of Myself." Not much else of interest to report—except the great Catholic effort to take over the government by labeling all Non-Catholics as fellow travelers.

As ever,
Malcolm

[AT TPCS]
[TO: ALLEN TATE]
[*no date*]

Dear Allen:—Ah doan no jes hwut ta say about Goyen. Terribly self-indulgent stuff and when it fails—as it does in "Old Somebody" —it falls flat on its face; but "Pore Perrie" really is a prose ballad, with a ritual self-castration. Let's say Sherwood Anderson reborn as a young man from East Texas, with a better education and more delicate wrists—willing to try anything in prose and capable of finding new things. [. . .]

M

[I]t would be more useful to exhibit serious foreign writing to Americans, to jolt us out of the self-satisfied world provinciality into which we are sinking.

Cowley to Edmund Wilson, March 22, 1952 [EW]

[NL TL/CC-I]
[TO: JAMES LAUGHLIN, NEW DIRECTIONS]
December 8, 1951

Dear Laughlin:

Thank you for sending me the proposal for a quarterly magazine on American materials.[49] There are several reasons why it seems to me useful and exciting.

The great reason is, of course, that the public in other countries gets a false impression of American life and literature from such exports of ours as movies, hard-boiled detective stories, comic books and magazines in which there is more advertising than text. Much or most of the serious work that is being done here is still unknown in Europe. Some of it was revealed in the American number of *Fontaine,* published in Algiers during the war.[50] The immense effect of that one issue of one magazine—which led, among other things, to new French translations of most of the authors who appeared in it—suggests how much could be accomplished by a well edited quarterly appearing in several languages.

But the proposed quarterly would also have an effect in this country that shouldn't be overlooked, even though its other function would be in the field of international relations. The fact is that serious American writers aren't having an easy time of it, in these days when the best of the literary magazines are in the midst of financial crises and when the whole book industry is having its crisis too. Even though the proposed quarterly wouldn't be distributed here, it would do two important things for our writers: it would furnish them with a little extra money, which is needed, and, more importantly, it would give them the sort of encouragement that comes from the assurance that some of their best work was being read and discussed in all countries.[51]

[...]

Cordially,
Malcolm Cowley

[JM TLS-1][NL TL/CC-1]
[TO: JOSEPHINE MILES]
February 18, 1952

Dear Miss Miles:

I thoroughly enjoyed your new collection of poems,[52] for the same reason that I enjoyed your early poems back in the days when I was literary editor of *The New Republic*—that is, I enjoyed them for their wit, their sharp observation, their ability to put usual objects and experiences under an unusual light. I suppose that people have told you often you are "like" Emily Dickinson. You aren't like her at all in the sense of being modeled after her, but you do have something of the same vision and sparseness. I like the special types of liberty you take with rhymes and I like most of the poems. Among the shorter ones my favorites were "Wreck," "Tally," "Exterior," "Ride," "Squirrel," "The Plastic Glass" and "Evangel."

The two long poems interested me as attempts to broaden your range. In "A Foreign Country" you were trying a subject that is extremely difficult, both because of your mixed feelings toward Russia—or rather, toward the conventional American view of Russia—and because of public taboos. I think you succeeded admirably in expressing the mixture of feelings, but I don't think that you succeeded at all points in turning public affairs into poetry. [...] I'd suggest that the poem would be improved as a whole by being purged of editorial matter. "Two Kinds of Trouble" isn't such a difficult poem and comes nearer to success as a whole; what I liked best in it was the passage about American faces.

I can't be very encouraging about the prospect of publication in book form. There has been a disturbing slump in the poetry market; we became painfully conscious of it at Viking when we published Horace Gregory's selected poems and when, in spite of very favorable reviews, they had an advance sale of less than 500 copies, with reorders going slowly. Five years ago they would have done twice as well. Moreover, there is this difficulty with your poems, that each of them has a separate life and that they don't contribute as much as they should to one another—sometimes they have more impact when read two or three at a time than when read in a larger group. I've always had the feeling that a book of poems should be a book rather than a simple collection—meaning that it should have an organic structure of its own; the poems ideally should be arranged so as to show some sort of progression toward some sort of goal, and at the very least they should be arranged in groups by subject matter. If I were you I should try rearranging the manuscript before sending it out. Perhaps it would be a good thing to shorten it to fifty poems instead of eighty, choosing those with the greatest emotional force.

Thanks for giving me the chance to read them. I spent some profitable and enjoyable hours with the manuscript.

Cordially,
Malcolm Cowley

[AB TLS-3] [NL TL/CC-3]
[TO: ALAN BARTH]
May 26, 1952

Dear Alan:

[. . .] What I chiefly wanted to talk about was your account of the prospects of the loyalty purge: I suspect that you were, as you feared, a little too optimistic. I have heard that the situation seems a little better in Washington, that Congress is getting bored with "revelations" that don't make the front pages, that the Un-American Activities Committee is being a little more polite to witnesses. [. . .] But I suspect that in spite of these happy auguries the purge will continue and will even grow worse—not in Washington but in what used to be called "the field." The point is that it is becoming institutionalized. There are now hundreds of persons interested in continuing and broadening the purge in order to assure the life of their own committees and their own jobs. As you know, purging has become a respectable activity that yields honors and emoluments. For some it has become a profitable racket.

I get interested in analyzing some of the forces behind the purge, for it's a complicated movement that involves a good deal of our culture. The fight against the New Deal was only part of it, though it seemed the biggest part in Washington. Out in "the field" there are other elements involved, including a great many class, religious and racial hostilities. Power in this country used to be held by Protestants of predominantly English descent; then other groups began to rise (Germans, Jews) in the economic scale without much disturbing the pattern; now it's the Irish who hold political power in many localities, without forgetting the snubs they had to suffer when they were poor—but the Irish in turn are being jostled by the Italians, the Poles, the French Canadians. The Irish at present are the chief purgers (McCarran, McCarthy, O'Neill, Fitzgerald) and one of the reasons is that the purge hits them least, there having been few Catholics who belonged to "subversive" organizations in the 1930s. I've even heard the loyalty purge described as the great Irish Catholic job-hunt. It's had that effect, at least, in the State Dept, in Hollywood, in television, I mean the effect of taking jobs away from Protestants, Jews, freethinkers and giving them to (mostly Irish) Catholics. The

Italians, Poles, and other new immigrant groups aren't getting so many jobs, but they certainly react to appeals against "the intellectuals" and "the long-hairs" and "the graduates of that Red law school," namely Harvard.

The Catholic hand in the purge is something I could talk about at considerable length, at the danger of overestimating it. [. . .]

Whittaker Chambers' book is wonderful for its tying in of Christianity with anticommunism (he says that all agnostics are potential communists) and for its attempt to arouse class hatred by identifying the friends of Alger Hiss with the people born on the right side of the tracks. That class element in the loyalty purge is becoming clearer—but never quite so clear as in *U.S.A. Confidential*, with its appeal to the rabble.[53] [. . .]

[. . .]

I'm not saying all these things to suggest what you could put into a new book[54]—my God, no, some of them shouldn't be said in a book and all of them should be handled with delicacy, if at all—but merely to show that the subject will still be a very big one after next November and that it merits a lot of hard thinking. [. . .]

As ever,
Malcolm

[NL TL/CC-1]
[TO: IRVING HOWE]
June 9, 1952

Dear Irving:

The joke is really on me. Strange as it seems, I hadn't known that you were the author of the article on *The Wild Palms*.[55] [. . .] I don't regard you as one of the surrealistic critics; the prime, the unsurpassed example of the genus is of course Richard Chase's *Melville*, and especially his chapter on *Pierre*, in which he completely disregards what the novel is to the reader, what it was to the writer, how and when it was written, what it really shows about Melville, and creatively transforms it into a scripture.

I think it's a mistake when writing about Faulkner not to bear in mind the distinction between what he does instinctively, out of his subconscious—of which he makes great and deliberate use—and what he does through conscious intention. Sometimes critics interpret his own books for Faulkner and he nods gravely and says, "Yes, I hadn't seen that." Sometimes critics, even fine ones like Cleanth Brooks, praise Faulkner's murkiest novels, tempted into overvaluing them by the fact that they offer the greatest opportunity to the explicator, who then becomes intoxicated with his own creation. My own standards are anything but Gothic—maybe I have an 18th century mind—and I prefer *Go Down, Moses* to *Absalom, Absalom* and "Old Man" to "The Wild Palms," I mean both the single story and the combined book. Yes, it does have interconnections and orchestral effects—almost any combination of two novels by the same author will present orchestral effects—but the 18th century mind prefers what is single and coherent. Valéry said, "I would infinitely rather write something weak, in full consciousness and in complete lucidity, than give birth to a masterpiece in a state of trance." I don't agree with him but I sympathize with his feelings.

When is your Faulkner coming out?

As ever,
Malcolm

On July 26, 1952, Nelson Algren asked Cowley to act as a reference for a Fulbright fellowship to France. Cowley wrote the following to the Fulbright Committee:

[...] [Nelson Algren] is a modest, friendly, rather witty Chicagoan with no mannerisms of the Great Writer and I am sure that Europeans would like him.

His literary work requires and deserves a longer discussion, for he occupies what I feel is a quite special place in American fiction. He started out as a poet and the early poems of his that I saw twenty years ago greatly impressed me by their fashion of turning Midwestern American speech into a poetic idiom and by their great imaginative power. Those same two qualities were shown in his prose when he began writing fiction; at that time, in a review,[56] I called him the poet of the Chicago slums. But his fiction had another special quality: it was in appearance naturalistic, but it wasn't merely external and observed, like most naturalistic writing; instead it was inspired by deep sympathy for the characters it presented: they were slum dwellers, but each of them had his special sort of self-respect— "You got your pride and I got my pride," one of them, a blind beggar, observes—and the result is that although the novels deal with what are apparently sordid situations, the final impression they give is not one of sordidness, but of a sort of wild poetry (in that respect they are like Sean O'Casey's early plays of the Dublin slums). In American writing there is nothing quite like them and I was deeply gratified when Algren's novel, *The Man with the Golden Arm*, won the National Book Award in 1950, over some pretty stiff competition; it was indeed the most distinguished American novel of the year.

From the point of view of his professional qualifications I should certainly say that Mr. Algren deserves any encouragement that your committee can give him. [. . .]

———————

[WK TLS-I][NL TL/CC-I]
[TO: WELDON KEES]
November 11, 1952

Dear Weldon:

There is nothing for me to do but repeat the letter that you have had from the publishers. Audience for poetry shrinks. Cost of production expands. Had grave disappointments with recent volumes of poetry on our list. Wonderful poems these. Don't see any chance this year of finding audience large enough to justify publication.

That's the letter and I know it by heart, almost. I want to add that from the moment I first read any of your poems I was impressed by their freshness, wit and accurate fancy. There are some beauties in this collection. I liked the Robinson poems and wish you would do more with that theme and character. There are some beautiful satirical pieces like "Problems of a Journalist." I think there is a loss of cumulative force in the collection because so many of the poems are based on special occasions and momentary perceptions. The style has more weight than the subjects and I am not sure that this particular book of yours justifies the quotation from *The Marble*

Faun—I mean that the poems descend into a lot of little caves instead of one dark cavern.

[...]

As ever,
Malcolm

———————

I'm heartbroken that when Random House gave the go-by and heave-ho to your ms you didn't bring it to me. I think I could have persuaded Viking that it was just the thing to publish and I'd love to work, not on the problem of selling your stories, which isn't a problem, but on that of establishing you as a front-line reputation [...]

Cowley to John Cheever, January 8, 1952 [1953][NL]

[NL TL/CC-I] [PARTLY *PMC* 496–497]
[TO: JOHN CHEEVER]
January 22, 1953

Dear John:

I enclose a little statement that you can send on to your publishers[57] and they can use it if they think it's worth using. I tried to express what I think has been the central virtue of your stories, or at any rate of your best stories—that of giving moments in which the Victim Tells All, or in which the narrator has a sudden feeling of heightened life (as at the end of "Goodbye, My Brother"). The best of all the moments—Joyce called them "epiphanies"—is the end of "Torch Song," which reminds me always of the end of "The Raven":

> "Take thy beak from out my heart and thy form from off my door."

Criticisms: for what they are worth. "Goodbye, My Brother" is finally ambiguous. The boys, meaning the critics, talk about the virtues of irony, and it is ironical that the narrator is as bad as Lawrence in his different way, but it is also troublingly uncertain, so that one wishes you had made your own point of view clearer. On the other hand, the emotional quality of the story is wonderful and the characters are solid. It is a story that you could expand into a novel, and my theory is that you'll have to write a novel that way, by starting with one short story and expanding it backward (into the past of the characters) instead of by looking for a "novel" plot, whatever that may be. When you start by looking for a novelistic plot, you'll always break it into complete and separate episodes, out of habit.

[...]

What next? Go abroad, for Christ's sake. Go abroad and write a novel or a play about these people. If you keep on writing short stories about them you'll reveal your irritation more and more. Read *The Lonely Crowd,* by David Riesman. I don't recommend it all down the line, but he's wonderful on what he calls the "other-directedness," by which he means the lack of inner conviction and the sensitivity to what other people think, of the American upper middle classes. They're the people you're writing about and Riesman has some new thoughts about them. But, to repeat, you're getting tired of living among them and need some new subjects for observation: therefore go abroad. And take the kids along, it will be good for them, and if you stay a year won't cost any more than living in Westchester. Among the middle-aged immature other-directeds.

Papa Cowley sacrificed five teeth this week to a theory about curing arthritis in its early stages. In older days he would have sacrificed a fat rhyme and burned a lock of his hair. A fat rhyme did I say? I meant a fat ram, but I'm still a little woozy with the gas they gave me when abstracting the sacrifice to the god of calcified joints. I'd better sign off now before I say something foolish. Before?

As ever,
Malcolm

[NL TL/CC-1] [SC 317–318]
[TO: KENNETH BURKE]
February 13, 1953

Dear Kenneth:

[...][One] of the little jobs that have been oppressing me all fall [...] was an article on the New Fiction that will lose me many friends among the New Fictionists and the New Critics. The real point of the article (outside of some funny stuff) was that the New Fictionists are trying to create a sort of pure or ontological fiction, which they call Moral Realism as opposed to Social Realism and which presents characters as existing independently of any human institutions and confronted only with "permanent" dilemmas of a moral nature. But our principal moral problems, today—as always— are in a context of institutions—so that Moral Realism is morally unrealistic. Result: novels that are like tidy rooms in Bedlam.[58]

This morning heard on the radio that the Pope is advising clemency for the Rosenbergs. What a situation, when the great anti-Communist himself is more merciful than our crusaders for human dignity. If he had spoken two weeks ago, Iron-Hewer[59] might have gathered up courage to make a sensible gesture. You are certainly right in your observations about the danger to the corporationists in accepting responsibility along with power. Meanwhile let us stay in our woodchuck holes and meditate until the winter is over.

As ever,
Malcolm

[NL TL/CC-1]
[TO: CONRAD AIKEN]
February 19, 1953

Dear Conrad:

[...]

I suppose you've heard about Bill Williams' tribulations with the Library of Congress.[60] He was attacked by a patrioteer in the *Lyric* for being a Communist sympathizer. That sent Fulton Lewis Jr.[61] around to the Un-American Activities Committees file, where he found that Bill's name was listed on "more than fifty cards"—apparently he had Signed Things (with, as you know, a complete innocence about politics). Result of the Fulton Lewis Jr. attack was that Bill's appointment was not confirmed and he fell into a most depressed state of mind, which he wouldn't have fallen into if he had been at all familiar with the political racket— but at his age to be called a subversive was more than he could bear. The Bollingen Committee at Yale tried to cheer him up by giving him the prize, with Archie MacLeish also getting it and Paul Mellon doubling the ante, so that each got $1,000. We figured that Bill mightn't be around to get the prize another year, for his health has been very bad since the second heart attack.

[...]

Love to you both, till I see you,

Malcolm

[NL TL/CC-2]

[TO: DAVID RIESMAN]

May 1, 1953

Dear Mr. Riesman:

[...]

It had taken me a long time to get round to reading *The Lonely Crowd,* but when I did get round to it I thought it was one of the most stimulating books I had read for ages. You work on a whole area of American life that is utterly familiar to us from experience yet almost utterly neglected by the sociologists,—perhaps because middle-class, semi-intellectual Americans, as part of their other-mindedness, are timid about describing their own experiences as in any way typical. Your studies are going to be very useful to novelists, and to sociologists too—but sociologically speaking the difficulty lies in reducing them to a quantitative and measurable basis (as I found when reading *Faces in a Crowd*).[62] Novelists don't have to worry about quantities and metrics, but just about truths, and God knows your picture is a true one.

Some remarks: Other-minded Americans, taught to say over and over, "There must be something in what he says," have a very weak equipment for resisting pressure groups, and that helps to explain the access of McCarthyism. The groups are pressure, not merely veto, groups. They don't merely say,

"You shall not make movies with such and such themes," they say, "You *shall* make movies with these other themes." The other movies are being made and middle-class Americans like myself are staying away from them in droves. The most active pressure–veto group—now being institutionalized, and salaried—is of course composed of what Alan Barth calls the Americanists; but the most powerful group year after year is the Catholic Church, and a dangerous feature of the present situation is the Catholic (or Irish-Catholic) support of the Americanists; for example, somebody ought to look into the religious affiliations of members of the Americanization Committees of the American Legion . . . To get away from this political theme, a great movement of the last thirty years is of urban Americans into the countryside. When they settle in little towns like this, they send their children to the local school, and class conflicts arise in new forms, between the bright middle-class children and the working-class or farmer children who are good at basketball. [. . .] Also some observations in *Faces in a Crowd* make me think that you should take a hard look at Exeter, which has become the great preparatory school for children of the intellectuals. It's a good school too, but rich in emotional complications. The relation of children to parents today and thirty years ago is another most fertile field [. . .]—for example I note that our son (only child; attended Sherman Public School and Exeter; now a freshman at Harvard) is immensely closer to his father and mother, immensely more willing to listen to what they say, than I was to my parents or my wife to hers. What's the reason for this situation, which seems to be general, and what results will it have? I am noting its literary results already and when I teach young writers I have to say, "For God's sake disagree with me instead of doing what I tell you to do." . . . For fiction about the other-directed, you might take a look at John Cheever's collection of stories, *The Enormous Radio;* it is full of observations and touches that round out your theme—but so are many other books.

I'd better stop, with the final observation that this letter is one example of the fashion in which your work sets people to putting their notes together into a new configuration.

Sincerely,
Malcolm Cowley

[GH TLS-I] [NL TL/CC-I]
[TO: GRANVILLE HICKS]
August 24, 1953

Dear Granville:

Yesterday I got to thinking about your treatment of the Rosenberg case, in your chapter on the doughface liberals,[63] and I began to wonder whether you had made your own position clear enough. Certainly you made it clear that you disagreed with those who claimed the Rosenbergs were innocent—but was everyone opposed to their execution a doughface liberal?

I was opposed to the execution, though I didn't sign any pleas. I hadn't any serious doubts that the Rosenbergs had betrayed atomic secrets to Russia or that they were justly convicted, but I did have doubts about the justice of the death sentence. Many official statements conveyed the idea that the sentence would be commuted to life imprisonment if the Rosenbergs would make a full confession. If that impression was correct, they were executed not so much for spying as for refusing to betray their accomplices. I don't think that should be a ground for execution and I think that the Supreme Court showed a sort of indecent haste in deciding the case (as Frankfurter said in his dissenting opinion).

In Europe almost everyone from the Pope to Rebecca West felt that the Rosenbergs should have been granted executive clemency. It may be that this European perspective of miles will prove to be the same as an American perspective of years—I mean that in 1963 or 1973 Americans too will feel that the execution was inhumane and harmful to the long-term ends of American policy. I would feel easier for your own discussion of the case if you had made it clear that one could oppose the execution on several grounds—as an anti-Communist, as a Catholic, as a Christian, as a humanitarian, as a patriot—without being a doughface liberal.

Well, that's off my mind. Today's my birthday and we had a big party last night, with dancing on the greensward after midnight, by moonlight, very gay and oh, today, my aching arthritic back. [. . .]

As ever,
Malcolm

[NL TL/CC-2] [*PMC* 497–500]
[TO: HOWARD MUMFORD JONES]
November 30, 1953

Dear Howard:

I do have some ideas about the 1890s,[64] and at one time I thought of writing a little book about the period, but that idea has long since been abandoned along with others. Your knowledge of the period is so much broader than mine that I hesitate to bring forth my story—thinking as I do that you'd mark it down from A- to B+ or even lower if you found it in a blue book. But maybe it does have the advantage of being based on a special point of view, that of the student of serious avant-garde writing. I ought to make some more apologies too, but any how here goes—

In literature the 1890s were an abortive renaissance, a sort of false spring in February. They were a renaissance—or close to being one—because our literature was fructified, or let us say inseminated—it stood to stud, but the operation didn't take—by the new literature in Europe, Tolstoy, Zola, Ibsen—only Herbert Spencer left a really wide imprint (or foal). The renaissance was abortive because the new authors never found a public to support them.

For me the period opens in 1887, I think it was, when young Hamlin Garland went to see Howells at the residence hotel in the Boston suburbs. That was a real laying on of hands, with Howells' influence passing over to the new generation, whether they called themselves Realists or Veritists or Naturalists, or whether they were trying to write perfectly balanced novels in the French fashion.

The battle between the Realists and the Idealists—climaxed at the Chicago Fair in 1893 (all the principal figures were there)—was lost by the Realists in 1895, for the illogical reason that Oscar Wilde was convicted of pederasty. Everybody opposed to the new literature tried to bury it under Wilde's infamy—while setting against it the pure idealism, so they called it, of Stevenson. No market for realistic books, or not much.

(Note that international copyright law in 1893 had shut off the free translation of naughty European books, though the earlier ones were still available at fifteen to twenty-five cents. When I was a boy you could still find *Germinal* and the *Kreutzer Sonata,* paperbacked, in second-hand stores.)

Howells was still the center of the battle and he didn't give up the fight in 1895. As a matter of fact, he was still doing very well financially—he needed a lot of money—and he was still encouraging young authors. Another scene in the drama was Frank Norris' visit to Howells shortly before he published *McTeague* and Howells' praise of the novel in *The Reviewer* (or was it *The Critic?* I'm dictating without notes). Another laying on of hands, another passing of *mana* from one generation to another. But when *Sister Carrie* appeared in 1900 that was too much for Howells. On his one meeting with Dreiser he said, "You know I didn't like *Sister Carrie.*"

Until that time Howells had been encouraging the new group of Naturalists, who had gone much further than the Realists. But the mood of the country had changed, for political and social reasons, about which you know vastly more than I. There was also a professional accident that helped to defeat the avant-garde writers and I hope you don't overlook it in your story. It was the bankruptcy of the great house of Harper, which had occupied the same position in relation to the new American writer that the NRF [*Nouvelle Revue Française*] did in France before World War II. Howells' entire income came from *Harper's*. He was relieved when J. P. Morgan put money into the firm and worry began when Morgan had it taken over by Colonel Harvey. There was another quietly dramatic scene when Harvey had Howells out for the weekend. Harvey told Howells that he should go on writing for *Harper's* at the same salary, but I think he took him off books at that time. Also he said, "The battle for realism is lost." Howells agreed sadly that the battle for realism was lost and quit defending the avant-garde writers.

Dreiser might have gotten off practically unscathed—except for having his first novel effectively if not technically suppressed—if the novel hadn't been published in England and very highly praised by English reviewers. That was the cause of resentment and scandal here, and the magazines— Dreiser had lived by writing for them—quit publishing his work, almost by common consent. Dreiser was on the manic depressive side and might have gone into a depressed period in any case, but the closing off of his magazine career certainly made the depression worse and he would have committed suicide if Brother Paul hadn't rescued him.

That was in 1902 and by that time almost all the leading figures of the abortive renaissance were dead or silenced. You can go over the list for yourself—Harold Frederic, James A. Herne, Crane, Norris, Kate Chopin (although I think she lived until 1904, but in silence), and without my notes I forget the others. Trumbull Stickney, of course. Almost the only survivors were Dreiser (after ten years out of the literary picture), John J. Chapman (after a nervous breakdown), and E. A. Robinson, and practically speaking these didn't reappear until after 1910.

That is my specialized story of the period and if you think it has any value or illumination, do what you will with it—and my apologies for setting it down so briefly and dogmatically. [...]

As ever,
Malcolm Cowley

[NL TL/CC-2]
[TO: JAMES THURBER]
December 16, 1953

Dear Jim:

It was nice of you and Helen to send me a copy of *Thurber Country*. I hadn't read most of the pieces when they were new-yorkered and reading them together makes them seem better (which is exactly the opposite experience to that of reading Sid Perelman, for example, who is wonderful in twenty-milligram doses, but poison in quantities of one gram or over). Essentially, says the critic, you are a writer, which means someone with the sense of words, a stylist, if you will. Maybe your defective vision is one of those concealed (or concealing) blessings for which those of us who have them should get down on our knees and thank the goddess Catastrophe. Blessings like those (sometimes I think my partial deafness is another) keep us from being distracted from the inner monologue, or dialogue. Writing then is a process of transcribing that unspoken dialogue, and revising it God how many times until it is right. The properly written piece is like a properly spoken incantation—if one word is wrong the incantation doesn't work, the kitchen maid doesn't turn into a princess.

[...] I read your work as if it were an authoritative textbook on easy (i.e., hard) writing. "There's a Time for Flags" is a wonderful comment on the loyalty purge (with nothing said about it). "The American Literary Scene" was something I had to read—it's not so good on the visiting Englishman, which is an old topic, but then your funny pieces are usually based on a large stock of observations and reflections that are accurate and responsible—the humor is a slant, distorting pane of glass, but behind the glass aren't show-window dummies, but people. To explain "I had to read..."—I'm trying to do a long, pretty serious piece called "A Natural History of the American Writer." It's slanted, too, as a sociological study, with a little jargon like Robert Lynd's and words like "provenience" and "affective" (instead of "origin" and "emotional"). Reading Thurber on the subject is part of my research. "The Interview" is one of those alcoholic pieces that you do better than anyone else [...]—but I noted how you worked in a lot of your perfectly serious ideas about Henry James. Getting back to style again, yours is better on the non-intoning level than that of any other American writer since Mark Twain (I think we should sometimes intone and when Faulkner does it he is very good about one-third of the time, even if the other two-thirds he is self-intoxicated). Did you ever read any of Twain's short pieces and occasional stuff? I doubt it and am convinced that you arrived independently at somewhat the same manner of saying things simply and accurately. Some other time I might insist on telling you what's wrong with Thurber. These remarks are just to put on record a few of the things that are right.

[...]

As ever,
Malcolm

❧ PART VIII ❧

Worker at the Writer's Trade, 1954–1960

In the winter months of 1954, a grant from the Newberry Library in Chicago allowed Cowley to work there on *The Literary Situation.* A "social history of literature in our times," the book drew on his observations of American writers, the writing profession, and the publishing industry. It adopted a broadly contextual approach in the obsessively text-focused era of the New Criticism. The book reflects Cowley's unease with the limitations of the New Criticism and his conviction that the literary canon it inspired was exorbitantly narrow. Not surprisingly, there was controversy: while fellow writers applauded the book, academic critics dismissed it as "middlebrow" or irrelevant because it exemplified a mode of "historical" criticism that focused on the cultural, social, and economic dimensions of literature. As his letters show, Cowley remained a critical observer of the New Criticism through the 1950s, defining his own practice as text oriented but pluralistic and sensitive to context. As he wrote to Newton Arvin on December 28, 1958:

> Intrinsic or "pure" criticism is largely a make-believe. As soon as the critic divulges (against his will) that Poem A by Author X was written earlier or later than Poem B by the same author, he is writing biographical criticism. If he also divulges that a given word in the same poem had a different meaning in the poet's time than it has today, he is writing historical criticism. If the word had a different meaning for the poet himself than for others of his time, and the critic makes that observation, he is writing psychological criticism. If he confesses that the poem was an answer to something written by another poet, or a publicist, he is writing social criticism. And if he makes none of those confessions, he is an absolutist ass. [Arvin]

In an "Age of Criticism," as Randall Jarrell called it, literature—rather than the discourse around it—remained Cowley's primary concern. Symptomatic was his support of *The Paris Review*'s policy of privileging the work of new, young writers over literary criticism. He doggedly plugged the seemingly unpublishable Nathan Asch and admonished the novelist Frederick Manfred to deepen his observations of human character. He championed conservative fictionists like Thornton Wilder and James Gould Cozzens and persuaded Wallace Stegner and Dawn Powell to publish with Viking. But he also offered editorial advice and encouragement to new and daring voices like James Purdy's and Ernest Gaines's, and he wrote a personal "fan letter" to Vance Bourjaily. Especially noteworthy were Cowley's efforts on behalf of Jack Kerouac, whose novel *On the Road* he successfully shepherded toward publication, and his supportive letters to Tillie Olsen, who in 1956 was a student in Cowley's writing class at Stanford.

The prior year Wallace Stegner had invited Cowley to teach at Stanford— the beginning of what would be a long friendship between the two writers. Cowley recurrently taught at universities across the country (in 1956, 1958, and 1959 at Stanford, in 1957 at Michigan) yet always considered himself, as he wrote James Thurber, "a spy and interloper" in academe, feeling more at home among writers and publishers.

Cowley's letters of the years 1954–1960 reflect the range of his multifarious activities as a worker at the "writer's trade." They also show his persistent concern over the effects of McCarthyism on the literary and political climate. The denial of passports to American writers was disturbing, as was the "creeping and galloping illiteracy" among readers of a younger generation.

From the midfifties on, Cowley was firmly a part of the literary establishment. In 1956 he was elected president of the National Institute of Arts and Letters. Many letters now came to reflect his preoccupation with Institute and Academy affairs, as he was called on to preside over annual ceremonies, dinners, committee meetings, elections, nominations, and awards. In his official capacity he sought financial relief for younger writers, Kerouac among them, and pleaded for ways to sustain older artists. When Yvor Winters relinquished his membership in the National Institute and Karl Shapiro refused election, Cowley defended the Institute's importance in maintaining standards of artistic merit against commercial encroachment. He argued for Pound's release from St. Elizabeths psychiatric hospital in Washington, D.C., where Pound was incarcerated for more than twelve years, and invited Faulkner to present the 1957 Gold Medal in Fiction to John Dos Passos.

Those who violated respect for language could count on Cowley's sharp rebuttal, as for example when he spoke out against the reductionism of psychoanalytical criticism or mocked the latinate jargon of sociologists. In his own writing he pursued the highest standards of craftsmanship, transparency, and persuasiveness. Yet occasionally readers, even sophisticated ones like Yvor Winters, mistook Cowley's limpidity of style for shallowness. At a time when writing, critical and creative, was more and more becoming the domain of academe, Cowley recurrently spoke up in defense of the unaffiliated professional writer.

Funded by a stipend from the Bollingen Foundation, Cowley spent the winter of 1957–1958 at the American Academy in Rome with his wife, where he worked on a translation of Paul Valéry's essays on Leonardo da Vinci, Poe, and Mallarmé. Though progress on the translation was slow, Cowley's output in the late 1950s was impressive: besides assorted essays and reviews, he wrote introductions to editions of Flaubert's *Madame Bovary,* Nathanael West's *Miss Lonelyhearts* (both 1959), Sherwood Anderson's *Winesburg, Ohio,* Ignazio Silone's *Fontamara,* and Tolstoy's *Anna Karenina* (all 1960). The publication of the letters of Thomas Wolfe (1956) triggered new insights in the psychology of this superb "writing man." But Cowley's most spectacular discovery was the miraculous freshness of Whitman's poetry in the first (1855) edition of *Leaves of Grass.* "I feel myself a crusader for an unadulterated early Walt," he wrote to Daniel Aaron on October 29, 1959. A new edition for Viking, prefaced by a critical revaluation that in James Miller's verdict "opened exciting new vistas in Whitman criticism" (October 12, 1959), won the 1960 Walt Whitman Award from the Poetry Society of America.

Cowley was now regularly consulted (and sometimes challenged) by a younger generation of scholars and critics. Ihab H. Hassan, then at work on an influential study of contemporary American fiction, solicited Cowley's advice about which of the "younger" authors merited serious examination. Late 1959 saw Cowley embroiled in an epistolary altercation with Leslie Fiedler over his iconoclastic reinterpretation of American writing, *Love and Death in the American Novel* (1960). In September 1960 Cowley took a firm stand in support of Newton Arvin, who was suspended from Smith College because of suspected homosexuality. That same year, as if to confirm his growing critical stature, Franklin and Marshall College, in Lancaster, Pennsylvania, awarded Cowley an honorary doctorate, the first of several to follow.

———

[NL TL/CC-2]
[TO: NATHAN ASCH]
c/o Newberry Library,
Chicago 10, Ill.,
January 10, 1954

Dear Nathan:

You write such damned good letters. *They* could be published, almost every one of them. [. . .] The query is why aren't your novels and your stories being published. Like you, like Auden, I think that being published is important.

[. . .]

What's wrong with your novels? Usually there's something wrong in the plot or structure—I've written you about that in specific instances and obviously I've made you angry, because you don't answer those letters, or answer them huffily. But there's something else wrong that I've also written you about, that the characters don't think, but only act and feel—and that the reader doesn't get any perspective on the characters, or gets the wrong perspective[. . .]. *You* have ideas [. . .] but your characters don't have them, even when they're the sort of characters (like the refugee girl in London) who in life would have ideas and express them—I too have known some of those girls and they talk about Life and Politics and People and the War and What Are We Doing Here at the least hint of an opportunity. Je ne propose pas, je ne dispose pas, j'expose. But what do you expose? People who don't live complete lives, but only the sentiment part of life; they have no bony structures.

Nevertheless you're good, and I think the real query is not, Why aren't you published? but What can be done to get you published? You'd better apply some hard thought to that topic. Let me have another crack at the

Day at the Dôme Chapter. I talked to Tom Guinzburg about it. He's one of the editors of *Paris Review,* which I think pays a little something for its material, and prints some good stuff. Tom was very eager to see it.[1]

[...]

As ever,
Malcolm

———

[NL TL/CC-I]
[TO: MARSHALL A. BEST]
Newberry Library,
Chicago 10, Ill.,
January 20, 1954

Dear Marshall:

[...]

The Newberry Library is a good place to work and I've been working hard, but writing a book is, oh, a slow job. Last week I did a section on the sale of hard and soft-cover books in the Near North Side—which doesn't sound like a great subject, but I was saying something about publishing and thought I should start with essentials. I hung around drugstores and watched people inspecting, sometimes buying, paperbacks. I had a long talk with Stuart Brent, a very forth-putting bookseller with likes and animosities. He didn't like *Augie March* too well, which was unlucky for Viking, because Brent is able to sell a thousand copies of a Chicago novel that he admires. [...] He told me confidentially that Nelson Algren's new novel has been refused by Ken McCormick—about two months ago—because McCormick thought it was too radical for these times. Ordinarily I would ask to see it immediately, but McCormick has taken more risks than most publishers and must have his reasons in this case. It would be better not to spread the story because Algren's prospects might be injured.

Last night we were about to entertain company and Muriel went to one of the hundred liquor stores in the neighborhood. She said to the proprietor, "I wish you'd tell me about these brands of Scotch, because I live in Connecticut and they carry different brands there." A man with a black shaggy dog on a leash was standing beside her and said to nobody in particular, "Just think, she lives in Connecticut and she comes to a dump like this." Muriel doesn't like Chicago and the remark delighted her. I like it when I'm feeling strong enough, but it's a town that you have to be strong to take. Nevertheless—a good place to work.

As ever,
Malcolm

———————

[NL TL/CC-2]
[TO: MORTON DAUWEN ZABEL, *POETRY*]
[Chicago] Sunday, February 21 [1954]

Dear Morton:

Before casting even a first ballot for three poets,[2] I decided to set down some thoughts about a few of them.

At present the most neglected of our major poets is Conrad Aiken. Last year his *Collected Poems* appeared in a big volume costing $10.50, which won't have any public sale. The volume was given the National Book Award for poetry, but the award doesn't carry any cash with it. He didn't get the Bollingen Award and his failure to get it was like a slap in the face. If he would be sure that he wasn't going to get the Pulitzer Prize this year, he should get this one. Is there any way to cast a provisional first vote for him?

After Aiken the poet who gives me most pleasure to read is Roethke. He is vigorous, inventive, has a fresh sense of language, and something to say. His greenhouse poems are marvelous, and so is the next group of poems about his childhood (although he wrote too many of these). In the past two years he has been writing Yeatsian poems, firm and polished, some of his best. I wouldn't vote for him if I were selecting the best character among the poets, considering his incurable exhibitionism. Also against him is the fact that he has received a great many of the minor awards (National Institute, Guggenheim, Ford Foundation),—not that these are minor financially.

John Berryman is continually productive and his long poem to Anne Bradstreet is far and away the most important thing he has done—it is major work. He hasn't received many honors.

Léonie Adams wrote two fine books of poems in the 1920s. I've been trying to get hold of her new book, but it hasn't yet been distributed for review, nor have I seen any of the new poems in magazines. What sets her down somewhat in my list is that I hate to vote for what I haven't seen.

I have considerable admiration for Yvor Winters, a masculine poet and a superb craftsman. The objection here is that he has written (or at least has published) only half a dozen poems since 1941.

Much admiration for Richard Eberhart, some for Richard Wilbur, much for Allen Tate (but he has been pretty widely honored). The others on your list I would strike out, either because they have had many prizes already (Jeffers, Auden, Ransom, Williams) or because they don't measure up in quality to those mentioned already. At present I'm inclined to cast my ballot in this order:

1. (Provisional on his not getting the Pulitzer) Aiken
2. John Berryman
3. Theodore Roethke
4. Léonie Adams
5. Yvor Winters

MC

[NL TL/CC-I]
[TO: CONRAD AIKEN]
Sherman, Conn.,
March 19, 1954

Dear Conrad:

Dated from Sherman but written in Chicago, on the eve of our departure, after two months and ten days. A moderately fruitful time. I wrote thirty thousand words, no less, of deathless (for six months) prose, including two sentences that I liked, and a few pages that weren't bad and gave me some pleasure. [. . .] As for Chicago—

It's easy to understand why Chicago is the fatherland and mother city of American naturalism. Naturalistic novels are full of types and so is Chicago. Everyone here is a type; everyone carries a sandwichboard with the words inscribed on it: I am a millionaire, I am a hoodlum, I am a fairy, I am down and out, I am cultured. Everyone is more so than in any other city:

the millionaires are richer, the hoodlums are tougher, the bums are hopeless, the fairies more homosexual, the people of breeding have the guts bred out of them. Here on North State Street where we live, everything comes together: on the one side the Gold Coast, and isn't it golden, on the other side the Clark Street honkytonks, and beyond them a Puerto Rican district, a Japanese district, a Mexican district, a Polish district, and some Negro slums that you've never seen anything more degraded.

We've been to several *Poetry* soirees.[3] Karl Shapiro has been away and the magazine has be[en] run by a replacement part named [Nicholas] Joost—yoost a fathead. The active spirit on the board of advisers or trustees is Ellen Stevenson, Adlai's ex-wife, and how she hates her ex-husband. She'll ruin herself with hatred, which will be a pity, for she's essentially a warm, sympathetic, and foolish, but not stupid woman. The poets here now are Elder Olsen, Reuel Denney, Henry Rago, all nice persons; I haven't read much of their work except some poems by Denney that weren't bad. The only novelist, practically speaking, is Nelson Algren, who isn't as bright as some novelists, but has a sort of warm solidity of character—he is what he is. All the other novelists move away and become flossy, in Mexico or Paris. The Newberry Library is full of first editions, incunabula, Shakespeare folios, Sherwood Anderson correspondence, and God knows what all. It's a shame that I hadn't time to look into its resources. I served on a jury to award the Harriet Monroe prize of five hundred smackers, which isn't going to anybody that I voted for—but I can't talk about that until the prize has been awarded.[4]

[. . .]

> Our very best love,
> Malcolm

―――――――――

> [NL TL/CC-2]
> [TO: CONRAD AIKEN]
> *July 31, 1954*[5]

Dear Conrad:

The book is out of the way—nothing to do on it now except read page proofs—and I can begin to try to be human again, so far as the weather permits. I wasn't human while I was reading galley proofs and writing the last chapter, and didn't even thank you for sending those issues of *Imago*.[6] They were just what I needed to introduce an article for *Harper's*,[7] which had promised to print that chapter [...] if I would take some of the heat off Dr. Bergler and apply the red-hot poker to other Bottoms. *Imago* gave me another Bottom the Weaver, alias Dr. Arthur Wormhoudt, of St. Cloud, Minnesota, Teachers' College, who did that wonderful analysis of Keats's "Urn" as a speaking breast. He's a disciple of Bergler's, which made it all the better.

Writing, Dr. Wormhoudt argues, is a form of oral regression, because writers use words, which are spoken with the mouth, QED. If we communicated with farts, writing would be on the anal level. Swedenborg reported from the spirit world that inhabitants of the Moon talked through their navels, which would put non-writers on the umbilical level of sexual regression. Drs. Bergler and Wormhoudt talk through their hats, or perpetasumate, if I may add a word to the vocabulary of science, on the longocapillary level.

[...]

I wonder what you'll think about Faulkner's new book,[8] on which he's been working for nine years. I wish he'd spent the years on another project than imagining that Christ was reincarnated in a corporal of the French Army in 1918, with a squad of twelve disciples. I liked his work better when it wasn't so holy, or willed, or fabricated, before he became a pillar. We just received an invitation to his daughter's wedding, which will obviously be the social even[t] of the decade in Oxford, Miss. Muriel sends her best love to both of you, with hopes that you're not sweltering like us.

As ever,
Malcolm

―――――

[NL TL/CC-2]
[TO: KENNETH BURKE]
August 28, 1954

Dear Kenneth:

[...]

Yesterday I heard that Josie Herbst[9] had been denied a passport. She asked that the news be regarded as confidential, so don't pass it along. A rich friend is paying a lawyer to fight the case. Her chief difficulty, she says, is being married to John Hermann, who was a Communist, though she was divorced fourteen years ago. Nelson Algren was denied a passport. Besides having belonged to left-wing organizations he had presided over a meeting held to protest the execution of the Rosenbergs. Arthur Miller was denied a passport, as you read in the papers—most of the denials are kept secret by the victims, who don't want to lose jobs or commissions. A lot of writers are being treated as second-class citizens, when most of them would so like to be respectable. "No," says the government, "we want to be sure that you're rebels."

[. . .]

As ever,
Malcolm

[NL TL/CC-2]
[TO: REUEL DENNEY][10]
August 30, 1954

Dear Reuel:

I'll set down some general remarks which might or might not carry the discussion further. It's an interesting and fruitful discussion. It might become even more fruitful if, besides following the sociological approach, you also considered the subject in terms of anthropology, mythology, and comparative religion. There's a lot of myth and religion in Hemingway.

He was an ambulance driver in World War I. See my chapter on the ambulance service in *Exile's Return,* where I make the point that the *ambulanciers* weren't participants in the war, but spectators. Their role had a moral value only when they risked their lives in it—so they ran unnecessary risks; Hemingway was badly wounded and gave himself up for dead. He was frightened, shell-shocked, and began to brood about the meaning of courage.

Spectators watch a spectacle, which, if it is serious enough, becomes a ritual, in other words, a dramatized myth or mystery, like that of Eleusis. The true spectator of a mystery is an initiate. As writer he is a *hierophant,* i.e., "an official expounder of rites of worship and sacrifice." Initiates and hierophants are of course more than mere spectators, since they have a necessary function in the sacred drama. Hemingway, the hierophant, is teaching spectators to become communicants.

Hemingway took up bullfighting as an emotional substitute for war—see the first chapter of *Death in the Afternoon,* which is an absolutely necessary key to the discussion. He tried to be a bullfighter himself and was very bad at it, because scared. Then he began brooding about the qualities that make a great sportsman or player. Courage, grace under pressure, skill, honesty, purity—there should be "nothing faked," i.e., nothing done merely to impress an audience. One should learn and follow the rules of one's metier. Writing too is a dangerous sport like bullfighting.

Many young men begin with an essential purity, in sport, but then they learn the tricks of the trade; they become "corrupt with age"—I forget where H. first used that phrase. One of his moral problems has been to find old men who were still pure in heart (like Anselmo, in *For Whom the Bell Tolls* and the hero of *The Old Man and the Sea*).

To drop Hemingway and go back to the social situation: in 1929 the Harvard-Yale and Yale-Princeton games were the great mass demonstrations of the bourgeoisie (wealth, motorcars, liquor in silver flasks, fur coats, beautiful women, all on display) and corresponded to the Communist May Day parades. Now, as I think Riesman pointed out, politics has become a spectator sport, exactly like baseball—people tuned out the Dodgers to watch the Army-McCarthy hearings. That contributes to the general point that Americans are condemned to be mere spectators of the great events, and that hence it is important to create a moral code of spectatorship.

Hemingway has helped to create that code (I didn't mention drinking as another sport and ritual and *ordeal of initiation*), but that hasn't been his primary interest. He always wants to be the player, the actor, the professional; he wants to excel in every sport that attracts him; and if he can't excel in it (as he couldn't in bullfighting) he wants to be the hierophant, the expounding priest. But now he too is becoming corrupt with age.

A damned interesting field you're opening up. [. . .]

As ever,
Malcolm

[NL TL/CC-I]
[TO: VICTOR WEYBRIGHT, NEW AMERICAN LIBRARY]
October 14, 1954

Dear Victor:

Seriously.

I wasn't trying to attack the paperback-book business.[11] Far from that, I think it is hopeful and wonderful. All I wanted to do was present it in the general context of American culture.

It has multiplied the potential audience for books by ten. But the potential audience for hard-cover books is only about a million persons. The potential audience for paperbacks is about ten million—but that is only one out of ten in the adult population. The other nine-tenths of the adults don't read books and, generally speaking, haven't enough education to make them able to read books.

Our real enemy—I mean the enemy of hard-cover publishers, soft-cover publishers, magazine publishers, and the writing profession—is the creeping and galloping illiteracy that is taking over this country. I think we'll all have to stand together to fight illiteracy, or we'll all be left without a livelihood. I mean that critics, authors, editors, publishers of books, and even Curtis, Luce, Crowell-Collier, yes, even Hearst and Roy Howard, must form an alliance in support of the reading habit.

I have one grief against the soft-cover publishers that I didn't mention in my chapters. It is that they have done very little to support the book industry as a whole—specifically by advertising their wares in book sections or in radio and television book programs. The book programs are disappearing, going off the air for want of support. The book sections are getting smaller for want of advertising. The whole literary industry is less important in the general economy than it was as recently as 1950.

[. . .]

Cordially,
Malcolm Cowley

[NL TL/CC-1]
[TO: GILBERT HARRISON, *THE NEW REPUBLIC*]
October 14, 1954

Dear Gilbert:

At first I couldn't think of anything to write for the anniversary issue.[12] [. . .] Then I wondered whether you'd be interested in a rather doleful piece, saying that American literature, after a brilliant period, is now more directly threatened than at any time since the Civil War. As I see it the threat takes four shapes or directions:

1.   The general atmosphere of anti-intellectualism, in Washington and throughout the country.
2.   The loss of an audience for light hard-cover fiction, which was the economic foundation of the publishing industry. (Because there aren't any more "Captains from Castille" or "Black Roses," a lot of promising first novels don't get published—the publishers can't afford to bring them out.)
3.   The tying up of literature with the universities—a phenomenon which, in the long run, makes it less interesting.
4.   The biggest threat is the decline of the reading habit, owing partly to TV but chiefly to the collapse of secondary education—high school students aren't learning how to read; they graduate without having read one complete book.

That would make a pretty interesting article, I think.[13] [. . .]

As ever,
Malcolm

[NL TL/CC-1]
[TO: JAMES STERN][14]
October 15, 1954

Dear Jimmy:

[. . .] In New York—except for lunch with William Faulkner and Bob Linscott[15]—I mostly autographed or consulted with the Viking publicity agent about *The Literary Situation*. It's going to receive a great deal of attention but the sales won't be brilliant, I fear—this is a rather disastrous autumn in the book business. [. . .] Here a favorite topic of conversation, as always, is passport troubles and the loyalty purge. I know a very learned critic, name omitted by request, who goes to France every summer. He is non-political, always has been, and is a Catholic convert. This summer his passport was very slow in coming through, though it finally did. Later he talked to a friend in the State Dept. Said the friend, dropping a word of advice, "You shouldn't write so much about Charlie Chaplin." . . . Horace Gregory has a son-in-law in the Navy. Last year he was suspended from duty for nine months because Horace had done some mild fellow-traveling in the 1930s. Anticommunism is the fashionable substitute for anti-semitism. The abhorred taint is considered to be inheritable, from father to daughter, from daughter to husband, and soon the question will be, "Are you completely loyal, or did you have one disloyal grandparent?"

[. . .] Incidentally the decline of McCarthy isn't the sort of good news it might have been, because McCarthyism has been adopted by the Department of Justice. [. . .]

As ever—

Malcolm

[VWB TLS-1] [NL TL/CC-1]
[TO: VAN WYCK BROOKS]
October 17, 1954

Dear Van Wyck:

Felicia[16] said in her letter that the Howells Medal for Fiction "is given every fifth year in recognition of the most distinguished work of American fiction published during that period. In other words, it is for a particular novel." That makes our problem difficult, unless we are privileged to change the terms of the grant. I admire Thornton Wilder and would ordinarily vote for him (though he received the Gold Medal, for fiction, in 1952). But his last novel, *The Ides of March,* was published in 1948. I'd also vote for James Gould Cozzens, but his last novel, *Guard of Honor,* was also published in 1948. What was the single great novel of the last five years? Answer, there wasn't any. Hemingway's *Old Man and the Sea* had a sort of greatness but wasn't a novel (and he had a special award last year). *The Adventures of Augie March* had a sort of greatness, or largeness. Thinking of authors who have published in those years we have Marquand, Steinbeck (no), Robert Penn Warren, Eudora Welty—who else? It's a really tough question. Farrell, no, O'Hara, no, Caroline Gordon, no for opposite reasons, Katherine Anne Porter, no because she hasn't published a novel, Carson McCullers, p-possible, Christopher Isherwood, no, Ham Basso, no—I go over the list with such little enthusiasm that I'm almost inclined to say, "Let's wait a year—or else break the rules and give it to Wilder or Cozzens."[17]

[. . .]

As ever,
Malcolm

────────

[HB TLS-I] [NL TL/CC-I]
[TO: HAMILTON BASSO]
October 21, 1954

Dear Ham:

Wednesday night after dinner I sat down with TVFPH [*The View from Pompey's Head*], intending to read it in two easy installments, but I couldn't put it down. Confession: I skipped the first hundred pages, because I remembered them clearly, but I read the rest of it that night, missing not a word, and not yielding to my old habit of looking at the last page first to see how the story would come out. The story line, the creation of expectancy, the little surprises, all hold one's attention; the book flows. [. . .]

The most important thing about TVFPH is that it carries your work to a new level of feeling and knowledge. It's as if you'd been climbing through woods and had reached a high meadow from which the view extended for many miles. I note with pleasure that all the reviewers have had this same feeling about the book—what nice things they've been saying about it: Obviously it's going to be the Big Book of this year, and I'll be surprised if the bookstore sale stops short of fifty thousand, even in this dark year for the book trade. Also the Literary Guild sales will go far beyond their initial guarantee. There will be a reprint sale, translations, a good press in England, perhaps a movie—so that your chief financial worry for the next two years will be the income tax. Time and leisure to write other books—you've never had time before. All this makes me happy for you.[18]

[...]

As ever,
Malcolm

———

[NL TL/CC-I]
[TO: CONRAD AIKEN]
November 2, 1954

Dear Conrad:

Election day. It's raining, a slow, cold, windless rain mixed with pellets of snow. Muriel is poll-watching at the town hall; she started at six and will be through a little after seven this evening; then she has a meeting of the school board. I'm alone in the house and feeling depressed, about the world (waste of feelings) and about the book [*The Literary Situation*]. I wrote it partly in an effort to break through the circle of loneliness and incomprehension that seems to surround writers in this country. I was addressing the average intelligent reader and trying to tell him how things operate in the literary world, putting in nearly everything, the topical (too much of that) and the permanent. By now it's evident that the book isn't going to break through the circle and that all I've done is to make enemies of the New Pundits without gaining a wider audience. I'd prophesy that the sales will be four or five thousand copies. Plus five thousand copies sold to the Book Find Club, which copies will be read but will yield only six cents apiece to the author. No miracles. Back to the treadmill.

Anyhow I had fun writing the "Natural History," and I'm glad it entertained you.

As ever,
Malcolm

———

[NL TL/CC-I]
[TO: WILLIAM CARLOS WILLIAMS]
November 22, 1954

Dear Bill:

That's a mighty nice send-off you gave to *The Literary Situation* and its enfeebled author. Thanks for listening.

Muriel and I are just back from a trip to Washington. The news from there, in govt circles, is that they've run out of communists and ex-near-communists to investigate. But the investigative outfits have to be kept busy and now they've turned their attention to sex, which is a broad and inexhaustible field. "You say you're not homosexual," they said to a Navy man, who wasn't. "*Give us the names* of twelve women you've slept with."

We're glad to be back in Sherman.

As ever,
Malcolm

———

[NL TL/CC-I]
[TO: ALLEN TATE]
December 22, 1954

Dear Allen:

George Ollendorf is younger than our lamented patron, Walter S. Hankel.[19] In fact George is the illegitimate son of Walter S. Hankel, and of Hemingway's Old Lady. The Old Lady's name was Maria Ollendorf. When found to be pregnant, she was expelled from a Mennonite seminary, and her wealthy parents sent her to travel in Europe, leaving the child behind. George grew up in the little town of Lititz, Pennsylvania, home of the genuine pretzel, or bretzel, as Lititzers prefer to call it. An early poem of his on bending pretzels, or pending bretzels—a surprising poem on three levels called "Bretzelstilskin, Let Down Your Hair"—attracted the attention of a wealthy patron, who sent him to Harvard. That's all, except that George, in middle life, acquired the habit of appropriating other persons' experiences. It was Van Wyck Brooks, not George, who recovered from a nervous breakdown when his wife received a pretty big legacy: hence, *The Flowering of New England.*

[...]

Yes, I was a little unfair in the little job on the *TLS* American number that I did for the *Saturday Review*.[20] As a matter of fact the specific article on Southern literature that I reacted against wasn't written by a Southerner, but by Fred Hoffman of Wisconsin, who has the gift of following a party line in whatever he writes about; he'd be a great success in the Russian Writers' Union. Southern literature has been amazingly rich in the last thirty years. Part of it has been written by fairies, Negroes, radicals, poor whites, an amazing assortment of people—they didn't do the best part, but they contributed their mites, and the general picture would be poorer without them.

[...]

Last night I spoke at an Institute dinner on "The Function of an Academy"—I was trying to make a realistic survey of what the Institute could do. Among other things I said that it should do a great deal more for the relief of aged and indigent artists, including its own members. I also said that the grants should be twice as large, and suggested that it wouldn't be unduly difficult to find more income for these purposes. The talk will be printed in the Proceedings. [...] I didn't get round to mentioning what in our society might be the principal function of the Institute. That is to provide some sort of center and focus for persons devoted to literature and the fine arts, some center relatively independent of government and mass opinion. Our society always tends to become totalitarian; the problem of freedom is to create and maintain other institutions that will make it more pluralistic— because freedom seems to exist chiefly in corners and interstices. There are no such corners in a society ruled by mass opinion.

Let me know when you and Caroline are coming East so we can get together. It's been a long time.

As ever,
Malcolm

{ ———— }

Jack Kerouac, 1953–1957

Between July 1953 (when he was first approached by Allen Ginsberg) and the fall of 1957 (when he traveled to Europe) Cowley made a concerted effort to expedite book publication for Jack Kerouac. Having persuaded Arabel Porter of *New World Writing* to publish an excerpt from *On the Road,* he referred to "John" Kerouac in his "Invitation to Innovators" in *The Saturday Review of Literature* as well as in *The Literary Situation,* and managed to interest *The Paris Review* in publishing another excerpt. He also appealed to the National Institute of Arts and Letters to relieve Kerouac's financial straits. But most effectively, after *On the Road* had been rejected by several publishers (including Viking), he renewed his endeavors to interest his fellow editors at Viking and this time, working in collusion with Keith Jennison, was successful: on April 8, 1954 he wrote an eloquent acceptance report to Viking Press that proved a prescient critical appraisal.

———————

I would like a chance to talk to you, if you are as interested in seeing Jack Kerouac published as I am.

Allen Ginsberg to Malcolm Cowley, July 3, 1953 [NL]

[AG TLS-1] [NL TL/CC-1]
[TO: ALLEN GINSBERG][21]
[New York, Viking Press]
July 14, 1953

Dear Mr. Ginsberg:
    You are right in thinking that I am interested in Kerouac and his work. He seems to me the most interesting writer who is not being published today—and I think it is important that he should be published, or he will run the danger of losing that sense of the audience, which is part of a writer's equipment. But the only manuscript of his that I have read with a chance of immediate book publication is the first version of ON THE ROAD. As

much of the second version as I saw contained some impressively good writing, but no story whatsoever. SAX [*Doctor Sax*] might be published by New Directions or Grove Press, but I am afraid that neither of them would be taken by any of the larger publishing houses.

I am generally free on Tuesday afternoons. Why not phone me on Tuesday morning before eleven at Viking? I will be very glad to see you.

Sincerely yours,
Malcolm Cowley

[NWW TLS-1] [NL TL/CC-1]
[TO: ARABEL J. PORTER, NEW AMERICAN LIBRARY]
November 14, 1953

Dear Miss Porter:

Thanks for the prompt check,[22] which will help me to make the local banker smile at me. Fact is, he always does smile, but often without good reason.

Today I was thinking about a manuscript recently rejected by Viking, to my sorrow. There are some passages in it that might be interesting to print in *New World Writing*. It's a very long autobiographical novel by John Kerouac, called *On The Road* (or alternatively, *Heroes of the Hip Generation*). It's about the present generation of wild boys on their wild travels between New York, San Francisco, and Mexico City—hitchhiking, bus riding, buying cars and wrecking them, stealing, smoking reefers, being cool and underground, sleeping with an assortment of cute tricks, singly or in batches, and wanting to write like James Joyce, but actually writing (Kerouac at least) more like Tobias Smollett. Of all that beat generation crowd, Kerouac is the only one who *can* write, and about the only one who doesn't get published.

I was thinking that there are two or three passages in the novel or narrative that would read very well by themselves. One is about the hero's affair, in California, with a Mexican chick named Terry. It's terrific as a transcript from life—maybe a little too dirty in spots, but could be censored. Another is an account of a San Francisco night in jive joints, not so dirty. A third, very wild and dirty, is an afternoon in a Mexican whorehouse.

[...]

I trust in your good judgment to dream up a biographical note for me. The notes I like best are full of inventions and inaccuracies and make the author feel that he has lived a triple or quadruple life.

Cordially,
Malcolm Cowley

[AA TLS-2]
[TO: FELICIA GEFFEN]
July 12, 1955

Dear Felicia:

I wonder if there is any chance of getting some money from the Artists' and Writers' Revolving Fund for my friend John Kerouac. He is a young novelist of really unusual talent. His weakness is that he hasn't much control over the talent. His work is uneven and much of it isn't publishable, but when he writes well, he writes, I almost said magnificently. His only published book is a long novel, *The Town and the City,* brought out some years ago by Harcourt Brace; it was well reviewed and had a good sale, but Harcourt rejected his next manuscript—mistakenly, I believe, for it's the best record I have read of what he calls "the beat generation." Lately a long section of that second book was printed in *New World Writing* (under the pseudonym of "Jean Louis"), and another section of it has just been taken by *Paris Review,* which, unfortunately, pays little and late.

At present Kerouac seems to be in desperate straits. He wrote me last week:

"Here is 'Ghost of the Susquehanna' and I hope the editor of *Paris Review* likes it and buys it because I need money, my two weeks in NY grew me a bloodclot biggern a baseball on my left ankle and I have to take expensive penicillin. . . . When you said, 'Jack, why don't you take a job for a while?' in the heat of our pleasurable drinks and dinners I forgot to tell you that there are mornings like this morning when I can't walk at all, and I couldn't hold down a steady job. That was why the court pronounced me Disabled. . . .

"It's been too long. I'm about ready not only to stop writing but jump off a bridge. The canoe is in the middle of the rapids and I don't even want to row."

I think that $300 would see him through his present crisis, from what I know of his story. I think there's a good chance that one of his book manuscripts will be accepted within the next three or four months, and then he would be entitled to an advance. Three years ago Kerouac came near being awarded a grant in literature—he ranked high on our list, but not quite high enough.

His case seems to me one of the emergencies that the Revolving Fund was specially intended to meet.

As ever,
Malcolm
[...]

───────────

[JK TLS-1] [NL TL/CC-1]
[TO: JACK KEROUAC]
[New York, Viking Press]
July 12, 1955

Dear Jack:

Paris Review is going to take "The Mexican Girl." Peter Matthiessen, the fiction editor, is enthusiastic about it. He is also bothered by the style in places, by adverbs like "frantically" and expressions like "her eyes were deep blue soul-windows." He wondered if you wouldn't want to revise and chasten the style. I told him not to bother you, that you would spare him a few adverbs, but that he shouldn't strike too many. The great trouble is that it pays little ($50 I'd prophesy) and on publication, not on acceptance. Still, it will be a good thing to get your name back in the public eye, and in a magazine that it's good to appear in. And you want to use your own name this time, don't you? There's no use signing Jean Louis if the court has absolved you from paying alimony—especially when John Kerouac is a better sounding name with one good book to its credit.

"On the Road" is still being considered by Dodd, Mead. If it comes back from them, Keith and I will take another crack at getting it accepted by Viking. I was thinking that Viking might consider it more favorably if I would write a brief foreword—what would you think of that?

I wrote to the National Institute and asked if they could make you an advance from the Writers' and Artists' Revolving Fund. [...] Let's keep our fingers crossed.

I'll try to do something with "The Ghost of [the] Susquehanna." Meanwhile don't get downhearted. Better times are coming. Meanwhile keep on writing, and try to have more control. You have a very fast curve, hard to hit, but it doesn't always go over the plate.

As ever,
Malcolm Cowley

———————

[JK TLS-1] [NL TL/CC-1] [PARTLY *PMC* 502–503]
[TO: JACK KEROUAC]
September 16, 1955

Dear Jack,

"On the Road"—I think that's the right title for the book, not "The Beat Generation"—is now being very seriously considered, or reconsidered, by Viking, and there is quite a good chance that we will publish it, depending on three *ifs*: *if* we can figure out what the right changes will be (cuts and rearrangements); *if* we can be sure that the book won't be suppressed for immorality; and *if* it won't get us into libel suits. The libel question is important, because I take it that you're dealing with actual persons. Most of them won't mind what you said about them—Dean Moriarty, for example—and Bill Burroughs for another example—but you run a risk when writing about anyone with a position of respectability to maintain, like the character you call Denver D. Doll; I wish you'd tell me more about him, so that I'd know whether the portrait had to be changed.

Are you sure you haven't used any actual names?

I've promised to do a short introduction if the book is published.

It's good news that you're writing again, and writing a lot on big projects. Also I think that the proper system for you is to write all in a breath, pouring out what you feel. But there are those two sides of writing, the unconscious and the conscious, the creation and the self-criticism, the expression and the communication, the speed and the control. What your system ought to be is to get the whole thing written down fast, in a burst of creative effort, then later go back, put yourself in the reader's place, ask whether and how the first expression ought to be changed to make it more effective. If you'd do that job of revision too, then most of your things would be published, instead of kicking around publishers' offices for years. And being published is what you need right now.

Give my regards to Allen Ginsberg and tell him I'm hoping to write him next week. And I'll write you again about "On the Road" when I've had time to go through the manuscript carefully, carefully.

As ever,
Malcolm Cowley

———

[JK TLS-I] [NL TL/CC-I]
[TO: JACK KEROUAC]
2120 Santa Cruz Ave.,
Menlo Park, Calif.———
(but that's only tonight's address.
Tomorrow's address is the old one.)
March 21, 1956

Dear Jack:

Some sort of malign fate is keeping us from getting together. First you'd left SF before I arrived, though I heard about you everywhere. Now your happy letter comes too late, on the very day we're packing to leave.[23] If you'd only known about your trip a little sooner! Then I could have waited a couple of days for your arrival—but now we have dates with people in Santa Fe and Lawrence, Kansas, and New York City, and I'll have to step on the gas to meet our schedule. And the worst of it is, you'll reach Palo Alto during their spring vacation, when there won't even be anyone around the university to tell you we've gone.

I think you have absolutely the right angle now for changing the characters in "On the Road"—those that have to be changed. My great worry is the Denver section, because some of the people mentioned there are the sort who get bothered if they're talked about and bring suits. Making Mr. Beattie G. Davies a bowling-alley tycoon would be marvelous, and funny too. I'll get a new look at the ms as soon as I'm back in NY—suggest the desirable cuts, mention the characters who need further disguise, then you can get to work on them in the High Sierras, which sound like a marvelous place to work.

Alan [*sic*] Ginsberg kept riding me about the book and all your other books when he saw [me] at a party at K. Rexroth's. Alan was loaded and kept scoring me off and I foolishly got mad and said more than I meant to say. But I do think, seriously, that he's very wrong when he keeps encouraging you to do nothing but automatic writing. Automatic writing is fine for a start, but it has to be revised and put into shape or people will quite properly refuse to read it—and what you need now is to be read, not to be exhibited as a sort of natural phenomenon like Old Faithful geyser that sends up a jet of steam and mud every hour on the hour. You've got the speed, but you also need the control.

I heard that Alan's poetry evening in Berkeley was a wild success. Wish I'd been able to go. Stanford kept me so busy for three months that there was no time to do anything at all except prepare lectures and read student manuscripts, some of which were not bad, not bad at all. And now in eight hours we're taking to the road again, in a beat-up Studebaker. I'll have time for "On the Road" as soon as I get back.

As ever,
Malcolm

[NL VIKING MEMO TL/CC-2]
DATE: 4-8-57
SPONSOR: MaC/KWJ[24]
Please Push Along for Wednesday's Meeting

MANUSCRIPT ACCEPTANCE REPORT

AUTHOR: Jack Kerouac   TITLE: ON THE ROAD
[...]

This is a narrative of life among the wild bohemians of what Kerouac was the first to call "the beat generation." It carries us from New York to Denver, from Denver to San Francisco, then back to New York (with a detour through the Mexican settlements of the Central Valley)—then New York, New Orleans, San Francisco, Denver again, Chicago in seventeen hours in a borrowed Cadillac, Detroit, New York, Denver once more, and a Mexican town—the characters are always on wheels. They buy cars and wreck them, steal cars and leave them standing in fields, undertake to drive cars from one city to another, sharing the gas; then for variety they go hitch-hiking or sometimes ride a bus. In cities they go on wild parties or sit in joints listening to hot trumpets. They seem a little like machines themselves, machines gone haywire, always wound to the last pitch, always nervously moving, drinking, making love, with hardly any emotions except a determination to say Yes to any new experience. The writing at its best is deeply felt, poetic, and extremely moving. Again at its best this book is a celebration of the American scene in the manner of a latter-day Wolfe or Sandburg. The story itself has a steady, fast, unflagging movement that carries the reader along with it, always into new towns and madder adventures, and with only one tender interlude, that of the Mexican girl. It is real, honest, fascinating, everything for kicks, the voice of a new age.

It has an interesting history. It was written in 1950 (incidentally on a continuous roll of Japanese drawing paper) and was, with some regret, rejected at the time by Harcourt, Brace, who had published Kerouac's first naturalistic novel (*The Town and the City*) with moderate success. It first came into our hands about two years ago—or was it three?—and was rejected at the time, but with the proviso that we'd like to see it again. When we did see it again, we decided to work on it to remove the two great problems of libel and obscenity. But while we held on to it, prevented from working on it by other projects that might take less time, Kerouac began amassing quite a reputation. The episode of the Mexican girl was printed in *Paris Review,* a jazz passage was used to lead off one issue of *New World Writing,* and a Mexican cathouse episode was accepted by New Directions, so that more of a groundwork seemed to be laid for publication of the book. Moreover, Kerouac changed the story to avoid most of the libel danger (as well as getting signed releases from four characters), and Helen Taylor[25] went over it taking out the rest of the libel, some of the obscenity, and tightening the story.

The book, I prophesy, will get mixed but *interested* reviews, it will have a good sale (perhaps a very good one), and I don't think there is any doubt that it will be reprinted as a paperback. Moreover it will stand for a long time as the honest record of another way of life.

[JK TLS-1]
[TO: JACK KEROUAC]
[New York, Viking Press]
July 16, 1957

Dear Jack:

The Viking edition of *On the Road* is very handsome—don't you think?—and very chaste; I don't know whether it looks more like a devotional work or a handbook of applied sociology. But that's just the appearance it ought to have if it is to receive the sort of serious attention it deserves and we want to get for it. Now we are waiting for the reviews. My hunch is that many of them will be unfavorable, but if it receives a few fair and sympathetic reviews that will be all it needs to get started. I know it will be read for many years to come.

And now there is the old question of what we should work on next.[26] I'm still of the opinion that DOCTOR SAX is the best of the present manuscripts and the one that would be easiest to put into shape for publication. I also feel, as I told you before, that it would be improved by being lengthened, and especially if you wrote into it some more scenes of your boyhood. Why don't you think about them now and write the scenes as soon as you have them clearly in mind—then send the manuscript here to Viking? I'd like to have it by October 1 if that isn't hurrying you too much, because I am hoping to go abroad toward the end of that month.[27]

Viking finally decided that the book didn't need an introduction by me or anyone else, and I was so busy out at Michigan all spring that I didn't get a chance to write the article. But I'll go to work on it soon.

That's a fine quotation from Mark 13.11.[28] If the Holy Ghost is speaking through you, fine, fine, let him speak. Sometimes he turns out to be the devil masquerading as the Holy Ghost, and that's all right too. Sometimes he turns out to be Simple Simon, and then you have to cut what he says. A good writer uses his subconscious mind and his conscious mind, one after the other, and uses them both as hard as they can be used.

As ever,
Malcolm Cowley

{ ——— }

[NL TL/CC-I]
[TO: J. ROBERT OPPENHEIMER,[29]
INSTITUTE FOR ADVANCED STUDY, PRINCETON]
January 22, 1955

Dear Mr. Oppenheimer:

It is years since I met you and Mrs. Oppenheimer at Princeton, when Kenneth Burke was at the Institute for Advanced Study and was having a social Saturday evening for his week-end guests, the Cowleys. Nevertheless I'm plucking up my courage to write—as hundreds of others must have written—about your lecture on "Prospects in the Arts and Sciences." Among its other virtues, it is one of the few serious and, let us hope, effective efforts to reestablish a "unity of knowledge" and a community of outlook in the separate arts and separate sciences.

As a writer I feel that its effectiveness lies in the tone and style of the lecture, almost as much as in the ideas you expressed. That is because unity of knowledge depends on the unity of the language in which all forms of knowledge are recorded. During the last fifty years each art or science has been developing its own language, or jargon, which is unreadable except by the author's colleagues. What a joy it is to find an American scientist—there are some in England, but no others here—who writes in English, in the language of Yeats and Churchill and Mark Twain, not in the jargon of the physicists or geneticists or sociologists or New Critics! That is already an effective step towards the unity of knowledge.

There isn't a word in the lecture about your own experiences. But I remember what Valéry said about his own apparently objective and impersonal writings: "Whoever so wishes can read my autobiography, *in the style.*" So I read the style, and your career and personality become apparent.

[. . .] I know that the Viking Press would be greatly interested in publishing any book you might plan to write or might collect from your past writings. It would be able to give such a volume a dignified and effective distribution, that being the good publisher's function—and, having looked over the field, I don't think there is any better publishing house than ours.

Sincerely,
Malcolm Cowley

[NL TL/CC-1]
[TO: LEONARD F. MANHEIM, CITY COLLEGE OF NEW YORK]
February 20, 1955

Dear Mr. Manheim:

The article in *Harper's* which you discuss in your letter ["Psychoanalysts and Writers"] was a condensed and rewritten version of a chapter in my book, *The Literary Situation.* [. . .] [My] position is by no means one of hostility to psychological interpretations of literature. I've done a good deal of psychological criticism, first and last, as note my introduction to *The Complete Walt Whitman* and my article in a 1948 issue of *Sewanee Review,* "Hawthorne in the Mirror." But I was angry—one always says *justifiably* angered—by the idiocies of Dr. Bergler and other more or less orthodox Freudians.

My thesis would run something like this: Literature is an art based on language. Language is a social product; in fact it is the basis or at least the distinguishing feature of human society. It is impossible to explain a work of literature, written in words, by the behavior of infants at a pre-verbal stage of development (that's exactly what Bergler tries to do). A psychologist who has no feeling for words (Bergler has none whatever) is disqualified from discussions of verbal competence. Words being a social product, they have to be socially accepted—or the author has to have the conviction that they will be accepted—before he becomes a functioning man of letters. The unaccepted writer is likely to be a blocked writer (although there are of course other causes of writer's block, the disease that Bergler claims to cure).

Beyond this thesis, or collection of judgments, about literature and language, I also have the feeling that the Freudians are wrong in believing that maladjustments due to the birth trauma or feeding difficulties or weaning difficulties are the sole explanation of neuroses. "The Freudians," here, is a loose term applying to the orthodox school of analysts, and not to Freud himself, who kept escaping from the rigidities of his own system. And I think the Freudians have done a bad job in their treatment of writers—in my own pretty wide circle of acquaintances I have never met what I would call a good writer who was measurably helped by analysis (some Broadway and slick-paper writers have been helped), and I have run into many writers who were definitely harmed.

[...]

Sincerely,
Malcolm Cowley

[NL TL/CC-I] [*PMC* 501–502]
[TO: JOHN CAWELTI][30]
February 20, 1955

Dear Mr. Cawelti:

[...]

I've often wondered what sort of critic I was. Primarily I have been a contemporary historian of letters rather than a critic. When, as often, I wrote essays that were primarily critical, they were likely to be biographical criticisms—in this sense, that I feel strongly that an author changes, that Hawthorne in 1837, for example, was not the same author as Hawthorne in 1860—and that most generalities about an author, when made on the basis of his life work, are meaningless. I am impressed by the effect on authors, not of broad social changes, but of social changes, sometimes much narrower, that directly affect his life—for example, Whitman was apparently not affected greatly by the panic of 1855, but he was greatly affected by losing his job on the Brooklyn *Eagle* in 1848. Writing about an author, I try to understand his life, and I also try hard to understand the actual nature of his achievement (at which point I do a good deal of *explication de texte*, but without carrying the procedure to the extremes of the New Critics). Great is language, but it is great because it is the medium and almost the basis of human society—so that I try never to lose sight of the connection between books and life. I feel that a critic who doesn't prove by his own style that he understands the art of using language is incompetent to discuss language as an art.—And what does all this make me? An eclectic?

Sincerely,
Malcolm Cowley

[NL TL/CC-I]
[TO: RUSSELL ROTH][31]
February 22, 1955

Dear Mr. Roth,

No, I can't take it. I can't take the imperative "Be an American!" any more than I can take the indicative "I am an American." What else are we, what else can we be? Like other generalities that seem to have no content, these imperatives and indicatives acquire a sneaking content—"I am an American" in practice has become a way of saying that Irish Jansenist Puritan Catholicism is the true Americanism and that Jeffersonian Americans are really Communistic traitors. That sounds like an extreme statement, but follow through the McCarthy speeches and the Hearst editorials and the security firing in Washington and you'll see what I mean. "Be an American!" becomes a way of saying, be rough and rural, show your muscles, speak as you think the buffalo skinners used to speak. It leads to show-off work like George Bellows' lithographs (the *good* artists of that school were Glenn Coleman and John Sloan). I find more sense in imperatives like "Be Midwestern" (if you were born and raised in the Midwest), "Be Southern!" or even "Be Suburban!" considering that the new Americans live in the suburbs. Why not simply "Be yourself"?

We are part of the great Atlantic culture, marked off from the great Asiatic culture by its passion for improvement or at any rate change.

Your jazz pieces are over my head. I belong to that ancient group who sang and played (badly) ragtime, back in the days when "jazz" was just a New Orleans–Chicago word for "fuck" ("I jazzed her good"). But there's a jazz expert in the family, namely my son, who used to write a jazz column for the *Exonian,* and I'll send him your interesting (even to me) piece on the origins of jazz to see what he says. [. . .]

Cordially,
Malcolm Cowley

[NL TL/CC-I]
[TO: WALLACE STEGNER]
May 13, 1955

Dear Mr. Stegner:

I look forward with pleasure to the prospect of coming to Stanford.[32] Of the two courses, the advanced course in the writing of fiction sounds like something that would be very interesting to teach. I've been impressed by the job that Archie MacLeish is doing at Harvard with just such a group (including my son), and have been wondering what improvements I could make on his methods. I might give the students more about the language itself (now woefully neglected), and more about using their imaginations. Archie's great trick is to make the students feel that they are a *very* selected group, entitled to meet the great men of literature. That sets them up, and they become very serious about their writing and about tearing to pieces one another's work.

I haven't so clear a picture of the course in the criticism of fiction, because of the mixed nature of the class. I wish you'd tell me more about it. In these days critics of fiction and writers of fiction are getting to be two different breeds; they don't even cross-fertilize any more. (I was thinking of that theory that *The Ambassadors*, *The Wings of the Dove*, and *The Golden Bowl* represent the natural, spiritual, and celestial worlds of Swedenborgianism. I was raised a Swedenborgian and I can't make the identification, and Henry James's notebooks don't, to the best of my memory, show any signs that he made it. But critics have stopped reading author's notebooks. They want to superimpose their own fictions on the fictions of the author.) [. . .]

I'm writing in haste to catch the afternoon mail. It will be a great pleasure to meet you in Palo Alto, if everything works out, as I have no doubt it will.—Just this morning I accepted a job at Yale this summer, giving fifteen lectures on American literature to a group of professors from French lycées; that sounds interesting.

Cordially yours,
Malcolm Cowley

I'm coming more and more to think that Whitman was our greatest poet. But he was our greatest poet in a book that is practically unknown to the public—I mean the first edition of *Leaves of Grass,* published exactly a hundred years ago, and at the moment unobtainable, even in facsimile. [...] It was the first edition that was the miracle.

Cowley to Robert Evett, *The New Republic,* June 6, 1955 [NL][33]

[NL TL/CC-I]
[TO: DAVID WATMOUGH, BBC, THIRD PROGRAM]
July 21, 1955

Dear Mr. Watmough,

[...] For the BBC talk, I thought of approaching *Leaves of Grass* from the standpoint of a reader who has heard a great deal about Whitman but is reading the book for the first time. What are the poems he might prefer, in this *omnium gatherum,* if his tastes are those of a reader trained in contemporary poetry? (No, I won't ask that as a rhetorical question.) The preferred poems turn out to be early ones; the early Whitman is the great Whitman, and he is great for different reasons than are usually given by Whitman enthusiasts; great as a lyrical poet, a realistic and intimate poet, who presented what he had seen and heard and touched in the Long Island countryside and the Manhattan streets, not—in those early poems—the landscapes of "Kanada, the prairies," which he had merely read about. "Song of Myself," his almost first and truly greatest poem, is an apocalyptic work, in the same great line as "The Marriage of Heaven and Hell," Emerson's essay "The Poet," Rimbaud's *Les Illuminations,* and *Also Sprach Zarathustra,*—but an apocalypse that starts with common daily experiences.

[...]

Sincerely yours,
Malcolm Cowley

[NL TL/CC-2]
[TO: NATHAN ASCH]
September 26, 1955

Dear Nathan,

[...]

The memoirs aren't bad or hopeless, or I would summon up cruelty to tell you so, and briefly. They are sometimes very good, but not entirely so, or I could write you an easy letter full of enthusiasm. Perhaps my first impression was that your intention of being perfectly honest hadn't produced the overwhelming result I had hoped for. Usually what it produced was the usually unwritten details of sexual intercourse, whether she took it in her mouth, whether or not you were able to function. That disappointed me, because I have fallen into the habit of asking a first question about any piece, "Can it be published," and in many of these pieces the answer is no, not ever, except in an edition privately printed in English in Paris. [...] The most important piece, of course, is the one on your father, and there your frankness and unself-protectiveness are really impressive. The account is so full of ambivalence that you could set up a wholesale establishment for dispensing ambivalence to people who need to keep their analysts interested. What a tough situation it is for anyone, anyone to have a distinguished father, especially if father is a writer! [...] But to be the son of a world-famous novelist who acted like a great opera singer—— No wonder you've taken so many years to grow up, and are you as yet completely grown?

You've put all this into the piece on your father, and yet it doesn't come off—not through lack of honesty but through lack of proportion. It's so big that it overshadows the other pieces and still isn't big enough. Some day after finishing this work you will have to revise it if you want it to appear in the future as a work of art. You're right to let it pour out—that's the only way to get these things going—but some day the pourings out will have to be measured into the right vessels. At that time you should either do a whole book about your relations with your father, or else you should kill that section as a section and distribute the episodes through the length of your memoirs in the proper chronological order. [...]

The memoirs are very good on Jews, and on how it feels to be a completely Westernized Jew whose father writes in Yiddish and is idolized by the ghetto. In speaking of the Yiddish-speaking Jews you reveal yourself as more of a snob than I had thought you to be. Perhaps you don't judge yourself severely enough—unless writing these memoirs is a form of judgment. Writing memoirs is very often a method of slaying one's former self, of symbolic suicide and rebirth. Yet I cannot feel, as you seem to do, that honest confession excuses and absolves one from the vice and sins that are being confessed.

And that's all I have to say about the memoirs, except, Go on with them. [. . .]

As ever,
Malcolm

[NL TL/CC-1]
[TO: FREDERICK MANFRED]³⁴
October 21, 1955

Dear Manfred,

Some day every writer who takes chances has to recognize that the last chance didn't pay off, he put his money on the even numbers and a seven turned up, or he started his bicycle across the slack wire just under the big top and it didn't reach the other side—there he is lying on his back in the net and the audience very silent wondering whether he has broken his neck. I think something like that happened with "Morning Red," and I can't tell you anything different because it wouldn't be the truth as it seems to me. Why it happened I don't know. Perhaps it is because in writing about Siouxlanders you're writing about your own people, and in writing about historical figures like Hugh Glass you have the documents to help and the reader accepts what you say—but in writing about these St. Paul and Minneapolis people you have to depend on observation and your observation hasn't gone deep enough—and that applies not only to the rich (or new rich) in the story but also to the gangsters and politicians. I can't say that out of any great knowledge of gangsters and politicians, I haven't been buddies with gangsters for thirty years, and then only with the small-timers south of Greenwich Village, Spanish Willie and his friends of the Louis J. Espresso Association, but as a reader I can feel when a character in the story is plausible and when he impresses you as being surface-observed or remembered from something the author read. [. . .] The best sequence is the long one about the cyclone in the Twin Cities—that's pretty terrific and completely imagined. You're weakest on all questions of social status, which are terribly important in this country where, on one level, everyone's as good as everyone else, but on another level everyone spends half his life worrying whether his children are recognized as being better than the Robinsons' children, as coming from a more cultured home with more expensive kitchen appliances and a two-inch-longer car. Fitzgerald was awfully good on those questions, no use saying he wasn't.

And don't tell me I don't know anything about the country west of Chicago. I get around a hell of a lot, and I was born on the west slope of the Alleghanies, where the Old West began. I didn't go east till I went to college and I still feel just a little foreign in New England.

Cordially,

Malcolm Cowley

[. . .]

[LB TLS-2]

[TO: LOUISE BOGAN]

2120 Santa Cruz Avenue,

Menlo Park, Calif.,

February 11, 1956

Dear Louise,

I've been wanting to write & tell you how glad I was that you accepted the secretaryship of our dear organization [National Institute of Arts and Letters]. A couple of days ago I received an official letter rubber-stamped "Louise Bogan" and it set me to thinking how we'd all been punk kids together in the Village, you and Allen and Léonie [Adams] and Kenneth and Rolfe [Humphries] (though I guess he didn't have a Village period) and now they've moved us to an institution on the far-upper West Side and embossed our signatures in rubber; I hope they haven't done the same for our personalities. You could have knocked me over with an adjective when Felicia telephoned at eight o'clock one morning last month to tell me that I'd been elected president of those marble halls. She'd forgotten that NY was three hours ahead of the Coast. After a few hours' reflection I discovered why I was qualified for the office from a negative point of view—that is, I was *not* a member of the art department, *not* involved in battles, *not* a woman (that was one complaint against Isabel Bishop), and deaf enough *not* to hear remarks made in an undertone, so that in meetings I could preserve the equanimity that is mistaken for benignity or magnanimity. But couldn't they have found someone even deafer and more ignorant of art and thus saved me a hell of a lot of trouble?

[. . .] I think SF is the most human city that I have so far visited in America, not too crowded yet, though that will come, and with everything on a man-sized, not a steam-crane-sized, scale. If a couple of good magazines and publishing houses would move out here, I'd rather live in SF than in New York.

[. . .]

As ever,
Malcolm

[NL TL/CC-1]
[TO: JOHN CROWE RANSOM, *THE KENYON REVIEW*]
May 7, 1956

Dear John,

These past two weeks I've been translating an essay by Paul Valéry that hasn't appeared in English, although it's one of the very best. For me it's part of a longer project, a volume composed of Valéry's writings on Leonardo, Poe, and Mallarmé, to be published by the Bollingen Series. Some of the essays in the volume have been translated before (three of them having been included in my translation of *Variety,* thirty years ago), but most of them are new. This particular essay, "The Existence of Symbolism," is different from the others.

It was originally a lecture that Valéry delivered in Brussels in 1936. He defined Symbolism for his new audience, at some length and with the rigor and ingenuity he so much admired, and then—what was new for him—he fell into a mood of reminiscence (never saying "I," always saying "the young Symbolist of 1886," but always meaning himself, and speaking with a personal warmth that I find very moving, partly because it is so restrained). Partly through the accidents of literary interests, the essay has become more timely now than it was in 1936—I think, for example, that it would be extremely helpful to all the teachers who mention Symbolism in their courses; it contributes some precisions.

The difficulty is that it's rather long, about 8,000 words. I'm writing you about it because I'd very much like to see it in *Kenyon,* and don't want to bother you with reading it unless there is a good possibility of publication.[35]

[...]

As ever,

Malcolm Cowley

[NL TL/CC-1]
[TO: CAROLINE GORDON]
September 12, 1956

Dear Cousin Carrie,

It was nice to get your letter, and your new red house in Princeton sounds marvelous.[36] [...]

I was sorry to miss the convocation of little magazinists at Cambridge. That week I was in Michigan, speaking to a group of social psychologists on "The Language of Sociology." I told them at great length that it was a barbarous jargon in which the nouns were enslaving all the other parts of speech— and ended with a heroic picture called "The Triumph of the Nouns"— drawn in a chariot by enslaved adjectives and vestigial pronouns and verbs that were dichotomized and feebly tottering—while the nouns spilled over the triumphal car, adorned with laurel branches and flowering hegemonies.[37] That was fun, or mild fun, but most of the summer I've been in a dumpsical state, obsessed by the passage of time and the work that doesn't get done. At this moment, having finished a long introduction to three novels by, hold your breath, Thornton Wilder, the man who abolished time,[38] I'm reading the letters of Thomas Wolfe, which I recommend to your attention. They

are completely concerned with Thomas Wolfe, the only character he succeeded in creating—no, that isn't fair, for he did a few marvelous portraits,
like those of Bascom Hawke (his uncle), and his sister Helen, and Max
Perkins—but this huge volume of letters is a record of the efforts of Thomas
Wolfe to be a genius, and they point a moral, though I'm not quite sure
what it is. One moral is that if you think about expressing yourself all the
time, you become manic depressive, which Wolfe was on a vast scale.

Muriel has been madly gardening. I tell her that she's never content to
let any plant stay in its place, to bloom and multiply—she must dig it up and
move it somewhere else; and her flower garden keeps encroaching on the
lawn, like a populous nation extending its territories by force and fraud and
the right of eminent domain.—Caroline, please, for the honor of the family
and the profession, get that book done for Viking.[39] You talk so well about
the novel that what you have to say, when put in print, will be useful and
used—and after those Kansas lectures it shouldn't be difficult to get the book
into shape between trips into the garden.

Jack Aldridge—between you and me it was a great comfort to have him
turn against me, in a book much of which was cribbed from the book he
was attacking.[40] It was awfully embarrassing to have him as a disciple. [. . .]

With love, as ever,

Malcolm

[HB TLS-1] [NL TL/CC-1]

[TO: HAMILTON BASSO]

September 23, 1956

Dear Ham,

I appreciated your thoughtfulness in sending me that series of Perkins letters.[41] What a grand editor he was, and what a grand person! There is nobody
like him today; there are only editors who calculate how much a book might
possibly earn. Reading the letters gives me twinges of conscience, because
there's a second-string Thomas Wolfe whose ms is now in my possession,[42]
and if I worked on it one-third, one-sixth as much as Perkins worked on
Of Time and the River, it would be published and its author would become
known as a second-string great man (but truly an original)—and I keep

putting off the job from week to month because I think my first duty is to get my own work done, slowly and laboriously, more slowly and more laboriously with the years.

And now the job is to write something about Wolfe, and it's not an easy job because Wolfe said so much about himself and so much of it is true. He was a writing man, I would almost say *the* writing man, except that there are other varieties of writing men. Wolfe was the writing man who depended on a stream gushing out from an inner reservoir which he at first thought was an inexhaustible and perennial spring. He had for equipment an immense and accurate memory, which he used in everything, and a fairly good intelligence, which he did not use on principle. There are these two sides to every writer, the memory transformed in the unconscious and the critical intelligence; nothing is accomplished without one *and* the other. Perkins served as Wolfe's critical intelligence—had to serve in that capacity, because Wolfe's theory of writing forbade him to use his own critical intelligence, except sometimes on other people's work. What terrible claptrap he put into *The Web and the Rock* when Perkins was no longer at this side to tell him to leave it out! Yet Perkins' critical intelligence *was* to some extent drying up the flood of uncensored and uncontrolled material that flowed from Wolfe's reservoir—that even more than DeVoto's snide remarks was why Wolfe felt it necessary to leave him. I suspect that the flood was beginning to dry up in any case—one can't keep up that type of writing after 40.

He was the writing man, in the sense that he thought with the fingers that held his pencil. If he wanted to say something truly candid and intimate, he put it into a letter. Sometimes, quite often in fact, he didn't mail the letter, but Elizabeth Nowell has now published them all, and the book is, as publishers say, a Reading Experience. For the last three days I've simply been taking notes on it. It gives me more affection for Wolfe, and respect, than I had felt before.[43]

[. . .]

Much love and luck to you,
Malcolm

[JP TLS-2]
[TO: JAMES PURDY]
November 22, 1956

Dear Mr. Purdy,

For a long time I have been meaning to write and tell you how much I enjoyed your book of stories.[44] You have a new way of telling them, and in West Virginia and Chicago and Allentown you have met some pretty unusual people. I especially liked the title story, and "Why Can't They Tell You Why," and "Man and Wife," and "A Good Woman." And I like the initiative and justified self-confidence that led you to have them printed and sent out to critics and others who might not read them. I'll bet that many of them did read and admire your work.

Last week your literary agent, Toni Strassman, submitted the stories and a novella to the Viking Press, where I am a literary adviser. Both books have been read with a good deal of interest—I might almost say excitement. [...]

The stories are ready for book publication, but there aren't enough of them to fill a hard-cover book. It would have to be pieced out with the novella. Unfortunately the novella, though a powerful piece of work, is not yet ready for trade-book publication—or at least that's how I feel about it.

The difficulty there is that when the novella ends with a bang—"You motherfucker"—it leaves a lot of questions hanging in the air. Why did Grainger (and by the way was that her married or her maiden last name?) and the nonwriting writer admire Fenton so much? In the novella Grainger has seen him only once, when she was owl-eyed, and the nonwriting nonwriter has seen him only twice. How did the nonwriting nonwriter find out what Fenton was doing?—My hunch is that you intended the novella to be longer, but that the scene of Fenton carrying Claire's decaying body upstairs was so powerful that you felt anything more would be an anticlimax. But then wouldn't your job be to fit in two or three more scenes—say between Grainger and Fenton in the Dream Palace—*before* what is now the final scene?

[...]—Then finally, for a trade book, there's the problem of bad language. You don't know how much trouble the simple word "fuck" can make for publishers—and not only in Boston!

So this letter is more or less in the nature of a query. How do *you* feel about the novella? Have you any notion of doing more work on it? Have you any other *good* material that could be used to round out a volume of stories? Are you now working on something longer? I might explain the questions by saying that, as a general rule, good publishers are not so much interested in finding separate books as they are in finding authors who, presumably, will produce more and better books.[45]

Sincerely yours,
Malcolm Cowley

[NL TL/CC-1]
[TO: JAMES THURBER]
January 16, 1957

Dear Jim,

A letter from George Plimpton says that you want to withdraw and expunge his interview with you from the book that the editors of *The Paris Review* are putting together from their files.[46] That's very bad news for the boys from *The Paris Review,* and I'd like to put in a word for them. Partly it's a word for myself too, but my interest in the book is incidental—I've promised to do some editorial work on it and write an introduction, but that's because I thought *The Paris Review* was doing a good job, and I'd like to help it along. I haven't even bothered to ask whether I'd be paid for the work, and believe me that shows a self-sacrificing temper on the part of a hard-scrabbling journalist, toward some younger hard-scrabbling editors.

The reason I think they're doing a good job is that they're printing good stories and poems by new people, and aren't printing any exegeses of texts or symbolic interpretations of *Moby Dick.* *The Paris Review* has actually been serving as a medium for younger writers, not for young Ph.D.'s on their hard road from an assistant professorship to an associate professorship. At present it's almost the only little magazine that isn't part of the so-called academic or bow-tie conspiracy.

I think the interviews have been valuable stories too. As I read them over it seems to me that the interviewers were serious about the questions they asked, and managed to get serious and often enlightening answers, answers with more candor than an interviewer usually deserves. One reason may have been that the interviewers actually read an author's books before going to see him, instead of just running over a file of clippings in the morgue. They worked. They weren't just trying to ride through the skies on somebody's coat tails. There are some very interesting pieces in the collection; in fact they're all worth reading except the very first interview, the one with Graham Greene, which I hope can be revised and thickened. The interview with Thurber is one of the best. I hope you'll find it in your heart to let it be used.[47] [...]

[...]

Did you ever see the review of *Further Fables for Our Time* that I did for *The Reporter?* I worked over it to get it running smooth. [...] Muriel and I are going out to Ann Arbor, Michigan, in two weeks, where I'm rejoining the academic conspiracy, as a spy and interloper. [...]

As ever,
Malcolm

[WFC TLS-1] [*FCF* 142–43]
[TO: WILLIAM FAULKNER]
March 2, 1957

Dear Bill,

I wonder whether you could do a little chore this year for the Academy and the Institute. I don't think those august bodies have bothered you in the past, but this is a rather special occasion.

This year Dos Passos is being awarded the Gold Medal of the Institute for Fiction. It is almost the highest honor that we award (the only higher one being the Howells Medal, which you received in 1950). Presentation is made by a member of the Academy at the annual Ceremonial, which takes place I think on Wednesday May 22.

I was very pleased when the medal went to Dos Passos, because in recent years his work hasn't been sufficiently recognized—but that's a formal and lukewarm way of putting it; the truth is that he's had to stand up under an intermittent hail of brickbats. Of course his recent work hasn't been up to the level of what he did in the twenties and thirties, but he did a lot then; he took chances; he put other novelists in his lasting debt. And now that he's being given a medal—the first, he says, since he was a boy in school—I'd like to see the occasion made just as big as possible, so that he knows the rest of us haven't forgotten him.

That's why I'm asking whether, as the most distinguished novelist in the Academy, you couldn't make the presentation of the medal.[48] [...]

[...]

As ever,
Malcolm

———————

[NL TL/CC-1]
[TO: WALLACE STEGNER]
June 13, 1957

Dear Wally,
    [...]
I had a pleasant surprise at the Viking office this Tuesday. A first book by an unknown writer was on the point of being accepted, and I found that the unknown writer was Dennis Murphy, the Menace.[49] Then I hastily read the novel and liked it even more than the others did. It seems that Murphy and his new wife are now in Mexico, and terribly broke, but it also seems that his book has won the Joseph Henry Jackson Prize of one thousand smackers. Dennis reported that he had been in jail for 18 days for taking a gun away from a man who was going to shoot him with it. He was always making such reports, and I've no doubt that most of them were reasonably true when they weren't false. But irresponsible as he is in life, he's very responsible as a writer—he works at it and reworks at it, and does a professional job.

Which talk of professional writing brings me back to the Hopwood lecture[50] and your wise comments on it. Look: the burden of what I was trying to say is that the present writing programs are either suffused with artiness and yearnings toward Creative Self-Expression, or else they are actually courses in critical analysis, fine for future teachers but fatal for many young writers. I'd like to see a writing program that was a *writing* program and not a critical program or a treatise on how to masturbate on the typewriter in ten easy lessons. Maybe the English Dept would boggle at some of the courses I suggested (notably the one on publication) (and perhaps the indoctrination

course too). But most of the English profs I talked to at Michigan were enthusiastic about the translation course and about the course in the Creative
Process (that's the title to sell it by). And I think I had something when I
suggested a *series* of writing courses—first verse, then drama, then narrative
fiction, then non-fiction. That's their historical order of development, and
each of these mediums, to be good, involves elements of the preceding medium. But whether any of these ideas could or should be applied at Stanford
is a question to which your answer would be based on a hundred times more
knowledge than mine.

[...]

As ever,
Malcolm

[ASCH TLS-1] [NL TL/CC-1]
[TO: NATHAN ASCH]
July 15, 1957

Dear Nathan,

I read about your father's death[51] when I was driving through Vermont,
after three days at Syracuse University and a night at Yaddo, both old haunts
of yours, and I wanted to write you at once, but there was no paper. Then,
back in Sherman I found your letter, and was moved by it—though I could
have guessed what you felt from what you had written before, in your memoirs. Though I never met your father, you made him such a vivid figure and
talked about your relations so accurately and honestly that I can feel with
you, now. It's a frightening experience to have a famous father, who was in
essence a good man though not a good father, and it's a painful experience
to lose him. But he had a good life and it's a comfort to think that your last
relations were close and understanding—yes, you came closer to him than I
ever did to my father, with whom I never succeeded in getting anything
said, so that sometimes I wake up at night and find myself explaining what
I never explained.

I think of you often. [...]

As ever,
Malcolm

[NL TL/CC-2]
[TO: YVOR WINTERS]
July 25, 1957

Dear Yvor,

To continue the letter I wrote you on Institute stationery, in my as you might say official capacity—to continue informally—

The diploma goes back to you.[52] It's yours, and we have no provisions for filing it. It was awarded in recognition of distinguished work in the arts, you can throw it away if you wish, or you can stash it away among the ribbons, blue and pink, won by dogs now defunct. But the distinguished work is not defunct.

I regret your decision, as I said before and will have occasion to say again. We need uncompromising voices like yours inside the Institute. Especially in this country where so much comes to depend on measure and quantity—so many copies sold, so much money earned, so high a price paid for a picture, so many performances for a symphony, so many inches of newspaper publicity—we need other standards of judgment, we need some institution that speaks for the artists themselves, and within that institution we need different types of informed opinion. We need to build up inner pressures to offset the outer pressures.

That's not to imply I think you're always right in your judgments. I think you're terribly wrong, for example, about the use of trochees in iambic lines (or inverted feet). I think you're wrong about the talent of Stanley Kunitz—when I read just two or three of his poems he seems wonderful, but then I read more poems (or additional versions of the same poem) and it seems to me that his talent is both narrow and diffused or diluted. I know that you're often unwilling to admit the possibility of your being wrong.

I often don't agree with your judgment, but I always respect it. And I'd have been much happier if you had elected to stay in the Institute and fight for your opinions. Not all of the fights would have been won, but some of them, in time, would have been successful.

Well, that's water over the dam now and we won't talk about it. [. . .]

As ever,
Malcolm

On the whole I think it would be a mistake for the Institute to give the
Gold Medal for Poetry to Ezra Pound. [. . .] Pound doesn't need a medal,
what he needs is freedom, and preferably freedom in Italy.

Cowley to William Carlos Williams, August 28, 1957 [WCW]

[AM TLS-1]
[TO: ARCHIBALD MACLEISH]
August 30, 1957

Dear Archie,

The poetry medal that Pound abundantly deserves is a special medal for
his catalytic effect on other poets. That has been marvelous, almost miraculous, but I've always had reservations about his own poetry—even about
Mauberley, good as it is; there's always been this trouble in my mind that I
liked the Mauberley poems better after learning a lot of information that
should be extraneous, for example the identities of Victor Plarr, Violet Hunt,
Lady Cunard, etc. As for the *Cantos*, they're being explicated and counter-
explicated, and turn out to be as full of meanings as the frieze of a Mayan
temple, but the central and always obvious meaning is nothing that throws
light on any real dilemmas, past or present—and where is the poetry, except
in a few passages like Pull down thy vanity? I would like to see that last
question argued at length.

But we're faced now with a more immediate problem. *If* Pound gets
the medal, we're going to have internal ructions at the Institute, which
I've been hoping to avoid. Among the outraged will be most of the Jewish
members, justifiably nervous about anti-Semitism, our one Negro member, and our many literary conservatives, like Bob Hillyer, who made such
a fool of himself about the Bollingen Award to Pound. Probably we
should have an external scandal too. I can't forget that the Bollingen
Award to Pound put the Fellows of the Library of Congress out of business and stopped any further literary or musical or art awards by the government. If such a scandal occurred this time, it would certainly delay
Pound's release [. . .].

About the Gold Medal for Poetry: in my purple book I can find only
records of its being given four times: to James Whitcomb Riley (!) in 1911,

E. A. Robinson in 1929, Robert Frost in 1939, and Marianne Moore in 1953. It is now being awarded every five years. We think it's a Big Thing.[53]

[...]

As ever,
Malcolm

Having been granted a stipend to translate a volume of Paul Valéry's essays for the Bollingen edition of the collected works, in November 1957 Malcolm and Muriel sailed to Europe, where, after a stopover in Paris and three weeks at Alexander Calder's house in Saché, in central France, they stayed at the American Academy in Rome.

[NL TL/CC-1]
[TO: MARJORIE GRIESSER, VIKING PRESS]
c/o Thos. Cook & Son,
2, Place de la Madeleine,
Paris 8e, France,
November 7, 1957

Dear Marjorie,

[...]

Paris so far has been a rather strange experience for me. The city has changed so much—not in architecture; that hasn't changed at all; but in atmosphere and above all in traffic. Perhaps it hasn't quite so many automobiles as New York, and they are smaller, but it seems to me they travel five times as much, at twice the speed of New York cars. It's no longer possible to stroll—FLANER—through the Paris streets, at least not until midnight, and even then strolling is a hazardous occupation. The insidious influence of America is spreading everywhere, into every detail of life: paper tablecloths, paper napkins (but not toilet paper), hot dogs (francfurters chaudes), hamburgers, milkshakes, juke boxes, blue jeans, pony tails, and Frigidaires. Yesterday afternoon I went to a publisher's cocktail party (Corréa). There was champagne instead of martinis, but otherwise everything was the same: the hopeful young authors, the critics being courted, the reputations being sapped, mined, and explored, the pretty girls who have written a novel and want you to read it, and if you mention Françoise Sagan, that familiar look of outraged pride: no, THEIR novel is in a different class from hers, THEY don't pander to the public. By eight o'clock tongues were getting thick and gestures becoming excessive.

[…] Meanwhile we're seeing dozens of people, new friends and old ones like Tristan Tzara and Sylvia Beach, who is busy writing her memoirs (any interest there?). I've so far been afraid—I make that confession—to accept delivery of our Renault; I just wouldn't know how to use it in Paris or where to park it in the crowded streets. But I'll pick it up some time next week, and then we'll set out for Sandy Calder's house in the country, with a large box of Scotch oatmeal in our baggage. [. . .]

As ever,
Malcolm

[NL TL/CC-2]
[TO: CONRAD AIKEN]
American Academy in Rome,
Via Angelo Masina, 5, Rome 28,
January 9, 1958

Dear Conrad,

This certainly is a Conrad Aiken year. No sooner had I heard that you had received the Gold Medal for Poetry, news which delighted me, than I also heard from Felicia that you had been given those five thousand smackeroos from the American Academy of Poets. Then Laurance Roberts[54] said that everything was arranged for you and Mary to come here in September. So things begin to pile up at last. God knows you had to wait for them, with about as little recognition as anyone could have and still keep working.

The Academy is a fine place to be. Let's tell you about it as if you had never heard of it. Location on top of the Giannicolo, or Janiculum [. . .]. Absolutely marvelous view across the domed city (every dome a church) to the Alban Hills, which are treeless mountains. Beyond them one can see a higher range covered with snow. I like to walk under palm trees & look up at snow. The Academy owns several acres of city property on both sides of Via Angelo

Masina. You will doubtless be given a place in the grounds of the Villa Aurelia, about three acres mostly of ilex trees all carefully tonsured—either with a Flat Top haircut when they shade a walk, or else trimmed into the shape of huge dark-green balloons, so that you expect them to tug loose from their roots and go sailing over the city. The place swarms with servants & gardeners, all of whom bow and smile when you pass. In the middle of the grounds rises the Villa Aurelia, a very handsome Renaissance structure with rooms as big as the common rooms in a Harvard House, where the Robertses live in state. The villa has dependencies where artists, musicians, scholars, and one or two stray writers live if they are married but have no children with them. One of the dependencies, higher than the others, is called the Villino, and there we live on the top floor with a magnificent exposure to the sun and also to the wind, especially if it's from the north. You and Mary may get that same five-room apartment, which is considered the best, although it has disadvantages, including the cold and a temperamental gas stove.

[...]

Once more congratulations on having all those honors & emoluments heaped on your sturdy shoulders. [...]

As ever,
Malcolm

I seem to sense a pro-American turn in Western European sentiment—they don't love America, but they are damned afraid of Russia, and Sputniks I and II had the paradoxical effect of making them [. . .] less anti-American than before—it was as if *their* big brother, whom they were jealous of, had taken a licking from somebody else's big brother.

Cowley to Gilbert Harrison, February 5, 1958 [NL]

[NL TL/CC-2] [PARTLY *SC* 330–331]
[TO: KENNETH BURKE]
American Academy in Rome,
Via Angelo Masina, 5,
February 9, 1958

Dear Kenneth,

The European venture is drawing to a close. In two weeks more we'll be leaving the Academy and Rome, then on March 2 we'll be sailing from either Genoa or Cannes on the Constitution [. . .]. In many ways the trip has been a disappointment—I waited too long and lost some of my power of adaptation, as well as too damned much of my sense of hearing. I won't forget arriving in Genoa at dusk in a rainstorm without a word of Italian and finding that for almost the first time in my life I was effectively lost. After a while I managed to buy a map, una pianta (I'd been asking for una carta, which is a sheet of paper), and couldn't locate our position on it. Then I crossed a busy highway and had the rear fender banged into by a streetcar. A crowd gathered, and fortunately someone in the crowd spoke English, so that I obtained directions from him, at the cost of twenty thousand lire to straighten the fender. That was the worst moment, but there was another bad one leaving Paris in the mist, when, with the tiny car loaded to the roof, other cars began flashing lights at us (they're not allowed to blow horns), and we found that one of the rear doors was gaping open. Later, in Tours, we discovered that Muriel's dress coat was missing, and also all the papers that certified our ownership of the car—without them we couldn't cross the border. Well, I got the papers replaced after a fantastic amount of correspondence, but I'd just as soon do my traveling in Europe by railway. And there has been some discomfort in Rome (though our living conditions here are superb) from the indirect effects of being not blacklisted but graylisted by USIS[55]—there's no red-carpet treatment for those on the gray list—but why the hell am I yammering? [. . .]

Thursday we drove to Naples, taking Francis Fergusson[56] along, and I gave a lecture there, not under USIS auspices, which means that I was badly paid. Friday we hired a guide to Pompeii and Herculaneum, Saturday morning we visited the Pompeian relics at the Naples museum. That was the high point of the trip for me, walking through those Roman streets, peering into Roman houses, and later seeing the collection of art objects and appurtenances of daily living that were found in the houses. It was seeing a civilization stopped and carbonized in full flight: this is exactly how it was on August 24, 79; here are the election scrawls on the walls, here is the phallus incised in the pavement to point the way to the whorehouse, and here is the whorehouse, with sixty-nine positions painted on the walls and comments by the guests scratched into the plaster. The painted frescoes, now in Naples, aren't very moving—rather dull colors, except for the reds and deep blacks, and a curious lack of depth that one associates, by way of Spengler, with the picture of a culture that lived entirely in the foreground—but the mosaics are incredible; perhaps the added difficulty of that form made the artists more venturesome. Certainly if our own civilization was turned to stone, it could show nothing in the nature of art that seemed to be so intimately connected with every moment of life.

And what *small* people they were. [. . .] They were five feet tall and slightly though gracefully built; I'd estimate the weight of the man at about a hundred pounds—they looked like American children of eleven or twelve. I pictured all Europe overrun by Roman midgets.

One favorite theme of painting and sculpture was this: a man with an enormous dong resting in one pan of a balance. The other pan holds a bag of gold, which weighs less than the dong. Obvious message: My dong is worth more to me than a whole bag of gold. Francis Fergusson thought that could go into your collection of sex-money symbols.

[. . .]

As ever,
Malcolm

[NL TL/CC-I]
[TO: HERBERT R. MAYES]
[Rome]
February 19, 1958

Dear Mr. Mayes,

[...] Your long letter of January 15[57] must have been sent to the Mediterranean by fishing smack, because it arrived only this afternoon. It is getting the promptest sort of reply.

In 1945 I was asked by *Time* to do a Horatio Alger story. I did a good deal of research on it, and of course I was helped by the Lucifer boys & girls. I wrote such a long piece that *Time* had room for only part of it, & the rest came out a couple of weeks later in *The New Republic*.[58] I don't think there was much reference to you in the *Time* section of the piece, though you might look it up.

Of course I got in touch with you—by telephone, not letter. We had a rather long conversation in which you evinced no particular eagerness to talk about Alger. You referred me to the Newsboys Home for the diaries.[59] I had various people there on the phone a couple of times, and sent the *Time* researcher down to see them, but no soap, not even bubbles. They reported that they had never heard of such a book and had no Alger material whatsoever.

I went to see one of the old Street & Smith executives who had been there for nigh on to fifty years. They used to be a wonderful source of the McCoy about dime-novel days. He was very skeptical about any prodigious sale for the Alger books, though he didn't have figures. Then after a while I said, "I've always had the idea that Street & Smith bought Alger's name, just as they bought or invented other names like Bertha M. Clay and Nick Carter, and signed it to books by other writers." There was a long pause, and then he said in a low but distinct voice, "Yes."—That confirmed something I'd been morally certain of in any case, because a lot of the Alger books came out after the author's death and departed from what I came to regard as the Alger formula for a plot: namely, the orphan son of a widowed mother, oppressed by the wicked Squire, who leaves home and finds a spiritual father at the end of the book. That story obviously answered to something deep in Alger's character, so when I found books without the myth, I concluded that someone else had written them—and I was right about it. (I doubt that Alger wrote anything at all during the period of ill health before his death, yet Alger books were still appearing in 1903 or '04.)

[...]

I'm glad to learn that there was—or rather were—Alger diaries, and if you succeed in tracking them down, I'd be most grateful for a chance to see them, though you know, to make a confession, I would have admired the kid that you once were if he'd had the nerve to make them up. Anyhow I'll be back in the States after March 10 and I'd enjoy talking to you about old Horatio, who I think is one of the most fascinating and completely misunderstood figures in—well, I can't say in letters, not exactly, but at least in the field of American mythology.

Sincerely yours,
Malcolm Cowley

{ ——— }

Tillie Olsen, 1958–1960

Cowley's acquaintance with the writer Tillie Olsen dated back to 1930s *New Republic* days, but they first met in person when Olsen was in Cowley's writing class at Stanford in 1956. Between the spring of 1958 and the summer of 1960 Cowley regularly offered encouragement and advice to Olsen, then at work on *Tell Me a Riddle*. He nominated her for a Ford Foundation Fellowship, negotiated a stay for her at Yaddo, and proposed to Viking that she be offered a contract for a novel. Though he did not succeed in signing her up for Viking, he promised Olsen that he would "keep making incantations, brewing magic potions, and burning sticks to see that you have fair winds and calm seas" (January 10, 1960).

[TO TLS-1] [NL TL/CC-1]
[TO: TILLIE OLSEN]
March 31, 1958

Dear Tillie,

Your story ["Tell Me a Riddle"] reached me with the first batch of held mail after I got back from Italy on March 10. [. . .] I think that the last few pages are terrific. You have that gift of extracting almost chemically pure emotion, so concentrated as to be almost unbearable, out of a complicated situation. I do think that in this case you waste pages at the beginning of the story by going inside your people too soon. Wouldn't a straight exposition and exterior narrative be more effective at that point? Were you in the writing class the day that Frank O'Connor gave hell to Denise James for wasting space in conversation at the beginning of her long story? He said something like, "Get it told the quickest way possible. Don't bother about the scenic method or interview monologues till you have the situation established"? I think his remarks would apply to "Tell Me a Riddle," because the reader gets a little confused at the beginning—you need that situation for background, but don't need so much of it, unless you're going to write a whole novel about these people, which I think you might do. It's after the cancer operation that the thing begins to build up and up.

I can't tell you how sorry I am to hear that you had to go back to a job after only three months of writing. If there's anything I can do to help, I will. From the Saxton people[60] I got the impression that they don't ever give fellowships for collections of short stories, so you'll have to cook up a novel one way or another. I shouldn't think that would be at all difficult, considering that almost all your stories have dealt with the same extended family—it would just be a question of fitting them together into a plot, or better, of taking one story and building it up to include all the other material. Actually I think you are essentially a novelist rather than a story writer. A story writer leaves things out to produce an effect; a novelist puts them in, and that's what you're always wanting to do. If you got a novel under way, I think I could get you something of an advance from Viking Press. We're just having quite a success with Dennis Murphy's book, which, my God, besides 16 thousand copies in print has also been sold to a reprint house and to the movies. Trouble is that publisher's advances aren't big enough these days to support even a bachelor writer, let alone a married one with four children. And you ought to be writing all the time.

[. . .]

As ever,
Malcolm Cowley

[TO TLS-1] [NL TL/CC-1]

[TO: TILLIE OLSEN, HUNTINGTON HARTFORD FOUNDATION]

490 Oregon Avenue,
Palo Alto, Calif,
February 13, 1959

Dear Tillie,

Dick Scowcroft phoned me two nights ago and told me the good news.[61] [. . .] It's really marvelous to have that happen—it means that your financial problems are solved for two years, even if other problems remain. Your first reaction should be, in Henry James's phrase, a large thankfulness to fate for having given you well no more than you deserve in return for those fine feelings you have put into your stories. And then the second reaction should be to work, work, and also to remember that your first duty is to your work. I suspect that sometimes you might be tempted to think of other duties instead, not because they are truly more important, but because they offer an escape (not too pleasant to offend your conscience) from the greater and sterner duty of putting words on paper. As a beginning of the new regime, you ought to stay at Huntington Hartford as long as possible. Try to put a book together. I am eager to have Viking publish it.[62]

[. . .]

As ever,
Malcolm

[NL-VIKING REPORT TL/CC-I]
[TO: PASCAL COVICI]
December 8, 1959

Tillie Olsen

I want to put the facts about Tillie Olsen on record.

I met her in the winter of 1956 when I was teaching the advanced writing course at Stanford. She held a creative writing fellowship for the year. She was a small dark woman about 40 years old with an interesting story. In 1934, when she was just out of high school, she had written a couple of stories that attracted wide attention. Then she married a labor leader. When publishers wrote offering her contracts for a book, she was in jail as a result of the San Francisco general strike.[63] After the strike she became a simple housewife, gave birth to four daughters, and disappeared from public view. Twenty years later, she took a course in writing at San Francisco State College and did such excellent work there that Stanford gave her a $2500 fellowship.

She was by all means the best writer in my course. Another student said to me, "I always hate the afternoons when Tillie reads one of her stories in class because I know that I'll get so discouraged about my own work that I won't be able to write for two months."

But the fellowship expired and Tillie had to go back to helping support her family. Her husband, black-listed as a labor leader, had become an apprentice printer in his forties and was earning very little money. In a year he would become a journeyman printer and then, Tillie thought, she could go back to writing. He did become a journeyman printer, but had a long spell of illness and Tillie became desperate. During the two years after leaving Stanford I think she finished only one long story, "Tell Me a Riddle." Meanwhile, Blanche Knopf had become interested in her work and offered her a contract—not an option contract, either. Tillie refused it on the ground that she had already at least half-promised a book to me when it was ready.

Last year she was one of I think ten authors to receive one of those huge Ford fellowships, of six or eight thousand dollars a year, I think, for two years. Blanche Knopf renewed her offer of a contract and Tillie made the same answer. She spent four months at the Huntington Hartford Foundation, starting a novel and writing much and easily. Then she went home in May and decided that what she had written wouldn't do, that she must start over again from the beginning and work at the novel slowly. My feeling is that she is essentially a novelist rather than a short story writer.

At present she is working at home on the novel and doesn't want to interrupt it to finish a volume of stories, but on the other hand, she is anxious to have a book published before her fellowship runs out, and accordingly she has sent me these four published or about to be published stories simply as samples of her work. The longest story, "Tell Me a Riddle," has been accepted by Sandy Richardson for publication in the new series of NEW WORLD WRITING. When this story appears I think she will get offers from more than one publisher. My feeling is that she is the best writer in this country who hasn't published a book.

I think we should offer her a contract before February, when NEW WORLD WRITING comes out [. . .]

Of course all this depends on whether others agree with me about the excellence of her work.

P.S. Other Tillie Olsen enthusiasts, besides Sandy Richardson, are Nolan Miller, the editor of NEW CAMPUS WRITING, and one of the editors of *The New Yorker*, who says she is the best short story writer in America. That's a lot of baloney, but she's good.[64]

{ ——— }

[NL TL/CC-I]
[TO: IHAB H. HASSAN]
April 2, 1958

Dear Mr. Hassan,

I read your critical essays with a good deal of interest.[65] They show, first, that you have read the books (a point not to be underestimated—Aldridge too often reads only his own mind), second, that you have read them with perception, third, that your critical judgments are sound. I think you should work to simplify the style, wherever it can be simplified without interfering with the accuracy of the perception. And I think you should quote more from the authors under discussion and less, much less, from other critics. Write as if nobody has ever discussed these authors.

As for your choice of authors to discuss, a truly important point, I should say that you are paying entirely too much attention to the homosexual group (McCullers, Capote, Bowles, half of your subjects) and too little attention, in fact none at all, to the big, sloshing, chance-taking novelists like Mailer, Jones, Styron, or the jive group like Kerouac, or to the emotional realism of John Cheever.

For further remarks on these: McCullers and Capote are writers, and gifted writers, but Bowles is too special for my tastes. Jones has a sort of raw talent that demands attention; the Thomas Wolfe tradition, but less literary. Styron has published a novel and a novelette, but has worked for years on another novel that should appear soon, and then would be the time to write about him. Mailer has talent and takes enormous chances and is important for what he tries to do. Kerouac might be only a footnote to Mailer, but is interesting for what he stands for (another book of his is now in the works, to appear next fall). Cheever is only beginning, in his forties, to come into his own.

Your important problem is not to miss the authors who will still be read twenty years from now. Bellow, Salinger, Capote, for example, are safe choices; Styron too, I think; Mailer and Jones chancy but not to be overlooked; McCullers, yes; but after that one is on more uncertain ground and has to ponder.

[. . .]

Cordially yours,
Malcolm Cowley

———

[NL TL/CC-1]
[TO: OSCAR CARGILL]
June 5, 1958

Dear Cargill,

I've been working on a long memoir of Hart Crane, and it made me think again about your piece in *The Nation*,[66] and how completely wet you were about Hart's relation to Allen Tate and Yvor Winters.

First Winters—not an extremely important question. Winters and Hart were never friends. I think they met once, when Hart was in California, and I'm not even sure about that. They had a long correspondence. Winters was enthusiastic about Hart's early poems, then he turned against him. There was no question of loyalty involved. Winters had a perfect right to turn against Hart or any other poet. In this case he did so on moral grounds, being outraged by Hart's homosexuality. He made what I think was a grave critical error, not the only one in his career, but the case against him rests on critical, not moral, grounds.

Then Tate, a more important question. Allen was the first enthusiast for Hart's poetry. They met in NY on what I think was Allen's first visit there, on June 24, 1924. For the next 2 years they were close friends in spite of Hart's homosexuality. Allen got married in the late summer of 1925 and soon afterward rented six rooms of Addie Turner's house on Tory Hill. Hart was out of work and desperate. The Tates offered him shelter, and Hart accepted the offer. But when he arrived in December he was no longer penniless; he had the first, or the remnants of the first, thousand dollars of Otto Kahn's beneficence. The situation was truly impossible. Caroline Tate was pregnant and was trying to finish a novel. Hart kept storming in and out of "the Tates' part," and finally there was a grand bust-up in April. I'm sure it was largely, in all probability mostly, Hart's fault, but nobody passed judgments; everybody thought of cabin fever.

Then Allen did a damned fine thing for Hart. Publication of *White Buildings* was hanging fire because Horace Liveright wouldn't publish it without an introduction by Eugene O'Neill, and O'Neill couldn't write the introduction. "I like the poems, but I don't know why," he complained. Allen wrote an introduction and offered to have it printed over Gene's signature, a truly generous gesture. But Gene wisely refused: "Everybody will know I couldn't write that," he said. Then Waldo Frank & Jimmy Light persuaded Liveright to go ahead with the introduction signed by Allen. Incidentally it was written as a gift, though the Tates (three of them by that time) badly needed money.

Hart couldn't help to get anything of Allen's published. Allen wasn't well known at the time, but he was much better known than Hart. It was the other way round: Allen's piece on "Voyages" probably got the poems, I mean the "Voyages," printed in *The Guardian*.

Hart had such a grand design for *The Bridge*, and did more than half of it with such brio and achievement, that nobody who had been familiar with the poem as it existed in 1927 could help feeling that the complete poem of

1930 was a failure *in terms of Hart's intentions.* (The precise weakness was the three poems written in the fall of 1929, when Hart had become alcoholic— "Indiana," "Quaker Hill," "Cape Hatteras.") I said so in the gentlest possible terms in my *New Republic* review. Allen said so a little less gently, and with complete accuracy, and Hart wasn't resentful, and in fact admitted the truth of what he said. The greatness of *The Bridge* is in its intention, and in the completed greatness of some parts—"Ave Maria," "The River," "The Dance," "Cutty Sark," "The Tunnel," which I think are the highest achievements short of what he planned for *The Bridge* as a whole.

Does that make me too a disloyal friend? Or just a critic trying to be accurate?

Sincerely,
Malcolm Cowley

[NL TL/CC-1
[TO: YVOR WINTERS]⁶⁷
June 26, 1958

Dear Yvor,

So now my sin is to have an easy and flowing style, indicative, so I gather, of ignorance and shallow thinking. My God, my God, what do you know about writing *prose* if you think that an easy and flowing style is a weakness to which one yields, as one might yield to any fleshy vice? I wish you could have a look some time at all the sentences, paragraphs, and pages that I reject in the course of making something sound as if it flowed from the tip of my tongue. Or watch me as I moon around the house and grounds and wander blindly down the road in the weeklong or monthlong effort to outline something so that it sounds like a natural, logical, and at the same time associational progress from the first sentence to the last. Writing easy, flowing—and correct—prose is my scholarship. It is a hard and constipated process. I think I must write more than sixty thousand words, sometimes much more than that, in the course of completing a six-thousand-word essay. [. . .]

I think the worst feature of American education today is the contempt for language as language. I'll absolve you of that sin as regards poetry, ah, most willingly absolve you. But why do you think that prose should not be easy and flowing?

[...]

As ever,

Malcolm

——————

[NL TL/CC-2]
[TO: DONALD HALL]
June 8, 1958

Dear Don,

[...]

Your letter about rhymes[68] [...] prompts me to two [...] pontifications, the first not about rhymes, but about syllabic verses in English. I'm skeptical about it, because it's so easy to confuse with the looser sort of four or five-stressed verse. For example, your two sonnets on Easter: I didn't guess they were syllabic, I thought they were loose pentameter, I thought you were taking liberties, not imposing another strict rule on yourself. To destroy that impression I would have had to actually count syllables. The possibility of misunderstanding has existed, in cold fact, for nearly 300 years. The English poets of the Restoration and early 18th century took over French prosody wholesale and *thought* they were writing decasyllabics, not five-stress lines (that explains all the "th'Eternal's" in Pope; he was getting rid of extra syllables for purposes of counting, though not in actual pronunciation). But I've always thought there was an element of syllable-counting (or consciousness of numbered syllables) in English heroic verse, except the verse based on Hopkins' sprung lines; it's one of the things that makes it so complicated.

So, for me syllabic verse doesn't *work* in English, except in combination with stress. The exception is Marianne Moore, who has constructed her own system of lines of unusual and arbitrary length: stanzas composed of one line 19 syllables, the next 17, the next 3, the next 19 again, the next 7; each stanza following the same arbitrary pattern; the reader doesn't count out the pattern, but he has the feeling of its being there, the feeling that the poet is doing something difficult. That *works*. I don't think Marianne's rhymes work; the reader simply disregards them. Anyhow she has her copyright on that system; anybody who copies it is a copycat.

Then about rhymes. I like what Owen was the first to call "slant" rhymes—wire, ware, weir; I like them even when the initial consonant is changed, as in air, wire, here. I hate off rhymes (on unaccented syllables), unless the syllable is good and strong: crackdown, town, and hearsay, way sound good to me. When the syllable is weak, especially when it contains a schwa, that indiscriminate sound of the unaccented vowel in English, it can't rhyme with any accented syllable truly, because the schwa doesn't exist in accented syllables. Awful doesn't rhyme with full or fool or fell or fall. Battle and rattle don't rhyme with monosyllables—the "tle" sound is merely a sort of click. "The" doesn't rhyme with anything, despite Marianne.

But scrimshaw-williwaw would be a nice rhyme in a poem about sailors, whalers.

Let's stick to the genius of the language, our language.

[. . .]

As ever,
Malcolm

<hr />

[NL TL/CC-1]
[TO: DAWN POWELL]
August 6, 1958

Dear Dawn:

Yesterday we talked about it at the meeting—some time I'll tell you about publishers' meetings, they're curious occasions—and the upshot was that Pat Covici was delegated to make an offer to your agent. [. . .] My feeling is that we could make *The Golden Spur* an occasion for getting a much wider recognition for your work in general. I'd be glad to contribute my modest efforts toward that end.

The beginning of *The Golden Spur* is very entertaining and promises well. The search for a father is one of the great themes, Jesus, from the beginning of the *Odyssey* down to Thos Wolfe, and because it's a great familiar theme it's also a marvelous vehicle for satire. I'd make one suggestion about those early chapters—I don't know whether you'll agree with me, but it's a simple and perfectly mechanical suggestion, and I think it's worth trying. The one trouble with them now is story line. The story starts with Jonathan, then starts again with Darcy and Lise, then starts again with Claire Van Orpen. Nobody minds your shifting from one character to another, that's almost always been your method; the suggestion is that you should prepare the reader for the shifts so that he'll be expecting them and feel that the story is moving ahead.

[. . .] That's something to think about when you're revising the book—the point now, as you know much better than I, is to work ahead and get a first draft without worrying too much about the beginning. Or are you one of those unfortunate souls who have to be sure that page one is right before they write page 2? Those are the bleeders, the damned souls.

[. . .]

As ever,
Malcolm

———

[NL TL/CC-1]
[TO: FRANCIS BROWN, *THE NEW YORK TIMES BOOK REVIEW*]
November 28, 1958

Dear Mr. Brown,

There is one little piece I could write for that page-two spot, but I had better query you about the subject before going to work on it. The subject is Bad Words and their degradation in current fiction. The point I wanted to make is that once there was a secret language used by adult males in our society, just as anthropologists report that there are other secret languages used by the males of various tribes in Melanesia. Powerful effects could be obtained in fiction simply by referring to the secret language in an oblique fashion—as, for example, by saying that a character uttered "a crimson flow of profanity," words not specified, though probably they consisted of two or three common oaths. Now those oaths are spelled out, and produce little effect of any sort. The secret language isn't secret any longer.

The difficulty in writing the piece would be that although the words have been degraded in fiction, they still retain their forbidden quality in the pages of the *Times*. I don't think I could even use "bitch" as an example, though the word used to have the force of a malediction, and now is scarcely more than a cute way of referring to a malicious female. I could of course use "bloody," since it belonged to the secret language only in England and was almost respectable in the USA. "Damn" and "hell" might be other by now respectable examples. But perhaps the whole point of the piece would lie in obtaining its effects *without* using any of the bad words it was talking about. It would lead to the question: When the bad words aren't bad any longer, how are novelists going to indicate that their characters are speaking under the stress of uncontrollable emotions? A whole range of effects has disappeared from fiction.

Do you think that would be worth saying in the *Times*?[69]

Cordially,
Malcolm Cowley

[NL TL/CC-1]
[TO: KARL SHAPIRO]
490 Oregon Avenue,
Palo Alto, Calif.,
February 15, 1959

Dear Karl,

Felicia Geffen tells me that you wrote refusing election to the National Institute. I wish you'd think it over and change your mind. The Institute is a damned good organization, one that doesn't take any more time from its members than they are willing to give—in fact takes no time, if they live far away from the NY area—and does not (unlike other organizations) commit them to any course of action or body of opinion that they are unwilling to adopt. It exists simply for the furtherance of art and literature in this country, and operates almost wholly by carefully choosing its members and by giving rather large cash grants (now $1,500 instead of the former $1,000) and gold medals to generally good people, including at one time yourself. It holds four dinner meetings each year, and two luncheons (to which the wives or husbands of members are invited), and an annual Ceremonial, all good affairs. In the last few years especially it has helped in this modest way to maintain standards of good writing and painting and composing, as against the purely commercial standards that are likely to prevail in this commercial country. And it can best maintain those standards if it has all the truly good people as members— every good man who isn't a member weakens its standing by the force of his virtue.

I must say that it *does* have almost all the good people, though it is sometimes slow in getting round to them. One thing sure is that the distinction of the artist is its chief and indeed its only criterion for membership—not popular reputation or social acceptability or any other damn fool criterion; that makes it pretty nearly unique. And it has a good endowment that enables it to give prizes without going around with its collective hat in its hand to get money from millionaires; it's independent of everything, including Congress, which chartered it. But it keeps strictly out of politics, another virtue in these days. It needs you; we all do.[70]

[...]

> Love to the Shapiros,
> Malcolm

Our writing, if not our art in general, is caught up in a period very heavily impregnated with the academic. There is little or no sense of risk. There is about the same amount of honesty. More and more of our sometimes writers compromise themselves, perhaps eventually their country's literature, by tumbling into graduate schools and preparing themselves for alternative careers. Turbulence is rare. What little we've seen in the San Francisco movement seems adolescent and not very intelligent. [...] Most important to me is the lack of risk in the personal as well as the aesthetic sense. Writer after writer, in the years when such things are crucial, elect the paths that provide for certain comforts, securities, alienation, sterility.

Richard Farina to Cowley, July 13, 1959 [NL]

[NL TL/CC-1]
[TO: RICHARD FARINA]⁷¹
July 18, 1959

Dear Mr. Farina,

I sympathize with your analysis of what has been happening to young writers, in fact it comes close to what I said five years ago in *The Literary Situation*. And I sympathize too with what you say about the contents of the quarterlies. There are a few little mags that do try to print hardly anything but fiction and poetry. There is *Paris Review,* printed not very regularly in Holland, there is *Quixote,* which has been printed all over—currently in Gibraltar, I think—and *Contact,* in SF (with an angel?) plans to pay more attention to fiction and poetry than to criticism—and of course there are the various little mags published in SF, New Orleans and a few other places that are done on electric typewriters and reproduced by offset, thus cutting the printer's bill by about half; but I don't gather that any of them [publish] work that doesn't represent little groups of admiring friends or outpourings of the libido of the beatniks. Any of the offset mags, I mean; *Paris Review* has printed some fine things, though there has been less good work in *Quixote*.

If you want to start a little mag without academic or foundation support⁷² you find an angel, or you find three or four young writers from prosperous families who share the same ambition of being editors. Then you find some way of reducing the printer's bill, which means going abroad (at the cost of copyright for any American work you print) or doing the job by offset, which makes it look amateurish, but what the hell. Then you try to find contributors with some talent, an enormous job in itself. Then you get somebody to design the magazine so that it looks good, and then you try to distribute it—a whole series of problems, but not insoluble ones, since little magazines do appear. *Paris Review* started as a sort of cooperative venture by a number of mostly Harvard graduates, all, I think, with some sort of income—then they got other young people to work for nothing distributing the magazine and getting subscription. One could do something like that in Rome, which is pretty full of young Americans. Maybe we could talk about this some time, I mean the whole question of starting a little magazine.

You're so right about that disinclination of young people to take financial risks. One has to lead a sort of monastic life of poverty and obedience, though not chastity, only nonpaternity, in order to be truly independent. Who's willing to do that now in the washing-machine era?

Cordially,
Malcolm Cowley

[ARVIN TLS-1] [NL TL/CC-1]
[TO: NEWTON ARVIN]
July 18, 1959

Dear Newton,

[...] I've been slaving over an introduction to a book Viking is doing late next fall, the 1855 text of *Leaves of Grass.* I'm crazy about the original text, which is completely different from and better than—I think—anything else that Whitman wrote. "Song of Myself" is the account of a mystical state that was the result (in the poem) of two (or three, to be accurate) ecstasies described in chants 5, 26, and 29. The mystical state or illumination encouraged Whitman to arrive at a whole aggregation of doctrines which are amazingly like some Brahman and Buddhist doctrines, notably those of the Mahayana Buddhists and the Tantric Brahmans—I dug up a series of parallels. But Whitman changed rapidly after 1855—he was already changing when he wrote the prose introduction to the first edition, even though he used one paragraph to announce his belief in something like karma. He returned part way toward his mystical beliefs after the Civil War (by which time he had actually read the *Bhagavad-Gita,* apparently), but this time with an admixture of his Personalism and of the Calamus doctrines. In 1867 and 1881, when he revised "Song of Myself," he changed it in various small fashions to make it accord better with his later beliefs (again I took some trouble to document)—the hero became Myself instead of the deeper Self or soul or transpersonal self, and God became the great Camerado, not simply Brahman or Oversoul. It's been a fascinating study for me to make.

In your own fine Whitman of years ago, I think you made a great mistake by going at the man topically instead of chronologically. Nobody in our literature changed oftener or more in the course of his lifetime. There is a whole series of Whitmans, strikingly different from one another except in the *apparent* form of their work. The style and texture of it kept changing from 1850 to 1874—after which I refuse to read what he wrote, except for purpose of reference. If anyone asked me, What did Whitman think about this or that? I should have to answer, "When?"

As ever,
Malcolm

[AA TLS-1]
[TO: GLENWAY WESCOTT]
September 17, 1959

Dear Glenway,[73]

Your letter about [Robert Penn Warren's novel] *The Cave* is a searching and splendid piece of criticism and makes me feel, once again, that novelists are the best critics of the novel. In some ways I'm tempted to carry your praise & blame of *The Cave* still father. I felt that it was truly poetic at times, and truly philosophical, and had a grand conception, and at the same time I kept saying of the characters, "I don't believe a word they say. They *wouldn't* say that. They're philosophical abstractions." Compare with Faulkner, whose characters are always true to North Mississippi, no matter how grotesque they become. I'm not against giving a Gold Medal to Warren, he's a man of true distinction in several fields, but I think that essentially he's a poet not a novelist—and secondarily a philosophical critic not a novelist.

Cozzens *is* a novelist. His best book, I suppose, is *Guard of Honor*, a magnificent piece of architecture and true all the way through, but some of his earlier work is admirable in his special way. (Same social subject as Marquand and O'Hara, and how much better.) *By Love Possessed* has fine things in it, and is fine as a whole, even though it has those two faults of being a short story about the present with extensions into the past, instead of a narrative, and of being written in a gnarled style as if he had spun a spider web and got caught in it. In spite of the faults it may be, in fact, the best American novel of the last five years, and Cozzens is possibly the best novelist we haven't honored in any way.

I suppose Nabokov is another serious contender, though I somehow don't feel we should be placed in the position of crowning *Lolita*. On the other hand Nabokov, an American citizen, should certainly be a member of the Institute. Shouldn't we nominate him on Monday?

[. . .]

As ever,
Malcolm

[NL TL/CC-1]
[TO: VANCE BOURJAILY]
November 7, 1959

Dear Bourjaily,

Would you like a fan letter? About the story in *The Dial?*[74] I thought that sexual intention was the most worked out, mined out, lumbered over, corned out, leached out, and eroded subject in American fiction. I thought that nobody could grow a new crop on this ruined soil. But you did find or produce a new growth, green and tender. Diarmuid Russell tells me that it's part of a new book, the confessions of U. S. D. Quincey, in which you treat his other initiations as well as the sexual one. It should be a hell of a good book.

Cordially,
Malcolm Cowley

[NL TL/CC-2]
[TO: LESLIE A. FIEDLER][75]
November 7, 1959

Dear Fiedler,

Just now, through a concatenation of circumstances, I happen to be reading the galleys of *Love and Death in the American Novel*. [. . .] I've only read about a third of them, but in that third I was impressed by the number of brilliant ideas you've turned up—the section on Charles Brockden Brown is especially good; it was something, it was a subject I've always intended to write about, and now you've foreclosed me by saying most of what I intended to say and a lot more besides. But I'm writing this letter now to correct you on another point, about Hawthorne. It doesn't weaken your main thesis, but it shows that one has to be careful to make qualifications and acknowledge exceptions.

Hawthorne didn't marry an invalid through fear of sex. He married an invalid and made a woman of her—for ten years, at least—and in so doing achieved a physically normal and more than normally happy sex life for himself during the same period. I told the story, leaving out its Freudian overtones, in a long article for *American Heritage* (December 1958). Briefly it was that Hawthorne during his lonely years had the usual vice of loneliness—if there aren't masturbatory overtones in many of the stories of that period, then I don't know how to read. When he courted Sophia Peabody he was trying to save himself as well as her, and there was no nonsense about purely spiritual love; he wanted to sleep with her, and maybe he did—Norman Pearson has never been able to make up his mind on that point, and Norman knows more about Hawthorne's private affairs than anyone else. You should read Hawthorne's *Love Letters,* with the passages inked out by Sophia after her husband died and later restored by Randall Stewart and an X-ray machine. Anyhow they were married after four years of courtship, and Sophia stopped being an invalid, worked hard, and they had a pretty intense sex life, to judge from some other letters. It lasted until Rose was born (1851? 52?—I'm not going to look up the date), when they decided to have no more children. They were Puritans, they didn't know about birth control, and I *think* that from Rose's birth their sex life slackened off or stopped completely, so that Hawthorne retreated once more into himself, and Sophia, though she didn't regress into invalidism, lost the splendid health of their early married years. Hawthorne was never her boy, and she never touched his work while he was living—her excisions in the letters and journals were made after his death. He was her divine lover (Psyche and Eros?), worshiped, obeyed (after one or two mild rebellions), husband and father—it was the best marriage in the annals of American writing; but she depended on him so much that after he died she was rudderless.

[...]

But what's the moral, for you, of the whole story? I think the moral might be that in Freudian or Jungian criticism of authors' psyches one can reach valuable generalities, but that one has to be careful about individual authors—one has to know more about their private lives than a general historian of literature often has time to learn about individuals, and sometimes more than has been left on record. That's one of the things that stopped me from writing a general history of American literature; I could never learn enough or read enough. But I think your volume (I haven't finished more than a third of it, as I said,) is going to be stimulating, new, and extremely valuable.

Cordially yours,
Malcolm Cowley

[NL TL/CC-2]
[TO: LESLIE A. FIEDLER]
November 17, 1959

Dear Fiedler,

Look, you can't have it both ways. If you're concerned with only that part of an author's life that he projects into his work—if you're not going to Paul-Pry into his private affairs—then you shouldn't make use of Hawthorne's most private observations on the death of his mother in order to interpret *The Scarlet Letter*. On the other hand, if you *are* going to do what is essentially, in this case, biographical criticism, then you are obligated to get the biography straight. You aren't allowed to say—I forget the exact words, but you aren't allowed to say or imply that Hawthorne married an invalid in order to escape the obligations of a mature sexual life when the truth is that he didn't do anything of the sort—he didn't marry an invalid—he had what seems to us now a mature sexual life, finally.

[. . .][76]

Some criticisms of your book. Eros and thanatos yield a good many illuminations, and I know you say in the introduction that there are many other valid approaches to criticism, but still you *do* give the impression of being too narrowly erothanatistic. It may lead to misinterpretations—of *Sanctuary*, for example, where eros and thanatos are on the surface and the deeper meaning is Southern nationalistic. George Marion O'Donnell was at least partly right about the book: Temple Gowan is the South and Popeye is industrialism, at least in some murky depth of Faulkner's psyche. I think you think "The Bear" is a short story. It's also part of a novel or near-novel, *Go Down, Moses,* which deals with incest and miscegenation in the McCaslin family, more impressively, to me, than Faulkner deals with the same subject in *Absalom, Absalom.* The book ends with the holy relic of the McCaslins, the silver horn, passing from the white to the colored branch of the family. There is no hint of repressed homosexual love between young Ike McCaslin and Sam Fathers—I should think the name Fathers would give you the hint; Sam is Ike's spiritual father. One thing you missed throughout your book was the Telemachus myth, the search for a spiritual father; it's very deep in the American psyche and is the true plot of Horatio Alger's books for boys (the hero *doesn't* make a fortune by his unaided effort; what the Alger hero always does is find a spiritual father, who is rich). It's the myth that Thomas Wolfe thought he was embodying.

Another criticism: because you're looking for archetypes, you sometimes (not always) are willing to hand too much to the writer who finds them. Having described the American genius as a talent for the Gothic (and why do you think Hemingway isn't Gothic?—considering that he's often a reversion to Charles Brockden Brown, with the same American mixture of neuroses and Indians) you aren't always just to the architectonic authors, the builders, as note your rapid dismissal of Cozzens. The kids in Pennsylvania used to say, "She was built square, like the little brick shithouse on the corner." I always think of that remark when reading a Cozzens novel—an unjust remark, since *Guard of Honor* is the most complicated piece of balanced architecture that any contemporary American author has produced. But look, Ma, no archetypes, no incest.

You won't mind these pokes and prods, because what they imply is that I enjoyed and was impressed by the book as a whole. It does force one to rethink and reread a good many of the American classics, and it does support one's instinctive feeling that the American novel expresses a talent, imagination, psyche, call it what you will, that is essentially different from what is expressed in English or French or German or Russian novels,—a different attitude toward love and death.[77]

Sincerely,
Malcolm Cowley

[NL TL/CC-I]
[TO: JAMES E. MILLER, JR.]
May 2, 1960

Dear Mr. Miller,

[...]

You and Karl [Shapiro] and Bernice Slote have done a valuable service for critics and teachers by showing that there is, beyond all argument, another tradition in American poetry—and English poetry too—besides the one that has been dominant for the last twenty years.[78] You are right in regarding Whitman as its principal source, its fountainhead, and I was particularly impressed by the chapters in which you explained D. H. Lawrence's enormous debt to Whitman, something that most critics have managed to disregard. Of course Crane acknowledged his own debt [...]. Certainly Dylan Thomas is in the tradition too, but here it isn't so much a question of literary debt as of a sort of fraternal sympathy. I liked Karl's chapters on Henry Miller and W. C. Williams—the first admittedly in the tradition, the second largely there, even while fighting against it.

I disagree with Karl when he talks as if T. S. Eliot were the central figure in a dire conspiracy. Eliot has been a man of very great personal authority ever since he was an undergraduate at Harvard. Much of the authority is due to the fact that even when we utterly disagree with him, we are unable to change a word of what he has written so as to make it more effective—I mean the authority is that of an incantation repeated without a single error. He's a magician but not a conspirator. The damage is done by all the little Eliots who try to repeat the incantations, and by all the professors who find that poetry in the Eliot tradition is teachable. Eliot is a religious man who tries to be humble. After "Song of Myself," Eliot's *Four Quartets* is the only long mystical poem written by an American, or former American.

[...]

Cordially yours,
Malcolm Cowley

[NL TL/CC-1]
[TO: MONROE K. SPEARS, *THE SEWANEE REVIEW*]
June 12, 1960

Dear Spears,

Could one of your throng of assistants [. . .] dig up the back issue of *Sewanee,* and a very back issue it is, containing [W. K.] Wimsatt's essay on the Intentional Fallacy? I enclose one plunk, not enough to pay for the service.

To explain: That phrase of Wimsatt's has *fait fortune,* has gone everywhere the Objective Correlative has gone, has been scrawled in toilets at faculty clubs, has been inscribed over doors leading to the administrative offices of English depts., has led to the acceptance or rejection of dissertations—and I think it's a dangerous phrase. I want to write an essay called the Unintentional Fallacy. My thesis would be that as soon as the author is robbed of all property in his work, it can be appropriated by any critic and deformed to his individual temperament. Of course the author's intention is not the final basis for judging a work. Of course all sorts of great works—*Huck Finn,* for example—are valued for reasons that have nothing to do with the author's intention. But to the extent that criticism is a judicial process, the writer is entitled to be heard, his testimony is of substantive value. And I propose to quote some examples of critical studies which, by totally disregarding the author and his process of composition, have become grotesque misreadings of all sorts of texts. Fiedler's homosexual *Huck Finn* is a case in point, but only one case among hundreds.

[. . .]

Cordially yours,
Malcolm Cowley

Cowley first met the young African-American author Ernest J. Gaines during his teaching stint at Stanford in 1959. On the basis of a novelette read by Cowley ("A Long Day in November") Viking offered Gaines an option contract for a longer novel. In several letters Cowley offered encouragement and extensive suggestions for revision of an early manuscript version of

Gaines's first novel, *Catherine Carmier* (published in 1964 by Atheneum). On June 20, 1960, Cowley reported to Gaines that, though his revisions greatly improved the novel, Viking could not offer him a further advance or a firm contract.

[NL TL/CC-1]
[TO: ERNEST J. GAINES]
June 27, 1960

Dear Mr. Gaines,

What I didn't manage to put into my letter was how deeply sorry I felt to be writing it. I believe in you as a writer. I feel that Jackson's dilemma is very close to your heart, that it could and should make a fine story. But still I had to tell you Viking's decision, made after several readings and a good deal of discussion, and I had to admit to myself that the decision was justified in the circumstances. [. . .]

[. . .]

Plotting is your great weakness at present. Good plotting means that nothing is introduced into the story—no character, no scene, no incident, no object—unless it contributes something to the central theme. Good plotting also means that there is some sort of preparation for every big scene and every big decision. Two examples of bad plotting in the present version are the revolver and Jackson's sudden decision to stay in Louisiana. The revolver is valuable as a symbol—granted—but once Aunt Charlotte finds it in Jackson's baggage some further use has to be made of it. I don't say it has to be fired, but at least Jackson should take it out, finger it, think *definitely* of using it (not vaguely, as in the present version), and then decide that the way of violence is not his way. As for Jackson's decision, there should be some good reason for it, besides Catherine and the fire—I mean, he should talk about farming with Brother, he should feel when he first sees the nook again (and do have him really *see* it) that it has a strong attraction for him, that his roots are there.

When I said that the novel had too big a canvas, I didn't mean that your theme was too big—I meant that you introduced perhaps too many characters and subsidiary themes, thereby losing your focus on Jackson himself and the big question he has to answer. There's a lot of rewriting to be done,

and I have faith that you'll end by making this book the sort of novel you
want to write.

Yours cordially,
Malcolm Cowley

In the summer of 1960 Newton Arvin, professor at Smith College and long-
standing advisor at Yaddo (where he had had an affair with Truman Capote),
was arrested on charges of "lewdness" and possessing homosexual erotica.
Arvin pleaded guilty, implicating two colleagues at Smith. Though friends
like Cowley, Hicks, and Daniel Aaron (a colleague at Smith) stood by Arvin,
he was eventually forced into retirement from Smith, removed from the
board of Yaddo, and hospitalized for suicidal depression. He died on March
21, 1963, having finished his *Longfellow: His Life and Work* (1963).

[NL TL/CC-1]
[TO: ELIZABETH AMES]
490 Oregon Avenue,
Palo Alto, Calif.,
October 30, 1960

Dear Elizabeth,

I've been thinking a great deal about Newton's tragedy and its bearing
on Yaddo. The question of public relations is an important one, and it has
different sides. One side is that of relations with the general public; another
is that of relations with our special public of writers, artists, and composers.
In that narrower but, for us, important public, the feeling is that Newton
has been persecuted, partly for obscure political reasons. Postmaster General Summerfield has been trying to build up a record for suppressing pornography. Massachusetts has a very zealous commission of that type, entirely composed of Catholic politicians. They are not unwilling to make
trouble for nonsectarian private colleges like Smith. Apparently Newton
was foolish enough to get his name on the mailing list of a dealer in homosexual pornography in Kansas City. Two younger Smith College professors
also had their names on that list (it wasn't Newton who turned them in,
though, in his state of utter shock and confusion, he may have made unwise

admissions about them to the sleuths who invaded his apartment). I've talked to many people about his case, members of the literary public, and they all felt that Newton's friends should stand by him. If they had wanted to ostracize him for being homosexual, they should have done so before he got into trouble. The arrest didn't reveal anything about him that wasn't known to his literary and academic colleagues.

All this presents Yaddo with a double problem. If we invite Newton for the winter, we do run some risk of unfavorable publicity (though not a great risk, I think). If we don't invite him, the members of the literary and artistic public will accuse us of cowardice and disloyalty. Balancing the two dangers, I think the second is the worse, especially as inviting Newton would be the courageous and honorable thing to do. I think back on other literary and academic scandals, for example on the very old (1912) story of Professor Harry Thurston Peck, discharged from all his positions and expelled from all his clubs as the result of a breach-of-promise suit—in lecturing on the period I've been bitter about the friends who deserted him, and now do I want to act in the same way? Also I think of a professor at Wooster College in Ohio, involved in this same Kansas City case, who committed suicide a couple of months ago. I worry about Newton and think I should help.

So, to summarize, I'm strongly in favor of inviting Newton for the winter.

[...]

My best love to you, as ever,
Malcolm

PART IX

The Sixties

The Sixties: Old Left, New Left, and the Community of Letters, 1960–1965

The Cowleys spent the 1960 fall term at their favorite academic venue, Stanford University. Cowley had taken over the Stegner Fellowship Class in Fiction, which that year included an exceptionally talented group of emerging writers: among his pupils were Larry McMurtry, Peter S. Beagle, and Ken Kesey, as well as a young Australian novelist, Christopher Koch. Cowley invited C. P. Snow to speak to his class, and he wrote to his contacts at Viking to report on the fresh new talent he was meeting. With the help of younger editors at Viking, Cowley got Ken Kesey a book contract for his landmark novel *One Flew Over the Cuckoo's Nest*. Other authors he prized for their daring were Doris Lessing, for her novel *The Golden Notebook*; Cormac McCarthy, for his first novel *The Orchard Keeper*; and Norman Mailer (with reservations) for his novel *The Deer Park*. Among the new poets he appreciated were Galway Kinnell and Laurence Lieberman.

The appearance of Daniel Aaron's *Writers on the Left* (1961) and the first serial publication of Alfred Kazin's memoir *Starting Out in the Thirties* in the *Atlantic Monthly* in May 1962 brought Cowley's embroilments in the factional politics of the 1930s once again before the public. In two revealing letters to Kazin, Cowley offered no apologies but wished to "set the record straight." Meanwhile, his own book on the 1930s was "going forward with almost psychopathic snailishness" (as he told Henry Dan Piper on January 13, 1963). Between 1962 and 1965 Cowley wrote several chapters—among them the confessional "The Sense of Guilt" (for *The Kenyon Review*). A symposium for *The American Scholar* (1966) revived memories of the 1935 First American Writers' Congress.

In May 1962 Cowley entered on a second term as president of the National Institute of Arts and Letters. In that capacity he wrote numerous letters as spokesman for the community of letters, an obligation he conscientiously fulfilled during his presidency—and beyond. More honors were to come: in May 1963 he was elected a fellow of the American Academy of Arts and Sciences, and in late 1964 he was "elevated" to the American Academy of Arts and Letters.

As often, the writing of books of his own was waylaid by countless smaller projects. Returning to an old but passionate interest, he collaborated with the historian Daniel P. Mannix on *Black Cargoes* (1962), a history of the Atlantic slave trade. For Bodley Head (which had published an English edition of *Exile's Return* in 1961) he prepared a new two-volume edition of stories by Fitzgerald (1963), and with his son, Robert Cowley, then assistant editor at *American Heritage,* he edited a research anthology for Scribner's, *Fitzgerald and the Jazz Age* (1966). *After the Genteel Tradition* was reissued in 1964, with the addition of much new material by Cowley. In 1963 Rizzoli's in Milan published an Italian translation of *Exile's Return,* and *The Literary Situation* appeared in German.

Ernest Hemingway's suicide on July 2, 1961, triggered complex and contradictory sentiments, voiced in letters to Conrad Aiken and Mary Hemingway. Over the years Cowley would advise Mary on how to care for her husband's legacy and reputation and would counsel her on the publication of unfinished manuscripts, including *A Moveable Feast* and *The Garden of Eden.* Speaking out publicly, he defended "the old lion" against the critical "jackals." With more and more of his literary friends suffering from ailments or passing away, Cowley came to feel as if an entire generation were being "swept off the board," as he told Elizabeth Ames (July 16, 1963). The deaths that hit him hardest were those of his neighbor and critical mentor Van Wyck Brooks; Pascal Covici, a beloved colleague at Viking; Hamilton Basso and Nathan Asch, both friends and correspondents since the 1920s; and Dawn Powell, "one of the bravest women I have ever known," as he told Elizabeth Ames (December 12, 1965). Writing to Allen Tate on the occasion of the death of R. P. Blackmur he observed: "all of us who started writing in the twenties had some curious feeling of closeness, of having shared in the same perilous undertaking. And we all seem diminished when one of us goes" (February 4, 1965). Like many, Cowley was deeply touched by the assassination of President John F. Kennedy. As president of the National

Institute of Arts and Letters he wrote a letter of condolence to First Lady Jacqueline Kennedy, expressing his admiration for her steadfastness but also for the Kennedys' support of the arts.

Inevitably, the political vicissitudes of 1960s America obtruded themselves. In late 1964 Cowley was invited to speak at the Southern Literary Festival at the University of Mississippi but worried about the segregated nature of the conference and consulted Robert Penn Warren about the principled thing to do. Back at Stanford for the winter quarter of 1965, he found himself in the midst of New Left political reaction against the Vietnam War and, exceptionally, joined 144 members of the Stanford faculty in signing a letter of protest against President Johnson's policies regarding Southeast Asia. Vietnam, however, generated less anxiety than man's capacity for destroying the environment: as Cowley told Burke, he was now "utterly convinced that the human race is going to extinguish itself by poisoning the soil, the water, the air, possibly even before it blows the world up."

Today the Negro scholars are so full of black nationalism that they want to blame everything on Europeans. But the truth about the slave trade is that it was disgraceful for everybody: Portuguese, Spanish, Dutch, English, French, Mandingos, Dahomeans, Efiks, Arabs, everyone that touched it. Perhaps the real blame is on the human race [. . .].

Cowley to Daniel P. Mannix, December 22, 1961 [NL]

[NL TL/CC-2]
[TO: DANIEL P. MANNIX][1]
Sherman, Conn.—or better:
490 Oregon Avenue,
Palo Alto, Calif.,
September 20, 1960

Dear Mr. Mannix,

Well, the answer to the question is "Make as few moral judgments as possible while telling your story." Moral judgments and historical generalities are what get one into trouble. The 18th century was a cruel time. Captains were cruel to their men, cruel to the black cargoes they carried, and cruel to white cargoes too, when they were transporting Irish immigrants. On the immigrant ships the mortality was sometimes as high as on the slave ships; you can find figures for that. The reasons for the mortality among the slaves were overcrowding, smallpox, ophthalmia, suffocation, suicide, etc. The—I believe—even higher mortality of the European crews was caused chiefly by malaria and yellow fever, on the Coast, and later by scurvy—not to mention floggings, drunkenness, and gunfights. The Negro traders on the Coast were as cruel to their own people as the whites were. You have to tell the truth in all cases, but if you tell the truth in terms of attested incidents, the sepia hagiographers won't be able to jump on you.

But your big problem, of course, is what to think about the Africans. Well, they were people like you and me. On the Guinea Coast, in Senegal and the Sudan—that is, in the areas where most of the slaves come from—they had developed a fairly high culture. There had been some pretty large Negro empires, most of which, in the Senegal-Niger region, were broken up by marauding Arabs. Many of the Negroes were skilful ironworkers. They had complicated systems of agriculture, land ownership, and government. Their religious notions, now being studied by anthropologists, were far from being primitive. Some of their sculpture was superb. They had no written literature, of course, but they had developed an extensive folklore, including fine poems that were handed down by word of mouth. Because they had learned how to cooperate, to work in groups—unlike the North American Indians—they made splendid agricultural workers, and in the South they were our unsung pioneers. It was the slave trade itself that demoralized and corrupted the Guinea Negroes, set them to warring with one another, turned their kings into drunken tyrants, and kept their society in an unstable state. Away from the Coast and away from Arab raiders, Negro life was much more peaceful, as Munro Park discovered when he pushed his way into the interior, depending on the kindness of the natives. So, the best policy is just to forget the color of their skins. Europeans might have acted in much the same way if faced with the same situation.

[...]

So speaks the pundit. [...]

Good luck,
Malcolm Cowley

[NL TL/CC-1]
[TO: C. P. SNOW]
490 Oregon Avenue,
Palo Alto, Calif.,
November 15, 1960

Dear Charles,

I am delighted that you and Lady Snow can come on December 15. I think you will be edified and amused by meeting the young writers in my class: item, the wild young man from Texas, expert in pornography, who had two novels accepted for publication during the last month; item, the soulful young man from Kentucky who is writing a novel longer than *Look Homeward, Angel;* item, the smooth and canny novelist from Australia; item, the skyblue-eyed Scotsman with a black-eyed and absolutely, impeccably beautiful wife from New York; item . . . but there will be perhaps ten of them and they're nice kids, some of them quite talented.[2]

[. . .]

Sincerely,
Malcolm Cowley

[NL TL/CC-2]
[TO: PASCAL COVICI]
490 Oregon Ave.,
Palo Alto, Calif.,
December 3, 1960

Dear Pat,

Greetings. Thought I'd better send you a report on my meetings with some of the young writers in my class and in the neighborhood.

Yesterday evening Peter Beagle[3] came to dinner. Muriel was entranced by him. He is serious, well read, fun loving, adventurous, and hasn't let his head be turned or his sense of economic reality be dimmed. So far at Stanford his one extravagance has been a motor scooter. He's having some trouble with the new novel, after a good first chapter, and maybe he's adopted too complicated a form [. . .]. My feeling is that I shouldn't interfere with him at this point, except to offer advice on minor matters, and that his first big problem is to finish a draft of the whole novel, as originally conceived. He's a good man and will solve his own problems as he goes along. [. . .]

Tillie Olsen came to lunch on Thursday. She's been working hard, but doesn't feel that she's ready to show me what she's written. She's a perfectionist, always gnawed by self-distrust; when she talks about herself she turns away her head, half-closes her eyes, and her voice becomes inaudible. When she talks about her white and black neighbors, she becomes animated and looks straight at you. We'll need to have patience with her, but she'll come up with something in the end—and when she's going good she writes like an angel.

I'm not so optimistic about *Ernie Gaines*. He's rewriting that novel once again while working half-time at the P.O. I'm not at all sure that he has solved his problems in the novel, divided as he is between nostalgia for the South and Negro patriotism. Tomorrow, Sunday, Dorothea Oppenheimer is taking us to his apt. for dinner with Ernie and his grandmother.

I'm interested in the work of a rough bird in the class named *Ken Kesey*. He wrote & submitted to Viking a novel about the SF beats, which I turned down without showing to the editors. Some of the chapters showed a marvelous storytelling ability, but the book as a whole had a weak story line, and the hero was unsympathetic, selfish, negative. I thought the novel had possibilities if he'd recast it completely. Now he's started and half-written the first draft of another novel laid in a mental hospital (he works in one). The narrator is a loony who pretends to be deaf & dumb, so that he is allowed to hear all sorts of private conversations. His delusion is that the mental hospital is a sort of electronic machine shop, in which the patients have electronic controls installed in their brains so that they can be released. One tough customer, not loony at all, comes into the hospital and tries to disrupt the system. The plot of the novel is this tough customer's battle with the head nurse, in which the reader feels certain that he'll be defeated. I suspect, but I'm not at all certain, that the book may turn out to be something rather powerful, and I've asked *Wally Stegner* to read the first 80 pages to check on my impressions.

Wally is of course delighted by the Literary Guild news, and worried lest the accolade should interfere with the critical reception of his novel. I too am a little worried about the critical reception—important to Wally, who wants to be a leading man of letters—but I'm much more confident about its popular reception. Wally is marvelous as a novelist of manners, and specifically of Pacific Coast manners. I hope, I hope we can get a movie sale and a big advance from the newsstand paperbacks. A SHOOTING STAR could easily become a jackpot book, and then we'd be certain of good sales for Wally's future work, beginning with his next book on is it Saskatchewan. The chief threat to Wally's big success as a writer is his success as an academic figure—he'll have to earn enough money by writing to pry him away from that other career. He's ambitious, clear headed, hard working, and not conceited. Viking should work hard to put this book over, big. Wally is delighted with what we have done with it—he says, "Compared with Houghton, Viking is a real publisher, I could feel it from the beginning."[4]

I'll write you later about the plans of author *Malcolm Cowley*. He wants to cut loose from the journalistic and academic life, or lives, and do some books. [...]

Pat, I hear nothing but praise of you on the Coast, you're a father figure for more authors than anyone else since Max Perkins.

My warmest regards, as ever,
Malcolm

[NL TL/CC-I]
[TO: PASCAL COVICI]
490 Oregon Ave.,
Palo Alto, Calif.,
December 17, 1960

Dear Pat,

I told you about Christopher Koch, a young Australian novelist here on a writing fellowship.[5] [...]

I'm also interested, perhaps more so, in a first novel by a young man named Ken Kesey, now about half written in first draft. I think I told you that the narrator is a schizophrenic in a state hospital, with delusions that the hospital is a place where electronic equipment is installed in the brains of the patients. After a while you begin to feel that the narrator isn't as crazy as all that—the electronic equipment is a delusion, but what is done to the patients amounts to destroying their personalities; the delusion becomes a symbol of real events. A man who's only pretending to be crazy comes into the hospital and has an epic battle with the head nurse, in the course of which the narrator becomes a good deal saner simply by taking sides. . . . Kesey went to the University of Oregon on a football scholarship. He hasn't ever learned how to spell, and didn't even begin reading for pleasure until he was an upper classman. He took a radio course with Jim Hall and produced so many interesting plots that Hall advised him to take up writing; then he won a Stanford scholarship; then a Saxton fellowship for a book that Harper turned down (correctly) when it was finished—I read it & think it can be salvaged if he wants to spend another six months on it. Last year Kesey nearly made the Olympic wrestling team—he has a 19-inch neck, like wrestlers. He's married, 1½ children, works in a state loony bin in this vicinity. Wally Stegner read 80 pages of the ms and also thinks that Kesey has something there, if he can carry it through to the end and then go back & tighten up the story.[6]

[. . .]

I've always suspected that when Donald Hall finished his book[7] we'd be unable not to accept it. Even in the first version, the best chapters had charm and authenticity—and a good subject too, an important subject, the absolute ruin and disappearance of rural New England. It's funny about Hall—one doesn't like him most of the time, he's an arriviste, a head hunter, a searcher out of fellowships, a self-advertiser; and then at a crucial moment he often comes across with something a good deal better than you've been expecting. I think he'll go far. I also think that my idea about having him do a prosody for us is sound and eminently and for a long time salable. There are several reasons, hard to explain, why he is the right man for the job. Auden won't ever do it.[8]

[. . .]

As ever,
Malcolm

[NL TL/CC-I]
[TO: EVAN THOMAS, HARPER & ROW]
490 Oregon Avenue,
Palo Alto, Calif.,
February 10, 1961

Dear Mr. Thomas,

Many thanks for your sending me galleys of John Cheever's new book.⁹ I read, or in most cases reread, the stories with fascination. It seems to me that Cheever has slowly and imperceptibly become one of this country's important writers. He's an accurate and realistic observer, but at the same time he is an apocalyptic poet of the prosperous middle classes. He catches his characters at the moment when they have been driven beyond endurance by the strain of being successful, intelligent, happily married, and just like everyone else in their highly restricted suburb.

Lately he has been developing a special quality of vision. The observation is as accurate as before, but now it's as if everything were being seen through slightly distorted lenses or moving water; the furniture is shaky, the walls are askew, the old people are dying in neighborhoods where death is strictly forbidden under the zoning regulations, the children are crying for love or bread, and pretty soon all these persons, places, and things are going to be exploded into a mushroom cloud, leaving nothing but Cheever's accurate and inalterable prose. I suspect him of being the H-bomb of the prosperous suburbs.

[...]

Cordially yours,
Malcolm Cowley

[NL TL/CC-2] [SC 340–341] [PMC, 509–510]
[TO: KENNETH BURKE]
490 Oregon Ave.,
Palo Alto, Calif.,
February 22, 1961

Dear Kenneth,

[. . .] Here I've been writing for forty-two years [. . .]. Forty-two years. Jesus Christ, I think of them and of the years still to come. I never forget that you and I were pretty obscure persons until we were fifty years old. I had an instinct or impulse or urge or drive, all the words are unsatisfactory, *not* to become a celebrity, but that was partly a conscious decision too. I'd seen too many talents ruined by an early success: what a price they pay for it in this country! I know you had that same instinct, and suspect that you made the same conscious decision, or series of little choices. Jesus X, ability isn't so widely distributed in our field that we both couldn't have been successful early by doing something only a little different from what we did. I feel now that the decisions were sound, though we were running the risk of bucket-kicking prematurely. Having survived into our sixties, things are a little easier and I'm no longer afraid of being well known or earning money—the big problem now is that with somewhat declining vigor (I'm speaking of mine not yours) [. . .] I still have to create or put together a body of work while there is still time. It can't be fiction any longer, and there's a question about poetry; most of it has to be history or criticism; but, by using my morning hours, as friend Emerson did (those mentions of Emerson are the result of my present seminar, but he *was* a marvelous administrator of his limited resources; that's the real burden of his essays, how a litry man can do good and lasting work in spite of deficiencies)—by doing what I can, I propose to gather that body of work. And the great advantage—this time for you as well as me—is precisely that we *were* obscure, that the vast fickle public didn't get tired of us, that now we have the experience and part of the freshness too.

[. . .]

As ever,
Malcolm

On July 2, 1961 Ernest Hemingway committed suicide in his home in Ketchum, Idaho.

[NL TL/CC-I]

[TO: CONRAD AIKEN]

July 7, 1961[10]

Dear Conrad,

[...]

I mourn for Hemingway. He could be as mean as cat piss and as sweet as a ministering angel. It's hard to think that so much vitality, vanity, unflagging zest, eagerness to excel in everything, willingness to learn and study and finally teach everything, ability to participate in other people's lives—that all this should simply vanish. Some time I'll tell you some of the curious things I found out about him that he didn't want the world to know. When he conquered certain weaknesses of character, when he stopped being a coward, when he became more or less the image he had created of himself—at that point he pretty well stopped being a writer. Let's nurse our vices and neuroses; it's dangerous to cure them.

As ever,

Malcolm

[NL TL/CC-I]

[TO: MARY HEMINGWAY]

July 15, 1961

Dear Mary,

I can't help writing to say how much I was saddened by Ernest's death. Even though we hadn't been exchanging letters for a long time, it was a comfort to me just to know he was *there*, standing for so much talent and vitality, so much enjoyment of life, so much interest in people, such a passion to study and master everything that isn't written in the books. I can't get over the feeling that he's still there. Some of the primitive tribes believe that immortality is a privilege granted only to a few, and only by virtue of what they were and did. Ernest won that privilege a long time ago.

It's a strange thing that several people wrote me as soon as they heard the news. They didn't know you or the boys, or didn't feel intimate enough to send you a letter, but they were so moved they had to put words on paper, and they addressed them to anyone they knew who had written about Ernest. One of them said, from a veteran's hospital, "I always felt he spoke for me." Another said, "He was the only writer living or dead that I've ever acknowledged in my heart of hearts was a better writer than I was." Many other people than I must have received letters like that.

The only thing I wrote about Ernest was a piece for the *Herald Tribune*,[11] as a favor to Belle Rosenbaum and Irita Van Doren, both old friends. [. . .] They prefaced it with an editor's note implying that I was one of Ernest's most lifetime friends. I hate that sort of guff, but you'll see if you read the piece that it is as accurate and unassuming as I could make it.

I keep reading what the papers say, and I've been impressed by your courage and dignity. [. . .] [I]f you ever want any errands run, literary or otherwise, don't hesitate to call on me.

As ever,
Malcolm

[NL TL/CC-I]
[TO: WALLACE STEGNER]
August 16, 1961

Dear Wally,

[. . .]

We've taken Ken Kesey's novel, ONE FLEW OVER THE CUCK-OO'S HOUSE [*sic*]. Much enthusiasm among the younger Viking editors. It's interesting how the judgments on that book divide along age lines—Kesey speaks for the younger generation and, liking his work too, I've been an exception among the gaffers.[12] [. . .] Regretfully we've turned down Chris Koch's book, which is a fine job of writing, but with small prospects of finding an American audience. It should do well in England. [. . .]

I keep telling people what a wonderful writing class Stanford had last year.
[. . .]

As ever,
Malcolm

[RPW TLS-1]
[TO: ROBERT PENN WARREN]
August 30, 1961

Dear Red,

I've been disturbed for a long time by the fact that nobody except the nonesteemed columnist of the *NY Sunday Times Book Review* seems to remember Elizabeth Madox Roberts in print. In the new generation of college students almost nobody has heard of her [. . .]. It seems to me a scandalous situation, considering that her best work deserves a place above the best of Willa Cather, for example.

With the warm cooperation of Marshall Best, I've at last persuaded Viking to reissue *The Time of Man* in paper. At least that will give professors a chance to place it on their list of assigned reading—if the professors themselves have heard about it. [. . .] To give it a fair chance, it needs an introduction by someone who can speak with authority, preferably by a fellow Kentuckian, and most preferably by yourself. Could you perform that act of piety?[13]

[. . .]

As ever,
Malcolm

[NL TL/CC-2] [SC 341–342]
[TO: KENNETH BURKE]
September 29, 1961

Dear Kenneth,

[. . .]

Tonight I reread "The Psychology of Literary Form"[14] for quite practical reasons. On October 11 I have to give a lecture on Art and Ethics at a Connecticut state teachers' college. Not only that, I have to write the lecture & give them the manuscript to publish (for a good fat honorarium of $525). Well, I have a reasonable number of things to say on the topic, and especially about the special ethic developed by writers. Very often the choice between two words is a moral choice, so that a work of literature becomes an aggregate of small moral decisions. Also, in one sense every story is a fable. A story is a situation that leads to an act, as a result of which *something is changed*. The nature of the change provides the moral of the fable. I have a good deal to say on both those topics, as well as on the function of art, the social function, I mean, which lies very largely in the domain of morals, since one of the functions is to provide archetypes of character and conduct. There will always be a conflict between artists and institutions, in so far as institutions quite rightly try to preserve themselves and artists, speaking for the unconscious minds of a new generation, are a threat to established institutions. That's easy to say, but what does it lead to in terms of social policies? I think it justifies censorship, and also justifies the resistance to censorship—the only answer I can find is that the conflict is dialectical, unending, and often fruitful. But how to make a lecture out of this material I don't yet know, and I'm reading to find hints or, better yet, something that makes me so mad I'll be impelled to answer it. Most of my writing—and yours? and almost everybody's—is also dialectical, an angry reply to somebody.

Anyhow, in your writing I find lots of hints, more than anywhere else, but nothing, or almost nothing, to make me rush to the typewriter with an angry retort. Obviously if a poem is a symbolic action and a strategy to encompass a situation, it falls at least partly into the field of morals; the action is "good" or "bad," as is its effect on the reader. But I don't think you have ever stated your notions of what a social policy toward literature might be. One trouble with censorship is that the state is a poor judge of what is "good" or "bad" for people.

It's too late at night for me to be verbalizing.

[...]

There'll be a frost tonight.

As ever,
Malcolm

Dear Allen,

I too was sorta disturbed when I read Matty's account of the janitor poet.[15] [. . .] The book is full of minor errors that could have been avoided. But what the hell, I said to myself, [. . .] it's all part of history, and history is always a mixture of true and false.

I've been running into these historical troubles in regard to my own past—for example, there's Dan Aaron's book, *Writers on the Left,* in which I play a pretty big part. Dan was perfectly fair, but Irving Howe did a hatchet job on me when he reviewed the book for the *Sunday Times.*[16] Reading the review I discovered that I was becoming indifferent to what was said concerning anything I did forty or thirty or twenty years ago— it wasn't *I* who did it, it was someone else about whom I have ceased to be sensitive. I'm not in the least ashamed or proud of what this other person did. I'd like the record to be straight, but for historical, not personal, rea- sons. If anyone wants to say that this someone else was a knave, a hero, or a fool, why, let him say it, and let another historian correct his errors; it's out of my hands now.

Matty's book is useful and entertaining when it deals with the Dada- ists and Surrealists, whom he knew better than did any other American writer. It is written in a comic spirit that often doesn't get across to the reader—one has to picture Matty speaking the words with gestures and with a roguish look in his eye. He has a habit of saying the wrong things, not only about you but about Kenneth and others. Muriel can't get over his referring to her as "a younger woman who, besides having other virtues, kept his household in beautiful order." His best story is the one at the end of the book, on the fire that nearly killed him—for it comes at the moment when his individual destiny coincided with the national destiny, and thus it serves as a fine synecdoche. What really disturbed me about the book, for Matty's sake and my own, was that a professional writer whom I had known for more than forty years could write so badly, with such disrespect for the language and for his profession.

[...]

As ever,
Malcolm

―――――――――

[NL TL/CC-1]
[TO: MARY HEMINGWAY]
January 20, 1962

Dear Mary,

I read the Paris book as soon as I got home, and I've waited all this time to tell you that it's good, it's wonderful, and must be published.[17] [...] It stopped much too soon. When Muriel read it after me, she said at the end, "I felt interrupted, as if a stranger had walked into the room when I was making love." You said that the book didn't end, it just tailed off. I don't think that's really so; it has more unity of subject than one thinks at first—it's only that the last four episodes in this particular manuscript (I don't know where they stand in the later manuscript) haven't yet been put into their proper order. It's a book, *the* book, about Ernest in Paris and the Vorarlberg learning to be a great novelist—the people who helped him, the people he hated, and Paris itself, which you can smell on every page, as if you were passing the window of a Paris bakery and smelling the good bread. The story begins when Ernest and Hadley and Bumby come back to Paris from Toronto in the winter of 1923–24 and decide to go to the Vorarlberg. It ends in the late winter of '26 in the Vorarlberg, when Ernest is revising *The Sun Also Rises* and Pauline moves in on him. I don't know whether it's fair to Pauline, but that's not our business; it's exactly what Ernest wanted to say, and he says it marvelously. I do think the published book ought to end there, when he says, "this is how Paris was in the early days when we were very poor and very happy." [...]

I keep thinking about the problem of handling that great pile of manuscripts for the good of you and the glory of Ernest. There's always the danger that the critics will start jumping on him with both feet, now that it seems safe to do so. The critics, of whom I have a low opinion taken as a group, never really liked Ernest except under compulsion. One way to provide that compulsion is to publish a good new book of his, and I hope and believe that the Paris book is what is called for. [. . .]

So I stop here, having said what I think—you're the CO and I'm just one of the staff officers, so long as you'll have me. [. . .]

Yours, as ever,
Malcolm

[NL TL/CC-2]
[TO: ALFRED KAZIN]
April 26, 1962

Dear Alfred,

It is always enlightening, and sometimes shocking, to find what someone thought of you at a given period, or thinks today. But there are some further remarks I ought to make about your piece in the *Atlantic*,[18] to set the record straight.

You were right to say that I was essentially interested in literary history, including trends of the moment, but quite wrong to say that I envisioned myself "in the lead."[19] I had the sort of imagination that works retrospectively. I almost never did things because they were the trend of the moment; I did them because I wanted to. But then, looking backwards, I sometimes discovered that scores or hundreds of other writers had been doing about the same things, at about the same time, so that my career in retrospect had become representative. That's what I tried to show in *Exile's Return,* and it seems to me that you are confusing what I wrote with what I said in conversation, or didn't say. I was never a great talker and only occasionally a good one. Try to remember honestly. If I ever told you anything about Hemingway or Dos Passos or Crane, it must have been in answer to direct questions.

The point about trends can be illustrated by an example you mention: Connecticut. I first moved here to Sherman in 1926, for the simple reason that I was country born and was never long at ease unless I could feel bare soil or pine needles under my feet. Later I found that moving to Connecticut had become a trend, but it wasn't one I had wanted to lead. I had enjoyed the country more when I was alone there, with two or three friends four miles away.

And then your point about picturing myself "in the lead" . . . There was a curious search for leaders all through the 1930s, with attempts to drape the toga on various reluctant shoulders: first those of Wilson, then of Dos Passos, then of Hemingway. On two or three occasions—notably at the first Writers' Congress in 1935—I was tracked down by toga-bearing emissaries, but I ducked and ran. The last thing in the world I wanted to be was a leader. Leaders, I felt, had too many responsibilities and too little freedom of action.

I was probably as lacking in ambition as anyone you met in the literary world. Again it was because of that backward-working imagination. I didn't look forward to picture myself in a commanding position, with money and a wide reputation. I was happy at *The New Republic*, where the work was exciting in the early 1930s, and I was content to let Bruce Bliven and George Soule run the paper. I had only two passions at the time: one was for the revolutionary movement and the other was for writing well and helping to get good work published. As the first passion faded away gradually after 1935, the second became stronger. I felt that anyone who wrote well was on my side, and the writers I worked hard to get, or get back, into the paper included Aiken, Wallace Stevens, Jim Thurber (who reviewed *Proletarian Literature in the United States*), Faulkner (I commissioned his only book review), Katherine Anne Porter (whose reviews were always late and three times as long as I asked for), Silone, and Yeats (after I rescued part of his *Autobiographies* from a pile of rejected manuscripts). Among reviewers my big trouble was with the party liners, most of whom wrote badly, but who needed money. I compromised by giving them shorter reviews, which I tried to edit into passably good English.

Among the young writers of the time whose first reviews or articles I managed to get published were, besides yourself, John Cheever, Robert Cantwell, Mary McCarthy, Eleanor Clark, Nathanael West (for his only review), Jim Farrell (I think), and Otis Ferguson. You were all wrong about the relation between me and Otis. After Wilson left the office, Otis was the other man on the paper with a primary interest in good writing. He kept razzing me about the young women who came into the office to ask for books and put their legs on my desk (Otis would illustrate obscenely) and about what he said was my habit of expecting him to read my mind. I could take the razzing, but was disturbed when his attacks on the pomposity of others turned, as they sometimes did, into attacks on serious artists. Still we were allies, and we trusted each other. When I was away on vacation or laid up with a broken arm, I had Otis take charge of the book department, and always found it in good shape when I came back. I did a good deal more than indulge him. Otis was at war with Bruce Bliven, whom he called Buster, and I had to stand between them. After I left the office in December 1940, it was only a few months before Otis was fired. . . . When is somebody going to do a collection of his articles?[20] They are perhaps the best work of the 1930s that is still to be recovered.

On these points I'm simply trying to set the record straight, while admitting that anybody has a right to like or dislike anybody he chooses to like or dislike. What I do resent in your article is the story about the lie-down strike at the Writers' Project, and for the one reason that it makes me responsible for something I didn't do or say or wish to have any part in. I thought the Writers' Project boys were acting like damned fools. I thought that they had a marvelous opportunity to show what they could do professionally, and to serve literature and the nation by writing good pieces for the Guides, while instead most of them were writing terrible junk, or nothing at all, and were building up their egos by acting as Communist Boy Scouts. When you imply that I indulged or condoned or would be happy to hear about their silliness, you make me feel as if a knife had been slipped into my back and turned.[21]

The turn of the knife is the placing of that story just before the news of the Russo-German Pact. I hope it wasn't what you meant to do, but the juxtaposition of the little story and the big event makes it appear that I was one of "These armchair ideologues of terror and deceit, these bookish exponents of mass murder" who went about explaining how clever Stalin was. Of course I did nothing of the kind. I was sick and revolted, like many others. I didn't say much for publication, but I wrote a lot of letters, some of which I reread two months ago, when I was preparing four lectures on the 1930s. The burden of all the letters was, "I want to get out of every God-damned thing." I did get out, and I've stayed there ever since, and now I do not feel grateful to you for reviving those vendettas and character assassinations of the 1930s. Think it over.

Sincerely,
Malcolm Cowley

[NL TL/CC-2]
[TO: ALFRED KAZIN]
May 18, 1962

Dear Alfred,

I'd better make some more remarks about the situation between us in 1934–39, because it needs to be cleared up. You were the youngest person reviewing books for *The New Republic* at the time, and perhaps the youngest since I had started reviewing in 1918, at about the same age. That gave me some sympathy for you, and what gave me more was that the reviews you wrote were printable without my slaving over them, as I had to do with the work of many reviewers. I should have liked to have given you more books, but sometimes it was hard to find them for you, because of the demand from the other editors—you must have run into it later[22]—for reviewers with reputations in special fields. No, I wasn't conscious at the time that you felt animosity toward me. I did feel that you were strenuously on the make, which amused me, and I suspected you of expressing safe opinions, at a time when "reckless" was my word of praise for a virtue I didn't always culti-vate. But I didn't mean to be surly toward you, and you must have gotten that impression from the fact that I was chronically tongue tied with you and almost everyone else. Note the complaint from Otis that I expected him to read my mind.

[. . .]

I've been searching my own memory and my conscience to see whether I *was* betting on what I thought was the wave of the future. I wasn't, to the best of my recollection. I was sincerely Marxian at the time, but without the optimism of the faithful. After 1933 I was much more exercised by the spec-tre of fascism than by the hope for a proletarian revolution. I had chosen a side, but feared it was going to lose.

Well, it's your autobiography, not mine, and I can't argue about what
you feel subjectively to be the truth, unless there is objective evidence to
disprove it. But I'd like to offer one warning, which is that you should be
careful not to fall into self-pity. I'm thinking about your rise from Brownsville and "from many early humiliations." What you fail to recognize is that
there is a Brownsville in every literary life. A writer should be grateful to his
Brownsville, or regretful that it wasn't Brownsville enough; the early hu-
miliation is what winds him up and keeps him going. In my life the Brownsville was East Liberty, a generally prosperous, semi-suburban area of Pittsburgh where my father was a pious Swedenborgian and a homeopathic
physician with a very small practice. The Cowleys were regarded as being
quite strange, if harmless, and too poor to clothe themselves properly. In the
Pittsburgh winters I didn't have an overcoat until I was fifteen. I went through
Harvard on scholarships, and at Harvard I was almost but not completely
an outsider; if I *had* been a complete outsider, I should have suffered fewer
humiliations. After Harvard and after starving in Greenwich Village, I
went to France on a fellowship; in that case I really was riding on a wave—
the fellowship wave—of the future. Except for two years as a proofreader
and underpaid copywriter for Sweet's Catalogue, *The New Republic* was my
first job. When you first came into the office, I had just published a book
that received generally scathing reviews meant to annihilate the author.
You had only a vague notion, and a false one, of what sort of man you were
meeting.

But that's just my own story. There are worse ones in the lives of others
you met or heard about at the time. Burke, Dos Passos, Anderson, Farrell,
Crane, Caldwell, Wolfe, and Max Lerner, to choose names at random, all
had their Brownsvilles, physically or emotionally squalid, and that helps to
explain their rage for putting justificatory words together. Edmund Wilson
was an apparent exception, although it was he who wrote "The Wound and
the Bow." He was of an established family, had gone to a good prep school
(the real division at the time was between prep-school and high-school boys),
had always been recognized for his ability, yet I suspected that he had a
Brownsville too, if one looked hard for it. Usually the rich boys like Jack
Wheelwright were the unlucky ones in literature; they hadn't enough to

drive them ahead and often declined into queerness or self-loathing. I think it's fine that you're trying to set down your own story candidly, at a time when, as you say, candor is rarer than ever, but part of the story is that Brownsville was your salvation as well as your sorrow, and that you rose from those early humiliations by force of ability, but also because they served you as a spring-board; give thanks for them. Another part of the story is that you weren't a sharp or a sympathetic observer of the sorrows of others.[23]

[...]

Sincerely,
Malcolm

[NL TL/CC-2]
[TO: ORVIL S. DRYFOOS, PRESIDENT, *THE NEW YORK TIMES*]
May 27, 1962

Dear Mr. Dryfoos:

This isn't a letter for publication. It is a letter of justified complaint, and it has to do with the *Times*'s story about the joint ceremonial of the National Institute and the American Academy of Arts and Letters, as carried in your issue of May 25.

I've been doing a slow burn about the story, and so, it appears from many conversations, has everyone else who attended the ceremonial. It was an exceptionally brilliant affair. On the platform among other distinguished members of the Institute were three winners of the Nobel Prize in Literature: Pearl Buck, William Faulkner, and Alexis Leger. Ten days earlier Faulkner had declined an invitation to dinner at the White House, on the ground that he wouldn't travel a hundred miles just for a meal. But he traveled three hundred miles for the ceremonial, where he was presented with the Gold Medal for Fiction. Eudora Welty made the presentation, and Faulkner responded with a short speech, which I am told was controversial. I didn't hear it because he read too fast, but there were copies of the speech if your reporter had asked to see it.

The other Gold Medal, for Victory, was presented by Allan Nevins and accepted by Samuel Eliot Morison, in a fine speech which I did hear. Earlier

Douglas Moore, the president of the American Academy of Arts and Letters, had opened the meeting by reading a telegram from President Kennedy. What Mr. Kennedy singled out as a particular cause for gratification was that the Institute's award for distinguished service to the arts was being given to Paul Mellon, then on the platform.

Aldous Huxley had come from Los Angeles to deliver the Blashfield Address, on "Utopias, Positive and Negative." Later, during the presentation of eighteen grants and four special awards in the arts, there was a fine moment when Abraham Walkowitz was presented with the Marjorie Peabody Waite Award, "to an older artist for his continuing achievement and integrity in his art." Walkowitz played a great part in the movement that liberated American painting during the first two decades of this century. Now eighty years old and blind, he is forgotten by much of the public, but his work is remembered by his fellow artists. When his niece led him up to the platform, first one member rose, then another; then everybody was standing, on the platform and in the audience, to honor the veteran.

I. A. Richards had some fine remarks to make in accepting the Loines Award not for his work in linguistics, but for his poems. Julie Harris, who received the medal for good speech on the stage, gave the last talk of the afternoon. It was a candid and engaging one, partly concerned with her great debt to Ethel Waters. I won't describe some other presumably newsworthy features of the afternoon; my only point is that not one of the features was mentioned in the *Times*'s story. That story consisted of nothing but a dewy-eyed report of some remarks by Alan Dugan, who scolded the Institute and the American Academy in Rome for giving him their Rome Fellowship. Speaking as if from an eminence, he said that he would take the money, in the hope that the academies would behave better in the future. The audience burst out laughing.

Your reporter, Miss Sanka Knox, did not report this laughter, and did not stay to find out whether Mr. Dugan's remarks were answered, or what happened in the second half of the program. As soon as Mr. Dugan finished speaking, she obtained a copy of his remarks and rushed back to the office to write her story. Before leaving, however, she informed the staff of the Institute-Academy that she was a friend of Mr. Dugan's; also she said rather grandly that the president of the Institute might phone her at the *Times* if he so desired.

The president of the Institute, not being a proud person and having a great respect for the *Times,* accepted her kind permission. He—but now we'd better change to "I"—told her what happened after her departure, and Miss Knox responded with some not-to-be-printed (nor, I think, believed) gossip about John Williams, the novelist who had been turned down for the Rome Fellowship by the American Academy in Rome. As at the Institute, she was very talkative, but not a good listener or observer.

Simply judged as a news report, the story she wrote for the *Times* seems to me vastly inferior to the story that appeared in the *Herald Tribune* that same morning. The *Herald Tribune*'s story also featured the Dugan incident (controversy is news), but it didn't imply that it was the only thing to happen all afternoon, and it did mention more important names and events, which Miss Knox completely disregarded. Her story, it seems to me, is an insult to William Faulkner, Eudora Welty, Allan Nevins, S. E. Morison, Aldous Huxley, I. A. Richards, Paul Mellon, Julie Harris, and everyone else, with one exception, who addressed the audience. The exception is her friend Alan Dugan, whom she presented as the star of the occasion, with everyone else as part of the anonymous mob. It seems to me that the Institute and *The New York Times* have both been victimized by arrogant and incompetent reporting.

Sincerely yours,
Malcolm Cowley
President

[NL TL/CC-I]
[TO: RAYMOND WALTERS, JR.,
THE NEW YORK TIMES BOOK REVIEW][24]
July 21, 1962

Dear Mr. Walters:

I'll pontificate, but I won't prophesy.

Nobody is going to take the place of Ernest Hemingway or that of William Faulkner, which of course were different places. Each truly good author has his separate niche, and nobody else can move his typewriter into it. But still, in ten or twenty years, there will be another Great American Writer, for the simple reason that the post has to be filled. There has to be someone who serves as international spokesman and chairman of the board, so to speak, for American writers as a group.

It's a high public office, and there are rigid qualifications that the Great American Writer must meet. He must have produced a considerable body of distinguished work. He must then be nominated by the critics and elected, as it were, by an enthusiastic body of readers who feel that he is speaking for *them*. It helps if he has an unusual character, photographs as well, and makes a lot of quotable remarks.

Nobody knows who will next hold the office. Twenty years ago Heming-way had fallen out of favor with the critics, and Faulkner was not only out of favor but out of print (except for *Sanctuary* and *The Hamlet,* the latter just published to a chorus of jeers). Scott Fitzgerald, dead in 1940, was practically forgotten. Edmund Wilson had been nominated for the office, but had refused to run. The general prediction was that either John Dos Passos or Thomas Wolfe, dead in 1938, would be regarded as the Great American Writer of his generation.

Prophecies made today are likely to be just as mistaken. It seems to me that hardly any writer now in his thirties or forties has *as yet* produced the considerable body of distinguished work that would qualify him for the office. But several authors are still in the running, and running hard, though I won't try to make a complete or considered list. Some obvious names are those of J. D. Salinger, Saul Bellow, John Cheever, William Styron, Robert Lowell (for the Great American Writer needn't be a novelist), and perhaps I should mention younger men like Philip Roth and John Updike.

Sincerely yours,
Malcolm Cowley

P.S. Robert Frost is still here.

[NL TL/CC-2]
[TO: KEN KESEY]
August 24, 1962

Dear Ken,

Since a long talk with the Viking lawyer three weeks ago, I hadn't kept up to date on Gwen Davis's libel suit.[25] When I got your letter and was stirred up by it, I went in to see Helen Taylor and ask her why the hell Viking had to settle a suit that was preposterous on the face of it. Helen was on the phone talking to the lawyer at the moment, and he explained to her once again the sad mathematics of the case.

Let's say that Viking decided to fight it out in court, what would have to be done? The lawyer would have to go to California to gather evidence in your behalf, talk to the people who would support you with affidavits, and later bring them to New York to testify. Viking would have to hire detectives to obtain all possible information about Gwen Davis both in California and New York. A preliminary hearing would be held at the Viking lawyer's office, where G.D. would answer questions under oath, and where representatives of Viking would answer questions under oath, and where representatives of Viking would be questioned under oath by her lawyer. The answers to all questions would become part of the court record. When the case would come up is anybody's guess, but probably it wouldn't be for more than a year from now, since the courts here are slow and crowded.

Sending a lawyer to California and hiring detectives are preliminary steps that couldn't be omitted, because the defense would have to be absolutely solid. The lawyer's guess is that Viking would win the case. His guess is also that total costs would run between $50,000 and $70,000, which you would be liable for by terms of the contract. (Incidentally that clause about authors' having to pay the costs of libel suits is part of every publisher's contract, put there in self-defense. Publishers are sitting ducks for libel suits.) I can picture you shelling out that big money, or rather I can't, and I can picture how happy the Viking stockholders would be when paying the bill for legal expenses. Of course if Gwen Davis did win the suit—and never underestimate the malignant power of a woman—there would be damages to pay as well.

So that's why lawyers almost always advise, "Settle the suit if you can, it's a lot cheaper." It does leave a bad feeling in the belly, but at least the business is over and finished and there's nothing worse to come. You can get back to work instead of wasting a year thinking about the trial.

[...]

So that's the discouraging report they gave me. About the only happy side of it is that G.D. will get God-damned little money out of her suit, even if the settlement should amount, as it probably will, to a good deal more than the $5000 you are being asked to pay. Her lawyer is likely to get most of it, and all she'll have is the satisfaction of having done you harm. That won't last long, and she'll go back to living in her G.D. private hell. My worry is about you and about whether this outrageous business will interfere with your finishing the novel. Viking is all on your side, and is doing its best to ease the financial burden on you, by going beyond the contract and assuming what promises to be more than half of the cost of defending the G.D. suit. I'm writing as a friend, not as an associate of Viking, but what we all hope and trust is that the new novel will wipe out all your obligations and make you prosperous for the first time—and no more roller washing for your wife.

As ever,

Malcolm Cowley

[NL TL/CC-1]

[TO: SEAN O'CRIADAIN, PUBLICITY DIRECTOR,

SIMON AND SCHUSTER]

September 29, 1962

Dear Mr. O'Criadain:

"O'Grady" would that have been, in the bad old days?

I want to thank you very belatedly for sending me a copy of Doris Lessing's THE GOLDEN NOTEBOOK. I'm slow to get round to reading long novels, but this one impressed me more than any book I have read for a long time, because it goes deep and is unfailingly intelligent. She's marvelous on such interrelated subjects as radical politics, bedroom hostilities, and the hysterical coolness of some Americans—though in this last case she seems to be basing her generalities on blacklisted Hollywood writers [...]. It's a marvelous mixed-up book in which the real theme is writer's block, and the cure for writer's block is presenting the notes for all the novels that one didn't get written—but what wonderful scenes from each of them, especially the African scenes. That pigeon hunt! And those nightmares at the end of the book!—I haven't read another novel in which the brink of madness was Leica-photographed and put on tape.

It's curious that the ex-Communist novel (which this is too) has never been done in this country with the same quality of moral imagination that one sometimes (but not often) finds in European writers—as note Koestler and what's-his-name who wrote *The Burning Bush*.[26] Compare this book with [Clancy Sigal's] *Going Away* or [Norman Mailer's] *Barbary Shore*, perhaps the two best American ex-Communist novels, and you'll see what I mean. Miss Lessing is in better control of her material, and I think she gets more of the truth told.

Well, it's too late for anything I say to furnish quotes for advertising, and perhaps too late for advertising the book, but I've been doing what I can to spread the word that THE GOLDEN NOTEBOOK has to be read.

Cordially yours,
Malcolm Cowley

[YUL TLS-1]
[TO: COMMITTEE ON ADMISSIONS, THE CENTURY ASSOCIATION]
January 3, 1963

Gentlemen,

Red Warren tells me that he and Archie MacLeish have nominated Ralph Ellison for membership in the Century. That strikes me as a very good idea, and I consider it a privilege to write one of the sponsoring letters.

Ellison, now in his late forties, is the author of only one novel, *The Invisible Man* [*sic*] (1952), but that is a very good novel which won the National Book Award and has become something of a contemporary classic. Besides publishing a good many stories and magazine articles, he tells me that he now has a second novel ready for publication; he is a slow and conscientious workman who wants all his work to be distinguished. He has taught on temporary assignments at many colleges and universities (Princeton,

Antioch, Bennington, among others), has served as vice president of P.E.N., and from 1955 to 1957 held the Rome fellowship of the American Academy of Arts and Letters. That last award proved to be a happy one both for the AAAL and for the American Academy in Rome, which sometimes has a hard time maintaining good relations among its talented but heterogeneous collection of fellows; Ellison was one man whom everybody liked and respected. I know that since then the American Academy in Rome has called on him for advice on at least one critical occasion.

So you can picture him as friendly, serious, witty on occasion, personally attractive (and with an attractive wife), soft-spoken, level-headed, and deeply devoted to the art of writing. I think he would make an admirable Centurion.

Quite properly Red Warren didn't say one thing in his nominating letter, [. . .] but I feel like using this private occasion to make some general remarks. We haven't any Negro members at present, and that fact has disturbed me. As a matter of principle we ought to recognize the achievements of Negroes in the arts (or better we should recognize that race is not a criterion of achievement). Also, on a lower and more practical level, the fact of not having Negro members leaves us open to embarrassment, as witness the front-page stories last year about the Cosmos Club in Washington. If something like that came up at the Century, which God forbid, the chances are that some of our members holding public offices might feel called upon to resign with a splash. Electing a Negro member now, and preferably more than one, would be a sort of insurance policy against the possibility of our being dragged into the prints.

In the field of literature Ellison is obviously the best choice (coming ahead of Langston Hughes, who also has much to recommend him). Besides strongly urging his election, I should also hope that the nomination could be processed with, if I remember the Court's phrase, "all judicious speed." Ellison would be in all ways a credit to the Century.

Sincerely yours,
Malcolm Cowley

[NL TL/CC-I]
[TO: RICHARD GEHMAN][27]
February 16, 1963

Dear Dick,

If I'm not too late with a comment on Mailer . . . try this on your pianola:

"Norman Mailer is a very talented writer who keeps flogging and spurring himself to produce a superequine burst of speed, as if he were both a racehorse and its jockey. Sometimes he does produce the burst of speed, as in parts of *The Deer Park,* and sometimes the horse stumbles. The danger is that it might founder. But either it will win a big race or the jockey will drop out of it. Never being content to ride a selling plater."

(What I mean—Mailer is very good by natural endowment, but not a genius like Auden in his early years or Faulkner until 1942. He's trying to get more out of himself than he is capable of giving, but sometimes, by God, he gets it.)

[. . .]

Yours, as ever,
Malcolm Cowley

[NL TL/CC-I]
[TO: WALLACE STEGNER]
May 10, 1963

Dear Wally,

[. . .] I'd been meaning to write you for a long time, though there's nothing special to report, and your letter was a welcome occasion for sitting down at the typewriter. Nothing special? Well, all those deaths, one after another, leaving great unhappy gaps in my acquaintanceship. Van Wyck's was especially painful, because the doctors knew he was an incurable case since last September. Gladys kept him alive by force of will, and nursing, and blood transfusions. We're fond of Gladys, a gay, spunky soul, frivolous still, as when she was a beautiful young woman, but now a great deal more considerate of others—we love her and wonder what she's going to do now. Administer the papers, I suppose. The funeral was impressive. Van Wyck's old friends had gathered from all over the East, some crawling out of dens where they existed in forgottenness, deaf, lame—others wearing success like a suit of Bond Street clothes—this was a gathering of the literary clan. Everybody remarked on how much Van Wyck's life in Bridgewater was like Emerson's in Concord. He received the same sort of adoration from his neighbors. After the services we crossed the street to the Brooks house, where a couple of hundred mourners were served a huge luncheon as an offering from the Bridgewater ladies.

[...]

As ever,
Malcolm

God damn it, they're wiping everybody out, and I'm beginning to feel like the last man alive on the raft.

Cowley to Robert Penn Warren, February 28, 1963 [RPW]

[NL TL/CC-I]
[TO: ELIZABETH AMES]
July 16, 1963

Dear Elizabeth,

These last two years have been the saddest I have known for illness and deaths among my friends. Hemingway, Faulkner, Thurber, Cummings, all gone as if a generation were being swept off the boards. And somewhat younger people too—I think I told you that Nathan Asch had an operation for lung cancer in the winter. He wasn't strong when I was on the coast last March, and hasn't answered a letter I wrote him shortly after; the best I can hope is that he's mad at me. Conrad Aiken had a heart attack in January and is still convalescing; we visited him on the Cape last week. Now Hamilton Basso is in a New Haven hospital; the doctors found a shadow on the X-ray of his lung and will probably operate. I'm going to see him tomorrow

morning. It's against this dreadful background that one thinks about Newton and Van Wyck Brooks.

[. . .]

As ever,

Malcolm

———

[NL TL/CC-2]
[TO: HARRY T. MOORE, EDITOR,
SOUTHERN ILLINOIS UNIVERSITY PRESS]
August 14, 1963

Dear Mr. Moore,

[. . .]

I was more pleased with the completed manuscript [of *After the Genteel
Tradition*][28] than I had expected to be. It seems to me that it is almost the
only history we have of the rebel generation of American writers after 1910
[. . .]. Outside of its value as literary history, the book also has some value as
a historical document, a record [. . .] of what the younger critics were saying
in 1937. For that reason I made a point, in the course of the revision, of not
changing the opinions I had expressed, and of not asking the other contributors to change theirs.

[. . .]

Revising the book set me to thinking about the nature and ideals of criticism in the 1930s. It was supposed to be social and political, and was indeed
that, as note Cantwell's judgment of Upton Sinclair. But to an even greater
extent it became moral criticism, the chief moral standard being (as we didn't
know then) Albert Schweitzer's: whether a work was life-enhancing or life-
diminishing (as note Trilling's judgment of O'Neill and Cather and Bishop's judgment of Hemingway's integrity); also there was the question
whether an author had faith, sympathy, love for the American masses and
hope for their future—pessimism was condemned almost as strongly as it
had been by the genteel critics twenty years before. My own slant [. . .] was
historical, but still applied these standards.

Another feature of criticism in the 1930s: With its interest in class
conflicts and the historical process and in authors as *representing* social

interests—with its emphasis on the meaning of moral decisions by the author—with its correct notion (though a lot of duffers never grasped the notion) that form and matter are interfused, or at least form and emotion, so that an author's withdrawal from society shows itself in the form of the work, as does his confusion or pessimism or faith—with these preoccupations it took broader views than criticism did in the 1950s and addressed itself to (though it did not always reach) a wider audience. It was weak on the connotative properties of language, though that weakness might have been counterbalanced if I had asked Kenneth Burke, for example, to contribute to the series.

[. . .] Now I have to get back to my book on the 1930s, which has progressed with all the speed of a semi-stationary starfish. [. . .]

Yours, as ever,
Malcolm Cowley

[NL TL/CC-I]
[TO: JOHN CHEEVER]
October 22, 1963

Dear John,

I read *The Wapshot Scandal* with pure delight—in your characters, in your firm and deceptively simple style, and most of all in your continual power of invention. Take the rector and his carol singers in the first chapter. It seems to me that nobody since Dickens has assembled such an outwardly commonplace but amazing group of people. You tell good stories one after another, and some you don't bother to tell; you throw them away like Honora passing out thousand-lira notes in Rome; you throw away more than most writers amass over the years by saving up their little inspirations, as if you didn't have to save, as if there were always more inventions coming from that inexhaustible store.

The terrible vision you have is of our daily lives in their emotional squalor and incongruity. You're getting angrier and angrier about them, so angry that you soar from the commonplace into the impossible, only stopping for an instant to twist the arm of coincidence. That riot of the housewives over the plastic eastern eggs: it's a Breughel vision of hell. I've been disturbed by the slowness of readers in realizing that your work is completely outside *The New Yorker* pattern or any other; that it's something unique in contemporary fiction. But they began to catch on in reading *The Wapshot Chronicle*, and with the *Scandal* I think they'll begin to realize that you're doing something special and entirely new.

[. . .] In fact I think the whole book is marvelous, and thousands and thousands of readers are going to feel the same way. [. . .]

As ever,
Malcolm

Jacqueline has been superb, like a Roman wife of Republican times, the only person in these sad proceedings who hadn't her eyes fixed on the TV cameras and who was utterly devoted to grief.

Cowley to Elizabeth Ames, November 29, 1963 [NL]

[AA ALS-I; DRAFT]
[TO: MRS. JOHN F. KENNEDY,
THE WHITE HOUSE, WASHINGTON D.C.]
November 27, 1963

Dear Mrs. Kennedy,

It is late now to express my shock and grief and horror at the President's death, or my admiration for your devotion and courage. There is something else, however, that will [never] be too late or early to put [on record]. Something not only for myself but for all the artists, writers, and composers in the Institute, and indeed for the country. I want to tell you how deeply grateful I am for what your husband did (and for the way you stood beside him) in giving a wider recognition for the arts in America. All of us, great and small, have benefited from his efforts, and each one of us now feels overwhelmed by a personal loss.

Sincerely yours,
Malcolm Cowley,
President, the Institute

[NL TL/CC-I]

[TO: FRANCIS BROWN, *THE NEW YORK TIMES BOOK REVIEW*]

August 3, 1964

Dear Francis,

With considerable hesitation I am sending you a short-enough answer to Frederick Crews' furious blast against James Gould Cozzens.[29] The hesitation is owed to your custom of sending along such letters to the reviewer for a simultaneous reply. Crews will simply use the opportunity to stick another knife into me, after setting me down as a literary and social conservative by implication, waiting for revenge on the avant-garde, and also by implication as a Goldwater Republican [. . .]—But I thought that I ought to say something, if only for the honor of the *Times Book Review*. My 1957 piece on Cozzens was a moderate one and a good one, and I'll stand by every word of it. [. . .]

As ever,

Malcolm Cowley

. . .

TO THE EDITOR:

Since I find myself in the line of fire of Frederick C. Crews's furious attack on James Gould Cozzens in your issue of Aug. 2, I had better answer some of Mr. Crews's allegations.

My review of *By Love Possessed* in these pages was not among the madly enthusiastic ones. I questioned whether *B.L.P.* was the best of Cozzens's 12 novels (my choice would be *Guard of Honor*). Among other reservations I said of his style that it "used to be as clear as a mountain brook: now it has become a little weedgrown and murky, like the brook when it wanders through a meadow."

I did not quote Mr. Cozzens's statement about his conservative beliefs "with seeming approval." I simply quoted it. For Mr. Crews's information, I do not recommend or agree with Cozzens's position. I am not a Republican or an Episcopalian or one of the landed gentry or "strongly antipathetic," as Cozzens says he is, "to all political and social movements."

I don't know how Cozzens will vote in the next election, but his conservatism seems to me quite far from Goldwater Republicanism (which is, of course, a political and social movement). The social class for which he speaks is composed of old-line families living near the Eastern seaboard and dependent for their incomes on such professions as medicine, the law, the ministry, or the Army. By contrast many of the Goldwater enthusiasts—those we regard as typical of the movement—are Southwestern businessmen with a great deal of new money. Also they are zealots "by love possessed," in the special sense that Cozzens has attached to the phrase: that is, they seem to be ruled by passion rather than reason. Where Cozzens is conservative, many of their proposals impress me as being appallingly radical.

Of course the real question is whether Cozzens should be convicted and sentenced to exile from American literature on the basis of his political opinions, his religious affiliations, his membership in an ethnical minority, the Wasps, and his alleged (sometimes on dubious evidence) prejudice against other groups—among which Mr. Crews mentions "Jews, Negroes, Catholics, middle Europeans, women, homosexuals, adolescents, and so on," a pretty wide-ranging list—or whether his accomplishments as a novelist should be more seriously considered before judgment is rendered. His books are as solidly built and filled with harvest as a Pennsylvania Dutch barn. *By Love Possessed* is not the best of them, but most of his fellow novelists would regard it as an enviably difficult achievement. . . . From a purely structural point of view, I don't know that any other American novelist has equaled it.

MALCOLM COWLEY
Sherman, Conn.

[NL TL/CC-I]
[TO: GALWAY KINNELL]
Yaddo, Saratogo Springs, NY,
October 8, 1964

Dear Galway,

Here at Yaddo for a couple of weeks, I remembered with a pain like gas on the stomach that I hadn't written to thank you for sending me *Flower Herding on Mount Monadnock*. It is something quite rare in contemporary literature, the poetry of a man who lives *alone*, who lives *in the woods*, and who projects himself into *whatever grows and dies*. By contrast most of our contemporary poetry is urban, mental, and lonely by accident, not by preference. There are several of your poems that I liked particularly, and it is a pleasure to set down their names:

"The River That Is East"	"Calcutta Visits," particularly the
"Doppelgänger"	first two stanzas
"Room of Return"	"Tillamook Journal" (magnificent)
"Spindrift" (beautiful for the way the dead things take life in the old man)	

—But there isn't much use specifying when the whole book, New England, New York, France, India, Japan (scene of what seem to me the weakest poems), and Oregon, is held together by the same style and vision.

Have you finished your Villon?[30] I'm eager to see it.

As ever,
Malcolm Cowley

———————

[NL TL/CC-I]
[TO: JOSEPH MITCHELL][31]
November 3, 1964

Dear Joe,

You can imagine that I read with fascination your two-part article on Joe Gould. I could have told you a few more stories about him, especially the one about his crucifixion on Christmas Eve at my flat (1920)—but that one's unprintable—and the very long story about the Blake and the fountain pens he stole from me. And his compliment to my then newly married wife: "Muriel, I'd rather have insomnia with you than sleeping sickness with the Queen of Sheba." And the time I was out of the *New Republic* office on account of a broken arm, so that there was a question about Joe's weekly dollar. Otis Ferguson, who took my place, said he wouldn't give Joe a dollar unless he brought in something to print on the correspondence page. So Joe brought a poem:

Dear God, save Malcolm Cowley from harm,
Or at least break his neck instead of his arm.

I wonder what was the moment or year when the Oral History changed
from being an honest project into a fraud and self-delusion. It was perfectly
serious in the beginning and had other chapters, probably many other chapters, than those you saw. Joe showed me a couple of his notebooks, and I remember a long chapter about the American Presidents, actually from oral
sources. But I thought the stuff was dull and worthless and didn't ask to see
other notebooks. How could he compile a history of the world from oral
sources when most of the time he didn't listen to anyone but himself? I
would guess that the Oral History became fraudulent at some time in the
period 1925–30. In 1930 Joe was off his rocker for a while and came near being put away; that may have been a turning point. After that his creative
work consisted of two-line poems, maybe enough of them to fill two printed
pages, and remarks, some of which are worth preserving. And you *have*
preserved a lot of them in your articles on Joe. Those future generations may
say that Joe Gould was a figment of your imagination.
  [. . .]

Yours, as ever,
Malcolm Cowley

———

[NL TL/CC-I]
[TO: ROBERT PENN WARREN]
November 23, 1964

Dear Red,
  Something has come up that I need your advice about. The Southern
Literary Festival at the University of Mississippi. They tell me you're invited
as one of the speakers, with Eudora Welty, Ruth Ford, and others, so I won't
go into the story of this Tribute to William Faulkner—except to say that
one of my former students, Robert Canzoneri, strongly urged me to accept
the invitation. He said that Evans Harrington, who issued it, was one of the
liberals on the Mississippi faculty. The question that bothers me is whether

the Festival will *in fact* be segregated. Snick[32] and other groups will probably make a fuss about it in any case. But if it's not a truly segregated affair—if even one Negro will be present—I'd say to hell with Snick in this case. It's a good thing, it's almost a moral duty, to support any efforts to reunite Mississippi with the rest of the world. I'll be at Vanderbilt the day before the Festival, so I could easily get to Oxford on April 23. I'll accept or refuse the invitation as a matter of principle, not of convenience. What do you think that principle dictates in this case?[33]

As ever,
Malcolm

———————

[NL TL/CC-I]
[TO: DAVID MADDEN, *THE KENYON REVIEW*]
(As of) 2301 Bryant St.,
Palo Alto, Calif. 94301,
December 24, 1964

Dear Mr. Madden,

[...]

What I was thinking about, vaguely, for *Kenyon* was another big horsd'oeuvre called "The Sense of Guilt" in which I tried to analyze as candidly as I could the sense of guilt that plagues many survivors of the 1930s, and its connections with the war, lost by both sides, between the so-called Stalinists and the so-called Trotskyites. One finds echoes of the war today in a good deal of critical writing, for example when Robert Brustein, a sort of second-generation Trotskyite, lams into Arthur Miller as an ex-Stalinist. I considered all this at some length, about 7000 words, and it might be something of interest to the readers of *Kenyon*. Incidentally it tries to be fair to everyone. Would you like to have a look at it?[34]

[...]

Cordially yours,
Malcolm Cowley

———————

[NL TL/CC-1]

[TO: ALBERT ERSKINE, RANDOM HOUSE]
2301 Bryant St.,
Palo Alto, Calif. 94301,
January 26, 1965

Dear Albert,

Cormac McCarthy is a new talent, and I congratulate you on finding him. Of course there are weaknesses in *The Orchard Keeper:* memories of Faulkner and too many strings of plot that haven't been knotted. But he tells a story marvelously, with a sort of baresark joy as he rushes into scenes of violence. He loves the countryside and makes us feel how a poor boy grew up loving it; everything comes alive. And he also loves language in the way that Faulkner did. I look forward with anticipatory pleasure to his next novel.

[...]

Yours, as ever,
Malcolm Cowley

I'm beginning to have a warm feeling about all us survivors of the 1920s. We've been through a hell of a lot together. We all belonged to the same chapter of the same fraternity, in the days when serious American writers weren't more numerous than the members and residents of a college fraternity house.

Cowley to Kenneth Burke, February 4, 1965 [NL]

[KAP TLS-2]
[TO: KATHERINE ANNE PORTER]
(As of) Sherman, Conn. 06784,
March 9, 1965

Dear Katherine Anne,

[. . .] I am distressed about your objection to what I wrote in *Exile's Return*.[35] Here is every word of the reference to you, to refresh your memory:

> "Each life has its own pattern, within the pattern of the age, and every individual is an exception. Katherine Anne Porter was a newspaper woman in the Southwest before she went to Mexico and worked for the revolutionary government; Mexico City was her Paris and Taxco was her South of France."

I only meant that the general pattern of the age was one of departure and return (or even, to use fancier words, alienation and reintegration. Yes, yes, you *were* moderately alienated from the American life of the time, in your own fashion, it's true, but still with a cousinly resemblance to the sense of alienation that the rest of us felt). But, to continue the exegesis, whereas most writers of the time went streaming to Paris and the South of France, you went to Mexico and did some serious work for the revolutionary government there.

I was completely wrong about Taxco; didn't mean to be; hadn't imagined that our ex-votoed trip there was your first (I wonder if that painting still exists).

Now, the difficulty in making corrections is that Viking will let me patch a plate or two, but would howl about changes that involved the resetting and replating of a dozen pages. So I'll have to do everything briefly. How would it be if I made the passage read:

> "Each life has its own pattern, within the pattern of the age, and every individual is an exception. Katherine Anne Porter was a newspaper woman in the Southwest before she went to Mexico and worked for the revolutionary government; she never thought of herself as one of the exiles."

There will be other printings in paperback of *Exile's Return,* and I hope they carry a reading that meets your approval.

[...]

As ever,
Malcolm

[NL TL/CC-1]
[TO: HIRAM HAYDN, HARCOURT, BRACE & WORLD]
June 10, 1967 [1965]

Dear Hiram:

[...]

Here's the story. Kenneth and I, thinking of our unrequited pasts, decided that the American Writers' Congress in 1935 was one of the key episodes. Perhaps it was the windrow on the beach that marked the high tide of radical sentiment among American writers in the 1930s. Both of us played considerable parts in the Congress. I was a member of the organizing committee. Kenneth read a paper on "Revolutionary Symbolism in America" that now seems to be the soundest thinking that came out of the Congress. He was reviled, excoriated, and utterly crushed by a chorus of radical critics, including Joe Freeman and Mike Gold—that was a dramatic episode—but a few months later the Communist Party Line veered round to his position.

[...] My notion was that the whole business could be set up as a symposium for *The American Scholar,* like that other, and successful, and often quoted, symposium on The New Critics.[36] The point would be to bring in a couple of other people, say Joseph Freeman and Granville Hicks, besides someone to act as moderator, either yourself or Dan Aaron. [...] I think we could produce something of interest to the 1960s. [...]

[...]

As ever,
Malcolm Cowley

[NL TL/CC-I] [SC 352]
[TO: KENNETH BURKE]
September 5, 1965

Dear Kenneth,

[. . .] [W]e're spending two days on the Cape. We had dinner yesterday with the Aikens, and in half an hour we're going there for lunch; the other guests will be Francis Biddle and his wife. Conrad is becoming grumpier in his convictions; at present he's supporting Johnson in the Vietnam business, and we have to keep away from that topic of conversation. Historical parallel: the argument in litry circles about the Philippines in 1900. Vietnam is worse than the Philippines, in its probable consequences, but for some reason I haven't been able to get excited. I must be losing my capacity for social indignation. Being utterly convinced that the human race is going to extinguish itself by poisoning the soil, the water, the air, possibly even before it blows the world up. I believe in Henry Adams's law of acceleration. Things are moving faster and faster—toward what, if not extinction?

[. . .]

As ever,
Malcolm

[NL TL/CC-I]
[TO: ROBERT CANZONERI][37]
December 1, 1965

Dear Bob,

[. . .] My little book is almost finished—"The Faulkner-Cowley File" is the tentative title—and it reprints the whole correspondence, except for two or three sentences that Estelle Faulkner wouldn't like, and I think it makes it clear that I did what Faulkner wanted me to do, and he wholly approved. If everything goes well, it will be out next summer.

[. . .]

Working with the letters, I come to have a greater & greater admiration for Faulkner as a person. His great problem was how to get his work done in spite of the "person on business from Porlock"—that's why he was sometimes rude; but he did the work. Even drinking was for him a form of self-defense. Now Porlock is trying to take him over.

[...]

Yours, as ever,
Malcolm Cowley

The Sixties: Retrospection and Consolidation, 1966–1970

With advancing age, Cowley felt new urgency to consolidate his literary legacy. On July 20, 1966 *The Faulkner-Cowley File* was published by Viking Press. It was widely and favorably reviewed. Coming twenty years after *The Portable Faulkner*, it served to bring Cowley's efforts on behalf of Faulkner to the attention of the public and, with English, French, and Japanese editions following shortly after, confirmed his international standing as one of America's preeminent literary critics. In early 1967 *Think Back On Us*, Henry Dan Piper's compilation of Cowley's 1930s pieces, was published by Southern Illinois University Press. Cowley was eager (and anxious) for the reviews: hoping for good ones, he also thought, as he wrote to Burke on January 7, that he could "hear the *Partisan* knives on the whetstone." Its publication led to critical self-reflections yet also appeared to confirm his belief that not all of his efforts at writing had been wasted. The publication strengthened his resolve to return to his book on the 1930s and to put his poems in final shape for a projected volume of collected poems.

As always, he promoted the work and reputation of friends and acquaintance he thought deserved greater recognition, like Burke and S. Foster Damon, and lobbied to get them elected to honorific bodies like the American Academy or the Century Association. He was particularly cheered when his longtime friend Burke was elected to the Academy in 1967. That same year, on the occasion of the fiftieth anniversary of America's entry into World War I, Cowley was asked by the National Institute to speak on the effects of the war on American literature. The talk he wrote became the opening chapter of *A Second Flowering* (1973). In late 1967, he was appointed chancellor of the American Academy. And as former Institute president he advised his successor, Allen Tate, about Institute affairs, insisting that the membership be made more representative and inclusive: "We are always in danger of becoming an Eastern and Southern Institute of Arts and Letters. People get elected to the literary department because their work has been favorably reviewed in the *Times Book Review*. Westerners don't stand much chance" (January 27, 1968).

From mid-January 1968 the Cowleys spent three months in Mexico, thanks to a National Endowment for the Arts fellowship. There Cowley revised old and composed new poems for *Blue Juniata: Collected Poems* (1968). The volume was well received and brought Cowley further kudos, including a poetry reading at the Library of Congress and, more memorable perhaps, a public performance, in August 1968, at the Sherman Playhouse, where he was honored with a silver plate for services to the town—not as poet but as chairman of the Zoning Board. Such honors were overshadowed by tragedy in Allen Tate's family, when one of his twin sons, eleven months old, choked to death on a toy.

As more and more members of his literary generation passed away, Cowley's letters reflect the growing belief that he was bound to his peers through an intuitive mode of understanding, whereas, he attested, empathy with younger writers demanded greater intellectual effort. Though he actively endorsed younger writers, like his former student Larry McMurtry and (with reservations) the poet Frank O'Hara, and responded with qualified enthusiasm to the Caribbean writer Paule Marshall's novel *The Chosen Place, the Timeless People* (1969), mostly he felt out of touch with the newer fiction and was disturbed by its self-exhibitionism and solipsism. To Conrad Aiken he observed on July 9, 1967: "In the litry world all the news appears to be hip, beat, or psychedelic. It's a new world in which the books themselves seem long-haired and bearded, and I don't know that I feel at home in it."

As the literary field was changing and new critical paradigms developing, Cowley continued to speak up in defense of his own (now often beleaguered) generation, in letters, lectures, and essays. At grumpier moments, he found it hard to sympathize with the New Left and the student rebellions in the universities, which he witnessed firsthand during teaching stints at the University of California at Irvine and Berkeley and at Stanford. A member of the establishment, now in his seventies, he was irked by their "high moral pronouncements" and driven into "an embittered conservatism," as he wrote to Aiken on July 23, 1969.

The year 1970 saw the publication of a second compilation of Cowley's more substantial essays, again edited by Piper, *A Many-Windowed House*. Work on the volume prompted Cowley to reflect on his own approach to literature and criticism and to consider the influences on his own writing, with Wilson, Burke, and Valéry looming large in his view. With Howard Hugo, Cowley compiled an anthology of famous passages from famous novels, *The Lesson of the Masters* (1971).

[NL TL/CC-1]
[TO: KENNETH BURKE]
April 5, 1966

Dear Kenneth,

[...] I feel happy about the prospect of time at home to get some work done. At our age that's the important thing—to get the stuff into books and the books on library shelves. [...]

I saw Allen [Tate] in town last week. He's divorced from Isabella,[38] but it isn't true, as the old biddies are saying at Princeton, that he seduced a nun. They had him tearing off her wimple and lifting her black serge skirts. Actually he did have, maybe still is having, and affair with an ex-nun, but she had long ago been released from her vows by the Pope. He doesn't plan to marry her; he says that 34 years of difference in ages are too many years. But isn't that old classicist the wildest romantic, even at 66?—The curious thing about Allen is that he has become so good (in another sense) during the last ten years. By goodness I'm thinking of the French *bonté*, the desire to do services for his friends and not-friends and casual strangers. He even makes a point of *speaking* kindly about people, something he never used to do; the suppression of malice takes the salt out of his conversation.

Yestreen I sat up until four o'clock doing a piece for *Book Week*.[39] The absolutely insane feature of that debauch of work—followed by Muriel's taking the piece into NY—is that I'm almost certain it is a wasted effort; the piece will be too late and too long. But I wanted to do some more work on Valéry in preparation for an introduction that I promised to write two years ago. Valéry is someone I don't think you read, and you ought to. You know the story: that he abandoned a literary career at the age of 21 and spent the next 20 years doing nothing but keeping notebooks (in addition to holding down a rather easy job). He worked on the notebooks from 6 to 10 every morning, and in the end there were 257 of them. The literary world forgot him—then suddenly he reappeared (at Gide's urging) in 1917 and began pouring out a flood of books. All his prose was written to order; he'd take a commission for so many characters (which the French count instead of words) and fill the commission without joy but with superb skill. The notebooks had given him a framework of ideas that were applicable to almost any subject. He should be the saint of all hack writers, the exemplar of the dream that they can do works of genius to order.

Page end. Letter ended.

As ever,
Malcolm

———

[NL TL/CC-I]
[CONRAD AIKEN]
July 21, 1966

Dear Conrad,

They held a funeral service for Delmore [Schwartz] on Monday. I didn't attend it, because of my bad knee, but I got an account of it from Catherine Carver, who was present and who talked with Delmore's friends and ex-friends. Nobody had seen him during the past year, except for casual brief meetings on the street. Apparently he was very far out. He stayed all day in his fleabag room and wrote. The printed account of his death produced a very old uncle and aunt, who took charge of the body. Several others besides yourself offered to help pay for the funeral, but the expenses were finally paid by New York University, where it seems that he taught for a time. The service was badly announced, so that there were only a few people present when it started, but others kept hurrying in, until the chapel was full. The rabbi was flowery and fairylike. Brief speeches were made by Fred Dupee, M. L. Rosenthal, and Dwight Macdonald.

Delmore's first wife, Gertrude Buckman, said a long time ago, "The trouble with Delmore is that he isn't Shakespeare." He wanted very hard to be Shakespeare. He was terrifyingly ambitious, not for himself, but for his work, and I used to feel that he drove himself crazy. For a long time he lived on a diet of alcohol, sleeping pills that didn't work, and Dexedrine, a dangerous mixture. He had a quantity of unprinted writing, including the enormous torso of an unfinished novel; I heard that there were two filing cabinet drawers full of manuscript, and I wonder what's going to happen to it.

[...]

Poor Delmore. Once I was instrumental in getting him the Bollingen Award, in a year that Cal Lowell had also published a book. I argued to the other jurors, "Look, Lowell will publish other books and he's certain to get the award some time, but this is Delmore's last chance." The award was for his impressive book of collected poems.

I'm sending you a copy of *The Faulkner-Cowley File.* You'll find your name mentioned several times in the course of the narrative, and I learned from various sources that you had a great influence on him; he started reading you very early. I didn't tell your story about his quoting "The Morning Song of Forslin"—no, it was "Music I heard with you was more than music," with your rejoinder. My story was getting solemn at that moment, with a funeral march being played offstage, and I felt that it wasn't the place for even a good joke.

[...]

Malcolm

[NL TL/CC-2]
[TO: MARY HEMINGWAY]
August 14, 1966

Dear Mary,

It was a funny correspondence I had with Faulkner. At the beginning of it I sensed that he was feeling pretty discouraged about his lack of recognition, and I fed him every nice remark that I heard about his work, in the effort to buck him up. That was something I never felt was necessary with

Ernest. I wanted Faulkner to write to Ernest; the exchange of letters would have been marvelous and it would have given Faulkner some of the reassurance that he needed at the time. They were curiously alike in some of their tastes—even in some of their subjects, as I said at one point—but with the polar difference that Faulkner was a small man physically, with a small man's distrust of the world in which he never knew who would turn out to be a bully. I wonder if that was one reason for his extreme courtesy—was he saying, in effect, "I'll be courteous to you, and you be courteous to me"? But he could also be damned rude to strangers, especially those he suspected of trying to invade his privacy. I was damned reticent in the book. Partly that was because the text had to be approved by Faulkner's daughter (who gets half the royalties), but mostly because of his extreme sense of privacy, which I respected even after his death, and because I was revolted by Hotchner's job on Ernest.[40]

[...]

I'm going to do a piece for *Esquire* on Hemingway in 1967. Not about Hotchner, but about some of the twerps who are attacking Ernest's literary reputation.[41] Some of them want to dismiss everything he wrote except a few short stories, after abolishing *For Whom the Bell Tolls* with a few bright remarks. Also they can't forgive Ernest for having lived a glamorous life, and when they speak of it they reveal a spiteful envy. I rather think I can have some fun with them—and I can do it without talking about the posthumous manuscripts.

About the unpublished manuscripts, I'm very eager to continue reading them, especially the Florida part of the big manuscript. What I want to find out for myself is whether it makes a continuous story that can and should be published as the next novel—leading up to and ending with the sea chase,—I keep thinking about that Garden of Eden manuscript which is so definitely unfinished. It contains not one but two marvelous long stories—the one about the boy in Africa you like so much, and the other, set in Hendaye, Andy's story about Nick and Barbara, leading up to Nick's accidental death and Barbara's suicide. I do think that both of those stories ought to be published in magazines and then in a new collection of Ernest's stories.[42]

If you invite me to lunch when you get back to NY, I'll accept like a shot.
[...]

As ever, ever,
Malcolm

———————

[NL TL/CC-I]
[TO: ROBERT COATES]
November 27, 1966

Dear Bob,

[...]

I never answered your long letter on Faulkner and Hemingway, principally because it would take so long to answer. Yes, Faulkner is pretty hard to
take until one gets used to him. I never said that *Pylon* was part of the
Yoknapatawpha story, and I never had much praise for it. *Sanctuary is* part
of the Yoknapatawpha story—the first part of it happens in the old Frenchman's place, marked on Faulkner's map of the country, and the trial and
lynching are in Jefferson, the county seat. I think it's a much better book
than you give it credit for being. But you haven't read two of the best books,
The Hamlet and *Go Down, Moses*. When I did the *Portable,* I was reacting
against the general neglect of Faulkner; that's why I didn't lay sufficient emphasis on his faults. Hemingway is a tougher problem. He was kind, generous, thoughtful, brave, and he was also (till about 1940) cowardly, and he
was also envious, spiteful, and on occasion mean as cat piss. I didn't say that
in the *Portable* or in the profile I did of Hemingway for *Life.* By that time I
had let myself get too damned involved with him, something a critic
shouldn't do. Somewhere around 1948–1950 he began to lose his sense of
reality. Why? We aren't ever going to know. It may have been drinking too
much, it may have been early senility, and I'm pretty sure that the process
was helped along by his getting knocked on the head so much, in one accident after another; he was punchy like an old fighter. The airplane accident
in Africa proved to be the final blow, but he seems to have made some apparent recoveries—for example, he had a good year in 1959, though when he
tried to write an account of that good year, he simply couldn't get it into

shape; he had lost his control. I conducted a great correspondence with him till 1951, but he was getting mean and suspicious, and I found that writing him letters was taking too much out of me. So I waited till he wrote me a beautiful letter, all griefs forgotten, and then I didn't answer it. Yet the funny thing is that everything nice ever said about him was true, was almost understated. I never met a more sympathetic, kind, understanding, perceptive, generous man. Or a meaner one when he was mean.

[...]

As ever,
Malcolm

———

[NL TL/CC-1]
[TO: KENNETH BURKE]
December 10, 1966

Dear Kenneth,

Just home from Academy luncheon. An enjoyable affair, as always for me. One sees a multitude of friends and wives of friends. This time a new wife, Allen Tate's—by maiden name Helen Heinz (Sister Helen?), who was a nursing sister and administrator when he met her; large, wide-apart, gray-green yellow eyes in a high-cheekboned rather Irish face. She was dispensed from her vows and remains a good Catholic, as Allen is a lapsed but still churchgoing Catholic. She is exactly ½ his age. [...] I like her and think this marriage has a better chance of success than the preceding one to Belle Gardner (of the blind Gardners, that is, without an "i," as Belle explained to me), who is, for all her excellent qualities, a fool and naive careerist.

Allen is a classicist, a traditionalist, an upholder of rigorous thinking, and at the same time the most incurably romantic character of our acquaintance. More romantic than Philip Roth, who got nicked for outrageous alimony, who loves beautiful *shickses*, but manages to resist most of those who besiege him. "Sometimes my head is harder than my cock," he explained to me, "but sometimes my cock is harder than my head." Allen's cock has been harder too damned often. At the same time he wants to be a good man. I said a long time ago of Allen and Caroline that Caroline was a Catholic but not a Christian, while Allen was Christian but a bad Catholic. Till forty he was as malicious as Caroline, almost, but then he began trying to be good to people. [. . .] Including you. Sadly he said that you have something against him, but of course, he added, you ought to be in the Academy—so he seconded your nomination and worked for your election and was as happy about it as he was about the election of John Ransom, with whom he has always been on excellent terms.

All this is a plea for you to nourish kindlier feelings toward Allen. It's a wonderful thing to have friends, or even old nonfriends, who you can be sure won't ever play you a dirty trick.

De Senectute was the theme of this year's elections to the Academy. Commager,[43] at 64, was the only adolescent. You are the next youngest. The other three are in their late seventies or early eighties. For next year we ought to look around for some representative of a slightly younger generation, and also, contrary to our professional instincts, for someone from another art than literature; painting, architecture, music. Self-interest, as opposed to the claims of friendship, requires that we make the membership of the Academy as distinguished as possible to confer honor on ourselves.

The one new subject introduced at the Academy meeting was a proposal to more or less amalgamate the Academy and the Institute, by making Institute members associate members of the Academy. The proposal comes from George Kennan,[44] who, as president of the Institute (and member of the Academy) has been somewhat appalled by the administrative complications of a double organization. On the other hand, I feel that it's good to have the smaller and more "elevated" organization as well as the larger one. [. . .]

Oh, hell, I'll stop at this point. I'm really happy about your election to the Academy. It's a reassuring tribute from one's colleagues, and it means that we can all have some fun together, if you'll just take some time out for having fun. I envy your projected trip home by boat. I look forward to seeing you in April and introducing you to half a dozen Centurions for afternoon drinks. It's only a formality. They'll elect you promptly unless you steal the spoons.[45]

I'll say, as in your telegram, your dear old friend.

As ever,

Malcolm

[NL TL/CC-I]
[TO: JOHN DOS PASSOS]
January 7, 1967

Dear Dos,

This letter on Institute Letterhead is a cry, not anguished, but still a cry for help. It seems that Allan Nevins[46] had a big idea, which was that the Academy should observe the Fiftieth anniversary of the First World War by having a paper written (and read) on the effects of the war on American literature. I became the sacrificial victim or little white goat by being invited to write the paper. It won't be long, but it will be illustrated by the reading of passages that reveal the effects of the war.

[. . .]

Some of them, I think, should be the absolutely familiar and obvious pieces like "I Have a Rendezvous with Death." Why not? As poetry it isn't much, but it helps to show that death, death was a central fact and determinant of emotion in the Great War and that the death wish and patriotism were often strangely confused. Then I might use a couple of Cummings' poems. There are early ones that expressed a purely aesthetic attitude to the war (did you feel it for a time in the ambulance service?), for example,

> at Roupy
> i have seen
> between barrages,
>
> the night utter ripe unspeaking girls,

and later ones that say to hell with aesthetics, like "i sing of Olaf." Then I think of your own statements, anger, hope, and mightn't one find as a constant thread your revulsion against the misuse of language by Meester Veelson and the four-minute orators? I think that determination to make the language clean explains a great deal about the literature of the twenties; your style, Hemingway's, even Wilson's critical prose.

[. . .] Can you, would you, suggest passages from your own work, or that of others, that I should read or have read?[47] [. . .]

As ever,
Malcolm

[NL TL/CC-I][SC 362–363]
[TO: KENNETH BURKE]
February 8, 1967

Dear Kenneth,

[. . .]

I humbly accept your comments on *Think Back on Us*[48] [. . .] I was accurate, but not profound. I had hold of one truth, which I overstressed, that we are all parts of one another; also that a good deal of one's energy is social energy, based on the consciousness of speaking for "us" and not only for "me." As you note in your letter, I understressed the other term of the dialectic, the "I." And I did not make the exagminations [*sic*] into meaning that I should have made. But now it's all part of the historical record.—Did you read my note at the end of the book? It sets forth my emphasis on construction, form, writing that led to (or was it compensation for?) a lesser interest in ideas.

[. . .]

Write me a poem!

As ever,
Malcolm

[NL TL/CC-I]
[TO: WILLIAM STYRON]
April 1, 1967

Dear Bill,

It was good of you to write me at length about *Think Back on Us*. I was happy to have a report from a novelist, and a good one, not just another damned critic. Seems to me that the critics have been running wild in recent years, not reporting on books, but trying to construct something else that will take the place of books. I was happiest when reporting what a novelist or a poet *did*, not what in my superior wisdom I thought he should have done. Every once in a while I slopped over in that other direction, and the results weren't good. The Thos Wolfe review, though it stated my honest opinion, could also be read as an exhortation to Wolfe to write about other people instead of just Thos Wolfe. He read it that way, he went up in the air (as I discovered from his letters), and he determined by God to show those critics and me in particular that he *could* write about other people. So, in his last two books, he killed off Eugene Gant (height, six feet eight) and made his new hero Monk Webber (height, five feet ten). But it didn't work. Monk Webber had all the perceptions of a six-foot-eighter, and the last books had all the faults of the early ones, with the added fault of something false in a hero. I guess a novelist (or a critic or a poet) can only be what he is, and if he *is* that completely, that's all we have a right to ask, and if what he is is a dolt, our only recourse is not to read him or report on his work except as a sort of Pure Food and Drugs label.

I don't mean by this that Wolfe was a dolt.

It was a happy experience for me to have somebody set to work collecting my old pieces and then to find after thirty years that they could still be read. I had pretty nearly killed myself writing them, figuratively, and in that falling-asleep episode, I pretty nearly killed myself unfiguratively. It seemed wonderful that all the work hadn't gone down the drain. Actually I like to think that I contributed something to the trade of book reviewing. It had been a pretty slapdash trade in the 1920s, and I like to think that by working harder at it myself I forced other people to work harder. Book reviewing in the 1960s is more sophisticated. Some damned good reviews are published. But also, as I said, the reviewers are taking too much pride in creation and are forgetting that they practice a secondary art, one that couldn't exist without novelists and poets worth writing about.

But thanks again for your letter.

As ever,
Malcolm

[NL TL/CC-I]
[TO: S. FOSTER DAMON]
April 11, 1967

Dear Foster,

I love you. And now I have a bad conscience about you, having put off the writing of that piece[49] month after month. [. . .] I rather hoped for a piece that I could also publish in a magazine, perhaps the *Saturday Review,* with its theme the fact that you have a genius for anonymity. But now I'll have to write memoirs, which come easier for me, with for theme the fact that you introduced one person after another, me included, to the delights and difficulties of modern literature (and music too, but I'm so incompetent in that field that I had better not intrude on it).

One of my guiding rules, often broken like others, has been never to offer excuses. But life itself, or age, is an excuse, isn't it? A bad knee, a tin ear, weakening eyes, arthritis, fatigue, all the rest of it—combined in my case with a weakness for taking on more jobs than I can ever finish. I'm working much harder and longer than I did when I was younger—why didn't I work harder then? I have to draw up schedules and assign priorities. The priority at present is Malcolm Cowley—not myself, but the person who signs my name to pieces that he painfully writes. I think that person should receive rather more credit than he has so far received, and so the other half of my divided personality tries to round out his work and get his books published. Then, with life smoked down to almost the butt and the remaining puffs rather bitter, I think of Muriel and my debt to her—I have to build up some sort of estate—and then I think of the people to whom I owe long-standing debts, yourself very high among them. I found a diary of 1918 in which some of our adventures were recounted. "September 16. Boston and Cambridge. Everyone was very much in the air. Foster invited me to Newton, but the first night I started to Dedham to stay with Jack [Wheelwright]. We had been dining at the Bourse and Jack was arrested and I spent the night with him in Brighton Jail, he turning the occasion to advantage with a poem. The next week I stayed with Foster and laid plans for the *Advocate*." I remember your room, and the piano with Satie on the rack, and the set of Casanova, one volume of which you read while standing naked in line waiting for your army physical. But how much I forget!

[...]

As ever,
Malcolm

[NL TL/CC-I]
[TO: LEWIS P. SIMPSON,[50] *THE SOUTHERN REVIEW*]
May 30, 1967

Dear Mr. Simpson,

I am a miserable correspondent. All during the month of May, which was a feverish one in this household, I was trying to finish a long piece about my old friend S. Foster Damon, for a *Festschrift* that is being presented to him on his umptieth or umpty-squillionth birthday. Everyone asks me, "Who is S. Foster Damon?" The answer is that he's the most self-effaced author in the country. He's the man who has never received credit for his work on Blake, which has been looted and pillaged by subsequent Blake scholars, or for his collection of American songs popular before the Civil War, again looted by every composer asked to do background music, and of course not for the years he spent on Thomas Holley Chivers. Foster's last book of poems was an absolute masterpiece of anonymity. Published in 1964, it has so far received not one review; it hasn't even been mentioned anywhere in "Books Received." Yet a number of better-known people—not only the Blake scholars, but E. E. Cummings, Virgil Thompson, John Brooks Wheelwright, myself, and others—are infinitely indebted to Foster. So I wrote about him at some length and eventually it came out as, I think, a very interesting piece—which again few people will read, buried as it will be in a *Festschrift*.[51]

[...]

Sincerely,
Malcolm Cowley

[NL TL/CC-I]
[TO: JACOB DAVIS]
June 1, 1967

Dear Jake,

I liked your candid letter, and I'll be just as candid in reply. Harvard when we went there was the most snobbish college in the country, at the end of its most snobbish period. Even Princeton was democratic by comparison, and Yale almost egalitarian. [...] Anti-semitism was the worst part of Harvard snobbery, but Jews weren't the only victims; the Irish were regarded in the same stand-offish fashion. Twenty years later an alumnus of the Fly Club raised a stink because the club had elected John F. Kennedy.

You had it, and I had it worse than you, because of a peculiar accident. An instructor named Freddie Schenk, very strong in the social world, developed a great enthusiasm for my work and passed down word that I should be cultivated. For one semester, spring of 1918, I *was* cultivated, though I wasn't elected to anything except the editorship of the *Advocate* and the Signet Society. But I was invited to the *Lampoon* punches and the *Crimson* punches and various other affairs that were actually amusing. Then I spent six months in Greenwich Village, got married, and was reputed to be a Red. When I came back to college, fall of 1919, I was treated as if I had smallpox. The powerful McVeagh family was after me and threatened to beat me up, just on principle. When I went to the Signet to eat because I had no money and could sign chits there, ice formed in the fireplace. Anyhow I had a complete view of the Harvard social system, going up and coming down. But it didn't leave me with a deep love for the class of 1919.

In a strange way I was grateful for the experience. I said to myself, "That's the way the world is. I'm glad I learned that at twenty instead of being an innocent all my life." But also I looked back nostalgically to our senior year at Peabody H.S., or rather the junior year [. . .]. Irish, Jew, Italian, Wasp, poor boy, rich boy, we didn't give a damn. It was certainly happier than Harvard.

[. . .]

As ever,
Malcolm

[RPW TLS-2]
[TO: ROBERT PENN WARREN]
July 9, 1967

Dear Red,

[. . .]

[. . .] I'm happy about the grant.[52] It means I can cut down on other work, appear less often at the Viking Press (maybe once a month), and finish some books. My God, did you know that I have a million words of uncollected

prose? [. . .] But I'm more interested at present in a collected volume of poems. The spirit hasn't stirred in me (as it stirs and earthquakes in you) to
write many new ones, but I have a curious mania for revising old ones, as if
I felt that each of the poems written long ago was begging me to chisel away
at the rough stone and give it a final form. I'm senilizing my juvenilia—or
would "senectutizing" be a nicer word?

[. . .]

[. . .] There is a new literary climate [. . .], long-haired and bearded in
prose and verse as well as in manners. I don't know that I feel at home in
it. I don't prospect any longer, I retrospect. I think the future of mankind
is short & getting shorter—we proliferate, we grow in bulk and stature
like some prehistoric species of animals on the brink of wiping themselves out by destroying their environment. Let's not think about it. Let's
enjoy the bounty that LBJ rains down on us along with the bombs on
you-know-where.

As ever,

Malcolm

[NL VIKING MEMO TL/CC-1]
[*September 4, 1967*]

A WESTERN READER

Frederick Manfred,[53] poor deluded giant, wrote me a long letter suggesting that I do a Portable Manfred. I squashed that idea. But he also sent
me a lot of material from small Western reviews, and that suggested another
idea that might be practicable.

The writers of the trans-Mississippi and cis-Sierran West—from Dakota
and Idaho south to Oklahoma and New Mexico—feel that they've been getting a dirty deal from Eastern publishers. They get together in conferences,
they publish papers, and they exalt their own serious achievements, mentioning great names like A. B. Guthrie, Vardis Fisher, Frederick Manfred,
Walter Van Tilburg Clark, Stegner (for some of his books), etc., etc. Well,
why not call their bluff by publishing a Western Reader, seriously edited, to
include the best of the writing about the prairies, the mountains, and the

desert—perhaps going back briefly to precursors like Cooper, Irving, Harte, but concentrating on Western writers of the present day? There would be a captive market for such a reader, not a big market, but a faithful one, consisting largely of state universities in the prairie and mountain states. It might do well later as a Portable.[54]

[. . .]

[GWA TLS-1]
[TO: GAY WILSON ALLEN][55]
Box 592, Hollins College,[56] Va. 24020,
September 29, 1967

Dear Gay,

It is heartening news that you are planning to do a life of Emerson. Rusk's big book[57] is so *dull*. I have to assign it to at least one student every time I give a seminar on Emerson, but I know he won't get anything out of it except facts. Rusk is good when he writes about the pears that Emerson raised. He is good enough on Emerson's last years, when he was as passive and benign as an October pumpkin, but no good at all, so bad as to be positively misleading, on the years of Emerson's first marriage, and his leaving the church, and his decisive trip to Europe. A real biography is needed, and you can do it.

When we both have time, I'd like to show you my notes on Emerson—they don't represent any original research (I read the *Journals* in the old edition), but they do reveal a considerable curiosity about RWE's mysticism and the extent to which he was influenced by Iamblichus, Proclus, and of course Plotinus, in Henry Taylor's translation. It comes to a sort of climax in a little-read essay, "The Method of Nature," which was an address delivered at Colby College on August 11, 1841, in which, several times, he uses the word "ecstasy" in its technical or mystical sense (yet I noted that he never laid claim to having had such an ecstasy). Until the middle 1840s he was a Neoplatonist in a pretty strict sense; why is that side of his thought always played down? After 1850 the practical Yankee began to take over; of course there were always those two sides to his nature.

But I'm merely trying to suggest one line of investigation, out of several. Your interest in the relation of an intellectual to the protest movements of his time is also very much to the point. The work on Emerson simply hasn't been done.[58]

[. . .]

Yours, as ever,
Malcolm

―――――

[NL TL/CC-I]
[TO: YVOR WINTERS]
Box 592,
Hollins College, Va. 24020,
November 18, 1967

Dear Yvor,

I greatly appreciate your generosity in sending me *Patterns for Discovery,* and it made me happy to learn that you had finished the book in spite of illness and every other interruption. Like every good book, it is first of all an act of courage. I have been reading it with steady interest and profit, and also with pained recognition of the gaps in my education. I'm weak, deplorably weak, in knowledge of the sixteenth-century lyric, and I felt that you were giving me a magisterial course in the poets from Wyatt to Donne. You wouldn't expect me to agree with you at every point, and to start with a big point, I think you are entirely too restrictive in your notions of what is good or lasting poetry. When you call on me to admire something by Gascoigne or Campion or Greville that I had never read, then I admire and feel grateful for your analysis. But when you dismiss something by Donne or Milton (as later almost everything by Pope, Shelley, Blake, Keats, Wordsworth, Whitman, Browning, the whole shebang), then I wonder whether you aren't impoverishing instead of refining the taste for poetry. There's a little too much of Dryden's character who

> So much despised the crowd, that when the throng
> By chance went right, he purposely went wrong.

For example, I can be persuaded to admire [Charles] Churchill's "Dedication," for all the qualities you find in it, but I can't be persuaded that it is better than the "Epistle to Dr. Arbuthnot."[59] It isn't, if I have to say so with all your bluntness. [. . .] [Y]ou have what seem to me blind spots, but also a wonderful way of saying that the emperor is naked when he *is* naked and everyone is praising the cut of his clothes.

[. . .]

As ever,
Malcolm

[BOYLE TLS-1] [NL TL/CC-1]
[TO: KAY BOYLE]
December 10, 1967

Dear Kay,

[. . .] I have read *Being Geniuses Together,*[60] in spite of your plea that I shouldn't. I read it with fascination, and with admiration for your share in it. McAlmon's share is rather saddening. He had a certain amount of raw talent, but he couldn't write prose, and on principle refused to learn. Nevertheless, what he says about people and events helps to round out what you say, so that the result is often a stereoscopic view in which things stand out with depth and solidity.

No, I didn't like him, and I like him rather less after reading his narrative. You keep stressing his generosity. There isn't any doubt that he helped dozens of people in admirably off-hand fashion, without asking for recompense, but the strange thing is that there isn't a shred of generosity in his narrative; there are only grudges and resentments. Of course he wrote the book at the beginning of an unhappy period in his life. Almost everybody he had known in Paris was becoming famous, while he was becoming obscure. He had been the patron of others, almost the Maecenas, and now he needed help, which nobody offered. It would have taken a great spirit not to feel resentful. McAlmon wasn't a great spirit. In some ways he was a man of the eighteenth century: realistic, shrewd, skeptical, but short-sighted. Some of his estimates are grotesque: note what he says about Fitzgerald and what he goes out of his way to say about Einstein. He lived among the great without ever knowing what made them great. My God, I don't in the least resent the little crack he made about me, in passing.[61] What saddens me are the cracks he insists on making about better people than I am.

His chapters are in utter contrast with yours. You write with imagination (of which he has hardly any) and real generosity of spirit, and especially at the end of the book I was deeply moved by your narrative. And yet—to repeat—the device of alternate chapters is effective, especially when you and McAlmon are describing the same events—truly, they come out in the round.[62]

[...]

I admire your courage in going to jail for your beliefs—and in California, not Paris....[63] [...]

As ever,
Malcolm

———————

Because the summer of 1968 promises—or threatens—to be a critical one in American life, we will be featuring articles on the role of language in general, and writers in particular, in the formation of national attitudes and policies. We will be featuring a symposium of prominent American writers addressing themselves to the old but lively question of "engagement." Given the current divisions and dilemmas in our country, do you—as an individual and/ or as a craftsman—expect to be spending the summer in any unusual (engaged) way? Participating in demonstrations? Preparing pamphlets? Writing novels of "social consciousness"? [...]

John Leonard [*The New York Times Book Review*] to Cowley,
April 19, 1968 [NL]

[NL TL/CC-1]
[TO: JOHN LEONARD]
April 29, 1968

Dear Mr. Leonard:[64]

It is dangerous for a writer not to be "engaged"—of course "enlisted" is closer to the meaning of the French word—at some period of his life in some cause bigger than himself. Otherwise he is likely to spend his days in a narrow world that centers on his own irritability. I envy Galway Kinnell, who enlisted in the cause of civil liberties, who went to jail in Louisiana, and who came back with a truly visionary poem, "The Last River." But then Kinnell is a special case: he even wrote a good poem about Vietnam, a theme on which many other poets were merely coining metaphors, so that their work makes me think of blood pudding topped with a fancy meringue. I couldn't hope to equal Kinnell in such undertakings, and besides I served my enlistment during the 1930s. Now I have a fantastic lot of work to do and not much time to do it in. For me no demonstrations during this summer of crisis, no pamphlets written (or even read), no novel undertaken to prove my social consciousness. If you don't find me at my desk, look for me in the garden.

Cordially yours,
Malcolm Cowley

[NL TL/CC-2]
[TO: CONRAD AIKEN]
May 23, 1968

Dear Conrad,

[. . .]

I read with admiration the interview with C. Aiken that appeared after five years in *The Paris Review.* [. . .] One statement I glommed onto—you have been making it for thirty years at least, but this time it was expressed so succinctly that I couldn't help quoting it, with proper ascription, in a review I finished last week for the *NY Times:* "That was always planned—that I should, as it were, give myself away, to such an extent as I could bear it, as to what made the wheels go round. Feeling that this was one of the responsibilities of a writer—that he should take off the mask." I quoted it apropos of Robt McAlmon, who wasn't really a writer and never took off the mask.

[. . .] Next Tuesday we go to NY for the Institute do. I'm curious about the figure Allen will cut on the platform when he hands out the grants; I think he'll be properly impressive. I saw him at the dinner in April and he was full of pride about the Gemini,[65] one of whom takes after him, the other, he says, after his lately defunct but once football-playing Brother Ben. We went to Yaddo for a director's meeting, and on the way home paid a visit to the Catholic Worker Farm, where Peggy, my ex-wife, has been ensconced for the last five years. She was in bed with two cats, six kittens, and a devotional book, and she announced that she was being baptized on June 1. A handsome priest, on leave from a Trappist monastery, is giving her instruction. She said she had thought of being converted for the last four years. He asked why she had waited. She said she was waiting for the right priest—and then, lest he become prideful, she added, "God sometimes chooses peculiar instruments." She is 77, looks 90, can hardly walk, but keeps her pecker up. I think I'll drive to Tivoli, fifty or sixty miles, for the ceremony on June 1.

And cross my heart, I'll write more letters.

With love, as ever,
Malcolm

[NL TL/CC-1]
[TO: GERALD FREUND, ROCKEFELLER FOUNDATION]
June 2, 1968

Dear Mr. Freund,

I saw a good deal of Larry McMurtry and his work when he was a student in the advanced writing course at Stanford in 1959 [1960]. He impressed me as an extraordinary character: Texas drawl, cowboy mannerisms, combined with an unusual knowledge of contemporary and seventeenth-century literature. Since his fellowship at Stanford wasn't large enough to support him and his wife, he supplemented his income by haunting the places where second-hand books are sold cheaply and picking up first editions for collectors.

In my class he was writing *Leaving Cheyenne,* a novel that went through several transformations before it finally appeared. In it he demonstrated a very firm grasp of Texas characters and speech; in fact, it was an unusually good book when it finally appeared, though it did not earn him much money. And the first book to appear, from which the movie *Hud* was made, was another good book that yielded less in cash returns than everyone thought it did; I think the movie rights went for a rather low figure.

Before *The Last Picture Show,* which I haven't read, he wrote another novel, concerned, in this case, with rodeo performers. I read it in manuscript and was disappointed. It seemed to me that he wrote with less enthusiasm and authority as soon as the book moved out of Texas. He is an Antaean writer; Texas is his native earth, and I am glad that he is teaching there.

Yes, I do think that he is a gifted and serious writer who is likely to contribute some new qualities to American fiction. [...]

Sincerely yours,
Malcolm Cowley

[NL TL/CC-1]
[TO: CONRAD AIKEN]
August 3, 1968

Dear Conrad,

I hope this note arrives on your birthday. [...] I hope all good things for you, thinking back on the years, fifty of them now, in which you have played a large part in my life and thought. On August 5 we'll break out a new bottle of djinn and drink to your health.

Djinn, djinn, djinni, you old Afreet.

[...]

[...] The saddest and most incredible event in the summer was the death of one of Allen's twins; he must have written you about it. Michael was his favorite, lively, in the best of health. Then, when they were out to dinner, Michael fell, got a toy lodged in his mouth, and when the toy was removed, started to vomit. The baby sitter, a middle-aged, supposedly responsible colored woman, left Michael on his back, completely lost her head, rushed out to the neighbors—and Michael choked to death on his vomit. It took a long list of accidents and blunders to cause his death—even down to the doctor's phone being out of order, so that it was too late when he reached the hospital for a tracheotomy. [...] We've been depressed by that catastrophe ever since it happened.

Can't I think of something more pleasant for a birthday letter? I looked at the shelf of your books and thought how much I owed to them and how they are belatedly receiving some of the attention and honors they deserve.

And I thought how fine it will be to see you and Mary. So love, love to you both, and special love for your birthday.

As ever,
Malcolm

[NL TL/CC-I]
[TO: KENNETH BURKE]
August 24, 1968

Dear Kenneth,

[. . .]

Today is my 70th annual appearance, a good day to write my oldest friend. Ah, Liberty School! Ah, Ruswinkle! Ah, Peabody! Aw, shit, let's think of today. The Blumes are giving me a pretty big party, which starts in a soixantaine of moments from this moment. Happen I'll get potted and stagger across the road at midnight to not sleep. I'll think of you and Libbie and wish you were here.

One thing I thought about was your giving the Blashfield Address, a big honor. Think of your predecessors: Forster, Frost, Madariaga,[66] Graves, Huxley, Bowra,[67] and Etcetera, a word that covers some duffers. I sat in on the c'tee meeting at which you were chosen. Allen Tate's argument was that the Blashfield [. . .] should get back to the original purpose of Mrs. Blashfield's gift, which was "to assist the American Academy of Arts and Letters in an effort to determine its duty regarding both the preservation of the English Language in its beauty and integrity, and its cautious enrichment by such terms as grow out of modern conditions."

Our dear, damned, degenerating, obese, but opulent English language! I think it was Glenway Wescott who first said that if we were going to listen to a talk about language, we should get you to do the talking. Everyone agreed with enthusiasm. [. . .] Anyhow display your ballocks and symballocks. Man is the ballock-using animal, rocked in the scrotum of the sea.

Cheez, my present job is reviewing a big book about the Great Stalin Purge. By Robt Conquest, who states what now seems to be the accepted view of the Purge, that it started when Stalin gave instructions to facilitate the assas-

sination of Kirov, and that it did not end until 5 percent of the Russian population had been arrested. Conquest thinks that 20 million people died as a result
of the purge, and of the 1932–33 famine, though most of them died in labor
camps. His figures seem large to me, but it's a horrible and revolting story. He
also thinks that all those shot, and all those sentenced to labor camps, were
innocent of the crimes for which they were convicted—though some of them
richly deserved to die, as notably Yagoda and his agents, of whom 3000 were
shot. It's a hell of a book for *me* to review, but conscience calls.[68]

With best septuagenarian love to you and Libbie.

Malcolm

[NL TL/CC-I]
[TO: LAURENCE LIEBERMAN]
September 22, 1968

Dear Larry,

[...]

I have a few basic ideas about writing poetry: how *I* should write it.
First, that every poem struggles to achieve its own form, which should be
fully achieved, at the cost of no matter how much revision (though the first
draft should be written rapidly). Second, that that form should be as unalterable as that of a mantra, a Hindu charm, which won't work unless every
word is repeated correctly. Third, that the poem should be an event, not a
picture—that the situation presented at the beginning of the poem should
be changed by the end of it; in that sense, even a brief lyric is a story. Fourth,
that the mantra or charm should be rememberable. Syllabics—if the line is
of more than seven syllables, don't seem to me remembrable. Fifth, that
poetry is audial more than visual; that the rhythms and tones are more important than the images. And sixth, that idea I passed on to you, that the
poem should be a recurrent pattern, with variations. All of which explains
why I don't admire a good deal of contemporary verse.

My best, as always,
Malcolm Cowley

[NL TL/CC-1]
[TO: KENNETH BURKE]
September 29, 1968

Dear Kenneth,

[. . .] My God, why shld you be downhearted abt yr work or the sort of recognition it has received?—which isn't as big as it ought to be, but still is a very satisfactory sort of recognition. I hardly open a litry paper without seeing yr name in some connection [. . .].

Kenneth, you and I have always been rivals of a sort, a little jealous of each other in the midst of friendship, but I think I'm outgrowing jealousy, or at least am getting too tired to feel more than faint twinges of it. So let me place on record that I've always thought you were better than I was. Not better in all ways, because I don't think you have equaled some of my special talents, e.g., for writing a sentence or constructing an essay or editing a manuscript or (as happened yesterday at Yaddo) chairing a difficult meeting and making everyone feel that he had gotten a fair shake. But I rank those talents as minor ones compared with the gift of seizing a new conception, dozens of new conceptions, and interweaving their implications. *That,* I should say, is the most important thing, and I don't think there is anyone living today who had laid hands on as many conceptions as you have gathered in by the armful. [. . .]

[. . .]

As ever,
Malcolm

———————

[NL VIKING MEMO TL/CC-1]
October 22, 1968

FRANK O'HARA, COLLECTED POEMS

Look, this isn't my kind of poetry. I go back to the age of dirt roads, outdoor privies and oil lamps. This is asphalt and neon and giggling together over tables in the back room of a Madison Avenue bar. "I have never clogged myself with the praises of pastoral life," O'Hara says, "nor with the nostalgia for an innocent past of perverted acts in pastures." That is in one of his most brilliant pieces, "Meditations in an Emergency." He is vigorous, candid, free (sometimes to the extent of being limp), proud of knowing selected people whom he calls by their first names, sometimes mystifying the uninformed reader. Metropolitan. In-group. Up to the minute as of 1956, 1959, 1966, which means that he'll be a minute or two late in 1970. He is not a poet of the stature of Roethke or Thomas—he is an "I" or lyric poet who doesn't often sing—but at the same time he is vastly entertaining in snatches, and I suspect that he will be a cult for some years to come. Therefore I am for publishing a volume of his work at $10. [...]

[NL TL/CC-2]
[TO: HENRY DAN PIPER]
March 10, 1969

Dear Dan,

[...]

Your introduction.[69] I feel some excitement about this, for nobody has written at length about my work except students doing papers. A few remarks about this:

It's always controversial to compare A with B and C to the disadvantage of B and C, but I rather hope to stay out of that kind of controversy. Thus, I don't see any use in talking about Trilling and Kazin. Wilson you'll have to mention, simply because I followed him at the NR—incidentally with a vast respect for his scholarship, his independence, and his ability to have opinions about everything and everybody. As I said in "Confessions of a Book Reviewer," I have some difficulty in reaching an opinion. I have to dig a lot before I decide whether the soil is fertile.

Wilson's mind is much quicker than mine (though mine is quicker than people think when they hear me talk. One reason I talk slowly is that I'm always jumping ahead to the answer to the answer to my answer to what has just been said). I think he has less poetry in him and less feeling for people

(I always objected to many of his friends, who were sucks or phonies). The man who reviewed *Think Back on Us* for *The Nation*[70] had some interesting things to say, in comparing MC and EW.

You are acute when you mention the difference in age. For the between-wars generation age counted a great deal. Yes, Wilson's class ('16) was in some respects prewar, and some members of my class ('19, not '20; I graduated in '20 on acct of wartime delays, but in three years of college) were postwar. It always seemed to me that the sentimentality of men just a few years older than I (Wilson, Dos Passos, Bishop) was different from mine, and I felt closer in that respect to Hemingway. But perhaps that was also due partly to being born west of the mountains, so that I *felt* often what Fitzgerald was feeling, though he too was older.

I often disagreed with Wilson, though always respectfully. He never had much effect on my writing. Among people my own age, in this country, the only one who influenced my writing was Kenneth Burke. When we were in high school we spent days yakking together. I greatly admired his early stories. I didn't follow him into the stage when he wrote his novel in the form of declamations, *Toward a Better Life,* but about 1930 he started working on critical theory (about which we had argued all during the twenties) and I thought his essay "The Psychology of Form"[71] was unanswerable. Kenneth and I are still yakking, after sixty years.

One other influence, the only master I was willing to acknowledge, was Valéry. I met him briefly in 1923 and translated his first prose book, *Variety I,* in 1926. I admired the marvelous fashion in which he put his essays together, and I admired the *availability* of his abstract thinking. He wrote on almost any given subject, at any given length, and yet, by intellectually mastering his subject and fitting it into his own system of thought, he made it his own, with not a cheap phrase from beginning to end. Last week I wrote a little piece on Valéry after rereading many of his essays and I saw how much I owed to him.[72] My work on *The New Republic* would have been different without his example of an independent mind approaching each subject as a totally new problem and each author as if nobody else had ever read him. It wasn't his opinions I accepted; I disagreed with many of them; what I admired was his method.

But I'm talking too much about myself. [. . .] Your introduction will be fine.

[. . .]

As ever,

Malcolm

[NL TL/CC-1]

[TO: KENNETH BURKE]

May 18, 1969

Dear Kenneth,

[. . .]

[. . .] I've been reading the enormous biography of Hart by John Unterecker;[73] he has dug up almost everything and quoted almost everything, usually with fairness to everybody (though Matty takes some licks in Hart's 1923–25 letters). You are in the background, but come out handsomely. It's extraordinary how much Hart did, how many people he met, how many letters he wrote, all in thirty-one years. How much vitality he had, and what a hard time he had killing himself (though that's what he was doing in effect and at almost every moment from the time he climbed out of his mother's window in Hollywood and never saw her again). Mother is the villain of Unterecker's story. He has had no trouble at all writing a book of 900 closely printed pages—five hundred thousand words, I should guess—without repeating himself. But the last two years of Hart's life make painful reading for me. I had given up on him in 1929 and decided that he was already doomed, already dead. Even then he surprised us at the end with one last good poem, "The Tower."[74]

[. . .] The sign of age with me is that work goes slower, slower, s l o w e r.

As ever,

Malcolm

[NL TL/CC-1]
[TO: A. C. SPECTORSKY, EDITORIAL DIRECTOR, *PLAYBOY*]

June 6, 1969

Dear Mr. Spectorsky:

Thank you for sending me Seymour Krim's confession "The American Novel Made Me."[75] It is forcefully if sometimes quite badly written, and it is the best sloganeering statement I have seen of the campaign to abolish art. The American novelists who "made" Mr. Krim were all of them artists after a fashion; some were superb artists. Besides expressing themselves and "telling what happened"—the phrase that has been replaced by "telling it like it was"—they also wanted to make something outside themselves: not Mr. Krim, but works of art with an organic structure and an independent life that would outlast their own lives. In other words, they expressed their personalities, but at the same time surrendered their personalities, sacrificing themselves *for the work* as a mother might do for her children.

In Mr. Krim's present condition—he has had other notions in the past— the work isn't worth the sacrifice, or any sacrifice. The work isn't action, which he craves; the work hasn't the immediate power over an audience that can be exerted by a raw confession, or boast: "Look, Ma, I've screwed them all! Look, Pa, I'm jerking off!" Power, not perdurability, is the goal he recommends. The hero-as-artist is to be replaced by the hero-as-exhibitionist and the hero-as-careerist. The work of art—novel, poem, play, what have you— is to be replaced by the raw confession torn from the id and slapped on the counter like a piece of boneless, quivering butcher's meat. After a while it smells.

Sincerely,
Malcolm Cowley

[NL TL/CC-I]
[TO: HIRAM HAYDN, HARCOURT, BRACE & WORLD]
July 1, 1969

Dear Hiram,

I haven't time to read many novels outside the line of duty. THE CHO-SEN PLACE, THE TIMELESS PEOPLE[76] is one that I shouldn't like to have missed. Still, I had the feeling that Miss Marshall had taken on too big a subject. A whole island—Barbados, I suppose—its history, its demography, its high society, its tourists, its peasants: combine this with American philanthropy trying to raise the standard of living of the peasants: then personify the island in an extraordinary woman of mixed blood and let her have an affair with a Jewish anthropologist while mourning for her African husband (and the anthropologist having a wife from the Philadelphia Main Line who in some ways personifies the power drive of American society)—all this becomes frightfully complicated.

But the writing has power, and the book is full of memorable scenes—especially the night at Sugar's, the whole story of Carnival, and all the scenes in which the people of Bournehills listen impassively to those who are trying to improve or mislead them. They are indeed "the timeless people," and nobody else has presented such a people more impressively. Paule Marshall is a writer of very real talent. Only, I wish she had simplified her story.

Yours, as ever,
Malcolm Cowley

Reagan is the Mao Tse-tung of the Right. Reading news from California is like reading news from China.

Cowley to Howard Hugo, January 22, 1967 [NL]

[NL TL/CC-1]
[TO: WALLACE STEGNER]
November 30, 1969

Dear Wally,

Dear God, what a picture you draw of graduate students at Stanford! And to think that these jerks, with their ignorance of everything that isn't "relevant"—i.e., that happened more than ten years ago—will soon be the faculties of American universities! Why do they enroll in courses about the Renaissance? Why do administrators bow down to them? I don't know what I'd do if I had to face ten of them at a table.

It's bad enough sitting here in my study and facing an uncooperative typewriter.

[...]

And chopping wood.

And putting the garden to bed.

AND READING *Middlemarch,* which reading is a profession in itself.

I think of you up in the hills trying to finish a big novel before going back on January 1 to face the great unwashed, unbarbered proletariat of graduate students. At least they've started to demonstrate about Ecology. Can't you grow sideburns in lieu of a beard and put yourself at the head of the protesters? Have a confrontation?

[...]

As ever,
Malcolm

PART X

Man of Letters, 1970–1987

Although advancing age began to affect his mobility and capacity for sustained work, until the mid-1980s Cowley continued to act out his multiple roles as one of America's leading men of letters: critic, historian, memoirist, poet, editor, publisher's advisor, writers' confidant, and literary "middleman." In the spring of 1980 he formally retired from Viking Press (since 1975 part of the Penguin Group) yet remained active as a literary consultant and (now less roving) scout for Viking. He took on teaching assignments at Hollins (1970), Minnesota (1971), and the University of Warwick in Great Britain (1973) and never wavered in his commitment to the (now amalgamated) American Academy and National Institute of Arts and Letters.

As he witnessed the declining health of friends, Cowley remained loyal to bonds forged in earlier times: in letters he offered encouragement and consolation, gave advice on how to beat back disease or ailments associated with old age, and reported on happenings in the literary world. Allen Tate's case was particularly poignant. In the wake of his son's tragic death, Tate's emphysema worsened and his eyesight dimmed. At almost eighty, Cowley traveled south from Sherman, to sit at Tate's bedside in Sewanee. "Your brother in age and affection," he signed one of his last letters. Tate's death on February 9, 1979, was one in a long litany of losses mourned in letters—among them Conrad Aiken ("a father figure"), Edmund Wilson, Matthew Josephson, John Cheever, Robert Lowell, and John Berryman. Often, such letters were resources for obituaries or public tributes.

Acting to consolidate his literary legacy, Cowley proved uncommonly productive in this final phase of his life: between 1970 and 1986 he saw into publication *A Many-Windowed House* (1970, edited by Henry Dan Piper), *A Second Flowering* (1973), *—And I Worked at the Writer's Trade* (1978), *The Dream of the Golden Mountains* (1980), *The View from Eighty* (1980), *Blue Juniata: A Life* (1985), *The Flower and the Leaf* (1985, edited by Donald W.

Faulkner) and *Conversations with Malcolm Cowley* (1986, edited by Thomas Daniel Young).

In *A Second Flowering* (1973) Cowley bade a last farewell to the generation of 1920s writers he now saw as "lucky" rather than "lost." Through the 1970s and 1980s his letters offer sensitive (re)considerations of contemporaries, exploring new dimensions, and correcting misapprehensions or perceived falsifications. As younger scholars challenged once pioneering and authoritative interpretations—as when feminist critics faulted Cowley for not having done justice to the female poets, critics, and editors of his own generation—he acknowledged oversights, and responded with percipience and historical sensitivity. As advisor for Viking he campaigned for new discoveries (John Glassco's *Memoirs of Montparnasse*), offered critical advice on biographies (Scott Donaldson's life of Hemingway), and in in-house memos passed verdict on new book proposals (Floyd Dell's letters to Edna Millay). By the late 1970s, as a younger generation of critics and scholars chipped away at the figures holding cultural power, Cowley felt uneasy about being looked on as a living monument to a quickly receding past. With typical self-irony, he consented to be the subject of a "Special Event" at the 1978 MLA convention in Chicago, offering himself up as a "sacrificial goat" to a cheering crowd of 600.

Unlike Burke, who continued to move in the frontlines of criticism, Cowley was uncomfortable with the predominance of literary theory in the universities. Movements like poststructuralism and deconstructionism were foreign to his literary intuitions and his axiomatic belief in the vital connection between literature and life. If he offered encouragement to the New Journalist and Beat writer Seymour Krim and could muster appreciation for the postmodernist fictions of Pynchon, Gass, and Coover (less so for Barth), he mostly disliked postmodernism's self-reflexive, ego-oriented tendencies. As he wrote to Reed Whittemore (June 12, 1972): "The kids are going crrrazy on self, self, self: self-aggrandizement, self-abuse, self-exhibition. [. . .] I suspect it has something to do with the drug culture. Alcohol, vice of the 1920s, was manic and social; the psychedelics are solipsistic and schizophrenic." As a counter-statement, he wrote a "defense of storytelling" and explored a generational method in literary historiography.

One of the last survivors of the World War I generation ("I knew them all"), Cowley was besieged in his old age with queries about writers he had known, sometimes intimately, sometimes professionally or hardly at all. Unlike Edmund Wilson, who gruffly declined such requests, Cowley mostly complied—often to the detriment of his own work. In countless letters he offered reminiscences and character sketches. Conjointly, these memoiristic letters—only exemplarily represented here—offer a gallery of cameo portraits of twentieth-century literary figures, both famous and forgotten: Djuna Barnes, Louise Bogan, Erskine Caldwell, Nilla Cook, Floyd Dell, Ramon Guthrie, Edna St. Vincent Millay, Nathanael West. In an offhand, often anecdotal way, the letters display Cowley's ability to evoke, often with a dash of nostalgia, but rarely without astute insight or telling detail, the color and mood of the historical moment, the flavor of a writer's personality, the link between character and work. Though Cowley jokingly complained of having become an unfunded National Scholarly Resource, such letters vividly bring the literary past to life. They also confirm his importance as both an actor in and observer of literary history.

His letters in this final phase reflect his uneasiness about the future of America under Nixon, Carter, and Reagan. "[Y]ou preside over a late-Roman world with the barbarians already inside the gates and elected to public office," he observed to Aiken on August 3, 1972; "For us old codgers the greatest pleasures are of memory." Writing from England in 1973 he offered doleful speculations about the effects of the international economic crisis, lamented the spread of American-style consumerism, and was disgusted by Watergate and Vietnam.

Cowley's strongest political passions were roused by his concerns for ecology and conservation. In letters and articles he lamented the destruction of the countryside by encroaching suburbanization and suggested ways of restoring farming to New England—an argument cited verbatim in the *Congressional Record*. A self-described "defeated agrarian," he wrote to congressional representatives, senators, and governors to protest what he felt was a disastrous suburbanization initiative in his region, WatersEdge. Into old age he worked to uphold Sherman's zoning laws and to keep the town, as he wrote in 1975, "neighborly and public-spirited," "a functioning community." As he told Christopher Lasch on June 2, 1983, "I am a Little American, and my life has been spent as a patriotic native first of Blacklick Township, Cambria County, Pennsylvania and for the last half century as a patriotic native of Sherman, Connecticut."

As Cowley struggled to complete his memoirs of the 1930s, the past came boomeranging back once again. His revaluations of the 1930s, in —*And I Worked at the Writer's Trade* (1978) and *The Dream of the Golden Mountains* (1980), brought laudatory letters and reviews. Yet they also embroiled him in the literary politics of the late 1970s and early 1980s and illustrated the persistence of the factional quarrels from the 1930s into the Reagan years, as for example when neoconservative critics like Sydney Hook and Kenneth Lynn took Cowley to task for misremembering the past and failing to speak out about his political misjudgments. In response to what he deemed an unfair review of his memoirs by Christopher Lasch, he tried to set the record straight in letters to Victor Navasky of *The Nation* and to Lasch himself. Cowley now acknowledged—in public—that he had been late in admitting the "utter villainy" of Stalin and confessed his "total misjudgment of the Moscow Trials in 1937 and 1938." When Allen Weinstein's controversial account of the Hiss-Chambers case appeared in 1978 under the title *Perjury* (Weinstein maintained Hiss was guilty of espionage), Cowley was angered enough by its distortions of the evidence to write to Alger Hiss and, at greater length, to the critic Benjamin DeMott about his own experiences with Chambers. In 1984 Cowley wrote a long essay in rebuttal to Kenneth Lynn's imputation that he (and Wilson) had traded in ideological and anti-American interpretations of American literature.

Lambasted by the "Neon-conservatives" (as Cowley called them) in these late years, he enjoyed the recognition and favors of southern critics and editors: Lewis Simpson (of *The Southern Review*), George Core (of *The Sewanee Review*) and Stanley Lindberg (of *The Georgia Review*) opened up the pages of their magazines to Cowley's work and published perceptive evaluations of his life and achievements. Younger scholars, too, offered sensitive interpretations of his long career, highlighting his endeavors to mediate between the serious writer and the general public. With critical recognition came public honors and encomiums. Harvard's Signet Society presented Cowley with a medal in 1976, and honorary degrees came from, among others, the University of Warwick (1975) and Indiana University of Pennsylvania (1985). In 1979, the state of Connecticut gave him an award from the Commission of the Arts; the Newberry Library in Chicago, home of the Malcolm Cowley papers, honored him at a dinner that included a moving tribute by John Cheever; and the Modern Language Association presented him with the Jay B. Hubbell Award for service to the study of American literature. And of special significance to Cowley, he was awarded the Gold Medal for Belles Lettres by the American Academy and National Institute of Arts and Letters in 1980. It was presented to him in a moving ceremony by Kenneth Burke, to a standing ovation. Last but not least, that same year Cowley was awarded the Who's Who in America Achievement Award.

Cowley's letters of his final years testify to a continuing struggle to find a shape and pattern to his life. "All our lives are dramas, after all, and one should look for a dramatic shape in them, with climaxes and recognitions and peripeties," he observed to his son, Robert, on February 23, 1984. In a 1983 statement for *Who's Who,* Cowley retrospectively defined the preoccupations governing his career: "to celebrate American literature and to defend American writers as a community within the larger community."

In 1980, at eight-two, Cowley published *The View from Eighty,* a testimony (based on an earlier essay for *Life*) to the particular challenges of living in "the country" of old age. No other book brought so many responses from so many readers. In his eighty-sixth year, he outlined in a letter a projected sequel to *The View from Eighty;* he eventually published part of that projected sequel in *The New York Times Magazine* in May 1985 ("Being Old, Old"). In September of that year he attended, with Kenneth Burke, a celebration in honor of James Sibley Watson, onetime editor of *The Dial*—his last public appearance—in Rochester, New York. A trip to New York, he told James Stern on September 1, 1985, now had "to be faced like an expedition to the Gobi Desert." As the infirmities of age proved forbidding, he spent most of his time in a reclining chair and under the care of nurses. His letters (now often limited to brief dictated responses) announced his forced withdrawal from the literary life. One of his last letters offered grandfatherly advice to his granddaughter Miranda, who was hoping to set out on a writing career. Writing to his oldest friend and correspondent, Kenneth Burke, he offered his "sad reflections" as "*messages d'outre tomb*": "At 87 my career in literature seems to have ended, with much less accomplished than I had hoped for." In May 1987, his reading mostly limited to Shakespeare, he belatedly discovered a role model in Samuel Johnson.

Malcolm Cowley died of heart failure in the New Milford hospital on March 27, 1989, at age ninety. The long voyage had ended.

[NL TL/CC-1]

[TO: CONRAD AIKEN]

June 30, 1970[1]

Dear Conrad,

Something I'll bet you didn't know about Brewster. Horatio Alger, Jr., was pastor of the Brewster Unitarian Church in 1865 and 1866. Well, maybe you did know that, but this I'm sure you didn't. In 1866 Horatio was called before a special parish investigating committee, which reported: "We learn from John Clark and Thomas S. Crocker [two boys] that Horatio Alger, Jr., has been practicing on them at different times deeds that are too revolting to relate. Said charges were put to the said Alger and he did not deny them." Indeed, he left town by the next train. The committee wrote to Boston and recommended that Alger be separated from the ministry of the Unitarian Church for "the abominable and revolting crime of familiarity with *boys*." Their italics. What a blow to the American ideal of success.

[...]

I'm still old-manfully taking care of a fairly large vegetable garden, though my knees creak as I kneel in the rows. [...] But now for the first time in ages I have a summer without a deadline, except those the garden sets for itself. Our best love to you and Mary.

As ever,

Malcolm

[NL TL/CC-1]

[TO: ERSKINE CALDWELL]

June 30, 1970

Dear Erskine,

Last [...] week I received a letter from William A. Sutton, of Ball State University, who says that he is doing a biography of Erskine Caldwell. I'll help him if I can. Searching my memory, I am dismayed to find how much I have forgotten—but I found one passage that might amuse you, in a piece I wrote about you and never tried to publish. Here it is:

"It must have been in the autumn of 1931, when *Tobacco Road* was waiting to be published, that Caldwell called at *The New Republic*. He was six feet tall, with a big square-cut head, broad shoulders, and enormous hands, but with little flesh on his bones. His orange hair was cut short and lay forward close to his scalp, so that he looked like a totem pole with a blob of orange paint on top. He complained that people thought he was a humorist; "I haven't ever tried to be funny," he said, and indeed he was as sober-faced as an Indian or a back-country farmer. He wanted to review books for *The New Republic*, as it seemed that everybody wanted to do in the depression years. I had been impressed by his book of stories, *American Earth,* as also by his contributions to *The New American Caravan.* I thought, and think, that he had a greater natural talent for telling stories than anyone else in his generation, and they seemed to come straight from life, without memories of how someone else would have written them. I told him—I forget what I said, but the point was that he shouldn't make his talent self-conscious by writing critical prose. Perhaps I was right in the long run, but I have often worried about that visit and thought that if I had known how penniless and hungry he was in those days, I would have sent him away with an armful of books to review. His narrative talent would have taken care of itself."[2]

—So that much I remember, outside of my pleasure in almost everything you wrote [. . .].

My best to you,
Malcolm Cowley

[NL TL/CC-2] [SC 376]
[TO: KENNETH BURKE]
November 14, 1970

Dear Kenneth,

[. . .] My God, I haven't any ideas about the Future of Criticism.[3] I have always avoided thinking about Criticism in my effort to think about the work being criticized and in trying to approach it without preconceptions. Criticism flourished during the 1950s; now it's less flourishing or even in a state of decay. That is because the methods developed in the 1950s or earlier were fruitful when applied to a work for the first or second or third time—on the fourth round they began to seem tired. One work after another was exhausted as a field for study—first *Moby Dick,* then *The Waste Land,* then *Absalom, Absalom, The Great Gatsby,* even *Ulysses* and *Finnegans Wake*—it was an exhaustion of resources like that of opened and receding frontiers. Either new subjects or new methods are required. Hence the wild divagations into Mythical Criticism, the Norman O. Brownholings, the efforts of the Critic to become an all-knowing psychologist and transform the work into a patient or even a corpse for dissection.

Could we go back to Aristotle and work with general forms of narrative: exposition, development, counterpoint, confrontation, restatement, coda (or as you early called it, tangent)? T. Mann did that superbly with his own work. But that too requires continually new subject matter; the critic is dependent on the artist. Unless he becomes like you a philosopher of symbolic action or of communication as the specifically human activity. . . .

[. . .]

As ever, with the sun shining for once in November,
Malcolm

[NL TL/CC-1]
[TO: JOHN CHEEVER]
May 14, 1971

Dear John,

As you lie back on the couch and free-associate, Dr. Cowley sits and listens, that bearded old Viennese bastard. What more can he-I do, for God's sake? I'm fourteen years older than you—I've been through a lot of this atrocious process of aging (would we were vintage wine)—and it gets worse with the years. Only somehow less painful, as the years anesthetize you while chopping off your limbs, and anoint the stumps with analgesic balm. Finally you can't get excited about anyone's disasters, including your own. It's true that the words & phrases don't come so easily, but they do come, and they can be saved like green stamps. You can't write twenty stories a year any longer, but patience takes the place of that early jizzum—you can write four or five and they can be damned good ones. (I've seen you losing patience with your characters for the last ten years or more. Wham, biff, zowie, you knock them over the head at the end of a story, so that I've always thought you were getting ready to move into a New Phase.)

About the drinking—hmmm, says Dr. Kaoli. I have two friends, Conrad Aiken (83 this summer) and K. Burke (74) who have kept on drinking nobly till this day and a lot of other nobly drinking friends who are under the sod. Me, I studied to be an alcoholic, but I flunked my exams, and now I take one big slug of bourbon per diem, at six P.M. If I take more I either get shaky on my pins or pay for it with a bout of indigestion. One thing you can say to yourself at the advanced age of 59 (on May 27). Nobody in God's world is going to help you or beseech you or argue with you to stop drinking—nobody but yourself (and Mary). It's completely up to you—and isn't that a relief? A focusing of responsibility? Why not join me in that one big sundown slug?

[...]

About the Institute, I think we have to pay attention to the General Critical Stock Market Quotation of authors; otherwise we'll be left on a limb, as the Institute was in 1930, when everything interesting in literature was being done by nonmembers. That's why I suggested Barth, Dickey, and

Gass, all of whose stocks are selling above par (though my opinion of Barth is candidly not so much higher than yours. He wrote what I thought was a hell of a good story, "Night Journey," but his novels seem to me show-offy. I found at a Grants Committee meeting that he isn't popular among writers). Well, let's forget him for the time being (though Eleanor Clark respects his work and might nominate him). Would *you* nominate Gass? If so, I'd second. We ought to give the members a chance to vote on those Famous Names.

As ever,

Malcolm

[NL TL/CC-2]
[TO: CONRAD AIKEN]
July 22, 1971

Dear Conrad,

[...]

I've just about stopped writing reviews, but I did take on one job for *Book Week* two years ago. I asked them to let me review the original manuscript of *The Waste Land* when it was published. I was and am full of curiosity about what Ezra did to it. I'd like to find—but doubt whether I shall— that *The Waste Land* was as good in the original version. Pound was a marvelous spotter of weak lines and his solution was usually just to omit them. Did that deprive the poem of any sequence, of every sequence? Pound didn't give a damn. His extraordinary mind was distinguished by an absolute lack of respect for sequence, especially narrative sequence—he sometimes said "therefore," but never said "and then ... and then." What he admired were discrete images and moments unconnected with other moments— and by God he imposed this special failing, this Zenonian disregard of motion, on a great sector of modern poetry. In his *Cantos*, Achilles never does catch up with the tortoise and the arrow is always in motionless flight. So I'd like to see just what he did to *The Waste Land*.[4]

[...]

[As ever,

Malcolm]

[NL TL/CC-1]
[TO: KENNETH BURKE]
August 2, 1971

Dear Kenneth,

[. . .] I've been trying to rewrite a lecture into a magazine piece, "A Defense of Story Telling." Story telling has been under attack for a number of years: "Plot, in the Dickensian sense, is obsolete," Hugh Kenner said in 1951, in celebrating the plotlessness of Pound's *Cantos*. The general effort seems to be to substitute spatial form for temporal form, pattern for process, image for event. In deploring that effort I reached a number of principles, some borrowed directly from you, with due acknowledgement. z.B.:

By emphasizing spatial form to the neglect of temporal form, some contemporary authors are entering a field in which materials and tools are more effective than language. They are operating in two or three dimensions instead of four.

Post hoc, ergo propter hoc is not only a logical fallacy but also an essential form of human thought, embodied in the myths of every culture.

A myth is the temporization of essence (this directly quoted from *The Rhetoric of Religion*).

In a story *something is changed*, irreversibly, and the change may be for better or worse. Hence every story becomes a fable with an implied moral.

Stories (i.e., characters involved in a series of events leading to something changed) occur in many types of literature—not only in fiction, drama, articles, newspaper columns, "nonfiction novels," but even in lyric poems. For example, Wordsworth's "A slumber did my spirit seal" is a complete story in eight lines.

Your principle in "The Psychology of Form" [*sic*] applies to all the temporal arts, though not to the spatial arts. The attack on form in the temporal arts is an effort to abolish the audience and let the author rule supreme.

Etc., etc. Anyhow I finally finished the piece in two versions, not one [. . .].[5]
[. . .]

'Zever,
Malcolm

———

[NL TL/CC-I]
[TO: KENNETH BURKE]
August 12, 1971

Dear Kenneth,
  [. . .]
I'm reading Sir Walter Scott. He seems more antiquated in technique
than Defoe or Fielding. Also a dreadful snob. But my God, what memory,
what imagination, what a pouring forth of persons and adventures! There
are fine scenes of low life in *The Heart of Midlothian.*—The requisites for a
writer are 1) memory, 2) vigor, 3) dreams, imagination, vision; 4) the need to
explain himself, 5) intelligence mixed with a little necessary stupidity.

As ever,
Malcolm

———

Why haven't we now, here, a good woman novelist, I mean better than
Joyce Carol Oates or Joan (early Hemingway) Didion? Has the consorority
dissolved? Was Virginia W. the last of the great line?

Cowley to Ellen Moers,[6] November 14, 1972 [Columbia]

[NL TL/CC-I]
[TO: BERNARD BERGONZI, CHAIR, ENGLISH DEPARTMENT,
UNIVERSITY OF WARWICK]
September 20, 1971

Dear Mr. Bergonzi,
  [. . .]
I've finished my blankety-blank book, *The Incorruptibles: Figures of the
Lost Generation* (though I hope to find a better subtitle[)].[7] [. . .] A mixture

of very old work, some of it familiar in anthologies, and new chapters such as those on American writers in World War I, Dos Passos, Cummings, Hemingway as image and shadow, and my farewell to the generation. I don't know what to think about the book, but at least it's out of the way. "Tomorrow to green fields . . ."

Meanwhile I have been reading with profit *The Situation of the Novel*. My God, how you do read (everything but the end of *The Sot-Weed Factor,* an omission for which Heaven has already forgiven you). I never even started it, and I bogged down night after night in *Giles Goat-Boy* till I said to myself, "This is spinach and to hell with it." I think you hand too much to the American black-humor-and-catastrophe novelists. A few, a very few of them are brilliant, Pynchon, for example, who has just turned in a new 960-page manuscript to the Viking Press.[8] It's about an American junior officer at the end of WWII who is either crazy or the world is crazy, or both. He thinks he has sensors that tell him exactly where the next V2 is going to fall in London—but I won't try to tell the rest of the complicated story as Pynchon's editor summarized it. The book is absolutely certain to receive a great deal of attention. Barth (or rather Barth's work) is thoroughly disliked by a large sector of the American literary community. I tried to get him nominated for the American Institute of Arts and Letters, not because I liked his work, but because I thought the membership should have a chance to vote on him. John Cheever (a more serious writer than is generally realized) promised to put him up, then wrote to me reneging on his offer. "I read a book of his again," Cheever said, "and I just can't do it." Several others had the same reaction, and he wasn't nominated at all. Some novelists who have interested me are Joyce Carol Oates, Thomas McGuane (*The Bushwhacked Piano*), Thomas Rogers (*The Pursuit of Happiness*), Harry Crews (who does wild novels about the new Florida, the latest one about a man who ate, but actually ate, a Chevrolet), Reynolds Price (of the Southern school, but he does write well), Robert Coover (who I think is better than Donald Barthelme).

[. . .]

I've run out of space. Best regards,
Malcolm Cowley

I have been mounting a little campaign to get attention for *Memoirs of Montparnasse,* a book of unusual interest and almost completely overlooked in the US.

Cowley to John Glassco, December 9, 1971 [NL]

[NL VIKING MEMO TL/CC-1]
November 2, 1971

MEMOIRS OF MONTPARNASSE, John Glassco

Thanks for sending me the Glassco book. If it is still on offer, I strongly suggest that it should be reconsidered by the Compass committee.

It is the liveliest and raunchiest of all the Montparnasse memoirs (more so even than TROPIC OF CANCER). When Glassco was a boy of 17 he left McGill, where he was already in his third year, left home, and paid his rent by hiring out his flat to friends as a place of assignation. That produced an allowance of $100 a month from his straitlaced father, who wanted to end the scandal, and the following year, 1928, Buffy Glassco and his friend Graeme Taylor went to Paris. Buffy was tall, slim, blond, and appeared to have an immense sophistication. In Montparnasse all the jaded lechers of all sexes seem to have converged on him crying, "Meat! Meat! Meat!" as cannibals used to do when they went into battle.

Buffy had no moral prejudices. He spoke French currently, and he met Everybody, including, among others, Joyce, Breton, Willa Cather (apparently, though he changes the name), George Moore, Gertrude Stein, Frank Harris, and Lord Alfred Douglas. Papa cut off his allowance and he sank through layers of society till he was sleeping under bridges; then he became a male prostitute, servicing elderly ladies. A beautiful, rich nymphomaniac took him in tow. After six months with her he was in the last stages of TB, and she shipped him off to the American Hospital at Neuilly, where one of his lungs was carved out. Then the American Hospital sent him back to Montreal for a thoracoplasty, an operation which, at the time, had a survival rate of one out of two. While waiting for the operation, at the age of twenty-two, he wrote these memoirs.

He did survive, fortunately, and moved to the Eastern Townships, where for a time he raised hackney ponies and wrote poems. At sixty-one, very frail, he is one of the lights of Montreal literary society, when he appears there. His memoirs couldn't have been published when written, not in the US or Canada, but he exhumed them and Oxford brought them out in 1970. The book had some very favorable reviews, I hear, but not much of a sale, even in Canada.

[. . .] Other books of Montparnasse memoirs are based on nostalgic memories. This one was written on the scene (the first three chapters) or immediately afterward, and truly, it's the McCoy.[9]

[. . .]

[NL TL/CC-I]
[TO: MARSHALL BEST]
Stanford Resort, 1765 Gulf Blvd,
Englewood, Fla. 33533[10]
February 5, 1972

Dear Marshall,

It's sad about Berryman.[11] When we saw him last winter he seemed in good shape, but rather subdued. The students crowded in to hear him, but he had no close friends in Minneapolis and felt cut off from the world. His wife (he has two daughters by her, one born last June) said that he had been depressed and had fallen off the wagon. He jumped off the university bridge connecting two campuses, east and west of the river, and his body was found on the ice. At Minnesota he *was* the department of Humanities and they have no one to replace him. Nor have we.

[. . .]

As ever,
Malcolm

[NL TL/CC-1]
[TO: ALLEN TATE]
Stanford Resort, 1765 Gulf Blvd,
Englewood, Fla. 33533
February 2, 1972

Dear Allen,

[...]

I'm working on a collection of mostly long-ago-written-and-published essays on writers of the 1920s, but with new chapters to write in an effort to round out the picture. I finished one on Dos Passos; now I'm doing one on Cummings, partly about his later period, when he reverted to Father and hearth and, my God, Emerson, whom he probably never read, but honest to goodness, there are things he says that would fit into Emerson's essays. Transcendentalism redivivus, if it ever defuncted. And a touch of Whitman too. But sometimes, after he has said a thing fifty, a hundred times—I love you, we together are wonderful, groups are unimportant, even despicable, there is no history, there is only Now—he finds just the right way of saying it again. There's no decline in Cummings, as alas there was in Dos Passos. He was alive till he died.

[...]

As ever,
Malcolm

[RPW TLS/1]
[TO: ROBERT PENN WARREN]
June 14, 1972

Dear Red,

How nice of you to write as Nature tries to restore you! And what a siege of it[12] you've had, aided not in the least by the grand achievements of modern medicine! You'd probably have recovered as fast in a lazar-house, anno 1472. Allen phoned from Sewanee to ask how you were and how he could get in touch with you. [...] Allen hadn't heard that Edmund Wilson was dead. That event saddened me; Edmund was the last of the glittering World War I generation (except from Thornton Wilder, who stood aside from it). Edmund was its Saint-Beuve, at least in the 1920s; after 1940 he showed less interest in what his contemporaries were doing, though occasionally he emerged from silence about them to pay tribute to Dawn Powell, for example, or Newton Arvin. But in the twenties he kept scanning the horizon for new talents, and wrote about each of them intelligently (about the novelists better than about the poets), and reproved them in judicial terms when they wandered off the right path. In loco parentis, he made each of them feel that he should always do his best work: "What would Bunny think about it?" they must have asked themselves when making a moral decision about their work. The pieces he collected in *The Shores of Light* are instructive reading today. . . .

[. . .]

As ever,
Malcolm

────────────

[NL TL/CC-1]
[TO: RUTH LIMNER][13]
June 18, 1972

Dear Miss Limner,

[. . .] I knew [Louise Bogan] from 1919 or 1920, when she first came to the Village; she used to call on my first wife and me when we lived in a tenement at 88 West Third Street. [. . .] Certainly Louise disapproved strongly of my political opinions during the 1930s. But the real incident for which she was years and years in forgiving me occurred in 1928 or 1929 when Allen Tate, who had been given a Guggenheim, was giving a big going-away party in a brownstone house somewhere in the Village. It was during the years when Louise was drinking too much. The Tates said, "No, she's fine." But then she did begin to ruin the party. I disremember how, and I decided (rather drunkenly too) that I would maneuver her to the door. I got her into the hall. "Louise," I said, "did anyone ever tell you that you were beautiful?" She *was* beautiful in those days. "Louise," I went on, gently nudging her toward the front door, "you're like a goddess. Not like Juno, Louise," I said as I opened the door, "but like Pallas Athena. Your forehead," I said as I guided her down the steps. "Your calm, open gaze. Why," I said, now on the sidewalk, "why can't you stay with us instead of flying back to Olympus."

Raymond Holden was waiting at the curb with a taxi. Together we pushed her in, and the taxi drove off. For years when Louise met me she would say, "You thought you were pretty smart. You had me." The atmosphere was chilly. But later, as you gathered, we became reconciled and had some good talks together. I had always admired her whether or not she sipped too much nectar when the gods' cupbearer passed it round. That stopped in her later years. In her work she was truly one of the incorruptibles. Meeting at the Academy, we felt like survivors from another time.

Cordially yours,
Malcolm Cowley

...it seems to me absolutely ridic and shameful to refuse [Pound] the Emerson-Thoreau medal on the ground of fascism and (I fear chiefly) anti-semitism. His services to literature are wiped out.

Cowley to Allen Tate, August 18, 1972 [AT]

[NL TL/CC-2]
[TO: HARVEY BROOKS, PRESIDENT,
AMERICAN ACADEMY OF ARTS AND SCIENCES]
September 4, 1972

Dear Mr. Brooks,

[...] The issues do have a "strong ideological content," I feel. [...]

Briefly, if it is to be an "Academy of Arts," as well as "Sciences," and if it is to give literary prizes, the prizes should be given for literary reasons. Not political reasons, not moral reasons. I detest Pound's support of Mussolini and his near-treason during the Second World War. I abhor his anti-Semitism. But for literary reasons that many others have stated at length, Pound deserves the Emerson-Thoreau Award. Once the committee named to choose a recipient had recommended him, the Council of an Academy of Arts should have accepted the recommendation.

Believe me, it is a dangerous precedent for the Council to refuse the award to an artist because of his politico-moral opinions. Are these abhorrently reactionary? The next step—or the step before—is to refuse the award to another artist because his opinions are dangerously radical. By politico-moral standards, Thoreau himself would have been ruled ineligible, if the prize were being awarded in the late 1850s; he had spent a night in jail. Emerson might have been turned down at the time because his abolitionism would have led to the resignation of pro-slavery members. Whitman? Of course he would not have been considered at the time, any more than Edgar Poe.

My very sad feeling is that the Council, by rejecting an award to Pound, has decided that the Academy is not to be "of Arts." Of Sciences, yes, and of Social Sciences Including Politics, and of Moral Sciences, and even of the Humanities (considering that there was something inhumane in Pound's opinions)—but of Arts, no. And if it is not to be an Academy of Arts, I have no place in it and am regretfully tendering my resignation.

Mr. Allen Tate, who had already decided to resign, subscribes to the feelings expressed in this letter. We have not corresponded with others, and we do not intend to make this letter public. We feel, however, that our place is no longer in the Academy.

Sincerely,
Malcolm Cowley

Sometimes I get bored with American literature. It's studied because the US [is] a powerful nation and must logically have antecedents. We find the sprouting seed of IBM in James and Howells. But where will our literature be when the country becomes relatively less powerful? Then Mao Tse-tung the poet will doubtless take the place of Whitman.

Cowley to Kenneth Burke, December 6, 1972 [NL]

[NL TL/CC-2]
[TO: ALLEN TATE]
December 19, 1972

Dear Allen,
Christmas, hell. No holly, mistletoe, feasting, benevolence. We've been picking and packing, yikking and yakking, toiling, moiling, boiling,

spoiling, and all to get off to England[14] December 26 (isn't that Boxing Day?). [. . .]

We'll spend eight or nine days in London, where I'll have a card (through the Century) to the Garrick Club and where I'll indulge in the childhood dream of ordering a suit in Bond Street. Reservations at the Wilbraham Hotel. Then to Coventry, where I'll be faced with the problem of what to say to bright English students of Amlit. My mind, if any, is an empty quarter. One of the first tasks will be talking about *The Golden Bowl,* which is not my favorite James novel—in fact, I bogged down twice in the early chapters. James got so damned wordy in his Major Phase; once I amused myself by going through a paragraph and striking out the unnecessary phrases: "in fine," "as one might say." Adam Verver is a truly impossible character: he had amassed millions by the age of forty, yet the fiercely competitive struggle had left no mark on him. He speaks a language that is not English, much less American: it is faintly German in the habit of inexorably shifting verbs to the end of the sentence; it is French in its quaint use of "then" in unexpected places ("donc" was the word that echoed in James's mind). Isn't language the heart of a writer's problem? And isn't James's language the token, no, the essence of his deracination, of his distance from any soil, whether American, English, or Continental?

This I say angrily, and then (*puis,* not *donc*), I admire more and more his architectonics, his building in scenes like huge granite blocs, and his economy not in words, but in materials.

[. . .]

KB, obsessed with the Demonic Trinity, loves to hunt for fecal images in what he calls *The Golden Bowel.* He points to Fanny Assingham as the character whose name encapsulates three pairs of buttocks. KB also, in a less stercoraceous mood, was delighted to hear that you thought of dedicating your memoirs to him & me—as I was delighted to.

[. . .]

As ever,
Malcolm

Here I cannot boast of conquests. The students at Warwick don't know me from Malcolm Bradbury or Malcolm X.

Cowley to Kenneth Burke, March 8, 1973 [NL]

[NL TL/CC-I]
[TO: KENNETH BURKE]
80 High Street, Kenilworth, Warks., England
4 May 1973

Dear Kenneth,

[...]

The English papers are delighted with the Watergate caper and give lots of space to it. They are disturbed too, because Shitty Dick's foreign policy has been better than his domestic policy and they need American support. But underneath they reveal a good deal of justifiable Schadenfreude. In most ways England is going the same way as America—consumerism, shoddy goods, high prices, conglomerate take-overs—they're just ten years behind us on the road to self-destruction, and they're racing to catch up. But in one good respect they're far ahead of us, that is, they're trying harder to preserve the environment. They're controlling urban sprawl by not releasing land for housing; there are farms right up to the corporate limits of English towns. One town, Bourton-on-the-water, has a trout swimming in it. That's because they spend money on pollution control. They spend money on education, too, and university students all have state scholarships that are supposed to pay all their expense. But, cheez, the crummy things with American trademarks that one buys in English stores!

[...]

Keep in there punching,
Malcolm

[RPW TLS-2]
[TO: ROBERT PENN WARREN]
14 August 1973

Dear Red,

[. . .] A crisis in Sherman: we have been invaded by a mixed band of do-gooders and real-estate speculators armed with bulldozers and apparently all the money in the world. They want to build a new town of 8000 people on 253 acres on the west shore of Candlewood Lake, just below that lovely island where we beached a canoe and swam. A racially mixed town, partly for low-income families. It's the word "black" that they hold over us, that they use to get money from foundations and play on the guilt feelings of liberals. Actually the blacks, with their intelligent leaders, will pretty soon learn that they are being used as pawns. There's no work here for low-income families, and the vast plans of the promoters mean that houses would be too expensive for them to live in. The real aim is to upset the zoning laws so that the big real-estate speculators can move in. The new town, called WatersEdge, couldn't pay for its own services, for education, fire and police protection, water, sewage disposal, garbage removal, snow plowing, and all that. Most of the money would have to come from other residents of Sherman and New Fairfield. The last farms would be taxed out of existence, the lake polluted, the countryside covered with strawberry boxes. It's all going to be threshed out in the courts, and I can picture the bulldozers drawn up in their battalions at the town line, waiting for a liberal judge. Suburban Action Institute. After strip mining, it's the biggest threat to what remains of the environment.

So I think about that and write pieces for the *Sherman Sentinel* instead of poems.[15]

[. . .]

I'm running head on into my 75th birthday in ten days. We'll have a big party here for positively the last time. I'm still going strong (if slow), but begin to feel that I ought to shave my bushy hair and don the saffron robes of a Buddhist monk. Breathe deeply, the preceptor will say, or the doctor. Say "Om" while I depress your tongue with a pine stick.

As ever,
Malcolm

Deep question: Would you be willing to second E. B. White for the Academy? I'm putting him up to rectify a long oversight.—M.

———————

[NL TL/CC-2]
[TO: RICHARD M. KETCHUM, EDITOR, *COUNTRY JOURNAL*][16]
August 16, 1973

Dear Mr. Ketchum,

I wish your magazine well, and I'd even subscribe to it, in spite of my horror at piling up more reading matter in this house ready to crumble under the weight of books. I'll write for it too, if we find there are points at which my interests and yours converge.

More and more I've been concerned with thoughts about trying to save the countryside. It's under pressure now, and the mere weight of money available to developers may leave us crushed to death, like a medieval witness who refused to testify. New England is particularly vulnerable because it is organized into hundreds of towns, and the developers can attack the towns one after another—each one is too small to resist. Sherman and New Fairfield at present are being attacked by Suburban Action Institute with a proposal to build a Planned Unit Development of 2500 apartments and row houses on the west shore of Candlewood Lake. [. . .]

We can fight such invasions, take some lickings, win a few cases, and lose the campaign. But something positive has to be done to restore the countryside. Of course farming is the answer—New England was what we wanted it to be when it was mostly farmed. That's a fear-frightful problem in itself, but one slight ray of hope on the horizon is the present shortage of meat. *Could New England go back to raising beef cattle and sheep?* There's plenty of land, but it's almost all too expensive to farm—when an owner dies, the inheritance taxes make his heirs sell the place. But what about the state's (or the town's or some foundation's) buying land and leasing it back to farmers? All the farmland bought up and wasted by interstate highways could be leased back at low rentals on condition that it be farmed—that would save maintenance costs. Meat growing is so profitable at present that I suspect that corporations could be formed to graze cattle and sheep on leased land. Sheep are a special problem on acct of dogs—but perhaps state laws providing that farmers would be reimbursed for sheep killed by dogs—say half by the town, half by the state—would pretty soon lead to the elimination of dogs running wild in packs.

Yeh, I've got a lot of ideas about the New England countryside, including smaller ideas—for little pieces about How to Grow Melons (as I've done every year until this one) and How to Start an Evergreen Plantation (on which conifers to plant). And there's the *Sherman Sentinel,* our mimeographed fortnightly town newspaper, which has now carried on and paid for itself for 25 years. Maybe you ought to have a department for little pieces of 1000 words or less—not everything spread over page after page. Flutes as well as kettledrums.

Before I forget it, Vermont Cheese is a good cheesy subject (not for me; I don't know enough about it, and I'm too old to do legwork). But one thing I do know: Plymouth cheese, from Cal Coolidge's hometown, is the best in the state and one of the few good varieties of native cheese. Drive up to Plymouth and see for yourself.

[. . .]

Cordially,
Malcolm Cowley

———————

[NL TL/CC-I]
[TO: NANCY MILFORD][17]
9 October 1973

Dear Nancy,

We might as well get down to business and first names.

"Generation gap" is partly the answer. Not "male chauvinism," though there may have been just a touch of that. We were the kids. Louise Bogan and Léonie Adams, among the women poets, were "on our side." Katherine Anne Porter was, too, although she was a coupla years older than Millay (she kept her age secret). The two generations were pre-war and war. Millay more or less allied herself with the prewar generation—not with Brooks, Frank, Rosenfeld, its leaders, but with Dell, Bynner, and what's-his-name, the major who wrote "Three Sisters."[18] Note the Spectrist hoax (and see the book about it by Wm Jay Smith). In poetry there was also a war between the idealists, romantics, and—so we called them—"conventional versifiers" and the rebels, realists, experimenters and female poets with three names; Lizette Woodworth Reese, Mary Caroline/ Dazies/ (I'm misspelling names). When you add the fact of her immense popularity, you can see that Millay wasn't "on our side." We—I—missed at the time her immense importance as a folk-singer of the sexual revolution and also her hard determination to be a great poet. We thought her classical sonnets were insufferably mannered. We said, tolerantly, "Bunny Wilson has no taste in poetry."

I'm spelling things out in primer-book fashion, but that's the way it was.

Cordially,
Malcolm

[NL TL/CC-I]
[TO: FRANZ DOUSKEY]
23 October 1973

Dear Mr. Douskey,

[. . .]

Seems to me that Pep [Nathanael] West was more "of the twenties" than "of the thirties" in spite of his probably having been a CP member. His friends were older men: Bob Coates, Faulkner, Fitzgerald, etc. Except for Sid Perelman, a real influence.

He was very quick to acquire the essential attitudes of the authors he admired. So the Dada-Surrealist-Paris influence was actually strong, even if he didn't spend much time in Paris.

That was an ethical influence, a stage in the religion of art. Épater les bourgeois, knock them off their pins. Trick them like Till Eulenspiegel. Don't be serious about yourself. Be serious about the work. Sacrifice yourself to produce a masterpiece and let it be right in every detail.

He played roles. He saw himself as an English gentleman, a great hunter, a boulevardier, a cynic. He was extremely afraid of being hurt and, with his sympathetic imagination, was also afraid of hurting others. In some ways he resembled Faulkner, though he could never be as cruel as Faulkner sometimes was to people he thought had no business prying into his life.

[. . .]

Bob Coates's *The Eater of Darkness* was another book he must have read carefully. He was one of the sweetest people I knew.

Sincerely,
Malcolm Cowley

Conrad Aiken died on August 17, 1973. "He had become for me a father figure," Cowley wrote to Mary Aiken on October 8, 1973. In dialogue with Tate, Cowley sought to weigh Aiken's life and career, preparatory to a tribute for the American Academy.

[NL TL/CC-2]
[TO: ALLEN TATE]
21 November 1973

Dear Allen,

[. . .] Funny, it's the WatersEdge battle that has mobilized my psychic energy more than literature or history. Sherman, to which I've become ivy-attached in the last forty years, is threatened all over its 13,000 acres with suburban developments; the next to go is the 200-acre farm just down the road. So I brood and fume and write angry pieces for the real-estate section of the *Times,* then I go back to reading Conrad Aiken's collected poems, collected novels, collected stories, collected criticism and to thinking about his collected life.

Yes, his relation with the Tsetse[19] was disastrous. They were on *The Harvard Advocate* together; Eliot was '10, Conrad '11, then together in England, where Conrad contributed a great deal to the relationship, but, as you say, nothing that caught the public imagination. The Tsetse was concentrated; Conrad was too diffuse. That's an impression I received again when reading over his poems. Not sufficiently inspissated. With his magnificent technical equipments, his mastery of the word, his active imagination, he wrote too easily for our present taste; that was part of his theory of writing poetry; go fast, take chances (but too many of the chances were of being conventional or of not getting the thing quite definitively said, so that the verse, instead of being opaque, was simply obscure, or again of simply going on too long because the flood of words and rhymes didn't stop). If "Tetélestai," to mention just one example, were half as long it would be twice as effective. I haven't time to reread all the "Symphonies." "The Coming Forth by Day of Osiris Jones" is a real tour de force—it helped Joyce with *Finnegans Wake*— but its publication received no attention whatever.

Conrad did have a world view and it emerges in his criticism. It is, to use a phrase that Matthiessen borrowed from him and used in his book on Henry James, the religion of consciousness. The development of consciousness in scope and refinement—the finding of the word that reveals a new facet of consciousness—is the great historical movement to which a writer should attach himself. But Conrad's great notion attracted little attention.

Will I wear you out just making you read this letter?—Conrad has some marvelous shorter poems, including a few in his randy, raffish, realistic mode, "Blind Date," for instance, and "The Lady in Pink Pyjamas." He has pious poems about Cape Cod; "Mayflower" is one of the best. But his attempt to present an American legend in "The Kid" (to show Hart Crane how it could be done?) is not interesting. What if the thousand pages of the *Collected Poems* were selected down to 200 pages; would the impact be greater? My wholehearted admiration is elicited more, this time, by the prose. Might it be that *Ushant* is his masterpiece? In one of the novels, *Great Circle,* the hero's long drunken monologue to a psychiatrist friend (Harry Murray?) is the most brilliant stream of semiconsciousness that I have read. Some of the stories, too. The book reviews are marvelous; one looks at the dates and wonders that such judgments could have been formulated and made final in 1919, 1925, 1929. A towering figure—but not so towering in age, say after 1960, when his disappointments gnawed at him and he began to excommunicate one person after another. I could see my own fate looming on the horizon for the last ten years.[20]

But I'm tiring you and giving you no oxygen. [. . .]

As ever,
Malcolm

[NL TL/CC-2]
[TO: PHILIP YOUNG]
10 December 1973

Dear Phil,

You meant it all for the best[21] and only kidded me a little, but, honest, those kid gloves were full of tacks & things. Or maybe they were velvet gloves and you stroked my back with them while slipping in the needle. I do come out like a dumb cluck. It seems I don't even know when somebody is putting me on, as in that story about there not being a café where us sadists can get together. Maybe I should have attached a name to the story; then you would have gotten the point of it. The remark was made by Willie Seabrook,[22] a professed sadist; his house in the French countryside was full of paraphernalia of the art, including a lion's cage on the roof in which he would persuade naked nonvirgins to let themselves be locked; then he'd go away for an hour and let them broil in the sun. One of them was a friend of mine, [*crossed out:* Ladine Young, known as the countess.] Anyhow, when Willie complained of there being no café where us sadists can get together, he knew he was saying something funny, but also he was more than half serious, he really *wanted* such a café. That's what made the remark really funny.

Willie Seabrook. Somebody ought to do a piece about his adventures. In one of his books he told about eating human flesh in West Africa. Maybe that was a put-on, but he just might have been telling the truth.

And then, for God's sake, that paragraph on the Harvard Aesthetes that I quoted from one of my 1932 reviews. [. . .] Those details of life among the Aesthetes were all remembered or retold from stories I had often heard. God knows, there's a lot of old stuff in *A Second Flowering,* but it's my own old stuff that has become familiar because other people copied it. I didn't put in the famous costume ball the Aesthetes gave that spilled over in to the Yard. It caused a scandal about homosexuality. Truth is that there were half a dozen homos among the Aesthetes, some of them later notorious (Stewart Mitchell, Kith-me-Cuthie (Cuthbert Wright), Bobbie Hillyer); you might have guessed as much from my paragraph; but most of the group were satisfactorily male.

In *A Second Flowering,* the writers of the wartime generation really did form a group, even if they didn't often meet together. The point is—one point is—that there weren't many serious young writers in those days, and they did come to regard themselves as brothers in arms. Some of them had actually been close friends in college (Dos Passos and Cummings, for instance, or Fitzgerald, John Peale Bishop, and Wilson). But principally they were all comrades in the same guerilla band, making forays against the establishment. Where'd you get the idea that five of the eight I treated in separate chapters weren't in the war? Five of them didn't get overseas, but three of those five were in uniform, including Fitzgerald and Faulkner, both of whom had such bold imaginations that they pictured themselves lying dead on the battlefield. Faulkner came home from elementary flight training and talked darkly of a nearly fatal wound (see the Sherwood Anderson story that has Faulkner as its hero). Only Wolfe and Crane were too young to be drafted, though Crane got his draft notice a week before the Armistice. Wolfe, Crane, Burke, Josephson worked in shipyards. I was thinking of a larger group than just those eight writers, and most of the others who fitted into the pattern had been soldiers.

Hemingway had no feeling for the group. Fitzgerald had a very strong feeling. So had Wilson, actually. The phrase was "my contemporaries." I could go on & on. I'm tempted to go on & on, to defend the concept of a generational history.

For the generous things you said, many thanks. I only wish you hadn't—like a Chinese cook planning a duck dinner—cut my throat while you were stroking my feathers.[23]

[. . .]

In mild disgruntlement,
Malcolm Cowley

[NL TL/CC-I]
[TO: ALLEN TATE]
25 July 1974

Dear Allen,

[. . .] I have to get back to doing a piece about Bob Coates. Southern Illinois University Press is republishing his *Yesterday's Burdens* (1933)—the presses are waiting—it's a better book than I remembered it to be, almost a classic of its time, beautifully written in a way that nobody writes today, a prose poem to country living and a farewell to city living and the self that lived in the city. Bob calls that self "Henderson" and kills him off. Bob was a funny mixture of city and country, classic and romantic (or rather nympholeptic), gregarious and solitary, sunny smile and a morbid unconscious that came out in much of his writing (in which he sympathetically presents child molesters, homosexuals on the prowl, and homicidal maniacs).[24]

[...]

As ever,
Malcolm

─────────

[NL TL/CC-2]
[TO: JAMES M. KEMPF][25]
23 November 1974

Dear Mr. Kempf,

My, oh, my, what a tumult of topics in your last letter! How can a contumacious obfuscator, a vacillating valetudinarian, find time to comment on all of them, especially when he's still aching and staggering with sciatica? Let's talk about Yaddo first. I've been going there almost every year since 1930, and early and late I've done a good deal of writing there. In youth it sheltered me/ And I'll protect it now. But also you're right: I've always felt that Yaddo was of great service to the literary community—helped to make it a community—helped to keep writers writing (and eating)—and hence deserved one's help and advice. I have been a director since when I can't remember—perhaps 1942—and vice president of the corporation since when?—1968 or 1970.

[...]

[...] I think you're right about my continuing effort to be a mediator, especially a mediator between serious writers and the public. My style shows the effect of that 18th-century ambition to write for the intelligent but unspecialized reader, the audience that Diderot had in mind for the *Encyclopédie*. One side of the mediating effort that you seem to have missed was that during the 1930s I made a quixotic attempt to fit the Communist movement into the general framework of American politics. I was vice president of the League of American Writers, founded under Communist auspices, and remained a vice president until after the Stalin-Hitler Pact. Then I tried to make the LAW an independent organization (we had a non-Communist majority on the board of directors), and failing in that effort I resigned in June 1940. Actually I resigned from political life at the time (and stayed resigned, except for such purely local activities as being for a long time chairman of the Sherman Zoning Board).

In 1949 I was elected to the National Institute of Arts and Letters. I was president of that organization 1956–59 and 1962–65. In 1964 I was elected to the American Academy of Arts and Letters, of which I have been chancellor (a fancy name for vice president) since 1968. Here is another activity for the literary community that has engaged a good deal of my attention. [. . .]

[. . .]

Cordially yours,
Malcolm Cowley

[NL TL/CC-2]
[TO: ALLEN TATE]
18 February 1975

Dear Allen,

[. . .] I give a lecture on Tuesday evening on Literary Generations, the lecture not written, though I've been reading & thinking about it for the last week. A rather fascinating subject for me. Why do writers (and artists and scientists) appear in clusters or constellations, with empty spaces between the clusters? How does one define a generation? Can one use generations as a model for literary history, which had seemed to me something impossible to write except as a succession of chapters on individual authors? (In other words, not a history at all, but a suite of critical analyses.) I mull over those questions and take notes. I take notes. Emerson (1803), Hawthorne (1804), Longfellow and Whittier (1807), Poe and Holmes (1809) composed our first cluster. Thoreau (1817), Whitman, Melville, Lowell (1819), Parkman (1823) were the second. In France Baudelaire and Flaubert were born in the same year (1821), as were Valéry and Proust (1871). Hart Crane and Hemingway were born on the same day (7/21/99), four months before A. Tate. It's something more than mere coincidence. Ortega Y Gasset is the most illuminating student of generations, but lets himself fall into the mysticism of numbers.[26]

[...]

As ever,
Malcolm

———

[NL TL/CC-1]
[TO: JAMES M. KEMPF]
20 April 1975

Dear Mr. Kempf,

[...] Look, I'm not a diplomat or ambassador of letters and bringing together the divergent interests of the literary community isn't my "chief virtue." My chief virtue is to have written well. Yes, I did have in mind the creation of a literary community. In the 1920s Allen Tate and I speculated about the possibility of putting out a magazine of sorts, to be called "News of the Republic of Letters." I was a contemporary historian of the fortunes of that republic. But the point was that I had to write well and sound to satisfy my conscience. How many nights I worked till the sun rose! Of course that was to meet a *New Republic* deadline, but also it was because I couldn't sign my name to anything awkward or unreadable. I also had in mind the 18th-century notion of the average intelligent reader. He was the man I wouldn't patronize, and he had to understand what I was saying, which at the same time had to be rigorously true. No jargon, but no shallowness.

In the 1930s part of my job was to see that *The New Republic* was well written. I read proof of it every week end—then on Tuesday morning I read and revised the editorial section, especially dipping my pencil into Bruce Bliven's editorial paragraphs, which were hastily written. I don't think he ever forgave me for recasting his sentences. Cheez, I was a busy man.

[...]

Cordially,
Malcolm Cowley

———

[NL VIKING MEMO/CC-2]
[TO: ALAN D. WILLIAMS]
May 12, 1975
LETTERS OF FLOYD DELL
Chiefly About Edna St. Vincent Millay
Edited by Miriam Gurko

I read this 600-page manuscript with a good deal of fascination [. . .]. In 1917 Dell met Edna Millay (he calls her "Edna" not "Vincent," as her family later took to doing) when he was already widely known as literary editor of *The Masses* (for $25 a week) and Edna was still a little-known poet, not quite starving, but not very well fed (or lodged or heated or dressed)—but, God, she had a face that nobody forgot. She was a passionate virgin with a lesbian background. Dell had a reputation as the Village Don Juan. He worked to convert her to heterosexuality and succeeded—after getting her to protect herself from men. The next time she came to his room she didn't wear the cross, and, Christ! what a night they spent together.

The affair lasted for ten or eleven months, with intermissions. Dell was undergoing analysis in the hope of being converted to monogamy, and *was* converted, and tried to convert Edna in turn, but she was obstinate. "I shall have many lovers," she said musingly after that first so-successful night together. At one stage Floyd and Edna were engaged. But she told him about her lecherous feeling for a young boxer and Floyd walked out and later gave her back her ring. She was crushed, he said. Soon afterward he fell in love with B. Marie Gage and married her and had children and remained faithfully married until he died in 1969 at the age of 82. But, in his dotage, he dreamed back over the incidents of his almost-a-year with Edna, and when he learned that Miriam Gurko was writing a young-adults life of Edna,[27] he wrote Gurko these hundreds of letters.

They are full of pretty scandalous details, many of which I have known about these many, many years, but which I have never seen in print. Floyd thinks that Edna's husband, Eugen (or Eugene) Boissevain was nearly impotent; in any case he did not object to her many love affairs. [. . .] There is talk about the alcoholism of her later years—Dell actually knows little about this, but he surmises that she drank and also took drugs for a time to calm the pain of a serious back injury; then she cold-turkeyed herself on her and Eugene's island off the Maine Coast. Yes, lots of scandals, including the night that Louise Bryant, then Mrs. Jack Reed, came home to the Reeds' cottage in Croton, found the door locked, then unlocked it to see Edna coming downstairs stark naked and holding a candle. But Dell doesn't like to make jokes about sex, and there aren't many of these funny stories.

[...]

Floyd Dell himself becomes a wistful character, plagued by serious illnesses, partly forgotten by the world (and himself growing forgetful). Appealing, in a way, but also deadly conventional in his judgments. This is truly his testament.

[...]

MaC

This is going to be a tearing-down book, not a building-up book. Okay. This means that there should be an introductory chapter to show that what you are tearing down is a considerable edifice, not merely a flimsy amusement park. Hemingway was the equivalent for the early 20th century of Byron for the early 19th century.

Cowley to Scott Donaldson, August 29, 1974[28] [NL]

[NL TL/CC-2]
[TO: SCOTT DONALDSON]
14 June 1975

Dear Scott,

I confess to being a little disappointed in the last chapter. Writing last chapters is always a problem—the writer wants to end with a bang; the reader expects him to do so, or at least to illuminate what has gone before by rolling it into one incandescent ball. There has been the foreplay and the friction; now comes the orgasm. Well, sometimes the orgasm isn't there and the writer can't be blamed for that, but at least he can summarize and build on what has gone before. The general fault of "The Man Who Would Be Master" is that it doesn't give sufficient sense of things ending. [...]

A couple of less sweeping criticisms. You start with a passage on Hemingway as a humorist, but in my book he wasn't a humorist at all; he was a wit. A distinction often made between humor and wit is that the humorist presents the ludicrous side of himself, or many people including himself; the wit makes jokes at the expense of other people. Satire, sarcasm, the put-down are forms of wit, and they were forms in which EH was often truly brilliant. He was never, or let's say almost never, a humorist like Jim Thurber, with a note of affection in his ridicule,—Incidentally, I wish you had found better or fresher examples of his wit. I seem to remember that some of his answers to questionnaires and his telegrams to *Time* magazine were really funny.

Later I think you spend too much space on his nevertheless real prejudice against Negroes and Jews. The prejudices were those of middle-class Americans in his time—as you say—and were about on a par with those of Fitzgerald, Edmund Wilson, T. S. Eliot, and others. They seem more heinous in our anti-racist age, when the word "nigger" has an entirely different value from what it had in 1930. It might be wise to do a little judicious cutting in that passage, for the book's sake.

[...] I also thought of some things you might have said in earlier chapters. One thought was that you didn't say enough about Hemingway's real virtues as a writer. One of them, not hard to illustrate by quotations, is the absolute freshness of his writings at its best. One could never mistake it for anybody else's writing. A single sentence I have always wanted to quote is that longest one from *Green Hills* [*of Africa*] about the garbage boats from Havana dumping their loads into the Gulf Stream. It was a high point for Hemingway, but there are other high points as late as *A Moveable Feast*. Or in *The Bell Tolls* El Sordo facing death while loving life. I think a few quotes of this nature would add to the strength of the book.

[...]

[...] Argue with me if you think I'm wrong—but I'm eager for this to be an impressive book.

[...]

Yours, as ever,
Malcolm Cowley

I like your effort to unzip yourself.

Cowley to Seymour Krim, October 30, 1975 [NL]

[NL TL/CC-1]
[TO: SEYMOUR KRIM]
31 October 1975

Dear Seymour,

More observations in scrimshaw-krimshaw after reading *You & Me*. I didn't put them into yesterday's letter.

Watch out, you are casting yourself into a role. It isn't one of the multitudinous roles you have dreamed of playing: ballad singer, gambler, best seller, Mafioso, and all that. Role playing, by the way, isn't such a universal or universally American characteristic as you think it is. I know one compulsive role player, Matthew Josephson, who has also been a biographer. Every time he started a new biography, he cast himself in the role of his subject. He was secretive about the book he was writing. We used to observe his behavior and guess who his new subject was. In turn he was Zola, Rousseau, Victor Hugo, and a robber baron. You stay in American life and find new types to celebrate. But watch out! Unconsciously you are casting yourself in another role, that of the Failure, the sad schlemiel, even of the schlemozzel who gets soup poured down his back by the schlemiel. Success looms ahead and your unconscious, or Ucs, forces you to stumble—because your Ucs wants you to achieve perfect success in another role.

It's time to recognize and frustrate that unconscious drive.

You have a real and rare gift for celebration. Especially for celebrating vital persons rejected by the intelligentsia: Breslin (your enemy), Mario

Puzo, and the like. The gift for celebration puts you in the line of Whitman, Thomas Wolfe (and Tom Wolfe too), Kerouac, Ginsberg, and a few others (but not so many others). If I were still a magazine editor, I would commission you to do a series called Celebrations and suggest subjects such as Coca Cola, drive-in restaurants, drag racing, communes, and TV personalities, as well as anything or anybody else that fired your imagination. Maybe some of that will go into your new book.

You've had Periods such as those reconstructed by archaeologists from their digs into a buried city. Instead of Archaic, Early Kingdom, late Kingdom, and the like, you've had Partisan-Intellectual, Early Beat, late Beat, Confessional, New Journalism, and now what? In the midst of all this you *have* been developing a style of your own, sometimes very effective, sometimes so clotted that it becomes hard to read. But it's best when it's dealing—as I said—not with Krimself, but with Krim in relation to other people. Whom you celebrate.

Enough of this.

As ever,
Malcolm Cowley

————

[NL TL/CC-2]
[TO: ALLEN TATE]
16 February 1976

Dear Allen,

[. . .]

I've been working intermittently on a long piece about Erskine Caldwell.[29] I thought (you don't) that his early work added something to American letters, a new sensibility, a vision of everyday country life as grotesque and, as Faulkner would have said, apocryphal. In the middle 1930s Faulkner and Caldwell were regarded by the movie studios and by many critics as almost interchangeable values. Why did their work diverge to such an extent in quality? "Faulkner's genius," one says immediately; but there was also the fact that they formed different self-images. Faulkner's self-image was that of a great writer, and by God he lived up to it. Caldwell's self-image was that of a little ol' country boy with a passion for writing stories. He didn't make demands on himself, except for earning money, and he did earn money. Watch out what you ask for, because God will give it to you.... It's taking me a long time to say all this, with documentation, and I don't know whether Caldwell is worth the time, in the end, but I do go back to his early stories with pleasure and mourn what happened to all that promise.

[...]

With all my arthritic best,
Malcolm

[NL TL/CC-1]
[TO: ERSKINE CALDWELL]
24 September 1977

Dear Erskine,

[...]

I was tough on you in the essay. I do think that, starting out with your extraordinary talent, you didn't ask enough of it, you weren't driven hard enough by the spirit of emulation; in fact, you refused to emulate. I like the early work best, when you were wilder and depended more on your unconscious; then there was something magical in your talent. Later you became more the observer and the reporter. But I hope my piece encourages others to write about you.

[...]

Yours, as ever,
Malcolm Cowley

[NL TL/CC-2]
[TO: MARTIN GREEN][30]
9 June 1977

Dear Martin Green,

Of course I remember you from Michigan, spring semester 1957, as a young English writer with a mind of his own. [...]

Nilla Cook. I knew her well, but only for a few weeks or months, late spring and early summer of 1926. I had known Jig and Susan, but only by sight, at the Provincetown Playhouse. They were Nilla's background, for she was one of the children of Greenwich Village rebels of 1910. Golly, they were an unfortunate generation. Raised in a casual fashion by unorthodox households, most of them had unhappy lives, unless they were reincorporated into bourgeois society and lost to sight. Mark Tobey's children, Hutch Hapgood's children, Mary Vorse's children, Gene O'Neill's children: almost the only survivor I have read about is Oona O'Neill, with her brood of eight. Oh, yes, there is Dorothy Day's daughter Tamar, also with eight children, whom she has supported by working as a practical nurse, her husband being insane. It would be worthwhile to examine the fate of that whole unhappy group.

Nilla had more spunk than the others and led an extraordinary life. You are exactly right to mention Isadora Duncan for Nilla had features and a body something like hers (to judge from photographs of Isadora, whom I didn't know) and had the same openness to experience. Openness? She was a yawning crater that swallowed up experience.

I first met her at one of the Sunday at-homes (to give them a flossy name) of Bill (William Slater) and Susan Jenkins Brown. They lived in a farmhouse or farm cottage that they called Robber Rocks, in the town (or township) of Pawling, New York: on one side their property was bounded by the state line. We used to gather at the Browns' for croquet on Sunday afternoons. My first wife Peggy Baird and I had just moved from Staten Island to another farmhouse (rent, $10 a month) four miles away in Sherman. Hart Crane had left for the Isle of Pines and the Tates were living in Addie Turner's barn of a house. I was 27 years old. Nilla shocked me a little by speaking of "Your generation" and "Our younger generation." "You talk about things," she said— our talk was free—"but we *do* things." And so she did.

Nilla was then about 16, a big, fresh-looking, soft-featured young woman (one didn't think of her as a girl) who still had her baby fat. Jig had died two years before in Greece (of glanders, people said with a chuckle). Susan Glaspell came to feel that Nilla was incorrigible and even thought—or so I heard, of putting her in an institution, but Fitzi came to the rescue. Fitzi was Eleanor Fitzgerald, a tall red-haired woman who had been the lover of Alexander Berkman. She was the treasurer of the Provincetown Players and raised money to keep them going. Somehow she had managed to buy a house for herself in Sherman—they were cheap then, about $4000 with acres of land—and she volunteered to give Nilla a home during the summer. Later Nilla was joined there by a thin, dark-haired friend whose name I forget, but we called her Lou, and by Lou's lover the trout fisherman Charlie Carpenter. Fitzi had a grindstone in her woodshed, and young men of the neighborhood used to come there to sharpen their axes. That's not a figure of speech, but one day I found Nilla alone in the house and forgot to sharpen my axe.

Of course we talked, or Nilla talked. She had no formal education, but had read pretty widely, had picked up some Greek, I suppose during father's travels, and had great misty dreams of producing Greek dramas and pageants. She never mentioned Isadora, who must, however, have been present in her mind as a model.

That's about all I remember of her. Except that one weekend Paul Robeson came to the Browns' with his wife Eslanda and there was a big party. Nilla led me outdoors into the night and told me that she had just fucked—that wasn't her word; what was it?—Paul and that it was wonderful. She called him her big chocolate drop, her black sugar baby. Not long afterward she left Fitzi's—for where? I don't know, for she never wrote me. But, through Fitzi, or reports that Fitzi passed on to the Browns, I continued to hear something about her adventures. She had married a young Greek of a prominent family, she had gone to Persia, I think (that was one of her dreams), and finally she had gone to India as a disciple of Gandhi. We all wondered how Nilla would adjust herself to Gandhi's laws of celibacy. But can't one say that, besides being a later avatar of Isadora, she also foreshadowed the eager young women of the 1960s? I don't remember how or when she died.

I'm writing this short memoir for you, but also for myself. [. . .] [T]here's hardly anyone but me who remembers those days [. . .].

Sincerely,
Malcolm Cowley

[NL TL/CC-1] [SC 407]
[TO: KENNETH BURKE]
21 June 1977

Dear Kenneth,

[. . .]

Right now I'm thinking about saying something that will illuminate my own attitude to the unbelievable 1960s, when a new generation came forward as different from past generations as anything can be and yet obeying a sort of historical alteration between diastole and systole—the age group of the 1950s had been systolic, contractive, uptight, so here appeared a new age group, open, full of illusions, and crazy. And here I was, feeling sympathy for most of the causes that engaged the youngsters—revolt against American business, black liberation, war against the war in Vietnam, back to the land, ecology, women's lib (not so much sympathy for that)—but dismayed by what they said and how they acted and especially by their innocent faith in the Coming Revolution; here I was, outside the littery life, no longer going to openings or publishers' cocktail parties, deaf, living in the country, getting my news from the newspapers, unable to read the new fiction, waiting for all the kids to be disillusioned, as they shortly would be (in 1972). How can I say all that in 1,200 words, which are all the words I want to write?[31]

So instead I write you a letter . . .

With all them best wishes and love,
Malcolm

No American wrote better than old Waldo did, unless it was Mark Twain.

Cowley to Carl Bode, 24 April 1979 [NL]

[GWA ALS-1]
[TO: GAY WILSON ALLEN]
22 August 1977

Dear Gay,

[…]

As I grow older, Waldo looms more and more as one of the master figures. And how well he *wrote*. I hope you have something to say about his hickory-tough, sinewy, wholly concrete style. Think of the contrast with the abstract nouns affected by so many of our contemporary thinkers, so many nouns like strings of the balloons.

As ever,
Malcolm

———

[AT TLS-2]
[TO: ALLEN TATE]
23 September 1977

Dear Allen,

I don't know what to say about Cal Lowell's death.[32] The heart attack must have been connected in some ways with his marital problems. He was returning from a hasty trip to Ireland to see his son. He was in a taxi bound probably for Elizabeth [Hardwick]'s apartment on West 57th Street. The newspaper account didn't say whether Elizabeth had met his plane. She was at the funeral in Massachusetts, weeping. So were Caroline and his little boy, weeping. Was he in an agony of indecision or remorse or whatever when he died? The egomania was there, something apparently essential to public acceptance as a Great Author. I suspect that it had destroyed his critical faculty: otherwise how explain those last poems? Yet one is very sorry to lose him.

[…]

I staggered through a review of [Edmund] Wilson's letters.[33] They are fascinating to me as a revelation of his personality, mostly on the warmer side, and my review was more an act of praise than I had intended it to be. It seems to me that he was, in a sense, our foremost critic, owing to his energy, curiosity, scope, conviction, production, but not owing to his depth. He was not our deepest critic, not by fathoms; you have been far deeper, and Kenneth far more original. Edmund was a Naturalist in all senses of the word, opposed to any sort of religious faith, persuaded that men are hardly different from other animals, and writing about love as if he were an ethnologist observing the sexual habits of chimpanzees. But he did have candor and shrewd perceptions on all but the deeper level. In his later years he was best on Russian writers—worked on them tremendously, read all their works in Russian (which he had learned in order to read Pushkin, as he had learned Italian to read Dante). As an irreligionist, he was a great student of the Bible, when he was 75 he puzzled through, with the help of a grammar, some apocryphal books of the New Testament that exist only in Old Church Slavonic. If I had had more space for the review, I would have said a lot more about him, not all of it encomiastic.

[...]

Malcolm

Somebody should have nominated you for the Nobel Prize before now.[34]

Cowley to Allen Tate, August 18, 1973 [AT]

[AT TLS-2]
[TO: ALLEN TATE]
11 November 1977

Dear Allen,

I look at the calendar and your 78th birthday is coming up in a few days—next Saturday, isn't it? Forgive me for birthday-writing a week in advance. We're among the hoary survivors. We've kept going, although these later steps have been more painful than the early ones—for you, more than for me. I'll confess to my share of pain, but just now I'm worried more about your eyes and am wondering what report you had from the oculist. Meanwhile I'll pass along what news I have.

[...]

I went to the Institute dinner on Wednesday evening. [. . .] the meeting was lively and argumentative, over familiar questions: whether each department should elect its own members; whether the Music Department should be enlarged; whether new radical poets should be elected. Allen Ginsberg spoke on this last topic, looking almost patriarchal and wearing, my God, a suit. Maybe he wore a necktie too, but if so it was completely concealed by his beard. He thought we were dastardly not to recognize William Burroughs, the author of *Naked Lunch.* He spoke of the candidates (four) qualified for election to the Department of Literature as "mediocrities." The four candidates qualified were John Malcolm Brinnin (who is a mediocrity), Galway Kinnell (who isn't), Donald Barthelme, and Joyce Carol Oates. At the dinner table there was a long discussion of an offer by somebody to give the Academy and Institute[35] a plot of land opposite the Metropolitan Museum. All we would have to do is to raise or contribute three millions to put up a building. That wouldn't leave us much money for grants or awards. People complained again about our inaccessible location. Suddenly the 55-year-old building seemed more attractive to me, and I contributed the jocular remark that we were in an ideal location for the older members, with the Presbyterian Hospital to the north of us and a cemetery across the street.

[. . .]

Allen, I think of you always with affection. The years since 1924 have made us brothers. I wish I could sit at your bedside and read to you. All our love to Helen. All our warmest hopes for you. And the book.

As ever,
Malcolm

[NL TL/CC-2]
[TO: WALLACE STEGNER]
14 December 1977

Dear Wally,

I'm tickled pink that you mostly liked the book [*WT*] & found it in your heart to send the publisher a few words about it. And I'm red-faced that you caught me up in an embarrassing piece of parochialism. Of course I've never, never had the delusion that cultuah flourishes only east of the Hudson. I come from Cambria County, Pa., which is the real beginning of the Midwest, just over the crest of the Alleghenies. The stream I fished in was Blacklick Creek, which finds its way west and south until its now polluted-with-mine-wash waters find their way into the Gulf of Mexico, mingled with waters from the Yellowstone. My friends in the twenties and thirties were mostly from the Midwest or the South. But they had come to N'yawk, and I lived in N'yawk at the time, and thinking back on the time I fell into the gaffe of saying that "young men of letters" traveled west of the Hudson or south of the Potomac "into regions they have never explored." I think *if* I can change "young men of letters" to "New York writers," it will become clearer that I was making fun of their parochialism. Actually Edmund Wilson had spent several months in Santa Barbara, but he was, at the time, firmly cemented into the haunts of the working class. Nathan Asch had traveled from Warsaw to Syracuse, where he was an undergraduate, but he knew little about the U.S. except for a couple of months of starving with his girlfriend in Texas. James Agee came from West Tennessee, but went to Exeter and Harvard and *Time-Life* as a graduate course. So, with many others, they all became tourists or trippers in the 1930s and wrote books about it.

Farrell was living in New York too, and Steinbeck moved there. Only Algren and Faulkner stayed faithful to their home towns.

I go along with your piece on *A Moveable Feast,* though I didn't *feel* the meanness of the book quite as strongly as you did. I took it more as an episode in literary warfare. I knew more than you, unfortunately, about Ernest's propensity for sticking a knife into one's back. In those last years he was a pretty sick ego. He couldn't ever forgive Fitzgerald for having helped him. Ford lied like blazes, but he was sweet and kind and helpful—Ernest couldn't forgive him for that. The story about Fitzgerald's prick was true, only it didn't happen in Paris; it happened in New York, 1934, at a time when Scott was having his crack-up. Ernest and Scott and Edmund Wilson got drunk together—Scott drunker than the others—and Scott began complaining about his being so small there. Ernest told him to measure the thing from below; it would seem longer. Wilson repeated the story to me the very next day, at the *New Republic* office. But even if the story is true, that's no excuse for Ernest's repeating it a quarter of a century later, after Scott was dead and famous again and Ernest had become very unsure of his own talent. As for writing, *A Moveable Feast* is a lovely book, as you say. I don't think Ernest was a *complete* son of a bitch. He suffered. He tried to do his best. But he could be mean as cat piss.

I'm sorting out a final batch of papers in preparation for shipping them to the Newberry Library. So far I have filled seven whisky cartons and I think there are still two to come. Newberry is going to appraise them. Another library might give me more for them, but Newberry has been good to me, and I want to get them out of the house while I still have strength to pack them. [...]

As ever,
Malcolm

[GWA TLS-1]
[TO: GAY WILSON ALLEN]
7 February 1978

Dear Gay,

[...]

In the *Second Series*, I have always been interested in another essay, "The Poet." Of course it merely sums up what Emerson says elsewhere, but sums it up magisterially and becomes the extreme statement of the inspirational view of poetry, that poetry comes from the unconscious and that conscious form is secondary. The opposite view is best expressed in Poe's essay "The Philosophy of Composition," written at almost the same time. I have always thought vaguely of doing a piece on the contrast between those two essays, something which became sharper during the next century. There's the Poe line in poetry—Mallarmé, Valéry, Eliot, Stevens, etc.—and there is the Emerson line—Whitman and all his followers down to Allen Ginsberg, the inspirationalists. "Doubt not, O poet, but persist. Say 'It is in me and shall out.' Stand there, balked and dumb, stuttering and stammering, hissed and hooted, stand and strive, until at last rage draw out of thee that *dream*-power which every night shows thee in thine own . . ." It was Emerson who italicized "dream."

[...]

As ever,
Malcolm

[AT TLS-2]
[TO: ALLEN TATE]
22 February 1978

Dear Allen,

We have been thinking & talking about you, and a hell of a lot of good that does when we are in Sherman and you are bedded in Nashville. I wish I were there to talk with you and read to you; there are so many memories to be summoned up. People come round here with tape recorders to tap, tap, tape my memories as if I were a National Scholarly Resource. The National Endowment for the Humanities ought to provide me with a secretary. I should be funded before being embalmed. [. . .]

I too try to act as if I were only 75, working doggedly on my memoirs of the 1930s [. . .] and going to New York every two or three weeks. I come home interviewed and exhausted. I try to walk a mile every day on the snowy roads, and then my legs ache like blazes. I write letters suggesting what the Institute and the Academy might do about electing new good members.[36] I'm sure Jacques Barzun files them away as if I were a junior member of his Columbia faculty. [. . .]

[. . .] No more of this babble. Allen, we love you and think of you every day.

Your brother in age and affection,

Malcolm

[NL TL/CC-1] [SC 413–414]
[TO: KENNETH BURKE]
13 March 1978

Dear Kenneth,

Matty died today suddenly, of a heart attack. He had spent the winter in Santa Cruz, as you know, and was coming back east tomorrow. Santa Cruz has a dreadful climate for Matty's chest condition; he had been ill for a time but had apparently recovered. Matty was 79 on February 15, not quite a year younger than I and two years younger than you. I wish I had been closer to him during these last years. But I had quarreled with him during Hannah's last illness; I think he was jealous because so many people came to see her; he was certainly distraught. So he attacked me, I mean shouted at me, on Bank Street in New Milford, and I shouted back. After that our relations were correct. Matty was a son of a bitch in some ways; he was stingy and cantankerous [. . .].

It hurts me that our friendship cooled over the years, when we were so close in the twenties and early thirties. And yes, you and Matty and I were at one time a triumvirate. Matty had an imagination that I respected and an enormous capacity for getting things done. He also had a bad habit of claiming credit for other people's achievements. He didn't really respect the language. He was a mild disaster on *The New Republic* when he took my place for two months. "But it wasn't so bad," Mary Updike told me—she was the book department secretary; "I didn't let him send out many books for review." I suppose that was when we began to be mildly estranged. Last summer he never came to see us; I went to see him once. [. . .]

Matty young was large-gestured, picturesque, admirable. I wonder how many of us take a slow nosedive after thirty or forty? Then feel somewhat embittered at lack of recognition? As Matty certainly did, though we have known many others.

I feel sad as I make these rough notes for an obit that will never be written.

[. . .]

Yours, sadly,
Malcolm

———

[NL TL/CC-3]
[TO: BENJAMIN DEMOTT][37]
6 May 1978

Dear DeMott,

I'm grateful for what you said about *The Writer's Trade* in the *Sunday Times Book Review*.[38] You picked out the good features of the book to praise, and your praise was heartening. But of course I demur at what you said at the end, about the Men of Good Will and their sense of guilt, and my own sense of guilt. You have misinterpreted what I said about Robert Brustein and the "greater sins" to which he demanded that the men of the 1930s should offer confession. Also you have a false notion of my testimony at the two Hiss trials, in 1949.

Brustein nowhere, "in the context" or otherwise, charged the Good Willers with espionage. He has too much sense to make a false accusation that couldn't be supported with evidence. He charged them with being Stalinists, including all the word implies with "reference to ideas, ideology, or power"; there lay what I regarded as the "greater sins." While trying to be utterly candid about myself, I set out to answer Brustein's charge, and I hope that I answered it effectively.

As for my testimony at the Hiss trials, it was a simple matter of repeating a 1940 conversation with Chambers that I had entered in my notebook on the day it occurred; the notebook was entered as evidence and was examined by the FBI, though later it was returned to me; I have the entry in front of me while writing this letter. I knew nothing about Alger Hiss and had never met him at the time of the first trial. About Whittaker Chambers I had heard a great deal, especially from our common friend Bob Cantwell; he was probably the most gossiped-about secret agent in the long history of espionage. I had met him only twice, but one of those two occasions was to have a lasting effect on my life.

Early in December 1940, I had a telephone call from *Time* magazine. A woman's voice explained that she was Whittaker Chambers' secretary, that Mr. Chambers was writing a story about writers who had jumped off the Moscow Express, and that she wanted to check some facts with me. I said that I wouldn't check the facts over the telephone, but that I'd be glad to see Mr. Chambers and talk with him. Later it was arranged by telephone that I should have lunch with him at the Hotel New Weston, across the street from *The New Republic*, on Friday, December 13.

So we had lunch together and talked about the world after the Hitler-Stalin Pact, and how one should reorder one's life, agreeing on many topics. But Chambers also talked about the Soviet underground—or two separate undergrounds, he explained—and what he said shook and depressed me. I went home to Sherman on the 4:32 train. After dinner I made a long notation on what he said, typing out about 600 words for my own eyes and memory. He hadn't once mentioned Alger Hiss. The man he said was center of an espionage ring in the State Department was Francis B. Sayre, Woodrow Wilson's former son-in-law.

Two of Chambers' remarks had impressed me. "My years in the party weren't wasted," he said. "I learned the technique of the movement, and now I am going to apply that technique to destroy it." "The counter-revolutionary purge is still to come," he said ominously. At the end of this memorandum to myself, I noted, "he paid for the luncheon, nearly $4 worth. It will cost me a great deal more when the article comes out."

The article came out in *Time*'s issue of January 6, 1941, and didn't cost me anything at the moment. Later I was to pay heavily for that luncheon.

When Chambers' allegations about Alger Hiss came into the open some years later, I told somebody about the long entry in my notebook. The somebody told Joe Liebling, who was in touch with Hiss's lawyers, and the lawyers asked me to testify. I said that I would if I were subpoenaed, but only about my notebook entry. That's in essence what I did. Afterwards I learned that several other persons who could supply evidence of value to the Hiss defense had been asked to testify, but had offered excuses for not appearing. It wasn't because they believed that Hiss was guilty; it was because they were afraid of the consequences to their own careers, in the climate of those times. I too was afraid of the consequences, and rightly, but, by God, if I had a piece of factual evidence that the jury should hear about, I wasn't going to run away and hide.

Immediately after I gave my testimony, Chambers was interviewed over the telephone by Victor Lasky of the *New York World-Telegram*. "The whole thing is patently absurd," he told Lasky when Sayre's name was mentioned. "I never said any such thing." The story in the *World Telegram* continues:

"Mr. Chambers does recall meeting Mr. Cowley for cocktails late in 1940. 'When I arrived,' Mr. Chambers said, 'it appeared to me Mr. Cowley had had quite a few. [Having 'quite a few' before talking to Chambers is a folly I would never have committed.][39] Robert Cantwell of *Time* was with me. [He wasn't] and as I recall it Mr. Cowley told quite a number of unpleasant and malicious stories concerning people on the Left Bank in Paris.' [The Left bank was never mentioned. But Chambers, having heard about *Exile's Return,* was trying to typecast me as an irresponsible bohemian.] ...

"Mr. Cowley had testified Mr. Chambers had wanted to talk with him about an article dealing with writers who had quit Communist ranks in disgust over the Soviet-Nazi pact.

"'I not only never contemplated such an article,' Mr. Chambers said, 'but I never wrote such an article. [He wrote it.] To the best of my recollection, Cowley had asked to meet me to ask about doing some part-time literary criticism for *Time.* Frankly, I never had trusted him and I vetoed the idea at the time.' [I didn't ask about doing work for *Time.* A few years later I was offered Chambers' former position as literary editor of *Time,* but turned it down.]"

Chambers' interview with Victor Lasky was calculated to damage me as much as possible, and it did damage me. A few years later, perhaps in 1953, I calculated that testifying in the two Hiss trials had cost me $40,000, in terms of lecture engagements, magazine assignments, and an appointment as full professor at the University of Minnesota. I'm not complaining; I survived and paid my debts. But the thing that angered me in Chambers' interview was that it didn't contain a word of truth from beginning to end. He knew he was lying; I knew he was lying; he knew that I knew he was lying, and there was nothing to be done. I thought of my experience with Chambers when reading one of Yeats's poems to Lady Gregory:

> Now all the truth is out,
> Be secret and take defeat
> From any brazen throat,
> For how can you compete,
> Being honour bred, with one
> Who, were it proved he lies,
> Were neither shamed in his own
> Nor in his neighbors' eyes?

I've gone on too long, writing more for myself, it must be confessed, than in any hope of changing your mind about aspects of the Hiss case. Some day I'll have to put my little part in the case on public record. As for the rest of the case, I have never gone into it deeply and have never read a book on the case from beginning to end. There's a reason for this. For years it has seemed to me that anyone who tried to puzzle out the truth about Hiss and Chambers was certain to become a little tetched. Weinstein is more than a little tetched, as one can see from his articles without reading the book.[40] I judge his bias from the fact that he went to the Newberry Library in Chicago and studied my correspondence, obviously with a view to impugning my testimony, but that he made no effort to see me or ask me questions. All he could find by way of impugnment was that I had received two letters from a character named Maus V. Darling when Darling was working on *Time,* just before he went into the armed forces. He had some very serious and justified complaints about Chambers, as did many, many people on the *Time* staff, but Weinstein doesn't mention them. Apparently he has been trying to prove a point rather than to arrive at the truth, if the truth can ever be found.[41] All I really know about the Hiss case is that, as a juryman, I wouldn't vote to convict a yellow dog on Chambers' unsupported testimony.

I hope that a man with the liberal virtues is also permitted to be testy and choleric.

Sincerely,

Malcolm Cowley

[. . .]

———————

[NL TL/CC-2]

[TO: BENJAMIN DEMOTT]

3 June 1978

Dear DeMott,

[. . .]

"The past is never dead," Faulkner's spokesman said. "It isn't even past." Weinstein's book is about the past living in the present. Implicitly it's a defense of the Cold War Liberals, who are at present in dire need of being defended. They sanctioned the Great Fear of 1950–56; you ought to read or at least skim through David Caute's book with that title, with its catalogue of people who suffered. The CWL's were ambiguous about Joe McCarthy— "We don't like his methods, but after all he's on our side," Hedda Massing told me. One of their central excuses for defending McCarthyism was that Whittaker Chambers was telling the truth and that Hiss had been an arch traitor. In the course of time, the Cold War Liberals have become the New York literary establishment, gathered round the *New York Review,* but their position is now threatened and, among other things, Weinstein is trying to shore it up by exonerating Chambers, who had served as their guru. Or that's how I read his book in its wider implications. I wish he had confined himself to the evidence in the case instead of playing for Columbia in a sort of football game against the, in the majority, Harvard men who hoped that Hiss would be proved to be innocent.

But I had promised myself to stop thinking or talking about the case, which seems to have the effect of tipping people off their rockers. "Keep your balance," I adjure myself. "Let the fanatics fall on their faces." [...]

With all my best,
Malcolm Cowley

[NL TL/CC-I]
[TO: DIANA KETCHAM][42]
24 May 1978

Dear Dr. Ketcham,

[...]

Your book has a timely theme. I didn't say enough about expatriate women in *Exile's Return.* There was a lesbian community in Paris that had its own leaders, some of them gifted—Djuna Barnes, Janet Flanner, Jane Heap, but of course and principally Natalie Clifford Barney and Gertrude Stein, both of them older. I knew some of them, but of course wasn't in their conclaves. Berenice Abbott was one of them—I knew her from Greenwich Village—so was Sylvia Beach, and I think Thelma Wood, whom I heard and forgot a lot about, but didn't know. John Glassco, who lives in Foster, Que., knows a lot more about the group. So does James Stern, who lives in England. And is writing a memoir of Djuna Barnes.

Everybody is getting very old. [...]

Almost everybody has written memoirs.

[...]

You seem to mix Englishwomen with Americans, perhaps more than they usually mixed. Mary Butts, for example. If you're going to bring in the English, what about Nina Hamnett? Mina Loy was much at home with Americans; her beautiful daughter Joella married Julien Levy, the art dealer. Later they were divorced. Nancy Cunard had a stormy affair with Louis Aragon. The story of Bryher, the other shipping magnate's daughter, is pretty well known.

It's a big field you're trying to cover. I haven't time to help, alas, alas.

Sincerely,
Malcolm Cowley

[NL TL/CC]
[TO: JAMES AND TANIA STERN]
7 August 1978

Dear Tanjim,

I've owed you a letter since almost forever—it was that damned busyness of the writer who has become a Survivor; you know about it. "I hate to bother you, but . . ." "I am writing a book (biography, dissertation, paper) on Blank, and I would appreciate any memories you can supply. Here is a list of questions I hope you can answer (three pages of single-spaced typing)." Meanwhile I was trying to finish a couple of writing jobs [. . .].

One of the jobs involved a trip to Oxford, Miss., Faulkner's home town. Faulkner has become the second industry of Oxford, ranking just after the university. I stood in a reception line in the 100° heat; I autographed books picked up in second-hand stores; I delivered my lecture, drenched in sweat; I was given a party and a birthday cake (and thank God a couple of drinks); and the following morning was driven to the Memphis airport, where I took a plane for Nashville to visit Allen Tate. Allen is 79, bedridden with emphysema, and nearly blind; he can't read, let alone writing. The worst of his afflictions is a wife (43) who has come to hate him and two little boys, aged eight and eleven, who wish he weren't there. He can talk, though, and it was a melancholy pleasure to people the Greenwich Village streets of fifty years ago, each of us contributing details.

[. . .]

Alfred Kazin's NEW YORK JEW is sharply written, with some brilliant character sketches that leave a bad taste in the mouth. Kazin has known the great and hasn't a good word to say for any of them except Edmund Wilson and Hannah Arendt, both of whom are safely defunct and hence no longer to be regarded as Kazin's rivals. Otherwise Kazin himself is the only exemplary character. The corpses of all the others litter his pages as the stage is littered at the end of *Hamlet*. The book is having a good sale. [. . .]

On 24 August I'll be 80. Can't believe that I made it when others are dropping by the way. Inside I'm only 26 until I try to walk downstairs. [. . .]

[As ever,

Malcolm]

[NL TL/CC-2]
[TO: THOMAS HORNSBY FERRIL][43]
30 August 1978

Dear Tom,

They gave me a party for my 80th birthday, you know, presents (mostly bottles), cards, letters, mailgrams, a cablegram (1), a cake with four candles (why?). I thought of a nice custom among the Northern Ojibway. In former times they were said to be very kind to their old people. When an old person became decrepit, they held a tribal feast. The old person sang a death song, in a cracked voice, and danced if he could. While he was still singing, his son came up behind him and brained him with a tomahawk. That was kind too, but would bruise our modern sensibilities. Instead we give the old person a sort of Bar Mitzvah, to mark his passage into that new stage in life, then set him apart with the problem what to do with his remaining years (6½ on the average, by actuarial figures).

He can do a lot of things of which one of the sweetest and most satisfying is not to do anything and not even try very hard to do nothing. Dozing in the sun, or in the shade on a hot day, is a pleasure that has never been properly celebrated. But the worm gnaws at us and we need the stronger stimulus of a project, of getting something done that is still within our powers or a little beyond them. I love the example of Yeats, who died at 73 the quitter, but still raged against age in some of his best poems:

What shall I do with this absurdity—
O heart, O troubled heart—this caricature,
Decrepit age that has been tied to me
As to a dog's tail?

Do? He went off and had the monkey-gland operation ("On both sides?" his Irish physician asked him, and Yeats nodded yes). That Steinach operation has been medically discredited, but it gave Yeats a great psychological lift, set him chasing after girls, apparently and writing randy poems like his "Lament to John Kinsella"—

What shall I do for pretty girls
Now my old bawd is dead?

He wrote his last poem, a good one, eight days before he died. Probably the operation shortened his life by putting an added strain on his heart.

But I won't emulate Yeats. I can't. I think one of the noblest projects for anyone in age is to find a shape in his life. It was a drama in how many acts. How can he make the last act worthy of the earlier ones? He is the author, the protagonist, the audience and the critic. He has to work under handicaps while the stage hands fidget and the audience is eager to go home. But perhaps he can succeed in acting out "I was" or even "I was *this*."

[...] What's wrong with being a regional poet? That's better than being a fashionable New York poet, isn't it?—in the long record of the years. Given time, everybody will hear about your work.

Yours,
Malcolm Cowley

———

[NL TL/CC-I]
[TO: ALGER HISS]
5 October 1978

Dear Alger Hiss,

Apologies for not answering your good note of 21 August. I was trying to write a big article in spite of phlebitis and other ailments and also I was hoping to hear more about your *coram nobis*[44] and about your success in obtaining documents from the FBI. I hope that process has moved ahead. Meanwhile I have been dismayed by the reception of Weinstein's book, that massive plea for the prosecution and for the Cold War liberals. If his treatment of Malcolm Cowley is a fair sample of how he treated other witnesses, the book should be thrown out of court. Here I had certain documentary evidence to show that Chambers was a liar. I was living within three hours' drive of Weinstein and was thoroughly accessible. He made no effort whatever to see me. Instead he traveled 800 miles to Chicago to go through my papers in the Newberry Library in the effort to impugn my testimony. He didn't find anything except a couple of letters from Maus V. Darling, whom he also made no effort to see. (Darling has died since then and his papers, if he kept them, have disappeared.) But he made the most of those letters, as if to prove that I was involved in a conspiracy against Chambers. [. . .]

[. . .] I feel the loss of Matty Josephson. As you know—and I knew, though Matty didn't talk about it to me—he was working on a book about the case,[45] but I don't think he made much progress with it after Hannah died in October '76—that was a blow that robbed him of his energy. [. . .]

The full story of what the FBI did in your case will never be revealed, I fear, but I hope you get enough documents to prove the important points. Keep on with the fight.

Sincerely,
Malcolm Cowley

Cowley's last letter to Allen Tate, who died on February 9, 1979.

[NL TL/CC-2]
[TO: ALLEN TATE]
8 January 1979

Dear Allen,

It's a tar'ble long time since I have written you a bulletin of happenings in the Snow Belt. To tell the truth, I don't know much about them. Since New Year's Day I haven't poked my nose outside the door. I had been in New York three days and nights of the preceding week, at

Viking and at the MLA convention, and that was too much for my aged frame. [. . .]

At the MLA I had to perform. "A Special Event: Malcolm Cowley Talks about the Lost Generation"[46] was the assigned subject, one that turned my stomach with its suggestion of Old Soldier Reminisces. I used the opportunity to answer that twerp Geoffrey Wolff, who had written a life of Harry Crosby in which he asserted that there was no such thing as a literary generation, that the term was a convenient fabrication; then to talk about Ramon Guthrie as a neglected but representative figure of the not "lost" but World War I generation. I had a big audience, people sitting on the floor. I went to two parties, at one of which I was supposed to be guest of honor (read: sacrificial goat), and I got home on Saturday exhausted [. . .].

[. . .]

Think I told you that I wrote a piece for *Life* magazine, "The View from Eighty." It came out in December and has been widely read—I never before had so many letters about a piece, all from old people. The eighty-year-olds, the octos, are frequently written about, but, at least in American magazines, they haven't done much speaking up for themselves. I listed some of the symptoms of being old and my correspondents all said, "I have most of those symptoms too." It's a cross, having a body all rags and bones and aches—and in my case, tonight, a chest that looks like a compote of cranberries and eggplant skins.[47]

All our love to you, Allen. I wish I could be there to talk with you.

As always, since the beginning,

Malcolm

[NL TL/CC-2]
[TO: ANDREW FIELD][48]
18 February 1979

Dear Mr. Field,

It must have been in 1918–1919 that Djuna Barnes lived with Courtenay Lemon on the top floor of 86 Greenwich Ave. at the corner of Eleventh St., the southeast corner. No. 86 was a sharp triangle, with a different tenant on each of the three upper stories. One tenant, I think on the middle floor, was a pianist, I think Australian; his name may have been Moskowitz. The top floor tenants were James Light and his then wife, Sue Jenkins; they had been in the class ahead of me at Peabody High School in Pittsburgh. Jimmy and Sue had come to NY in 1917, I think; Jimmy had gotten himself a job as a city news reporter for the now long defunct *Herald*. They had lived next door to the Provincetown Players on MacDougal St. and Jimmy had become connected with the PP's before they moved to 86 Greenwich. It was the house where Clemenceau had lived for a time during his American years. Later it was torn down, with the other houses in the block, for a big cinema. The cinema too was eventually torn down and the block is now an empty lot.

I think Djuna and Courtenay sublet from Jimmy. For a time they occupied the triangular room at the tip of the house; then I think they moved to a larger room before separating and moving away. They didn't mix with visitors to the apartment; they were quiet, the others were noisy. Djuna was a handsome woman who wore tricorn hats. She had written a play produced by the PP's, Irishly poetic in its language; I think it was inspired by Synge. [...]

For a time Djuna (subsequently) was squired around by Jimmy Light. I took it that they were having an affair. I was very young, brash, and known among friends for my collection of dirty limericks. Djuna was said to be forthright in her language. I met Djuna and Jimmy at an Italian speakeasy and sat at their table. I argued with Djuna that men were superior in equipment to women because they could piss standing up and write their initials in the snow. Djuna said, "I can make a period." Conversation continued. I may have been objectionable, speaking bad French. Djuna said something that offended me. I said, "Fuck you, Djuna." She took umbrage, deep umbrage, rose and swept out of the restaurant, carrying Jimmy with her. After that we avoided each other; I didn't see her at all in Paris, or many of the Lesbian group that she consorted with; they had their own café. Natalie Clifford Barney was their high priestess. They weren't invited to Gertrude Stein's, and in fact Gertrude didn't much associate with avowed lesbians, though many of her habitués were male homosexuals.

People have a bad habit of dying, thus closing off your sources. [...]

Sorry, but this is all the help I can be, or have time to be.

Sincerely,
Malcolm Cowley

[NL TL/CC-1]
[TO: WILLIAM PLUMMER, *QUEST*/79]
29 May 1979

Dear Mr. Plummer,

I was heartened by your extraordinarily kind letter. It arrived, though, when I was buried in things to do, as in a deep stratum of volcanic ashes. I'm still buried, but I'm slowly clawing my way toward the surface, and perhaps I'll catch a glimpse of sunlight by midsummer.

[. . .] There's one piece, however, that I *could* do [. . .] Let's play a few snatches from it and see if it would interest you.

It's about my lifetime friend Ramon Guthrie, who died a few years ago.[49] Ramon had all the experiences that one associates with the Lost Generation and a few more besides. He went abroad as a volunteer with the American Field Service—drove an ambulance in France and then at Saloniki (without having graduated from high school)—enlisted in American aviation—was the sole survivor (with his pilot) when his whole squadron was shot down by the Red Baron's flying circus. That's all documented and it's just a beginning.

After the war he walked out of an Army hospital and got a job as a private eye. Went back to France, mostly on his disability pay, and attended the University of Toulouse. Still without a high-school diploma he earned a doctorate there. Married a French wife. Came home and wrote two novels, then succumbed to writer's block. Eventually became a professor at Dartmouth, where for 31 years he gave a famous course on Marcel Proust. Took a couple of years out to serve as a lieutenant colonel in OSS. Went back to his first love, poetry.

At 70 he became despondent. He still hadn't produced a great poem, a masterpiece, and he was, the doctors thought, dying (cancer of the bladder). One day he [woke] up in the intensive care ward, in a maze of plastic tubes—and there, mentally, he put the masterpiece together, a book-length poem called *Maximum Security Ward* that sums up his life and his aspirations. Survived to see the book published: it received some rave reviews, but didn't make a dint on the public. Received an honorary doctorate from Dartmouth. "Ramon," I told him, "you should have asked them for a high-school diploma."

I'd like Ramon to be remembered, and you can see that I know his story. It would probably take 3000 words to tell. Any interest on your part?[50]

Yours,
Malcolm Cowley

[NL TL/CC-I]
[TO: JOHN CHEEVER]
29 November 1979

Dear John,

I haven't written to tell you how grateful I was to you for making that trip to Chicago and for what you said at the dinner.[51] To tell the truth, I was tongue-tied with embarrassment. You gave me credit for being better than I was. Kind, was I? I hadn't ever before met a boy of seventeen who could speak honestly about himself, and in English. I never afterward met another. I wasn't so much kind as grateful to you for being yourself.

[...] I had a glow of pleasure at having you recall things that happened almost fifty years ago. I had completely forgotten that cocktail party at which Peggy and I served manhattans and something greenish. Poor Peggy. She died about 1970 in Dorothy Day's Catholic Worker farm in Tivoli. Before dying she became a Catholic convert. Dorothy Day said skeptically, "Peggy just wants a place to be buried." The priest who instructed her couldn't confirm her; he had been sent to a refuge for alcoholic priests. The services, at which I was the only old friend present, were conducted by a hippy priest with long dirty hair.

[...]

The Newberry people are very nice. They've been wonderful about my papers.

[...]

Yours, as ever,
Malcolm

[NL TL/CC-1]
[TO: LILLIAN HELLMAN]
29 February 1980

Dear Lillian,

[...]

I thought that Mary McCarthy's attack on you was unpardonable.[52] I wonder, though, whether it was a good move to bring suit against her. The courts haven't shown any disposition to help us, ever. Isn't it curious how the antagonisms of the late 1930s and of the 1950s, the scoundrel time, have persisted in the literary world? Every once in a while I'm accused of being responsible for the Moscow trials. I say nothing, being convinced that the scoundrels will end by hanging themselves.

Yours, as ever,
Malcolm

[NL TL/CC-1]
[TO: LAWRENCE H. SCHWARTZ][53]
29 October 1980

Dear Dr. Schwartz,

[...] I am not in sympathy with the implied thesis of your Faulkner book. What it seems to imply is a conspiracy among publishers, critics, and academics to create Faulkner's vast reputation. There was no conspiracy. The reputation was created by Faulkner's work, ultimately. It was created against some ponderable obstacles raised by critics, publishers and academics. On the other hand, the situation was ripe for the growth of a new American literary reputation. Why it was ripe might be the subject of an interesting study. But conspiracy there was none, as I can assure you from personal memories.

Publishers did not conspire. Random House had permitted all of Faulkner's books to go out of print. They had sacrificed the copper plates of two or three of his books to the war effort (a serious matter in those days before offset printing; any new issue of these would have to be set into type). I think *Sanctuary* was technically OS, out of stock, not OP, out of print.

Liveright's warehouse had a few copies of *Mosquitoes*. I had the devil's own time persuading the Viking Press to issue a *Portable Faulkner*. No correspondence with Harold Guinzburg, but some with Marshall Best and perhaps Pascal Covici. It was Harold who made the deal with an unenthusiastic Bennett Cerf. I had talked with Max Perkins and suggested that he take over Faulkner if Random House didn't really want him—but Max said flatly, "Faulkner is finished."

Critics didn't conspire. They were almost all against Faulkner, and some left-wing critics were especially hostile: Hicks, Geismar, Kip Fadiman. Humanist critics were savage. In academia Faulkner had only two supporters: Warren Beck and Joseph Warren Beach. For a time I seemed to be waging a one-man crusade. And I did wage it, in 1943–46. I had some leisure on acct of that subsidy from Mary Mellon (1944) and had undertaken to write a history of American literature. My interest in Faulkner had been growing over the years, and I decided to start with him and then work backward, one author at a time. Then I became rapt in the Yoknapatawpha cycle.

I found that several novelists, creative writers, had a deep admiration for Faulkner. Red Warren. Caroline Gordon. Evelyn Scott. Conrad Aiken—those are the important ones—but also poet-critics such as George Marion O'Donnell and Allen Tate. R. N. Linscott, a new editor in chief at Random House, lent a sympathetic ear. Hal Smith, then publisher of the *Saturday Review*, had been Faulkner's publisher early on, and was still amazed by him. I wrote that very long essay on Faulkner and managed to get it published in sections (though it was turned down by *Harper's* and the *Atlantic*). Marshall Best and Pat Covici changed their minds about the Portable—and then, for a wonder, some of the novelist-enthusiasts charged in and the book was widely reviewed. Conspiracy? My God, no, unless you want to cast me in the role of arch conspirator. It was Red Warren himself deeply influenced by Faulkner (see the first 100 pages of *All the King's Men*) who attracted the interest of the academics. Warren has always had a very high standing in the academic community.

So there's the story, with a couple of details that didn't fit into *The Faulkner-Cowley File*. [...]

Sincerely yours,
Malcolm Cowley

[NL TL/CC-1]
[TO: LEWIS P. SIMPSON]
24 June 1981

Dear Lewis,

George Core did indeed send me your essay on the undersigned,[54] and I was a little abashed by it. You went so deeply into my feelings about America and Europe, and about revolution in literature as opposed to or conjoined with revolution in society that you left me gasping to understand myself. America and Europe, the colony that was once a place of redemption, then a colony again (in terms of the literary life), then once more a forerunner (in terms of industry and advertising), then finally a part of the Old World, more powerful than other parts but doomed to decline with them (as it *has* declined in our lifetimes)—all that is part of history, if a complicated part, and my own changes in attitude are sufficiently explained by changes in the objective situation of America and Europe. But my change in attitude toward the dream of revolutionary brotherhood is a still more complicated story, and harder for me to explain to myself. Briefly, my central aim in the later 1930s wasn't revolutionary at all; it was defensive and ultimately fearful. I thought that Hitler and his state were the immediate danger and were fated to triumph unless the Western democracies formed a grand alliance against him and unless the alliance included Soviet Russia. So I rather averted my eyes from Stalin's crimes—until he formed that alliance with Hitler. The years from 1937 to 1942 were the blackest in my life—not only in my public life, but in my private life as well. In the end I decided that instead of announcing new political opinions I would simply withdraw from political expression, having been wrong about it in the later 1930s. Yes, as you suggest, that did involve a loss of faith in the social power of the literary man.

I'm trying to deal now with that period of my life, and it involves me in some painful rethinking. Your essay has been a help to me, and a spur.

I'm working now on one chapter that might be of interest to *Southern Review*. It's called "[No] Homage to Catalonia" and it's a reconsideration of George Orwell's book on the subject. I was in Catalonia a few days after Orwell escaped by train over the French border and my reactions were completely different from his. Orwell and I were then on different sides as regards Spain; he was a revolution-firster and I was a victory-firster. He supported POUM[55] and the Anarchists; I followed the Communist (or in those days conservative) line. He was right about the Communists, but wrong about the 1937 situation in Spain and what seemed then to be the only chance for a Loyalist victory. In the chapter I consider Orwell's book as it seems to me in 1981. Is there any chance that *Southern Review* would be interested?[56]

[. . .]

Yours,
Malcolm

I keep wondering why [the Neo-conservatives are] determined to hang my scalp in their tepee. [. . .] What makes my position difficult is that I now hate Stalin and his deeds as much as anybody. But, I'm like Cummings's blond Olaf: "there is some shit I will not eat."

Cowley to Kenneth Burke, 1 July 1981 [NL]

[TO: VICTOR S. NAVASKY, EDITOR, *THE NATION*]
22 July 1981

Dear Mr. Navasky,[57]

[. . .]

At the present moment I have almost the whole pack of Neo-Conservatives, Making-It-Bigs, and Trotskyrights on my trail. Does that sound like paranoia? You'd believe it was a reasonable statement if you read a group of belated but very long and abusive reviews of *The Dream of the Golden Mountains.* You may have had a similar experience with *Naming Names,* which, by the way, I greatly admired. In my case Alfred Kazin and Dan Aaron had earlier written favorable reviews of *The Golden Mountains.*[58] Both of them have been receiving stern letters designed to bring them back into line.

There have been similar episodes involving others of the Commentarians, and I now wonder what I have done to become the object of such abuse

for things I did or didn't do forty years ago. One thing I did, which they
seldom mention, was to testify in the two Hiss trials. The Neo-Conservative
ideology depends partly on rewriting history to offer their own picture of
the 1930s, which they present as a mythical structure in which everybody
who supported the People's Front was a potential or actual traitor. For this
structure they require an arch villain, and of course he is Alger Hiss: wasn't
his guilt proved in court? They also require a St. George or angel of light
and truth, and of course he is Whittaker Chambers. Now, I don't know a
damned thing about the career in Washington of Alger Hiss, but I do have
pretty convincing evidence, only part of it produced in court, that Chambers
was a scrupulous liar. That's why Alan [*sic*] Weinstein spent days or weeks at
the Newberry Library reading my correspondence in the effort to cast my
evidence in doubt. He never once got in touch with me. Then recently the
whole controversy was renewed when I talked at some length for John
Lowenthal, in the film he made about the Hiss case.[59]

So, the Commentarians are after me as a threat to their mythology.
[...]
  [...]

In my own troubles with the Sidney Hooks and Joseph Epsteins,[60] it
would be nice to have a little help, and it can't be said that I've been getting
much from *The Nation*. Christopher Lasch's review of *The Golden Mountains* was a masterpiece of misrepresentation.[61] I'm used to unfavorable reviews and never answer them, but Lasch wasn't merely unfavorable; he turned
my life upside down through distorting pieces of evidence. For example, in
another book I had noted the rise of a new class during the 1920s, composed
of the designers and stylists of prefabricated dreams. I disdained this new
class, but at the same time pitied them for their neuroses. Lasch makes me
out to be one of them, a high priest of consumerism. My God, since I was in
high school (as I note from a poem written in 1916) I have been a conservationist and an enemy of consumerism; that has been a thread running
through my life. In the 1920s I was a free lance never earning as much as
$3000 a year. On that I somehow bought an abandoned farm with a pump
in the kitchen. Consumerism? I didn't consume much except beans and
coffee and hard cider. From my account of a summer in the 1930s he picks
up the unfortunate phrase "and feasting on lobsters." It was unfortunate

only because I didn't add that in the summer of 1933 lobsters were 25 cents a pound at the Niantic fish market. We boiled them in the seawater over a two-burner kerosene stove. We lived in a quarryman's cottage that had an outhouse and rented for $150 a season. Consumerism? Most of my close friends had the same ideal of Spartan living—for example, Kenneth Burke wouldn't install electricity until 1948 even though a power line ran fifteen yards from his door. When he finally yielded it was because, he said, he couldn't buy good kerosene any longer. Consumerism? We were all trying to live on the shore of Walden Pond.

[. . .]

Yours cordially,
Malcolm Cowley

[NL TL/CC-I]
[TO: CLAUDE & JUDY RAWSON][62]
7 January 1982

Dear Claude and Judy,

[. . .]

If we got together we could debate the question: Resolved: That Reagan is worse than Thatcher (or vice versa). Reagan is more of a danger to the world, with all his MX missiles and B1 bombers. He's a gun-slinging cowboy. He is also reducing all expenditures for social services, at a time when the country is sliding into a depression that threatens to be as bad as the 1930s. Reagan takes money from the poor and gives it to the rich, by cutting their taxes. His policies are like Herbert Hoover's and the year 1982 threatens to repeat the year 1930 (if without a Wall Street crash). We're feeling prosperous this year, but God pity the unemployed. Reagan's administration is full of right-wing fanatics who make the English Conservatives sound like Progressives.

[. . .]

Yours, as ever,
Malcolm

I'm not proud of having failed to realize the extent and barbarity of Stalin's purges.

Cowley to Hope Hale Davis, November 20, 1981 [NL]

[NL TL/CC-1]
[TO: KENNETH BURKE]
20 July 1982

Dear KB,

[...] I have reached a painful passage in my memoirs and I'm stuck dead on it. I have to explain how I totally misread the Moscow trials, through not being willing to admit to myself the utter villainy of Stalin. I was still Marxist enough to believe that the masses controlled their own destiny, that followership was more important than leadership, that the leader (even Stalin, whom I never admired) embodied the policies that were demanded by history. But Stalin, having attained supreme power, set out to hold it at the expense of the masses. There's a big, appalling book by Robert Conquest, *The Great Terror,* that tells the whole story in a convincing fashion. God, how blind we were in the 1930s. Now I'll have to face up to my own errors, and that without encouraging the Cold Warriors.

[...]

As ever,
Malcolm

———

[NL TL/CC-1]
[TO: GEORGE CORE, *THE SEWANEE REVIEW*]
3 August 1982

Dear George,

I've been thinking things over, and I'd like to do for you a short tribute to John Cheever.[63] It will be a hard piece to write because John and I were close for many years. Then John's daughter Susie, whom I never liked, married my son, and after that relations were more distant. Especially after the divorce. I continued to like and respect John, even though I couldn't follow him into the Episcopalian Church (too much kneeling) or into the Big Money. He was truly a *good* man, intensely loyal to his family and his old friends, brave in his battle against alcoholism and cancer, with a New England sense of duty and guilt, and (in this respect like Faulkner) with a powerful imagination that transformed everything he saw into wonderful and monstrous shapes.

His writing changed at a certain point, I think with the writing of *The Wapshot Chronicle.* Until that time he had been regarded as the typical *New Yorker* storywriter, but he wasn't ever that. He pushed his *New Yorker* stories behind him and began writing magical fairy stories— "Metamorphoses," he called some of them, and that was a key word. Perhaps he became an Ovid of the New York suburbs. *The New Yorker* wouldn't print his stories any longer; they were too fabulous and grotesque, but some of them were masterpieces. And his narrative prose made me feel when reading it that I had groped beneath roots in a stream and taken a live trout in my hands.

[. . .]

As ever,
Malcolm

[NL TL/CC-2]
[TO: CHRISTOPHER LASCH]⁶⁴
29 December 1982

Dear Mr. Lasch,

For almost two years I have intended to write about your review of *The Dream of the Golden Mountains* (*The Nation,* July 5, 1980). It disturbed me, and not because it was unfavorable. I didn't expect you to link arms with others and sing hosannas. You have always had a thing about *The New Republic* and its editors during the 1930s. I remember that in your first book⁶⁵ you pictured them as sitting smugly in their "pine-paneled offices"—my God, you should have seen those shabby offices or had a first-hand account of them. You have a pictorial imagination and a right to prejudice. What disturbed me in your review was that it condemned me for being exactly what I am not, playing a social role that I detest even more than you, and for being the sort of person that I have always disliked and pitied.

I am and have always been a country boy, a little uneasy in the company of urban intellectuals (which doesn't mean that I don't understand them). I grasp ideas and can express them well, that being my business, but have always been moved by feeling more than by intellection. Those are grave limitations and they have led me into egregious errors, for which I don't resent my being condemned. But I hate to be condemned as a tool of American consumerism or as helping to create a market for sales policies and intellectual fashions. I am not and have never been a consumerist; I have always been the opposite of that, a conservationist attached to the land.

[...]

One of my first published poems, in 1916, was a lament for the ruined countryside around Belsano, where I was born. Sixty years later I wrote a long poem of age that ended with a prayer:

> I pray for this:
> to walk as humbly on the earth as my father and mother did;
> to greatly love a few;
> to love the earth, to be sparing of what it yields,
> and not to leave it poorer for my long presence;
> to speak some words in patterns that will be remembered,
> and again the voice be heard to exult or mourn—
> all this, and in some corner where nettles grew in the black
>   sail,
> to plant and hoe a dozen hills of corn.

Corny, you'll say, but it isn't consumerism. So go right ahead abusing me, but don't gang up with the Neon Conservatives and abuse me for what I'm not. You're essentially honest, but do get your facts straight.

Sincerely,
Malcolm Cowley

[NL TL/CC-1]
[TO: LEWIS P. SIMPSON, *THE SOUTHERN REVIEW*]
23 May 1983

Dear Lewis,

Here is a piece that I am eager to have placed on record. It is about an episode I'm not proud to remember, that is, my total misjudgment of the Moscow Trials in 1937 and 1938. I have been blamed for that rightly, no more than I blame myself. Now I feel that all the circumstances should be set forth honestly. It's personal history, and ancient history, but it shouldn't be forgotten; it casts light on issues in the world today.[66]

[…]

As ever,
Malcolm Cowley

———

[NL TL/CC-1]
[TO: STANLEY W. LINDBERG, *THE GEORGIA REVIEW*]
January 8, 1984

Dear Mr. Lindberg,

Would you like to consider a rather long essay I have written on Hemingway's wound and its consequences for American literature?

[…]

The occasion for it was Kenneth S. Lynn's very long review (*Commentary*, July 1981) of Hemingway's *Selected Letters*. Lynn isn't a mental giant; he has a talent for getting things wrong. In this instance, however, his angle of attack on Hemingway, on me, and on Edmund Wilson represents a general contention of the Neo-Conservatives that appears in *Commentary, The American Scholar, The New Criterion,* and other right-wing periodicals. They hold that American authors present a false picture of the country, thus weakening us in the Cold War, and that much of American criticism is a growth of "poisonous weeds."

Lynn's indictment of Wilson and me is based on the contention that we misinterpreted Hemingway's story "Big Two-Hearted River" in the effort to strike at the moral basis of capitalism. It's utter balderdash. In my very extensive correspondence with Hemingway, never printed, there is firm evidence that the hero of "Big Two-Hearted River" is a man home from the war and still traumatized by his wound. Passages from the correspondence have lost their "natural copyright"—enough of them to permit me to make my point.[67]

[. . .]

Cordially,
Malcolm Cowley

———————

[NL TL/CC-2]
[TO: RICHARD H. UHLIG][68]

May 30, 1984

Dear Mr. Uhlig,

[. . .]

Alcohol and the writer is a fascinating subject, but please leave me out of it. I have never been a compulsive drinker. I used to be a party drinker, which is something different. I liked to get drunk at parties and do outrageous things and these gained me a reputation, but I went back to work the next morning. For some years now I have been pretty abstemious, on doctor's orders—nothing till dinnertime and then only a glass or two of wine. That hardly qualifies me for your survey.

The best overall survey of the interwar generation of writers is my book *A Second Flowering* [. . .]. Of the eight authors who received a full-scale treatment in *A Second Flowering,* all were heavy drinkers at some period of their lives and four of them died as alcoholics: Fitzgerald, Hart Crane, Faulkner and Hemingway in his last years; before that time he had been simply a heavy drinker. Fitzgerald and Faulkner were possibly congenital alcoholics; both their fathers were old soaks. Crane and Hemingway applied themselves manfully to becoming alcoholics. Cummings stopped drinking on doctor's orders: Arthritis.

To include some other names of writers not treated at length, Jack London, Sinclair Lewis and Booth Tarkington were alcoholics, though Tarkington went off the sauce in his forties, again on doctor's orders. James Thurber, Katherine Anne Porter, Conrad Aiken, Kenneth Burke, Thornton Wilder and Edmund Wilson were among those who were heavy drinkers for all their lives without becoming clinically alcoholic. One test for true or clinical alcoholism is the question, do you drink before breakfast? These writers didn't, although they drank the rest of the day.

But I am missing something. Alcohol isn't really the professional deformation of writers. Their real trouble is the manic depressive syndrome, this being a state that is congenital with some of them but is encouraged in others by the nature of their work. They have to work intensely and often under strain; then after working they have to relax or fall into a depressed mood and alcohol is the great depressant. It is interesting that the manic depressive syndrome should be so characteristic of writers, considering that it is usually a malady of extroverts. The truth is that writers are usually extroverted, not introverted. But this could be the subject of a long discussion.

There is a freemasonry of heavy drinkers and it is rather a pleasure to belong to it. If a writer stops drinking, as I have done like many others, he feels a little cut off from pleasant companionship. But I won't expand on this subject, on which I could talk for hours. Instead I'll have to sign off after this one letter. Good luck with your undertaking, but please don't expect anymore help from the undersigned.

Sincerely,
Malcolm Cowley

I can do so little traveling that I feel like an old horse tethered to a stake. [. . .] We're all getting too damned old, but let's take age by the throat and twist its neck.

Cowley to James and Tania Stern, December 10, 1984 [NL]

[NL TL/CC-3]
[TO: PETER BRAESTRUP, EDITOR, *WILSON QUARTERLY*]
20 December 1984

Dear Mr. Braestrup:[69]

[...]

Five yours ago I published a little book, *The View from 80,* that was widely read by my coevals. Several of them said, "We're waiting for you to write a sequel, "The View from 90." I can't do that yet—perhaps I can never do it—but I might offer some observations from the intervening vantage point of 86. How does it *feel* to enter the second half of one's ninth decade?

Sometimes it feels terrible. "After 70," a friend told me, "if you wake without pains, you're dead." Infirmities accumulate, as they have a habit of doing, and little daily tasks become harder to perform. The aged man or woman has to learn new methods of doing everything, as if he were starting over in early childhood. How to get into bed and out again—how to stand—how to walk (yes, even to crawl)—how to sit in what chair—each of these becomes a new problem. Here are some items of advice from my recent experience.

The first item is to have a companion. A wife is best in every way and a daughter comes next, but any woman in the house is better than none, if she can cook and make beds. I am thinking here about the household of an old man. Women seem able to live indefinitely with no companions (except too often the bottle), but men are more fragile. It is a distressing trait of widowers that they die off rapidly, to the immense disappointment of lonely widows in the neighborhood.

A second item of advice is to consult a physical therapist, who will usually be a woman. She won't make you strong again, but at least she will retard the process of muscular deterioration.

Item three is always to make a mental survey of any strange room you may occupy. Keep a light burning all night in the bathroom. That is the room where most falls occur, and falls are the greatest hazard of the aged. I have noted that shower stalls and bathtubs never have enough handgrips within easy reach, especially if the bather is bending over to wash his feet.

Here are some other items for those willing to become as children and undertake the process of relearning:

—*How to get into bed and out of it.* If the bed is high, sit on the edge of it and swing both legs under the covers. If it is a low couch, lean on it with both arms and bring one knee forward as far as it will go; then swing the other leg over it. When both legs are parallel, collapse on the pillow. Getting out of bed is psychologically more difficult, since bed is such a comfortable spot, but be sure to place both feet firmly on the floor. Bend forward from the hips and grasp anything—a chair, a doorknob—that will help you to stand erect.

—*How to stand.* Keep your feet apart to preserve your balance. Lean against something—the wall, the back of a chair—if you feel in danger of losing it.

—*How to get dressed.* For a man of uncertain balance, pulling on his pants is the greatest problem. That can't be done in the middle of a room without danger of falling. Stand next to a wall, or better still in the angle formed by a wall and a bureau so that you can steady yourself with an elbow while standing precariously on one leg. For putting on shoes, a long-handled shoehorn is almost essential.

—*How to negotiate stairs.* Grasp the railing firmly and take one step at a time. If there is no railing, have your bed moved downstairs.

—*How to sit.* The problem here is choosing a seat from which it will be easy to rise. Stoutly made hard-bottomed chairs are the safest. Deep, comfortable overstuffed chairs or sofas may become prison cells for the aged person, but still he can escape from them if they have at least one strong arm. Grasping the arm he inches forward, then pushes himself to his feet, taking a sideward step to keep his balance.

—*How to walk.* This is the crowning achievement for a person with weak legs, besides being the best form of exercise. Have your feet wide apart, raise each of them in turn to avoid stumbling (don't shuffle), and move forward in a sort of duck waddle; it isn't pretty, but it is safer. Avoid sudden steps and be slow in changing direction. Always have a cane in your hand even when you aren't using it. Pause often. If you are on a traveled road, walk on the extreme left to face approaching traffic. Wear a white scarf and let it hang down in back so that drivers can't fail to see you.

All these are bothersome instructions and doubtless you will invent still others. There is a reward for following the instructions, which is that you will survive longer as an independent person. Each new day in this endlessly fascinating world will be a miracle granted by grace from above, but also partly achieved though your own efforts.[70]

Malcolm Cowley

[NL TL/CC-I]
[TO: B. F. SKINNER][71]
22 August 1985

Dear Mr. Skinner,

The 87th birthday is almost here—day after tomorrow—and I'm grateful for your note of condolence. I also have to thank you for your book on enjoying age, which I read with attention and with profit, too. I should have profited more if it hadn't been for one deplorable feature of being old, namely, the loss of mental as well as physical vitality. Behavioristically, how does one get up gumption enough to change one's daily habits, self-destructive as these are proving to be? I give you seven years to find the answer, while wishing you and all of us luck.

Cordially yours,
Malcolm Cowley

[NL TL/CC-2]
[TO: KENNETH BURKE]
December 16, 1985

Dear Kenneth:

Eleven in the morning and I'm still sleepy after a rather bad night (but not the worst, by any means). Sitting at the typewriter for the first time in two or three weeks and trying to collect my thoughts such as they are. [. . .]

I hadn't much to report except a steady slow process of deterioration. At 87 my career in literature seems to have ended, with much less accomplished than I had hoped for. Nothing much remains except to put my papers in order. I can't summon up enough mental or physical energy to undertake anything new and I read with envy your account of projects half finished and new obligations accepted for next spring. How the hell do you do it all at almost 89? It's beyond my present aspirations, which have woefully diminished during the past three months.

I'm lonely for almost the first time in my life. I live mostly upstairs in my study, separated even from Muriel by 18 steps. The steps are now rather painful to negotiate and are even dangerous late at night when I can't sleep and can't lie peacefully in bed. Once at three in the morning I slipped and fell heavily on my left wrist, cracking a bone. For five weeks arm in a cast, I couldn't even type, though I could still make entries in my daybook or nightbook, mostly having to do with fresh infirmities. I suffer from two incurable diseases. One is cancer of the prostate, which isn't even life-threatening so long as I control the size of my prostate. [. . .] The other disease or condition is cerebellar atrophy, which I didn't think would bother me if it left my mind active even while impairing my ability to navigate. [. . .] Sometimes late at night I'm tempted just to give up and sign out, but that would require a conscious decision and I don't feel capable of making it. Non sum qualis eram. You can regard these sad reflections as messages *d'outre tombe.*

I sound more dispirited than I am in reality. [. . .] As writers we fall into the habit of living in our next book, not the one recently published, and now I rather doubt that there will be a next, even though it would be easy to put one together by copying out passages from my intermittent daybooks. Perhaps I've said my say and am receding into the past.

God damn it, I'll keep on struggling after a fashion; there's nothing else I can do. In practical ways I haven't been doing badly. My work seems to attract some continuing attention—not so much as *your* work, not by a damned sight, but more than I presently feel it deserves. There won't ever be a Malcolm Cowley Society or a Malcolm Cowley Chair: why should there be? But two or three of my older books are being reprinted at an actual profit to their author. What pleased me was that my poems are being paperbacked under a new title: BLUE JUNIATA: A LIFE (and this after being out of print for a dozen years). [...] News about your multifarious activities cheers me up and somewhat relieves my loneliness. So write again at length if you can find an hour to spare, and don't be depressed by my tale of physical and spiritual woes. It's the common fate of old men, though miraculously you seem to be escaping it. Keep so busy that you don't have time to brood.

Yours, from the dumps,
Malcolm

[NL TL/CC-2]
[TO: MIRANDA COWLEY]
6 May 1986

Dear Mandy,

We didn't get a chance to talk when you were here last weekend. It's time for me now to talk, and talk on paper, as I have always done more easily. It's also time for me to put on my long white whiskers and give you advice in grandfatherly terms. Silence, a prolonged silence. Dear Mandy, you don't need advice. You have always followed your own advice, driven by your urge to excel, something you displayed already at the age of six. So far your own advice has proved to be excellent.

The grandfather finds a few words. There has never been a time in the literary trade when more opportunities were offered to bright young women. [...]

You are thinking about my own field of freelance writing. I go back over my own career and wonder where I went wrong, at least financially. My great mistake or great achievement was spending too much time with each new job of work. I wanted each thing I wrote to be permanent and that is a good ambition but it forces one to spend too much time on the writing at the expense of time spent on gathering material. I was always weak on reporting, which at present is the most vendable talent. So my first advice to you as a freelance writer would be to gather a helluva lot of material by asking the right questions. [...] A general aim for you would be to get your name before the public—and before the editors of other magazines so that in your letters suggesting articles you wouldn't have to waste time explaining who you are, the editors would have heard of you and have seen your name in tables of contents. Each article printed means that the next article will be printed more readily.

[...]

You can be certain that we are proud of you and mention you often in conversations over the breakfast table. That's all that has to be said on this bright Spring afternoon while I try to enjoy it from my wheelchair and wish you were here. [...]

Your loving G-Parent,

[Malcolm]

My days are as empty as the Sahara now that I don't write. [...] It's a torture to be useless.

Cowley to Ruth Nuzum,[72] March 22, 1987 [RN]

[GWA ALS-2]

[TO: GAY WILSON ALLEN]

May 9, 1987

Dear Gay,

—I was happy to hear from you and to learn that the Crèvecoeur[73] is at last put to rest. [...]

I have little to report, being a prisoner in my comfortable room, living mostly in a reclining chair, with few visitors and nurses round the clock. I read the newspapers & think that Reagan is one of our national disasters, like the San Francisco earthquake or Pearl Harbor (and lasting in its effects). I read the classics: Shakespeare and currently Dr. Johnson (on whom I now find that I modeled myself). [...]

Malcolm

Malcolm Cowley died of a heart attack on March 27, 1989. On December 9, 1983, aged eight-five, on learning that he had been selected as a finalist for one of the *Who's Who in America Achievement Awards,* he had sent in the following retrospective evaluation of his work and career:

A STATEMENT

Looking back at a long career, I hope to be excused for setting forth what I have tried to do, even if those aims far exceed my limited achievements. The aims, so it seems to me, have always been to celebrate American literature and to defend American writers as a community within the larger community.

My efforts started long ago, when I was an undergraduate during World War I. In the poems I wrote at the time I was trying to express "what you really felt"—as Hemingway would later say— "rather than what you were supposed to feel, and had been taught to feel." Gradually I learned that others in my wartime generation had the same genuine feelings. I then turned from poetry to prose and wrote *Exile's Return* to explain as well as to judge their common aspirations. Some of my coevals—notably Faulkner, Hemingway, Fitzgerald, and Hart Crane—had been seriously misestimated, and I wrote various studies to restore the balance between their real worth and their public standing.

The next step was extending my field of study to earlier American writers, whose work I approached in the same spirit. I was joining in the search for what Van Wyck Brooks called "a usable past"—usable, that is, as a foundation on which to build the future. Since that future would depend on very young writers, I tried to hold them to high standards while helping them to find a public. I tried to set them an example by writing honest prose. I told them that a writer is a man or a woman *with readers*, and sometimes I scolded them for frightening readers away by lapsing into pretentious jargons.

Most often a young writer's central problem is how to keep alive while doing his best work. That fact led me into studies of the changing situations in publishing and bookselling as they affected the writer's trade. It is clear that my efforts were being exerted in various fields. I was—not always by turns—poet, critic, keeper of chronicles, literary historian and scholar, editor, and teacher. I could change my working clothes so long as it was all in the service of literature, the reading public, and the writers' community.

All this is written by an old man looking back at his career with mixed emotions. Yes, he finds things to boast about, but he must also admit to having made blunders and to having suffered from periods of discouragement. There was a time not so long ago when his work was generally neglected or disparaged. Most of his books—with others still to come—have been published since he was seventy. It is only of recent years that he has been pretty widely honored. He has enjoyed the honors, whether or not they were deserved. Especially he was pleased by the last sentence of a citation read at the public university of his own state, Connecticut, on the occasion of his being granted another honorary degree. The sentence was: "Our national cultural life continues to be enriched by the perspectives of this man, who not only writes our literary history but also makes it."

Malcolm Cowley

Notes

꙰

1. HARVARD, WORLD WAR I, GREENWICH VILLAGE, 1915–1921

1. Cowley had written three poems and submitted one to *The Smart Set,* one to *The Harvard Monthly*. Both were rejected.

2. Against Cowley's hopes, Burke had decided to enter Ohio State University, where he studied with Ludwig Lewisohn (1882–1955), the American Jewish author, critic, and translator, who introduced him to the work of Remy de Gourmont and Thomas Mann.

3. W. S. Gilbert (1836–1911), English dramatist and librettist, best known for the comic operas he wrote in collaboration with the composer Sir Arthur Sullivan.

4. Cowley was spending the summer at the family farm in Belsano and, at Burke's urging, was reading Thomas Mann's first novel, *Buddenbrooks* (1901).

5. Both Cowley's father and his grandfather were devout Swedenborgians.

6. After a year at Ohio State, Burke was spending the fall in New York. In February 1917 he entered Columbia University.

7. On November 11, Cowley added: "I know you don't like my show of snobbishness, and you ought to know that I love to irritate you with it."

8. Royall H. Snow, freshman poet from Chicago, who later—with Cowley—contributed to *Eight More Harvard Poets* (1921). In an earlier letter Cowley had described him to Burke as "pleasing of face, not troublesomely moral, and a capable poet. […] He is very youthful in appearance, but seems to pass through every test of membership to our coterie" (November 11, 1916).

9. John Gould Fletcher (1886–1950), American Imagist poet, associate of Amy Lowell and Ezra Pound. *Goblins and Pagodas* had appeared in 1916.

10. Cowley's and Burke's elementary school teacher.

11. James Light (1894–1964), a fellow student at Peabody High School, was editing a little magazine, *Sansculotte,* from Ohio State University. Cowley and Burke were regular contributors. Light later became director of the Provincetown Playhouse in Greenwich Village.

12. "From the Diary of a Restoration Gentleman" appeared in *The Harvard Advocate* of February 28, 1917.

13. Barrett Wendell (1855–1921), noted lecturer and professor of literature at Harvard, author of *A Literary History of America* (1901).

14. Robert S. Hillyer (1895–1961), at the time a rather well-known Harvard poet. His *Collected Verse* won the Pulitzer Prize for 1934. In 1949 he notoriously attacked the awarding of the Bollingen Prize to Ezra Pound in the *Saturday Review*.

[699]

15. Cowley had signed up with the American Ambulance Service and expected to depart for Paris in May.

16. A Harvard instructor who had taken a liking to Cowley's work.

17. G. B. Kirk, an instructor at Peabody High.

18. Charles Townsend Copeland (1860–1952), poet, popular professor of literature at Harvard, and influential mentor of writers and poets such as T. S. Eliot, Conrad Aiken, Van Wyck Brooks, John Dos Passos—and Malcolm Cowley.

19. In a later letter, Cowley gave his precise location, in the northeast of France: "We are at Dommiers, a village about eight miles south of Soissons, almost straight south, or rather south by west. As soon as I am out of training camp [...] I shall go to Jouaignes, a little town almost due east of Soissons. [...] The camp there is within range of the German shells" (June 11, [1917]).

20. William Henry Irwin (1873–1948) achieved fame as a reporter on the *San Francisco Chronicle* before moving to New York to write for *Collier's* and, as one of the first American correspondents on the war, for *The Saturday Evening Post.*

21. *Sansculotte,* the literary magazine published by James Light, with the help of Burke, at Ohio State.

22. Robert Alexander Cunningham, a classmate from Harvard, served in the American Field Service with Cowley.

23. Cowley's sister, adopted by his parents when he was twelve.

24. Pennsylvania river that runs southeast of Pittsburgh.

25. Cowley wrote up the celebrations in "Fourth of July in the Old T.M." for the *American Field Service Bulletin*, no. 51 (June 29, 1918), n.p. Reprinted as "Fourth of July, 1917" in *History of the American Field Service in France, Vol. 3* (Boston and New York: Houghton Mifflin, 1920), 91–96.

26. Coningsby Dawson (1883–1959), an Anglo-American novelist and a soldier in the Canadian Field Artillery during World War I.

27. The *New Yorker Staats-Zeitung,* nicknamed "The Staats," a German-language weekly newspaper in the United States.

28. A *marraine* (or "godmother") was a young female companion, often escorted by an older protectress, who provided material and other comforts to a soldier at the front, called *filleul* (or "godchild").

29. A. Piatt Andrew (1873–1936), head of the American Field Service in France. A recipient of the Legion of Honor from the French government and the Distinguished Service Medal from the U.S. army, Andrew later served as Republican congressman from Massachusetts in the House of Representatives.

30. Published as "Last Night We Held Great Argument" in *The Harvard Advocate* of February 1918.

31. *A Rebours* (1884), novel by Joris-Karl Huysmans, often seen as the bible of the decadent movement.

32. George Alfred Henty (1832–1902), English author of popular boys' adventure stories, many set in historical times and in faraway places, including *Redskin and Cowboy, A Tale of the Western Plains* (1892).

33. Elihu Root, Cowley's fellow chauffeur, also from Harvard.

34. *Bubu de Montparnasse* (1901), novel by Charles-Louis Phillipe (1874–1909), based on the author's liaison with a prostitute. An English translation by Laurence Vail, with a preface by T. S. Eliot, appeared in 1932.

35. *Jean-Christophe,* cycle of ten novels by Romain Rolland (1866–1944), published between 1904 and 1912. Rolland had won the Nobel Prize in Literature in 1915.

36. Marthe Gouttefangea was a *marraine* who had adopted Cowley as her *filleul.* Cowley had met her on an earlier trip to Paris. For a while, she continued to write him letters and postcards after his return to the United States.

37. Cowley was writing from the Wallace Building in Pittsburgh, where his father, Dr. William Cowley, ran a practice as a homeopathic physician.

38. Published in *Youth: Poetry of Today,* October 1918.

39. John Masefield (1878–1967), British novelist, poet, and playwright who served as a hospital orderly in World War I and in 1918 lectured in the United States to soldiers waiting to be sent over to Europe.

40. Eugene O'Neill would use some of the characters witnessed by Cowley in his play *The Iceman Cometh* (1940).

41. Louis Wilkinson (1881–1966), British novelist, author of *The Buffoon* (1916) and *A Chaste Man* (1917). Wilkinson early encouraged Burke and introduced him to Theodore Dreiser and the *Others* circle of Walter Arensberg and Alfred Kreymborg.

42. Edna St. Vincent Millay (1892–1950), poet and playwright, known for her frank exploration of female sexuality, and her two sisters, Norma and Kathleen. Norma Millay was an actress with the Provincetown Players.

43. Franz Grillparzer (1791–1872), Austrian dramatist.

44. Romanie Marie's cafés were popular taverns and salons for bohemian intelligentsia in Greenwich Village.

45. S. Foster Damon (1893–1971), one of the Harvard Aesthetes and a member of the circle of young poets around Amy Lowell. A close friend of Cowley during his Harvard days, Damon introduced Cowley to Laforgue and countless modern writers. Author of *The Moulton Tragedy* (1971), he wrote the definitive biography of Amy Lowell (1935) and became a distinguished Blake scholar.

46. Sigma Alpha Epsilon, a prestigious Harvard student association.

47. "The White Oxen," a short story by Burke, the title story in his first published collection (1924).

48. Mitchell Kennerley (1878–1950), American publisher. Sherman French was a Boston publishing firm.

49. *Sansculotte,* the little magazine published at Ohio State by James Light, had folded in 1917.

50. Harriet Monroe (1860–1936), founder and editor of *Poetry.* William Stanley Braithwaite (1878–1962), American poet, critic, and editor; from 1913 to 1929 he edited the annual *Anthology of Magazine Verse.*

51. Shortly afterward, Cowley sent Burke a detailed plan for "a post-bellum Sansculotte." "Editors suggested are Damon, Aiken, Snow, Wilkinson, Amy Lowell, Edna [St. Vincent Millay], Floyd Dell, [Charles] Ellis, [James] Butler, Stuart Davis, Burke, Light, and Cowley—as many of these as can contribute $25[...]. The magazine shall have no political creeds, and damned few artistic."

52. Susan Jenkins, a fellow student from Peabody, then the wife of James Light.

53. Charles Ellis, Village artist, at the time in love with Norma Millay, whom he would later marry.

54. Pound's influential article "A Study in Modern French Poets," *The Little Review* 4, 10 (February 1918), 3–61, introduced many of the French Symbolist poets to an American audience. Among the fourteen poets discussed and presented by Pound were Jules Laforgue, Tristan Corbières, Arthur Rimbaud, Laurent Tailhade, and Francis Jammes.

55. Sara Teasdale (1884–1933), American lyric poet, winner of the 1918 Pulitzer Prize.

56. "Moonrise," "Barn Dance" and "Danny" were published in *Poetry* in November 1919.

57. A volume of poetry by Lowell, published in 1918.

58. Cowley had applied for the Field Artillery Central Officers' Training School at Camp Zachary Taylor in Louisville, Kentucky; he spent only a brief period there, until Armistice Day, November 11, 1918.

59. Cowley to Jackson R. Bryer, February 5, 1964 [NL]. "Sunday Afternoon (After Jules LaForgue)" appeared in *The Little Review* 6 (July–August 1919), 61–62.

60. Dorothy Day (1897–1980), pacifist and suffragist Village friend of Peggy, was then in an affair with Lionel Moise, a reporter on the *New York American.* Day worked on the staff of *The Masses* and *The Liberator,* and was the author of a semi-autobiographical novel, *The Eleventh Virgin,* which Cowley reviewed in 1924. In 1917 Peggy Baird had joined Day in picketing the White House in support of women's rights; they had been arrested and jailed and had gone on a hunger strike. Day later founded the Catholic Worker movement, which provided a home for Peggy in her old age.

61. To make money Cowley was writing $1 "briefers" for the fortnightly *Dial,* whose then literary editor, Clarence Britten, was a friend of Peggy.

62. Matthew Josephson (1899–1978), American critic, editor, and biographer. Burke had first met Josephson at a poetry reading at Columbia University in November 1916 and shortly afterward introduced him to Cowley. In the 1920s they came to form a triumvirate of young rebellious writers centered around the "little magazines" *Broom* and *Secession.* Despite diverging interests and temperaments, they remained lifelong literary companions.

63. Harold Bell Wright (1872–1944), a former minister who became a popular American novelist and reputedly was the first to sell a million copies of a novel.

64. Burke had recently married Lillian Mary Batterham.

65. Peggy had returned to New York while Cowley remained in Cambridge, struggling to graduate.

66. Joseph Ferdinand Gould (1889–1957) was a legendary and eccentric character in the Village, often homeless and for years on end reputedly at work on a (never finished) "Oral History of the World."

67. Cowley tried to attain the effect described here in a prose sketch indebted to F. T. Marinetti's Futurism, "Race between a Subway Local and a Subway Express," published in *transition* in January 1928.

68. "Day Coach" was published in the opening issue of *Secession* (Spring 1922).

69. Cowley was now working as a copy editor at *Sweet's Architectural Catalogue* and *Export Trade*.

70. Cowley and Burke cooperated on the writing of a satirical play titled "Hamlet: For an Operetta." It remained unfinished and partially survives in manuscript.

71. The Provincetown Players, experimental theater group in Greenwich Village initiated by George Cram Cooke and Susan Glaspell in 1915 in Provincetown. It was an important force in launching the careers of Eugene O'Neill and Susan Glaspell.

72. Van Wyck Brooks (1886–1963), prominent American literary critic, biographer, and historian. In 1920 he was best known as one of the cultural critics associated with the magazine *The Seven Arts* (1916–1917) and the author of *America's Coming of Age* (1915), a controversial and influential probing of the "failure" of American culture to provide a sustaining milieu to the literary artist. Between 1936 and 1952 Brooks explored a "usable past" for American literature in a five-volume history of the development of American writing, *Finders and Makers*. Brooks's biographical-historical criticism and lively, anecdotal prose set him apart from the increasingly dominant New Criticism. Cowley became a loyal but not uncritical supporter. In the 1930s both men worked together in the League of American Writers. After World War II they were near neighbors in Connecticut.

73. Brooks had recently launched *The Freeman* (1920–1924).

74. Francis Hackett (1883–1912), literary editor of *The New Republic* from 1914 to 1922.

75. Scofield Thayer (1889–1982), former editor of *The Harvard Monthly* who, together with James Sibley Watson, Jr. (1894–1982), had launched the newly refurbished *Dial* in January 1920.

76. In *America and the Young Intellectual* (1921) Harold E. Stearns (1891–1943) had urged young writers to turn their backs on a desiccated American culture and seek salvation in expatriation. In 1922 he would edit *Civilization in the United States,* a collective indictment of American life and culture by thirty intellectuals, including Van Wyck Brooks, H. L. Mencken, and Lewis Mumford. Stearns would be a recurrent butt of Cowley's satire in the 1920s.

77. Ivan Opffer (1897–1980), artist, painter, and Village acquaintance of the Cowleys. He drew the illustrations to a series of interviews with French writers that Cowley did for *The Bookman* from France.

78. William Slater Brown (1896–1997), American novelist, biographer, and translator of French literature. A friend of E. E. Cummings, he appears as the character "B" in *The Enormous Room* (1922). He later married Susan Jenkins. Brown joined the editorial board of *Broom* in the fall of 1923. His best known novel is *The Burning Wheel* (1924).

79. Mary Reynolds (1891–1950), artist, bookbinder, and longtime partner of Marcel Duchamp. With Djuna Barnes, she had a reputation as one of the great beauties of 1920s Montparnasse.

2. PILGRIMAGE TO HOLY LAND—FRANCE, 1921–1923

1. The Battle of Malplaquet, one of the major battles of the War of the Spanish Succession, took place on September 11, 1709.

2. Paul Poiret (1879–1944), influential French fashion designer.

3. Poet and fiction writer Robert McAlmon (1895–1956) became a prominent publisher in 1920s expatriate Paris, where he established Contact Editions in 1923. He was instrumental in publishing Joyce's *Ulysses* and Hemingway's first volume of poems and short stories and, largely through the fortune of his wife, Bryher, was a benefactor to (and publisher of) many expatriate American writers, including Mina Loy, H.D., Gertrude Stein, William Carlos Williams, and Djuna Barnes.

4. Mina Loy (1882–1966), the modernist poet and artist, was a Village friend of Peggy.

5. Lorimer Hammond, a writer and translator, was a colleague copywriter of Cowley at Sweet's Catalogue Service.

6. Cowley had reviewed Lowell's *Legends* for *The Dial,* August 1921.

7. Together with S. Foster Damon, Berenice Abbott, and Burke, Cowley had played a literary prank on several poets, including Witter Bynner, Amy Lowell, and Conrad Aiken, by composing and forwarding to their attention the poems of the fictive rural poet Earl Roppel. Cowley wrote up the hoax in *WT* 39–43.

8. John Brooks Wheelwright (1897–1940) was a Harvard poet of Boston Brahmin descent, whom Cowley had befriended through Foster Damon in Cambridge. Wheelwright became notoriously involved in the imbroglios surrounding *Broom* and *Secession* and in the 1930s became a committed socialist. He died in 1940, after being hit by a car at a Boston intersection.

9. "The Journey to Paris," published in *Gargoyle,* October 1921. The short-lived *Gargoyle* was edited by Arthur Moss (1889–1969) from August 1921 to October 1922.

10. "Three Americans in Paris," satirical portraits in verse of Harold Stearns, Ezra Pound, and Sinclair Lewis, appeared in *The Literary Review* of the *New York Evening Post* of January 14, 1922. "This Youngest Generation," published in the issue of October 15, 1921, marked Cowley's first appearance as self-appointed chronicler of his generation. Defining the "youngest" generation (besides Burke and himself, Cowley named Cummings, Damon, Dos Passos, and William Slater

Brown), he credited them with "a new interest in form" and high ideals of literary craftsmanship inspired by Flaubert and De Gourmont, and described their aesthetic "catchwords"—"Form, simplification, strangeness, respect for literature as an art with traditions, abstractness."

11. Malcolm Vaughn was a minor poet Cowley had known at Harvard.

12. "Rabelais Returns to His Own Home Town" appeared in the *New York Tribune,* November 21, 1921.

13. A 1920 play by Alfred Kreymborg, put on by the Provincetown Players. It was included in *Plays for Merry Andrews* (1920).

14. Francis Picabia (1879–1953), French painter associated with Cubism, Dada, and Surrealism. Between 1913 and 1915 he helped to promote modern art in New York, visiting the Armory Show and exhibiting in Alfred Stieglitz's gallery 291. Picabia contributed doodles and drawings to Tristan Tzara's Dada manifestoes.

15. Tristan Tzara (1896–1963), French-Romanian poet, who was a founder and leading figure of the Dada movement. He was known for his eccentric personality and provocative performances as an artist. Wearing his trademark monocle, he figured prominently in Dada's iconoclastic pranks and became embroiled in its factional conflicts. In 1922–1923 Cowley befriended Tzara in Paris and was taken up in the Dada ranks. He translated several of Tzara's poems, and Tzara reciprocated by translating Cowley's poem "Valuta."

16. Brooks had responded to Cowley's essay "This Youngest Generation" in his "Reviewer's Notebook" in *The Freeman* of November 9, 1921, critiquing the generation outlined by Cowley as artistically naïve, ignorant, and superficial.

17. Nicolas Boileau-Depréaux (1636–1711), one of the leading theorists of seventeenth-century French classicism, especially in his *Art Poétique* (1674).

18. Floyd Dell (1887–1969), midwestern novelist and playwright who promoted Chicago writers including Dreiser, Anderson, and Sandburg before relocating to New York in 1913. He became a leading figure in prewar Greenwich Village bohemia, an editor of *The Masses,* and a fervent proponent of Freudianism, which earned him the mockery of Burke and Cowley, who referred to him as "Freud Dell."

19. Lowell had managed to sell "Mountain Valley" to *The Dial* (December 1921).

20. Cowley had solicited Lowell's criticism of his poems. On October 29, 1921, Lowell had reported her verdict that many of Cowley's poems were "dangerously like prose" and "not quite rhythmical enough" and suggested that Cowley most needed to learn the skill of "teasing a poem up, and then teasing it up some more, until [he had] wrung the final essence out of it, all the subject will bear and all its implications" [NL].

21. A little magazine edited by William Carlos Williams and Robert McAlmon, to give expression to Williams's conviction (developed in opposition to expatriates like Eliot) that art should emerge from an artist's local roots. *Contact* appeared irregularly between December 1920 and June 1923 and was revived briefly in 1932.

22. Stewart Mitchell (1892–1957) had been editor-in-chief of *The Harvard Monthly;* he had contributed to *Eight Harvard Poets* (1917) and become managing editor of *The Dial*. He was spending the winter of 1921–1922 in Montpellier.

23. Harold A. Loeb (1891–1974), New York business-man with literary leanings who, after having run the Sunwise Turn Book Shop in New York, joined forces with the poet Alfred Kreymborg to found *Broom* (1921–1924), one of the influential "little" magazines devoted to the international avant-garde in the early 1920s. Tensions between Kreymborg and Loeb about the course of *Broom* led to Kreymborg's dismissal as editor in early 1922. Under Loeb, *Broom* would sail a stronger course of cultural nationalism. Cowley recorded his impressions of Loeb in a letter of September 10, 1922, to Burke (included here). Loeb went on to become a novelist, publishing *Doodab* (1925), with Cowley's help, and then *The Professors Like Vodka* (dedicated to Cowley) in 1927. Hemingway used Loeb as his model for Robert Cohn in *The Sun Also Rises* (1926).

24. Arthur Machen (1863–1947), British author of tales of fantasy and horror.

25. *Fir-Flower Tablets* was a book of Chinese poems, translated by Florence Ayscough and Amy Lowell, which Cowley reviewed both for *Gargoyle* and for *The Dial* of May 1922.

26. Munson had recently launched *Secession*. In a letter to Cowley he had referred to "This Youngest Generation" as a "prospectus" for the magazine.

27. Conrad Aiken had resigned two years earlier, as had the Irish poet and playwright Padraic Colum (1881–1972).

28. At the insistence of Bynner, Cowley decided to accept membership in the Poetry Society after all.

29. Henry Murger (1822–1861), French novelist and poet, best known for his *Scènes de la vie de bohème* (1847–1849). "A Brief History of Bohemia" appeared in *The Freeman* of July 1922; reworked, it became part of *Exile's Return*.

30. Cuthbert Wright (1899?–1948), with Cummings, Damon, and Dos Passos, one of the original *Eight Harvard Poets* (1917). In the 1920s Wright regularly contributed criticism to *The Freeman* and *The Dial*.

31. John U. Nef (1899–1988) was a classmate of Cowley at Harvard. An economic historian, he later cofounded the Committee on Social Thought at the University of Chicago.

32. One of the rare Cowley letters to Josephson to survive the 1930 fire in his New York apartment. The first issue of *Secession* (Spring 1922) had featured two of Tristan Tzara's poems translated by Josephson, who used the pseudonym "Will Bray." In a subsequent essay, "Apollinaire: Or Let Us Be Troubadours," Josephson had enthusiastically greeted the new, effervescent, and ultramodern work of the young French Dadaists (Louis Aragon, André Breton, Phillipe Soupault, Tzara). In an April 12 letter to Burke, Cowley had denounced Will Bray as a "galloping young genius" whose opinions were diametrically opposed to theirs: "let me repeat that our ideals are really reactionary. We are not classicists, but distinctly we are anti-romantic." Cowley's poem "Day Coach" had appeared in

the same debut issue of *Secession,* and a note from Munson referred readers to Cowley's essay "This Youngest Generation" as "an important origin and a general program" for the magazine. Cowley was extremely ambivalent about being so closely associated with a magazine that expressed great enthusiasm for the Dadaists.

33. In "Exposé No. 1," an editorial in the opening issue of *Secession,* Munson had denounced *The Dial* for its unadventuresome and indiscriminating catholicity of taste.

34. In a May 3, 1922, letter to Cowley, John Brooks Wheelwright, who had recently met Brooks in New York, reported that Brooks had praised the "Gallic clarity" of Cowley's essays. The two articles, a review of a biography of Wycherley and the essay on "A Brief History of Bohemia," appeared in *The Freeman* of June and July 1922.

35. A satirical portrait of a young man befuddled with aesthetic ideas, published in *Broom,* October 1922.

36. Louis Untermeyer (1885–1977), poet, critic, and anthologist, whose genteel impressionism and old-fashioned taste in poetry roused the satirical anger of Cowley and his friends.

37. Percy Winner was a friend of Josephson.

38. Henri Barbusse (1873–1935), French novelist, author of *Under Fire* (1916), whose humanism and social consciousness appealed to Cowley (Barbusse became a communist in the 1920s); Paul Fort (1872–1960), French poet, part of the circle of Verlaine and Apollinaire; André Salmon (1881–1969), French poet and art critic who shared Cowley's sensitivity to generations.

39. John C. Farrar (1896–1974), Yale poet who edited *The Bookman* until 1927, when Seward Collins took over. In 1929 Farrar cofounded the publishing house Farrar and Rinehart; after World War II he was a cofounder of the firm Farrar, Straus and Giroux.

40. George Duhamel (1884–1966), French novelist and editor of *Mercure de France.* His experiences as an army surgeon during World War I were reworked into *Civilisation,* for which he won the prestigious Prix de Goncourt in 1918.

41. Jules Pascin (1885–1930), Bulgarian-born painter and watercolorist. He moved to Paris in 1905 but spent the years 1914–1920 in the United States, painting the "American" watercolors Cowley was so taken by.

42. Waldo Frank (1889–1967), novelist, cultural critic, and historian of Spanish and Latin American literature. He was an editor of *The Seven Arts* (1916–1917) and, with Randolph Bourne and Van Wyck Brooks, an avid sponsor of its cultural nationalism. In *Our America* (1919) he articulated his belief in America's power of spiritual regeneration. A student of mysticism and spirituality, Frank wrote an opaque and impressionistic prose, which made him the frequent target of Cowley's satire and critique. In the 1930s both men worked together in the League of American Writers, of which Frank served as the first president.

43. "Pascin's America" appeared in the January 1923 issue of *Broom*.

44. Kathleen Cannell (1891–1974), a dance and fashion correspondent who, in the 1920s, lived with Harold Loeb and became a well-known member of the American expatriate community in Paris. Hemingway, somewhat unfairly, used her as the model for Frances Clyne in *The Sun Also Rises* and based the character of Helen Ferguson *(A Farewell to Arms)* on her. She contributed translations from the French to *Broom* and short fiction to *transition*. In later life she was married to the French poet Roger Vitrac. Cowley took a particular liking to her and for a time may have been in love with her.

45. John Frederick Mowbray-Clarke (1869–1953) was a sculptor; his wife, Mary Horgan, was an art critic and instructor who for a time ran the Sunwise Turn Book Shop in New York.

46. Ananda Kentish Coomaraswamy (1877–1947), Indian philosopher and art historian, an influential interpreter of Indian art and culture to the West.

47. Georges Duthuit (1891–1973), French art historian who became an authority on Byzantine art and on the painter Henri Matisse, whose daughter he married.

48. "The Book of Yul," a short story by Burke that appeared in the second (July 1922) issue of *Secession*. Cowley's poem "Day Coach" had led off its first (Spring 1922) issue.

49. Burke's short story "First Pastoral."

50. In "The Mysticism of Money" Loeb had pleaded for an American culture unadulterated by European ideas or traditions. Genuine artistic expression in America, he held, was rooted in an American religion of business and moneymaking. The manifestations of U.S. business and technology—architecture, machinery, advertising, the popular arts—had "an aesthetic value of no mean order." Loeb's essay appeared in the September 1922 issue of *Broom*.

51. Robert Coady's little magazine *The Soil* (December 1916–July 1917). Loeb had explicitly credited *The Soil* as an important precursor of *Broom*'s new editorial line.

52. The Cowleys aimed to spend three weeks in Berlin, from October 3 to 23, 1922. "Young Mr. Elkins" appeared in *Broom* in December 1922.

53. Louis Lozowick (1892–1973), Russian émigré lithograph artist who moved to America in 1906. He had contributed to James Light's magazine *Sansculotte* at Ohio State, before residing in Europe (Paris, Berlin, Moscow) from 1919 to 1924, when he returned to New York. He became associated with Constructivism and joined the editorial board of *The New Masses* in 1926.

54. Lola Ridge (1873–1941), feminist and anarchist poet who worked at the New York office of *Broom*.

55. Cowley's translation of Aragon's story "The Extra" appeared in *Broom,* November 1923.

56. A novel by André Salmon, published in an English translation by William Slater Brown as *The Black Venus* (Macaulay, 1929).

57. A novel by Pierre MacOrlan, four parts of which, translated by Cowley, appeared in *Broom* in August 1923. The full text of Cowley's translation was published by Boni & Liveright as *On Board the Morning Star* in 1924, illustrated with woodcuts by Jean-Gabriel Daragnès.

58. Cowley's article on readers' responses to *Ulysses* appeared in *The Bookman* for July 1924. His own impression of Joyce, he wrote to Farrar on November 12, might be "summed up in two words 'intolerable genius'" [JCF].

59. Cowley was developing the ideas that would go into "A Monument to Proust," published in *The Dial* in March 1923.

60. Cowley quoted this paragraph in *Exile's Return* (1951), 135–136.

61. Burke had become an assistant editor of *The Dial*.

62. Robert M. Coates (1897–1973), expatriate avant-garde American writer, later art critic for *The New Yorker* (where he coined the phrase "abstract expressionism"). Coates was the author of five novels, among them *The Eater of Darkness* (1926), *Yesterday's Burdens* (1933), and *Wisteria Cottage* (1948). He became part of Cowley's intimate circle of literary friends. Coates married his first wife, Elsa, in February 1927.

63. Published in revised form as "Voices from Home: 1923" in *Blue Juniata: Collected Poems* (New York: Viking Press, 1968), 68. "Portrait by Leyendecker" appeared in *Broom,* March 1923.

64. A review of two volumes of poetry by Aiken and Sandburg published in the November 1922 *Dial.* Cowley had advanced that there was "no poetry so deeply rooted in our soil and tradition that a foreigner can never understand it.... America remains a thing seen and not a manner of seeing."

65. *Littérature,* a magazine edited by Louis Aragon, André Breton, and Philippe Soupault in Paris, from 1919 to 1924.

66. John Marin (1870–1953), American modernist painter of abstract landscapes and watercolors; a protégé of Alfred Stieglitz.

67. André Suarèz (1868–1948), French poet and critic, associated with *Nouvelle Revue Française.*

68. James Oppenheim (1882–1932), novelist, poet, and founding editor of *The Seven Arts* and an early follower of Jung.

69. Cowley quoted this paragraph in *Exile's Return,* 106–107.

70. Harold Stearns had edited *Civilization in the United States: An Inquiry by Thirty Americans* (1922), a collection of essays analyzing what Van Wyck Brooks, one of the contributors, had called "the failure of American culture."

71. Clive Bell (1881–1964), English art critic and member of the Bloomsbury group.

72. Gilbert Seldes (1893–1970), American writer and cultural critic, editor and drama critic of *The Dial,* author of *The Seven Lively Arts* (1924).

73. Sylvia Beach (1887–1962) ran the English-language bookstore Shakespeare & Company in Paris; it was a famous gathering place for American expatriates and French writers. Shakespeare & Company was also the first publisher of Joyce's *Ulysses* (1922).

74. Peggy was making a series of drawings of American and French artists, for an exhibit at Galérie Six, a Paris art gallery run by the wife of Philippe Soupault.

75. A poem by Cowley published in *Broom,* November 1922. *Les feuilles libres* (1918–1928) was a magazine edited from Paris by Marcel Hubert Raval; contributors included André Salmon, Max Jacob, Philippe Soupault, Blaise Cendrars, Roger Vitrac, Jean Cocteau, Tristan Tzara, and others.

76. Roger Vitrac (1899–1952), French Surrealist playwright and poet. Cowley translated his "Poison" for *Broom,* November 1923. Vitrac later married Kathleen Cannell.

77. Philippe Soupault (1897–1990), French poet, critic, novelist, and coeditor of *Littérature.* Cowley translated "My Dear Jean" for *Broom,* January 1924.

78. The poet Paul Éluard (1895–1952) and Georges Ribemont-Dessaignes (1884–1974), poet and painter, both sympathized with the Dadaist movement.

79. Hippolyte Jean Giraudoux (1882–1944), French writer and diplomat, internationally known as a dramatist.

80. The poet Hart Crane (1899–1932), whom Cowley would meet on his return to New York and who would become one of his closest but also most complicated friends. Cowley was aware of Crane's poems, which had appeared in both *Broom* and *Secession,* as well as in *The Dial* and *The Little Review.*

81. Jean Toomer (1894–1967), poet and novelist, who was an influential figure in the Harlem Renaissance. Several sections of his book *Cane* (1923) were prepublished in *Broom.*

82. Glenway Wescott (1901–1987), expatriate novelist of fame in the 1920s and 1930s, author of *The Grandmothers* (1927) and *Goodbye, Wisconsin* (1928). In his letters of 1923–1924 Cowley consistently misspelled his name.

83. Yvor Winters (1900–1968), modernist poet and critic, whose early work appeared in both *Broom* and *Secession.*

84. A little magazine edited from New York by Norman Fitts.

85. Of all the French writers Cowley met in France in the early 1920s, Louis Aragon (1897–1982), the famous poet, novelist, and editor, had the strongest personal impact. Cowley befriended Aragon on his visits to Paris and spent time with him in Giverny. After his involvement with Dada and Surrealism in the 1920s, Aragon would move on to become a prominent literary presence in the French Communist movement and later in the French Resistance. Cowley closely followed Aragon's literary and political development, which partly paralleled his own, and kept in personal touch. He met Aragon again in Paris in 1937, when he was on his way to Spain to report on the Spanish Civil War, and translated a volume of Aragon's wartime poetry in 1945.

86. Jacques Rivière (1886–1925), French man of letters, who was editor of *Nouvelle Revue Française* from 1919 until his death in 1925 of typhoid fever.

87. Cowley used this paragraph in *Exile's Return,* 163.

88. Cowley's essay on Racine appeared in *The Freeman* in two installments, October 10 and 17, 1923. He also had it privately printed as a booklet, *Racine* (1923).

89. Cf. *ER*, 162.

3. THE CITY OF ANGER—NEW YORK, 1923–1929

1. George Moore (1852–1933) was an Irish novelist, poet, and critic, whose *Memoirs of My Dead Life* (1906) Cowley had enthused over at Harvard; Arthur Schnitzler (1862–1931) was an Austrian dramatist whose "modern" plays Cowley and Burke had relished as early as Peabody High School.

2. Cowley used this paragraph in *Exile's Return* (1951), 179.

3. Agnes Boulton (1892–1968), a successful writer of "pulp fiction," O'Neill's second wife. In 1957 Cowley would write an article about a weekend spent with O'Neill for *The Reporter*, later included in *AMWH* 191–200.

4. *Tulips and Chimneys*, Cummings's first volume of poems.

5. The quarrel between Josephson and Munson had ended in a fistfight, refereed by the art historian William Murrell Fisher. Cowley wrote up the incident, helping to give it anecdotal notoriety, in *Exile's Return*, 183–185.

6. Cowley quoted part of this paragraph in *Exile's Return*, 204.

7. Cowley incorporated these maxims into his notebooks. Some of these would remain truths for him for the rest of his life.

8. In December 1923 Cowley and Brown wrote an open letter to *The Dial*, challenging its decision to present its 1923 award to Van Wyck Brooks, a critic of established reputation, rather than to an important new talent like Cummings. In mock retaliation, Cowley and Brown announced a *Broom* award of $2 to "a young American writer who, in our opinion, has done a significant service for American letters"—Sinclair Lewis.

9. Cowley used parts of this letter and that of February 19 (*SC* 158–159) in *Exile's Return*, 202–203.

10. Paul Elmer More (1864–1937), American philosopher, a leading proponent (with Irving Babbitt) of the New Humanism. Best known for his *Shelburne Essays* (1904–1936).

11. Josephson's brother-in-law, Maxwell Geffen, a banker who was willing to sponsor *Broom*.

12. Robert Alden Sanborn, poet and prose writer whose work appeared in *Others, Poetry,* and *Broom;* presumably Peggy Guggenheim (1898–1979), a rich cousin of Harold Loeb, who became a famous socialite and art collector; Susan Jenkins, then wife of James Light; Wilfrid H. Bendall, who had published "Sixth Poem" in *Broom*, October 1923.

13. Cowley was trying to find a publisher for Loeb's novel *Doodab;* it was published by Boni & Liveright in 1925.

14. George Ivanovich Gurdjieff (1866?–1949), Greek-Armenian mystic and spiritual teacher who lived in France. Among his American disciples were G. B. Munson, Waldo Frank, and Jean Toomer.

15. A little magazine edited by the poet and critic Edwin Seaver from July to December in Woodstock, New York. In the 1930s Seaver became a prominent critic and writer on the left; he was active in the League of American Writers and a regular contributor to *The Daily Worker, The Liberator,* and *The New Masses.*

16. Isidore Schneider (1896–1976) had published poems in *Broom* and *The Dial* and would go on to write a novel, *Doctor Transit* (1925), and become an editor at *The New Masses.* In 1924 he worked for Boni & Liveright.

17. Heywood Broun (1888–1939), drama critic and journalist for the *New York Tribune* and the *New York World;* Ernest Boyd (1887–1946), Irish-born American critic and translator, whose *Portraits: Real and Imaginary* (1924) would soon rouse Cowley's satirical wrath; Henry Seidel Canby (1878–1961), critic and editor who had recently stepped down as editor of *The Literary Review* of the *New York Evening Post* to found and edit *The Saturday Review of Literature* (1924–1936).

18. Waldo Frank, "Seriousness and Dada," *1924* 3 (September 1924), 70–73.

19. Cowley's open letter led to an epistolary altercation with Frank in the pages of *1924* (reprinted in part in Frank's collection of essays *In the American Jungle* [New York: Farrar & Rinehart, 1937], 128–135). The debate was continued in private correspondence.

20. Frank had ended his open letter of November 3 as follows: "The one statement in your letter which has the force of relevance is that in which you volunteer to be considered an American Dada. Of course, one must accept you so, since you insist upon it. I admit however that I, for one, could accept you in this guise with less regret, had not my acquaintance with your poetry convinced me that you will be fit for better things when you achieve the moral courage to confront the reality of our world, and the spiritual energy to take issue with it; instead of permitting yourself to be flung off by its centrifugal action, in the fond belief that because you fly off into nothing in a graceful pirouette and with a foreign oath upon your lips you are being any the less booted about and beshat and befooled by the very elements of life which you profess to despise" [NL; reprinted in *In the American Jungle,* 134].

21. Cowley had first met Allen Tate during a memorable evening in Brooklyn in June 1924, with Hart Crane. Cf. Cowley's account in *ASF* 193–194.

22. Contributors were Burke, Brown, Crane, Josephson, Schneider, Tate, Wheelwright, and Williams. The painter Charles Sheeler designed the cover.

23. Princes Bay is the official name of the post office; the neighborhood's name is alternatively spelled "Prince's" or "Princess Bay." Cowley mostly uses Princes Bay, though later he reverted to Princess Bay.

24. In the winter and spring of 1925–1926 Jane Heap, who was coeditor with Margaret Anderson of *The Little Review,* prepared a special joint French-American issue of the magazine (Spring–Summer 1926). She had asked Cowley to help with the

issue by translating some of Tristan Tzara's poems. Cowley also translated a piece by Michel Leiris on Joan Miró. The issue was the occasion for another group manifestation in the mode of *Aesthete 1925*. Besides his translations Cowley contributed "Anthology," a collection of poems on his friends (Burke, Coates, Crane, Josephson, Cowley himself, and the fictitious Walter S. Hankel).

25. Leonie Sterner was the wife of Harold Sterner (1895–1976), an American artist, later an architect, best known for his surrealist paintings. Both were friends of Wheelwright, who dedicated one of his poems to the Sterners.

26. On December 31, 1925, Williams had invited Cowley to submit some of his poems, "such especially which seem to you tentative toward new forms" [NL]. Cowley sent Williams "Anthology" and "Leonora."

27. *Brentano's Book Chat* (started in 1922) was the bimonthly in-house publication of the bookseller and publisher Brentano's. Under the editorship of Bellamy Partridge it had literary ambitions beyond the promotion of new books. Cowley served as contributing editor, with Gilbert Seldes and Samuel Ornitz.

28. In response, the Scribner's editor Maxwell Perkins put Cowley in touch with Lardner.

29. Besides those mentioned in his letter, Cowley wrote portraits of H. L. Mencken, Edwin Arlington Robinson, Conrad Aiken, Carl Sandburg, and Ernest Hemingway. They were published in *Brentano's Book Chat* between March and April 1926 and September and October 1928.

30. Boyd had invited Cowley to contribute a volume in a series of critical biographies on classic writers of the nineteenth century, analogous to the "English Men of Letters Series."

31. *Charm,* "The Magazine of New Jersey Home Interests," was published by L. Bamberger & Company, a publishing company in Newark, New Jersey. Between 1924 and 1928, for all his skepticism about such "hack" work, Cowley wrote a regular book page for *Charm,* on an assortment of topics, ranging from New Jersey history to Christmas books. For its first few years *Charm* was edited by Elizabeth ("Bessie") Breuer, a Village friend of Peggy, who had edited the women's department at the *New York Tribune,* been an expatriate consort of Kay Boyle in 1920s France, and who published a number of novels in the 1930s without attaining much recognition. Breuer was succeeded by Lucy Taussig, an editor who gave Cowley more freedom to write on topics of his own choosing. In the fall of 1927 Taussig was succeeded by Elizabeth D. Adams, who discontinued the magazine's book page, thereby depriving Cowley of an assured $50 a month.

32. The Tates were living at Addie Turner's, five miles from Sherman, Connecticut.

33. Paul Valéry (1871–1945), prominent French poet and essayist, sometimes regarded as the last of the French Symbolists. In *Exile's Return* Cowley portrays Valéry as one of the "saints" of modernism (Eliot, Pound, Proust, and Joyce are others) whose adherence to a "religion of art" he decried. Valéry exerted a strong influence on Cowley, primarily through his intellectual methodology. In his introduction to his translation of *Variety* (1927) Cowley praises Valéry's essays as exercises

of an "instrumental mind" capable of mastering any subject of enquiry and still retaining its unity and independence.

34. Lewis Galantière (1895–1977) was a well-known translator of French literature, based in Paris. In November 1925 Cowley had favorably reviewed his translation of Jean Cocteau's first novel *Le Grand Écart* (1923)/*The Grand Écart* for *The Saturday Review of Literature*.

35. Learning of Cowley's predicament, Galantière gallantly withdrew as a translator and diplomatically negotiated with Valéry on Cowley's behalf.

36. In May 1926 Cowley moved to the area around Sherman, Connecticut (postmarked Gaylordsville), which would become his lifelong home, leading for now a pendulum lifestyle, summering in the country, wintering in the city.

37. Monroe had agreed to print seven poems by Cowley in *Poetry* (November 1926): "Bones of a House," "Chestnut Ridge," "Laurel Mountain," "Empty Barn, Dead Farm," "Bill George," "The Urn," and "The Streets of Air."

38. In October 1927 Cowley was awarded *Poetry*'s Salmon O. Levinson Prize for the group of poems "Blue Juniata." He used the bulk of the money as a down payment on a farmhouse.

39. Baudelaire remained a critical preoccupation in Cowley's reviews of the 1920s and 1930s, but his biography of the poet was never written.

40. George Cram Cook (1873–1924), poet and playwright who, with Susan Glaspell, founded the Provincetown Players in 1915.

41. Cowley expanded the idea of "the instrumental mind" in his introduction to *Variety* (1927), published as "Towards a Universal Man" in *The New Republic* of December 8, 1926.

42. *The Principles of Literary Criticism* (1924), by the British critic I. A. Richards, one of the founding books of the New Criticism. Richards developed the notion of "practical criticism," a pedagogical method of "close reading."

43. Eugene Jolas (1894–1952) would found *transition* in 1927. He had mistaken Cowley's sequence of poems about his friends—which had appeared in *The Little Review* as "Anthology"—for an anthology of poems by them.

44. Cowley had sent Tate a draft version of "French Poetry and the New Spirit," an early attempt to define what was shared by the contradictory manifestations of modernism. It was published in *The Saturday Review of Literature*, May 7, 1927.

45. One of the books Cowley had expressed a strong interest in reviewing was Hervey Allen's biography *Israfel: The Life and Times of Edgar Allan Poe*.

46. The poet Marianne Moore had become managing editor of *The Dial* in 1925; the year after, on Scofield Thayer's resignation, she became editor-in-chief, until the magazine's demise in 1929. Moore's meticulous criticism of Cowley's work led to frictions in their relationship.

47. A spate of recent Poe biographies, including Joseph Wood Krutch's book, had linked Poe's genius to psychological, social, and sexual maladjustments. Edmund Wilson, Allen Tate, and Cowley had each in their different ways taken issue and emphasized Poe's conscious artistry. The review appeared in *The Dial* of August

1927. Cowley wrote at greater length on Poe in a 1928 article published in *The Outlook*.

48. Trader Horn was the nickname of Alfred Aloysius Horn, a late-nineteenth-century British Ivory Coast trader whose reminiscences, *The Ivory Coast in the Earlies,* edited by the South African novelist Ethelreda Lewis, and with a foreword by John Galsworthy, were published in 1927. It went through eleven printings between July 1927 and February 1929 and was reissued in October 1930 as *Trader Horn.*

49. Published in the January–February 1928 issue.

50. Amy Lowell had died in May 1925.

51. Louis Bromfield (1896–1956) served in the American Field Service during World War I and was awarded the Croix de Guerre and Legion of Honor. The author of several novels, including the 1927 Pulitzer Prize–winner *Early Autumn,* he lived in France from 1925 to 1938.

52. Lieber was a successful New York literary agent whose clients included Langston Hughes, Erskine Caldwell, and left-wing writers of the 1930s. Later, as agent and coconspirator of Whittaker Chambers, Lieber would be forced to live outside the United States from 1950 to 1968.

53. A review of Walter Edwin Peck's *Shelley: His Life and Work.* The review appeared as an essay, "Alastor," in *The Dial* of June 1928.

54. On April 28, 1928, René Taupin, writing from the Department of Romance Languages at Columbia University, where he was working on a study, "The Influence of French Symbolism on Modern American Poetry," asked Cowley to comment on the influence of French poets on his own and other modern poets' work.

55. *Le Calumet* (1910) by André Salmon.

56. Both Doubleday, Doran and Harrison Smith, who had recently gone into partnership with Jonathan Cape, offered to publish the book.

57. As early as 1919 Cowley had written occasional book reviews for *The New Republic* under Francis Hackett, but his long-term connection with the magazine did not properly start until the late 1920s, after Edmund Wilson had become an associate and then, in 1928, its literary editor. In October 1927 Wilson had invited Cowley to become a regular contributor.

58. *I Thought of Daisy* (1929) was being considered by Scribner's.

59. Tate's review of *Blue Juniata,* "A Regional Poet," appeared in *The New Republic* of August 28, 1929. Tate praised "the discipline of craftsmanship" in Cowley's verse and rated him a better poet than critic: "His mind is basically concrete and unspeculative; he brings to facts and observations an even emotional tone that is the mark of a genuine style; but in criticism Cowley's instinct for exact definition is not strong." *Blue Juniata* was uniquely valuable, Tate thought, as "the record kept by a member of this generation who broke with his past, witnessed the moral collapse of Europe, and returned to make the best of the confused intellectual life of post-war New York."

60. Wilson's first wife, Mary Blair, a classmate of Cowley at Peabody and an actress with the Provincetown Players. Wilson and Blair were divorced in 1930.

61. Irita van Doren, editor of *Herald Tribune Books,* had invited Cowley to be "visiting critic" for the fall. The series of six essays he wrote in effect formed the beginning of the critical-historical evaluation of the achievements of his generation that would grow into *Exile's Return.*

62. Burke had made his own evaluation of the literature of the past ten years in "A Decade of American Fiction," published in *The Bookman* for August 1929.

63. A book of short stories by Glenway Wescott (1928). His first novel, *The Apple of the Eye,* was published by the Dial Press in 1924.

64. Novel by Elizabeth M. Roberts, published in 1927.

65. Morley Callaghan (1903–1990), Canadian novelist and short story writer, companion of Hemingway and Fitzgerald in Paris in the 1920s.

66. A novel by Maurice Barrès, which Cowley had translated for Macaulay's in 1929.

67. Cowley's observation proved prescient: *Blue Juniata: Collected Poems,* which incorporated Cowley's second booklet of verse, *The Dry Season* (1941), appeared in 1968; a last expanded edition, *Blue Juniata: A Life* in 1985.

68. Tate was in Europe (London and Paris) on a Guggenheim fellowship.

4. The Depression Years—Literature and Politics, 1930–1940

1. [NR] indicates a letter (often dictated) written from Cowley's editorial desk, on *New Republic* stationery.

2. Louise Bogan (1897–1970), American poet and a regular contributor to *The New Republic*; poet laureate consultant to the Library of Congress in 1945.

3. *The New Republic* was planning a series of essays on individualism.

4. John Dewey, preeminent American philosopher, was on the *New Republic* payroll as a contributing editor.

5. Newton Arvin (1900–1963), a professor of English at Smith College, was a pioneering critic of American literature, the author of groundbreaking biographies of Hawthorne, Whitman, and Melville. In the 1930s he was actively involved on the left, and, like Cowley, an advisor of Yaddo. From 1930 on, he regularly wrote for *The New Republic.*

6. On a brief vacation Cowley and Peggy had traveled to the South to visit the Tates in Clarksville before visiting Katherine Anne Porter in Mexico.

7. *I'll Take My Stand: The South and the Agrarian Tradition,* by Twelve Southerners (1930). Tate's introduction to the symposium was published in abbreviated form in *The New Republic.*

8. Andrew N. Lytle (1902–1995), southern novelist, dramatist, critic; with Tate and Robert Penn Warren, he was one of the driving forces of the Southern Agrarians, and from 1961 to 1973 editor of *The Sewanee Review.*

9. Ralph Borsodi, author of *This Ugly Civilization,* which Cowley had reviewed for the *New York Herald Tribune* in 1929. Borsodi, an economic theorist, had offered

a critique of "machine-age America" and suggested a remedy might be found in self-sufficient homesteading.

10. Wilson published his famous essay "An Appeal to Progressives," suggesting that communism be taken away from the Communists, in *The New Republic* of January 1931.

11. Contributors to *I'll Take My Stand*. Nixon's essay was entitled "Whither Southern Economy?"

12. Samuel Ornitz (1890–1957), screenwriter and novelist, one of the "Hollywood Ten" blacklisted under McCarthy.

13. Raymond Holden (1894–1972), publisher, poet and writer of mystery and detective fiction, who worked and wrote for *The New Yorker, Fortune,* and *Newsweek*. Holden and Bogan had married in 1925; they divorced in 1937.

14. Léonie Adams (1899–1988), American poet who in 1928 had had a brief affair with Wilson; poet laureate consultant to the Library of Congress in 1946; winner of the Bollingen Prize in 1954.

15. Irving Babbitt, with Paul Elmer More, advocated the New Humanism, a conservative literary philosophy; among its adherents were T. S. Eliot, Seward Collins (editor of *The American Review*), Norman Foerster (editor of a New Humanist symposium), and G. B. Munson. In an essay for *The Critique of Humanism* (1930), an anti–New Humanist symposium edited by C. Hartley Grattan, Cowley had objected that the New Humanism failed to consider "man in relation to society" and envisioned "the lamest utopia ever imagined." "Has it any validity for the mill-hands of New Bedford and Gastonia, for the beet-toppers of Colorado, for the men who tighten a single screw in the automobiles that march along Mr. Ford's assembly belt?"

16. Luis Angel Firpo (1894–1960), legendary Argentinian boxer, who famously challenged world champion Jack Dempsey, a fight that was painted by George Bellows in 1924.

17. John Chamberlain (1903–1995), journalist, editor, and regular contributor to *The New Republic;* later worked for *Fortune* and *Life,* and turned from left-wing sympathies to the right.

18. Henry Allen Moe (1894–1975), secretary, later president, of the Guggenheim Foundation.

19. Cowley wrote a tribute to this American woman, "killed from ambush" by Mexican revolutionaries in 1924: "Rosalie Evans' Ranch," *The New Republic,* February 18, 1931.

20. Kay Boyle (1902–1992), novelist, short-story writer, and poet and a prominent member of the American expatriate community in 1920s Paris. From 1932 to 1943 she was married to Laurence Vail, with whom she had three children. Among her friends were Harry Crosby, who published her first book with Black Sun Press, and Eugene Jolas, editor of *transition*. She coauthored *Being Geniuses Together* (1968) with Robert McAlmon. A victim of McCarthyism in the 1950s, she became involved in political activism during the Vietnam War and was imprisoned for her beliefs.

21. Peter Blume (1906–1992) was a Russian-born American painter and sculptor who used elements of surrealism and magical realism in his work. Cowley had met Blume in 1929 in the Village. He and his wife, Grace "Ebie" Douglas Craton, would be lifelong neighbors and friends of the Cowleys in Sherman.

22. Burke had complained about the magazine's treatment of his contributions.

23. John Brooks Wheelwright and Evan Shipman were also invited. Evan Shipman (1904–1957) had befriended Hemingway in Paris in 1924 and later became a journalist dedicated to horse racing. The sessions at Yaddo signaled the beginning of *Exile's Return.*

24. Sidney Hook (1902–1989), American philosopher and public intellectual. A supporter of Communism in the early 1930s, Hook turned against the Soviet Union at the time of the Moscow Trials and became a fervent supporter of Trotsky. Later he became a virulent anticommunist and in the Cold War era was one of the founders of the Congress for Cultural Freedom. He became one of Cowley's bitterest opponents. During his summer 1931 stay at Yaddo, Hook reputedly converted several guests, among them Diana and Lionel Trilling, to Communism.

25. Morris R. Cohen (1880–1947), philosopher, lawyer, and legal scholar, author of *Reason and Nature* (1931). He contributed regularly to *The New Republic.*

26. Robert Cantwell (1908–1978) made a name for himself in the 1930s as a writer of proletarian fiction (*Laugh and Lie Down,* 1931; *Land of Plenty,* 1932). Later he fell under the influence of Whittaker Chambers, turned against left-wing politics, and worked for *Fortune, Time,* and *Sports Illustrated.* Cowley had the highest hopes for him in the 1930s and enlisted him as a reviewer for *The New Republic.*

27. Cowley's letter was broadly circulated and led to a formal letter of protest to the Chinese minister, signed by many of the leading figures of the time. See also Cowley's "Twenty-Four Youngsters," *The New Republic,* July 8, 1931.

28. Cowley's "battle" with Ernest Boyd over Boyd's "Aesthete: Model 1924" is described in *Exile's Return,* 190–196.

29. Yaddo is located near Saratoga Springs, New York, famous for its horse racing.

30. Nathan Asch (1902–1964), Jewish-American writer of Polish descent, son of Sholem Asch. Asch had lived in Paris in the early 1920s, published in expatriate little magazines, befriended Hemingway, and by 1931 had published three novels, *The Office* (1925), *Love in Chartres* (1927), and *Pay Day* (1930). Cowley and Asch were lifelong friends and correspondents.

31. Burke's *Counter-Statement* appeared in 1931.

32. Granville Hicks (1901–1982), literary critic and editor, was a regular contributor to *The New Republic* under Cowley's editorship. An influential literary presence on the Communist left, Hicks wrote *The Great Tradition* (1933), a Marxist interpretation of American literature since the Civil War. In his review for *The New Republic* of November 29, 1933 ("To a Revolutionary Critic" [*TBOU* 47–51]) Cowley expressed his personal sympathy with Hicks's radical position but faulted his book for displaying "harshness, narrowness, dogmatism." Hicks joined the

Communist Party in 1934 and became editor of *The New Masses* in 1935. In 1939 he was one of many who resigned from the Party in the wake of the Nazi-Soviet Pact. From 1942 he was an advisor for Yaddo, often working in tandem with Cowley.

33. Chard Powers Smith (1894–1977), American poet, novelist, and critic.

34. Asch was working on the stories collected in *The Valley* (1935).

35. Cowley's editorial, "Death of a Poet," appeared in *The New Republic* of May 11, 1932.

36. Crane had sent the poem to Cowley from Mexico on Easter 1932, asking for his "honest appraisal." Now generally acknowledged to be one of his finest later poems, it was inspired by Crane's new love for Peggy.

37. Crane's poem "The Broken Tower" appeared in *The New Republic* of June 8, 1932, together with Wheelwright's poem "To Hart Crane."

38. *Contempo* was a short-lived little magazine edited from North Carolina by M. A. Abernathy and A. J. (Tony) Buttita.

39. Samuel Putnam, "If Dada Comes to America," *Contempo* 2 (July 15, 1932), 1, 3, 5. Putnam, critic, publisher, and well-known translator of Cervantes, related a different version of the incident, as it had been narrated to him by Louis Aragon, in his memoir *Paris Was Our Mistress* (1947), 148.

40. On his way to the Tates at Cloverlands, where he hoped to finish writing *Exile's Return*, Cowley had visited Scott and Zelda Fitzgerald in Baltimore. He had taken notes on Fitzgerald's remarks. He later incorporated an account of the visit into *DGM* 187–191.

41. George Anthony Weller (1907–2002) was an American novelist, playwright, and Pulitzer Prize–winning journalist for the *New York Times* and *Chicago Daily News. Not to Eat, Not for Love,* a novel about undergraduate life at Harvard, was published in 1933.

42. Blackmur, who was preparing to review *Exile's Return* together with T. S. Eliot's book *After Strange Gods*, wrote to Cowley on April 27, 1934, asking him to clarify his position on the social and political obligations of the artist. The ideas Cowley advanced in his response are the genesis of the epilogue to the original edition of *Exile's Return: A Narrative of Ideas* (1934), entitled "Yesterday and Tomorrow." He finished the epilogue on May 1, 1934, "with a brave feeling of doing my part for the Rrrrevolution," as he wrote to Warren Susman on March 8, 1965. The gist of the epilogue appeared as "Art Tomorrow" in *The New Republic* of May 23, 1934 (collected in *TBOU* 56–62). For the 1951 revised edition of the book Cowley replaced the original epilogue with a new one (see Part VIII). Blackmur's review, "The Dangers of Authorship," appeared in *The Hound & Horn* 7 (1934), 719–726.

43. Cowley had articulated his attitude toward the New Humanism at length in "Angry Professors," *The New Republic,* April 9, 1930 (collected in *TBOU* 3–13). In expanded form it appeared as "Humanizing Society" in Grattan, *Critique of Humanism,* 63–84.

44. Fitzgerald had inscribed Cowley's copy of the novel: "Dear Malcolm: Please don't review this—I know how you'd do it. Put a young man on it—oh hell—use your own judgment, as you will anyhow. Ever Yours, Scott."

45. *The New Republic* was running a listing of unjustly neglected books.

46. Cowley's review, "Breakdown," appeared in *The New Republic* for June 6, 1934 (*TBOU* 225–228). It contained the germ of the controversial revision of the novel's structure that he undertook in 1951.

47. Bernard DeVoto (1897–1955), literary critic, authority on Mark Twain, and Pulitzer Prize–winning historian of the American West. In "Exiles from Reality" (*Saturday Review of Literature,* June 2, 1934), DeVoto had offered a trenchant critique of *Exile's Return* from a Freudian and a sociological perspective. He challenged Cowley's thesis of deracination and dismissed his book as "the apologia of a coterie." Cowley discussed the 1934 reception of *Exile's Return* in *DGM* 227–232.

48. On August 20, 1934, Caresse Crosby, then residing in France, had written to Cowley objecting that he had not asked her permission for the use of Harry Crosby's diaries in *Exile's Return.*

49. Lewis S. Gannett (1891–1960) for thirty years wrote a daily book review column for the *New York Herald Tribune,* "Books and Things." From September 15 to 26, 1947, Cowley substituted for Gannett as guest reviewer.

50. The gist of Cowley's letter was printed in the *New York Herald Tribune* of August 17, 1934.

51. Maurice Zolotow (1913–1991), then a student at the University of Wisconsin, Madison, later achieved a reputation as a writer on theater and film celebrities. He was known as "the Boswell of Broadway."

52. A reference to Eliot's poem "Morning at the Window," from *Prufrock, and Other Observations* (1917).

53. Zolotow had charged that there was a Communist cabal on *The New Republic.*

54. Cowley had published Cheever's very first short story, "Expelled," in *The New Republic* (October 1, 1930), 171–174, in effect launching the eighteen-year-old writer on his career. Cheever would become closely associated with Yaddo.

55. Muriel was pregnant with their son, Robert Cowley.

56. Wilson was writing *To the Finland Station,* parts of which were being serialized in *The New Republic.*

57. *The Birth and Death of David Markand,* a novel by Waldo Frank; Cowley's review, "Pilgrim's Progress," appeared in *The New Republic* of October 17, 1934. He praised Frank's novel but was disturbed by his understanding of Communism as a mystical state of religion instead of a practical way of revolutionary action. In *The New Republic* of November 21 Frank faulted Cowley for approaching the novel on ideological grounds yet failing to properly define his terms. Cowley's response (which here appears in its original draft) was printed in *The New Republic* in abbreviated form.

58. Robert Herrick (1868–1938), American novelist, professor of English at the University of Chicago from 1893 to 1923. Herrick wrote seventeen realistic social novels critical of American society, including *The Web of Life* (1900) and *The Memoirs of an American Citizen* (1905).

59. Arvin's article appeared in *The New Republic* of March 6, 1935.

60. Cf. Dos Passos to Cowley, November 13, 1934, in *The Fourteenth Chronicle: Letters and Diaries of John Dos Passos,* edited by Townsend Ludington (Boston, 1973), 450. For Dos Passos's angry response to Cowley's printing of the letter, see *The Fourteenth Chronicle,* 453.

61. Max Eastman (1883–1969), novelist, poet, and editor of the socialist magazines *The Masses* (1911–1917) and *The Liberator* (1918–1924). With Floyd Dell and others, he was a key figure in Greenwich Village, a proponent of Freudianism, and an advocate of free love. He was committed to socialism through the 1920s and 1930s but critiqued Stalin and the Soviet system and developed a friendship with Trotsky, whose *History of the Russian Revolution* (1932) he translated into English.

62. Dos Passos had written to Cowley that he was getting "thoroughly sick of every little inkshitter who can get his stuff in a pink magazine shying bricks" at Hemingway (*Fourteenth Chronicle,* 456).

63. On December 12, 1934, Tate sent Cowley Cleanth Brooks's "Metaphysical Poetry and the Ivory Tower," the last of three essays by Brooks on modern poetry published in *The Southern Review* in 1935, with the comment that it was "nearly the last word on the propaganda vs. art controversy." In his essay Brooks insisted on the need to "prize poetry as *poetry,* not as doctrine or science" (571) and critiqued the "essential naiveté" of the Marxist position on literature: "in insisting on art as propaganda, the Marxists have merely revived and restated the oldest and stubbornest heresy of criticism—the didactic theory. [. . .] [T]he truth of the doctrine enunciated in a poem cannot in itself make the poem good" (572, 574).

64. Tate had taken Cowley to task for allowing the "the steady deterioration of the [magazine's] literary department." "For not less than three years I have heard from many people [. . .] that you have steadily tried to exclude from *The New Republic* those writers over whom you could not feel an easy supremacy. [. . .] Invariably this opinion [. . .] has been accompanied by astonishment that one of the ablest stylists in America could tolerate such a low standard of thinking and of expression." Tate gave warning: "You are now in a position where criticism of the casual, frank kind that we passed around ten years ago, only with difficulty reaches you" [NL].

65. Robert William Cowley was born on December 16. On December 19, Cowley wrote to Robert Herrick: "At nine o'clock last Sunday morning Mrs. Cowley gave birth to a large, healthy and—if I must admit it—damned ugly baby which is going to be called Robert William. She had a hard time of it, but is recovering quickly and feeling very happy indeed. I hope you will regard yourself as one of the baby's godfathers" [RH].

66. Ignazio Silone (1900–1978), Italian writer, author of *Fontamara* (1930; an English translation appeared in 1934). A founding member of the Italian Communist Party, Silone settled in Switzerland in 1930, turned against Stalin, and was expelled from the International Communist Party. Later he joined the Congress of Cultural Freedom. After his death historians unearthed controversial evidence that in the 1920s he had been an informant for the Fascist police.

67. Cowley had reviewed Silone's *Fontamara* in *The New Republic* for October 10, 1934 (included in *TBOU* 237–240). A 1960 edition of *Fontamara* published by Atheneum Press in New York contained a foreword by Cowley.

68. From April 26 to 28, 1935, the First American Writers' Congress was held at the Mecca Temple and the New School for Social Research in New York City. It aimed to bring together as many writers as possible to support the Popular Front policy of the American Communist Party and was the occasion for launching the League of American Writers, in which Cowley was prominently active, as a member and vice president.

69. Dos Passos declined. On behalf of the American Organizing Committee for the Congress, Cowley wrote a similar letter of invitation to Katherine Anne Porter, Sherwood Anderson, Sylvia Beach, and others.

70. *The New Republic* had been printing short anthologies of the new English poets, California poets, proletarian poets, and southern poets. Cowley had recently asked Zabel to prepare an anthology of New England poets.

71. Cowley was asking Arvin about the First American Writers' Congress. Cowley had read a paper, "What the Revolutionary Movement Can Do for a Writer." It was published in *The New Masses* (May 7, 1935) and reprinted in the proceedings of the conference, *The American Writers' Congress,* edited by Henry Hart (New York: International Publishers, 1935), and included in *TBOU* 87–94.

72. In his speech at the First American Writers' Congress, "The Writer as Technician," Dos Passos had insisted that even in the face of revolutionary pressures of power and bureaucracy the writer must "be free to give rein to those doubts and unclassified impulses of curiosity that are at the root of invention and discovery and original thinking" and had put in a fervent plea for the upholding of "liberty, fraternity and humanity." Hart, *American Writers' Congress,* 80, 82.

73. Joseph Freeman (1897–1965), writer and editor on *The New Masses* from 1926 to 1937, and one of the founding editors of the early, Communist *Partisan Review* (1934–1936).

74. Fred E. Beal (1896–1954) was a former Communist labor union organizer who had become disillusioned with Party tactics during the 1929 Gastonia strike and escaped a U.S. prison sentence for murder by fleeing to the Soviet Union. In 1933, horrified by Stalin's regime, he went underground in the United States to write his autobiography, *Proletarian Journey* (1937). In 1938 he was captured, imprisoned, and deprived of his U.S. citizenship. In 1948 his citizenship was restored, and he famously proclaimed: "I would rather be an American prisoner than a free man in Russia."

75. Cowley was eagerly anticipating Wilson's forthcoming book on his travels through the USSR, *Travels in Two Democracies* (1936), parts of which were prepublished in *The New Republic*. On February 21, 1936, Cowley praised the "feeling of absolute candor" in Wilson's account [EW]. Cowley reviewed the book in two parts, in *The New Republic* of June 3 and 10, 1936 (*TBOU* 115–122).

76. Though Cowley had known Conrad Aiken since he had arranged to meet him in Cambridge in 1918, the earliest surviving letter is dated December 3, 1935. Aiken was then residing at Jake's House, Rye, Sussex.

77. In "The Poet's Privacy" (*The New Republic*, September 18, 1935; included in *TBOU* 101–104) Cowley had challenged Aiken's conception of the poet—individualist, entitled to freedom, privacy, and anonymity—as "based on a questionable theory of art and politics."

78. "Poem for Amy Lowell" appeared in *The New Republic*, January 6, 1936 (*TBOU* 278–282).

79. In 1936 and 1937 Cowley published a series of essays in *The New Republic* on American writers who between 1910 and 1930 had revolted "against gentility." Contributors included Arvin (on Sandburg), Hamilton Basso (on Thomas Wolfe), John Peale Bishop (on Hemingway), Cantwell (on Upton Sinclair and Sinclair Lewis), Cowley (on Dos Passos), Bernard Smith (on Van Wyck Brooks), Lionel Trilling (on Eugene O'Neill and Willa Cather), and others. The series was published as a book, *After the Genteel Tradition: American Writers since 1910* (Norton, 1937), edited by Cowley, who also wrote the introductory essay, "The Revolt against Gentility" (collected in *PMC* 191–205).

80. With Isidore Schneider, Harold Rosenberg, and Marjorie Fischer, Cowley was actively involved in organizing a lecture series under the auspices of the League of American Writers.

81. Alexander Trachtenberg (1884–1966) was a leading figure in the American Communist movement. He was the founder and manager of International Publishers, a radical publishing house, and a member of the Central Control Committee of the U.S. Communist Party.

82. Cowley is referring to two of Hicks's books, *The Great Tradition: An Interpretation of American Literature since the Civil War* (1933) and *John Reed: The Making of a Revolutionary* (1936).

83. "A Game of Chess," published in *The New Republic* of April 29, 1936.

84. Philip Horton was writing the first biography of Hart Crane (published in 1937), and Tate was considering an edition of Crane's letters for the Equinox Press.

85. Anthony Eden (1897–1977), British foreign secretary during the time of the Spanish Civil War, later (1955–1957) prime minister.

86. Trilling was contributing an essay on Willa Cather, as well as one on Eugene O'Neill, to the series dedicated to American writers who revolted "against gentility."

87. V. F. Calverton (born George Goetz) (1900–1940), author and reformer, best known as founder and editor of *The Modern Monthly*, formerly *The Modern Quarterly*, in which he pursued an independent Marxist course.

88. Michael Gold (1894–1967), editor of *The Liberator* and *The New Masses,* was a vociferous critical voice on the Communist left. The author of a popular autobiographical novel, *Jews without Money* (1930), he became cultural commissar of the Communist Party and wrote a daily column for the *Daily Worker.*

89. Josephine Herbst (1892–1969), writer and journalist who was active on the Communist left. She is best known for her trilogy of "proletarian" novels, *Pity Is Not Enough* (1933), *The Executioner Waits* (1934), and *Rope of Gold* (1939).

90. Fred B. Millett (1890–1976), professor of English at the University of Chicago and subsequently (from 1937 to 1958) at Wesleyan University. He authored bio-bibliographical surveys of contemporary British and American writers.

91. Edmund Wilson, *Letters on Literature and Politics, 1912–1972,* selected and edited by Elena Wilson (New York: Farrar, Straus and Giroux, 1977), 286–287.

92. In its issue of April 18, 1936, the *New Militant* published a scathing attack on Cowley by Felix Morrow, a political activist prominent in the Trotskyite movement. In "Malcolm Cowley: Portrait of a Stalinist Intellectual," Morrow berated Cowley for uncritically espousing Stalinism in *The New Republic.* Morrow faulted him for an inability to handle ideas and for attacks on Trotsky marked by "malicious dishonesty" and symbolic character assassination. "He is a minion of the law of Stalin," Morrow concluded, "a cop patrolling his beat in the book review section of *The New Republic* with readymade memoranda drawn up for him by his Stalinist masters." The attack hurt, and for several years reverberated through Cowley's correspondence. In an April 1936 note to Burke, Cowley wrote: "This Morrow article is a bad one, bad because there is enough truth in it to make it damaging—he takes the qualities I have been working for—definiteness, simplicity, ideas in terms of character—and makes terrible vices out of them"; he added on April 27, 1936: "They are out after you too, they are out after all of us, and picked me first as the easiest target."

93. In late 1937 Cowley traveled to Pennsylvania to attend the funeral of his mother, Josephine Hutmacher Cowley, who had died at seventy-two.

94. Samuel Sillen, "Authors of Surrender," *The New Masses,* October 8, 1940, 4–7.

95. Malraux's *L'Espoir* (*Man's Hope*) was reviewed by Cowley under the title "Apocalypse" in *The New Republic* of March 2, 1938.

96. Wilson had recently married the novelist Mary McCarthy.

97. The Munich Pact, permitting Nazi Germany to annex Sudetenland (then part of Czechoslovakia), was negotiated and signed on September 30 by Germany, France, Britain, and Italy.

98. *Letters on Literature and Politics,* 309–310.

99. In "Partisan Review" (*The New Republic,* October 19, 1938) Cowley faulted *Partisan Review* for no longer being "a nonpartisan literary monthly" but conducting a "grand anti-Russian campaign"—"Put a green cover on it and today you could hardly tell it from *The American Mercury.*" He pleaded for a new magazine in the tradition of *The Dial,* "devoted primarily to literature." In response, the editors

of *Partisan Review* accused Cowley of having launched "a malicious and politically motivated attack masquerading as a matter of literary differences," in which he engaged in "Red-baiting, C.P. style." Cowley in turn called for a truce but only fanned the controversy; see "Red Ivory Tower" (November 9, 1938) and "Partisan Review Finale" (December 21, 1938).

100. Dwight Macdonald (1906–1982), American writer, film critic, social critic, and political radical, edited *Partisan Review* from 1937 to 1943, leaving the magazine to start his own journal *Politics* (1944–1949), which featured work by James Agee, Daniel Bell, John Berryman, Albert Camus, André Gide, Irving Howe, Mary McCarthy, and Marianne Moore. In the 1950s he would become America's vocal critic of mass culture, whose defining features he saw as vulgarity, kitsch, homogeneity, and standardization.

101. F. W. Dupee, "André Malraux," *Partisan Review* 5, 4 (March 1938), 24–35.

102. Cardinal Pacelli (later Pope Pius XII) in 1933 had signed a treaty with Germany on behalf of Pope XI that helped to give moral legitimacy to the Nazi regime shortly after Hitler's rise to power.

103. In May 1938 Cowley signed a statement by "American Progressives on the Moscow Trials" in *Soviet Russia Today* denouncing the Trotskyites and supporting Russia's "drastic defense" against its internal dangers. That same month he wrote two articles for *The New Republic* (May 18 and 23, 1938) in which he evinced skepticism about the justification for the trials and argued that, even on the assumption that the defendants were guilty as charged, the trials gave a morally bleak picture of the Soviet Union and left him with "a new respect and affection for the political virtues of the old-fashioned liberals."

104. "Hemingway: Work in Progress," *The New Republic,* October 20, 1937. In his letter of October 20, 1938, Wilson had wondered: "I was thinking a year ago that something must have gone very wrong with you when you could get yourself into a state of mind to praise Hemingway's Popeye-the-Sailor novel—though I am sure that your natural instincts must have told you that it was mostly lousy and actually represented Hemingway in pieces!" *Letters on Literature and Politics*, 310.

105. Hamilton Basso (1904–1964), southern novelist, author of eleven novels, including *The View from Pompey's Head* (1954). For much of his life Basso oscillated between the South and New York City. Cowley had known Basso since the late 1920s, but his earliest surviving letters to Basso date from the late 1930s. Basso was a frequent contributor to *The New Republic* under Cowley's editorship. Cherishing his independence, he freely criticized Cowley's politics but valued his critical advice on his novels. Both men were lifelong friends and correspondents. On Basso's death, Cowley wrote a tribute for *Saturday Review* (June 27, 1964), "The Writer as Craftsman: The Literary Heroism of Hamilton Basso."

106. A series of revaluations by leading *New Republic* contributors on nonfiction books of the last forty years that had influenced American ideas. Edited by Cowley and Bernard Smith, the series was published in 1940 by Doubleday, Doran as

Books That Changed Our Minds. It included appraisals of books by Henry Adams, Thorstein Veblen, John Dewey, Charles Beard, V. L. Parrington, Benedetto Croce, Oswald Spengler, Sigmund Freud, and others. Cowley contributed a foreword and "An Afterword on the Modern Mind."

107. *Grand Hotel,* a star-studded 1932 film produced by Paul Bern and Irving Thalberg, based on a novel by Vicki Baum and featuring Greta Garbo, John Barrymore, and Joan Crawford, introduced the "Grand Hotel formula"—the bringing together of unrelated characters into a single setting. *Days Before Lent* was made into a film entitled *Holiday for Sinners* (dir. Gerald Mayer, 1952).

108. *Cinnamon Seed,* published in 1934, was Basso's second novel. *Days Before Lent* (1939) was his fifth.

109. Basso's note: "Let's wait and see." Basso's notes were scribbled in the margin of Cowley's letter on July 15.

110. Tom M. Girdler (1877–1965), manager of Republic Steel Corporation, 1930–1937. Basso's note: "NUTS!"

111. "Such faith, Malcolm, such faith! As if the monolithic state couldn't falsify figures!" [Basso's note].

112. "RATS! Nonsense!" [Basso's note].

113. "More blind faith! Damn it, why can't Malcolm do his own thinking!" [Basso's note].

114. "This sort of thinking is going to cost M.C. dear some day." [Basso's note].

115. Heywood Broun (1888–1939), American journalist and founder of the Newspaper Guild, converted to Catholicism before his death in December 1939.

116. "Quien sabe?" [Basso's note].

117. Brooks had resigned from the League on October 17, 1939 and had written to Cowley on November 1: "I think the League will have to be reorganized under some other control and that it will fail utterly unless this happens. The die-hard Stalinists will be left high and dry and the American writers will be somewhere else. I think the League is trying to unite impossibles, because it gives primary emphasis to European questions. [. . .] It ought to be chiefly concerned with domestic questions on a broadly democratic American basis." [NL] Franklin Folsom was executive secretary of the League of American Writers from 1937 to 1942.

118. Jean Giono (1895–1970), French novelist and essayist whose pacifist convictions led to his imprisonment. Aragon's and Giono's fates were representative of the difficulties experienced by Communists and pacifists during the so-called Phoney War, the tense and uncertain military and political situation between the declaration of war on Germany by France and Great Britain in September 1939 and the start of the Battle of France in May 1940.

119. The House Committee on Un-American Activities, established in 1938, under the chairmanship of Martin Dies, Jr., hence known as the Dies Committee. In January 1942 Dies would denounce Cowley, then recently appointed to the

Office of Facts and Figures, in Congress as one of many radicals seeking to infiltrate the U.S. government, and "one of the most ardent Communist intellectuals in this country." Dies's speech appears in the *Congressional Record* vol. 88, 1 (77th Congress, 2nd session), 15 January 1942, 407–411.

120. Max Lerner (1902–1992), journalist and author, editor of *The Nation* (1936–1938) and, later, of *PM* (1943–1948). Lerner consistently held liberal political and economic views. In the 1930s he supported the New Deal and the Popular Front; and in the wake of the Nazi-Soviet Pact he organized several meetings of progressives to discuss a new orientation for radical liberalism.

121. Brooks had written: "I have just reread *Exile's Return*. You don't know how deeply I feel at one with that book. It is absolutely thrilling." Van Wyck Brooks to Cowley, November 1, 1939 [NL].

122. Joseph North, journalist for the communist *New Masses* and *Daily Worker*.

123. Arvin had already decided to resign from the League.

124. Berryman suggested adding "After Breughel" to the title, and the poem was accepted. Cowley had earlier recommended Berryman for a stay at Yaddo, referring to him as "a young poet of some real talent who went to Oxford and is now recovering from that misfortune in a state of poverty." Cowley to Newton Arvin, April 21, 1939 [Arvin].

125. In the 1930s Cowley sent out dozens of such requests on a weekly basis, only a fraction of which survives. Cowley reviewed *Native Son* in *The New Republic*, March 18, 1940. Included in *TBOU* 355–357.

126. *Letters on Literature and Politics*, 357–358.

127. Benjamin Stolberg (1891–1951), author and journalist on labor issues, was a member of the Dewey Commission, which investigated the charges against Leon Trotsky. In various essays and in his book *The Story of the CIO* (1938) he had lashed out against the role played by Stalinists in various CIO unions.

128. Eugene Lyons (1898–1985), American journalist and writer. A former fellow traveler, Lyons moved to the political right and famously authored *The Red Decade: The Stalinist Penetration of America* (Indianapolis: Bobbs-Merrill Co., 1941), an exposé of intellectuals who had allowed themselves to become infatuated with Soviet Communism. Echoing Felix Morrow's 1936 attack, Lyons denounced Cowley for having been "outspokenly Stalinist [. . .] the Number One literary executioner for Stalin in America" (134).

129. José Robles Pazos was a friend (and translator) of Dos Passos who fought with the Loyalists in Spain but was arrested in late 1936 and executed by the Communists as a Fascist spy. Though Dos Passos tried hard to establish the precise reasons for his friend's death, much remained unclear. Hemingway, who was with Dos Passos in Spain to work on Joris Ivens's film *The Spanish Earth*, believed that Robles, as the Communists asserted, had been involved in espionage for the Fascists. Hemingway's stance led to a break with Dos Passos. In reviewing Dos Passos's *Adventures of a Young Man* (*The New Republic*, June 14, 1939) Cowley had taken

Hemingway's (and the Communists') side and proclaimed: "People who ought to know tell me that the evidence against [Robles] was absolutely damning." In reply, Dos Passos had written to the editors of *The New Republic*, outlining what he believed were the actual circumstances of Robles's execution and challenging Cowley to reveal any concrete evidence he might have. Cf. *Fourteenth Chronicle*, 527–529.

130. Minister of foreign affairs on the Republican side in the Spanish Civil War. Dos Passos was convinced Del Vayo had lied to him about the circumstances of Robles's death.

131. Juan Negrín, Franco's predecessor as prime minister of Spain, from May 1937 to February 1939, controversially allowed his government to be infiltrated by the Communists.

132. In *The New Republic* of January 22, 1940, Cowley had reviewed *In Stalin's Secret Service*, a book by W. G. Krivitsky, a former spy of Stalin who had defected to the West. Basing his judgment in part on information received from anonymous inside sources Cowley believed to be "trustworthy," he denounced Krivitsky as a spinner of fables and falsities who in any case, on the basis of his own story, was an opportunist, coward, and traitor to former friends.

133. Nicholas Dozenberg (1882–1954) was a Soviet spy who was arrested in late 1939 on charges of passport fraud. In January 1940 he had pleaded guilty and been sent to prison. Because he cooperated with the investigations of the FBI and the House Un-American Activities Committee, he was released after one year and a day.

134. Morrow's attack had appeared in the *New Militant*.

135. As the letter is dated February 2, Cowley in all likelihood took two days to write it.

136. In "Archibald MacLeish and 'the Word'" (*The New Republic*, July 1, 1940; reprinted in *Classics and Commercials* [1950], 3–9) Wilson had taken issue with Archibald MacLeish's recently published attack (in *The Irresponsibles*, 1940) on the writers of the 1920s for not taking an active stand in support of democracy and for having sailed a defeatist course. MacLeish's piece had been prepublished in *The Nation* of May 18, 1940.

137. Stuart Chase (1888–1985), American economist and engineer. A regular contributor to *The New Republic*, Chase wrote on a wide assortment of topics, from single tax and birth control to planned economy. In *The Tyranny of Words* (1938) he popularized the theory of "general semantics."

138. C. Hartley Grattan (1902–1980), a historian, critic, and economic analyst, later an authority on Australian history and literature. In 1930 he had edited *The Critique of Humanism*, the proceedings of the anti–New Humanist symposium, which included Cowley's "Humanizing Society."

139. Edmund Wilson had published a scathingly satirical poem, "The Omelet of A. MacLeish," in *The New Yorker* of January 14, 1939.

140. Cowley quoted a substantial part of his letter (paragraphs 3 through 7) in "In Memoriam," his review of *Fighting Words,* Donald Ogden Stewart's account of the Third American Writers' Congress of June 1939, in *The New Republic* of August 12, 1940. See also the League's response, and Cowley's reply, in "More Fighting Words," in *The New Republic* of August 26, 1940.

5. THE WAR YEARS, 1940–1944

1. Unless indicated otherwise, all letters in this section are written from Gaylordsville, Connecticut, the postal office for Sherman.

2. Henderson (1882–1942), British ambassador to Germany from 1937 to 1939, supported Chamberlain's appeasement policy toward Hitler at the time of the Munich Pact. In "The Other England," his review of Henderson's *Failure of a Mission: Berlin 1937–1939 (The New Republic,* April 29, 1940), Cowley lashed out against Henderson as a betrayer of Western democracies and appeaser of Fascism.

3. A new literary magazine recently launched by Thompson and Brown that ran for two years before both editors enlisted in the U.S. army. Thompson (1918–1975) published a volume of poetry in 1943 (*Poems*) and a novel, *The Dove with the Bough of Olive* (1942).

4. Philip Rahv (1908–1973), influential literary critic at midcentury, and, with William Barrett, a founding editor of *Partisan Review.* Rahv joined the Communist Party in 1932 but broke with it at the time of the Moscow Trials and turned sharply against fellow-traveling liberals (like Cowley), whom he castigated for selling out Western culture to Stalin. He operated at the center of a powerful circle of New York intellectuals that included Dwight Macdonald, Mary McCarthy, Alfred Kazin, and Lionel Trilling. Rahv's paradigm-setting essay "Paleface and Redskin" appeared in the summer 1939 issue of *The Kenyon Review.*

5. Burke had objected to Cowley's prospective outline, arguing that the book tended to become "too much journalism and diarism, and not enough criticism," "not so much *literature* as *finagling among literary politicians.*" He urged Cowley to aim to make the issues larger than merely local, personal, or political. *SC* 231–232.

6. The GPU, a forerunner of the KGB, was the Soviet Union's secret police organization from 1922–1934.

7. On December 13 Cowley had had his notorious lunch with Whittaker Chambers in which Chambers had warned him that "the counterrevolutionary purge is still to come." Notebook III, January 1, 1939–September 13, 1942, entry for December 13, 1940, p. 67 [NL].

8. "The People's Theatre," Cowley's review of *Arena,* appeared in *The New Republic* of January 13, 1941 (*TBOU* 184–188); "Death of a Hero," his review of *For Whom the Bell Tolls,* in *The New Republic* of January 20 (*TBOU* 361–364).

9. Lewis Mumford (1895–1990), historian, sociologist, and literary and cultural critic, well known for his writings on technology, cities, and urban architecture. In "Shipwreck," his review of Mumford's book *Faith for Living* for *The New Republic* of September 9, 1940, Cowley had faulted Mumford for coming dangerously close to fascism in his search for a "new religion of humanity." Cowley signed a subsequent letter to Mumford "Yours for beating Hitler."

10. Cowley had reviewed Frederick L. Schuman's *Night over Europe: The Diplomacy of Nemesis, 1939–1940* in *The New Republic* of February 3, 1941.

11. In "Poets as Reviewers" (*The New Republic,* February 24, 1941) Cowley praised Conrad Aiken's sonnet sequence *And in the Human Heart* while lamenting the "disheartening" state of poetry reviewing. He particularly faulted Randall Jarrell for writing poetry reviews as "a form of art in which the technical skill and the attitude—the dandysme—of the reviewer are more important than his subject matter. Poetry enters them only as a target. The poet who gets a going-over by Mr. Jarrell is like the scared Negro at a county fair who sticks his head through a sheet while people throw baseballs at it, three balls for a dime." Cowley also observed that in *The New Yorker* Aiken's book had been "used by Louise Bogan as one of the texts for a sermon against the grand poetic manner."

12. Cowley responds to Bogan's supposition that Aiken had used her as a model for a character in his novel *Conversation, or: Pilgrim's Progress* (1940).

13. Freeman had left the Communist movement shortly after publishing his autobiography *An American Testament: A Narrative of Rebels and Romantics* (1936), which prompted Communist Party officials to denounce him as "an enemy of the people." He publicly broke with the Party after the 1939 Hitler-Stalin pact. Cowley had reviewed *An American Testament* in the October 28, 1936, issue of *The New Republic,* characterizing it as an uneasy synthesis of bohemian and revolutionary worlds.

14. Martha Dodd (1908–1990), daughter of William Dodd, U.S. ambassador to Germany from 1933 to 1937. Later Martha Dodd colluded with Soviet intelligence and in the 1950s fled to Prague.

15. In a letter of March 7, 1941, Bogan had observed to Cowley that "hatred is the psychic coloring of our day; but if there is hatred, there is also great capacity for love. [. . .] AMOR, in the depths of the spirit, is both." Cowley quoted from her letter in "Marginalia" (*The New Republic,* July 7, 1941).

16. Archibald MacLeish (1892–1982), Pulitzer Prize–winning modernist poet, critic, and dramatist. MacLeish had been an ambulance driver in World War I and between 1923 and 1928 was part of the American expatriate community in France. Cowley critically reviewed MacLeish's work through the 1930s, and in September and October 1933 he and MacLeish debated the legacy of World War I in the pages of *The New Republic* (see *TBOU* 35–47). MacLeish served as Librarian of Congress from 1939 to 1944.

17. Cowley had asked MacLeish to write to Russell "Mitch" Davenport, the managing editor of *Fortune,* on behalf of Joseph Freeman, who, much like Cowley, was being "blackballed" by both Communists and anticommunists and had difficulty finding employment as a freelance writer (Cowley to Freeman, April 22, 1941 [JF]).

18. Cowley had agreed to contribute an essay to *Whose Revolution? A Study of the Future Course of Liberalism in the United States,* edited by Irving DeWitt Talmadge (New York: Howell, Soskin, 1941). It contains essays by Roger Baldwin, Alfred Bingham, James Burnham, John Chamberlain, Lewis Corey, Malcolm Cowley, Granville Hicks, Hans Kohn, Eugene Lyons, and Bertram D. Wolfe that evaluate the prospects of liberalism after the failure of political radicalism in the 1930s. In "Faith and the Future," Cowley worked out his interpretation of Communism as a religion. The essay was reprinted as "Communism and Christianism" in *FL* 12–24.

19. Dillon accepted the four poems—"Roxane," "The Lost People," "Restaurateur with Music," and "Seven"—which were published as a group entitled "The Lost People" in *Poetry* in December 1941.

20. In October 1941 MacLeish had been appointed by FDR to lead the newly formed Office of Facts and Figures, a precursor of the Office of War Information. On October 8 and 9, at MacLeish's invitation, Cowley participated in a conference in Washington on the future of the Federal Arts Program. Shortly thereafter, Macleish invited him to join the Office of Facts and Figures, asking him to come at his earliest convenience.

21. On November 13, 1941, Congress had repealed the 1939 Neutrality Act by a narrow ten-vote margin.

22. Cowley appended a list of names of people he thought might usefully be invited to work for the Office of Facts and Figures, among them Hamilton Basso, Christopher LaFarge, Max Lerner, Felice Swados, and Norbert Guterman.

23. *Opinions of Oliver Allston* was reviewed by Cowley in two installments for *The New Republic* (November 24 and December 1, 1941) as "Mr. Brooks Dissenting."

24. Cowley had reason to believe that it was the *Time* editor Whittaker Chambers, former Soviet spy turned anticommunist, who was responsible for moving the review of *The Dry Season* to a prominent place in the magazine where it could do more damage. Chambers's manipulation was one of several factors that eventually led Cowley to resign from the Office of Facts and Figures.

25. In its March 16, 1942, issue *Time* published, in abbreviated form, a letter from Cowley that recapitulated many of the points he had made in his private letter to MacLeish. *Time* added a title—"Frantic and Fanatical"—and a concluding comment: "TIME cheerfully concedes that ex–Literary Editor Malcolm Cowley is no danger to the country. —ED."

26. Cowley was investigated by George J. Gould, chief of investigations of the Office of Emergency Management, on February 5, 1942. As chief information analyst,

Cowley had access to potentially sensitive information. The interrogation intended to establish the precise extent of Cowley's radical affiliations. The text of the interrogation, reprinted in abbreviated form in *CMC,* was not made available to Cowley until 1985.

27. Westbrook Pegler (1894–1969) was a right-wing syndicated newspaper columnist. A sharp critic of the New Deal, he won the Pulitzer Prize for reporting in 1941 for exposing corruption in Hollywood labor unions. In his column "Fair Enough" for January 30, 1942, he had denounced Cowley as a former Communist and contributing member of the staff of the *Sunday Worker.*

28. Louis Weiss (1894–1950) was a lawyer at the international law firm of Paul, Weiss, Rifkind, Wharton & Garrison, a firm committed to fighting anti-Semitism and protecting human and civil rights. He worked with Eleanor Roosevelt on issues of children's rights and race relations.

29. Max Lowenthal (1888–1971) was political advisor to various U.S. senators and, later, President Truman.

30. On February 24, Weiss replied that he was shocked by Cowley's revelations; he considered it "one of the extreme cases which points the moral." There was "nothing specific" he could do on Cowley's behalf, but he did ask permission to show Cowley's letter to Mrs. Roosevelt [NL].

31. Dorothy Dudley Harvey (1884–1962) contributed to *Poetry* and wrote an early biography of Dreiser, *Forgotten Frontiers* (1932). She spent much of her life in France, befriending Gertrude Stein and Matisse. In 1937 she wrote reviews for *The New Republic* but withdrew because of political differences with Cowley over Stalin and the Moscow Trials.

32. Cowley thought he had recognized the testimony of Sidney Hook.

33. Paul Wohl (1901–1985), a German-Jewish refugee who had participated in the 1921 German revolution and worked for the League of Nations. He was a friend (and literary agent) of Krivitsky and in 1939 had sought out Cowley on *The New Republic,* hoping for book review assignments. Malcolm Cowley to Hans Bak, February 17, 1983.

34. Davis had recently been appointed head of the Office of War Information. Cowley reported on Davis and his new responsibilities in "The Sorrows of Elmer Davis" in *The New Republic* of May 3, 1943.

35. Massing (1902–1979) was a German sociologist who was involved in Soviet intelligence, with his wife, Hede Massing.

36. Poet and painter Weldon Kees (1914–1955) enjoyed Cowley's consistent support and encouragement. In the summer of 1942 Kees spent time at Yaddo and in May 1943, with the help of Cowley, got a job on the editorial staff of *Time;* but he left the magazine after several months, relieved to no longer serve under Whittaker Chambers. Cowley was dismayed by Kees's mysterious disappearance, presumably a suicide, in San Francisco in 1955.

37. On February 6, 1943, MacLeish had invited Cowley to participate in a panel discussion at the Library of Congress on April 13 on "the relation of Mr. Jefferson's

general position to the problem of this present racked and riven world." The Bicentennial was organized by the Library of Congress and the National Gallery.

38. Jarrell added a note in the margin: "Southey's *Politics Explained for the Young* is the title of *this*."

39. Hans Arp (Jean Arp) (1886–1966) was a German-French sculptor, poet, and painter who had been a founder of the Dada movement in Zürich in 1916.

40. Cowley's profile of Max Perkins was published as "Unshaken Friend" in two installments in *The New Yorker* of April 1 and 8, 1944 (included in *FL* 55–66). It was reissued as a separate booklet in 1985.

41. Cowley was exploring the possibility of writing a follow-up profile for *The New Yorker* on Henry Allen Moe and the Guggenheim Foundation. Partly for lack of cooperation by Moe, the profile never materialized.

42. Hoffman, then at the Department of English at Ohio State University in Columbus, was doing research for his book *Freudianism and the Literary Mind* (1945).

43. Isidore Schneider (1896–1976), American novelist who had worked for Macaulay publishers in the 1920s and joined forces with the left in the 1930s, serving as an editor on *The New Masses* and becoming active for the League of American Writers. He was assembling material on American humor and had asked Cowley what he thought were the best pieces of humorous writing in America.

44. Otis Ferguson (1907–1943), pioneering if idiosyncratic film and jazz critic on *The New Republic* in the 1930s, where he rose to be assistant editor. "Nertz to Hertz" had appeared in *The New Republic* of April 5, 1934. Ferguson had volunteered with the Merchant Marine and died in action in 1943, when his ship was hit by a radio-guided German bomb off the coast of Salerno. Cowley's memorial tribute, "For Otis," was published in the magazine on November 1; it was later revised by Cowley to serve as the foreword to *In the Spirit of Jazz: The Otis Ferguson Reader,* edited by Dorothy Chamberlain and Robert Wilson (New York, 1982).

45. Alfred Kazin (1915–1998), the Jewish-American literary critic and memoirist, had published *On Native Grounds: An Interpretation of Modern American Prose Literature* in 1942, at age twenty-seven. He was a longtime admirer of William Blake and in 1946 edited *The Portable Blake* for Viking Press.

46. V. L. Parrington's three-volume history of American letters, *Main Currents in American Thought* (1927), won the Pulitzer Prize in 1928. The historian Merle Curti won the Pulitzer Prize in 1944 for *The Growth of American Thought*.

47. Cowley had reviewed Warren's novel in *The New Republic* of August 23, 1943.

48. On April 8, 1944, Warren acknowledged that he had indeed read *Butterfield 8* and "actually [. . .] had had feelings much like yours about the book. But in the course of writing *At Heaven's Gate* I wasn't conscious of the suggestion which might very well have come from the other book" [NL].

6. THE MELLON YEARS, 1944–1949

1. Stanley Young (1906–1975), publisher, playwright, and managing editor of the Bollingen series, had been chosen by Mary Mellon to administer her "Five Year Plan" of scholarships to writers, no strings attached. The stipend was granted through the Bollingen Foundation, which had been established by the philanthropist and art collector Paul Mellon, son of the banker Andrew Mellon, together with his wife Mary. The winners agreed to spend all their working time on creative work, to assign Mary Mellon a 20 percent interest in any literary property undertaken during the five years, and to submit a semiannual report. Besides Cowley, three others were beneficiaries of Mary Mellon's plan: Denis de Rougemont, John Hyde Preston, and Stanley Young. William Maguire, *Bollingen: An Adventure in Collecting the Past* (1982), 79.

2. Unless indicated otherwise, all letters in this section are addressed from RFD Gaylordsville, Conn., the post office for Sherman, Conn.

3. Cowley may have been embellishing here; I have found no record of his having attended the Sorbonne as an international student.

4. The letter goes on to list Cowley's book publications and translations.

5. Cowley's essays on French literature remain mostly uncollected.

6. *Aragon: Poet of the French Resistance* (New York: Duell, Sloan and Pearce, 1945) was edited by Cowley in collaboration with Hannah Josephson. Cowley wrote an introductory essay ("Poet of This War"; included in part in *FL* 77–88), and was mostly responsible for the poetry section, the bulk of which he translated (often in cooperation with Rolfe Humphries; other poems were rendered by Kenneth Muir, Louis MacNeice, Sally Wood, William Jay Smith, George Dillon, Stephen Spender, and others). Cowley also translated "The Martyrs," which, in a shorter anonymous version, had been published in May 1942 in *Life* as "They Died for France."

7. Cowley's translation, *Imaginary Interviews,* by André Gide, was published by Alfred A. Knopf in 1944. "A Footnote on French Prosody" first appeared in *The New Republic* of May 22, 1944, and was reprinted as an appendix to the book.

8. In *The New Republic* of April 24, 1944, Cowley spoke up "in defense of the 1920s" in rebuttal to the critic Bernard DeVoto, who in *The Literary Fallacy* had faulted the writers of the interwar years for indulging in disillusionment, cynicism, and nihilism and misrepresenting American life and society. Included in *FL* 179–184.

9. Archibald MacLeish, in *The Irresponsibles* (1940), and Van Wyck Brooks, in *Opinions of Oliver Allston* (1941), had likewise attacked the writers of the 1920s.

10. Paul Rosenfeld (1890–1946), American critic of literature, art, and music, affiliated with *The Seven Arts* (1916–1917) and *The Dial*. With Waldo Frank, he had been a favorite punching bag of Cowley and his friends in the 1920s because of his flowery, impressionistic style.

11. Cowley was responding to "The Three Periods of Louis Aragon" by Paul Rosenfeld, which appeared in the *Saturday Review* of April 29 [not 15], 1944, 8. Rosenfeld

had implied that Aragon's "new politics" were in sympathy with the collaborationist Vichy regime: "His voice now was regularly heard on the Vichy radio, broadcasting to the strains of the Marseillaise."

12. A group of French collaborators with the Fascists, named after Jacques Doriot (1898–1945), founder of the anticommunist French Popular Party.

13. In subsequent correspondence with Rosenfeld, Cowley reiterated his plea not to endanger the life of "one of the bravest, most loyal people I know," but Rosenfeld was not persuaded to retract his charges of collaboration (Cowley to Rosenfeld, May 8, 1944 [NL]). Some nine months later, the debate resumed publicly in the *Saturday Review:* see Cowley's reaction in "The Truth about Louis Aragon," *Saturday Review of Literature,* January 6, 1945, 28, 30. There, Cowley repeats the gist of his argument. In a response in the January 20 issue of the *Saturday Review,* 23, Rosenfeld refused to publicly retract his charge, criticizing Cowley for making a "sentimental appeal" without presenting adequate evidence.

14. Raymond William Postgate (1896–1971), a British socialist journalist, editor, mystery novelist, and gourmet. A founding member of the British Communist Party, Postgate broke with the Party in 1922 to become a leading ex-Communist radical.

15. Liston M. Oak (1895–1970), Communist journalist and political activist who, after repudiating Communism in the late 1930s, became an editor at *The New Leader* (1943–1948) and worked for Voice of America; V. J. Jerome (1896–1965), Polish-American novelist, critic, and editor of the *Communist* (later *Political Affairs*) from 1935 to 1955. A theorist and cultural spokesman for the Party in the 1930s, Jerome was later prosecuted and convicted under the Smith Act and served a sentence in prison between 1954 and 1957.

16. The New Economic Policy, introduced by Lenin in 1921 and boosted by a strong propaganda campaign. In 1928 the NEP was replaced by the first of Stalin's Five Year Plans.

17. Cowley had written to Faulkner in February, but the letter does not survive.

18. "But I thought in a distant way of Scribner's, since I felt (and feel) that Max Perkins was a great editor. Not long afterward I talked to Max about Faulkner; he was not interested. 'Faulkner is finished,' he said unemphatically" [MC's note].

19. In Cowley's letters to Faulkner, bracketed phrases in italics indicate passages or phrases that appear in the original letter but not, or in variant form, in the version as edited by Cowley for publication in *FCF.*

20. Clifton P. Fadiman (1904–1999), author, critic, editor at Simon and Schuster, and book review editor for *The New Yorker;* he later worked for radio and television. In his reviews, Fadiman had objected to Faulkner's morbidity, obscurity, and sensational melodrama and to his concern with the "more horrifying aspects of sex" (*The Nation,* November 5, 1930).

21. "Geismar is not a professor" [MC's note].

22. "More errors on my part. Of course the critic was George Marion O'Donnell, who had been the first to recognize that Faulkner was a moralist, and his essay

had been published in *The Kenyon Review* (1, Summer 1939), not in *The Southern Review*. Cleanth Brooks's compendious and level-headed study of Faulkner's work had not been started at the time, and would not be published for twenty years" [MC's note].

23. F. O. Matthiessen (1902–1950), literary critic and scholar of American literature at Harvard University, whose *American Renaissance: Art and Expression in the Age of Emerson and Whitman* (1941) defined the canon of nineteenth-century American writing for the next three decades (it was Matthiessen who coined the expression "the American Renaissance" for the flowering of mid-nineteenth-century American literary culture). As Cowley's letter shows, Matthiessen's book influenced Cowley's interpretations of contemporary writers like Hemingway and Faulkner. Matthiessen had regularly reviewed for *The New Republic* under Cowley's editorship.

24. "Hemingway at Midnight," the introductory essay to *The Portable Hemingway,* was included in *FL* 169–178. See also *PMC* 317–326.

25. Cowley's "piece" on Frost appeared in two installments: "Frost: A Dissenting Opinion" (*The New Republic,* September 11, 1944) and "The Case against Mr. Frost: II" (*The New Republic,* September 18, 1944). Together they appeared in *AMWH* 201–12.

26. In writing on Auden's book *For the Time Being* ("Virtue and Virtuosity: Notes on W. H. Auden," *Poetry,* January 1945, 202–209; *FL* 269–274) Cowley had been impressed by Auden's knowledge of prosody and made the poet's technical skill into the focus of his review.

27. "The Return of Henry James" and "The Two Henry Jameses" appeared in *The New Republic* of January 22, 1945, and February 5, 1945; included in *AMWH* 89–99.

28. The protagonist of James's story "The Next Time," whose fineness of imagination prevents him from writing a commercially successful novel.

29. On April 26, 1945, the poet Charles Olson, a government employee since Pearl Harbor, wrote to Cowley to inquire if he knew of any action being undertaken in the case of Ezra Pound, who had come under scrutiny for his profascist radio broadcasts in Italy. Olson thought he might be able to help "save the scoundrel's skin" [NL].

30. Cowley goes on to ask a number of questions about his selections. See *FCF* 28–29.

31. Peter De Vries (1910–1993), novelist, editor, and wit, was editor of *Poetry* from 1938 to 1944 and served on the staff of *The New Yorker* from 1944 to 1987.

32. *Poetry* did not take up Cowley's suggestion for a special issue on Aiken, but Cowley would prove a persistent champion of Aiken's work.

33. Cowley goes on to suggest Kenneth Burke, Granville Hicks, Alfred Kazin, James T. Farrell, or Maxwell Geismar.

34. In 1947 Cowley's reflections on naturalism were "beefed" and published in *The New Republic* and *The Kenyon Review* before they appeared integrally in *Evolutionary Thought in America* (1947), edited by Stow Persons.

35. Spiller, general editor, had asked Cowley's advice on who might write a concluding chapter on the impact of American books abroad.

36. Cowley's enthusiastic response prompted Spiller to invite him to do it. On March 20, 1945, Cowley answered: "the chapter I might be able to write would *not* be historical, and would have as its principal thesis that American literature has recently become one of the world literatures in its own right, like English and French and German and Russian, instead of being regarded merely as a branch of English literature." He enlisted the help of Archibald MacLeish, then assistant secretary of state, and collected firsthand information from Upton Sinclair, Margaret Mitchell (see letter included here), Pearl S. Buck, Sinclair Lewis, Jean Paul Sartre, and a wide range of publishers, scholars, and authors from Europe and Japan.

37. Arvin was responding to "Walt Whitman: Poet of America?" (*The New York Times Book Review,* February 24, 1946); "Walt Whitman: The Miracle" (*The New Republic,* March 18, 1946), and "Walt Whitman: The Secret" (*The New Republic,* April 8, 1946). On June 30, he had observed to Cowley: "you somewhat exaggerated the *mysteriousness* of Whitman's sexual 'inversion'; I mean the extent to which it had been suppressed and glossed over, since in fact it has been public property for forty years. [. . .] I myself think that the special quality of Whitman's work [. . .] depends very profoundly on the fact that his erotic nature was what it was [. . .] I thought there was just a suggestion, in your piece, of regret or apology or concession, and I see no need for any." The latter two of Cowley's pieces on Whitman were incorporated in "Whitman: The Poet and the Mask," *AMWH* 35–75.

38. Warren's editor at Harcourt, Brace and Company.

39. Allan Dowling, a businessman with literary leanings, proposed to finance a revival of *The Dial* and approached Cowley for advice and a possible role as editor.

40. After much deliberation Cowley declined Dowling's invitation to be the editor of the "new" *Dial,* giving priority to his own writing. A year later, Dowling put his money behind *Partisan Review.*

41. Mary Mellon had unexpectedly died on October 11, 1946.

42. "Ten Little Magazines," published in *The New Republic* of March 31, 1947.

43. Francis Biddle (1886–1968), U.S. attorney general under presidents Roosevelt and Truman, from 1941 to 1945; he served as the primary American judge during the 1945–1946 Nuremberg trials.

44. At Macdonald's suggestion Cowley wrote an anonymous article on his FBI dossier for *Politics.*

45. At Cady's invitation Cowley had agreed to lecture at Syracuse on June 9 and 10, 1947.

46. Cowley had earlier contracted with George Soule's firm Pilot Press to edit one or more volumes in a new American Classics series. In 1948, at Cowley's

suggestion, Pellegrini & Cudahy published a two-volume edition of *The Complete Poetry and Prose of Walt Whitman,* edited, with a critical introduction, by Cowley. In 1953 the firm of Pellegrini & Cudahy was taken over by Farrar, Straus & Co.

47. Ella Wheeler Wilcox (1850–1919), popular poet of sentimental, optimistic verse, best known for her poem "Solitude," included in *Poems of Passion* (1883).

48. After U.S. air force service work in London and Paris, Asch had relocated to California, with his second wife, Carol, to work on a novel, "Paris Is Home," featuring the protagonist Kranz as Asch's alter ego. The book remains unpublished, though Cowley helped to get two fragments published in magazine form: "The Nineteen Twenties: An Interior" appeared in *Paris Review* in 1954, with an introduction by Cowley, and "My Father and I" appeared posthumously in *Commentary* in 1965. Some of Cowley's observations on the American writer in *The Literary Situation* (1954) were based on the life and career of Asch. He continued to offer criticism and advice on Asch's manuscripts until Asch's death in 1964.

49. In a long middle section Cowley offered detailed criticism of Asch's novel.

50. With his wife, Muriel, and son, Robert, Cowley had spent twelve days with Hemingway in Havana, on assignment for *Life.*

51. Among others Cowley consulted were Otto McFeely, childhood friend of Hemingway in Oak Park, about specific memories of Hemingway in his high school football days; Brigadier General C. T. Lanham, for biographical information on Hemingway in World War II; and Spruille D. Braden, U.S. ambassador in Colombia (1939–1942), Cuba (1942), and Argentina (1945), about Hemingway's antisubmarine activities off the coast of Cuba. Through Norman Holmes Pearson of Yale University, Cowley gained access to Hemingway's correspondence with Gertrude Stein and Sherwood Anderson.

52. For a while Cowley seriously entertained the idea of writing a full-length biography of Hemingway and negotiated with Scribner's (who were hesitant) and (through Harold Strauss) with Alfred Knopf. When the *Life* portrait appeared in January 1949, Hemingway was disturbed by the choice of photographs as well as by Cowley's treatment of his Oak Park years and his antisubmarine activities off the coast of Cuba and so declined further cooperation with Cowley on a biography. Cowley abandoned the idea, instead advising others (Philip Young, Carlos Baker, Scott Donaldson) on their critical and biographical studies of Hemingway.

53. Cowley's interpretation of Hawthorne's "secret guilt" appeared as "Hawthorne in the Looking-Glass" in the autumn 1948 issue of *The Sewanee Review.* At the express request of the editor, John Palmer, Cowley substituted "auto-eroticism" for "masturbation" as a phrase more acceptable to *Sewanee*'s readership. Cf. "Hawthorne in Solitude," *AMWH* 3–34.

54. Faulkner's *Intruder in the Dust* (1948) was reviewed by Cowley in the October 18, 1948, issue of *The New Republic.* The novel about World War I he refers to is *A*

Fable, not published until 1954. Cowley reviewed it in the *New York Herald Tribune Book Review* on August 1, 1954.

55. Gorky (1904–1948) was an Armenian-American modernist painter who had come to the United States in 1920 after fleeing the Armenian genocide of 1915. An important precursor to the Abstract Expressionists, he had settled in the Sherman area in 1945 and become a close friend of Cowley and Blume. Cowley composed a more formal letter of commemoration for the *New York Herald Tribune,* printed in its issue of September 5, 1948: "Arshile Gorky—A Note from a Friend."

56. Cowley had sent Hemingway a section from Asch's manuscript on the Paris expatriate café, the Dôme, later published in *The Paris Review.*

57. Cowley's review, "The European Travel Diary of a Humanist," had appeared in *New York Herald Tribune Books* of September 12, 1948.

58. Faulkner spent two days at Sherman, on October 25 and 26. Cowley made long entries on Faulkner's visit in his notebook, parts of which he later incorporated in *FCF* 103–114.

59. After the success of his portrait of Hemingway, Cowley had been asked by *Life* to write such an essay. It was not published until 1962, in a much revised version, in *The Saturday Review of Literature.* Cowley's thoughts on myths would have constituted a leading unifying motif in his projected but never finished History of American Literature.

60. Norman Holmes Pearson (1909–1975), professor of English and American studies at Yale University, was an important force in establishing American studies as an academic discipline after World War II. Cowley had consulted Pearson extensively while working on *The Portable Hawthorne.* Pearson later collaborated with Auden on the six-volume *Poets of the English Language,* published between 1950 and 1977. Cowley writes to Pearson about the Hart Crane letters he had presented as a gift to Yale University Libraries; in 1949 and 1962 he also made Yale a gift of his William Faulkner letters.

61. Faulkner had categorically refused his cooperation on a biographical essay for *Life.*

62. Hermann Hagedorn's *Edwin Arlington Robinson: A Biography* (1938) combines memoir and biography.

63. Cowley worked closely and laboriously with Moore to fine-tune her translations of *The Fables of La Fontaine,* which were published by Viking in 1954.

64. Leonora Speyer, Lady Speyer (1872–1956), was a Pulitzer Prize–winning American poet and a violinist.

65. Ridgeley Torrence (1874–1950) had been poetry editor at *The New Republic* from 1920 to 1933, when Cowley took over.

66. Percy MacKaye (1875–1956), American dramatist and poet.

67. *The Complete Poetry and Prose of Walt Whitman,* with an introduction by Cowley, had appeared in 1948.

7. Literature and Politics in Cold War America, 1949–1954

1. Leonard Ehrlich (1905–1984), novelist with leftwing sympathies, best known for *God's Angry Man* (1932), a fictional portrayal of John Brown. Ehrlich and Ames were lovers.

2. All subsequent letters in this chapter are written from Sherman, Connecticut, unless otherwise indicated.

3. Tate had reported that Lowell's behavior on visiting the Tates in Chicago had exemplified clear and disturbing symptoms of delusional paranoia.

4. Cowley went on to describe how in subsequent directors' meetings Elizabeth Ames was cleared of political charges and it was decided to leave the question of prolonging or renewing invitations in the hands of an admissions committee. The precise nature of the reorganization of responsibilities and selection procedures at Yaddo was lengthily debated in subsequent correspondence between Cowley, Hicks, and Arvin.

5. James Vincent Forrestal (1892–1949) served as secretary of defense under President Truman, from 1947 to 1949. After disagreements over Truman's economizing defense policy and public attacks by the muckraking columnist Drew Pearson, Forrestal was asked by Truman in March 1949 to resign. He was hospitalized for severe depression and fell to his death from a sixteenth-floor window on May 22, 1949. The precise circumstances of his death remain unclear.

6. Smedley, who had moved to England in November 1949, had died of acute circulatory failure on May 6, 1950.

7. Cowley had participated in a writers' conference at the University of Kansas and had taught at Bennington College in Vermont.

8. Cowley had testified at the first Hiss trial in June 1949.

9. A. J. Liebling (1904–1963) was a longtime writer for *The New Yorker* and a war correspondent who had covered the landings at D-Day. He was a friend of Alger Hiss and a critic of the House Un-American Activities Committee.

10. Auden was working with Norman Holmes Pearson on *Poets of the English Language,* a multivolume anthology published by Viking. Cowley was writing in his new capacity as advisory editor for Viking.

11. Julian Wadleigh (1904–1994), American economist and State Department official who in the 1930s had passed on information to the Soviet Union through Whittaker Chambers. He had recently testified in the Hiss prosecution.

12. Alan Barth (1906–1979), a journalist best known for his writings on civil liberties, from 1942 to 1972 worked as an editorial writer for *The Washington Post.* In 1941 Barth had worked for the Office of War Information. Cowley made a similar proposal to A. J. Liebling, but Liebling declined.

13. With two books on the Hiss case forthcoming, Barth suggested a new book that focused on the loyalty purge in government circles. Over the next two years Cowley worked with Barth on *The Loyalty of Free Men* (1951), pouring many of

his own ideas and worries over "the age of suspicion" into his editorial correspondence.

14. Robert Hillyer had written two articles in the *Saturday Review* attacking the decision by the Fellows of the Library of Congress to give the Bollingen Award to Ezra Pound. Hillyer's articles led to an explosion of outrage in the literary world; Cowley joined the fray with "The Battle over Ezra Pound" (*The New Republic*, October 3, 1949; collected in *FL* 99–106).

15. Lillian Hellman had adapted *Montserrat* (1949) by the French-Algerian playwright Emmanuel Roblès (1914–1995), a play about hostages who gave their lives to protect Simon Bolívar. In late 1948 Hellman had consulted Cowley about the feasibility of translating and adapting the play.

16. Brooks had written on October 1, 1949, to express his appreciation for Cowley's essay "The Literary Atmosphere of Two Eras" (*New York Herald Tribune Book Review*, September 25, 1949), but took issue with his "concluding thesis: that the critical achievement has acted to divert writers from or strangle the creative." Brooks adduced as counter-examples himself, Ransom, Eliot, Tate, Warren, Jarrell, and Lowell—writers who had produced both fine poetry or fiction and criticism: "One activity has not seemed to inhibit the other."

17. Cyril Connolly (1903–1974), eminent English literary critic, author of the unclassifiable *The Unquiet Grave* and editor of *Horizon* (1940–1949).

18. Cowley had voted for the Communist Party candidates in 1932 and 1934. In 1936 his vote went to FDR.

19. The university president Raymond B. Allen was prepared to make the issue of Cowley's appointment a test case for academic freedom and saw that Cowley's letter was published in the local newspapers.

20. A former student of Theodore Roethke at Bennington, who acted as an unofficial agent for the poet.

21. Carey McWilliams (1905–1980), American writer, editor, journalist, sharply critical of anticommunism, defender of the Hollywood Ten, and editor of *The Nation* from 1955 to 1975. McWilliams had written to Cowley on March 20, 1950, inviting him to join a National Committee on Behalf of the Constitutional Rights of the Hollywood Ten.

22. F. O. Matthiessen, a committed socialist whose homosexuality was an open secret, jumped to his death from a Boston hotel window on April 1, 1950. His suicidal depression was widely believed to have been aggravated by the Cold War political climate.

23. Murdock was chairman of the Committee on Higher Degrees in the History of American Civilization, at Harvard.

24. Louis F. Budenz (1891–1972) was a notorious ex-Communist who had turned Catholic and FBI informant. He had recently been denounced in the Senate by Dennis Chavez, Democratic senator from New Mexico.

25. Cowley's review of *Across the River and into the Trees* appeared in the *New York Herald Tribune Book Review* of September 10, 1950.

26. Fulton J. Sheen (1895–1979), Catholic radio priest, later a bishop. He was one of the first televangelists.

27. Marshall A. Best (1901–1982), editor at Viking Press; he had worked with Cowley on the Hemingway and Faulkner Portables and would become one of Cowley's most beloved and trusted colleagues at Viking.

28. Rather than reprint and contextualize the original epilogue as a matter of historical record, for the revised edition Cowley chose to write a new, depoliticized one that he may have felt was more in accordance with the zeitgeist of the early 1950s and offered better sales possibilities. Some readers see his replacement of the original epilogue as an attempt to rewrite (his personal) history. In 1967 Cowley reprinted "Art Tomorrow" (the gist of the original epilogue as published in *The New Republic,* May 23, 1934) in *TBOU* (56–62). See also *PMC* 275–281. In 1994 Donald W. Faulkner appended the full text of the 1934 epilogue to the Viking/Penguin edition of the 1951 version of *Exile's Return.*

29. John W. Aldridge (1922–2007), critic, scholar, teacher, then at the University of Vermont, where he organized a series of writers' conferences in the early 1950s. Following in the footsteps of Wilson and Cowley, whom he befriended, he was one of the first younger critics to seriously consider postwar American writing. His first book, *After the Lost Generation* (1951), was inspired by Cowley's *Exile's Return.* Cowley's friendship with Aldridge cooled after Aldridge wrote a highly critical review of *The Literary Situation.* See "The Question of Malcolm Cowley," in Aldridge's *In Search of Heresy; American Literature in an Age of Conformity* (1956), 166–176.

30. Cowley's collection, *The Stories of F. Scott Fitzgerald,* containing twenty-eight stories "of *all* periods," appeared in 1951. Cowley also consulted Edmund Wilson on the selection.

31. Arthur Mizener (1907–1988), professor at Cornell University, was at work on his biography of Fitzgerald, *The Far Side of Paradise.* Cowley had offered an extensive critique of an earlier version of the manuscript.

32. Cowley also consulted the Fitzgerald scholar Henry Dan Piper on his projected revision of the novel's structure. Piper later wrote *F. Scott Fitzgerald: A Critical Portrait* (1965) and in 1967 and 1970 edited compilations of Cowley's essays for Southern Illinois University Press.

33. Gilbert A. Harrison (1915–2008), critic and biographer, editor of *The New Republic* from 1953 to 1974.

34. The myth of Fitzgerald as a tragic failure in the grip of alcoholism was established in Budd Schulberg's best-selling novel *The Disenchanted* (1950), later a successful Broadway play, about a young screenwriter who collaborates on a screenplay with a dissolute, once famous novelist.

35. "The Scott Fitzgerald Story," *The New Republic* (February 12, 1951).

36. Cowley's 1951 edition of "the author's final version" was controversial, but it remained in print in the United States from Scribner's until 1959. In 1960,

after much heated critical debate, the original 1934 edition was brought back. In 1953 the Cowley edition was published in England; between 1955 and 1978 it remained available as a Penguin paperback. In 1997 Penguin Popular Classics reprinted the 1951 edition, without acknowledging it was Cowley's revision.

37. Cowley offered the essay, which served as an introduction to *The Great Gatsby* in the 1953 omnibus edition of three of Fitzgerald's novels, for first serial publication in *The Western Review*. "F. Scott Fitzgerald: The Romance of Money" appeared in its summer 1953 issue. It was incorporated in the chapter on Fitzgerald in *ASF*.

38. Ironically, an earlier manuscript version revealed that the "potato-faced poet" referred to Cowley himself.

39. *Ernest Hemingway,* by Philip Young (1918–1991), based on his 1948 dissertation, was published in 1952 by Rinehart & Company. In 1966, five years after Hemingway's death, Young brought out a revised edition, *Ernest Hemingway: A Reconsideration,* which incorporated the story of his difficult negotiations with Hemingway during the writing of the book. Young went on to become a notable Hemingway scholar and was professor of American literature at Pennsylvania State University from 1959 till his death.

40. Lillian Ross, "Portrait of Hemingway," first published in *The New Yorker* of May 13, 1950. Hemingway had been irritated by Ross's portrayal, as he had been earlier by Cowley's portrait for *Life.*

41. Hede (or Hedda) Massing, the wife of Paul Massing, was an Austrian-born Soviet intelligence operator in the 1930s who was particularly active as a Soviet spy recruiter among New Deal liberals. She later turned against Communism and testified at the second Hiss trial. In 1951 she published *This Deception.*

42. John K. Hutchens (1905–1995) was book critic for the *New York Herald Tribune* from 1948 to 1963.

43. Harvey Breit (1909–1968), critic and interviewer for *The New York Times Book Review* from 1940 to 1965; he coauthored the screenplay based on Budd Schulberg's novel *The Disenchanted.*

44. Cowley briefly recapitulated his dealings with Young's manuscript as detailed in his letter of May 9, 1951. In several letters written between July 19, 1951 and January 28, 1952, Cowley had continued to pacify Hemingway's objections to Young's book.

45. *Red Channels: The Report of Communist Influence in Radio and Television,* published by the right-wing magazine *Counterattack* in 1950, effectively blacklisted 151 employees in the entertainment industry. Presumably Cowley refers to the magazine's two editors, Theodore C. Kirkpatrick and Francis J. McNamara.

46. As a sequel to *Exile's Return,* Cowley had proposed to Viking a book on the writers of his age group, but "critical rather than historical and objective rather than personal." The book became *A Second Flowering* (1973).

47. On April 30, 1951, Cummings answered: "The ER [Enormous Room] wrote itself as a(n however microscopic) gesture of thankfulness toward my father. [...] B & I were together at the writing, which sans his memory of events would have proved impossible. [...] as for the 'big change': (1) our unhero wrote for a literary mag called *The Harvard Monthly,* not for a social sheet called The ditto *Advocate* [...] (2) perhaps, & here's hoping, I just growed" [NL].

48. William Goyen (1915–1983), Texas-born American novelist, short story writer, and playwright.

49. On November 23, 1951, James Laughlin of New Directions had sent Cowley a four-page document, "Proposal for a Quarterly Magazine on American Materials for Distribution Abroad"; the magazine was later titled *Perspectives USA.*

50. *Fontaine* was a French journal edited by Max-Pol Fouchet and published during the occupation in Algiers. It became the voice of French Resistance poetry in North Africa. *Fontaine* 27/28 (June/July 1944) celebrated American writers and poets: Gertrude Stein, Robert Frost, William Carlos Williams, Wallace Stevens, T. S. Eliot, Sara Teasdale, Robinson Jeffers, Conrad Aiken, Lola Ridge, Archibald MacLeish, Horace Gregory, Louise Bogan, Carl Sandburg, Allen Tate, E. E. Cummings, Hart Crane, Langston Hughes, Frederic Prokosch, Marianne Moore, James Agee, Kenneth Patchen, James Laughlin, and Vachel Lindsay. It was republished in Paris in 1945.

51. At Laughlin's invitation Cowley guest-edited *Perspectives USA* 5 (Fall 1953). He included contributions by the architect Hugh Morrison, Kenneth Burke, Conrad Aiken, Henry A. Murray (on Aiken), Otis Ferguson, John Cheever, Richard Gay, and David Riesman and book reviews by Edmund Wilson and the French critic Mrs. Claude-Edmond Magny. Cowley wrote an introductory essay on "the literary situation."

52. On October 30, 1951, writing from Berkeley, Miles had offered a book of poems called "Two Kinds of Trouble" to Cowley for possible publication by Viking.

53. Whittaker Chambers's autobiography *Witness* was published in 1952. *U.S.A. Confidential* (1952) was a compilation of the popular "Confidential" series written by journalists Jack Lait and Lee Mortimer which offered a salacious exposé of crime, corruption, sex, and communism in American life and society.

54. Cowley had suggested Barth write a sequel to *The Loyalty of Free Men.*

55. In his "Marginalia" page for *The New Republic* of May 26, 1952, Cowley had taken critics to task for being overly creative or imaginative in their interpretations of an author's work: "They should be writing surrealistic novels." Targeting an article on Faulkner's book *The Wild Palms,* Cowley failed to register that it had been written by Irving Howe, whose *William Faulkner: A Critical Study* appeared in August 1952.

56. Cowley reviewed Algren's second novel, *Never Come Morning,* for *The New Republic* of May 4, 1942.

57. On December 29, 1951, Cheever had written to Cowley that Funk & Wagnalls had accepted his collection of fourteen stories for publication after the manuscript had been rejected by Bennett Cerf. *The Enormous Radio and Other Stories* appeared in January 1953.

58. "A Tidy Room in Bedlam" was published in *Harper's* in April 1953.

59. President Eisenhower.

60. Williams was to become consultant to the Library of Congress but lost his appointment as a result of supposedly procommunist sentiments expressed in his poetry.

61. Fulton Lewis, Jr. (1903–1966), conservative radio broadcaster, avid anticommunist, and loyal supporter of Senator Joseph McCarthy.

62. *Faces in a Crowd: Individual Studies in Character and Politics,* by David Riesman in collaboration with Nathan Glazer (1952), is a sequel and companion volume to Riesman's earlier landmark study of conformity, *The Lonely Crowd* (1950), in which he developed the concept of "other-directedness."

63. At Viking, Cowley was working with Hicks on his memoir of the 1930s, *Where We Came Out* (Viking, 1954).

64. Howard Mumford Jones (1892–1980), then professor of English at Harvard University, was engaged in writing a book on the 1890s and in late November 1953, at the suggestion of Marshall Best, asked Cowley for his ideas on the literary decade.

8. WORKER AT THE WRITER'S TRADE, 1954–1960

1. "The Nineteen Twenties: An Interior," part of Asch's (unpublished) novel "Paris is Home," appeared in the summer 1954 issue of *The Paris Review,* prefaced by a note by Cowley; it was one of Asch's rare late publications. Earlier, on November 2, 1951, Cowley had offered the chapter to Irving Kristol at *Commentary:* "[Asch] has a real feeling for language and I think that pretty soon he will be rediscovered. It would be nice if that could be in *Commentary.*" Another part of Asch's manuscript, a memoir of his father, Sholem Asch, appeared posthumously in *Commentary* in 1965.

2. With Zabel and Babette Deutsch, Cowley served as a member of the jury for the Harriet Monroe Award in Poetry in 1954, given out by *Poetry.*

3. In 1954 the Newberry Library was the home of *Poetry.*

4. The Harriet Monroe Award for 1954 went to Léonie Adams. Cowley liked the Newberry so much that, at the suggestion of the librarian Stanley Pargellis, he deposited part of his papers there, the start of a lifelong connection.

5. Unless indicated otherwise, all letters in this section are written from Sherman, Connecticut.

6. *American Imago,* founded in 1939 by Sigmund Freud and Hanns Sachs, is a journal of psychoanalysis and the arts and sciences.

7. "Psychoanalysts and Writers" appeared in the September 1954 issue of *Harper's*. Cowley had exposed the reductive implications of the psychoanalytic theories of Dr. Edmund Bergler (1899–1962), who defined the writer as an "orally regressed psychic masochist."

8. *A Fable* (1954).

9. Josephine Herbst (1892–1969), the author of a trilogy of "proletarian" novels, had known Whittaker Chambers in the 1930s during his days as an underground agent of the Communist Party. She had cooperated with Alger Hiss's lawyers at the time of the 1948 trials. Reputedly, Herbst's ex-husband, John Herrmann, had introduced Hiss to Chambers during a lunch in 1934.

10. Reuel Denney (1913–1995), American poet, sociologist, and critic of popular culture; coauthor, with David Riesman and Nathan Glazer, of *The Lonely Crowd* (1950). In his letter Cowley responded to a draft of an essay by Denney on the ethos of the spectator in Hemingway that Denney later incorporated into *The Astonished Muse* (1957).

11. Cowley had written on the merits of hardbacks versus the new phenomenon of paperbacks in two articles for *The New Republic* (April 26 and May 3, 1954), later included in *The Literary Situation*.

12. *The New Republic,* launched in 1914, was celebrating its fortieth anniversary in 1954.

13. The essay was published as "Some Dangers to American Writing" in *The New Republic* of November 22, 1954. Included in *FL* 112–118.

14. James Stern (1904–1993), Anglo-Irish writer of fiction and criticism, and a close friend of the Cowleys. With his wife, Tania, he had lived and worked in New York from 1939 until the early 1950s, when they returned to Great Britain. Among his literary friends and correspondents were W. H. Auden and Djuna Barnes.

15. Robert N. Linscott (1886–1964), Faulkner's editor at Random House. Cowley had worked with Linscott on *The Portable Faulkner.*

16. Felicia Geffen, administrator at the National Institute and American Academy of Arts and Letters, sister of Hannah Geffen, wife of Matthew Josephson.

17. The Howells Medal for 1955 went to Eudora Welty's novel *The Ponder Heart.*

18. On October 23, 1954, Basso replied that he was "very touched" by Cowley's letter: "As you know, there are only a few people whose opinion one really cares about, and to have such appreciation from you is a true reward."

19. On November 30, 1954, Tate responded to *The Literary Situation,* wondering "who is this guy Ollendorf?" (a fictive persona used by Cowley in *The Literary Situation*), and continued: "It's a *very* good book. [. . .] I find myself in almost complete agreement with you in your first chapter: an excellent job. But I can't think we're to blame for the Alexandrianism of the 'newer' critics. Isn't the failure of nerve theirs?"

20. "English Eyes upon Us," a review of a special issue of the *Times Literary Supplement* titled "American Writing Today," appeared in *The Saturday Review of Literature* of October 30, 1954.

21. Ginsberg, acting as Kerouac's informal agent, was sounding out various publishers on Kerouac's behalf.

22. Porter had earlier accepted "The Time of the Rhetoricians" for *New World Writing* 5 (1954); it was part of the first chapter of *The Literary Situation*.

23. At Wallace Stegner's invitation Cowley had been teaching at Stanford during the winter quarter. Kerouac wrote to Cowley on February 10, expressing regret that he had left California for the East Coast before Cowley's arrival. When Kerouac received no reply, he wrote again on March 16, to announce his forthcoming return to California. Cowley's March 21 letter did not reach Kerouac until April 19. A few days earlier, unhappy with the pace of the editing, Kerouac had sent Cowley a postcard containing, in red pencil, the one word: "BOO!" [NL].

24. In-house abbreviations for Malcolm Cowley and Keith W. Jennison.

25. Helen K. Taylor, senior editor at Viking; she worked, among others, with Kerouac, Dawn Powell, and Ken Kesey.

26. On July 4, 1957, Kerouac sent Cowley an excerpt from "Visions of Neal." He was eager to see *Doctor Sax* in print, and willing to write a second part of *Desolation Angels*.

27. In the late fall Cowley traveled to Europe. On December 9, 1957, Kerouac wrote to Cowley that he had just completed a new novel, *Dharma Bums*. In Cowley's absence Kerouac worked with Helen Taylor at Viking. "Kerouac looked like Gregory Peck," Cowley wrote on the inside of his Kerouac folder.

28. In a PP.SS Kerouac had added: "Incidentally, from Mark 13.11,—'Take no thought beforehand what ye shall speak, neither do you premeditate; but whatsoever shall be given you in that hour, that speak ye: for it is not ye that speak, but the Holy Ghost.' (spontaneous language)."

29. J. Robert Oppenheimer (1904–1967) was a theoretical physicist who, with Enrico Fermi, developed the first nuclear arms. He was an early proponent of nuclear arms reduction and in 1954 had his security clearance repealed because of his outspoken comments during the McCarthy red scare. He was politically rehabilitated under Kennedy and Johnson.

30. John G. Cawelti (b. 1929), pioneer critic of American popular culture and author of *The Six-Gun Mystique* (1970). In 1955 he was a graduate student at the State University of Iowa, engaged in research on "the attitudes of four American critics [Van Wyck Brooks, Cowley, Hicks, and Aldridge] towards America, the world, and the place and responsibilities of the writer in society." Cawelti to Cowley, February 14, 1955 [NL].

31. Roth, thirty-three in 1954, was the author of several published war stories, an unpublished war novel, and articles on writing and jazz. He had sent Cowley extensive responses to "Invitation to Innovators" and *The Literary Situation* and on February 14, 1955, had expounded his conviction that "the only salvation for the contemporary American writer would be to think more strenuously about 'being American.'" He also enclosed a number of his jazz writings.

32. On May 11, 1955, Stegner had invited Cowley to come to Stanford for the winter quarter of 1956, to teach two courses, one to an advanced group on the writing of fiction, the other to a group of undergraduate and graduate students on the criticism of fiction. The invitation was the start of a long friendship.

33. Cowley compiled a selection of passages from the first edition in "Whitman: A Little Anthology," *The New Republic*, July 25, 1955.

34. Frederick Manfred (1912–1994), Iowa-born American novelist of partly Dutch descent, who published his first novels under the name of Feike Feikema. On October 7, 1955, Manfred had written in angry response to criticism of his novel *Morning Red* from Viking and had asked: "what makes you an expert on the country west of Chicago?" *Morning Red* was published by Alan Swallow in 1956.

35. Cowley's translation was published in the Summer 1957 issue of *The Kenyon Review*.

36. Allen Tate and Caroline Gordon had divorced in 1945 and remarried in 1946. Their second marriage was strained and unstable, rocked by Tate's recurrent infidelities. In 1956 they were living apart, Tate in Minneapolis and Gordon in Princeton. They divorced a second time, and permanently, in 1959. Cowley tried to remain on good terms with both, but was always closer to Tate, who had invited him to participate in a symposium on little magazines in Cambridge earlier that year.

37. "Sociological Habit Patterns in Linguistic Transmogrification" appeared in *The Reporter* of September 20, 1956. Cf. *FL* 218–223.

38. Cowley had written an introduction to *A Thornton Wilder Trio*, a reissue of three of Wilder's novels: *The Cabala, The Bridge of San Luis Rey*, and *The Woman of Andros* (New York: Criterion Press, 1956). In revised form, the introduction became chapter 6 of *ASF*.

39. Gordon was at work on *How to Read a Novel* (1957), based on lectures she had given at the University of Kansas in Lawrence.

40. A propos of *The Literary Situation*, Aldridge, a onetime disciple, had critiqued Cowley in his book *In Search of Heresy* (1956) for evading his responsibilities as a critic and for displaying faults that he thought were endemic to "the historical method" in criticism. Aldridge's critique led to a cooling of their friendship.

41. Basso had sent Cowley the letters Perkins wrote to him in the period he was writing *Days Before Lent*.

42. Cowley is referring to Kerouac's novel *On the Road*.

43. Cowley reviewed Wolfe's letters in *The New Republic* of November 19, 1956. In 1957 he published two further essays on Wolfe: "The Miserly Millionaire of Words" (*The Reporter*, February 7, 1957) and "Thomas Wolfe: The Professional Deformation" (*The Atlantic Monthly*, November 1957). Together, the three articles became the chapter on Wolfe in *ASF*.

44. Purdy's first two collections of fiction had been privately published in 1956, through William-Frederick Press in New York: *63: Dream Palace: A Novella*, and *Don't Call Me by My Right Name and Other Stories*.

45. A first commercial edition, encompassing both the novella and the book of stories, came out in 1957 in London (Victor Gollancz) as *63: Dream Palace.* It was published in the United States by New Directions as *Colors of Darkness* (1957).

46. *Writers at Work: The Paris Review Interviews,* published by Viking in 1958, was edited and introduced by Cowley. It was the first in a long-running series of collected interviews from the magazine and helped to establish the genre's reputation and prestige.

47. Cowley's plea was effective: Thurber consented.

48. Faulkner accepted the invitation and presented the Gold Medal for Fiction to Dos Passos at the ceremonial of May 22, 1957, presided over by Malcolm Cowley.

49. Murphy, a Stanford graduate, in 1957 won the Joseph Henry Jackson gold medal for a first novel in progress; *The Sergeant* was published by Viking in 1958 and was the year's literary sensation and an international best seller; it was made into a movie in 1971.

50. During his semester at the University of Michigan in the spring of 1957 Cowley had been asked to deliver the prestigious Hopwood Lecture. In "The Beginning Writer in the University" (included, in slightly revised form, in *PMC* 554–569) he offered practical suggestions for "how writing might be taught," based on his long experience with writers and writing.

51. Asch's father, the writer Sholem Ash, had died on July 10, 1957. Cowley had earlier spoken admiringly of Asch's memoir of his father; see his letter of September 26, 1955.

52. On June 13, 1957, Winters had written to Cowley: "I wish to resign my membership in the National Institute," offering to return his "diploma and boutonniere." As a consequence of its democratic procedures, Winters felt, the membership was too large and "predominantly undistinguished"—"The Institute, so far as I can see, imposes a penalty upon distinction and places a premium upon mediocrity" [NL].

53. With Cowley's strong support, the 1958 Gold Medal for Poetry went to Conrad Aiken. Other contenders were Louise Bogan, E. E. Cummings, Archibald MacLeish, and William Carlos Williams. On April 16, 1958, speaking on behalf of members of the Institute, Cowley wrote to the attorney general of the United States pleading that Pound be released from St. Elizabeths psychiatric hospital into the custody of his wife and be allowed to travel to Italy.

54. Laurance Page Roberts (1907–2002), Orientalist and museum director; director of the American Academy in Rome from 1946 to 1960.

55. United States Information Service, the overseas branch of the United States Information Agency (USIA), a public diplomacy agency dedicated to fostering understanding of the United States abroad through spreading information and organizing cultural and educational activities.

56. Francis Fergusson (1904–1986), prominent critic and theorist of drama, best known for his influential book *The Idea of a Theater* (1949).

57. Herbert R. Mayes, magazine editor at *Good Housekeeping* and *McCall's* and author of a largely fictionalized first biography of Horatio Alger (*Alger: A Biography without a Hero*, 1928), had inquired into the background of Cowley's 1945 articles on Alger.

58. "Holy Horatio" appeared in *Time,* August 13, 1945; "The Alger Story" in *The New Republic,* September 10, 1945.

59. Mayes's 1928 biography took a great many liberties with Alger's life; it was allegedly based on diaries and letters that later turned out to have been imagined by the author. In 1945 Cowley was one of the first to correct persistent misapprehensions about Alger.

60. On September 6, 1958, Cowley recommended Olsen to the Eugene F. Saxton Memorial Trust, calling her "possibly the best unbookpublished author in the country."

61. Richard P. Scowcroft, professor of English and director of the Creative Writing Program at Stanford, had informed Cowley that Olsen had received a two-year Ford Foundation fellowship. Cowley had nominated her.

62. In early 1959 Cowley also wrote to Marshall Best and Pascal Covici urging Viking to option Tillie Olsen.

63. At the suggestion of Lincoln Steffens, Tillie Lerner (Olsen), then active in the San Francisco Youth Communist League, wrote an account of her arrest, "Thousand-Dollar Vagrant," which was published in *The New Republic* of August 29, 1934. "We're trying to build some backfires here in the East against the California terrorists," Cowley wrote to Steffens's wife, Ella Winter, on August 16 [Columbia]. To Olsen, he wrote on September 17, 1934: "Here in the East the story of your arrest, coming simultaneously with the efforts of half a dozen publishers to get hold of you, was one of the most effective bits of propaganda against the San Francisco Terror. It happened that you were working for the cause even while in jail" [TO].

64. *Tell Me a Riddle,* a collection of four short stories, was published in 1961 by Lippincott.

65. Hassan, then at Wesleyan University, Middletown, Connecticut, had sent Cowley early versions of chapters from what became *Radical Innocence: Studies in the Contemporary American Novel* (1961).

66. In "Hart Crane and His Friends" (*The Nation,* February 15, 1958), the critic Oscar Cargill had faulted Tate for misunderstanding the theme and symbolism of *The Bridge.*

67. On June 17 Winters had responded to Cowley's Hopwood Lecture on the teaching of writing: "You have what my students sometimes call an easy and flowing style, and you touch on many topics. But I don't think you understand the main issues."

68. On May 16 Donald Hall had asked Cowley to fulfill the role of a "critical second consciousness" to his poems, and submitted a number of problems in rhyme for his consideration. As an offshoot of their correspondence on rhyme, on Novem-

ber 3 Cowley asked Hall to write a book on prosody for Viking. Hall, like Auden before him, did not rise to the bait.

69. "Speaking of Books" appeared in *The New York Times Book Review* of June 28, 1959.

70. Cowley's letter was effective. On March 2, 1959, Shapiro wrote to Cowley that he had decided to accept membership.

71. Richard Farina (1937–1966), American writer (author of *Been Down So Long It Looks Like Up to Me* [1966]) and folksinger, was part of the countercultural Village circle including Bob Dylan and Joan Baez. He died in a motorcycle accident in 1966.

72. Farina had asked Cowley's advice on how to launch "another *Broom*" that could serve as "a kind of atelier" for writers outside the academic world.

73. Wescott had succeeded Cowley as president of the National Institute of Arts and Letters, and served from 1959 to 1962, when Cowley was reelected. Cowley and Wescott are discussing potential candidates for the 1960 Howells [not Gold] Medal in Fiction, which was awarded to Cozzens for his novel *By Love Possessed*.

74. Vance Bourjaily (1922–2010), American novelist who from 1957 to 1980 taught creative writing at the Iowa Writers' Workshop. "The Poozle Dreamers," which appeared in *The Dial* (Fall 1959), was included in Bourjaily's fourth book, *Confessions of a Spent Youth* (1960).

75. Leslie A. Fiedler (1917–2003), iconoclastic and singular critic of American literature who championed genre fiction and explored classic American texts in terms of mythography, psychology, and implied or unspoken homoerotic bonding. In his most influential book, *Love and Death in the American Novel* (1960), Fiedler argued that American literature shies away from sexuality and possesses a pathological obsession with death.

76. In a long middle section of the letter Cowley expanded on his interpretation of Hawthorne's marriage, the gist of which he had given in his previous letter to Fiedler. See also Cowley's essay "The Hawthornes in Paradise," *American Heritage* 10 (December 1958), 30–35. Included in *FL* 121–139.

77. Cowley's review, "Exploring a World of Nightmares," appeared on the front page of *The New York Times Book Review* of March 27, 1960 (*FL* 236–240). In his review he offered sharp criticisms—sharper, perhaps, than he had expressed in his letters to Fiedler—but also reiterated his conviction that the book presented stimulating and new insights. In a public letter to *The New Leader,* Fiedler took Cowley to task for not saying in public what he had expressed in private correspondence. Granville Hicks wrote in, coming to Cowley's defense: "There is no discrepancy: although Cowley makes some sharp criticisms, his review says plainly enough that he found the book 'stimulating, new and extremely valuable.'"

78. Cowley had received proofs of *Start with the Sun: Studies in the Whitman Tradition* (1960), edited by Miller, Karl Shapiro, and Bernice Slote.

9. The Sixties

1. Journalist, historian and filmmaker Daniel P. Mannix (1911–1997) wrote on a wide variety of topics, including gladiators and big game hunting, and performed as a stage magician, fire eater, and sword swallower. He had solicited Cowley's advice and cooperation on a book on the slave trade, a subject Cowley had thoroughly researched in the 1920s for his 1928 edition of *Adventures of an African Slaver*. *Black Cargoes: A History of the Atlantic Slave Trade, 1518–1865* (with extensive revisions and three chapters by Cowley) was published by Viking in 1962.

2. The writers listed in Cowley's letter are: Larry McMurtry, who had recently sold two novels to Harper & Brothers and was at work on a third that, Cowley told Marshall Best on November 5, 1960, promised "to outMailer *The Deer Park*" (most likely Cowley refers to *Leaving Cheyenne,* the novel McMurtry was writing in Cowley's seminar); Wendell E. Berry, who had recently finished his novel *Nathan Coulter* (1960); Christopher Koch, who would become one of Australia's foremost writers; Robin MacDonald from Scotland; and Joanna Ostrow, author of *In the Highlands* (1970).

3. Peter S. Beagle (1939), writer of popular fantasy fiction. His best known book is *The Last Unicorn* (1968). In 1960 he had published his first novel, *A Fine and Private Place,* with Viking.

4. The year before Cowley had brought Stegner to Viking.

5. Koch was working on *Across the Sea Wall* (1965).

6. For Cowley's published reminiscences, see "Ken Kesey at Stanford" in *FL* 324–327.

7. *String Too Short to Be Saved* (1961), a nostalgic evocation of boyhood summers Hall spent on a family farm in New Hampshire.

8. Despite Cowley's repeated urgings, Hall did not write the book.

9. *Some People, Places and Things That Will Not Appear in My Next Novel* (1961).

10. Unless indicated otherwise, all letters in this chapter are written from Sherman, Connecticut.

11. "One Man's Hemingway" appeared in the *New York Herald Tribune Books* of July 9, 1961.

12. For Cowley's in-house report on Kesey's novel, see *PMC*, 507–508.

13. Warren consented. His introduction first appeared as an essay, "Elizabeth Madox Roberts: Life is From Within," in *Saturday Review,* March 2, 1963.

14. Cowley is mixing up the titles of two of Burke's publications: *Philosophy of Literary Form* (1941) and "Psychology and Form" (first published in 1925, later part of *Counter-Statement* [1931]).

15. Tate had taken offense at Josephson's portrayal of him in his memoirs of the 1920s, *Life Among the Surrealists* (1962).

16. In his review, "High Hopes that Led to Disillusion" (*The New York Times Book Review,* November 12, 1961), Howe (in part quoting Aaron) referred to Cowley as

"an extremely talented literary critic who throughout the Thirties 'quite consciously but somewhat uneasily allowed himself to be used as a front man by the party.' The chapter on Cowley is especially interesting as a study of an intelligent man struggling with doubts, forcing himself to say and do things he knew to be dubious [. . .], and then finally regaining his independence."

17. *A Moveable Feast* was posthumously published in 1964, edited by Mary Hemingway; in 2009 a "restored edition" was issued.

18. Cowley is responding to Kazin's essay "The Bitter 30's: From a Personal History" (*Atlantic Monthly,* May 1962, 82–99), which contained memories of Cowley in the 1930s that ambivalently mixed admiration and resentment.

19. Emphasizing Cowley's barometric sensitivity to changes in "the literary weather," Kazin observed: "To Cowley everything came down to the literary trend, to the forces that seemed to be in the know, and to himself in the lead." In the article he presented himself as a young ambitious writer "on the make," facing "critics in power" like Cowley, who condescendingly doled out books for review to a poor, Jewish boy excluded from the circles of privilege.

20. In 1982 Dorothy Chamberlain and Robert Wilson edited *The Otis Ferguson Reader,* with an introduction by Cowley.

21. Kazin removed the implied association in the book version.

22. Kazin served as literary editor of *The New Republic* from August 1942 to May 1943, when he accepted a job at *Fortune.*

23. Cowley's letters prompted Kazin to revise his portrait of Cowley for the book edition of *Starting Out in the Thirties* (1965), correcting errors and removing some of the more egregious accusations. Cowley and Kazin enjoyed cordial relations in their later years. In late 1989, when Kazin was inducted into the American Academy of Arts and Letters, he was elected to fill the seat of Cowley, who had taken Van Wyck Brooks's seat in 1964.

24. On July 20 Walters had asked Cowley to respond to the question "Who do you see on the horizon who may in time take the lately vacated places of Hemingway and Faulkner as the internationally recognized 'greats' of American letters?" [NL].

25. Gwen Davis, a novelist of sexually explicit books, was notorious for bringing libel suits against authors. Kesey and his wife, who knew Davis from Palo Alto, sued Davis in 1962 when they thought they recognized themselves in *Someone's in the Kitchen with Dinah,* a novel about "wife swapping." When *One Flew Over the Cuckoo's Nest* appeared, Davis, in turn, threatened to sue Kesey for what she thought was his unflattering portrayal of her in a plump Red Cross character named Gwendolyn. Kesey and Davis settled out of court. In subsequent editions Viking made Kesey change the character to a man called the Public Relation.

26. A 1932 novel by the Norwegian author Sigrid Undset.

27. Richard Gehman (1921–1972), American novelist and nonfiction writer, affiliated with magazines like *Esquire, Cosmopolitan,* and *Playboy.*

28. The revised edition of *After the Genteel Tradition*. Cowley had added essays on John Dos Passos and Edward Arlington Robinson and expanded the prologue, the afterword, and "A Literary Calendar, 1911–1930."

29. In *The New York Times Book Review* of August 2, 1964, the critic Frederick C. Crews had spoken of the "popular acclaim" of James Gould Cozzens's novel *By Love Possessed* (1957) as "a kind of mass delusion." Crews denounced the novel for, among others, being governed by "a considerable latent appeal to miscellaneous prejudices—against Jews, Negroes, Catholics, middle Europeans, women, homosexuals, adolescents, and so on" in order to show that "status before one's neighbors is a grave and wonderful thing." He had attributed the book's popularity in part to Cowley's laudatory review, implying that Cowley appeared to be in general agreement with Cozzens's conservative social and political beliefs. Cowley's letter in rebuttal to Crews was printed in *The New York Times* of September 13, 1964. For Cowley's 1957 review see *FL* 285–288.

30. Kinnell was at work on a translation of the poems of François Villon, published in 1965.

31. Joseph Mitchell (1908–1996), American journalist-writer known for his *New Yorker* portraits of eccentrics. His best known books are *McSorley's Wonderful Saloon* (1943) and *Joe Gould's Secret* (1965). In his review of the former (*The New Republic,* July 26, 1943) Cowley had spoken of Mitchell as "the best reporter in the country" in his chosen field. Cf. *FL* 261–264.

32. The Student Nonviolent Coordinating Committee, one of the principal organizations of the American civil rights movement in the 1960s.

33. Cowley wrote a similar letter to Evans Harrington, president of the Southern Literary Festival Association, emphasizing that, unless the festival was in fact desegregated, he would decline the invitation. Harrington offered convincing reassurance that the conference would de facto be desegregated (he invited African-American students to participate). Cowley attended and gave a talk titled "The Literary Situation, 1965," published in *University of Mississippi Studies in English* 6 (1965), 91–98.

34. "The Sense of Guilt" appeared in *The Kenyon Review,* Spring 1965. It was included in *WT.*

35. In a letter of March 3, 1965, Katherine Anne Porter had objected to being included in Cowley's generational paradigm: "You remarked in effect that Mexico was my Paris, and Taxco my South of France, and I said not at all. There was nothing to stop me from going to the real Paris and the real South of France if I had wished. I was where I chose to be, and Mexico was my Mexico, my beloved city . . . I never was an exile anywhere" [NL].

36. "American Scholar Forum: The New Criticism" had appeared in *The American Scholar* 20 (1950–51); "Thirty Years Later: Memories of the First American Writers' Congress," a symposium moderated by Daniel Aaron and involving Cowley, Burke, Hicks, and William Phillips, was published in the Summer 1966 issue.

37. Robert W. Canzoneri (1925–2010), a former student of Cowley at Stanford, was a critic, writer of fiction, and memoirist as well as a professor of English and director of the Creative Writing Program at Ohio Sate University.

38. Isabella Gardner (1915–1981), a cousin of Robert Lowell and great-niece of the art collector Isabella Stewart Gardner, was the author of four volumes of poetry. "Belle" Gardner was married to Allen Tate from 1959 to 1966. After her divorce from Tate (her fourth husband), Gardner led a life marked by tragedy: alcoholism, a daughter's collapse into insanity, and a son's murder. Tate subsequently married Helen Heinz, a former nun and student of his at Minnesota.

39. "Gide as Friend and Colleague," a review of the Gide-Valéry correspondence and a volume of interviews with Gide, appeared in *Book Week* on May 1, 1966.

40. A. E. Hotchner's *Papa Hemingway* (New York: Random House, 1966), an adulatory personal memoir, was based on fourteen years of friendship with Hemingway. Mary Hemingway had refused Hotchner permission to quote from personal correspondence.

41. "Papa and the Parricides" appeared in *Esquire* on March 11, 1967.

42. In a much abridged version *The Garden of Eden* was published in 1986.

43. Henry Steele Commager (1902–1998), prominent liberal intellectual and historian of American liberalism, author of *The American Mind: An Interpretation of American Thought and Character since the 1880s* (1950).

44. George F. Kennan (1904–2005), influential diplomat, advisor, historian, and leading authority on the Cold War. Succeeding Cowley, he served as president of the National Institute from 1965 to 1968, when Allen Tate took over.

45. With Robert Penn Warren as his seconder, Cowley had nominated Burke for nonresident membership in the Century Association.

46. Allan Nevins (1890–1971), prominent American historian of the Civil War and Pulitzer Prize–winning biographer of Grover Cleveland, Hamilton Fish, Henry Ford, and John D. Rockefeller. His *Ordeal of the Union* won the Gold Medal for History and Biography from the National Institute of Arts and Letters in 1957.

47. Cowley also wrote for suggestions to Archibald Macleish, Robert Penn Warren, Allen Tate, and others. He later expanded his talk into the opening chapter of *ASF*.

48. On February 2 Burke had commented that Cowley's 1930s reviews held up "impressively well" and had praised his "sense of good judgment and good placement," which made "the pieces serve exceptionally well to recover the nature of the times." He had also objected that "the Iron Laws of Dialectics sometimes lead you to an overstress upon the society side of the relations between the author and his tribe" [*SC* 361].

49. Cowley had been invited to contribute to a festschrift for his old Harvard friend the poet and scholar S. Foster Damon, edited by Alvin H. Rosenfeld.

50. Lewis P. Simpson (1916–2005), literary critic and cultural historian of the American South; he was professor of English at Louisiana State University and editor of *The Southern Review* from 1965. Among the best known of his books are *The Man of Letters in New England and the South* (1973), *The Brazen Face of History* (1980), *The Dispossessed Garden* (1983), and *Mind and the American Civil War* (1989). Simpson wrote some of the finest critical appreciations of Cowley.

51. The essay, "The Self-Obliterated Author: S. Foster Damon" (later included in *WT*), first appeared in the Winter 1968 issue of *The Southern Review*.

52. Cowley had been awarded $10,000 by the National Endowment for the Arts. Other recipients that year were Louise Bogan, Kenneth Patchen, John Crowe Ransom, and Yvor Winters.

53. Frederick Manfred (1912–1994), midwestern author whose novel *Morning Red* Cowley had criticized in his letter of October 21, 1955.

54. Viking published a *Portable Western Reader,* edited by William Kittredge, in 1997.

55. Gay Wilson Allen (1903–1995), biographer and leading authority on Whitman. Cowley had reviewed Allen's books *Walt Whitman Handbook* in 1946 and *The Solitary Singer: A Critical Biography of Walt Whitman* in 1955, both for *The New York Times Book Review.* As Viking editor Cowley had worked with Allen on his biography of William James (1967).

56. In the fall of 1967 Cowley was writer-in-residence at Hollins College in Virginia.

57. Ralph L. Rusk, *The Life of Ralph Waldo Emerson* (1949).

58. Over the next thirteen years Cowley worked intensively with Allen on his Emerson biography. When *Waldo Emerson* appeared in 1981, Allen dedicated the book to Cowley.

59. Winters had praised "Dedication to Warburton," a poem by the eighteenth-century English satirist Charles Churchill (1732–1764) as one of the greatest poems of the century, superior to Alexander Pope's better known "Epistle to Dr. Arbuthnot."

60. *Being Geniuses Together,* by Robert McAlmon, revised and with supplementary chapters by Kay Boyle (Garden City, N.Y.: Doubleday, 1968).

61. McAlmon had referred to Cowley as a young intellectual "who could be duly ponderous" and "fairly slow on the uptake." (42)

62. Boyle tried to dissuade Cowley from reviewing the book, but without success. Cowley's review appeared on the front page of *The New York Times Book Review* of June 9, 1968 (*FL* 243–247). On June 22, 1968, Boyle wrote to Cowley to say she was "deeply saddened that [Cowley] chose to get back at McAlmon in this way" and pointed out what she thought were inaccuracies in his review. Cowley responded on June 26, again emphasizing Boyle's "generosity of spirit" but wondering: "For heaven's sake, Kay, why can't you admit that Bob McAlmon, for all his winning qualities (not winning to all), was radically incapable of writing the English language?" Cowley and Boyle continued to bicker over the merits of

McAlmon into November 1968. In later years, they grew mellower toward each other and commiserated over shared infirmities of age.

63. In 1968 Kay Boyle was jailed for thirty-one days for demonstrating against the Vietnam War at the Oakland Induction Center in California. Cowley had spent a night in a Paris jail in 1923, for punching a café proprietor in the jaw.

64. John Leonard (1939–2008), left-wing activist and influential literary, cultural, and media critic; in 1967 he had joined *The New York Times Book Review* as critic and later became its editor.

65. On August 30, 1967, Helen and Allen Tate had become parents of twin boys.

66. Salvador de Madariaga (1886–1978), Spanish diplomat, writer, and historian.

67. Cecil Maurice Bowra (1898–1971), English classical scholar and academic, renowned for his wit.

68. Cowley's review of Robert Conquest's book *The Great Terror: Stalin's Purge of the Thirties,* "The Soviet Socialist Republic of the Dead," appeared in *Book World (The Washington Post, Chicago Tribune),* on September 22, 1968.

69. Piper was writing his introduction to *AMWH* (1970).

70. Leonard Kriegel, "Art and the Book Reviewer," *The Nation,* June 5, 1967.

71. Burke's essay was titled "Psychology and Form." It had first appeared in *The Dial* 79 (July 1925), 34–46.

72. "Paul Valéry," a short literary biography commissioned by Louis Kronenberger for *Atlantic Brief Lives* (1971).

73. Cowley reviewed John Unterecker's *Voyager: A Life of Hart Crane* (1970) for the Winter 1970 issue of *The Sewanee Review:* "Hart Crane: The Evidence in the Case."

74. In 1932, shortly after Crane's death, Cowley had published Crane's last poem, "The Broken Tower," in *The New Republic.*

75. Seymour Krim (1922–1989), Jewish-American author, critic, and editor, often associated with the Beat Generation. As a journalist he was a practitioner of the New Journalism, writing for magazines like *Village Voice* and *Playboy.*

76. Third novel by Barbados-born Paule Marshall (b. 1929), published in 1969. Her first novel, *Brown Girl, Brownstones,* had appeared in 1959.

10. MAN OF LETTERS, 1970–1987

1. Unless indicated otherwise, all letters in this section are dated from Sherman.

2. Cowley elaborated his memoir of Caldwell for "Georgia Boy," included in *WT.*

3. On the occasion of the publication of *AMWH,* Henry Dan Piper had invited Cowley and Burke to Carbondale, Illinois, for a symposium titled "The Future of Criticism." Cowley also gave a lecture on "The Last Years of Ernest Hemingway," later reworked into a chapter for *ASF.*

4. In 1971, the facsimile and typescript of the original drafts of Eliot's poem, prior to Pound's changes, was published as *The Waste Land: A Facsimile and Transcript of the Original Drafts Including the Annotations of Ezra Pound.* Cowley's review,

"Editing Eliot's 'Waste Land,'" appeared in *Book World (The Washington Post)*, November 7, 1971; included in *FL* 314–318. Despite his reservations about Pound, Cowley acknowledged that, with the possible exception of Pound's handling of "Death by Water," his deletions to Eliot's typescript had been judicious ones and his editing "brilliant."

5. An early version appeared as "Storytelling's Tarnished Image" in *Saturday Review* 54 (September 25, 1971), 25–27, 54. A longer version, "A Defense of Storytelling," appeared in *WT*.

6. Ellen Moers was writing *Literary Women: The Great Writers* (1976), a feminist study of Jane Austen, George Sand, Colette, Simone Weil, and Virginia Woolf.

7. An early title for *ASF*. Bergonzi had invited Cowley to teach at the University of Warwick in 1973. He had published *The Situation of the Novel* in 1970.

8. *Gravity's Rainbow*, published by Viking in 1973.

9. The book was published by Viking in 1973. Cowley reviewed it for *The New Republic* of December 25, 1971 (included in *FL* 247–251).

10. The Cowleys were spending the winter months in Florida, together with Kenneth Burke.

11. On the morning of January 7, 1972, Berryman had committed suicide by jumping off the Washington Avenue Bridge in Minneapolis. Cowley had last met Berryman during his winter term at the University of Minnesota.

12. Warren was recovering from hepatitis.

13. Limner edited *Journey Around My Room: The Autobiography of Louise Bogan: A Mosaic*, published by Viking in 1980.

14. Cowley had been invited to teach American literature during the spring semester at the University of Warwick in Great Britain.

15. Cowley wrote numerous letters in protest of the WatersEdge project, among others to the National Endowment for the Arts and to the Democratic congresswoman Ella Grasso.

16. Editor and cofounder (with William S. Blair) of Blair & Ketchum's *Country Journal*, a monthly magazine launched in 1974. "Is There Still Hope for Farming in New England?" was published in the journal's August 1974 issue. It was reprinted in toto in the *Congressional Record*, at the request of Senator Thomas J. McIntyre of New Hampshire. In 1974 and 1975 Cowley wrote four other articles for *Country Journal*.

17. In the wake of her biography of Zelda Fitzgerald, Nancy Milford (b. 1938) had begun work on a life of Edna St. Vincent Millay. She had interviewed Cowley about Millay but in a subsequent letter of September 26, 1973, probed more deeply into the reason for the "critical disregard" of Millay by her male contemporaries: "very few of the men who were writing well, and who were any good, took her seriously as a working poet. [. . .] Was it because she was a woman, or is that pushing it?" [NL].

18. "The Three Sisters" is a poem written by Arthur Davison Ficke (1883–1945), published in *Poetry*, February 1913. In 1916 Ficke, a conservative poet and a lawyer,

with the poet Witter Bynner had played a literary hoax by inventing a new "Spectrist" school of poetry, which in turn inspired the Earl Roppel hoax perpetrated by Cowley, Burke and Berenice Abbott in 1918. See *WT*, 39–43. During World War I Ficke served as a major in the U.S. army. In the late 1910s he and Millay had a brief but intense affair.

19. Aiken's name for T. S. Eliot.

20. Cowley's tribute was published as "Priest of Consciousness" in *Quest* 2 (March /April 1978); collected in *FL* 333–338.

21. Apropos of *ASF*, Philip Young had written a tribute, "For Malcolm Cowley: Critic, Poet, 1898–" for *The Southern Review* (Autumn 1973), 778–795, mixing praise and condescension.

22. William Seabrook (1884–1945), American explorer and journalist, with an occultist interest in Satanism, voodoo, and sadism.

23. Young did not answer Cowley's letter.

24. In expanded form Cowley's introduction was incorporated, as "Figure in a Crowd," into *WT*.

25. James Kempf was writing a doctoral dissertation on Cowley. It was published in 1985 by Louisiana State University Press as *The Early Career of Malcolm Cowley: A Humanist among the Moderns*.

26. Cowley's lecture became the opening chapter to *WT*: " 'And Jesse Begat . . .' A Note on Literary Generations."

27. Miriam Gurko was the author of *Restless Spirit: A Life of Edna St. Vincent Millay* (1962). Dell's letters to Gurko are in the Newberry Library, Chicago. They remain unpublished.

28. Donaldson was writing a thematic biography of Hemingway, *By Force of Will: The Life and Art of Ernest Hemingway* (Viking, 1977).

29. "Georgia Boy: A Retrospect of Erskine Caldwell" first appeared in *Pages: The World of Books, Writers and Writing*, vol. 1, edited by Matthew J. Bruccoli and C. E. Frazer Clark, Jr. (1976), 62–73. Included in *WT*.

30. Martin Green (1927–2010), English-born writer and literary and cultural critic. Green had studied with F. R. Leavis at Cambridge University and met Cowley in 1957 during his stint at the University of Michigan, where Green was taking his Ph.D. Among his many books are *Cities of Light and Sons of the Morning* (1972), *Dreams of Adventure, Deeds of Empire* (1979), *Tolstoy and Gandhi: Men of Peace* (1983), and *The Great American Adventure* (1984).

31. "Reconsiderations—The '60s" appeared in *The New Republic,* August 20 and 27, 1977.

32. Lowell had died on September 12. He was married to Elizabeth Hardwick for twenty-three years, but in 1970 left her for the British author Lady Caroline Blackwood, with whom he had a son, Sheridan.

33. Cowley's review of Wilson's *Letters on Literature and Politics, 1912–1972,* appeared in *Saturday Review* of October 29, 1977. Included in *FL* 328–332.

34. On July 19, 1977, writing to the Swedish Academy as chancellor of the American Academy of Arts and Letters, Cowley had nominated Tate for the Nobel Prize in Literature.

35. In May 1976, after ten years of debate in which Cowley had played an active role, the American Academy and National Institute of Arts and Letters had been amalgamated by a vote of the joint membership.

36. On December 30, 1977, Cowley had written to President Jacques Barzun, urging the nomination of a higher proportion of younger members, "more representation to new forces in the arts, and [. . .] more nominations for Midwesterners, Westerners, women, blacks, and other underrepresented groups so as to make the Academy and Institute more truly national."

37. Benjamin DeMott (1924–2005), writer, cultural critic, and professor of English at Amherst College.

38. DeMott's review appeared in *The New York Times Book Review* of April 30, 1978. After praising Cowley for displaying "the liberal virtues—tolerance, considerateness, the sense of fraternity, openness to experiment, antipathy to dogma, and contempt for commercial cant," he criticized Cowley's analysis of "the sense of guilt" as a "tormented but still [. . .] evasive version."

39. Insertions between square brackets in this story quoted from the *World-Telegram* are Cowley's own.

40. Speaking of Cowley's testimony at the Hiss trials, DeMott had referred readers to Allen Weinstein's recently published book *Perjury*, which claimed that Hiss had been guilty of espionage.

41. Weinstein's research remains controversial: he has been criticized by Victor Navasky of *The Nation* for misquoting and distorting evidence; others, including Daniel Aaron, Sidney Hook, and Alfred Kazin, have supported his scholarship.

42. Critic and essayist who wrote on architecture, literature, and historic landscapes.

43. Thomas Hornsby Ferril (1896–1988), American poet, essayist, and journalist from Colorado.

44. In the 1970s, in the wake of the Watergate scandal and the discrediting of Nixon, Alger Hiss, who in 1950 had been convicted of perjury for lying under oath about having spied for the Soviet Union in the 1930s, sought correction of justice by filing for a writ of *coram nobis* (an appeal to a higher court to correct a previous verdict in the light of new evidence), after the FBI had released records that showed, Hiss felt, that he had not received a fair trial. The petition was denied by a federal court. Cowley had first met Hiss in 1950, for lunch after the June 1949 trial, and once again in 1960, at a dinner party in New York. The letter printed here is the only one he ever wrote to Hiss.

45. In 1974 Josephson had set out to write a book on Alger Hiss, whom he believed to be the innocent victim of the witch hunts of the postwar years. He hoped to expose the investigation and trials as a miscarriage of justice. Hiss had offered his

cooperation, but the writing of the book was disrupted by the death of Hannah Josephson.

46. The special session had been organized by Donald G. Parker and Warren Herendeen, editors of *The Visionary Company: A Magazine of the Twenties* (formerly the *Hart Crane Newsletter*). In 1987 they published a special double issue devoted to Cowley.

47. Cowley had suffered a hematoma, a ruptured blood vessel that overspread his chest with a huge purple blotch. His essay won *Life*'s National Magazine Award. "The View from Eighty" was published as a book in 1980. Cowley wrote a tribute to Tate for the annual meeting of the American Academy of Arts and Letters on December 7, 1979. It was published in *Georgia Review* (Spring 1980) and collected in *FL* 339–343.

48. Field was at work on a biography, *Djuna: The Life and Times of Djuna Barnes* (Putnam, 1983).

49. Ramon Guthrie (1896–1973), American poet, novelist, critic, and professor of French literature at Dartmouth College. Guthrie received a Silver Star for service in the U.S. air force during World War I. He was involved with the little magazine *S4N* (1919–1925). Cowley had known Guthrie since the 1920s and over the years paid him many visits in Dartmouth. Guthrie contributed a chapter on Proust to *The Lesson of the Masters* (1971).

50. A brief note on Ramon Guthrie, "A Resurrected Masterpiece," was published in *The Sewanee Review* 93 (January–March 1985).

51. In the fall of 1979 the Newberry Library in Chicago staged an exhibition of Cowley's papers, "Sharing the Literary Feast," and hosted a dinner in Cowley's honor, with John Cheever as stellar speaker, at Chicago's Drake Hotel. In his speech Cheever recalled attending a party at the Cowleys' in New York in the early 1930s. "My Friend, Malcolm Cowley" was included in the Library of America edition of John Cheever, *Collected Stories and Other Writings* (2009).

52. In January 1980 Mary McCarthy, interviewed by Dick Cavett on his TV-talk show, had denounced Hellman as an overrated and dishonest writer ("every word she writes is a lie, including 'and' and 'the.'") Hellman subsequently sued McCarthy. Hellman's *Scoundrel Time,* an autobiographical account of her experiences in the 1950s when she was summoned to appear before HUAC, had come out in 1976.

53. Schwartz was writing on the mechanics by which critics and institutions had conjointly created Faulkner's reputation in the early Cold War years; his book *Creating Faulkner's Reputation: The Politics of Modern Literary Criticism* was published in 1988.

54. Simpson's long review of *DGM,* "Cowley's Odyssey: Literature and Faith in the Thirties," had appeared in the Fall 1981 issue of *The Sewanee Review.*

55. POUM (*Partido Obrero de Unificación Marxista*) was a Spanish communist political party heavily influenced by the thought of Leon Trotsky and critical of Stalin and the Comintern. In *Homage to Catalonia* (1938) George Orwell recounts

his experiences with POUM. Orwell's book was not published in the United States until 1952.

56. "No Homage to Catalonia: A Memory of the Spanish Civil War" appeared in the January 1982 issue of *The Southern Review*.

57. Cowley was writing to Navasky to explain why he thought it was better not to lend his support to the American Writers' Congress.

58. Among the "abusive" reviews was Sidney Hook's, "Disremembering the Thirties," in *The American Scholar* of August 1980. And Kenneth S. Lynn excoriated Cowley in his review, "Malcolm Cowley Forgets," which appeared in *The American Spectator* in October 1980. Kazin and Aaron offered sympathetic appraisals in *The New York Times Book Review* and *Washington Post Book World*. Navasky's book *Naming Names* (Viking, 1980) frankly explored the practices of Hollywood blacklisting. It won the 1982 National Book Award for Nonfiction.

59. John Lowenthal, a professor of law at Rutgers University, in 1980 released "The Trials of Alger Hiss," a feature-length documentary in which Cowley was interviewed.

60. Epstein was editor of *The American Scholar* from 1974 to 1998.

61. Christopher Lasch's review, "Alienation à la Mode," appeared in *The Nation* of July 5, 1980. Cowley wrote to Lasch on December 29, 1982 (included here).

62. Claude Rawson, professor of eighteenth-century English literature at Yale University. Cowley had first met Rawson and his wife, Judy, during his stay at the University of Warwick in 1973. The Rawsons remained lifelong friends and correspondents of the Cowleys.

63. Cheever had died on June 18, 1982. "John Cheever: The Novelist's Life as a Drama" appeared in the Winter 1983 issue of *The Sewanee Review*. Included in *FL* 360–374.

64. Christopher Lasch (1932–1994), acerbic and iconoclastic critic of American culture, best known for *The Culture of Narcissism: American Life in an Age of Diminishing Expectations* (1979). Lasch decried the politics of progress, spoke out loudly against institutions that served to undermine communities and families, and warned of the dangers of consumerism and a "culture of narcissism."

65. *The New Radicalism in America, 1889–1963: The Intellectual as a Social Type* (1965).

66. "Echoes from Moscow: 1937–1938" appeared in the January 1984 issue of *The Southern Review*.

67. "Hemingway's Wound—And Its Consequences for American Literature" appeared in the Summer 1984 issue of *The Georgia Review*. Reprinted in *PMC* 417–435. Lynn's critique of Cowley (in "Hemingway's Private War," *Commentary*, July 1981) was reprinted in *The Airline to Seattle* (1983).

68. Richard H. Uhlig (1923–2002), clinical psychologist affiliated with the School of Social Work at the University of North Carolina at Chapel Hill.

69. The *Wilson Quarterly* had recently printed a number of essays on the topic of "The Elderly in America."

70. "Being Old Old" appeared in *The New York Times Magazine* of May 26, 1985.

71. B. F. Skinner (1904–1990), American psychologist famous for his experimental theories of radical behaviorism. In 1983 he had published *Enjoy Old Age: A Program of Self-Management,* with M. E. Vaughan.

72. Ruth Nuzum (1918–2006) was a passionate collector of Cowley's works and related items. She knew and befriended Cowley during the last ten years of his life and often asked him to inscribe books for her. She bequeathed her collection of Cowleyana to the Newberry Library.

73. Allen was collaborating with the French Americanist Roger Asselineau on *St. John de Crèvecoeur: The Life of an American Farmer.* It was published by Viking Penguin in September 1987.

Acknowledgments

This volume has been long in the making. It had its origin in my early explorations of Cowley's voluminous papers at the Newberry Library in Chicago in 1979–1980, in preparation of *Malcolm Cowley: The Formative Years* (1993), and owes much to the trust and encouragement of Malcolm Cowley himself, whom I was fortunate to have known during the last ten years of his life. In personal meetings—in Chicago, in Sherman—and in many letters, an aging Cowley, with unflagging energy, patience, and generosity, answered pertinent (and impertinent) queries from a fledgling Dutch scholar, illuminating the layered dimensions and complexities of a long life in the service of American literature. First and last, then, I owe a debt of gratitude to the late Malcolm and Muriel Cowley, for hospitably receiving me and my wife, Ella, into their home and at their dinner table, and giving me carte blanche permission to deal with his story and his legacy in the way I saw fit.

In the years since Cowley's death I have been equally lucky in finding my ongoing explorations of his long voyage supported and expedited by Robert Cowley, his father's literary executor. His trust and patience have equaled if not surpassed those of his parents. Over the last two decades, in letters, emails, telephone conversations, and personal meetings—in New York, in Sherman, in Newport—he has shared his rich fund of memories and reminiscences of his father (worthy of a book in their own right) and offered his experienced editorial advice on what at times must have seemed an interminable project. I am deeply grateful to Robert and Didi Cowley for their trust, help, and hospitality. All Cowley letters in this book are published with the permission of the Malcolm Cowley Estate.

Over many years I have painstakingly examined and assembled Cowley's letters at numerous libraries and institutions in the United States and, to a lesser extent, in Europe. The primary and indispensable collection of Cowley letters is at the Roger and Julie Baskes Department of Special Collections at the Newberry Library in Chicago. From 1954, when Cowley made the library a first gift of his pre-1940 archives, the Newberry has periodically acquired supplementary installments, processing shipments of papers (sometimes packed in whisky boxes) from Sherman, Connecticut, recognizing its unique value for scholars of twentieth-century American literature and culture. In more ways than one, this is a Newberry book. First, I thank Newberry for materially supporting my research with a 2004 short-term Lester J. Cappon Fellowship in Documentary Editing. Not only have the vast majority of the letters in this volume been edited from originals or carbon copies in the Malcolm Cowley Papers, during many research visits over the years the library has offered a hospitable, friendly, and stimulating home-away-from-home to its editor. Without exception the staff at Newberry—from its formidable scholars to its volunteer pagers—has been unfailingly helpful and encouraging. I thank in particular Richard H. Brown, Paul Gehl, James Grossman, Janice Reiff, and long-time Newberry scholar-in-residence Bruce Calder for taking personal interest, for allowing me to participate in the library's stimulating research sessions, and for making me feel part of an international community of scholars at Newberry. But I owe a special word of thanks to the staff of the library's Special Collections department, who for many years have kindly accommodated a visiting scholar from the Netherlands in their fourth-floor reading room and generously and cooperatively answered his inexhaustible store of queries and requests. Over the years the help of Carolyn Sheehy, Diana Haskell, Margaret Kulis, and Martha Briggs has been invaluable. I owe a personal word of thanks to Alison Hinderliter, who has gone far beyond the call of duty in her assistance to the project. With miraculous efficiency and an uncannily precise knowledge of the Cowley archive, she has helped me circumvent its many pitfalls and been infallibly effective and insightful in solving queries. Thanks for taking personal interest and making the transatlantic gap between Nijmegen and Newberry a smooth electronic highway.

In addition, I owe much to the help of curators and librarians at the many institutions that host Cowley's letters in their collections. Special thanks go to the staff of the manuscript divisions and special collections departments of the libraries and institutions that I have personally visited, for providing me with copies of Cowley materials and, where required, granting me permission to publish Cowley's letters: the archives of the American Academy of Arts and Letters, New York City; the Bancroft Library, University of California,

Berkeley; the Henry W. and Albert J. Berg Collection of English and American Literature and the Manuscripts and Archives Division, New York Public Library; the Butler Rare Book and Manuscript Library, Columbia University, New York; the University of Chicago Special Collections Research Center; the Manuscripts Division, Library of Congress; the John Hay Library, Brown University; the Houghton Library, Harvard University; the John F. Kennedy Presidential Library and Museum, Boston; Manuscripts Division, Department of Rare Books and Special Collections, Princeton University Library; the Harry Ransom Humanities Research Center, University of Texas at Austin; the Jacques Doucet Literary Library, Sorbonne University, Paris; the Special Collections Research Center, Syracuse University Library; Special Collections and University Archives, Jean and Alexander Heard Library, Vanderbilt University; the Viking Press Archives, New York; the Yale Collection of American Literature, Beinecke Rare Book and Manuscripts Library, Yale University; and Manuscripts and Archives, Sterling Memorial Library at Yale University Library.

I also thank the many other institutions that have helped in significant ways, by providing copies on xerox or microfilm, and granting permission to publish: Amherst College Archives and Special Collections, Amherst, Massachusetts; Archives and Special Collections, Thomas J. Dodd Research Center, University of Connecticut Libraries, Storrs; Hoover Institution Archives, Stanford University; Huntington Library, San Marino, California; University of Illinois Rare Book and Manuscript Library, University of Illinois, Urbana-Champaign; Special Collections, University of Maryland Libraries at College Park; Literary Manuscripts Collection, University of Minnesota Libraries, Minneapolis; Morris Library, Southern Illinois University, Carbondale; the Jane Pope Geske Heritage Room of Nebraska Authors, Lincoln City Libraries, Lincoln, Nebraska; the Poetry Collection of the University Libraries, University at Buffalo, the State University of New York; University of Pennsylvania Rare Book and Manuscript Library, Philadelphia; Rare Books and Manuscripts, Special Collections Library, Pennsylvania State University Libraries; David M. Rubenstein Rare Book and Manuscript Library, Duke University Libraries, Durham, North Carolina; Mortimer Rare Book Room, Smith College, Northampton, Massachusetts; Manuscripts Division, Green Library, Stanford University; Louise Pettus

Archives and Special Collections, Winthrop University, Rock Hill, South
Carolina; Archives Department, University of Wisconsin-Milwaukee Libraries. In the "Abbreviations" I have listed all manuscript collections used,
with proper citations. I thank Mrs. Kate Donahue Berryman, executrix of
the Berryman Estate, for permission to publish a letter from Cowley to
John Berryman (January 10, 1940) and also Ronald Poteat, a private collector, for making available the letters Cowley wrote to his parents from
France in the early 1920s. A special word of thanks is for the late Gay Wilson Allen, who generously received me in his home in Oradell, New Jersey,
and made his entire correspondence with Cowley available to me; it is now
part of the Gay Wilson Allen Papers at the David M. Rubenstein Rare Book
and Manuscript Library of Duke University, Durham, North Carolina. A
selection of Cowley's letters to William Faulkner (edited from their originals) is reprinted here from *The Faulkner-Cowley File* (copyright 1966 by
Malcolm Cowley and The Estate of William Faulkner) by permission of
Viking Penguin, a division of Penguin Group (USA) Inc. A selection of
Cowley's letters to Kenneth Burke, edited from their originals, is reprinted
from *The Selected Correspondence of Kenneth Burke and Malcolm Cowley,
1915–1981*, edited by Paul Jay (copyright 1988 by Kenneth Burke, Malcolm
Cowley and Paul Jay) by permission of Viking Penguin, a division of Pen-
guin Group (USA) Inc. I also thank University of Washington Press for
permission to reprint selected Cowley letters from *Robert B. Heilman: His
Life in Letters*, edited by Edward Alexander, Richard J. Dunn, and Paul
Jaussen (Seattle & London: University of Washington Press, 2009).

Besides the Newberry Library, material support for research on the Cowley letters was granted by the Netherlands Organisation for Scientific Research (NWO), the Netherlands Research School for Literary Studies (OSL),
the Netherlands America Commission for Educational Exchange (Fulbright
program), and the Institute for Historical, Literary and Cultural Studies
(HLCS) of the Faculty of Arts of Radboud University Nijmegen, the Netherlands. I thank the Faculty of Arts for granting me leaves of absence in the
fall of 2003 and the summer of 2009 to push the project forward.

Over the years, many of my students in the Department of English and
American Studies at Radboud University, Nijmegen, have helped to digi-
talize or otherwise research Cowley's letters. They will be surprised to find

that only a fraction of their immense labors is represented in the selection of letters included in this volume. With luck, the vast remainder will see the light in other, perhaps digital form in the future. Here I should like to thank (in roughly chronological order of their labors): Martine van Poucke, Elke van Cassel, Irene Vrinte, Laura Maessen, Linda Mous, Martijn Visser, Maarten van Gageldonk, Saskia Bak, Marieke van Eijk, and Wilco Versteeg. I also thank my Nijmegen colleagues in American literature Mathilde Roza and Jaap van der Bent for critically reviewing parts of the manuscript and suggesting effective ways of selecting and eliminating. I thank Heather Hughes, editorial assistant at Harvard University Press, and Kimberly Giambattisto, production editor at Westchester Publishing Services, for their expert assistance in guiding me through the final stages of production. Last but not least, I thank my editor at Harvard University Press, John Gregory Kulka, for his patience and encouragement and for the meticulous precision with which he helped to sharpen and polish my prose. Whatever infelicities or errors remain are mine.

This project could not have been realized without the moral and social support of many. I thank my Chicago friends Elspeth Revere and Bruce Calder for generously putting me (and my family) up at their beautiful Chicago home, for initiating me into the cultural, political, and culinary delights of a miraculous city, and for sharing the delights of Euro-American friendship. I thank Rob Kroes, John Raeburn, Werner Sollors, and Kristiaan Versluys for their interest in and support of my Cowley work, and my friends Eric and Sue Sandeen for offering good counsel and sharing many exhilarating distractions, from Laramie to Nijmegen, from Izmir to San Juan. Many of my good friends and relatives, and many of my colleagues at Radboud University and beyond, have patiently suffered my absences, physical and mental, as I struggled to round off a project that seemed to have no end; some have despaired if it ever would make the finish line. I thank them all for cheering me on and keeping the faith. My ultimate thanks go to my wife, Ella, and my daughter, Saskia, who have suffered more than their fair share of my absence and stubborn persistence but never stopped believing. Their unstinting love, shrewd advice, and enduring support have been priceless. I dedicate this book to them.

Index

Note: numerals in boldface and italics indicate the page on which a letter *to* the person cited begins. References to books, essays, poems or other works *by* a person cited appear under the heading of the person's name.